Clinical
Behavior Therapy

Clinical
Behavior Therapy

Adults and Children

Michel Hersen

John Wiley & Sons, Inc.

Library of Congress Cataloging-in-Publication Data:

Clinical behavior therapy : adults and children / [edited by] Michel Hersen.
    p. ; cm.
    Includes bibliographical references and index.
    ISBN 0-471-39258-8 (cloth : alk. paper)
    1. Behavior therapy. 2. Behavior therapy for children. 3. Psychology, Pathological. I.
Hersen, Michel.
    [DNLM: 1. Behavior Therapy—methods. 2. Mental Disorders—therapy. WM425
C6404.2002]
    RC489.B4 C578 2002
    616.89′142—dc21

                                                                    2001058148

Printed in the United States of America.

10 9 8 7 6 5 4 3 2 1

To Vicki, Jonathan, Nathaniel, Helen, and Susan

Preface

The genesis of this book lies in the supervisory relationship in practicum, internship, and residency settings. Given the clinical field's increased emphasis on accountability, assessment, clear conceptualization, and treatment effectiveness, this multiauthored text is designed to answer the most frequently posed questions by students of all disciplines (psychology, psychiatry, counseling, and social work) in doing psychotherapy with both adults and children. Among these questions are: How do I describe the case succinctly? What is there about this client's history that is particularly important? What is the best method to assess this client? What kind of consultation will I need? How do I conceptualize the case? What is my rationale for the treatment I have chosen? How do I deal with complications during the course of treatment? What are the important therapist-client factors (i.e., the therapeutic relationship)? How do I deal with termination? How do I follow up to ensure continuation of therapeutic gains? How is managed care a factor in my choice of treatment? How do I assess overall effectiveness?

Although casebooks such as this one have been published in the past (including a few by the present editor), they now are dated, have dealt only with adults or with children, and have not considered the more contemporaneous issues such as managed care, case conceptualization, and rationale for treatment choice. I firmly believe that it is critical for all clinicians (certainly in the formative years) to be able to deal with both adults and children and adolescents with a fair degree of expertise. There obviously is time for specialization later in their careers. Therefore, in this book, coverage is provided for several age groups.

Clinical Behavior Therapy: Adults and Children is divided into two parts. In Part I (Adults), the first chapter, "Behavioral Case Conceptualization for Adults," is followed by 11 chapters that detail important adult disorders and problems. In Part II (Children and Adolescents), the first chapter, "Behavioral Case Conceptualization for Children and Adolescents," is followed by 12 chapters that detail important childhood and adolescent disorders and problems. Chapters 2 through 12 and 13 through 25 follow an identical format:

1. Description of the Disorder
2. Case Description
3. Chief Complaints
4. History
5. Behavioral Assessment:
   Behavioral
   Self-Report
   Physiological

 6. Medical Consultation
 7. Case Conceptualization
 8. Rationale for Treatment Choice
 9. Course of Treatment (including detailed descriptions)
10. Therapist-Client Factors
11. Course of Termination
12. Follow-up
13. Managed Care Considerations
14. Overall Effectiveness

Many individuals have contributed to having this book published. First, I thank my esteemed colleagues, whose expertise has metamorphosed into heuristic outlines for graduate students in the clinical and counseling fields. Second, I thank Carole Londerée, my administrative assistant, who, as always, saw to it that things kept on track. Third, I thank Jennifer Simon, my editor at Wiley, who understood the relevance and timeliness of this project. Fourth, I thank Angelina Marchand and Alex Duncan for their very able technical assistance. Finally, I thank my students over the many years, who have taught me how to be a better clinical supervisor.

MICHEL HERSEN

Forest Grove, Oregon

Contributors

Ron Acierno, PhD
National Crime Victims Research and
    Treatment Center
Department of Psychiatry and
    Behavioral Sciences
Medical University of South Carolina
Charleston, South Carolina

Tina W. Billmeyer, MA
Department of Psychology
West Virginia University
Morgantown, West Virginia

Gary R. Birchler, PhD
VA San Diego Healthcare System and
    Department of Psychiatry
School of Medicine
University of California, San Diego
San Diego, California

Deanne Zotter Bonifazi, PhD
Department of Psychology
West Chester University
West Chester, Pennsylvania

Clara M. Bradizza, PhD
Research Institute on Addictions
University at Buffalo
The State University of New York
Buffalo, New York

Michelle G. Craske, PhD
Department of Psychology
University of California, Los Angeles
Los Angeles, California

Joseph P. DeCola, PhD
Department of Psychology
The Ohio State University
Columbus, Ohio

Keith S. Dobson, PhD
Department of Psychology
University of Calgary
Calgary, Alberta Canada

Kelly L. Drake, MA
Department of Psychology
University of Nevada, Las Vegas
Las Vegas, Nevada

Michel J. Dugas, PhD
Department of Psychology
Concordia University
Montréal, Québec Canada

Paul M. G. Emmelkamp, PhD
Department of Clinical Psychology
University of Amsterdam
Amsterdam, The Netherlands

William S. Fals-Stewart, PhD
Research Institute on Addictions
University of Buffalo
The State University of New York
Buffalo, New York

Sharon M. Flicker, MS
Center for Family and Adolescent
    Research
The University of New Mexico
Albuquerque, New Mexico

Mary F. Flood, PhD
Department of Psychology
University of Nebraska
Lincoln, Nebraska

Edna B. Foa, PhD
Center for the Treatment and Study of
    Anxiety
Department of Psychiatry
University of Pennsylvania School of
    Medicine
Philadelphia, Pennsylvania

Martin E. Franklin, PhD
Center for the Treatment and Study of
    Anxiety
Department of Psychiatry
University of Pennsylvania School of
    Medicine
Philadelphia, Pennsylvania

Kurt A. Freeman, PhD,
Behavior Analysis Track
Pacific University
Portland, Oregon

David M. Garner, PhD
River Centre Clinic for Eating
    Disorders
Bowling Green State University
University of Toledo
Toledo, Ohio

Brian C. Goff, PhD
Portland Dialectical Behavior Therapy
    Program
Portland, Oregon

Matt J. Gray, PhD
National Center for PTSD
Boston University School of Medicine
    and VA Boston Healthcare System
Boston, Massachusetts

Alan M. Gross, PhD
Department of Psychology
University of Mississippi
Oxford, Mississippi

David J. Hansen, PhD
Department of Psychology
University of Nebraska
Lincoln, Nebraska

Michel Hersen, PhD, ABPP
School of Professional Psychology
Pacific University
Forest Grove, Oregon

Eugenia Hsu, MA
Department of Psychology
University of Nebraska
Lincoln, Nebraska

Stephen D. A. Hupp, MA
Department of Psychology
Louisiana State University
Baton Rouge, Louisiana

Christa Holland Johnson, PhD
Department of Pediatrics
University of Oklahoma Health
    Sciences Center
Oklahoma City, Oklahoma

Cynthia R. Johnson, PhD
Autism Center
Children's Hospital of Pittsburgh
Pittsburgh, Pennsylvania

Jan H. Kamphuis, PhD
Department of Clinical Psychology
University of Amsterdam
Amsterdam, The Netherlands

Christopher A. Kearney, PhD
Department of Psychology
University of Nevada, Las Vegas
Las Vegas, Nevada

Nasreen Khatri
Department of Psychology
University of Calgary
Calgary, Alberta Canada

Soonie A. Kim, PhD
Portland Dialectical Behavior Therapy
    Program
Portland, Oregon

M. Krijn, MA
Department of Clinical Psychology
University of Amsterdam
Amsterdam, The Netherlands

Cristina G. Magana, MA
River Centre Clinic for Eating
    Disorders
University of Toledo
Toledo, Ohio

John S. March, MD, MPH
Department of Psychiatry
Duke University Medical Center
Durham, North Carolina

Sara G. Mattis, PhD
Department of Psychology
Boston University
Boston, Massachusetts

Barry W. McCarthy, PhD
Washington Psychological Center
Washington, D.C.

Daniel W. McNeil, PhD
Department of Psychology
West Virginia University
Morgantown, West Virginia

Catherine A. Miller, PhD
Counseling Psychology Program
Pacific University
Portland, Oregon

J. Scott Mizes, PhD
Behavioral Medicine and Psychiatry
West Virginia University School of
    Medicine
Morgantown, West Virginia

Tracy L. Morris, PhD
Department of Psychology
West Virginia University
Morgantown, West Virginia

Larry L. Mullins, PhD
Department of Psychology
Oklahoma State University
Stillwater, Oklahoma

Thomas H. Ollendick, PhD
Department of Psychology
Virginia Polytechnic Institute and
    State University
Blacksburg, Virginia

David Reitman, PhD
Center for Psychological Studies
Nova Southeastern University
Fort Lauderdale, Florida

William M. Reynolds, PhD
Department of Psychology
Humboldt State University
Arcata, California

C. Nannette Roach, PhD
Department of Psychology
University of Mississippi
Oxford, Mississippi

Kenneth J. Ruggiero, PhD
Department of Psychology
West Virginia University
Morgantown, West Virginia

Moira Rynn, MD
Mood and Anxiety Disorders Section
Department of Psychiatry
University of Pennsylvania School of
    Medicine
Philadelphia, Pennsylvania

Joseph R. Scotti, PhD
Department of Psychology
West Virginia University
Morgantown, West Virginia

Georganna Sedlar, PhD
Department of Psychology
University of Nebraska
Lincoln, Nebraska

John T. Sorrell, MA
Department of Psychology
West Virginia University
Morgantown, West Virginia

Paul R. Stasiewicz, PhD
Research Institute on Addictions
University at Buffalo
The State University of New York
Buffalo, New York

Paula Truax, PhD
Counseling Psychology Program
Pacific University
Portland, Oregon

Kevin E. Vowles, MA
Department of Psychology
West Virginia University
Morgantown, West Virginia

Holly Barrett Waldron, PhD
Center for Family and Adolescent
  Research
The University of New Mexico
Albuquerque, New Mexico

C. Eugene Walker, PhD
Department of Psychiatry and
  Behavioral Sciences
University of Oklahoma Health
  Sciences Center
Oklahoma City, Oklahoma

Julie Wolfgang, MA
Department of Psychology
West Virginia University
Morgantown, West Virginia

Contents

PART I   ADULTS

1 Behavioral Case Conceptualization for Adults   3
  Paula Truax

2 Major Depressive Disorder   37
  Keith S. Dobson and Nasreen Khatri

3 Panic and Agoraphobia   52
  Joseph P. DeCola and Michelle G. Craske

4 Specific Phobia   75
  Jan H. Kamphuis, Paul M. G. Emmelkamp, and M. Krijn

5 Social Phobia   90
  Daniel W. McNeil, John T. Sorrell, Kevin E. Vowles,
  and Tina W. Billmeyer

6 Posttraumatic Stress Disorder   106
  Matt J. Gray and Ron Acierno

7 Generalized Anxiety Disorder   125
  Michel J. Dugas

8 Bulimia Nervosa   144
  J. Scott Mizes and Deanne Zotter Bonifazi

9 Borderline Personality Disorder   160
  Soonie A. Kim and Brian C. Goff

10 Alcohol Abuse   181
   Paul R. Stasiewicz and Clara M. Bradizza

11 Sexual Dysfunction   198
   Barry W. McCarthy

12 Marital Dysfunction   216
   Gary R. Birchler and William S. Fals-Stewart

PART II   CHILDREN AND ADOLESCENTS

13 Behavioral Case Conceptualization for Children
   and Adolescents   239
   Kurt A. Freeman and Catherine A. Miller

14 Childhood Depression   256
   William M. Reynolds

15 Obsessive-Compulsive Disorder 276
  Martin E. Franklin, Moira Rynn, John S. March,
  and Edna B. Foa
16 School Refusal and Separation Anxiety 304
  Sara G. Mattis and Thomas H. Ollendick
17 Social Phobia 326
  Christopher A. Kearney and Kelly L. Drake
18 Anorexia Nervosa 345
  David M. Garner and Cristina G. Magana
19 Posttraumatic Stress Disorder 361
  Joseph R. Scotti, Tracy L. Morris, Kenneth J. Ruggiero,
  and Julie Wolfgang
20 Conduct Disorder 383
  C. Nannette Roach and Alan M. Gross
21 Attention-Deficit/Hyperactivity Disorder 400
  David Reitman and Stephen D. A. Hupp
22 Mental Retardation 420
  Cynthia R. Johnson
23 Elimination Disorder 434
  Christa Holland Johnson, Larry L. Mullins,
  and C. Eugene Walker
24 Child Sexual Abuse 449
  Eugenia Hsu, Georganna Sedlar, Mary F. Flood,
  and David J. Hansen
25 Alcohol and Drug Abuse 474
  Holly Barrett Waldron and Sharon M. Flicker

Author Index 491

Subject Index 505

PART I

ADULTS

CHAPTER 1

Behavioral Case Conceptualization for Adults

PAULA TRUAX

INTRODUCTION TO CASE CONCEPTUALIZATON

THE PRIMARY GOAL of this chapter is to provide an overall framework for applying the scientific method to the clinical setting through developing and testing hypotheses about clinical concerns of adult clients. In the most general sense, this process of providing "a clear, theoretical explanation for *what the client is like* as well as *why the client is like this*" (Berman, 1997, p. xi) is termed *case conceptualization*. More specifically, behavioral case conceptualization implies that the theory employed is derived from behavioral principles that emphasize observable behaviors to describe *what* the client is like and learning principles to describe *why* the client is like this. The basic assumption in behavioral theory is that both adaptive and maladaptive behaviors are acquired, maintained, and changed in the same way: through the internal and external events that proceed and follow them. This means that behavioral case conceptualization involves a careful assessment of the context within which a behavior occurs, along with developing testable hypotheses about the causes, maintaining factors, and treatment interventions.

The recent proliferation of empirically supported treatments coupled with managed care demands has significantly increased recent attention to conceptualizing adult cases from a behavioral perspective. A contemporary focus for clinical outcome research has been to identify interventions with empirical support for specific concerns. This has catalyzed a movement toward establishing common criteria for defining treatments as being *empirically validated* (Division 12 Task Force, 1995) or *empirically supported* (Chambless & Hollon, 1998). According to the American Psychological Association Division 12 Task Force, "well-established treatments" require at least two randomized controlled clinical trials (by more than one research group) or a series of single-subject designs demonstrating either superiority over a placebo or effectiveness comparable to another well-established treatment. Additionally, the research should employ a treatment manual and clearly defined subjects. Based on these criteria, 22 well-established treatments were identified for 21 different disorders. Of these treatments, 19 were behavioral or cognitive-behavioral. Although such preponderance of behavioral interventions in the well-established treatments category may be partially due to the fact that behavioral interventions are researched more frequently than other therapies, these findings both mirrored and spurred a heightened interest in behavioral case conceptualization. The enhanced availability of treatment manuals resulting from these clinical trials has made state-of-the-art behavioral interventions more accessible.

Managed care also has had an important role in broadening the use of behavioral case conceptualization. First, and probably of most concern to clinicians, are the imposed session limits that encourage therapists to use the most cost-effective interventions available. Current research suggests that behavioral interventions may offer both the briefest and the most effective treatments available for a variety of client concerns. According to recent cost-effectiveness analyses, behavioral therapy may be even more cost-effective than medication (Antonuccio, Thomas, & Danton, 1997). Second, nearly all managed care organizations require that treatment plans include behaviorally specific symptom descriptions and treatment targets, regardless of the therapist's theoretical orientation. Third, therapists who are able to present a cohesive treatment plan using empirically supported interventions when petitioning for additional sessions with managed care review boards may have a greater chance of having their requests approved (Castonguay, Schut, Constantino, & Halperin, 1999). In the state of Oregon, for example, behaviorally specific treatment plans are required by law for clients treated through the public health care system, the Oregon Health Plan (OHP; Oregon Administrative Standards 309–032-0001, 2001). In turn, those agencies that meet or exceed the state's requirements for specificity and comprehensiveness are more likely to obtain or maintain contracts to provide services to those on the OHP. Thus, clinicians who couple the necessary behavioral descriptions with behavioral interventions and measurements may have a leg up on clinicians who rely on nonbehavioral conceptualizations. Finally, managed care review boards often are not composed of mental health professionals. Instead, administrators may be involved in decisions about health care. Behavioral descriptions of problems and interventions may be more comprehensible and even more plausible than descriptions from other theoretical orientations. This all may translate into an increased probability that requests for clients and session increases will be granted (Hoyt, 1995).

APPLYING THE SCIENTIFIC METHOD IN THE CLINICAL SETTING

Although the pragmatic issues make a compelling case for simply describing cases and interventions behaviorally, behavioral proponents emphasize the importance of grounding behavioral case conceptualization in its theoretical roots. Behaviorism is not only a theoretical perspective to explain behavior and treatment; it is also a philosophy about the importance of scientific inquiry (Plaud & Vogeltanz, 1997). Whether behavioral theories are being tested in the laboratory or the clinical setting, data gathered through hypothesis testing are necessary to justify any conclusions. Clinical decisions should be based on data rather than assumptions or guesses.

Even though the average clinician does not have the same experimental controls as a laboratory scientist, the endeavor of developing and testing hypotheses in the real clinical setting is much like that of the scientist. According to Stricker and Trierweiler (1995), the ideal model for a clinician is that of a "local clinical scientist," in which the clinician applies the scientific method to the clinical setting. Traditionally, the generic scientific method has been defined as involving five steps: (1) *observing* a phenomenon; (2) *developing hypotheses* to explain the phenomenon; (3) *testing the hypotheses* through experimentation; and (4) *observing the outcome* to evaluate the predictive validity of the original hypotheses. If the hypotheses are not supported by the outcome, then Step 2 is revisited based on the additional information from the hypothesis test. For the clinician, the steps in behavioral case conceptualization parallel those of the scientific method (see Figure 1.1). The steps are briefly described next and will be further elaborated in the next section.

1. *Observation* is akin to assessment or the initial interview phase of therapy. This is when the clinician identifies the target problem, its topography (i.e., frequency, intensity, duration), and its remote and current context.
2. *Developing hypotheses* is the treatment-planning phase of case conceptualization. Here, the clinician develops hypotheses about the factors causing and maintaining the client's behaviors. From this, hypotheses are developed about interventions likely to be helpful to the client. These general hypotheses are then translated into testable hypotheses through developing a treatment plan with specific goals, interventions, and outcome measurements.
3. *Testing hypotheses* represents the treatment phase, in which the treatment plan is carried out and the hypotheses developed in Step 2 are tested.

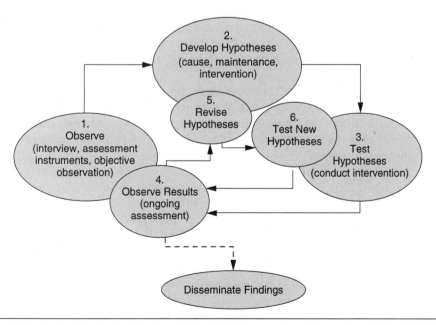

Figure 1.1   Scientific Method in the Clinical Setting

4. *Observing the outcome* parallels the treatment review phase of therapy in which therapist and client evaluate treatment progress according to the treatment plan developed in Step 2.
5. *Revising hypotheses* refers to changes in the treatment plan based on data collected in Step 3.

OBSERVATION: ASSESSMENT

Accurate behavioral case conceptualization hinges on a comprehensive assessment of the client's concerns and strengths. This section addresses a variety of methods for collecting information, identifying observable treatment targets, operationally defining treatment targets, and assessing the behavioral context.

DATA COLLECTION METHODS

Strictly speaking, observation refers to the direct objective visual inspection of a phenomenon or behavior. Although this may be the data collection method of choice for children or adults with a resident caregiver, there are a number of challenges to direct behavioral observation of typical adult outpatients. First and foremost, any observation by an outsider, such as the therapist, is likely to be intrusive and undesirable to the client. Second, even if the client agreed to have the therapist observe his or her behavior, the therapist's presence would effectively modify the context of the behavior. In all likelihood, this modification would change the behavior enacted and the data collection would be inaccurate until the client habituated to the observer. Third, the client's problematic behaviors are likely to occur in a variety of contexts that would be difficult to duplicate in the laboratory or observe naturalistically. Finally, direct observation is time-intensive and expensive, especially when a lengthy habituation period must precede baseline data collection. In combination, these challenges often preclude direct observation as a primary clinical assessment tool for adult clients. Instead, a number of alternative data collection methods are often used, including the clinical interview, self-report questionnaires, self-monitoring, and naturalistic video- or audiotaping.

Clinical Interview   The clinical interview is the most common method by far for assessing the presenting concerns of adult clients. Compared to direct behavioral observation, it is often more desirable, feasible, and cost-effective. It also has the advantage of allowing therapists to observe in-session behavior and begin establishing necessary rapport through mutual reinforcement. The primary drawback of the clinical interview is that interrater reliability tends to be quite low, especially for unstructured interviews. These findings suggest that the behavior being *observed* in the clinical interview is often not consistent over time, situations, or interviewers. They also point to the fact that interviewers participating in a clinical interview are neither consistent in their behavior nor objective in their assessment of clients. It is important to note, however, that reliability is substantially increased with widely used structured interviews such as those listed below (cf. First, Spitzer, Gibbon, & Williams, 1997a):

- Structured Clinical Interview for the *DSM-IV* (SCID-I; First, Spitzer, Gibbon, & Williams, 1997b): The SCID is a semistructured diagnostic interview that combines specific closed- and open-ended questions to yield Axis I diagnoses. The primary advantage of this instrument is its reliability and comprehensiveness in identifying pertinent symptoms and assigning diagnoses. The primary disadvantage for behavioral case conceptualization is that it provides little information about the factors that maintain the current symptoms.

- Functional Analytic Interview (Cormier & Cormier, 1998): The Functional Analytic Interview consists of a set of questions designed to elicit the client's perceptions of the functional antecedents, consequences, and potential secondary gain of target behaviors. Although this type of interview provides potentially valuable information about the pivotal variables that may be targeted in treatment, little is known about interrater or test-retest reliability.

In combination, these diagnostic and functional assessments offer a valuable clinical picture of symptom clusters and important environmental factors. Because most of the empirically supported treatments are based on diagnostic categories, the diagnostic interview can aid the clinician in deciding on a treatment manual. The functional analysis may then aid in tailoring the treatment foci.

Standardized Self-Report Instruments   The observation phase of behavioral case conceptualization often includes the use of self-report questionnaires. These usually ask the client to make quantitative ratings in response to specific questions. On the Beck Anxiety Inventory (BAI; Beck & Steer, 1993), for example, clients rate the extent to which they experience anxiety symptoms such as "numbness or tingling" from 0 (not at all) to 3 (severely). Some of the concerns regarding the subjectivity of the clinical intake are at least partially circumvented with the use of such standardized questionnaires. First, in contrast to the clinical interview, self-report questionnaires represent stable stimuli and clinician subjectivity is minimized. Questions are asked in the same way each time and the scores are typically computed through systematic scoring algorithms. Second, standardized self-report instruments have the advantage of allowing clinicians to compare their clients' scores with those of normal and/or clinical populations. This helps to take some of the guesswork out of assessing the client's level of severity relative to the population. Finally, self-report instruments are practical. A great deal of information can be collected in a short amount of time, often at little cost.

Some of the drawbacks include the fact that, although test-retest reliability is better than interrater reliability for the clinical interview, it is far from perfect. For example, a client's report of mood may change due to increased awareness as a result of therapy rather than as a result of an actual change in mood. Likewise, the validity (i.e., the extent to which the questionnaire measures what it is intended to measure) of self-report questionnaires often is challenged. Because clients must complete the form independently, they do not have the opportunity for clarification and may misinterpret items. When there are multiple applications of the same instrument, clients may begin to respond out of habit rather than thoughtful self-assessment. Perhaps the greatest drawback to using questionnaires is one of preference. Neither clinicians nor clients like to complete these instruments on a regular basis. Some theorists propose, however, that attitudes toward using such outcome assessments may be enhanced when clients get regular feedback regarding the results of these instruments (Halperin & Snyder, 1979).

Self-Monitoring   Although observation by an objective observer may be impractical and problematic, teaching clients to be observers of their own behavior may be a good substitute. Self-monitoring usually involves having the client track variables such as the intensity, frequency, duration, context, and timing of a target behavior. Examples of common forms of self-monitoring include rating the daily intensity of a mood such as depression from 0 (not at all depressed) to 10 (most depressed imaginable); tracking of daily frequency of a behavior such as nail-biting or anger outbursts; recording the duration of target behaviors such as time in bed spent sleeping; and monitoring the antecedents and consequences of target behavior. Having clients observe their own behaviors is inexpensive, practical, and may also be therapeutic. Baker and Kirschenbaum (1998) found, for example, that intensive self-monitoring of food intake may increase weight loss in overweight individuals. Of course, self-monitoring may be biased as well. Lack of compliance, concerns about social desirability, and impaired awareness of the behavior's occurrence may affect the accuracy of self-monitoring. Some research findings suggest that the accuracy of therapy directives such as self-monitoring may be enhanced through focused training, in-session rehearsal, and regular in-session reviews (Stickler, Bradlyn, & Maxwell, 1981).

Other Assessments   Other, less frequently used methods of assessment include naturalistic or laboratory taping of behaviors and physiological measures of behavior. John Gottman, a renowned marital researcher and therapist, routinely combines the use of videotape and physiological measurement for evaluating laboratory interactions in maritally distressed couples. Couples are asked to reenact a recent argument while the interaction is videotaped and physiological variables (e.g., heart rate reactivity) are simultaneously assessed. Although these methods have yielded some provocative and robust findings suggesting that divorce within the succeeding two years can be predicted by the male's level of physiological arousal during marital conflict (Gottman et al., 1995), such methods may be infeasible for the average clinician.

Taping of target client behaviors may be conducted in clinical or naturalistic settings. For example, therapists may tape in-session behavior for later review, or they may instruct clients to set an audio- or videotape to record during high-risk times for problem behaviors at home. Taping like this may be used for externally observable behavior to increase the information available to the therapist and the client regarding the behavioral chain and its antecedents or consequences. A client with trichotillomania, for example, may be asked to place a video camera in the room where hair pulling occurs and to turn it on whenever he or she enters the room. This video may help the therapist assess possibilities for interrupting the behavioral chain.

CASE EXAMPLE FOR BEHAVIORAL CASE CONCEPTUALIZATION

The following case is discussed in the context of behavioral conceptualization.

Mr. X., a 27-year-old unemployed, married father of three young children, presented with a primary problem of 10 to 15 daily episodes of feeling very panicky and tearful, accompanied by hyperventilation, heart racing, nausea, sweating, shaking, dizziness, and feeling that he is going crazy. A secondary problem was a five-year history of ongoing depression. He requested help with resolving the panic and was ambivalent about treatment for depression.

Panic attacks began about six months previously and had increased in severity and frequency since then. He could not identify anything unusual about the time that the panic began. He stated that onset, as well the daily occurrences, seemed to "come out of the blue." Events that were likely to elicit panic attacks were being somewhere where escape was difficult (e.g., mall, store, theater, bus, tunnels), and having very negative thoughts about himself (e.g., "I am worthless"; "I am crazy"; "I am a bad father"). He reported that his most effective coping strategy had been to leave the evocative situation or distract himself as quickly as possible. He reported that the desire to escape was intense and the relief after escape acute.

The depression also had no clear precipitating event other than some reported general difficulty dealing with the "human tragedies" that accompanied his previous job as a police officer. He had been involuntarily retired from his job after being hospitalized for depression four years earlier. He stated that his depression had been constant since that time, but that it had worsened since onset of the panic and that over the past month he had sat at home because he "feels too depressed to move." He reported depressed mood most of the day nearly every day accompanied by low interest, difficulty sleeping, feeling very guilty most of the time, low energy, difficulty concentrating, increased appetite, and visible slowing of speech and movements. He admitted to suicidal ideation four years earlier when hospitalized, but denied any current ideation, plan, or intent.

He was participating in current psychotropic treatment (Wellbutrin) for his depression and anxiety when he presented for treatment. He reported that the medication had helped to reduce his depression to a "tolerable level" but that the panic had not been helped.

According to the Beck Depression Inventory-II (BDI-II; Beck, Steer, & Brown, 1996) and the Mobility Inventory (MI; Chambless, Caputo, Jasin, Gracely, & Williams, 1985), Mr. X.'s depression (BDI-II = 50) and agoraphobic avoidance (MI = 4.3 for activities done alone) were both in the severe range. Similarly, baseline self-monitoring data indicated that the average daily intensity for anxiety and depression was an 8 (on a 0–10 scale, with larger numbers representing greater severity) with an average of 11 daily panic attacks.

IDENTIFYING TARGET BEHAVIORS

Although the scientific method begins with observation of a phenomenon, the exact phenomenon of interest in the clinical environment can be difficult to define. Most adults begin treatment with a variety of strengths and weaknesses. Mr. X., for instance, was having difficulty with depression, generalized anxiety, panic attacks, and occupational functioning. Despite these symptoms, however, he was performing adequately as a parent and a spouse, according to his report. This client's treatment would be shaped by the foci chosen for interventions. Prochaska and Norcross (1999) point out that a meaningful advantage to having a cohesive theoretical framework is that it "delimits the amount of relevant information, organizes that information, and integrates it all into a coherent body of knowledge that prioritizes our conceptualization and directs our treatment"

(p. 5). Conceptualizing from a behavioral perspective helps to limit the number and type of relevant treatment targets. Both the types and the topography of treatment targets are addressed in the following sections.

Early behavioral theorists emphasized the importance of focusing on only observable behavioral targets. Internal experiences were discounted in lieu of externally observable behavior. Thus, for a client who reported feeling depressed, the treatment targets might be to reduce the frequency of crying, oversleeping, and inactivity rather than to reduce depressed mood. More contemporary behavioral theorists, such as Aaron Beck (Beck, Rush, Shaw & Emery, 1979) and David Barlow (1988) have added internal experiences, such as mood and thought, to the list of important behavioral treatment targets, especially for adult clients.

Cormier and Cormier (1998) outlined both *overt* and *covert* behavioral treatment targets. Overt treatment targets include verbal, nonverbal, and motoric behaviors. Examples of verbal behavior include reduced production of speech, cursing, or unassertiveness. Nonverbal behavior is communicative behavior without the verbal component; examples are frowning, crying, or sitting with a slumped posture. Motoric behaviors are visible behaviors that are not expressly communicative, such as eating a bag of cookies. Cormier and Cormier's covert treatment targets include thinking or believing, feeling, imagining, and physical sensations. The depressed client may be thinking "I am a failure! Nothing I do will ever be enough!", feeling very depressed, imagining rejection in social situations, and experiencing physical feelings of fullness from consuming the bag of cookies. Either internal or external behaviors may be targeted for treatment from a behavioral perspective.

For Mr. X., examples of overt behavioral targets include decreased speech (verbal), flat facial expression and lack of hand gestures (nonverbal behavior), leaving or avoiding anxiety-provoking situations, and sitting at home alone (motoric). Covert behavioral targets include thoughts regarding danger of panic symptoms (e.g., "I am going to die"; "I am having a heart attack"; "I am going crazy") (cognitive); feeling very anxious and depressed (emotional); imagining himself dead with his family weeping over him or being institutionalized and burdening his family (imaginal); and hyperventilation, heart racing, nausea, sweating, shaking, and dizziness while panicking (physical).

TOPOGRAPHY OF TREATMENT TARGETS

Behavioral case conceptualization may involve either internal or external treatment targets; the one caveat is that all treatment targets must be *operationalized* or described in terms of their observable, specific, measurable aspects. Assessing the "lay of the land" or the topography of a treatment focus requires an operational definition of the client's concerns, a time line, and appropriate diagnosis.

Operational Definitions A hallmark of behavioral case conceptualization is the focus on observable, specific, measurable treatment targets (i.e., operational definitions). Specific behaviors (i.e., what the client *does*) are described rather than labels or traits (i.e., what the client *is* or *has*). So, even for internal behaviors such as mood or thought, externally observable signs become the focus of treatment. In the case of Mr. X., the therapist may operationalize his panic attacks through querying him about the behavioral manifestations and impacts, as well as the frequency, intensity, and duration of the depression. This way, even internal states have external, measurable, observable referents. Questions such as the following may be used to glean behaviorally specific treatment targets. Mr. X.'s responses are in italics following each question.

1. Behavioral manifestations
   - How would I know by looking at you that you were feeling panicky?
     I would become very quiet and start to pace and sweat.
   - What have others told you they have observed about your behavior while you were feeling panicky?
     No one has really said they have noticed anything other than that I have suddenly left some business meetings.
   - How has feeling panicky affected the way you take care of yourself?
     I avoid being closed in the shower, so I shower less often and only when no one else is home so I can leave the door open. Also, I don't do fun things like go to movies anymore.
   - How has feeling panicky affected the way you communicate with others?
     I try to avoid others mostly, especially emotional conversations because feeling emotional can bring on an attack. I am also afraid the others will figure out that I am losing control and I don't think I could bear that. So, I just try to avoid conversations about anything other than the weather.
   - How has feeling panicky affected your relationships with family or friends?
     My wife is concerned about me and suggested that I come see you. I do talk to her about what is going on, but I don't let anyone else know. I don't think my parenting has been affected much, though, but I am worried that I might die and not be there for my kids (begins to cry).
   - How has feeling panicky affected your work?
     I don't have a job right now. I don't feel strong enough to even look for one. I would like to get a job in the criminal justice system once I get a grip on myself.
2. Frequency, intensity, and duration of internal state
   - How would you rate your anxiety on a scale of 0 to 10, with 0 being the least anxious you can possibly imagine feeling and 10 being the most anxious you can image feeling:
     - On *average* over the past week (intensity)?
       Around an 8.
     - At the *worst* times over the past week (intensity)? How many of these have there been (frequency)? How long have they lasted (duration)?
       That would be during a panic attack. These have been a 10 over the past week. I have had seven or eight attacks at an intensity of 10 lasting 10 to 30 minutes over the past week.
     - At the *best* times over the past week? How many of these have there been? How long did they last?
       In the evening when I read my kids a story, it's like life is back to normal for a few minutes. I get involved in the story and forget briefly about my problems. I would say my anxiety is about a 4 at those times. That happens every night for about 30 minutes.

Time Line   A second step in understanding the topography of the presenting concern is to establish a *time line*. Once the problem is defined in the present, the clinician should assess how long the problem has existed and what the course has been over time. One method that aids both client and clinician in visualizing the peaks and valleys of the target concern is to collaboratively draw a time line with a severity scale on the vertical axis and time on the horizontal axis (see Figure 1.2). The severity scale is idiographically defined depending on the type of concern:

- *Intensity:* Behaviors best depicted by intensity, such as moods or feelings, may be characterized by a 0–10 intensity scale. Combined very high and very low moods may be depicted by –10 to +10, for example.
- *Frequency:* Behaviors best depicted by frequency, such as thoughts or overt behaviors, may be characterized as the average frequency per day or week during that time period.

The initial date represents the first time the problem occurred and the final date is typically the current date. Intervals are defined based on the nature and course of the presenting problem. If the problem had existed for a short time with many fluctuations, briefer intervals would be appropriate (e.g., weeks or months), whereas, if the concern was chronic with few ups and downs, longer intervals would probably be adequate (e.g., one- to five-year intervals). Instrumental events or symptoms can be penciled in to begin to establish clues about precipitants and functional variables. Multiple presenting concerns also may be presented on the same time line using different ink colors or symbols to increase understanding of

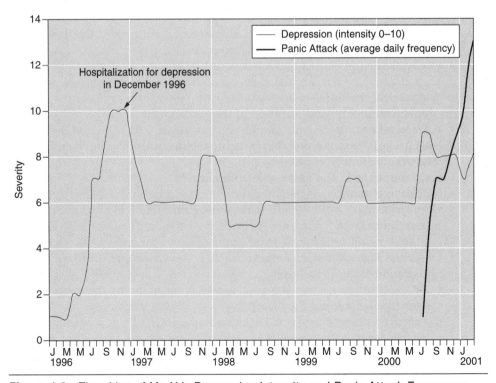

Figure 1.2   Time Line of Mr. X.'s Depression Intensity and Panic Attack Frequency

the interrelationship among symptoms (see Figure 1.2 for Mr. X's combined image of depression and anxiety).

Diagnosis A third step in describing the problem is to decide on the best-fitting diagnostic category. It should be noted, however, that diagnosis is one of the most controversial aspects of behavioral case conceptualization. Although diagnosis is typically a required element in treatment planning, there is little consensus among professionals about its usefulness in accomplishing its purported goals of communication, treatment direction, and prediction. Behavioral theorists, in particular, have lamented the limited utility of the current diagnostic classification system, the *Diagnostic and Statistical Manual of Mental Disorders* (*DSM-IV*; American Psychiatric Association, 1994). Some of the most vehement complaints have involved *DSM-IV*'s diagnoses and categories based on similar symptom topography rather than on the function of the target behavior (Follette & Houts, 1996). In the *DSM-IV*, depression and anxiety, for example, are considered entirely different disorders because they look different from one another. Follette, Houts, and Hayes (1992) argue, however, that diagnosis would be more valuable if the behaviors were classified according to the types of variables that control them. In such a system, depression and anxiety would be similarly classified if they were both maintained by negative reinforcement, for example (e.g., an increase in the target behavior [anxiety, depression] leads to a decrease in an aversive stimulus [working at a stressful job]). Other theorists and clinicians argue that diagnoses may be not only unhelpful but harmful. Some of these concerns include negative stigma and attributions for those with mental health diagnoses; negative effect on client job or insurance opportunities; unfavorable impact on clients' beliefs about themselves; inconsistent messages from different providers because of low diagnostic reliability; and minimization of the uniqueness of each client. Perhaps most detrimentally, diagnoses (which are simply descriptions of symptoms) are often used tautologically as the reasons for clients' behavior.

Although diagnosis remains debatable, it is required by most agencies and third-party payers. For this reason, some basic guidelines for conscientious diagnosis that maximize the potential for benefit and minimize the potential for harm are listed below:

1. Involve the client in the process.
   - Help the client to understand how and why you will be making a diagnosis.
   - Emphasize that diagnosis represents hope through increasing knowledge about treatment options and makes more possible use of state-of-the-art research findings.
   - Explain how diagnosis will facilitate communication with other providers.
   - Describe diagnoses as here-and-now (not lifelong) descriptions of symptoms rather than disease labels.
   - Note that the existence of a diagnostic category for the client's concern means that he or she is not alone.
2. Make accurate, careful diagnostic decisions.
   - Use structured interviews such as the SCID-I whenever possible.
   - Make sure that all diagnostic criteria are fully met before making a diagnosis.
   - Take client's cultural issues into account.

3. Never use diagnoses as names for clients (e.g., "I am seeing my borderline today").

For Mr. X., the following diagnoses were determined based on the SCID interview:

Axis I:	300.21	Panic Disorder with Agoraphobia
	296.33	Major Depressive Disorder, Recurrent, Severe without Psychotic Features, without full interepisode recovery
Axis II:	V71.09	No diagnosis
Axis III:		Noncontributory physical problems
Axis IV:		Unemployment due to depression and panic
Axis V:		50

ASSESSING THE CONTEXT

The final key assessment area for the observation phase of behavioral case conceptualization is the context within which the target behaviors occur. Context includes past as well as current factors that contribute to the cause and maintenance of the presenting concerns. According to behavioral theory, an understanding of the instrumental variables that precede and follow the target behaviors is essential to developing an effective treatment intervention.

Remote Context   The remote context refers to the historical context, especially biological, psychological, or social events that may have *causal* properties for the behavioral target. Although the concept of what actually causes a problem is elusive because it can never be truly known or tested, developing hypotheses about how the past or remote context has *set the stage* for the current behavior may be pivotal in treatment choices. All aspects of the biopsychosocial assessment are relevant for understanding this historical context, including learning and modeling, life events, genetics, physical factors, drugs or substances, and sociocultural factors.

LEARNING AND MODELING   The client's learning history may be central to understanding current behavior. For Mr. X., the clinician would want to learn whether there were any other family members who experienced similar anxiety or depressive symptoms to assess the possibility that he modeled that behavior. The clinician would also want to learn more about his vicarious (i.e., observed) and actual (i.e., experienced) reinforcement and punishment for panicky and depressive behaviors. Mr. X. reported that his mother had spent some time in the hospital for a "nervous breakdown" after his sister was born and that his father had been "a very cautious person." According to Mr. X., both parents had strict rules and frequently worried about his safety (e.g., curfews, frequent calls to make sure he was okay). He reported not knowing his one sibling (a sister, four years his junior) very well due to the age difference and the fact that she lived across the country and did not fly due to a plane phobia.

LIFE EVENTS   Both recent and past life events may play a significant role in setting the stage for the current behavior. These events may occur only once or repeatedly and may be either traumatic or pivotal in some way. Although one can never be absolutely certain that any one event or series of events *caused* the client's current condition, knowledge of salient events that may have involved important learning may help to generate hypotheses for interventions. Knowledge of significant events may alert the therapist to important antecedents or consequences of the current behavior. If a woman who experienced panic attacks cued by the sight of men with beards had also experienced child sexual abuse by a man with a beard, treatment may take a different direction than if no such history existed. In this case, the therapist may wish to focus more on the escape having been adaptive at one time.

Mr. X. reported that his childhood was stressful because his parents were so strict, but he denied any specific events or overt abuse. Instead, he reported having found his work as a police officer traumatic. He said that he dealt with tragic situations (e.g., hopeless people, car accidents, murders, domestic violence) that he felt powerless to control. He relayed that he had felt "more and more depleted" at the end of each day.

GENETIC FACTORS   Research in the area of genetics is increasing daily. Still, definitive connections between mental health concerns and genetic heritage are lacking. Nevertheless, most research indicates that the likelihood of developing mental health concerns increases when first-degree relatives also have mental health difficulties. Although some of this variance is accounted for by the behaviors and coping skills learned from a disordered parent, even children raised separately from parents with mental health concerns have a greater chance of developing mental health concerns themselves (Kendler & Robinette, 1983). Thus, it is important to assess the client's familial history of psychological and substance abuse problems. It is also important to assess the extent to which clients believe that their conditions are genetic. This may help to ascertain a treatment direction. Some research suggests, for example, that depression with a probable genetic or endogenous component responds better to psychotropic medication than to psychotherapy (Jarrett, 1995).

As noted above, Mr. X. said that both parents had showed some anxious and depressive behaviors. Only his mother had ever received treatment for the "nervous breakdown." When asked to elaborate, Mr. X. said that he had been 4 years old at the time and did not remember much about what behaviors may have constituted the breakdown.

PHYSICAL FACTORS   Any number of physical factors may be involved in causing, maintaining, or exacerbating the client's presenting problems. Depression, for example, may be sequelae of endocrine dysfunction such as hyper- or hypothyroidism. Panic Disorder may be caused or worsened by heart conditions such as mitral-valve prolapse. A more comprehensive list of the various medical conditions that may be related to psychological disorders is provided in Morrison's (1995) *DSM-IV Made Easy: The Clinician's Guide to Diagnosis.* An initial evaluation that includes thorough questioning about possible physical conditions coupled with a recent physical examination and medical records is essential so that serious or complicating physical factors are referred for the appropriate care.

Mr. X. reported that, although he was convinced there must be something wrong with him physically, none of myriad medical tests (e.g., ECG, EKG, CAT scan, blood workup) had revealed any physical problems. He said he had mixed feelings about the lack of findings. On the one hand, it meant that he might not be dying; on the other hand, his only other explanation for his panic attacks was that he was going crazy or that he had some fatal condition that had not been detected yet.

DRUGS OR SUBSTANCES   A variety of substances, including alcohol, prescription drugs, illegal drugs, over-the-counter drugs, and alternative medications, may be related to mental health conditions. Thorough assessment of current medications in all of these categories is vital to evaluating the extent to which a recent increase, decrease, initiation, or discontinuation may fully or partially account for the client's current symptoms.

Mr. X. denied any alcohol or illicit drug use. He said that until the panic began, he would have about three beers a week. After the panic began, he became concerned that the alcohol would bring on an attack and had avoided it since. He did note that he was taking Wellbutrin as prescribed for his depression and anxiety. He reported some relief from the severe anhedonia and sleep problems, but denied any other significant relief from the anxiety or depression.

SOCIOCULTURAL FACTORS   Clients' sex, age, ethnic heritage, religion, socioeconomic status, and education may all be related in idiosyncratic ways to presenting concerns. Behavioral theorists are most interested in the ways that social and cultural factors may affect the learning history and available punishers, reinforcers, models, and beliefs. Such information may help to form hypotheses about behavioral and cognitive interventions that may be especially helpful.

For Mr. X., being a young, middle-income, professional Caucasian male experiencing depression and anxiety along with recent unemployment has led to some punishing responses from family and peers who expect a man of his age and status to be successfully earning a wage. He also reported some beliefs about himself based on his perceptions of cultural values for young, professional men: "I must be the primary breadwinner in my family"; "A sign of economic failure is a sign of personal failure"; "I should deal with this alone and not let anyone see how distressed I am."

Recent Context   Recent context refers to the current antecedents and consequences that are *maintaining* the target behavior. More specifically, the context of most interest in behavioral case conceptualization is the functional relationship between internal and external events that precede and follow the target behavior. To assess these variables, a functional assessment interview is typically conducted with adult clients. The focus of this interview may be behaviors as they *usually occur*, or a *recent, specific* example of the behavior. The former is likely to provide information about clients' theories about causes for their depression; the latter may provide more concrete information about a specific episode. Both may be important in developing hypotheses about treatment and should be assessed.

It is essential to note here that clients may not always be good observers or reporters of these contingent relationships. There are at least three ways that clients' verbal reports of contingent relationships may be suspect. First, some clients may lack awareness of the actual contingencies. Clients with panic attacks, for example, may report that escaping from an anxiety-provoking situation and receiving subsequent support from family members is helpful in reducing their panic, whereas these very consequences may be maintaining and exacerbating the severity and frequency of their panic. Second, clients' verbal reports may be influenced more by the in-session environmental contingencies than the actual events they are reporting on. Thus, clients may be unsure about the contingencies and unwittingly base their responses on actual (e.g., head nods, "uh-uh's") or anticipated (e.g., beliefs about social desirability) therapist reinforcements. Third, clients' beliefs about consequences of reporting contingencies may also deter them. For example, clients who receive disability payments due to their mental health concerns may not reveal to their therapist (or acknowledge to themselves) that these payments provide a positive reinforcement for their avoidance, while the avoidance is further negatively reinforced by relief from the discomfort of being in the work environment. Taken together, these problems highlight the importance of approaching functional analytic interviewing as a hypothesis-generating endeavor rather than a fact-finding mission.

ANTECEDENTS   The events that immediately precede target behavior and increase the probability that the behavior will occur are labeled antecedents. They are not considered causal in the strictest sense, but they do increase the probability that the target behavior will occur. Skinner (1974) remarked that if human behavior were simply reflexive responses to stimuli, then "An organism would have much of the character of a puppet, robot, or machine. But stimuli do not *elicit* operant responses; they simply modify the probability that the responses will be emitted" (p. 245). Instead, a stimulus becomes an antecedent when the behavior has been reinforced immediately following the antecedent in the past. The antecedent is strengthened with each resultant reinforcement. The antecedent then becomes a signal that reinforcement is likely to occur when the target behavior is performed. If the target behavior is picking up the phone and saying "Hello," the antecedent is the phone ringing. The ringing signals an increased probability that answering the phone will be reinforced with a response. Most people do not answer the phone when it is not ringing because reinforcement is unlikely. If, on the other hand, an individual has received a number of telemarketing calls in the past hour, he or she may perceive that the probability for a reinforcing interaction has diminished and opt to not answer succeeding rings. Hence, the phone's ringing does not *cause* phone answering, it simply increases the probability that the phone will be answered and that reinforcement will follow.

Much like behavioral targets, antecedents for psychological issues may be internal or external. Internal antecedents may be physical, emotional, or cognitive; external antecedents may be behavioral or environmental (e.g., situation, location, people). After identifying the target behavior as described above, the next step in functional analytic interviewing is to identify antecedents that increase the probability that the target behavior will occur. As noted above, the focus of this interview may be on either a recent prototypical example or the client's impressions of what usually happens. Questions that may elicit clients' observations of pertinent antecedents are listed below. See Table 1.1 for the results of this functional analysis with Mr. X. The target behavior for the following interview questions is the panic attacks with a *recent severe panic* as the focal period. An assessment of *what usually happens* prior to a panic attack may follow this assessment.

- When was your most recent severe panic attack (i.e., greater than an 8 on a scale of 0 to 10)?
- What was happening *around you* right before that attack? (environmental)
  - Where were you? (location)
  - Who was with you? What were they doing? (people)
  - What was going on? (situation)

Table 1.1
Results of Mr. X.'s Functional Analytic Interview

Behavioral Target	Antecedents	Consequences		
		Exacerbating Factors	Mitigating Factors	Secondary Gain
Panic Attacks	**Overt** • Being in any situation in which escape might be difficult if a panic attack were to occur. **Covert** • Emotional: increased anxiety and depression. • Cognitive: predicting that a panic attack will occur (e.g., "Oh my God! I am going to have a panic attack!"). • Physical: sweaty, light-headed.	**Overt** • Staying in the situation. • Others asking if okay. **Covert** • Cognitive: catastrophic predications about the consequences of panicking (e.g., "This is going to be the big one"; "I'm really going to go crazy this time").	**Overt** • Leaving the situation. • Staying at home. • Taking deep breaths. **Covert** • Cognitive: reassuring thoughts (e.g., "I haven't died yet, there's no reason to think it will happen this time").	• Wife is supportive and understanding when he experiences panic. • Does not have to take on responsibility of occupational or domestic tasks.
Depressed Mood Greater than an 8	**Overt** • Home alone. • turns down social engagement. **Covert** • Emotional: increased anxiety. • Cognitive: berating self for inability to resolve panic (e.g., "I am such a weak person!"). • Having just had a panic attack.	**Overt** • Inactivity. • Turning down opportunities to do things with family because afraid of panic attacks. **Covert** • Cognitive: continued berating self for inability to resolve panic. Thinking about all the things he used to do before developing depression and panic.	**Overt** • Staying in bed. • Having wife say she understands. • Spending time with family. **Covert** • Cognitive: normalizing (e.g., "It is normal for people to feel depressed once in a while"; "I don't have to be perfectly responsive at all times").	• Wife is supportive and understanding when he experiences panic. • Does not have to take on responsibility of occupational or domestic tasks. • Depressed mood makes it easier to avoid anxiety-provoking situations.

- What were you *doing* right before the attack? (behavioral)
- What was happening *inside of you* right before the attack? (internal)
    - What were you feeling physically? (physical)
    - What emotions or feelings were you having? (emotional)
    - What thoughts were going through your head? (cognitive)

CONSEQUENCES   The instrumental events that follow the target behavior are labeled consequences. Consequences are those internal or external events that either increase or decrease the probability that the behavior will occur again. At the most basic level, consequences that increase the target behavior are called *reinforcers;* those that reduce the target behavior are called *punishers.* At a more technical level, either reinforcement or punishment can be divided into positive or negative depending on whether an increase or decrease in the consequence leads to a change in the target behavior. See the examples below in the context of Mr. X.'s panic attacks and agoraphobic avoidance:

- *Positive reinforcement:* An *increase* in a consequence (e.g., wife's nurturing support after a panic attack) leads to an *increased* probability that the target behavior (e.g., panic attack) will occur in the future.
- *Negative reinforcement:* A *decrease* in an aversive consequence (e.g., reduced anxiety after avoiding an anxiety-provoking situation) leads to an *increased* probability that the target behavior (e.g., avoidance) will occur in the future.
- *Positive punishment:* An *increase* in a consequence (e.g., increased anxiety in places where escape may be difficult) leads to a *decreased* probability that the target behavior (e.g., staying in car on crowded freeway) will occur in the future.
- *Negative punishment:* A *decrease* in a consequence (e.g., decreased positive self-talk following anxiety-provoking situations) leads to a *decreased* probability that the target behavior (e.g., staying in anxiety-provoking situations) will occur in the future.

In practice, when the target of the functional analysis is an undesired behavior, positive and negative punishment are often grouped under the more global heading of *mitigating factors.* Positive reinforcement often is termed an *exacerbating factor,* and negative reinforcement is sometimes termed *secondary gain.*

Consequences, like antecedents and target behaviors, can be internal (physical, emotional, and cognitive) and external (behavioral and environmental). Questions that may elicit responses from clients to aid in forming hypotheses about consequential functional variables are listed below. See Table 1.1 for the results of Mr. X.'s functional analytic interview.

1. Exacerbating factors
   - What happens *outside of you* that makes the situation *worse?* (e.g., What do you do and say? What do others do and say? What about the situation makes it worse?).
   - What happens *inside of you* after the panic that makes the situation *worse?* (e.g., What do you feel emotionally, and physically? What do you say to yourself after you have a panic attack?).
2. Mitigating factors
   - What happens *outside of you* that makes the situation *better?* (e.g., What do you do and say? What do others do and say? What about the situation makes it worse?).
   - What happens *inside of you* after the panic that makes the situation *better?* (e.g., What do you feel emotionally, and physically? What do you say to yourself after you have a panic attack?).
3. Secondary gain
   - Is there any relief from any other *external* activities as a result of this problem? (e.g., Have your work or home responsibilities changed? Have others

changed their demands on you? Have you changed your demands on yourself? Are you getting any compensation as a result of this problem?).

- Is there any part or any time in this problem that you experience some relief from something uncomfortable *inside of you?* (e.g., Do you experience any physical or emotional relief at any time during this problem? Is there anything uncomfortable that you think about less as a result of this problem?).

Again, it is important to note that clients may not be aware of the functional relationships that are maintaining their behaviors. It is unlikely, for example, that clients would recognize that staying in an anxiety-provoking situation during a panic attack could be a mitigating factor because they feel worse in the moment. This is where it is important for the therapist to have a good grasp of behavioral theory and some probable types of consequences that may be maintaining a behavior to augment the information offered verbally by the client. (See the section on Hypotheses about Maintenance for common types of functional relationships with certain presenting concerns.) Nevertheless, even inaccurate information from clients can represent useful clinical tools. Reports of contingencies often reveal salient beliefs that may be keeping the client stuck (e.g., "The only thing that keeps me from dying is getting out of the stressful situation right away!"). This gives the therapist clues about beliefs that can be dispelled through education, experimenting with alternative hypotheses (e.g., trying out new behaviors such as staying in the situation), and self-monitoring (e.g., so client learns that immediate relief does not transfer into long-term gain).

Observation is classically considered the first phase of the scientific method. For practicing scientist-clinicians, however, this process continues throughout therapy, as will be evident in the later discussion on testing hypotheses and revising hypotheses.

DEVELOPING HYPOTHESES: TREATMENT PLANNING

The observation phase is followed by the developing hypotheses phase of the scientific method. Once the phenomena or the presenting concerns are observed or assessed in behavioral case conceptualization, then testable hypotheses as to cause, maintenance, and treatment are developed. The goal here is for the clinician to consolidate the following information: client observations of self, therapist observations of the client, therapist knowledge of behavioral theory, empirical findings with this client (e.g., self-monitoring), and empirical findings with other clients with similar concerns.

HYPOTHESES ABOUT CAUSE

Behaviorists often have shied away from the concept of cause, focusing instead on currently observable variables. Although the value of current behavior and contingencies cannot be underestimated, hypotheses about the client's history may provide important hints about salient contingencies and genetic endowments that might not be immediately apparent in a functional assessment based only on the present. The variables typically addressed in hypotheses about cause include those assessed in the biopsychosocial assessment, specifically: learning and modeling, life events, genetic factors, physical factors, substances and drugs, and sociocultural factors.

Given the biopsychosocial assessment for Mr. X., it appears that learning/modeling, genetic factors, life events, and sociocultural factors may play causal roles. Examples of hypotheses about cause that may be generated for Mr. X. include the following:

- Mr. X. learned at an early age, through modeling and reinforcement, that the world is dangerous (e.g., parent's concerns about safety were modeled) and that cautiousness is rewarded (e.g., he was reinforced when he engaged in safety behaviors).
- Simultaneously, his family history of depression and anxiety may have genetically predisposed him to manifest his responses to stress in similar ways.
- While he was a police officer, he witnessed traumatic events that challenged his central beliefs regarding the importance of safety and the role of control (e.g., "As long as I am always careful, I and others can always be safe"). Instead, he learned that there are some events over which he has no control. This leads to feelings of panic when not in control.
- The majority of men in his ethnocultural group are employed and do not have depression or anxiety disorders. The societal expectation is that young married men will contribute financially to their family and maintain a modicum of mental health. Mr. X. may have experienced feelings of shame and fear as a result of not living up to society's expectations of him. These expectations may be contributing to the cause of his current intractable depression.

HYPOTHESES ABOUT MAINTENANCE

Embedded in the behavioral case conceptualization are hypotheses about current factors that are maintaining the client's presenting concerns. The functional analytic interview is the centerpiece for hypotheses about maintenance. However, because clients may not always be accurate observers of the contingencies of their own behavior, behavioral theory, the empirical literature, and any additional self-monitoring data also are important in generating these hypotheses.

Behavioral theory posits that a reinforcer increases the probability that the behavior will occur again, whereas a punisher decreases the probability that the behavior will occur again. Likewise, effectively modifying either the functional antecedents or consequences should change the target behavior. Thus, the only way to know if the correct contingencies have been identified is to monitor the target behavior and the contingencies. If Mr. X.'s proposal—that escaping an anxiety-provoking situation is a mitigating factor—is correct, then the more he escapes, the less anxiety he will experience. On the other hand, if his anxiety gets worse and worse with continued escape, this behavior may represent a negative reinforcer that keeps the behavior going. In addition, if Mr. X. begins staying in the anxiety-provoking situation and the panic attacks begin to diminish, then it is likely that the escape response is being extinguished.

There is an extensive empirical literature on the factors that tend to maintain certain types of presenting concerns. Because depression and anxiety are the most common reasons that people seek help in outpatient psychology clinics (Kelleher, Talcott, Haddock, & Freeman, 1996), those will be addressed briefly here. (See Chapters 2 through 7 in this text for more detailed information on depression and anxiety and Chapters 8 through 12 for eating disorders, personality disorders, impulse control disorders, and sexual and marital dysfunctions.) Through observation of factors that tend to worsen depression and anxiety as well as strategic modification of certain variables, common patterns emerge (see Table 1.2). Depression tends to be maintained with behavioral factors, such as a reduction in pleasurable or mastery activities or a preponderance of aversive activities (e.g., difficult social interactions, lack of contingent relationship between behavior and outcomes). Behaviors that tend to reduce depression are the reverse of these behavioral deficits or excesses. Cognitive variables that tend to increase depression are unrealistic predictions, labels, or standards about self, others, or the world that focus on themes of helplessness, hopelessness, and worthlessness. Anxiety, in contrast, tends to be maintained by the negative reinforcement inherent in escape; when individuals escape the anxiety-provoking stimulus, they experience profound relief. Such relief then increases the escape response and reinforces beliefs that the stimulus is catastrophic (e.g., "It was so bad, I had to get out of there or I would have died"; "If I hadn't avoided thinking about it, I would have completely lost it"). Having knowledge of the empirical findings regarding common contingencies of presenting concerns may help the clinician evaluate accuracy of clients' reports. Mr. X.'s contention that his depression is helped by staying home in bed all day does not match the empirical findings that inactivity tends to exacerbate depression, whereas high levels of pleasurable and mastery activities reduce depression. However, he may experience less aversive activity (i.e., fewer panic attacks) when he avoids activity. Also, his statement that the best way to reduce his panic is to get out of the situation is inconsistent with the data on what improves panic in the long run; instead, he may have been reporting on the short-term benefit of escape.

Taken together, the functional analytic interview, behavioral theory, the empirical literature, and pertinent hypotheses about cause lead to the following hypotheses about maintenance for Mr. X.:

- Mr. X.'s panic is worsened by:
  - The occurrence of antecedents in which he has little control.
  - Beliefs that he will die while having a panic attack (e.g., at the first physiological sign of an attack, he says to himself, "Oh no! I really am going to die this time!").
  - Beliefs that he must be in control at all times.
  - Negative reinforcement (relief) he experiences when he escapes an anxiety-provoking situation.
  - Negative reinforcement (relief) he experiences when dismissed from household and parenting responsibilities.
- Mr. X.'s depression is worsened by:
  - The occurrence of panic attacks.
  - A reduction in pleasurable and mastery activity due to avoidance of anxiety-provoking activities (interaction between anxiety and depression) and low motivation.
  - Beliefs that he should not be experiencing "weak" emotions such as anxiety and sadness and that he should be gainfully employed.
  - Positive reinforcement he experiences when his wife inquires compassionately about his sadness.

Table 1.2
Common Functional Variables for Depression and Anxiety

	Common Exacerbating Factors	Common Mitigating Factors
Depression	*Behavioral* (see Leahy & Holland, 2000, for a review)	
	Reduction of positive and rewarding behavior.	Increasing pleasurable activities, mastery activities and exercise (Lewinsohn & Gotlib, 1995).
	Behavior that has become less rewarding.	
	Lack of self-reward.	Increasing self-reward.
	Skill deficits.	Improving social skills (Bellack, Hersen, & Himmelhoch, 1996).
	Lack of assertion.	Increasing problem-solving skills (Nezu & Perri, 1989).
	Exposure to aversive situations.	Reducing aversive situations (Lewinsohn & Gotlib, 1995).
	Poor problem-solving skills.	Increasing problem-solving skills (Nezu & Perri, 1989).
	Noncontingency of behavior and outcomes.	Increasing awareness of relationship between behavior and outcomes (McCullough, 2000).
	Relationship conflict.	Improving marital satisfaction (Jacobson, Dobson, Fruzzetti, Schmaling, & Salusky, 1991).
	Cognitive	
	Self-defeating thoughts about self, others, and the world focused on themes of worthlessness, helplessness, and hopelessness (cf. Beck, Rush, Shaw, & Emery, 1979).	Realistic, moderate, constructive predictions, labels, and standards about self, others, and the world (cf. Dobson, 1989).
Anxiety	*Behavioral*	
	Anxiety is typically exacerbated by some element of escaping an anxiety-provoking situation. The relief experienced after escape negatively reinforces (strengthens) the escape response (Barlow, 1988).	
Panic	Avoidance of physical symptoms of panic (Craske & Barlow, 1993).	Exposure to physical symptoms of panic (Schmidt et al., 2000).
Phobias	Avoidance of trigger stimuli (Barlow, 1988).	Exposure to feared situations (Oest, 1989).
PTSD	Avoidance of reexperiencing of trauma (Keane, Zimering, & Caddell, 1985).	Exposure to alarming images and memories (Foa et al., 1999).
GAD	Worry that functions as avoidance of visualizing feared catastrophic images (Stavosky & Borkovec, 1987).	Exposure to visualizations of feared images (Borkovec & Costello, 1993).

(continued)

Table 1.2   *(Continued)*

	Common Exacerbating Factors	Common Mitigating Factors
Anxiety	*Behavioral*	
OCD	Compulsions that function as avoidance of obsessions (Riggs & Foa, 1993).	Exposure to obsessions and feared stimuli (Abramowitz, 1997).
	Cognitive	
	Beliefs are often focused on cata-strophic predictions about the fu-ture that lead to attempts to avoid or escape (Barlow, 1988).	Realistic, moderate, constructive beliefs that emphasize the client's ability to cope and de-emphasize the dangerousness of anxiety (Chambless & Gillis, 1993).

Note: PTSD = Posttraumatic Stress disorders; GAD = Generalized Anxiety Disorder; OCD = Obsessive-Compulsive Disorder.

- Negative reinforcement (relief) he experiences when dismissed from household and parenting responsibilities.

Because behavioral intervention hinges on an accurate understanding of the functional relationships between the target behaviors and contingencies, hypotheses about maintenance lay the foundation for hypotheses about treatment.

HYPOTHESES ABOUT TREATMENT

The final step is to develop hypotheses about treatment. Such hypotheses should flow logically from information collected in the observation phase as well as the hypotheses developed about cause and maintenance. In the behavioral tradition of empiricism, developing hypotheses about treatment also should take into account the empirical literature on effective treatments. Furthermore, from a pragmatic perspective, good hypotheses about treatment should address cost-effectiveness, affordability, therapist competence, client preference, and client stage of change.

Functional Relationships   First and foremost, the functional relationship between the target behaviors and the potential contingencies should be seriously consid-ered. It was noted above that one of the central features of behavioral theory is that a change in an important antecedent or consequence should also modify the target behavior. If changing hypothesized contingencies does not lead to a change in the targeted behavior, then the hypotheses regarding the contingent relationships are probably in error. Hence, sound hypotheses about antecedents and consequences that are maintaining the behavior are fundamental to the treatment plan. If, for ex-ample, a client is depressed and the functional analysis suggests that primary an-tecedents for feeling more depressed are negative social interactions and primary exacerbating consequences are verbally abusive interchanges, then social interac-tions and social skills would probably be targeted for intervention. For Mr. X., hypotheses about maintenance point to the importance of catastrophic beliefs and avoidance for his panic attacks. Although his depression is more long-standing, it appears that the panic attacks may account for the recent exacerbation through the side effects of anxious avoidance (i.e., reduction in activity, unemployment, and reinforcement of beliefs about worthlessness). Treatment, therefore, should address both behavioral (i.e., avoidance) and cognitive (i.e., catastrophic beliefs) variables.

Empirical Literature   The second step in deciding on a treatment direction is a literature review of effective treatments specific to the client's presenting condition. As described above, the American Psychological Association's Division 12 Task Force (1995) has developed criteria for defining treatments as empirically supported or validated, emphasizing the role of well-controlled group or single-subject designs to establish a treatment's efficacy. Inherent in these criteria is the expectation that clinicians maximize a client's opportunity to improve by using treatments with empirical support. A comprehensive, critical literature review for every client may be beyond the capability of many practicing clinicians, but some excellent resources effectively summarize empirically supported interventions for an array of presenting concerns (cf. Nathan & Gorman, 1998). Even though a common criticism of the tightly controlled research is that subjects and therapists are not representative of real clinical settings (Goldfried & Wolfe, 1996), an increasing body of literature suggests that community applications of empirically validated treatments yield results similar to those from randomized controlled clinical trials (cf. Sanderson, Raue, & Wetzler, 1998; Wade, Treat, & Stuart, 1998). An additional benefit to seeking empirically supported treatments is that, by definition, the research treatments must have been conducted by a manual. This means that step-by-step instructions should be available for duplicating the interventions used in these studies. Sources of such treatment manuals focused on adult clients include *The Clinical Handbook of Psychological Disorders*, 3rd ed. (Barlow, 2001) and *Sourcebook of Psychological Treatment Manuals for Adult Disorders* (Van Hasselt & Hersen, 1996). Although clients often have idiosyncratic concerns or multiple problems that are not adequately addressed through available empirically supported treatments, these manuals, or components within, may provide important ingredients to a behavioral intervention.

With regard to Mr. X.'s presenting problems, empirically supported interventions exist for both panic attacks and depression. Based on a meta-analysis of 43 controlled clinical trials for Panic Disorder with Agoraphobia, Gould, Otto, and Pollack (1995) concluded that treatment packages, including education, relaxation, cognitive restructuring, and exposure to the physical symptoms of panic (interoceptive exposure), were the most effective interventions available. These typically resulted in 87% of clients achieving a panic-free state at the end of 15 weeks of treatment. Results of this meta-analysis also indicated that interventions including interoceptive exposure were superior to medication or cognitive-behavioral therapy without interoceptive exposure. Recent reviews of depression interventions suggest that cognitive-behavioral and interpersonal treatments are similarly efficacious in reducing depressive symptoms. Typically, these interventions lead to approximately 60% of clients reaching clinically significantly improvement by the end of 12 to 20 sessions of therapy (cf. Craighead, Craighead, & Ilardi, 1998). Although antidepressant medication is also an effective treatment for depression, a number of studies indicate that it may not be as durable as cognitive-behavioral therapy (Evans et al., 1992). The treatment outcome literature on comorbid Panic Disorder and depression indicate that depression symptoms do not appear to deter panic treatment (Black, Wesner, Bowers, Monahan, & Gabel, 1995; McLean, Woody, Taylor, & Koch, 1998) and may be ameliorated during the course of the panic treatment (Lidren et al., 1994; Wade et al., 1998). The role of panic in depression treatment, on the other hand, is less well understood, although some literature suggests that anxiety in general may hinder progress in depression treatment (Brent et al., 1998).

Pragmatic Concerns   An essential element in successful treatment planning from any theoretical orientation is a consideration of pragmatic concerns. The most elegant conceptualization and plan are of little utility if they are not feasible or acceptable to either the client or the therapist.

For a treatment to be feasible it must address priority concerns while being cost-effective, affordable, and within the therapist's range of competence. Cost-effectiveness refers to the ratio of effectiveness to cost. Treatment choices should aim to maximize effectiveness while minimizing cost. Second and relatedly, the proposed treatment must be feasible given the client's financial and time constraints. If a client has eight sessions through his or her managed care organization, the treatment plan should not exceed this without an agreement with the client about how payment for the additional sessions will be handled. Third, clinicians must have adequate training and/or supervision in the approaches they use. If the most effective treatment available for a client's presenting concern is outside the therapist's repertoire of skills, a referral should be made to another clinician or the necessary supervision should be obtained.

A treatment should be plausible, attractive, and tailored to clients' readiness to change. If it is not, the client may be unlikely to either stay in or benefit from therapy (Steenbarger, 1994). Plausible, attractive interventions often are those that are consistent with clients' conceptualizations. If a client wishes to resolve a nail-biting problem and the therapist maintains that an exploration of childhood relationships is the best route to its resolution, the client may not see the proposed intervention as plausible or helpful. Thus, treatment plans should address clients' primary presenting concern first in the absence of factors that may contraindicate it (e.g., significant risk issues such as suicidal ideation, homicidal ideation, violence, and substance abuse, which need immediate attention). Similarly, clients' readiness for change should be considered in the choice of interventions. McConnaughy, DiClemente, Prochaska, and Velicer (1989) developed five stages of change pertaining to psychotherapy: precontemplation, contemplation, decision making, action, and maintenance. Precontemplative individuals either do not perceive that they have a problem or believe that others or the environment need to change. Those in the contemplative stage recognize that they have a problem but are unsure whether the benefits of change outweigh the costs of changing. Those in the decision-making or preparation stage recognize the problem and have made some preliminary steps toward change. Individuals in the action stage have made substantive steps toward change, and those in the maintenance stage have already achieved their goals and would like to maintain the changes. Prochaska and Norcross (1999) have proposed a transtheoretical model of intervention that suggests different interventions will be more successful at different stages of change. Clients in early stages of change may benefit most from interventions that focus on increasing awareness of problem behaviors such as giving feedback about assessments or self-monitoring; clients in later stages of change may make the most change through action-oriented interventions such as goal setting and cognitive restructuring. At least one study suggests that premature psychotherapy dropouts can be differentiated from therapy completers based on the match between stage of change and interventions (Brogan, Prochaska, & Prochaska, 1999).

For Mr. X., among the most cost-effective interventions are 12- to 20-session cognitive-behavioral treatments (cf. Antonuccio et al., 1997). They are feasible within his insurance allotment of 20 sessions yearly and the therapist's primary training is in cognitive and behavioral interventions. Mr. X. identified a strong preference for targeting his panic symptoms first. He felt that the panic was more debilitating and urgent than the depression. Although his depression was severe, he was not experiencing suicidal ideation or other conditions that would mandate priority attention. He also believed that the panic was ultimately exacerbating his underlying depressive symptoms. He expressed tentative interest in later addressing the depressive symptoms if they did not remit in the course of panic treatment. His stage of change was informally identified as preparation. He had begun making some changes in his life to reduce his panic symptoms, including seeing a psychiatrist, beginning regular relaxation practice, and reading self-help books about panic attacks, but he had not made the sweeping behavioral changes that would place him in the action stage.

Hypotheses about Mr. X.'s Treatment   After reviewing the functional relationships between the target behavior and the contingencies, the empirical literature, and pragmatic concerns, hypotheses about treatment should be generated. The hypotheses about Mr. X.'s treatment follow:

- Mr. X.'s panic attacks exacerbate and maintain his depression through reaffirming beliefs of worthlessness and reduced satisfying activity due to anxious avoidance.
- Treatment will be effective if panic treatment precedes depression treatment due to the client's preference and empirical evidence supporting the effectiveness of panic treatment with comorbid panic and depression.
- Panic treatment will be effective if it addresses the hypothesized functional relationships between panic and contingencies. Specifically, interventions should focus on reducing the catastrophic beliefs that are escalating the panic and extinguishing the escape response that is currently negatively reinforced by relief.
- Panic treatment that includes education, relaxation, cognitive restructuring, and exposure to the physical symptoms of panic (extinguishing the escape response) will effectively reduce Mr. X.'s panic symptoms because it:
  - Is consistent with the hypothesized pertinent functional relationships.
  - Has the best data to support its effectiveness with panic symptoms.
  - Is unlikely to be negatively impacted by the depressive symptoms.
  - Is cost-effective and feasible for client and therapist.

- Addresses the client's priority concerns first with action-oriented interventions to meet him in the preparation stage.

DEVELOPING A TREATMENT PLAN

After hypotheses about cause, maintenance, and treatment are generated, a treatment plan that defines specific goals, interventions, measurements, and a time line and is endorsed by client and therapist is developed. It is vital that this process involve close collaboration between therapist and client. Client involvement in treatment planning is essential to its accuracy and feasibility. A client who has contributed and agreed to a treatment plan may be more likely to actively participate in treatment, continue in treatment during difficult interventions (e.g., exposure), and complete the treatment plan. This collaborative treatment plan should enable clinician and client to test the hypotheses regarding treatment.

Goals   The treatment plan should include goals that are consistent with hypotheses regarding treatment and are sufficiently specific to allow for evaluation of the treatment hypotheses. The goals should meet the following SMART criteria (see Figure 1.3 for Mr. X.'s treatment plan):

- *Specific:* Goals should target specific variables with observable referents that are relevant to the client's presenting concerns (e.g., intensity of depressed mood, frequency of panic).
- *Measurable:* Goals should include an observable, objective scale of measurement that is meaningful to the client (e.g., on a scale of 0 to 10; daily frequency).
- *Anchored:* To assess whether sufficient progress was made, goals should include the current level and the client's desired level at the end of treatment (e.g., intensity of depressed mood will be reduced from a daily average of 9 to a daily average of 5).
- *Realistic:* Goals should be realistic given client's current and past functioning as well as available treatment time.
- *Time line:* Goals should include a target date for goals to be accomplished.

Interventions   To assess whether the hypotheses about treatment are correct, an intervention plan should be outlined with a clear relationship between goals and interventions. The interventions should target the hypothesized functional relationships and be grounded in the empirical literature, if possible. See Figure 1.3 for an outline of Mr. X.'s interventions as they relate to his goals.

Measurements   Assessment of client progress is essential to both ethical practice and hypothesis testing. Without measurement, clinicians cannot adequately evaluate whether progress is being made. Here again, the measurements should have an objective, observable component and directly reflect the client's goals. Both standardized (e.g., BDI-II) and idiographic measurement (e.g., depressed mood rated on self-defined 0 to 10 point scale) are recommended to assess clients' outcome relative to the population and themselves. See Figure 1.3 for measurements related to Mr. X.'s goals.

Client: Mr. X.   Primary Therapist: Dr. Truax   Current Date: 1/5/01   Target Date: 3/23/01

Primary Presenting Concerns:

Panic attacks, anxiety, and depression. Mr. X. presents with a 5-year history of recurrent depression without interepisode recovery and a 6-month history of generalized anxiety and panic attacks. Current average intensity for both anxiety and depression is an 8 (0–10 point scale, with larger numbers representing greater severity) and he averages 11 panic attacks daily. As a result, his occupational functioning is severely impaired (i.e., he is unemployed) and he avoids nearly all activities that involve leaving the house.

Diagnoses:

Axis 1:	300.21	Panic Disorder with Agoraphobia
	296.33	Major Depressive Disorder, Recurrent, Severe without Psychotic Features, without full interepisode recovery
Axis II:	V71.09	No diagnosis
Axis III:		Noncontributory physical or medical problems
Axis IV:		Unemployment due to depression and panic
Axis V:		Current functioning = 50

Primary Goals:

1. Reduce frequency of panic attacks from 11 times daily to 3 times daily.
2. Reduce intensity of daily anxiety from an average of 8 to an average of 5.
3. Reduce severity of avoidance from the severe range to the mild range.

Secondary Goals:

4. Reduce intensity of depressed mood from daily average of 8 to an average of 4.
5. Reduce severity of depression from the severe range to the mild range.

Interventions:

1. Relaxation Training: diaphragmatic breathing, progressive muscle relaxation, cue-controlled relaxation, and recall relaxation (Goals 1 & 2).
2. Cognitive Restructuring: identifying activating events, alarming beliefs, consequences, more reassuring beliefs, and more adaptive coping (Goals 1–5).
3. Interoceptive Exposure: developing a hierarchy and conducting graded exposure to physiological symptoms of panic (Goals 1, 2, & 3).
4. In vivo Exposure: developing a hierarchy and conducting graded exposure to avoided situations due to panic (Goals 1–5).

Measurements:	Schedule
Self-monitoring of frequency of panic attacks (Goal 1)	Daily
Self-monitoring of average daily intensity of anxiety on a 0–10 scale (0 = no anxiety, 10 = most anxiety imaginable) (Goal 2)	Daily
Mobility Inventory (Goal 3)	Monthly
Self-monitoring of daily intensity of depression on a 0–10 scale (0 = no depression, 10 = most depression imaginable) (Goal 4)	Daily
Beck Depression Inventory-II (Goal 5)	Monthly

(continued)

Figure 1.3   Mr. X.'s Treatment Plan

Agreement:

By signing this plan, I agree to complete the above outlined treatment plan. this will entail participating in weekly therapy sessions and regular completion of tasks outside the session. If either client or therapist is concerned about the progress of therapy, the concerned party will address the issue in-session as soon as possible.

Prioritized summary and timeframe:

12 weekly sessions targeting goals 1–3 (Sessions 1–8: Relaxation Training and Cognitive Restructuring; Sessions 5–12: Interoceptive Exposure, Sessions 8–12: In Vivo Exposure)

Client Signature: _____   Therapist Signature: _____

Figure 1.3   (Continued)

TESTING HYPOTHESES PHASE: IMPLEMENTING THE TREATMENT PLAN

The final stage of behavioral case conceptualization involves testing hypotheses by conducting the treatment and measuring the outcome according to the plan. If the data suggest that the hypotheses were incorrect or that the methods are insufficient to test the hypotheses, client and clinician return to the observation phase to develop new hypotheses and a revised plan. Clinicians also should carefully educate clients about extinction-based interventions that are designed to temporarily increase distress so that successful interventions are not abandoned prematurely. A brief synopsis of Mr. X.'s hypothesis test follows. Per the treatment plan, 12 sessions were conducted. See Craske and Barlow (1993) for details of interventions.

IMPLEMENTING THE TREATMENT PLAN

Sessions 1 to 8
- *Education:* Throughout the course of treatment, Mr. X. was educated about the physiology of anxiety and relaxation, the role of escape in maintaining anxiety, and the role of exposure in extinguishing escape response.
- *Relaxation training:* Mr. X. learned and implemented relaxation techniques through education, modeling, and in- and out-of-session practice of diaphragmatic breathing, progressive muscle relaxation, cue-controlled relaxation, and recall relaxation.
- *Cognitive restructuring:* Mr. X. learned to challenge the beliefs that preceded increases in his anxiety through education, modeling, and in- and out-of-session practice of identifying triggering events, alarming beliefs, problematic consequences, more reassuring alternative beliefs, and the consequences of revised beliefs.

Session 5
- *Developed interoceptive exposure hierarchy:* Mr. X. participated in 10 different exercises designed to elicit physiological symptoms related to his panic (e.g., breathing through a thin straw for one minute, spinning in a chair for one

minute). He then rated the intensity of his physiological responses, the similarity to his panic symptoms, and his anxiety. Then a hierarchy was developed from least to most severe. (See Craske & Barlow, 1993, for details about developing an interoceptive exposure hierarchy.)

Sessions 6 to 12
- *Conducted the interoceptive exposure exercises:* For Mr. X. to habituate to the physiological symptoms of panic, he gradually and deliberately exposed himself to the panic symptoms. He began with the least anxiety-provoking physiological symptom on his hierarchy and intentionally elicited that symptom between three and five times daily by vigorously repeating the interoceptive exercises. He continued exposure with that item until he could not get his anxiety higher than a 3 during the exercise. Then he moved on to the next item up the hierarchy.

Session 8
- *Developed in vivo exposure hierarchy:* Because Mr. X. avoided a number of situations due to fears of panic, a hierarchy of avoided situations was developed.

Sessions 8 to 12
- *Conducted in vivo exposure exercises:* Mr. X. conducted daily exposure exercises, gradually working his way from the bottom to the top of the hierarchy as he habituated to the items.

Session 12
- *Reviewed progress:* Based on data in Figure 1.4, reviewed Mr. X.'s progress in therapy.

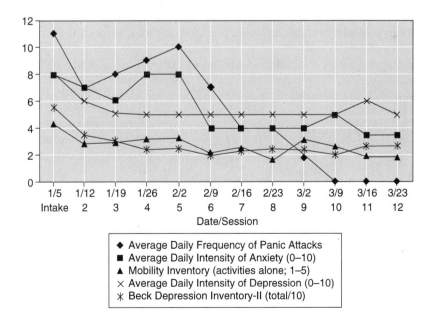

- ◆ Average Daily Frequency of Panic Attacks
- ■ Average Daily Intensity of Anxiety (0–10)
- ▲ Mobility Inventory (activities alone; 1–5)
- × Average Daily Intensity of Depression (0–10)
- ✳ Beck Depression Inventory-II (total/10)

Figure 1.4   Mr. X.'s Progress in Therapy

OBSERVING THE OUTCOME

Mr. X.'s treatment proceeded according to the treatment plan, and the hypotheses about anxiety and panic were supported; however, the hypotheses about depression were not. Consistent with the hypotheses, application of cognitive-behavioral interventions targeted at reducing panic attacks effectively eliminated his panic attacks, agoraphobic avoidance (Session 12 MI score of 1.8 was within one standard deviation of the nonclinical population; Chambless et al., 1985), and average daily intensity of anxiety. Contrary to the hypotheses, although his depression scores diminished somewhat over the 12 sessions, his depression was moderately severe at the conclusion of the treatment plan (Session 12 BDI-II score of 25 was in the moderate range of depression; Beck et al., 1996; see Figure 1.4). Taken together, these findings suggest a need for revising the predictions about depression.

REVISING THE HYPOTHESES

The final phase of the scientific method is often iterative. As results of hypotheses tests are reviewed, new hypotheses may need to be generated. Typically, this involves returning to the observation phase to collect additional information about target concerns and relevant contexts. New hypotheses are developed and the treatment plan is revised. The new treatment plan is then carried out and the new hypotheses are tested (see Figure 1.1). For Mr. X., the hypothesis about responsiveness of his depression to interventions targeted at panic was unsupported. Therefore, the functional analysis of depression was reviewed. Mr. X. reported that his depression had returned to its baseline level for the preceding four years. A subsequent functional analysis of the current depression suggested that important antecedents to worsened depressed mood were inactivity and self-depreciating thoughts regarding competence and unemployment. Based on this functional analysis, Mr. X.'s preferences, and a review of the empirical literature, new hypotheses regarding his depression were generated:

- His depression is exacerbated and maintained by a paucity of pleasurable and mastery activities (especially unemployment).
- His depression is exacerbated and maintained by thoughts of incompetence and ineptitude.
- Depression treatment will be effective if it addresses the hypothesized functional relationships between depression and contingencies. Specifically, interventions should focus on increasing pleasurable and mastery activities while reducing self-depreciating beliefs.
- Cognitive-behavioral treatment that includes education, increasing activity through goal setting, career counseling, and cognitive restructuring will effectively reduce his symptoms of depression because it:
  - Is consistent with the hypothesized functional relationships.
  - Has data to support its effectiveness with depression (Dobson, 1989).
  - Is cost-effective and feasible for client and therapist.

These hypotheses are then incorporated into a treatment plan and the interventions implemented. The results are reviewed and revised, if necessary.

SUMMARY

This chapter is designed to provide a framework for behavioral case conceptualization through applying the scientific method to the clinical setting. Much like scientists, clinicians must assess their clients (observation phase), develop treatment plans (developing hypotheses phase), implement those treatment plans (testing hypotheses phase), assess clients' progress (observing the outcome phase), and revise treatment plans if necessary (revising hypotheses phase). Through conscientious, compassionate attention to pinpointing concerns, understanding their contexts, and systematically implementing empirically supported interventions, therapists offer their clients the maximum opportunity for meaningful improvement in psychotherapy.

REFERENCES

Abramowitz, J. S. (1997). Effectiveness of psychological and pharmacological treatments for Obsessive-Compulsive Disorder: A quantitative review. *Journal of Consulting and Clinical Psychology, 65*(1), 44–52.

American Psychiatric Association. (1994). *Diagnostic and statistical manual of mental disorders* (4th ed.). Washington, DC: Author.

Antonuccio, D. L., Thomas, M., & Danton, W. G. (1997). A cost-effectiveness analysis of cognitive behavior therapy and fluoxetine (Prozac) in the treatment of depression. *Behavior Therapy, 28*(2), 187–210.

Baker, R. C., & Kirschenbaum, D. S. (1998). Weight control during the holidays: Highly consistent self-monitoring as a potentially useful coping mechanism. *Health Psychology, 17*(4), 367–370.

Barlow, D. H. (1988). *Anxiety and its disorders: The nature and treatment of anxiety and panic.* New York: Guilford Press.

Barlow, D. H. (2001). *The clinical handbook of psychological disorders* (3rd ed.). New York: Guilford Press.

Beck, A. T., Rush, A J., Shaw, B. F., & Emery, G. (1979). *Cognitive therapy of depression.* New York: Guilford Press.

Beck, A. T., & Steer, R. A. (1993). *Beck Anxiety Inventory manual.* San Antonio, TX: Psychological Corporation.

Beck, A. T., Steer, R. A., & Brown, G. K. (1996). *Beck Depression Inventory* (2nd ed.). San Antonio, TX: Psychological Corporation.

Bellack, A. S., Hersen, M., & Himmelhoch, J. M. (1996). Social skills training for depression: A treatment manual. In V. B. Van Hasselt & M. Hersen (Eds.), *Sourcebook of psychological treatment manuals for adult disorders.* New York: Plenum Press.

Berman, P. S. (1997). *Case conceptualization and treatment planning: Exercises for integrating theory with clinical practice.* Thousand Oaks, CA: Sage.

Black, D. W., Wesner, R., Bowers, W., Monahan, P., & Gabel, J. (1995). Acute treatment response in outpatients with Panic Disorder: High versus low depressive symptoms. *Annuls of Clinical Psychiatry, 7*(4), 181–188.

Borkovec, T. D., & Costello, E. (1993). Efficacy of applied relaxation and cognitive-behavioral therapy in the treatment of Generalized Anxiety Disorder. *Journal of Consulting and Clinical Psychology, 61*(4), 611–619.

Brent, D. A., Kolko, D. J., Dirmaher, B., Baugher, M., Bridge, J., Roth, C., et al. (1998). Predictors of treatment efficacy in a clinical trial of three psychosocial treatments for adolescent depression. *Journal of the American Academy of Child and Adolescent Psychiatry, 37*(9), 906–914.

Brogan, M. M., Prochaska, J. O., & Prochaska, J. M. (1999). Predicting termination and continuation status in psychotherapy using the transtheoretical model. *Psychotherapy, 36,* 105–113.

Castonguay, L. G., Schut, A. J., Constantino, M. J., & Halperin, G. S. (1999). Assessing the role of treatment manuals: Have they become necessary but nonsufficient ingredients of change? *Clinical Psychology: Science and Practice, 6*(4), 449–455.

Chambless, D. L., Caputo, G. C., Jasin, S. E., Gracely, E. J., & Williams, C. (1985). The Mobility Inventory for Agoraphobia. *Behavioral Research and Therapy, 23,* 35–44.

Chambless, D. L., & Gillis, M. M. (1993). Cognitive therapy of anxiety disorders. *Journal of Consulting and Clinical Psychology, 61*(2), 248–260.

Chambless, D. L., & Hollon, S. D., (1998). Defining empirically supported therapies. *Journal of Consulting and Clinical Psychology, 66*(1), 7–18.

Cormier, S., & Cormier, B. (1998). *Interviewing strategies for helpers: Fundamental skills and cognitive behavioral interventions.* Pacific Grove, CA: Brooks/Cole.

Craighead, W. E., Craighead, L. W., & Ilardi, S. S. (1998). Psychosocial treatments for Major Depressive Disorder. In P. E. Nathan & J. M. Gorman (Eds.), *A guide to treatments that work.* New York: Guilford Press.

Craske, M. G., & Barlow, D. H. (1993). Panic Disorder and Agoraphobia. In D. H. Barlow (Ed.), *Clinical handbook of psychological disorders* (2nd ed.). New York: Guilford Press.

Division 12 Task Force. (1995). Training in and dissemination of empirically validated psychological treatments: Report and recommendations. *Clinical Psychologist, 48,* 3–23.

Dobson, K. S. (1989). A meta-analysis of the efficacy of cognitive therapy for depression. *Journal of Consulting and Clinical Psychology, 57*(3), 414–419.

Evans, M. D., Hollon, S. D., De Rubeis, J. J., Piasecki, J. M., Grove, W. M., Garvey, M. J., et al. (1992). Differential relapse following cognitive therapy and pharmacotherapy for depression. *Archives of General Psychiatry, 49,* 802–808.

First, M. B., Spitzer, R. L., Gibbon, M., & Williams, J. B. W. (1997a). *User's guide for the Structured Clinical Interview for DSM-IV Axis I Disorders: Clinician version.* Washington, DC: American Psychiatric Press.

First, M. B., Spitzer, R. L., Gibbon, M., & Williams, J. B. W. (1997b). *User's guide for the Structured Clinical Interview for DSM-IV Axis I Disorders: Clinician version (SCID-CV).* Washington, DC: American Psychiatric Press.

Foa, E. B., Dancu, C. V., Hembree, E. A., Jaycox, L. H., Meadows, E. A., & Street, G. P. (1999). A comparison of exposure therapy, stress inoculation training, and their combination for reducing Posttraumatic Stress Disorder in female assault victims. *Journal of Consulting and Clinical Psychology, 67*(2), 194–200.

Follette, W. C., & Houts, A. C. (1996). Models of scientific progress and the role of theory in taxonomy development: A case study of the *DSM. Journal of Consulting and Clinical Psychology, 64*(6), 1120–1132.

Follette, W. C., Houts, A. C., & Hayes, S. C. (1992). Behavior therapy and the new medical model. *Behavioral Assessment, 14*(3/4), 323–343.

Goldfried, M. R., & Wolfe, B. E. (1996). Psychotherapy practice and research: Repairing a strained relationship. *American Psychologist, 51*(10), 1007–1016.

Gottman, J. M., Jacboson, N. S., Rushe, R. H., Hortt, J. W., Babcock, J., La Taillade, J. J., et al. (1995). The relationship between heart rate reactivity, emotionally aggressive behavior, and general violence in batterers. *Journal of Family Psychology, 9*(3), 227–248.

Gould, R. A., Otto, M. W., & Pollack, M. H. (1995). A meta-analysis of treatment outcome for Panic Disorder. *Clinical Psychology Review, 15*(8), 819–844.

Halperin, K. M., & Snyder, C. R. (1979). Effects of enhanced psychological test feedback on treatment outcome: Therapeutic implications of the Barnum effect. *Journal of Consulting and Clinical Psychology, 47*, 140–146.

Hoyt, M. F. (1995). *Brief therapy and managed care: Readings for contemporary practice.* San Francisco: Jossey-Bass.

Jacobson, N. S., Dobson, K., Fruzzetti, A. E., Schmaling, K. B., & Salusky, S. (1991). Marital therapy as a treatment for depression. *Journal of Consulting and Clinical Psychology, 59*(4), 547–557.

Jarrett, R. B. (1995). Comparing and combining short-term psychotherapy and pharmacotherapy for depression. In E. E. Beckham & W. R. Leber (Eds.), *Handbook of depression* (2nd ed.). New York: Guilford Press.

Keane, T. M., Zimering, R. T., & Caddell, J. M. (1985). A behavioral formulation of Post-traumatic Stress Disorder in Vietnam veterans. *Behavior Therapist, 8*, 9–12.

Kelleher, W. J., Talcott, G. W., Haddock, C. K., & Freeman, R. K. (1996). Military psychology in the age of managed care: The Wilford Hall model. *Applied and Preventive Psychology, 5*, 101–110.

Kendler, K. S, & Robinette, C. D., (1983). Schizophrenia in the National Academy of Sciences–National Research Council twin registry: A 16-year update. *American Journal of Psychiatry, 140*, 1551–1563.

Leahy, R. L., & Holl, S. J. (2000). *Treatment plans and interventions for depression and anxiety disorders.* New York: Guilford Press.

Lewinsohn, P. M., & Gotlib, I. H. (1995). Behavioral theory and treatment of depression. In E. E. Beckham & W. R. Leber (Eds.), *Handbook of depression* (2nd ed.). New York: Guilford Press.

Lidren, D. M., Watkins, P. L., Gould, R. A., Clum, G. A., Aterino, M., & Tulloch, H. L. (1994). A comparison of bibliotherapy and group therapy in the treatment of Panic Disorder. *Journal of Consulting and Clinical Psychology, 62*(4), 865–869.

McConnaughy, E. A., DiClemente, C. C., Prochaska, J. O., & Velicer, W. F. (1989). Stages of change in psychotherapy: A follow-up report. *Psychotherapy: Theory, Research, Practice, Training, 26*(4), 494–503.

McCullough, J. P. (2000). *Treatment for chronic depression: Cognitive behavioral analysis system of psychotherapy.* New York: Guilford Press.

McLean, P. E., Woody, S., Taylor, S., & Koch, W. J. (1998). Comorbid Panic Disorder and Major Depression: Implications for cognitive-behavioral therapy. *Journal of Consulting and Clinical Psychology, 66*(2), 240–247.

Morrison, J. (1995). *The DSM-IV made easy.* New York: Guilford Press.

Nathan, P. E., & Gorman, J. M. (1998). *A guide to treatments that work.* New York: Oxford University Press.

Nezu, A. M., & Perri, M. G. (1989). Social problem-solving therapy for Unipolar Depression: An initial dismantling investigation. *Journal of Consulting and Clinical Psychology, 57*(3), 408–413.

Oest, L.-G. (1989). One-session treatment for specific phobias. *Behaviour Research and Therapy, 27*(1), 1–7.

Oregon Administrative Standards. (2001, January). Department of Human Services, Mental Health Development Disability Services Division, Division 32, Community Treatment and Support Services 309–023-0001.

Plaud, J. J., & Vogeltanz, N. D. (1997). Back to the future: The continued relevance of behavior theory to modern behavior therapy. *Behavior Therapy, 28,* 403–414.

Prochaska, J. O., & Norcross, J. C. (1999). *Systems of psychotherapy* (4th ed.). Pacific Grove, CA: Brooks/Cole.

Riggs, D. S., & Foa, E. B. (1993). Obsessive Compulsive Disorder. In D. H. Barlow (Ed.), *Clinical handbook of psychological disorders* (2nd ed.). New York: Guilford Press.

Sanderson, W. C., Raue, P. J., & Wetzler, S. (1998). The generalizability of cognitive behavior therapy for Panic Disorder. *Journal of Cognitive Psychotherapy, 12*(4), 323–330.

Schmidt, N. B., Woolaway-Bickel, K., Trakowski, J., Santiago, H., Storey, J., Koselka, M., et al. (2000). Dismantling cognitive-behavioral treatment for Panic Disorder: Questioning the utility of breathing retraining. *Journal of Consulting and Clinical Psychology, 68*(3), 417–424.

Skinner, B. F. (1974). *About behaviorism.* New York: Vintage Books.

Stavosky, J. M., & Borkovec, T. D. (1987). The phenomenon of worry: Theory, research, treatment and its implications for women. *Women and Therapy, 6*(3), 77–95.

Steenbarger, B. N. (1994). Duration and outcome in psychotherapy: An integrative review. *Professional Psychology: Research and Practice, 25*(2), 111–119.

Stricker, G., & Trierweiler, S. J., (1995). The local clinical scientist: A bridge between science and practice. *American Psychologist, 50*(12), 995–1002.

Strickler, D. P., Bradlyn, A. S., & Maxwell, W. A. (1981). Teaching moderate drinking behaviors to young adult heavy drinkers: The effects of three training procedures. *Addictive Behaviors, 6*(4), 355–364.

Van Hasselt, V. B., & Hersen, M. (1996). *Sourcebook of psychological treatment manuals for adult disorders.* New York: Plenum Press.

Wade, W. A., Treat, T. A., & Stuart, G. L. (1998). Transporting an empirically supported treatment for Panic Disorder to a service clinic setting: A benchmarking strategy. *Journal of Consulting and Clinical Psychology, 66*(2), 231–239.

CHAPTER 2

Major Depressive Disorder

KEITH S. DOBSON and NASREEN KHATRI

DESCRIPTION OF THE DISORDER

MAJOR DEPRESSIVE DISORDER (MDD) is recognized in current diagnostic nomenclature as a mood disorder, which is characterized by two or more major depressive episodes (MDE), without a history of manic, mixed, or hypomanic episodes. Though no single symptom is diagnostic of depression, to be considered part of a clinical syndrome, an MDE must last at least two weeks and include:

1. Sad or irritated mood, or a loss of interest in or pleasure from usual activities.
2. At least four out of nine accompanying symptoms, that can include cognitive (e.g., difficulty concentrating or making daily decisions), affective (e.g., sad mood and feelings of hopelessness), and vegetative (e.g., difficulty with sleep, appetite, and motor functioning) symptoms.
3. The symptoms cause clinically significant distress or impairment in social or occupational functioning (see *Diagnostic and Statistical Manual of Mental Disorders* [*DSM-IV*], American Psychiatric Association [APA], 1994, 2000, for complete criteria for MDE and MDD; see Tables 2.1 and 2.2).

MDD is the most common form of mental disorder treated in outpatient clinics. An MDE can last from several weeks to months, although most untreated episodes remit within six months. However, untreated episodes are associated with morbidity and mortality through general medical conditions such as cardiovascular disease and most clearly through suicide. Most people who experience an episode (approximately 70%) will return completely to premorbid functioning. However, at least half of all people who experience one episode of depression will go on to have at least one more episode during their lifetime, and depression has a recurring course for many individuals. Moreover, the experience of each additional episode increases the chances of having a subsequent episode.

Table 2.1
Criteria for Major Depressive Episode

A. Five (or more) of the following symptoms have been present during the same 2-week period and represent a change from previous functioning; at least one of the symptoms is either (1) depressed mood or (2) loss of interest or pleasure.

Note: Do not include symptoms that are clearly due to a general medical condition, or mood-incongruent delusions or hallucinations.

  1. Depressed mood most of the day, nearly every day, as indicated by either subjective report (e.g., feels sad or empty) or observation made by others (e.g., appears tearful).
     Note: In children or adolescents, can be irritable mood.
  2. Markedly diminished interest or pleasure in all or almost all activities most of the day, nearly everyday (as indicated by subjective account or observations made by others).
  3. Significant weight loss when not dieting or weight gain (e.g., change of more than 5% of body weight in a month), or decrease or increase in appetite every day.
     Note: In children, consider failure to make expected weight gains.
  4. Insomnia or hypersomnia nearly every day.
  5. Feelings of worthlessness or excessive or inappropriate guilt (which may be delusional) nearly every day (not merely self-reproach or guilt about being sick).
  6. Diminished ability to think or concentrate, or indecisiveness, nearly every day (either by subjective account or as observed by others).
  7. Recurrent thoughts of death (not just fear of dying), recurrent suicidal ideation without a specific plan, or a suicide attempt or a specific plan for committing suicide.

B. The symptoms do not meet criteria for a Mixed Episode.

C. The symptoms cause clinically significant distress or impairment in social, occupational, or other important areas of functioning.

D. The symptoms are not due to the direct physiological effects of a substance (e.g., a drug of abuse, a medication) or a general medical condition (e.g., hypothyroidism).

E. The symptoms are not better accounted for by Bereavement (i.e., after the loss of a loved one), the symptoms persist for longer than two months or are characterized by marked functional impairment, morbid preoccupation with worthlessness, suicidal ideation, psychotic symptoms, or psychomotor ideation.

MDD is diagnosed twice as often in women as it is in men. The reasons for this imbalance have been posited by various researchers as related to reproductive events, roles as caregivers, other biological factors, the stress caused by the multiple roles that women play in society, and the disadvantaged position they have had financially and socially as compared to men. It is most likely that women and men are diagnosed with depression at different rates due to some combination of biological and social factors. In terms of the general population, the lifetime risk for developing MDD is between 10% and 25% for women and 5% and 12% for men.

This chapter describes the assessment and cognitive-behavioral treatment of an individual with Major Depressive Disorder. In recent years, considerable research has been conducted on the efficacy of cognitive-behavioral therapy for MDD, which demonstrates that cognitive-behavioral therapy is as effective for this disorder as medication.

Table 2.2
Criteria for Major Depressive Disorder, Recurrent

A. Presence of two or more Major Depressive Episodes.

 Note: To be considered separate episodes, there must be an interval of at least two consecutive months in which the criteria are not met for Major Depressive Episode.

B. The Major Depressive Episodes are not better accounted for by Schizoaffective Disorder and are not superimposed on Schizophrenia, Schizophreniform Disorder, Delusional Disorder, or Psychotic Disorder Not Otherwise Specified.

C. There has never been a Manic, Mixed, or Hypomanic Episode.

 Note: This exclusion does not apply if the manic-like, mixed-like, or hypomanic-like episodes are substance or treatment induced, or are due to the physiological effects of a general medical condition.

CASE DESCRIPTION

Sarah W., a 37-year-old White married homemaker, was referred by her family physician to her husband's Employee Assistance Program (EAP) for 10 sessions of cognitive-behavioral therapy for depression, following what was only a partially successful treatment using medications. Ms. W. had a history of major depressive episodes dating back to her college years. She had noticed that she was feeling distressed, teary, and unable to keep up with household and social obligations. She sought help without prompting from friends or family, but with the knowledge and urging of her husband.

CHIEF COMPLAINTS

Ms. W. requested treatment for depression, stating that she was sad and crying much of the time. A homemaker, her current level of functioning was quite poor, such that she largely left housework undone, except for required tasks such as grocery shopping. The home, by her report, was a "disaster," and she believed that she was for the most part "failing" in her responsibilities. She stated that since her eldest of two children had left for college three months earlier, she could not concentrate on daily tasks and felt empty and unable to enjoy daily life. She reported that although her marital relationship was "okay," she felt that of late she was a disappointment to her husband, and that they were noticeably less romantic and intimate than earlier in their relationship.

HISTORY

Ms. W. was the eldest daughter in a family of four in a small town in Ontario, Canada. Her father was a general physician, with the heavy demands that such a position encompassed. Her mother did not work out of the house, and although Ms. W. recalls some social activity in the home, it was not excessive. Ms. W. reported that her mother had seemed quite contented with a quiet life involving the house, her children, and a passion for needlework. The children were expected to excel at school (which they all did) and to comport themselves consistent with their perceived station in town. Ms. W. recalled feeling a considerable amount of pressure to behave properly, and withdrew from social events where alcohol or "rough" teens might be. Social activity largely consisted of small parties with a circle of close female friends she developed. When not socializing with her friends or studying, Ms. W. spent a great deal of time with her mother, shopping, helping around the house, and working on hobbies together. She described her mother as overprotective but meaning well. For example, her mother insisted on meeting all her friends before "approving" of them to become a part of Ms. W.'s social circle. Father, when home, was mostly quiet and in the background.

Given her excellent grades, Ms. W. was given admission with a scholarship to several universities. Initially, her mother had cautioned her about going too far from home and listed the advantages of attending a school closer to home. Ms. W. finally selected one some distance from home, and began studies in science there. Although diligent in school, her social life was meager. She dates her first depression to this time. She found it difficult to get out of bed in the morning to make it to class on time. In addition, she found herself feeling unbearably homesick, crying in the hallways on the way to science labs and feeling more and more isolated. At this time, she did not seek help for her depression. Within a few weeks, her mood began to improve and she "threw herself into her work" and was able to push herself through the first semester with As and Bs. She persisted socially and by the end of the first year had developed a few friends.

She met her husband, Richard, who was one year ahead of her in university, in her second year and they dated intermittently through that year. In her third and Richard's last year of university, they dated more seriously, and finally agreed to marry at the end of the year, when Richard was offered a position in Calgary, Alberta. Following Richard to his new job, Ms. W. never did complete her degree in science. Instead, she became pregnant about six months after their marriage. Her second depression, which slowly remitted, came on the heels of her daughter's birth, which also coincided roughly with the sudden death of her father due to myocardial infarct. At the time of the second depressive episode, she did seek help from her family physician, who suggested mild exercise, mood monitoring, and some grief counseling. Ms. W. found this treatment somewhat helpful. She did not want to try drug therapy, as she nursed her daughter for the first year of the child's life. In summary, Ms. W. had suffered through her first two episodes of depression without any systematic psychotherapy or drug treatment.

BEHAVIORAL ASSESSMENT

BEHAVIORAL

Ms. W. presented as a quiet, sad woman, who spoke quietly during the intake interview and expressed considerable pessimism about the possible outcome of treatment. She made little eye contact with the therapist and, when discussing emotional topics, such as her daughter's beginning college, would tear up, sigh, and have trouble speaking. She was well groomed and dressed neatly but had a hunched posture and unsmiling demeanor that did not change, except briefly, during the interview.

Ms. W. reported that all activity at home, besides lying on the couch and watching television, took a great deal of effort on her part. She felt guilty that some of the housework had to be parceled out to a maid and, when possible, aided by her husband and 16-year-old son. She was unable to get motivated to work and reported that most mornings, she returned to bed or napped on the couch after her son and husband had left for the day.

SELF-REPORT

When asked to describe how she felt, Ms. W. stated that she felt that "the world has gone from color to black and white." She described her overriding emotions as sadness, loneliness, and a lack of purpose. She stated that she had difficulty concentrating, could not organize herself, and found herself staring into the distance and daydreaming about the things her daughter and she used to do together, even though she felt that she had tasks around the house that she must get done. She stated that she felt guilty and self-reproachful and even had fleeting thoughts of suicide but had not made a plan and had no history of previous attempts. Her verbal self-report was reinforced by her Beck Depression Inventory (BDI-II) score of 34, which placed her in the moderately to severely depressed range (see Figure 2.1).

PHYSIOLOGICAL

Ms. W. reported having little appetite. She had lost 15 pounds in the past month, without dieting. She was a slight woman, and at the time of the interview appeared gaunt and exhausted. She also reported having trouble staying asleep at

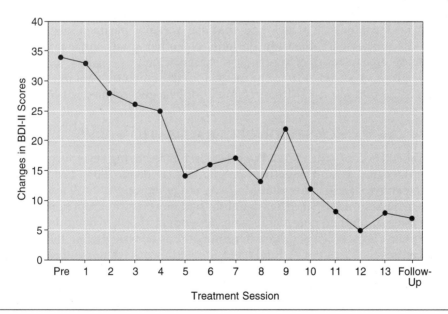

Figure 2.1 Changes in BDI-II Scores during the Course of Cognitive-Behavioral Therapy

Note: A score of 13 or more indicates mild depression, while a score of 20 or more indicates at least moderate depression.

night, and tossing and turning most of the night. She reported that some nights she would rise and try to sleep in her daughter's vacated bed, as a way to minimize the negative impact on her husband. During the day, she was anxious and fidgety but lacked almost all energy to complete household tasks and would instead nap fitfully throughout the day. She had a markedly reduced interest in sex. It is important to note that none of her three episodes had occurred at the same time of year; therefore, no seasonal pattern could be established.

On review, she met criteria for a diagnosis of Major Depressive Disorder, Recurrent. Her current symptoms included sad mood, decreased interest in activities, loss of energy, fatigue, decreased appetite and weight loss, decreased sexual desire, self-criticism, pessimism, and occasional thoughts of suicide (without a formalized plan). Complicating issues such as alcohol or substance abuse were not present; however, there was a history of anxiety (both Agoraphobia and Generalized Anxiety Disorder) and two past episodes of depression.

MEDICAL CONSULTATION

Ms. W. underwent a complete physical examination, although she had not been physically ill just prior to the start of her most recent depressive episode. Her family physician, being aware of her current depression, conducted the examination to determine if Ms. W. was experiencing any general medical condition that may have better accounted for symptoms than a diagnosis of MDD. All laboratory results returned negative for blood and urine pathologies. In addition, it was discovered that Ms. W. had no long-standing medical conditions, such as hypertension, diabetes, hypothyroidism, or cardiovascular disease, that may have contributed to and/or exacerbated the symptom profile observed in depressed individuals. Considering that Ms. W was 37 years old, she also was examined for signs of perimenopausal symptoms; it was found that she was not perimenopausal, as she continued to experience monthly periods. No other gynecological difficulties were discovered as a result of her medical examination.

Overall, it was concluded from the medical consultation that Ms. W. was suffering from MDD that was not better accounted for by a general medical condition.

CASE CONCEPTUALIZATION

The therapist conceptualized Ms. W.' s depression as having several components: behavioral, cognitive, and affective (Persons & Davidson, 2001). From a behavioral perspective, it was clear that Ms. W.'s range of activity and sources of reward were quite limited. Since her daughter had moved away from home, she had lost the roles of mother, confidante, and dependent that her daughter had provided for her. Her son did not share her interests, as he was often involved in outdoor activities and was not as interested in needlework, chats, and shopping as her daughter had been. Further, it appeared that her relationship with her husband was impoverished, and he was not able to provide the support and intimacy she had previously enjoyed. As such, it was clear that she needed activities that would fill the void left by her daughter's departure for college, to increase her sense of efficacy, to allow for positive reinforcement from other people, and to boost her flagging self-esteem.

The cognitive aspects of the case were notable. Although Ms. W. had slowed down her activity level only recently, the thoughts and beliefs that led to that slowing were probably in place much earlier than her lethargy and lack of productivity. It seems that she had grown up in a home where there were very strict criteria for proper behavior and an emphasis on achievement. She likely internalized these standards to mean that one had to do extremely well in school, in relationships, and as a parent to be deemed acceptable. Those demanding, if not somewhat perfectionistic standards may have led Ms. W. to become depressed when she felt that she could no longer carry out her role as homemaker "perfectly," even for a very good reason. Thoughts such as "I must be productive, even if I feel down" and "I need to always do things right" promoted the kind of self-criticism that would lead to and maintain depressogenic beliefs, behaviors, and emotions. It was notable that Ms. W. first became depressed when she started college away from home. It may be that, in addition to her own separation from her daughter, she harbored concerns about the same type of depression experience awaiting her daughter as happened to her.

Ms. W. was clearly depressed, anxious, and very distressed at the time of the assessment. According to cognitive theory, it was the second piece, her negative and distorted thinking, that led to her distraught emotional state and limited productive behaviors in her daily life.

RATIONALE FOR TREATMENT CHOICE

The treatment choice for Ms. W. was based on several factors. First, although she did manifest many of the vegetative symptoms of depression (e.g., weight loss, sleep disturbance, fatigue) that may well have responded to antidepressant medication, she stated that she would prefer to pursue psychotherapy treatment. Her reasons for wanting to engage in psychotherapy were that it would give her a chance to openly express herself to a nonjudgmental listener on a consistent basis, and that she may find new ways of looking at her situation that would be helpful both now and in the future.

We also discussed her history of depressive episodes and decided mutually that we would be present-focused in the therapy. We would focus on what precipitated the current depressive episode, how to move toward wellness, and how to prevent relapse. The therapy that presented itself in light of a psychotherapeutic, short-term, present-focused treatment for MDD was cognitive-behavioral therapy (Dobson, 2001). Cognitive therapy is a well-tested, theory-based treatment, which holds the premise that what affects our thoughts and behaviors is the way we think about ourselves, our future, and the world around us (Beck, Rush, Shaw, & Emery, 1979). In addition, cognitive theorists posit that distortions in thinking (e.g., "I must be perfect all of the time") may lead to the development and maintenance of depressogenic states. It is these distortions in thinking and the beliefs that underlie them (e.g., "I'm not good enough") that are targeted in cognitive-behavioral therapy through a multimodal approach to changing thoughts and behaviors to positively impact emotional states.

As mentioned earlier, cognitive-behavioral therapy for depression has been demonstrated to be at least as efficacious as pharmacotherapy, with much reduced relapse rates compared to drug therapy once treatment is discontinued (Jacobson

& Hollon, 1996). Cognitive-behavioral treatment can be tailored to the individual's needs and progress in therapy can be monitored in a systematic way. In the case of Ms. W., it was decided to first monitor and increase her activity levels, then to talk about the negative thoughts and beliefs that she held, and use the BDI-II (Beck, Steer, & Brown, 1996) to track the remission of her depressive symptoms.

COURSE OF TREATMENT

Therapy began with weekly sessions. The first session was focused on explaining the rationale for cognitive-behavioral therapy, the need for therapist and client to work together in a collaborative partnership, and the necessity of homework assignments. During the second and third sessions, although Ms. W. was still experiencing quite low mood, we reviewed her BDI-II scores and activity records (see Table 2.3) and began a mutually agreed upon behavioral plan to improve her functioning. Cognitive-behavioral therapists often focus on behavioral change first because it is easier to change one's behaviors than it is to change thoughts and beliefs. Also, positive behavioral change often naturally leads to an acknowledgment that there are more positive ways to think about the situation.

The therapist and Ms. W. began behavioral therapy by assessing her daily routines. It quickly became apparent that most of Ms. W.'s day was spent unproductively. Although she would get up in the morning and see her husband off to work and child off to school, she often would return to bed after they left the house. Much of this time was spent in intermittent sleep, punctuated by periods where she was self-critical for not being awake. Her afternoon would be spent in a combination of some housework, some television watching, and some errands. It did appear that she obtained some pleasure from gardening, but quickly tired and often left it uncompleted, feeling demoralized as a result.

It was agreed that more structure to her days would be helpful. The therapist and Ms. W. worked out a plan to return the house to a "reasonable" state of cleanliness by identifying and prioritizing all of the work that she needed to do. Similarly, a list of errands outside of the home (e.g., repairing some damaged screen windows) was generated. Finally, a list of garden work was made. It turned out that one garden job in particular was quite distressing to Ms. W. This was a large job that she had assigned herself, of digging up a patch of grass, building a retaining area, and then preparing and planting a strawberry patch.

The plan for Ms. W. began with small, manageable steps. She agreed not to return to bed each morning, but instead to use that time for cleaning. She first focused on visible parts of the house (e.g., entrance, living room, and kitchen) and set targets for each day. She was encouraged to take a short rest or to read if she fatigued, but not to return to bed or to watch television. If she found it difficult to do a task, she also was asked to pay attention to her internal dialogue. In addition, she was asked to make a schedule of contact with her daughter so that she would feel less estranged from her. Ms. W. and her daughter made a plan about telephone contact, e-mails, and visits that would fulfill both mother's and daughter's needs for closeness without impinging on the daughter's burgeoning independence. According to Ms. W., her daughter was "relieved and happy" to have some ground rules about contact that they could agree on. Apparently, the daughter was secretly worried that her mother was not going to be able to adjust well to her move away from home.

Table 2.3
Activity Chart

Time	Day 1	Day 2	Day 3	Day 4	Day 5	Day 6	Day 7
6–7 A.M.							
7–8	Wake up/dress A = 2 P = 0						
8–9	Eat breakfast A = 3 P = 1						
9–10	Nap						
10–11	Watch TV A = 0 P = 2						
11–12	Nap						
12–1 P.M.	Lunch/make sandwich A = 2 P = 2						
1–2	TV A = 0 P =2						
2–3	TV A = 0 P =2						
3–4	TV A = 0 P =2						
4–5	Talk to son A = 1 P = 3						
5–6	Greet husband/help with dinner A = 3 P=3						
6–7	Call sister A = 1 P = 4						
7–8	Nap						
8–9	Go to bed						
9–	Sleep						

Note: A = Accomplishment (0–10); P = Pleasure (0–10).

By the fourth session, with some of the basic behavioral work underway, the therapist and Ms. W. both agreed that she was highly self-critical, and that it would be helpful if she could learn to be less so. The therapist offered that there were certain techniques that she could learn in this regard. Finally, the therapist offered the hypothesis that Ms. W. held certain beliefs that contributed to either

her becoming or staying depressed. Although the therapist was tentative in this suggestion at this early stage of therapy, it was suggested that some of these beliefs might be in the area of putting other people's interests ahead of her own and having perfectionistic standards.

As Ms. W. began to undertake more tasks, it became clear that her negative thoughts included ideas such as those listed in Table 2.4. The therapist discussed ways to respond to these thoughts with coping alternatives, designed to maintain her desire to do these projects and to provide some positive reinforcement for success. As Ms. W. was able to accomplish some of her behavioral and cognitive goals, she was surprised to notice that her family was responding more positively toward her. Her husband commented on how she seemed to be getting "better," and her son asked her to do things that he had not asked for recently, such as baking things he liked. Although on the one hand, Ms. W. appreciated their response, she was also aware of another negative set of thoughts related to having "demands" put on her.

By the fifth session, the therapist used Ms. W.'s increasing awareness of negative cognitions to have her begin to record her negative thoughts using a Daily Record of Dysfunctional Thoughts (Beck, 1995). In the therapy session, several examples of negative thoughts were discussed in detail. The evidence for these cognitions was examined, and it was discovered that Ms. W. often made negative assumptions about the intentions of others. Further, it became clear that part of her automatic response to these requests put herself in a one-down position. It was agreed that a more healthy response would be for her to not assume this position and to begin to express her wants and needs to others. For example, she was able to learn how to ask her family how to make requests of her that were not seen as demands. She began this process with her family, who initially resisted her requests, but did generally comply.

As Ms. W. began the process of being more assertive, she realized that she experienced her wishes in only a vague manner. The therapist and she began to

Table 2.4
Thought Record

Original Negative Thought	Coping Alternative
(Before undertaking some work):	
"There is too much to do. This is just a little part of it."	"I can do it if I break this down into manageable steps and take breaks when I have to."
"Why clean up this room, it will just get dirty again?"	"If I clean it up well now, it will be easier to clean in the future."
(When she had completed some work):	
"I should have done this a long time ago. I made it more difficult that it actually was."	"Although I might have preferred to do this earlier, I am depressed. I have to pace myself, and give myself credit for what I do accomplish."

explore her hopes and wishes, both in the short and long term. She realized she was lonely, and wanted at least one good friend, now that her daughter had moved away. Although anxious about the prospect of "too much" social contact, she realized that part of her relative isolation was due to a fear of inadequacy and concerns about standing up to the demands of others. Using the skills taught to her to deal with negative automatic thoughts, though, she signed up for a quilting course, which she enjoyed immensely. One of the other women in her course asked her out for coffee one day, which led to a nascent friendship.

By the eighth session, Ms. W. had accomplished several goals. Her house and yard were generally under control, and what was not getting done was less of a burden. She was in touch with her daughter, who reported that she was doing fine at college, on a fairly regular basis. Her son and her husband were more helpful around the house, and she felt more entitled to make requests of them. She was able to regularly enjoy her needlework projects. Her BDI-II score, which was being monitored on a weekly basis, had improved considerably, dropping to a new low of 13.

By the ninth session, during the regular review of Ms. W.'s BDI-II scores, the therapist noticed that the score had risen to 22, clearly in the depressed range. Just as the therapist and she were about to prepare for the termination of therapy, it seemed that Ms. W. was once again experiencing depressive symptoms. On further examination, Ms. W. stated that she was aware that her husband's EAP funded only 10 therapy sessions and that she was distressed that she would not be ready to end therapy after only a single additional session.

At this point, the therapist elected to spend the rest of the session discussing Ms. W.'s concerns about the termination of therapy. As they reviewed the gains that she had made in therapy, they both agreed that overall, she had met her behavioral goals concerning becoming productive and establishing a comfortable pattern of contact with her daughter, and her emotional goals in terms of decreasing her depressive symptoms. In addition, she had begun to identify and challenge her negative and dysfunctional thoughts and beliefs. In light of this progress, it was mutually decided that the therapist would discuss adding three follow-up sessions with the EAP (see Managed Care Considerations, next). Ms. W. agreed that if the EAP company would not pay for these sessions, she would pay out-of-pocket to ensure that there would be follow-up sessions to help her maintain her therapy gains.

As it turned out, the EAP company did agree to fund the extra three appointments. These were provided to Ms. W. at increasing intervals (i.e., the time between the tenth and eleventh appointments was two weeks, the gap until the twelfth session was three weeks, and the final session took place one month after session 12). During this time, she was able to practice more of the skills she had learned in therapy and to further consider her future goals. One issue she recognized as having improved without much direct attention was her marital relationship. Through session 10 until the end of treatment, however, time was spent encouraging Ms. W. to express to her husband her wishes and desires related to intimacy. One of the successes she reported as a consequence of this work was that she and her husband had had her mother baby-sit while they went off for a romantic weekend together. In general, she reported that although her relationship was not ideal, it was significantly better than at the beginning of therapy.

THERAPIST-CLIENT FACTORS

This case represents the need to attend to the typical processes in cognitive therapy for depression. As discussed in treatment manuals (Beck, 1995; Beck et al., 1979), the therapist-client relationship was a collaborative one, which was focused on here-and-now problems with a positive orientation toward problem solution. When the therapist introduced new topics, it was always done in a psychoeducational manner. Typically, each method was introduced in the following manner:

1. The therapist would identify an important clinical issue.
2. The therapist would suggest that there might be a technique that could help (e.g., the Daily Record of Dysfunctional Thoughts).
3. The method was introduced and discussed using examples from Ms. W.'s life.
4. An application was identified by both therapist and patient.
5. Specific homework was collaboratively assigned.

Ms. W. was asked about her reactions to specific sessions at several points in the course of therapy, and in general about the treatment a few times. At every inquiry, she was very positive in her response, so much so that the therapist wondered if perhaps she was reporting as she thought she was "supposed" to react rather than what she really thought and felt about the treatment. The therapist encouraged statements about limits of the treatment and concerns, but was unsuccessful in eliciting these thoughts. The only relationship "problem" that emerged was at session 9, where Ms. W. had increased depression scores associated with her pending termination. In this session, the therapist was able to elicit thoughts such as "I can't do this on my own" and "You [the therapist] are quitting too soon." These thoughts were used to identify two underlying related themes of personal ineffectiveness and premature "abandonment." The therapist was able to help Ms. W. to see these thoughts in the context of her own life history (i.e., to adopt a cognitive conceptualization of these thoughts) and encouraged her to have more faith in her own competence. The therapist's willingness to obtain the further three treatment sessions, though, was seen by Ms. W. as a reasonable compromise to her concerns. By the end of treatment, she was able to express her willingness to strike out on her own.

COURSE OF TERMINATION

In part due to the remission of Ms. W.'s depression (her BDI-II scores returned to the nondepressed range), her behavioral gains, and her own sense of awareness of her issues underlying her depression, it was agreed to terminate individual therapy for depression. A review of the major techniques used in the case (activity scheduling, graded tasks, identifying and countering negative automatic thoughts, challenging negative core beliefs, awareness of personal wishes) was conducted in session 12, and Ms. W. wrote these down so that they could be reviewed in the final session and used if needed in the future. Remaining tasks and threats to her self-esteem were discussed, and several relapse-prevention strategies were developed. Ms. W. agreed to a follow-up appointment six months after termination, although she was encouraged to call for other individual sessions, if needed in the future.

FOLLOW-UP

Ms. W. attended the scheduled follow-up session, during which she remained remitted. This session was used to review her strategies to prevent relapse and to continue to challenge her negative, dysfunctional thinking with evidence gathering from her daily life and other strategies she had learned in therapy. She also talked about her behavioral goals, combining her interests in needlework with working with others. She stated that she was confident that she could continue to use her relapse-prevention strategies. Indeed, she shared with the therapist her idea for beginning a small needlework shop with a friend.

MANAGED CARE CONSIDERATIONS

The treatment described in the current case was financed as part of an EAP, an employee benefit that the patient's husband had; fortunately, this plan also applied to other people in the household. The structure of this plan was such that referral from a physician was sufficient qualification for the benefit. As such, the funding for this treatment was primarily nonproblematic.

The major funding issue that did emerge was when it became clear that the session entitlement was not going to be quite sufficient for the treatment to be successfully concluded. The psychologist in this case was compelled to seek approval for an extra three sessions, which were approved based on a fairly brief verbal report and request by telephone. This approval mechanism is quite different in other settings. For example, in many publicly funded health settings in Canada, psychological services are provided by salaried professionals who do not need to have their treatment plan approved or monitored. Some psychological services are provided in private, fee-for-service offices with direct payment from patients (sometimes with insurance copayment). Managed care as it exists throughout the United States is largely nonexistent in Canada. Thus, had this case been conducted in the United States in the context of managed care, it is likely that the psychologist would have been compelled to provide a written treatment plan before funding would begin, and a written detailed report before additional sessions would have been approved (assuming they were approved!). Psychologists and other mental health service providers are compelled to ensure quality of care for those who receive services, as well as to attend to their own financial well-being by staying conversant with managed care and other financial reimbursement schemes (Drum, 1995; Miller, 1996).

OVERALL EFFECTIVENESS

As documented above, this case was largely successful in meeting the needs of the patient and reducing her overall depression. But how successful is cognitive therapy in general? Cognitive therapy was first written about in the early 1970s, although the first evaluations of its effectiveness did not emerge until the latter part of that decade. Since then, hundreds of evaluations have been done on cognitive therapy, many in the area of depression. Indeed, enough studies have been done to warrant two meta-analyses (Dobson, 1989; Gloaguen, Cottraux, Cucherat, & Blackburn,1996). These analyses reveal that cognitive therapy is significantly better than no treatment, waiting-list comparisons, drug therapies, and other therapies, except perhaps behavior therapy. Gloaguen et al. (1996) reported that the success rate for cognitive therapy is about 67%, which is roughly the same success rate reported for pharmacotherapy for depression, but that the relapse rate at one year following treatment is less than that for drug therapy.

Although continued research is warranted related to the above claims (Jacobson & Hollon, 1996), the evidence to date seems to substantiate that on average, cognitive therapy is at least as effective as alternative treatments for depression. The American Psychological Association Division 12 Task Force (Chambless et al., 1996) for evaluating and disseminating psychological treatments has recognized it as an empirically supported therapy. Although many questions remain about cognitive therapy, including the mechanisms of change, the predictors of change (patient, therapist, and relationship), the mitigating effects of comorbid conditions on outcome, the stability of outcome, and the integration of cognitive therapy methods with other techniques and approaches, the literature to date is certainly sufficient to warrant the consideration of cognitive therapy as a first line of treatment for cases of clinical depression.

The case described here did not involve the combination of the psychological treatment with any other form of therapy. It is not uncommon in clinical practice, however, for patients with depression to be referred for cognitive-behavioral therapy after already being prescribed an antidepressant medication. From the patient's perspective, this combination can be advantageous. Certainly, we recognize the benefits of a rapid reduction of symptoms following pharmacotherapy. What can be problematic, however, is the attribution patients make for overcoming depression. We have seen patients who did very well in cognitive therapy and who, in our estimation, likely would have recovered without medication. However, because they were also on medication, the attribution they made for change was biochemical. Our general practice has therefore evolved to include explicit discussions with patients about the mechanisms of change they have experienced and their causal explanation for it. To the extent it seems accurate, we encourage patients to accept responsibility and credit for their mental health. We believe that this method encourages improved self-esteem and enhances the likelihood that they will use the techniques they learned in cognitive therapy in the future, if the need should arise.

In summary, cognitive-behavioral therapy is a well-developed and empirically supported treatment for depression. While the field evolves and as practice guidelines continue to be written, we encourage the training and practice of this approach for MDD.

REFERENCES

American Psychiatric Association. (1994). *Diagnostic and statistical manual of mental disorders* (4th ed.). Washington, DC: Author.

American Psychiatric Association. (2000). *Diagnostic and statistical manual of mental disorders* (4th ed., text rev.). Washington, DC: Author.

Beck, A. T., Rush, A. J., Shaw, B. F., & Emery, G. (1979). *Cognitive therapy of depression.* New York: Guilford Press.

Beck, A. T., Steer, R. A., & Brown, G. K. (1996). *BDI-II manual.* San Antonio, TX: Psychological Corporation.

Beck, J. S. (1995). *Cognitive therapy: Basics and beyond.* New York: Guilford Press.

Chambless, D. L., Sanderson, W. C., Shoham, V., Bennett Johnson, S., Pope, K. S., Crits-Christoph, P., et al. (1996). An update on empirically validated therapies. *Clinical Psychologist, 49,* 5- 18.

Dobson, K. S. (1989). A meta-analysis of the efficacy of cognitive therapy for depression. *Journal of Consulting and Clinical Psychology, 57,* 414- 419.

Dobson, K. S. (Ed.). (2001). *Handbook of cognitive-behavioral therapies.* New York: Guilford Press.

Drum, D. J. (1995). Changes in the mental health service delivery and finance systems and resulting implications for the national register. *Register Report,* 20(3) & 21 (1), 4- 10.

Gloaguen, V., Cottraux, J., Cucherat, M., & Blackburn, I. (1996). A meta-analysis of the effects of cognitive therapy in depressed outpatients. *Journal of Affective Disorders, 49,* 59- 72.

Jacobson, N. S., & Hollon, S. D. (1996). Cognitive therapy versus pharmacotherapy: Now that the jury's returned its verdict, it's time to present the rest of the evidence. *Journal of Consulting and Clinical Psychology, 64,* 74–80.

Miller, I. J. (1996). Managed care is harmful to outpatient mental health services: A call for accountability. *Professional Psychology: Research and Practice, 27,* 349- 363.

Persons, J., & Davidson, J. (2001). Cognitive-behavioral case formulation. In K. S. Dobson (Ed.), *Handbook of cognitive-behavioral therapies* (pp. 86–110). New York: Guilford Press.

CHAPTER 3

Panic and Agoraphobia

JOSEPH P. DeCOLA and MICHELLE G. CRASKE

DESCRIPTION OF THE DISORDER

PANIC DISORDER WITH Agoraphobia is characterized by recurrent panic attacks, usually perceived by the individual as uncontrollable, unpredictable, and dangerous. These frightening episodes of acute distress often result in the development of fear and avoidance of places where escape may prove difficult or help is unavailable if an attack occurs. The disorder can be debilitating, producing large economic and personal losses to both the individual and society. Panic Disorder has been best conceptualized as a fear of fear, because the individual develops an intense fear of the physical symptoms of anxiety or panic attacks.

The fourth edition of the *Diagnostic and Statistical Manual of Mental Disorders (DSM-IV)* defines a panic attack as a discrete episode of intense fear or discomfort accompanied by 4 or more of 13 physical and cognitive symptoms (American Psychiatric Association [APA], 1994). These symptoms include heart palpitations, chest pain or tightness, shortness of breath, dizziness, depersonalization, sweating, trembling, feelings of choking, nausea, chills or hot flushes, numbness or tingling sensations, and fear of death, going crazy, or losing control. A panic attack begins abruptly and quickly reaches peak intensity within 1 to 10 minutes.

Panic attacks may occur in the context of a variety of anxiety disorders. A diagnosis of Panic Disorder is only given in the presence of recurring, unexpected panic attacks followed by at least one month of persistent worry or concern about having the attacks or a significant change in behavior as a result of the attacks. Panic attacks are considered "unexpected" if they are not associated with any specific situational triggers, that is, if they occur "out of the blue." Individuals with Panic Disorder also often experience "situationally cued" panic attacks, which occur when exposed to situational triggers that have been paired with panic attacks. Additionally, many individuals experience "situationally predisposed" panic attacks, where a particular situation increases the probability of experiencing an attack but does not inevitably trigger the immediate onset of a panic attack.

Panic Disorder may occur with or without Agoraphobia, the fear that develops about places and situations from which escape may be difficult, where help is unavailable, or where an attack may prove embarrassing (APA, 1994). Hence, these situations are avoided or endured with great discomfort. Agoraphobic situations include large crowds, malls, movie theaters, waiting in line, traveling by car or public transportation, and simply being outside the home alone. The degree of impairment in functioning due to the avoidance ranges from mild to severe. The individual with mild Agoraphobia might avoid driving long distances alone but can drive alone to work on most days. He or she may feel uncomfortable in large crowds but will occasionally attend concerts and go to movies but will sit on the aisle to be closer to an exit if a panic attack occurs. A person with moderate Agoraphobia may limit driving to a few miles close to home, never drive on freeways or on unfamiliar streets, may drive on freeways only when accompanied, and may avoid shopping malls and large supermarkets. Those with severe Agoraphobia may be virtually housebound, require a companion to leave the house even for a short trip to the store, and can no longer work due to the disorder.

The commonly used cognitive-behavioral treatment for Panic Disorder and Agoraphobia was developed during the past 15 years and was based primarily on the biopsychosocial model of panic (e.g., Barlow, 1988). In this model, the initial panic attack is conceived of as a "false alarm" or misfiring of the fear system that can take place in biologically and psychologically vulnerable individuals. This initial panic attack often occurs during a period of stress or following a significant life change, such as the death of a loved one, job- or school-related stress, and positive but demanding events like a marriage or the birth of a child. It is hypothesized that a neurobiological overreactivity may contribute to the origin of the initial panic attack. Theoretically, a lowered threshold for stress may be one predisposing factor for development of Panic Disorder. In the second part of the model, this physiological overreactivity interacts with a psychological vulnerability, which results in development of key features of the disorder. The psychological or cognitive factors are conceptualized as a set of danger-laden beliefs about bodily sensations (e.g., "Heart palpitations mean I could be having a heart attack") and about the world in general (e.g., "I cannot control what happens to me"). Together, these two concepts of anxiety sensitivity (Reiss, Peterson, Gursky, & McNally, 1986) and uncontrollability (Barlow, 1988) form the central feature of the cognitive schema or filter that is considered critical for the acquisition and maintenance of Panic Disorder. The individual with Panic Disorder is prone to believe that bodily sensations are not normal but are signs of a serious illness or simply are dangerous. In support for this model, anxiety sensitivity has been shown to predict the occurrence of future panic attack following the natural environmental stressor of military training (Schmidt, Lerew, & Jackson, 1997, 1999).

In the biopsychosocial model of Panic Disorder, experience of an unexpected panic attack in a vulnerable individual leads to development of learned associations among internal and external cues present during the attack. For example, in the case illustration discussed in this chapter, Sue experienced dizziness during her initial panic attack; therefore, when she later experienced slight dizziness after taking an over-the-counter cold medication, she feared that she was having another panic attack. As a result of simple associative learning, normal fluctuations in Sue's balance as well as taking any medication have now become conditioned cues or "learned alarms" for panic. Following the initial panic, vulnerable individuals develop hypervigilance for internal sensations, becoming highly sensitive to any innocuous somatic response or change. Indeed, natural variations in physiology that go unnoticed by most people can trigger a conditioned panic response. This learned response is the result of the Pavlovian conditioning of interoceptive cues, otherwise called internal sensations. This form of associative conditioning has been shown to be a very rapid and stable form of learning (e.g., Razran, 1961). Sue, for example, avoided medication and exercise following her initial attack. External cues present at the time of the attack may also become associated with panic, beginning the cycle of agoraphobic avoidance. Internal and external cues may generalize over time so that the range of triggering sensations and avoided situations becomes increasingly broad.

Individuals with Panic Disorder develop an anxious apprehension about having future panic attacks, which often is at the source of their disabling agoraphobic avoidance. Such apprehension stems from the perceived unpredictability and uncontrollability of panic attacks ("When will it happen again and how will I end it?"), and the apprehension in turn generates more physical tension as well as vigilance for bodily cues, which together trigger more panic attacks. Moreover, unexpected autonomic arousal tends to generate fear, which intensifies the sensation because fear produces more autonomic arousal. This process results in an escalating spiral of fear: the fear-of-fear cycle. Often, individuals are not aware of the initiating internal sensation; thus, they perceive the attacks as unexpected or out of the blue. The interoceptive cues and resulting panic attacks are viewed as unpredictable and uncontrollable, which results in elevated levels of chronic anxious apprehension and increases the likelihood of further panic attacks.

CASE DESCRIPTION

Sue was a 34-year-old, recently divorced woman, who was working as a commercial actor. Although she recalled experiencing anxiety attacks in her early 20s, they seemed to her to be quite different from the ones that currently troubled her. She remembered that those episodes usually occurred at large parties or when she was on stage, and consisted of slight shaking, tightness in her chest, and blushing. She always thought of them as a mild form of stage fright and not particularly troubling. The first panic of this recent episode occurred about two years earlier while at an audition for a commercial. At that time, Sue's main symptoms included shortness of breath, heart palpitations, dizziness, unreality or depersonalization, and a fear of going crazy.

The day of her first panic attack was proceeding fairly normally except for a relatively high level of stress. She had to make a frantic race across town in heavy traffic to arrive at her audition just in time. She had skipped breakfast, but she did stop for an extra cup of coffee before getting on the freeway. After checking in with the receptionist, she went to the waiting room, which was filled to capacity, quite warm, and uncomfortable. While waiting, she tried to review the script, but had trouble concentrating due to the room conditions and recurring thoughts about the financial importance of her getting this job. She recalled that when her turn to audition arrived, everything began well. However, soon after she started reading, symptoms emerged and quickly rose to a peak. She had trouble breathing, became quite lightheaded, and felt very strange, with a weird out-of-body experience. She fumbled over a few words, blurted out something about having the flu, and excused herself from the room. Thinking that there was something terribly wrong, she abruptly left the building and phoned a friend, who drove her to an emergency room. At the hospital, after a series of tests revealed no medical cause for her symptoms, she was offered a sedative, which she refused, and was discharged home.

The initial panic attack that triggered this episode of Panic Disorder was perceived as out of the blue and its impact was significant and immediate. After returning home from the emergency room, Sue canceled the rest of her appointments for that week. When she finally started to venture out, she did so quite tentatively and preferred to be accompanied by a friend. She found that her subsequent panic attacks were triggered by situations in which she felt trapped and potentially compromised by embarrassment. At first, this was true only for auditions and professional situations; however, it later generalized to other social situations like dating and she occasionally avoided family gatherings if she anticipated that there would be a large group. In these situations, she began to feel anxious when she anticipated having an attack. Often, this thought acted as the catalyst, which began the cycle of anxiety that realized her fear. The thought usually preceded a hypervigilance for body sensations, which increased the likelihood that she would experience a sense of depersonalization or a dizzy sensation. Typically, these sensations gave quick rise to a full-blown panic attack and her rapid escape from the situation.

In the six months following her first attack, frequency of her panic attacks grew steadily. They reached a peak frequency that corresponded to a period when she stopped driving, and then they tapered off to a steady level for the six months prior to the start of treatment. In the period prior to her intake interview, despite her relatively high degree of avoidance behavior, Sue has averaged about 5 panic attacks and about 10 to 15 limited-symptom attacks per month.

When Sue sought treatment at the clinic, she displayed a moderate level of Agoraphobia. She avoided crowds and unfamiliar places or endured them with discomfort. She avoided most airline travel and would get on a plane only for a short flight if absolutely necessary. Her social activities were restricted to friends and family, as she still felt uncomfortable with strangers. Indeed, she reduced her frequency of attendance and participation at AA meetings and went to only small, familiar meetings. She drove on surface streets but avoided most freeway driving, attempting only the most familiar routes, avoiding rush hour, and usually accompanied by a friend. Immediately after her first attack she drove without anxiety for a brief period. However, as her frequency of attacks increased, she began slowly to restrict her driving after she experienced a number of panic attacks while driving. In fact, there was a short period when she did not drive at all and relied on taxis and friends for transportation. Motivated by the great difficulty she experienced getting around town, she started driving again and gradually increased her driving range slightly. She was able to increase her comfort zone to the point where she could do some limited travel on her own.

CHIEF PRESENTING COMPLAINTS

Since that first panic attack, most of Sue's attacks began with her noticing a slight feeling of dizziness. This often happened when she exercised or simply walked up a flight of stairs. The first attack in the audition left her with a hypersensitivity to dizziness, fainting, feelings of unreality, or simply feeling slightly off balance and falling. She recalled that during that first panic, her immediate concern was fainting in front of all of those important people. One reason these sensations scared her was that they seemed to have no origin and felt so unusual. All of a sudden she noticed this vague sense of being out of her body. Her arms and legs seemed heavy, slightly larger than normal, and felt almost as if they were floating at her side. It was then that she noticed the ringing in her ears and the dizziness. By the time she left the room, her heart was pounding and the room was spinning. She was convinced that she was either going crazy or having a stroke—but that the way she felt was definitely not normal.

During the initial diagnostic interview, Sue reported that her primary problem was worrying about the attacks and the fear that something was seriously wrong. After her first panic, she received some literature from her general practitioner about panic attacks. Also, she had read some self-help manuals about anxiety and recognized that these "dizzy spells" probably were panic attacks. However, she was not fully convinced that she did not have something seriously wrong with her brain. She had the recurring thought that she might be different from everyone else, that she was going crazy, or was having a stroke, or had some sort of brain damage. She believed that perhaps her years of substance abuse had damaged her brain and now there was nothing anyone could do to help her.

In addition to the problem with auditions, she also had begun to have difficulties in most social situations. Until recently, she had always enjoyed socializing and had started to date again following her divorce. However, soon after the panic attacks started, she noticed that when she was in any social situation where she felt vulnerable to scrutiny, she became anxious. She worried about the consequence of panicking in these situations, and that quickly brought on a slight dizziness and the feeling of unreality. This pattern was also the primary problem with auditions. It was the anticipation of developing symptoms that often precipitated a panic attack and inhibited her ability to perform.

In addition to restricting social engagements and exercise, Sue had developed a pattern of avoidance of certain driving situations. She found that she became quite anxious at the thought of having an attack while driving on the freeway. She believed that the dizziness made it dangerous to drive and commented, "Well, it's common sense that if I get dizzy while driving on the freeway, I could cause a serious accident."

Her general practitioner offered to prescribe a benzodiazapine and a selective serotonin reuptake inhibitor (SSRI) to help reduce the severity of the anxiety symptoms, both of which are routinely prescribed for Panic Disorder. However, due to her history of substance abuse, she refused the benzodiazapine and only reluctantly tried the SSRI. She stated that the medication made her "feel funny," and she quickly stopped taking it. Currently, she is reluctant to take any medication, even over-the-counter cold preparations, as she is hypersensitive to any small side effect or sensation they might produce. She has even stopped taking the antiallergy medications that she took for years, which has caused a resurgence of allergy symptoms.

HISTORY

Two years prior to this episode, Sue had undergone some major changes in her life situation. Over the past 10 years, she had gradually developed a serious problem with drugs and alcohol as well as significant marital conflict with her husband. After separating from her husband, she entered and successfully completed a drug rehabilitation program. A few months after gaining her sobriety, she initiated a divorce from her husband. She was quite happy with her new life, although it was a significant change from the past.

Although moderately successful as a commercial actor and model, money from her husband's family business had supplied the majority of their household income. They had no children, traveled often, and routinely entertained her husband's business clients in their large house near the beach. As part of the process of her recovery from drug and alcohol abuse, she decided that she wanted a complete break from the lifestyle that contributed to her abuse. Therefore, she did not request alimony and instead settled for a small, one-time monetary payment, which she used to set up an apartment near her old neighborhood, where she regularly attended AA meetings. She planned to support herself by working as an actor.

Sue reported a family history of anxiety, mood disturbance, and substance abuse. She described her mother as a very anxious person who constantly worried about the health and welfare of all the family members. Her mother and father frequently consumed alcohol, and Sue believed that both were alcoholics. Additionally, although he never received treatment, in retrospect she believes that her father suffered with depression.

BEHAVIORAL ASSESSMENT

Like most successful psychological treatments, an effective cognitive-behavioral treatment for Panic Disorder and Agoraphobia requires thorough and reliable assessment procedures. The process of behavior change must start with a complete assessment of the problem areas before treatment can proceed. Continued assessment during and after treatment not only allows for monitoring of progress and evaluation of treatment effectiveness but, more important, it supplies client and therapist with the necessary information to design and modify the treatment procedures.

An intake interview serves a number of important functions that aid the course of treatment. Initial diagnosis of Panic Disorder is best determined through the use of a clinical interview that offers a reliable and nonambiguous result. The Anxiety Disorders Interview Schedule for *DSM-IV* (ADIS-IV; Brown, DiNardo, & Barlow, 1994) is a widely used clinical interview that was designed specifically for the assessment of anxiety disorders. This semistructured instrument follows the *DSM-IV* diagnostic criteria for the anxiety disorders and takes approximately 1.5 to 2.5 hours to administer, depending on the severity of symptoms and experience of the interviewer. The ADIS-IV provides a reliable means for obtaining the information necessary to establish a differential diagnosis among the anxiety disorders as well as diagnose other comorbid *DSM-IV* Axis I disorders that may be present. The lifetime version gathers information on past diagnoses. For Sue, the initial interview established the current diagnosis of Panic Disorder with Agoraphobia and Social Phobia as well as a past diagnosis of Polysubstance Dependence in sustained full remission. Sue also exhibited features of Generalized Anxiety Disorder and Major Depression, however, both with symptoms below clinical severity. Another benefit from using a structured diagnostic instrument is that the data are available in a format that allows for a clear distinction between clinical and subclinical problems.

Ongoing self-monitoring is another important aspect of assessment and treatment. A clinical interview provides important information but is always subject to retrospective recall biases. Self-monitoring forms and self-report instruments offer more objective feedback on current frequency and intensity of symptoms. At the intake interview, Sue was given a pack of panic attack records that she used to record intensity, duration, situational context, and symptom profile for each panic attack. Recording was initiated prior to treatment to establish a baseline and was continued throughout treatment. These forms provided immediate feedback for Sue to help identify triggers for each attack and rate the effectiveness of any intervention that she employed. This method also helped her develop an objective, "scientific" self-awareness with regard to her anxiety symptoms. During the two-week baseline period between intake and the first session, Sue experienced 4 full-blown and 10 limited-symptom attacks. As previously mentioned, an attack is classified as a full-blown panic attack if the episode includes 4 or more symptoms from the list of 13. A limited-symptom attack is defined as one that follows the same temporal pattern but has 3 or fewer symptoms. This is a useful distinction for the client to learn, as it can be helpful to establish an objective focus. Teaching clients to view their symptoms more objectively is a fundamental goal in this treatment method and facilitates the process of identifying triggers.

Sue was asked to rate a number of aspects about her mood and anxiety on a daily basis. Items included the average and maximum levels of anxiety during the day, her preoccupation with panicking, percent chance of panicking the next day, and average level of depression. Sue recorded these ratings on retiring each night on a Weekly Record of Anxiety and Depression. To monitor degree of agoraphobic behavior, she also monitored activities by logging daily excursions in a diary and checking off activities completed on an Agoraphobia checklist.

Standardized self-report inventories are used prior to and following treatment to provide information for treatment planning as well as to assess therapeutic change. Sue completed a series of inventories that assessed a number of important factors that contribute to and/or identify key features of Panic Disorder and Agoraphobia. These included degree of avoidance as indexed by the Mobility Inventory Questionnaire (Chambless, Caputo, Gracely, Jasin, & Williams, 1985). The Anxiety Sensitivity Index (ASI; Reiss et al., 1986), the Agoraphobia Cognitions Questionnaire (Chambless, Caputo, Bright, & Gallagher, 1984), and the Body Sensations Questionnaire (Chambless et al., 1984) are used to assess the degree to which specific bodily sensations are feared. To further assess the physical and cognitive symptoms of both anxiety and mood, the Beck Anxiety Inventory (BAI; Beck, Epstein, Brown, & Steer, 1988) and the Beck Depression Inventory (BDI; Beck, Ward, Mendelson, Mock, & Erbaugh, 1961) were included. Information from these instruments, the self-monitoring forms, and the ADIS-IV was used to help construct exposure hierarchies for both the in vivo and interoceptive exercises.

Behavioral tests provide an objective measure of avoidance of specific situations that may differ from individuals' subjective impressions of what they can accomplish. Although these tests traditionally are the tools solely of research scientists, they can provide useful information in a clinical setting. These tests may be standardized or tailored to the individual. Standardized behavioral tests typically involve walking or driving an established route. Anxiety levels are rated at regular intervals and the actual distance traveled is recorded. For Sue, we established a battery of three individualized tasks; two involved driving alone on two different freeway routes and one challenged her to go alone to a crowded movie theater. These were selected, with Sue's help, to be from moderate to high difficulty to establish a significant goal for treatment. Maximum levels of anxiety and extent of approach (i.e., refused, attempted but escaped, or completed) were recorded for each task. Although Sue attempted all three tasks prior to the first session, she was not able to complete them. Nevertheless, she discovered that her predicted anxiety was far higher than the level she actually encountered for the two driving tasks.

Standardized behavioral tests are useful to assess fear of bodily sensations. Indeed, these exercises to induce interoceptive sensations are a key element of the cognitive-behavioral treatment for Panic Disorder. These tasks are useful as part of the intake process to help establish the degree of impairment. In our clinic, we use spinning in a circle for one minute, breathing through a straw for two minutes, and hyperventilation for 30 seconds as assessment tasks. Anxiety levels before and after each task as well as task duration are recorded. These three exercises constitute our standard battery. Sue attempted these three tasks at pretreatment. She was able to complete the spinning but ended the straw breathing at 30 seconds and stopped hyperventilation after 15 seconds.

Monitoring of physiology is a useful assessment tool in the treatment of Panic Disorder and Agoraphobia. In addition to providing a good objective measure of treatment gains, physiological monitoring can be useful to help challenge some of the cognitive and perceptual errors that are common in Panic Disorder. Hypersensitivity and hypervigilance to internal sensations are two key perceptual characteristics found in virtually all individuals with Panic Disorder. Providing corrective feedback as to the actual range of physiological function can be useful in reversing these misperceptions. For example, in our clinic, we use a heart rate monitor during the interoceptive behavioral tasks. At the time of her initial assessment, Sue perceived that her heart rate was in a dangerous range during the hyperventilation task; she was surprised to see that her actual heart rate was only slightly elevated and well below that typical for mild exercise.

MEDICAL CONSULTATION

It is often the case that clients who seek cognitive-behavioral treatment for Panic Disorder and Agoraphobia simultaneously receive pharmacological treatment. Historically, the benzodiazepines and tricyclic antidepressants were the drugs of choice; however, recently, the SSRIs have become widely prescribed for the pharmacological treatment of Panic Disorder (e.g., Gitlin, 1996). Also, it is not uncommon for that treatment to be managed by a family or general practice physician rather than a psychiatrist. Regardless of the specialty of the prescribing physician, it is good practice to confer. Consultation can increase client's compliance with both psychological and pharmacological treatment if it can result in a unified message being delivered to the client. Additionally, consultation may provide the transfer of valuable clinical information between practitioners. In the era of managed care, the extensive structured assessment done in cognitive-behavioral therapy likely exceeds the degree allowed in a medical setting and will be a welcome additional tool for the physician.

Early studies indicated that there was a benefit from exposure-based behavioral therapies delivered in combination with drug therapy (e.g., Marks et al., 1983). However, recently, a number of studies have indicated that addition of drug treatment to behavior therapy may produce deleterious effects on outcome (e.g., Otto, Pollack, & Sabatino, 1996). The possible reasons for this effect are diverse (for review, see Craske, 1999), but there are a number of factors that are important in terms of the present case presentation. The addition of a drug can often increase anxiety by means of increased bodily sensations from side effects, which can reduce compliance with treatment. Additionally, there is a possible negative effect on motivation from the addition of a drug when the individual attributes treatment success to the drug rather than developing new learning or skills. It has been argued that this effect may increase the probability of remission. More important, the most widely accepted mechanisms of action that have been proposed for behavioral exposure predict a negative effect with the addition of drug therapy. However, despite these potential downsides, many clients achieve significant clinical improvements with combination treatments and find behavioral exercises to be more tolerable with a reduction in arousal due to pharmacological therapy.

Medical consultation is a necessity prior to the start of treatment to rule out possible physical causes that might underlie the panic symptoms and to identify possible health factors that might be exacerbated by treatment. These conditions include hyperthyroidism, heart disease, diabetes, adrenal tumor, inner ear problems, stroke, hypoglycemia, mitral valve prolapse, and pregnancy. In our research clinic, we require each participant to have had a complete physical within the prior year and to complete a detailed medical screening questionnaire. Sue reported absence of these conditions. She had a complete physical as part of her substance abuse treatment prior to developing panic symptoms as well as a complete physical following the initial panic attack. Her physician reported that she was in good health, supported her entering cognitive-behavioral treatment, and expressed a preference for it to be combined with pharmacological treatment. As previously stated, Sue discontinued drug therapy due to her sensitivity to physical sensations and history of drug abuse.

CASE CONCEPTUALIZATION

Similar to a common pattern for development of Panic Disorder, Sue originally experienced an anxiety attack while in her early 20s. This is a time when it is common for the number of life stressors to increase with the many changes that often occur at this age. For Sue, this included an end to the security of home and college life, the pressure to succeed at a new career, and the challenges of finding a life partner. She described a period in her early 20s when she experienced panic-like attacks in social and performance situations, which could be a feature of either Panic Disorder or Social Phobia. Establishing a differential diagnosis can be difficult when relying on retrospective data alone. Even though the symptoms of these attacks from this early period were somewhat different from those of the more recent attacks, these events clearly could be classified as panic attacks. However, there was a critical difference in the focus of her anxiety during the earlier period. At that time, she did not develop a true fear-of-fear pattern, as she expressed no concern about the sensations per se except for the effect they had on how people viewed her. She developed symptoms only in social situations and did not fear the effects of the sensations outside of a social context; her concerns centered entirely on the fear of negative evaluation. Therefore, the more parsimonious diagnosis for Sue's anxiety at that time was Social Phobia rather than Panic Disorder.

Sue reported a reduction in the intensity of her social anxiety, which was due in large part to the self-medication of her anxiety with drugs and alcohol, and a gradual decline in the frequency of panic attacks. She began her use of substances to alleviate the anticipatory anxiety and to decrease the tension she experienced in social and performance situations. During her 20s, she escalated her substance abuse, which was negatively reinforced by a reduction in her social anxiety and was aided by her husband's drug use. By the time she turned 30, her problem with social anxiety was a distant memory but was replaced by the more pressing and self-destructive behaviors associated with substance abuse.

As mentioned previously, Sue's recovery from substance abuse preceded her acquisition of Panic Disorder with Agoraphobia. Clearly, her sobriety facilitated the many positive changes she was making in her life and to a large extent reduced the stressful demands she had experienced in her former life. However, these changes also provided a vehicle for the formation of new demands and challenges, which may have had an incubating effect on the development of Panic Disorder. Sue remembered that she spent an increasing amount of time worried about her dwindling bank account and diminishing job prospects. Moreover, the day of the panic attack at the commercial audition, she was feeling acute stress due to being stuck in traffic while traveling to the audition, which was compounded by an excessive intake of caffeine that morning. Caffeine can stimulate autonomic activity and produce the panic-like sensations of heart palpitations, sweating, and trembling. It is likely that this contributed to onset of Sue's symptoms on that day.

Since that first episode, Sue observed that she often felt panicky when she was rushing to an appointment and had skipped lunch. Since the day of her first panic attack, she had gradually stopped drinking coffee. She had noticed that coffee drinking often preceded development of a panic attack. It is likely that the stimulating effects of the caffeine acted as a conditioned stimulus, which triggered a panic reaction. Other conditioned stimuli included fatigue, bright lights, and other elements that increased her sense of feeling unreal. In a similar fashion, her anxiety often was precipitated by a tough audition or by the realities of her difficult financial situation.

Sue expressed severe apprehension over having her next attack. The idea of experiencing an attack was frequently on her mind and she was unable to plan activities without considering how she would escape or cope with an attack. Whenever a full-blown attack hit, she would do whatever she could to escape the situation and return to the security of her home. Her avoidance was clearly motivated by anticipation of another panic attack. However, the specific type of thought generating this anticipatory anxiety differed with each type of situation. Her avoidance of work and social situations stemmed primarily from a fear of negative evaluation. Her avoidance of physical arousal from exercise, coffee, or medications was centered in fear of the sensations they produced and their potential danger. She avoided places where escape might be difficult if she had a panic attack, and similarly, she avoided driving as she thought it was dangerous to drive if she had a panic attack.

It was clear that her fear of sensations associated with panic and anxious arousal were at the center of her dysfunctional behavior and emotional stress. This fear was the ultimate cause of her anxiety, which was mediated and modulated by her beliefs. She firmly held on to the idea that she was somehow prone to physical illness, and this notion motivated her hypervigilance of her body. During therapy, she recalled that her mother was very concerned about illness and colds. When Sue was a child, her mother would constantly warn her about the dangers of getting wet or cold when playing and monitored her physical well-being closely. This modeling and instruction by her mother seemed to facilitate the development of Sue's hypochondriac-like belief set. She seemed to notice any small fluctuation in her body and tended to view any new sensation as a sign of illness or the start of some physical danger. This propensity toward catastrophic thinking concerning physical sensations fueled her Panic Disorder symptoms and helped develop her avoidance behavior. It would also be one of the more difficult cognitions to be challenged during therapy.

RATIONALE FOR TREATMENT CHOICE

The National Institute of Health (NIH, 1991), following a review of all the available treatment outcome studies on Panic Disorder, has determined that cognitive-behavioral therapy and pharmacological therapy are the treatments of choice. Their review found that a standard cognitive-behavioral regimen resulted in approximately 80% of subjects becoming panic-free and 52% with significant clinical reductions in anxiety at the end of treatment. The latter figure increases to over 70% at follow-up. This continued gain following termination demonstrates the benefit of a skill-based, behavioral-exposure therapy in that improvement can continue following the end of treatment when the client continues to apply the principles and skills learned in therapy.

Sue contacted our research clinic to take part in a 12-week treatment program for individuals with Panic Disorder and Agoraphobia. She had heard about the program from a public service announcement that was broadcast on a local radio station. Following the initial screen and diagnostic interview, she was offered a standard group treatment protocol that was based on the Panic Control Treatment (Barlow & Craske, 1989, 1994). This treatment was being administered in the context of a large research study, where each group was conducted by a well-trained therapist and followed a structured treatment manual. However, like most cognitive-behavioral protocols, it was possible for the therapist to individualize the treatment to some degree to fit each participant while remaining true to the basic method and procedure. Although a good protocol allows adjustments to match the specific clinical requirements of each client, structured treatment protocols have been shown to be more effective than unstructured formats (e.g., Chambless, 1996). A group format can offer the added benefit of group support and vicarious learning. Observation of another group member's success can increase motivation and serve as a catalyst for positive change. Many of the published clinical trials that demonstrated success with cognitive-behavioral treatment for Panic Disorder employed group designs (Craske, 1999).

A cognitive-behavioral treatment approach contains several components that target the physiological, cognitive, and behavioral aspects of Panic Disorder and agoraphobic avoidance. Each component is designed to attack one or more key features or symptoms of the disorder and is used for both theoretical and practical reasons. These techniques have a strong foundation in experimental and clinical psychology, and there are numerous laboratory and clinical findings that support their use. As typically executed, the treatment is brief, commonly completed within 10 to 20 weeks, and highly effective, with approximately 76% of clients panic-free following treatment and 78% at follow-up (for a complete review, see Craske, 1999).

Sue received a 12-session group treatment for Panic Disorder with Agoraphobia. The treatment began with education about the nature of anxiety and instruction on the physiology of panic. This educational component served to help her understand that her symptoms were part of a normal anxiety response and not dangerous to her body. In the next phase, she was taught a breathing technique that helped her relax and start the process of gaining some control over her physiological symptoms. This breathing technique offers the client an active strategy to cope with the panic and anxiety when it occurs. The treatment then shifted to cognitive restructuring, which included identifying anxiety-based thoughts and systematically challenging them. The process of identifying triggers and labeling thoughts as anxious helps create an objective focus that can facilitate anxiety reduction and decrease hypervigilance of internal and external threats. In the cognitive restructuring segment, thoughts that are based on threats and danger arising from Sue's panic symptoms were analyzed and challenged. For example, dizziness would often trigger her to jump to the conclusion that she would faint. She was taught to challenge that thought by looking at the evidence directly—specifically, that she has felt this way many times before but has never fainted. During this part of the treatment, Sue began to keep careful records of her thoughts, noted each situation when they occurred, and generated alternative thoughts based on a realistic examination of the evidence. These first three components of the treatment—education, breathing retraining, and cognitive restructuring—offered Sue a means to take control over her symptoms and manage her anxiety. This prepared her for the next treatment phase, behavioral exposure, and gave her the necessary skills to manage anxiety generated by the exposures.

All components of the treatment are important, but interoceptive exposure can be thought of as the core element of the treatment. Its purpose is to reduce or replace the associations between internal sensations and panic. Through repeated confrontation with the feared sensations, Sue gradually learned that the sensations were harmless. For example, because she was particularly fearful of dizziness, she was instructed to slowly spin in a circle and experience the sensation. Gradually, she was able to tolerate the dizziness without triggering a panic attack or becoming anxious. This technique is a powerful tool to change dysfunctional associations, but, understandably, it is difficult for the client to face the feared sensations. The preceding components—education, breathing retraining, and cognitive restructuring—gave Sue skills to help her manage the anxiety arising from these difficult exposures. In the last phase of treatment, Sue was instructed to gradually confront the situations and places that she feared and avoided. Similar to interoceptive exposure, in vivo exposure directly challenges feared associations and establishes new learning.

COURSE OF TREATMENT

The major components of cognitive-behavioral therapy target the cognitive distortions and dysfunctional behaviors that stem from a fear of internal sensations and external situations. Treatment can be administered in an individual or group format. In our clinic, group treatments are limited to four to six individuals, are

90 to 120 minutes in length, and always employ a cotherapist to assist with the exposures and management of homework. Sessions are highly structured and focus on current symptoms and thoughts associated with recent panic attacks. Historical material is considered only when directly relevant to current symptoms. Clients are taught that although discussion of symptom origins can sometimes offer insight into current problems, it is not a necessary component of successful treatment. They are told that one can successfully change behavior by understanding what maintains it, without knowing the details of its acquisition.

Homework assignments are given each session throughout treatment and practices are carefully monitored. Typically, each session begins with a review of the prior week's homework. This includes an inspection of panic attack records, weekly record of anxiety, cognitive monitoring forms, and the record of exposures performed. Each client is given feedback on all of the homework material, with particular attention to correcting any problems with practices and reinforcing good performance. The effective completion of homework is critical to produce behavior change. Problems with homework completion should be targeted as a behavior requiring change and not as a failure.

Collaboration between client and therapist is emphasized, but clients are encouraged to avoid relying completely on the therapist's observations and to develop the skill of objective observation of their symptoms. They are instructed in a general method that they will continue to use following treatment, so the ultimate goal is for them to become their own therapist. That process starts with the notion of the "personal scientist," developing the ability to objectively analyze one's own behaviors, thoughts, and feelings, provide self-corrective feedback, and generate alternative thoughts and behaviors to use in future situations. One goal of therapy can be to make the therapist redundant; by the end of treatment, clients have enough skill to guide themselves with continued practices as needed.

In the first two sessions, the client is provided with education about the nature of panic and anxiety. These sessions are primarily didactic in nature. However, some time is spent on introductions and briefly identifying each subject's key panic symptoms and goals for treatment. Panic Disorder and Agoraphobia are defined, and individuals are informed that fear is a natural response to danger and is actually part of the body's fight-or-flight system. That system is a primitive part of our autonomic nervous system, which is triggered in reaction to an actual or perceived threat. The physiological basis of panic and anxiety is explained in detail; particular attention is paid to a review of the key aspects of respiratory physiology and the autonomic nervous system in general. The goal is to normalize the fear response and provide a scientific explanation for arousal and anxiety. Each of the physical symptoms of a panic attack is explained in terms of its physiological origin and evolutionary adaptive value. For example, when a potential threat is identified, the brain sends a signal to increase the heart rate as a means of getting more blood to the limbs so that a quick escape can be executed.

The myths about panic also are discussed and debunked in detail. Common misconceptions, such as "I have anxiety because there is an imbalance in my brain chemicals," are revealed as false. Clients are taught that when the brain detects danger, the autonomic nervous system initiates a number of physiological changes, which may result in an increase in blood flow, rate of breathing, heart rate, sweating, and more. Although the proximate cause for these responses is a neurochemical change, there is no reason to believe that a chemical imbalance is the ultimate cause of anxiety. This was particularly important for Sue to hear, as she believed that her brain was not functioning properly. Another misconception corrected for her was that feeling dizzy or lightheaded means that she will faint, and she was informed that fainting tends to occur only in people with a particular physiological vulnerability. Therefore, the fact that she did not have a history of fainting meant that, in all likelihood, she never would faint in response to anxiety.

Through this discussion about anxiety, the adaptive nature of fear and the autonomic nervous system is emphasized. That is, a highly reactive fight-or-flight system served an important adaptive function that was necessary for survival during our early evolutionary history (for review, see Fanselow & Lester, 1988). Indeed, it is still important today: If one steps off the curb, hears a horn blast, and looks up to see a truck barreling closer, a well-functioning fight-or-flight system will help one quickly respond and jump out of the way. Thus, the goal of treatment is not to eliminate all anxiety, but rather to learn effective ways of managing extreme and inappropriate expressions of anxiety. Prediction and control of anxiety are stressed rather than the elimination of anxiety. Eliminating anxiety in not only impossible but also dangerous, as it protects us in times of real danger.

Another important concept in these first sessions is the three response systems that function in the expression of anxiety. This notion is presented to help explain the functioning of anxiety and also to offer clients a means to objectively categorize their symptoms. It is explained that anxiety, like all emotions, can be delineated into three separate, but not independent, response systems: cognitions, physiology, and behavior, or to think, to feel, and to do. All panic and anxiety symptoms can be categorized as being constructed of a thought, a physical sensation, and/or an action. Clients are instructed on how the interaction among these three systems is a key component in the elicitation of anxiety. Sue reported that when she felt dizzy, she believed that she might faint. In this case, the feeling of dizziness triggered a cognition or interpretation, fear of fainting, which then intensified the arousal and produced an action, escape from the situation. This example of the fear cycle demonstrates how interactions among the three response systems can produce escalation of anxiety symptoms.

In these initial sessions, this notion of a fear cycle is further developed into a general model for the etiology of panic. This model emphasizes the role of thoughts and actions in the development and maintenance of panic. It is explained that a panic attack is basically a physiological response, which may be triggered at inappropriate times and can be uncomfortable, but is fundamentally harmless. When no external stimulus is readily available to explain these strange sensations, the normal tendency is to search internally for an explanation. For individuals who may be predisposed toward anxiety, such as Sue, some malignant internal cause like "I have a brain tumor" or "I'm going crazy" is often deemed the source of these symptoms. These misappraisals result in an intensification of the symptoms, and this increased arousal can act to confirm the initial misappraisal, which leads to escape. The urgency to flee in turn contributes to accelerating arousal, and so on. The notion that anxiety symptoms are normal and time-limited in nature is discussed and represents an initial step toward correcting misappraisals, which are more formally targeted later with cognitive restructuring.

Breathing retraining is introduced in the third session as a method of relaxation and symptom control. This component begins with a hyperventilation or overbreathing demonstration to illustrate the potential role of hyperventilation in the development of panic symptoms. Clients are asked to stand and breathe deeply and rapidly, as if they were blowing up a balloon. The therapist first models the task and then joins the clients in performing the exercise. Following the exercise, sensations elicited and the similarity to panic symptoms are noted and discussed. Similar to the reaction of some clients, Sue had an immediate and strong response to the exercise. She had to stop hyperventilating after 20 seconds due to feelings of panic. She reported a sense of lightheadedness and depersonalization, which began shortly after starting to overbreathe. The therapist was able to assist her recovery by helping her to identify her anxious thoughts and reassure her that the feeling would dissipate soon and was not dangerous. During the exercise, the sensations triggered the thought that she would panic and not be able to stop. This demonstration and Sue's recovery became a valuable example for her and the other clients. It vividly demonstrated the relationship between hyperventilation and panic, the role of triggers for panic, and the benefit of breathing control and cognitive restructuring.

Following the overbreathing exercise, the role of hyperventilation in panic was discussed in detail. Hyperventilation is presented as a process that may occur subtly, without conscious awareness, and that occurs naturally when an anxiety response begins. The need to escape from danger results in an increase in the body's requirement for more oxygen to produce more energy for the working muscles. The physiology of hyperventilation is presented in detail. The client is told that hyperventilation occurs when more oxygen is taken in than can be used by the body, and the result is a lowered amount of carbon dioxide dissolved in the blood relative to the amount of oxygen. The physiological effect of this hyperventilation is to increase the alkalinity of the blood, which causes oxygen to bind tighter to the hemoglobin molecule and constrict the blood vessels. These events lead to the sensation of dizziness, lightheadedness, and a tingling in the extremities when there is a temporary reduction in the amount of oxygen available at the tissues. However, the emphasis is placed on the harmless nature of these sensations and that this is a normal function of the body's defense system. In times of real danger, when fight or flight is required, hyperventilation helps ready the body for action.

Breathing retraining or slow diaphragmatic breathing is presented as a tool to use when hyperventilation occurs during a panic attack and to correct the habit of chronic overbreathing that develops in some people with Panic Disorder. Additionally, there is a meditational component to the exercise that facilitates relaxation and calmness. Sue was instructed to breathe slowly and deeply from her diaphragm rather than her chest, because shallow chest breathing contributes to hyperventilation. The meditational component places the focus of attention on the process of counting during the inhalation and on repeating the word "relax" with each exhalation. Sue was instructed to count starting with 1 and, with each new breath, proceeding to 10 and then back down to 1 in a continuous cycle. She had difficulty with the meditation at first; when she tried to clear her mind of thoughts and focus on the counting, she experienced intrusive, random thoughts. She was told that this is common and to let these thoughts simply pass through her mind, not to fight them, and that she would gradually improve with practice. Breathing was practiced in-session this week and for the next three weeks. Sue was asked to practice slow diaphragmatic breathing as homework at least twice a day for 10 minutes. She was instructed to begin practicing in a quiet, undisturbed place, but to gradually introduce distractions to facilitate generalization. Eventually, this technique would become a useful control strategy when she experienced anxiety or panic. After each week of practice, the rate of breathing was gradually slowed until the target of about 10 breaths per minute was achieved. Sue was instructed that each inhale and exhale should last for about three seconds, so that a full cycle was six seconds long.

Training in cognitive restructuring starts in the third session with an introduction of the notion that anxiety is often automatically generated by maladaptive thoughts (Beck & Emery, 1985). In Panic Disorder, these cognitions often take the form of interpretations of bodily sensations as a sign of some underlying danger or threat. These thoughts are automatic in that they occur habitually, are often triggered by stimuli without awareness, and reflexively result in behavioral consequences. Clients are introduced to the concept of cognitive filters, which help determine the particular interpretations and perceptions we construct for events that occur in the world. Some examples of automatic thoughts that Sue engaged in were thinking that she needed a "safe" seat on the aisle in a theater to allow escape, assuming that dizziness will always lead to fainting, and thinking that any body sensation was a sign of an illness or abnormality. Cognitions may be discrete events that change with the cues generated by particular situations. In terms of Sue's fear of fainting, when she was alone, the thought took the form of a fear of hitting her head and dying; however, when she was in a social situation, her thoughts focused on embarrassment. Identifying the specific cognition requires detailed and careful questioning by the therapist. The goal is to get the client to focus on a specific event rather than generalities so that the true basis underlying the fear can be identified.

Once a specific thought is identified, it is categorized as either a probability overestimation or a catastrophization. Overestimation is defined as jumping to conclusions or inflating the likelihood of a negative outcome. Catastrophizations are defined as blowing events out of proportion or viewing them as disastrous and unmanageable. Categorizing the thought allows the client to begin to restructure the thought. If it is a catastrophic thought, clients learn to challenge the underlying assumptions; if it is an overestimation, clients learn a process of questioning the evidence. The therapist helps clients engage in this process with the Socratic method of inquiry, an empirical, hypothesis-testing approach, asking such questions as "What is the evidence that you will faint?" or "How many times have you fainted before?" Using this technique, the therapist teaches clients how to focus on relevant data like health status and explore alternative explanations like attributing the dizziness to a skipped meal or too much coffee. Perhaps the best way to counter a catastrophization is to simply teach the client that anxiety is time-limited and manageable. An important strategy toward that goal is to help the client examine the realistic consequences of negative events and establish concrete strategies for dealing with these events should they occur. For example, much of Sue's anxiety stemmed from her fear that she might faint in public. The therapist was able to use a series of questions to restructure her thoughts and introduce alternatives: "How bad would it really be if you fainted?" "What would you do if it actually happened—how would you cope?" These questions led Sue to realize that not only is it unlikely to happen, but that if it did happen, people would most likely be understanding, helpful, and sympathetic. They would assume that she had the flu or low blood pressure. She would quickly recover and the consequences would be minimal. These new alternatives became Sue's ammunition at times when she found herself faced with the old automatic thoughts. She practiced repeating these new, nonanxious alternative cognitions, and they eventually achieved a dominant status among her beliefs.

Success with cognitive restructuring and slow diaphragmatic breathing sets the stage for the introduction of interoceptive exposure during the sixth session of this particular protocol. Sue now possessed two effective coping methods that allowed her some control over anxiety and increased her willingness to face her fear of internal sensations and learn that these sensations are harmless. Interoceptive exposure is introduced to weaken or disrupt the associations between specific internal cues and panic reactions. The role that learning has in the panic attack cycle that was introduced in the initial sessions is elaborated on and a simple model of Pavlovian conditioning is presented. It is pointed out that repetition is the key to all learning. When these internal sensations and external events are repeatedly paired with panic and anxiety, we can then learn this relationship and begin to expect one event to follow the other. Examples like touching a stove or learning to avoid certain foods after becoming ill are used to explain this concept. The notion that a panic attack can be triggered by a sensation as the result of a process of learning thus is introduced to the client.

During this interoceptive exposure phase, a number of tasks are used that were designed to induce sensations similar to those experienced during a panic attack. First, all clients attempt each task and then rate the intensity of any sensations produced, similarity to naturally occurring panic sensations, and the maximum anxiety experienced while performing each exercise. The therapist then uses this information to construct a hierarchy of exercises that reliably induce sensations that mimic the panic symptoms. During this phase, Sue practiced this set of tasks, which included hyperventilation, spinning in a circle, running in place, breathing through a straw, and holding her breath. These tasks were ranked according to anxiety levels elicited, starting with the least anxiety-provoking. The exercises were repeated until anxiety decreased to a mild level, and then the next task in the hierarchy was performed. Sue was instructed to experience the sensations completely and try not to engage in any distraction during the task. Rather, she should tolerate the sensations for at least 30 seconds after first noticing them and thus provide herself a means to learn that they are not dangerous and that the catastrophes predicted will not occur. Cognitive restructuring and slow diaphragmatic breathing strategies were employed after each exposure trial as a means to help return to baseline, and then the task was repeated. Sue was instructed to conduct interoceptive exposures at least three times before the next session, repeating each task three to five times or until no anxiety was generated. Following completion of this interoceptive hierarchy, Sue identified natural activities that also induced feared internal sensations. Tasks like drinking coffee, exercising, and watching scary movies, all of which she had been avoiding, produced sensations that she feared and often triggered panic reactions. A hierarchy was established for these tasks and she was then instructed to practice these exercises repeatedly at least three times a week.

Sue, like many other clients, demonstrated significant agoraphobic avoidance that developed in response to her panic attacks. The treatment of choice for Agoraphobia is in vivo exposure, which is typically conducted as the last intervention. Similar to the preceding treatment component, a hierarchy of relevant agoraphobic situations was generated and exposure was conducted in a graduated manner. Sue was instructed to practice these tasks at least three times per week. The difficulty of some of these tasks was managed by manipulating relevant safety signals. Such safety signals as the presence of friends, carrying a cell phone, and carrying water were added and removed from tasks as needed to move up the hierarchy. For example, Sue began her freeway driving exercises with a friend, then she drove alone with a cell phone, and finally alone without a cell phone. Additionally, an interoceptive component was occasionally introduced to increase the task demand. For example, at the top of her hierarchy, to induce dizziness while driving, Sue practiced freeway driving with the windows rolled up and the heater turned on. Like interoceptive exposures, she was directed to refrain from distraction during the exposures and to focus her attention completely on the task. In vivo exposure exercises included confronting and challenging anxiety-laden thoughts that occurred during the exposure with cognitive restructuring techniques. Additionally, slow breathing was used as needed to cope with anxiety during exposures. Sue planned and rehearsed in vivo exercises with her therapist at each weekly session. Together, they reviewed the prior week's practice, modified strategies, and identified areas for improvement. They tried to anticipate potential problems and develop cognitive and behavioral coping strategies in advance of the upcoming week's exercises. Whenever practical and consistent with the hierarchy, the therapist can accompany the client on in vivo exercises during the session.

THERAPIST-CLIENT FACTORS

The primary issue relevant to this topic is the problem of noncompliance with treatment. Similar to other psychiatric disorders, individuals with Panic Disorder do not seek treatment immediately after onset. Typically, they delay seeking psychological intervention until their disability has reached a critical threshold. At this point, the avoidance behaviors and dysfunctional coping strategies are well developed and intervention is often difficult to initiate. Although clients may wish relief, many of the interventions produce a short-term rise in their anxiety and discomfort. Therefore, to motivate clients to engage in these difficult interventions, it is critical to offer some relief early in treatment. Perhaps the best relief arises from a sense of hope that recovery is possible, which can be instilled by the therapist during the initial education component. Disseminating information with a positive, supportive voice can increase clients' belief that this treatment will work for them. The degree to which the therapist can be viewed and trusted as an "expert" by the client will facilitate this process; a warm, supportive, and informed expert will facilitate clients' acceptance that this treatment may produce relief. If clients accept the rationale for the treatment, they will be more motivated to engage fully with the interventions, even if they produce some immediate discomfort. In the case of Sue, she expressed a belief that this treatment would work for her. She identified with the specific examples used and was able to understand the mechanism for each intervention that was to be used during the treatment. This understanding, instilled by the therapist as teacher, was the keystone supporting all of her treatment gains.

Noncompliance with treatment may arise in clients who have an intense level of fear and Agoraphobia. For such individuals, the therapist must take care to conduct the exposures in a more graduated fashion. Additionally, these people may benefit from additional practice with cognitive restructuring and relaxation techniques. The therapist needs to view treatment noncompliance as merely another behavior to be changed. The key to the problem is often obtained by identifying the underlying reason for the noncompliance. It is often based in an intense fear or firmly held belief that the treatment intervention is dangerous. Usually, the therapist can alleviate the problem by identifying a less fearful task for the client to perform.

Noncompliance may arise from a lack of credibility in an intervention's usefulness. For example, originally, Sue believed that she was different from other people with panic because she perceived her symptoms during the interoceptive exposures to be more intense than that experienced by the others in the group. Therefore, she was reluctant to continue, as she believed that the intervention was dangerous and would not be helpful to her. These beliefs were explored through cognitive restructuring and were successfully challenged by the therapist.

COURSE OF TERMINATION

A cognitive-behavioral treatment approach for Panic Disorder always begins with an eye toward termination. Treatment is designed as a short-term intervention with a major goal being teaching clients to become their own therapist. This goal dictates that a good therapist be like a teacher or coach who is helping students to develop skills that they can use following the end of therapy. All of the interventions should be applied in a fashion that fades out therapist involvement. The large reliance on homework and the active participation of clients in the development of hierarchies are essential parts of this educational process. The therapist should take every opportunity to allow clients to answer their own questions by redirecting them and employing the Socratic style. This approach, along with the structure of a time-limited treatment protocol, makes the end of treatment seem more like a graduation than a termination.

Occasionally, therapy can be structured so that the end is approached in a graded fashion. This is done by gradually increasing the time between sessions or by employing a few follow-up sessions at three-month intervals. As a research protocol was being used in the present case, these options were not available for Sue. However, despite this limitation and the difficulties that she experienced over the course of treatment, she felt confident in her ability to continue to apply the techniques that she learned. She expressed some regret that she did not achieve all her treatment goals but was prepared to continue to work toward those goals. In Sue's case, the research protocol brought a slightly premature end to her treatment; however, managed care and the increasing cost of health care has made this a more common feature of therapy. Despite the reason, an early termination can sometimes be used to the client's advantage: Having discrete treatment goals that requires clients to continue to apply the interventions can function to reinforce and consolidate their skills.

FOLLOW-UP

Similar to the rational for the gradual fading of treatment sessions, the majority of clients benefit from periodic clinical follow-up after termination. These contacts can be formally scheduled as part of a fading procedure, beginning with office visits every three months and gradually fading to periodic phone contacts as needed. As part of our research protocol, each participant is contacted monthly for a brief phone interview to assess clinical status and to collect data on progress. Follow-up is important not only for clinical intervention but also for the assessment of functioning from both a research and a clinical perspective. Maintenance of treatment gains can be properly validated only by repeated administration of assessment instruments. In clinical treatment outcome research, maintenance of gains can be calculated as a percentage of the sample or in regard to the individual subject. Recently, it has become popular to combine measures into a composite variable to assess improvement at treatment end and at follow-up. This approach offers a more reliable and valid assessment of a broad clinical improvement and may be a useful technique for a clinical setting. Additionally, assessment at follow-up may be relevant to identify problems or conditions that were masked by the prominent Panic Disorder symptoms.

Sue participated in an assessment session six months following treatment termination. At that time, she underwent another ADIS-IV diagnostic interview, which indicated continued improvement following treatment. She had not had a panic attack since the end of treatment, she experienced virtually no worry about future attacks, and the frequency of limited-symptom attacks remained at or below one to two per month. Additionally, the Social Phobia that triggered much of her substance abuse also seemed to be in partial remission. Additionally, she demonstrated virtually no signs or symptoms of the subclinical depression and General Anxiety Disorder that she had displayed at intake. The findings from the standardized instruments confirmed this diagnostic picture, as did her daily reports of anxiety, mood, and agoraphobic avoidance.

MANAGED CARE CONSIDERATIONS

Managed health care is having an ever-increasing impact on the type and course of treatment that is available for individuals with Panic Disorder and Agoraphobia. It is now recognized that the majority of individuals with Panic Disorder are seen initially by their primary care physicians or by emergency room personnel and not by mental health professionals. Panic Disorder causes a substantial burden to the individual and to society. Individuals with Panic Disorder and Agoraphobia evidence high rates of unemployment and disability and use medical services at a higher rate than do most other patients (for review, see Craske, 1999). The high prevalence rate for Panic Disorder requires the use of effective and efficient treatments, such as Panic Control Treatment (Barlow & Craske, 1989, 1994), to alleviate this large resource burden on managed health care. A related problem is the education of primary care physicians and emergency room personnel regarding the efficiency and availability of these treatments. Sue turned to our research clinic after failing to identify a source for treatment. Managed care could rectify this problem if greater resources were directed to specialized mental health care.

Rapaport and Cantor (1997) have described specific strategies for dealing with managed care in regard to the treatment of Panic Disorder and Agoraphobia. They propose that to work effectively within managed care, the clinician must first understand the benefit plan structure. Understanding the specificity of the mental health benefits and identifying the "gatekeeper" for mental health benefits as well as the criteria used for evaluating treatment success are important to develop a positive relationship. They argue that clinicians potentially could increase the level of care delivered if they created a dialogue with the plan administrator, which could facilitate referrals and increase positive decisions regarding future care delivery. Additionally, Rapaport and Cantor advocate that clinicians establish themselves as expert consultants for managed care plans. In this capacity, clinicians can educate other professionals about the social and economic cost of Panic Disorder and Agoraphobia and how effective treatments can reduce the use of medical services and increase patient satisfaction and quality of life. This is especially relevant for Panic Disorder and Agoraphobia given the high rate of effectiveness and the brevity of treatment. Greater use of this treatment protocol would have a positive effect on overall costs and simultaneously provide quantifiable data on outcome, which is needed for developing algorithms for care delivery.

OVERALL EFFECTIVENESS

Individual clinical effectiveness can be determined only with an objective assessment, which should be included as part of the treatment plan in all clinical settings. Documentation of gains and identification of problem areas are difficult without reliable, objective assessments. Despite the limited resources of a clinical practice, this can be accomplished simply by repeating a subset of the standardized instruments given at intake. As a participant in the research study, Sue underwent a thorough assessment before and after treatment. The ADIS-IV clinical interview, completed by an independent assessor, found that her severity rating for Panic Disorder decreased from a 6 (on a 0–8 scale) with moderate Agoraphobia, to a 2 with mild Agoraphobia by posttreatment. This degree of change is highly significant in that it represents a change from a severe level of disability to a subclinical level that displays a few mild features of Panic Disorder. Frequency of panic attacks that she experienced declined from an average above 5 full panics and over 15 limited-symptom attacks per month before treatment to no full attacks and only 3 limited-symptom episodes reported in the month preceding the posttreatment assessment. Sue reported only occasional worry about a future panic attack, which resulted in very little interference with her day-to-day life. After treatment, she engaged in many of the activities that she previously had avoided. She was once again exercising, socializing, and attending auditions, and her freeway driving improved greatly. She was still limiting the amount of time she spent out of the rightmost lane, but she could now negotiate most freeways and avoided only a few difficult interchanges at busy times of day. She also realized significant decreases in the scores on all of the standardized instruments previously described, with her ASI and BAI scores dropping below the level associated with clinical severity.

Efficacy of cognitive-behavioral treatment has been documented in numerous clinical outcome studies. Craske (1999) reviewed 20 independently conducted controlled studies that measured success by the percentage of panic-free clients at termination or in a panic-free state accompanied by reductions in maladaptive anxiety. Although these results are quite promising, they were, in most cases, observed with subject samples drawn from populations displaying moderate to low levels of Agoraphobia. This selection bias may limit the generalizability of these findings to the entire population of individuals with Panic Disorder, many of whom exhibit severe Agoraphobia. However, despite its limitations, the overall effectiveness of cognitive-behavioral treatment for Panic Disorder and Agoraphobia places it among the best treatments that psychology has to offer. Clearly, there is a need for further development of techniques as well as new strategies for treatment delivery. Fortunately, research continues to identify new methods and broaden the sophistication of treatment application.

REFERENCES

American Psychiatric Association. (1994). *Diagnostic and statistical manual of mental disorders* (4th ed.). Washington, DC: Author.

Barlow, D. H. (1988). *Anxiety and its disorders: The nature and treatment of anxiety and panic.* New York: Guilford Press.

Barlow, D. H., & Craske, M. G. (1989). *Mastery of your anxiety and panic.* New York: Guilford Press.

Barlow, D. H., & Craske, M. G. (1994). *Mastery of your anxiety and panic: II.* San Antonio, TX: Harcourt Brace.

Beck, A. T., & Emory, G. (1985). *Anxiety disorders and phobias: A cognitive perspective.* New York: Basic Books.

Beck, A. T., Epstein, N., Brown, G., & Steer, R. (1988). An inventory for measuring clinical anxiety: Psychometric properties. *Journal of Consulting and Clinical Psychology, 56,* 893–897.

Beck, A. T., Ward, C. H., Mendelson, M., Mock, J., & Erbaugh, J. (1961). An inventory for measuring depression. *Archives of General Psychiatry, 5,* 561–571.

Brown, T. A., DiNardo, P. A., & Barlow, D. H. (1994). *Anxiety Disorders Interview Schedule for DSM-IV (ADIS-IV).* Albany, NY: Graywind.

Chambless, D. L. (1996). In defense of dissemination of empirically supported psychological interventions. *Clinical Psychology: Science and Practice, 3,* 230–235.

Chambless, D. L., Caputo, G., Bright, P., & Gallagher, R. (1984). Assessment of fear in agoraphobics: The Body Sensations Questionnaire and the Agoraphobia Cognitions Questionnaire. *Journal of Consulting and Clinical Psychology, 52,* 1090–1097.

Chambless, D. L., Caputo, G., Gracely, S., Jasin, E., & Williams, C. (1985). Assessment of fear in agoraphobics: The Mobility Inventory for Agoraphobia. *Behaviour Research and Therapy, 23,* 35–44.

Craske, M. G. (1999). *Anxiety disorders: Psychological approaches to theory and treatment.* Boulder, CO: Westview Press.

Fanselow, M. S., & Lester, L. S. (1988). A functional behavoristic approach to aversively motivated behavior: Predatory imminence as a determinant of the topography of defensive behavior. In R. C. Bolles & M. D. Bacher (Eds.), *Evolution and learning* (pp. 185–212). Hillsdale, NJ: Erlbaum.

Gitlin, M. J. (1996). *The psychotherapist's guide to psychopharmacology* (2nd ed.). New York: Free Press.

Marks, I., Grey, S., Cohen, S. D., Hill, R., Mawson, D., Ramm, E., et al. (1983). Imipramine and brief therapist-aided exposure in agoraphobics having self-exposure homework: A controlled trial. *Archives of General Psychiatry, 40,* 153–162.

National Institute of Health. (1991, September 25–27). *NIH Consensus Development Conference on Panic, 9,* No. 2.

Otto, M. W., Pollack, M. H., & Sabatino, S. A. (1996). Maintenance of remission following cognitive behavior therapy for Panic Disorder: Possible deleterious effects of concurrent medication treatment. *Behavior Therapy, 27,* 473–482.

Rapaport, M. H., & Cantor, J. J. (1997). Panic Disorder in a managed care environment. *Journal of Clinical Psychiatry, 58,* 51–55.

Razran, G. (1961). The observable unconscious and the inferable conscious in current Soviet psychophysiology: Interoceptive conditioning, semantic conditioning, and the orienting reflex. *Psychological Review, 6,* 81–147.

Reiss, S., Peterson, R., Gursky, D. M., & McNally, R. J. (1986). Anxiety sensitivity, anxiety frequency and the prediction of fearfulness. *Behaviour Research and Therapy, 24,* 1–8.

Schmidt, N. B., Lerew, D. R., & Jackson, R. L. (1997). The role of anxiety sensitivity in the pathogenesis of panic: Prospective evaluation of spontaneous panic attacks during acute stress. *Journal of Abnormal Psychology, 106,* 355–364.

Schmidt, N. B., Lerew, D. R., & Jackson, R. J. (1999). Prospective evaluation of anxiety sensitivity in the pathogenesis of panic: Replication and extension. *Journal of Abnormal Psychology, 108,* 532–537.

CHAPTER 4

Specific Phobia

JAN H. KAMPHUIS, PAUL M. G. EMMELKAMP, and M. KRIJN

DESCRIPTION OF THE DISORDER

ONE OF THE most widespread anxiety disorders is specific phobia. The term specific phobia refers to a wide range of fears associated with specific stimuli or situations. According to the diagnostic criteria of the *Diagnostic and Statistical Manual of Mental Disorders* (*DSM-IV*; American Psychiatric Association, 1994), specific phobia (*DSM-IV* Code 300.29) should be diagnosed in the case of a persistent excessive or irrational fear of a circumscribed stimulus (object or situation), which is avoided, or endured with intense anxiety. To meet diagnostic criteria, the fear or the avoidance behavior has to interfere significantly with the person's normal life. As well, the fear-related stimulus of specific phobia has to be different from Panic Disorder/Agoraphobia or social phobia stimuli and unrelated to the content of the obsessions of Obsessive-Compulsive Disorder or the trauma of Post Traumatic Stress (PTS). *DSM-IV* distinguishes four types of specific phobias: (1) animal type (e.g., spiders, dogs, cats, and snakes); (2) natural environment type (e.g., storms, heights, or water); (3) blood-injection-injury type (e.g., dental phobia); and (4) situational type (e.g., tunnels, bridges, elevators, flying, driving, or enclosed places).

CLINICAL PICTURE

Specific phobia can lead to intense panic and extreme avoidance of the associated cues. Patients often are very creative in avoiding phobic confrontations and they therefore rarely seek treatment. In some cases, this can have severe consequences, such as when a blood phobic avoids medical treatment, or when a claustrophobic refuses to have a necessary medical scan taken. When specific phobics do seek treatment, it is often because they anticipate that circumstances will force confrontation with a dreaded cue stimulus.

When specific phobics are confronted with the phobic object or situation, this immediately induces extreme distress and panic. When the phobic stimulus is removed, anxiety decreases. Confrontation with the phobic stimuli also leads to a sympathetically mediated increase in blood pressure and heart rate. In contrast, blood-injury phobics show a very short sympathetic activation followed by a parasympathetic activation (i.e., a drop in heart rate and/or blood pressure; Öst & Hellström, 1997).

Specific phobias develop only around a limited array of stimuli (i.e., objects or situations). Surprisingly, some phobias never occur, like gun phobia, electric outlet phobia, car phobia, grass mower phobia, or hammer phobia, even though many people have had dangerous or life-threatening experiences with these stimuli. The preparedness theory attempts to explain this phenomenon. According to this perspective, most phobias are based on a genetic disposition (or preparedness) to develop fear of those objects and situations (e.g., snakes, spiders, enclosed places) that posed a threat to the survival of our prehistoric ancestors. Although a number of experimental laboratory studies have tested this theory, results are at present inconclusive (Merkelbach & de Jong, 1997).

PREVALENCE, COURSE, AND PROGNOSIS

In the past decade, several epidemiological studies investigated the prevalence rate of simple phobia according to the *DSM-III* (e.g., see Chapman, 1997; Kessler et al., 1994). Specific phobia is the most common anxiety disorder, with a mean lifetime prevalence of just over 10%. Highest point-prevalence rate was observed for the situational and the natural environment types (13%), followed by animal phobias (8%) and blood-injection-injury phobias (3%). Specific phobias are more prevalent among women than among men. This difference is strongest for animal phobias and the situational/natural environment phobias (Frederikson, Annas, Fisher, & Wik, 1996). In general, there is a considerable overlap between anxiety and affective syndromes. Such comorbidity is not seen among specific phobics. For example, only 9% of patients with specific phobia reported past depressive episodes (Monroe, 1990).

The mean age of onset for animal phobia and blood-injury phobia is about 8 years old (Öst & Hellström, 1997), 12 years old for dental phobia, and 20 years old for claustrophobia (Öst, 1987). In young children (2 to 6 years), specific phobias (mostly fears of animals) often improve "spontaneously" without any treatment. Those with phobias that continue into adulthood seldom recover spontaneously. Specific phobias are especially responsive to behavioral treatment (Emmelkamp, 1994). However, there may be practical problems in arranging exposure for less approachable stimuli (e.g., storms).

CASE DESCRIPTION

The present case is concerned with acrophobia, or specific fear of heights. Rarely does one encounter case descriptions of specific phobia in the clinical literature, presumably because there is consensus about appropriate treatment (i.e., exposure in vivo). Moreover, exposure in vivo is a well-documented and relatively simple procedure, with good prognosis among phobics; a number of publications have even documented treatment success within one session. However, as this case illustrates, things are not always as simple as they seem.

The history of chief complaints and its present assessment pre- and posttreatment are described, as well as several complications encountered over the course of treatment of a 50-year-old bank employee (referred to as Albert) with severe fear of heights. Albert had been married for over 20 years and had no children. As will be discussed in more detail, no other psychopathology was evident. Interpersonally, Albert was a cooperative and friendly patient to work with.

CHIEF COMPLAINTS

Albert presented with severe fear of heights. Any open space higher than 10 feet posed a problem for him, especially when it involved open-depth views, but even lower heights could cause him significant distress. This meant that while he had no problem flying, getting onto the airplane's staircase was a major problem. Likewise, working on the eighth floor of a high-rise bank building with a window view was not a problem; getting on the stairs to go from one floor to the next was. His main concerns were losing his steadiness, falling, or being drawn to the depth and jumping. Situations Albert avoided included stairs and escalators (especially going down), open balconies, multilevel parking lots, elevated train stations, and (tourist) towers. Situations became more challenging when they included "open space," without railings to hold. When in the phobic situation, Albert reported suffering from excessive sweating and stiff, trembling muscles in his legs. He had always recognized his fear as excessive, but decided to mention his problems to his general practitioner when the fear-related avoidance started to significantly interfere with his holidays (e.g., getting on stairs of airplanes) and transport to work (e.g., cycling over bridges).

HISTORY

Albert had a difficult time pinpointing when his specific phobia for heights had started, but he believed it to be about 30 years earlier. His fear of heights had fluctuated somewhat over time, but the extent of his problems was "masked" because he had become such a self-proclaimed master of avoidance. For example, he carefully planned his routes when going to work or shopping, such that no bridges or other elevations had to be crossed. He described how he lately had become increasingly preoccupied with the possibility of having to face heights when taking trips abroad. He had finally decided to seek treatment after his rather traumatic holiday in Argentina. He had felt quite incapacitated and unable to enjoy the trip because even relatively minor height differences in the hilly scenery caused him great anxiety and stress; things came to a peak when he was terrified to climb the small set of stairs leading up to a cruise boat. Upon returning home, he noticed that he now had serious trouble riding his bicycle to work because of a ditch (± 3 feet) alongside the road demanding his anxious attention. When visiting his general practitioner, he was told that there were some "training programs" that the doctor believed could benefit him. Albert had not realized there were such "programs," nor was he aware that he met criteria for a formal diagnosis (i.e., specific phobia for heights; *DSM-IV* Code 300.29).

BEHAVIORAL ASSESSMENT

Behavioral

Meeting him at the reception desk, the therapist (JHK) thoughtlessly invited Albert to follow him to the second floor, where the outpatient clinic was located.

Without complaining, Albert followed the therapist onto the first open staircase, when the therapist came to realize his oversight. Albert managed to climb, but did so by walking in a straight line behind the therapist and keeping his focus on the therapist's back as he anxiously climbed the staircase, relying on its railing.

A more formal Behavioral Assessment Test (BAT; Emmelkamp et al., 2001b) was conducted before treatment started. Phobic stimulus was the emergency metal staircase along the outside back wall of a commercial building (maximum height approximately 38 feet). Albert was instructed to climb it as high as his fear permitted, at a steady pace and continuously looking at ground level. He was told that he had to stay at his maximum height for one minute.

INTERVIEW AND SELF-REPORT

As part of the formal assessment, the Structured Clinical Interview for the *DSM* (SCID-I; First, Spitzer, Gibbon, & Williams, 1996) was conducted. Albert did not meet criteria for any disorder except his specific phobia for heights (*DSM-IV* Code 300.29). The only noteworthy comorbidity was significantly elevated anxiety about public speaking, but not such that this posed problems for him in his daily life.

In addition to the SCID, Albert filled out several self-report measures, including the Acrophobia Questionnaire (AQ; Cohen, 1977), the Attitude toward Height Questionnaire (ATHQ; Abelson & Curtis, 1989), and the Symptom Check List 90 Revised (SCL-90; Derogatis, 1977). A brief description of these measures follows here:

- *Acrophobia Questionnaire:* The AQ has two subscales: anxiety (range 0–120; Cronbach alpha .80) and avoidance (range 0–60; Cronbach alpha .70).
- *Attitude toward Heights Questionnaire:* The ATHQ contains six questions assessing attitude toward heights (range 0–60; Cronbach alpha .81).
- *Symptom Check List 90 Revised:* This widely used 90-item questionnaire was included to screen for additional psychopathology. Psychometric properties are good.

PROCESS MEASURES

In addition, to elucidate the process of treatment and potential obstacles, the following measures were used:

- *Acrophobic Cognitions Inventory (ACI):* The ACI is a newly developed inventory that consists of two subscales measuring positive self-statement/coping-oriented cognitions (e.g., "I can do this"; "Nothing can happen to me") and negative threat-oriented cognitions (e.g., "I won't manage"; "I might jump") while in the phobic (height) situation. Normative data and psychometric properties currently are unavailable, but this did not pose a major problem given our within-subject application.
- *Physiological Arousal:* Heart Rate (HR) Measurement: Continuous HR measurement was conducted during two exposure in vivo sessions using an ambulatory heart rate monitor (Polar system). The unit consists of an electrode belt worn around the chest that transmits HR signals to a wrist receiver, where the data are stored during each exposure trial. HR was sampled every five seconds.

Table 4.1
Albert's Baseline Scores on Selected Indices of
Acrophobia Compared to Means and Standard
Deviations of Acrophobic Patients

Domain/Scale	Albert Score	Patients with Acrophobia	
		Mean	SD
Behavioral			
BAT (in steps)	12	11.76	4.20
Self-report			
AQ-Anxiety	57	58.6	14.78
AQ-Avoidance	17	14.67	4.59
ATHQ	47	44.76	8.42

Source: Based on Emmelkamp et al., 2001b.

As can be seen in Table 4.1, Albert's scores were generally in the normative range for acrophobic patients, both behaviorally and via self-report. The only noteworthy exception was his somewhat elevated score on avoidance (which fit well with his spontaneous self-description of "master of avoidance"). Compared to clinical norms, his scores on the SCL-90 subscales were low or very low, indicating absence of other major sources of psychopathology. The only exception was an above-average score on agoraphobic avoidance, but on closer inspection this elevation was entirely due to endorsement of items that involved heights. On the behavioral test, Albert climbed the first set of stairs (eight steps) to the first plateau (± 6 feet) and added four more steps before stopping because of high anxiety (subjective units of discomfort [SUDs] = 8; ranging from 0 to 10), at an approximate height of 8 feet (see Table 4.1: Baseline assessment).

MEDICAL CONSULTATION

Albert was referred by his general practitioner. He did not use medication, except for a beta blocker to control his blood pressure. This medication likely influenced his heart rate reactivity, as measured by the ambulatory instrument. He had not received prior psychological treatment for his fear of heights or any other problem or disorder.

CASE CONCEPTUALIZATION

Originally, behavior theorists held that specific phobias were acquired through a process of conditioning, in which conditioned stimuli (CS) and unconditioned stimuli (UCS) became paired through possibly traumatic learning. In height phobia, the person might have experienced or witnessed some traumatic event related to falling or jumping from great heights (UCS) and have feared similar cues since (CS). No such traumatic experiences were reported by Albert, and he had no idea what had initiated his fear of heights. He did remember gradually becoming more and more adept at avoiding situations that involved high, open spaces, which he thought explained the persistence and increase of his fear. This involved outright avoidance but also more subtle safety strategies (see, e.g., Kamphuis & Telch, 1998). He spontaneously identified several safety strategies, such as scanning the environment for side railings, planning his routes in advance, looking at people's back rather than looking down when going up or down stairs, obstructing his view, holding onto objects, and walking sideways to increase his balance.

Albert's account is particularly consistent with the second component of Mowrer's (1960) two-factor theory of fear and avoidance. Consistent with previous theorizing, the two-factor theory states that phobias arise as a result of a classically conditioned association of a phobic stimulus and an aversive consequence (i.e., Factor 1). The acquired phobias fail to extinguish because avoidance or escape behavior prevents or shortens the occurrence of potentially therapeutic exposure to the feared stimuli, in turn preventing habituation and long-term fear reduction. Persistence of avoidance behavior is accounted for by negative reinforcement (i.e., Factor 2), with "anxiety relief" acting as the negative reinforcer.

Exposure is often explained in terms of habituation. Habituation refers to a decline in fear responses, particularly the physiological responses, over repeated exposures to fear-provoking stimuli. Several studies have provided supportive evidence for a role of habituation in exposure therapy: Self-reported fear and physiological arousal show a declining trend within and across exposure sessions consistent with habituation (e.g., Emmelkamp & Felten, 1985; Kamphuis & Telch, 2000; van Hout, Emmelkamp, & Scholing, 1994).

The conditioning model of fear acquisition cannot adequately account for the accumulated research data (e.g., Emmelkamp, 1982). It has become widely accepted that many factors other than the experienced pairings of CS and UCS can affect the strength of the association between these events. These factors include cognitive representations, such as beliefs and expectancies about possible danger associated with a particular CS, possibly reflecting culturally transmitted information about the CS-UCS contingency (Davey, 1997; Reiss, 1980, 1987). Particularly notable in this context is the expectancy theory of Reiss and McNally (1985), which emphasizes the role of danger and anxiety expectancies. Danger expectancy refers to the degree to which one has learned that the feared stimulus reliably signals external danger. Thus, acrophobic persons are not afraid of heights per se, but of what they believe might happen when they encounter heights (e.g., "I might fall"). The association can be established through various pathways, including classical conditioning, covert conditioning, and cognitive learning. Every fear has its specific danger expectancies, and the strength of the expectancy is usually measured in the frequency of the occurrence of the threatening thoughts. Anxiety expectancy is the anticipation of becoming anxious when a certain stimulus is encountered (e.g., "I will feel anxious when I . . ."). As such, acknowledgment of a fear implies an anxiety expectancy. For Albert, the fear of falling or being drawn to the depth and jumping were the most salient dimensions of his threat appraisal, and he clearly had strong anxiety expectancies related to heights. Several studies have investigated the cognitive processes underlying exposure in vivo, but a detailed discussion exceeds the scope of this chapter (see, e.g., Kamphuis & Telch, 2000; van Hout et al., 1994).

RATIONALE FOR TREATMENT CHOICE

The following techniques were considered for Albert's treatment of acrophobia: exposure in vivo, virtual reality exposure, pharmacotherapy, and cognitive restructuring.

EXPOSURE THERAPY

Exposure therapy consists of exposing patients to the cues and situations they fear. Exposure can be carried out in two principal ways: (1) in imagination, in which patients must imagine themselves to be in a fearful situation, or (2) in vivo, in which patients are really exposed to this situation. Exposure in vivo is usually more effective than exposure in imagination (for review, see Emmelkamp, 1994). With specific phobics, the treatment of choice is usually exposure in vivo (Emmelkamp, 1994). Craske (1999) summarized 10 controlled studies that reported clinically significant change. In some of these studies, applied relaxation or modeling was added to exposure. After a mean of five hours of therapy, over 75% of the patients were rated as clinically improved. One three-hour session of prolonged exposure in vivo was equally effective as five one-hour sessions (Öst, Alm, Brandberg, & Breitholz, 2001). *Massed exposure* sessions are expected to be related to higher dropout rates, more return of fear, and more stressfulness in comparison to spaced sessions. However, research into the optimal format of exposure does not provide firm evidence to justify this expectation. For example, for specific phobics, no differential effect was found between spaced and massed exposure in relapse rate or dropout rate. Exposure in vivo was found to be effective in treating acrophobia (Emmelkamp & Felten, 1985).

VIRTUAL REALITY EXPOSURE

A recent development is the application of virtual reality (VR) in clinical psychology. VR integrates real-time computer graphics, body tracking devices, visual displays, and other sensory inputs to immerse individuals in a computer-generated virtual environment. VR exposure has several advantages over exposure in vivo. Treatment can be conducted in the therapist's office instead of forcing therapist and patient to go outside for exposure exercises in real-life phobic situations. Hence, treatment may be more cost-effective than exposure in vivo. Further, VR treatment can be applied with patients who are too anxious to attempt even low-intensity exposure in vivo.

A few case studies reported on the effectiveness of exposure provided by VR. Such case studies have been reported on fear of flying, acrophobia, claustrophobia, spider phobia, and agoraphobia. Recently, Emmelkamp, Bruynzeel, Drost, and van der Mast (2001a) evaluated effectiveness of two sessions of low-budget VR versus two sessions of exposure in vivo in a within-group design among acrophobics. VR exposure was found to be at least as effective as exposure in vivo on both anxiety and avoidance. However, VR exposure as the first treatment was already so effective that a ceiling effect occurred, thus diminishing the potential effects of exposure in vivo. The aims of a subsequent study by Emmelkamp et al. (2001b) was to compare the effectiveness of exposure in vivo versus VR exposure in a between-group design with acrophobic patients. To enhance the comparability of exposure environments, locations used in the exposure in vivo program were exactly reproduced in virtual worlds used in VR exposure. Again, VR exposure was found to be as effective as exposure in vivo on both anxiety and avoidance as well as on attitudes toward heights, and treatment gains were maintained at six-month follow-up. In sum, there is now considerable evidence that VR exposure is an effective treatment for patients with acrophobia.

PHARMACOTHERAPY

A few studies in the 1970s investigated whether benzodiazepines combined with exposure in vivo might enhance effectiveness of exposure in vivo alone in patients with specific phobia, but results were inconclusive (Craske, 1999). More recently, the high-potency benzodiazepine Alprazolam was found to increase rather than decrease anxiety in flight phobics. A combination of exposure in vivo plus Alprazolam was less effective than treatment by exposure alone (Wilhelm & Roth, 1997). To our knowledge, no studies have specifically investigated the efficacy of benzodiazepines in treating acrophobia.

COGNITIVE THERAPY

In controlled outcome studies, there is no consistent evidence that cognitive techniques potentiate the effects derived from exposure (Emmelkamp & Felten, 1985; Getka & Glass, 1992). However, two recent analog studies showed that adding a cognitive threat appraisal intervention to exposure in vivo may enhance emotional processing of fear cues (Kamphuis & Telch, 2000; Mohlman & Zinbarg, 2000). Finally, the differential efficacy of exposure in vivo and cognitive therapy was tested among claustrophobic subjects, and no significant differences were obtained (Booth & Rachman, 1992; Öst et al., 2001).

Given the success of VR exposure among patients with acrophobia and the cost-effectiveness of this treatment, we decided to treat Albert with VR exposure. If this treatment was unsuccessful, then graded exposure in vivo would be the second option. Given the high success rate of exposure in vivo, a combination with pharmacotherapy was not considered. Further, because cognitions also change as a result of exposure in vivo (van Hout & Emmelkamp, 2001) and there is no *specific* evidence that cognitive therapy enhances the effects of exposure in vivo among patients with acrophobia (Emmelkamp & Felten, 1985), cognitive therapy was not added to the treatment program.

COURSE OF TREATMENT

VIRTUAL REALITY

Initially, Albert's treatment followed the protocol developed for VR exposure for acrophobics (Emmelkamp et al., 2001a, 2001b). VR was provided in a dark laboratory room at the Department of Clinical Psychology of the University of Amsterdam. The virtual worlds were generated using an ordinary Pentium Pro 233 MHz computer with 64 Mb RAM, 4 Gb hard disk, and two Intergraph Intense 3D Pro 2200 graphic cards, with 16 Mb texture memory. The software used was Sense 8 WorldUp R4, a commonly used VR modeling and visualization toolkit. Overall, the system was able to generate the display at a rate of about 15 to 20 frames per second. The worlds were displayed using the Cybermind Visette Pro. Projection was stereographic. Tracking was done with Ascension Flock of Birds. To give the individual an enhanced feeling of height, a railing the user could hold onto surrounded the patient.

First, Albert was acquainted with VR by watching a VR environment for a few minutes. Treatment then included exposure to three different virtual environments that were especially created for this project: (1) a mall in Amsterdam

(Magna Plaza), consisting of four floors with escalators and balustrades; (2) a fire escape in the center of Amsterdam (height approximately 50 feet); and (3) a roof garden on a university building (height approximately 65 feet), with a view on the Magna Plaza building and a street. In general, when the patient's anxiety diminishes, the therapist introduces a more difficult exercise in the virtual environment. Patients are first exposed to the mall, then to the fire escape, and finally to the roof garden. The VR exposure is gradual and the therapist controls the exposure by means of the keyboard and joystick connected to a personal computer. The world seen by the patient is displayed on a monitor to the therapist. During VR exposure, the therapist gives verbal guidance (patients are continuously instructed to look over the railing to ground level) and encouragement. Patients can look around freely and walk around on 1m² (3 square feet). Patients rate their anxiety level (SUDs) at regular times during the VR exposure exercises on a 0 to 100 scale. Standard protocol includes three sessions in which patients, contingent on fear reduction, are exposed to one, two, or three virtual environments.

Albert's SUDs ratings showed very limited evidence of habituation, and after three sessions, he had been exposed to only one VR environment. After three sessions of VR exposure, a formal evaluation was held. Albert showed only minimal improvement on the AQ: His anxiety had decreased from 57 at pretreatment to 48 at the end of the three sessions, and avoidance had decreased from 17 to 14. The behavioral assessment indicated no gains at all, as is evident from the maximum height of 12 steps before and after VR treatment.

EXPOSURE IN VIVO

Given the slow progress achieved with VR exposure, treatment was continued using exposure in vivo. Treatment activities used the same three locations (i.e., the fire escape stairs, the Magna Plaza shopping mall, and the roof garden) as in the VR treatment. As with VR exposure, exposure in vivo was gradual and verbally guided by the therapist. If necessary, the therapist accompanied the patient, but assistance was kept minimal. Albert had to rate his anxiety level at regular times during the exposure exercises on a 0 to 100 scale (SUDs). When the anxiety had diminished, the therapist encouraged Albert to do a more challenging exercise.

After two sessions of exposure practice at the fire escape stairs, we decided to switch practice targets even though only minimal habituation had occurred. The shift of focus was therefore not because the stairs were no longer feared. It also reflected some concerns about the patient's motivation to continue treatment when progress was so piecemeal and removed from everyday utility. Hence, it was decided to try the escalators at a large Dutch department store; these are long escalators that provide a very open view over the complex. The patient declined to try this challenge, visibly shaken by the prospect. After some discussion, it was decided to try a different department store with less-threatening escalators first.

Given the influence of Albert's fearful predictions, we decided to distinguish SUDs ratings of predicted and actual fear. A number of researchers investigated the overprediction of fear in a series of laboratory studies, in which they asked the subjects to rate their *predicted* fear before they were exposed to a threatening situation, and to indicate their *reported* fear (i.e., reflecting their actual experience) just after the exposure trial. Overprediction of fear led to avoidance and anticipatory anxiety because subjects expect to be more fearful during exposure than turns out to be accurate in reality. Most support for the match-mismatch model derives from studies performed in a laboratory setting with relatively mildly phobic subjects (reviewed by Rachman, 1994), but van Hout and Emmelkamp (1994) by and large replicated these findings in a clinical population during exposure in vivo therapy.

Accordingly, at the start of every escalator ride, up or down, Albert was asked to indicate his level of confidence and predicted fear on a scale from 1 to 100 (SUDs/-self-efficacy). After completing the ride, he was asked to indicate the actual fear level on a similar scale. Again, very little habituation was evidenced, as well as minimal increments in confidence; in Albert's case, predicted fear almost perfectly matched his appraisal of self-efficacy. To illustrate, the most fear-provoking escalator, a very open view going down from the third floor, initially resulted in a rating of 70, which came down to "between 40 and 50" after eight trials up and down. Behaviorally, meanwhile, Albert seemed rather more relaxed, looking down, bending his knees, and looking around. A second session was needed before the patient mastered the "low impact" escalators, when he reported a 30 out of 100 tension. However, Albert still did not have the confidence to try the more threatening escalators. Using the mall's elevator instead, a view of the mall from the second floor induced intense fear leading to a panic attack.

Treatment was in somewhat of an impasse. It was unclear what hindered more profound habituation. A few specific hypotheses were considered. First, it seemed that Albert tried to keep his anxiety under control as best he could, and instead of reaping threat disconfirmation, he slowly lost his grip on the situation and anxiety increased instead of deceased. Second, the issue of desynchrony between fear response systems was raised (Lang, Melamed, & Hart, 1970). It seemed quite unlikely that the patient did not experience physiological habituation after the repeated trials. Perhaps his subjective appraisal differed in timing from his physiological response? Accordingly, a number of changes were introduced: (1) emphasizing the "antiphobic spirit" ("daring the anxiety on") to the patient; (2) continuous HR measurement; and (3) prolonging the exposure time. Continuous HR measurement was performed using the Polar system. Sessions were extended to three hours. These adaptations proved to be effective. His subjective fear response slowly gave way and he subsequently mastered all three phobic situations, reporting a fear level of 40 out of 100 or lower.

Treatment Process

Figures 4.1 and 4.2 show the decrement in HR and fear reduction (indexed as SUDs, ranging from 0 to 100), as well as the associated cognitive change. In support of the desynchrony hypothesis, decrement in Albert's subjective fear showed a latency with the decrease in HR, while it marched in concert with his threat appraisal. It appears that it took protracted physiological evidence before Albert's cognitive appraisal of threat decreased (ACI-negatives) and fear reduction (SUDs) was obtained. Of note, the increase in Albert's self-reported positive self-statements/coping thoughts (ACI-positives) seems to be characteristic of an intermediate phase in treatment. Low scores on the ACI-positives either reflect very low or very high confidence of people who are terrified or totally unaffected by the situation, respectively. High (or increasing) scores on the ACI-positives indicate that the person is actively coping with a situation that is perceived as challenging.

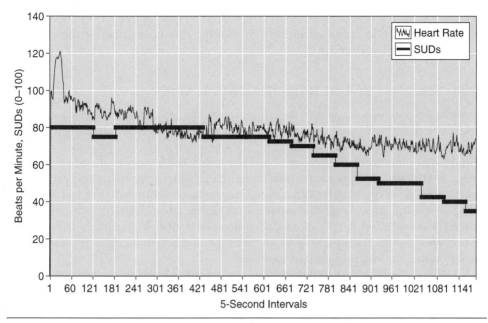

Figure 4.1 HR and SUDs over Time

THERAPIST-CLIENT FACTORS

Albert was punctual in appearing for treatment. He generally pushed himself to perform the exposure exercises, but to a point. He initially refused to start the escalator rides, saying, "Perhaps one day I may be ready to try this, but not today!" This statement did not reflect avoidance or resistance to treatment; rather, it seemed to indicate a fairly accurate appraisal of his ability to cope. He

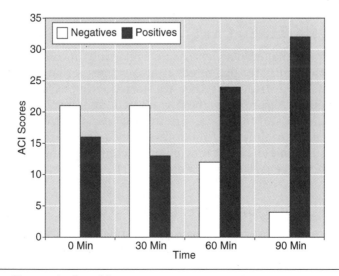

Figure 4.2 Change in Cognitions

exercised at high levels of anxiety (at times, to the point of panic), spontaneously increasing the difficulty of situations by looking down, leaning on the railings, or increasing the heights.

COURSE OF TERMINATION

Termination date was made contingent on improvement. Possible setbacks and relapse were discussed with the patient. Albert requested some written guidelines to rely on in case this were to happen. The one-page memo emphasized that potential future increases in avoidance or fear were to be conceptualized as cues for exposure (instead of cues for relapse or failure). It further explained that the exposure had to be of sufficient duration, emphasized the importance of the "antiphobic spirit," and described specific exercise sites. Finally, our telephone number was included if Albert needed more assistance. In addition, a follow-up session was planned two months following termination, to ascertain whether fear reduction had maintained and generalized.

Asked to reflect on his experience of treatment, Albert reported that the VR exposure had been useful in helping him take "the first step of trying the exercises at all." And, although he had found the VR exposure surprisingly credible, he still felt that "the real thing" was significantly more frightening.

FOLLOW-UP

At 3 month follow-up, an informal assessment was conducted. Albert's report suggested that he had maintained his gains, without gaining or losing significantly. When interviewed, he had just returned from another trip to Argentina. In contrast to pre-treatment, he had not suffered at all from anticipatory anxiety about the height situations and had not run into any problematic situations either. He was planning to continue self-guided exposure practice to further increase his level of comfort beyond 30 feet, and spontaneously quipped the "fear is my friend" self-instruction as his guide.

MANAGED CARE CONSIDERATIONS

This report illustrates that even an *a prima facie* relatively uncomplicated case can take more time than initially budgeted. It also suggests that, for this patient, treatment began to have effect only when we started with *prolonged* sessions (i.e., more than two hours). Accordingly, the current treatment involved three VR sessions of one hour each and nine exposure in vivo sessions; these initially were scheduled for 90 minutes, but the final four sessions were extended to between two and three hours. In general, it may be more clinically- and cost-effective to schedule fewer and longer sessions (Öst et al., 2001).

OVERALL EFFECTIVENESS

Table 4.2 compares Albert's scores on acrophobia-related indices over the course of treatment, as well as with those of patients with acrophobia. These scores reflect major improvement across domains but are not indicative of total recovery. At the end of treatment, Albert was able to climb an open staircase and overlook

Table 4.2
Albert's Scores on Acrophobia-Related Anxiety and Avoidance, and
Attitudes at Pretreatment, Post-VR Exposure, and Postexposure In Vivo

Domain/Scale	Pretreatment	Post-VR Exposure	Postexposure In Vivo	Patients with Acrophobia	
				Mean	SD
Behavioral					
BAT (in steps)	12	12	27	11.76	4.20
Self-Report					
AQ-Anxiety	57	48	42	58.6	14.78
AQ-Avoidance	17	14	9	14.67	4.59
ATHQ	47	36	25	44.76	8.42

the environment (± 38 feet), take the escalators of a high-rise large department store in Amsterdam, and remain at a roof garden overseeing the inner city. Moreover, in his daily life, he had begun to resume activities he had long ceased to do because of anxiety, including cycling alongside the canal to work, shopping in high-rise department stores with his wife, and making holiday excursions that involved heights. Accordingly, although his fear response had not yet remitted completely, his level of fear no longer met diagnostic criteria. He understood, however, that he could maintain and extend his gains by continuing the exercises combined with the "antiphobic spirit."

REFERENCES

Abelson, J. L., & Curtis, G. C. (1989). Cardiac and neuroendocrine responses to exposure therapy in height phobics: Desynchrony with the physiological response system. *Behaviour Research and Therapy, 27*, 556–561.

American Psychiatric Association. (1994). *Diagnostic and statistical manual of mental disorders* (4th ed.). Washington, DC: Author.

Booth, R., & Rachman, S. (1992). The reduction of claustrophobia-I. *Behaviour Research and Therapy, 23*, 207–221.

Chapman, T. F. (1997). The epidemiology of fears and phobias. In G. C. L. Davey (Ed.), *Phobias: A handbook of theory, research and treatment* (pp. 416–434). New York: Wiley.

Cohen, D. C. (1977). Comparison of self-report and behavioral procedures for assessing acrophobia. *Behavior Therapy, 8*, 17–23.

Craske, M. G. (1999). *Anxiety disorders: Psychological approaches to theory and treatment.* Boulder, CO: Westview Press.

Davey, G. C. L. (1997). A conditioning model of phobias. In G. C. L. Davey (Ed.), *Phobias: A handbook of theory, research and treatment* (pp. 301–318). New York: Wiley.

Derogatis, L. R. (1997). *SCl-90-R: Administration: Scoring and procedures manual-I for the revised version of other instruments of the Psychopathology Rating Scale Series.* Baltimore: Johns Hopkins University of Medicine, Clinical Psychometrics Research Unit.

Emmelkamp, P. M. G. (1982). *Phobic and Obsessive-Compulsive Disorders.* New York: Plenum Press.

Emmelkamp, P. M. G. (1994). Behavior therapy with adults. In A. E. Bergin & S. L. Garfield (Eds.), *Handbook of psychotherapy and behavior change* (4th ed.). New York: Wiley.

Emmelkamp, P. M. G., Bruynzeel, M., Drost, L., & van der Mast, C. A. P. (2001a). Virtual reality treatment in acrophobia: A comparison with exposure in vivo. *CyberPsychology and Behavior, 4,* 335–339.

Emmelkamp, P. M. G., & Felten, M. (1985). The process of exposure in vivo: Cognitive and physiological changes during treatment of acrophobia. *Behaviour Research and Therapy, 23,* 219–223.

Emmelkamp, P. M. G., Krijn, M., Hulsbosch, L., de Vries, S., Schuemie, M. J., & van der Mast, C. A. P. (2001b). Virtual reality treatment versus exposure in vivo: A comparative evaluation in acrophobia. *Behaviour Research and Therapy.*

First, M. B., Spitzer, R. L., Gibbon, M., & Williams, J. B. W. (1996). *Structured Clinical Interview for DSM-IV Axis I Disorders.* Washington, DC: American Psychiatric Association.

Foa, E. B., & Kozak, M. J. (1986). Emotional processing of fear: Exposure to corrective information. *Psychological Bulletin, 99,* 20–35.

Frederikson, M., Annas, P., Fischer, H., & Wik, G. (1996). Gender and age differences in the prevalence of specific fears and phobias. *Behaviour Research and Therapy, 34,* 33–39.

Getka, E. J., & Glass, C. R. (1992). Behavioral and cognitive-behavioral approaches to the reduction of dental anxiety. *Behavior Therapy, 18,* 3–16.

Kamphuis, J. H., & Telch, M. J. (1998). Assessment of strategies to manage or avoid anxiety among Panic Disorder patients: The Texas Safety Maneuver Scale. *Clinical Psychology and Psychotherapy, 5,* 177–186.

Kamphuis, J. H., & Telch, M. J. (2000). Effects of distraction and guided threat reappraisal on fear reduction during exposure-based treatments for specific fears. *Behaviour Research and Therapy, 38–12,* 1163–1181.

Kessler, R. C., McConagle, K. A., Zhao, S., Nelson, C. B., Hughes, M., Eshleman, S., et al. (1994). Lifetime and 12-month prevalence of *DSM-III-R* psychiatric disorders in the United States. *Archives of General Psychiatry, 51,* 8–19.

Lang, P. J., Melamed, B. G., & Hart, J. H. (1970). A psychophysiological analysis of fear modification using an automated desensitization procedure. *Journal of Abnormal Psychology, 76,* 220–234.

Merkelbach, H., & de Jong, P. J. (1997). Evolutionary models of phobias. In G. C. L. Davey (Ed.), *Phobias: A handbook of theory, research and treatment* (pp. 323–348). New York: Wiley.

Mohlman, J., & Zinbarg, R. E. (2000). What kind of attention is necessary for fear reduction? An empirical test of the emotional processing model. *Behavior Therapy, 31,* 113–133.

Monroe, S. M. (1990). Psychosocial factors in anxiety and depression. In J. D. Maser & C. R. Cloninger (Eds.), *Comorbidity of mood and anxiety disorders* (pp. 463–543). Washington, DC: American Psychiatric Press.

Mowrer, O. H. (1960). *Learning theory and behavior.* New York: Wiley.

Öst, L.-G. (1987). Age of onset in different phobias. *Journal of Abnormal Psychology, 96,* 223–229.

Öst, L.-G., Alm, T., Brandberg, M., & Breitholz, E. (2001). One vs five sessions of exposure and five sessions of cognitive therapy in the treatment of claustrophobia. *Behaviour Research and Therapy, 39,* 167–183.

Öst, L.-G., & Hellström, K. (1997). Blood-injury-injection phobia. In G. C. L. Davey (Ed.), *Phobias: A handbook of theory, research and treatment* (pp. 63–80). New York: Wiley.

Rachman, S. (1994). The overprediction of fear: A review. *Behaviour Research and Therapy, 32,* 683–690.

Reiss, S. (1980). Pavlovian conditioning and human fear: An expectancy model. *Behavior Therapy, 11,* 380–396.

Reiss, S. (1987). Theoretical perspectives on the fear of anxiety. *Clinical Psychology Review, 7*, 585–596.

Reiss, S., & McNally, R. J. (1985). Expectancy model of fear. In S. Rachman & R. R. Bootzin (Eds.), *Theoretical issues in behavior therapy.* New York: Academic Press.

van Hout, W. J. P. J., & Emmelkamp, P. M. G. (1994). Overprediction of fear in Panic Disorder patients with Agoraphobia. Does the (mis)match model generalize to exposure in vivo therapy? *Behaviour Research and Therapy, 32*, 723–734.

van Hout, W. J. P. J., Emmelkamp, P. M. G., & Scholing, A. (1994). The role of negative self-statements in agoraphobic situations: A process study of eight Panic Disorder patients with agoraphobia. *Behavior Modification, 18*, 389–410.

van Hout, W. J. P. J., & Emmelkamp, P. M. G. (2001). Exposure in vivo therapy. In M. Hersen & W. Sledge (Eds), *The encyclopedia of psychotherapy.* New York: Academic Press.

Wilhelm, F. H., & Roth, W. T. (1997). Acute and delayed effects of Alprazolam on flight phobics during exposure. *Behaviour Research and Therapy, 35*, 831–841.

CHAPTER 5

Social Phobia

DANIEL W. McNEIL, JOHN T. SORRELL, KEVIN E. VOWLES,
and TINA W. BILLMEYER

DESCRIPTION OF THE DISORDER

SOCIAL PHOBIA IS defined by the text revision for the fourth edition of the *Diagnostic and Statistical Manual of Mental Disorders* (*DSM-IV-TR;* American Psychiatric Association [APA], 2000) as an excessive, irrational social or performance fear in which the person expects evaluation by others and, as a result, experiences significant functional impairment, anxiety, or panic when exposed to the situation, and/or behaves to avoid or escape from such social or performance situations. Recently, these problems have been referred to as "social anxiety disorder" in the literature (see McNeil, 2000). Before a formal diagnosis of Social Phobia can be met, the *DSM-IV-TR* specifies particular exclusion criteria to be considered, such as general medical conditions, substance abuse, and other anxiety disorders (e.g., Panic Disorder and Generalized Anxiety Disorder). Individuals with Social Phobia experience difficulties in one or any combination of Lang's (1979) triple response systems. For example, when anticipating or encountering a feared social situation, an individual may have ruminating thoughts of embarrassment and humiliation, heightened physiological reactivity such as increased heart rate, sweating, and respiration, and/or ultimately engage in avoidance or escape behavior from social arenas.

Settings most frequently found to produce heightened social anxiety are formal and informal public speaking, being observed by others performing some work or social task, interacting in small or large social groups, attending parties, and interacting with authority figures (see Beidel & Turner, 1998). Although it is common for individuals to report concerns across situations (i.e., generalized Social Phobia), manifestations of the disorder may be limited to specific situations as well (i.e., referred to in the literature as Circumscribed, Specific, or Nongeneralized, Social Phobia). Recent attention has focused on conceptualization of specific subtypes of Social Phobia (e.g., McNeil, 2000). For example, research has shown that individuals diagnosed with Circumscribed Social Phobia versus Social Phobia Generalized Type respond differently to stressful social situations (Boone et al., 1999; McNeil, Ries, Taylor, et al., 1995). Also, research suggests Avoidant Personality Disorder may be a severe instantiation of Social Phobia, generalized type (Reich, 2000). These findings indicate there is merit to the conceptualization of Social Phobia subtypes and, hence, differential treatment approaches as a function of these categories of Social Phobia diagnoses may be required.

Another important feature of Social Phobia is its cultural component, meaning that the manifestation of this disorder is dependent, in some large part, on the social demands of the particular culture within which the individual lives. For example, in some cultures, gaze aversion and passivity in the presence of elders or authority figures may be seen as appropriate and respectful, whereas similar behaviors may be considered odd and even "abnormal" in cultures in which eye contact and assertiveness are socially mandated. Moreover, there are different cultural forms of social anxiety and phobia, including *Taijin Kyofusho*, seen primarily in East Asian cultures, which involves concern about disturbing other people through inappropriate behavior or offensive appearance (Kleinknecht, Dinnel, Kleinknecht, Hiruma, & Harada, 1997). Thus, knowledge of a patient's cultural background is essential in considering a diagnosis of Social Phobia.

CASE DESCRIPTION

The present case description is that of a client (referred to here as Derek) who sought treatment from the Quin Curtis Center for Psychological Service, Training, and Research (QCC) which is a training clinic in the Department of Psychology at West Virginia University. Derek was initially seen by a female therapist trainee for 10 sessions (who then graduated and so left the clinic staff) and then was seen by two male therapist trainees for 9 sessions, collectively totaling 19 sessions over 11 months. The case was supervised by a licensed clinical psychologist (DWM).

IDENTIFYING AND BACKGROUND INFORMATION

At the time of intake, Derek, an African American male, was 19 years old. He was self-referred to the QCC, where he received treatment for problems consistent with a principal (and sole) diagnosis of Social Phobia. Derek was living with his biological mother, biological father, and three brothers in an urbanized but small town in West Virginia, approximately a 40-minute drive from the QCC. He had graduated from high school one year prior and was working part time at a fast-food restaurant in his hometown. Although he had some romantic relationships during high school, he was single and not dating at the time of the initial evaluation. From his self-report, he met all developmental milestones on time and without complication. Further, he did not report that he currently took any medications nor that he had any remarkable health history problems at the time of intake or while growing up. Derek also denied prior mental health evaluation or treatment, or alcohol or other drug use, and he reported minimal daily caffeine consumption (e.g., two to three caffeinated sodas per day). Derek also reported that there was no history of mental health problems in his family.

CLIENT PRESENTATION

Derek arrived on time at the clinic for his initial evaluation and was appropriately dressed in brown leather sandals, blue jeans, and a gray, short-sleeved polo-style shirt. His height was approximately 6 feet, and he weighed about 175 pounds. Upon greeting, the therapist shook Derek's hand, and noticed that it was moist with sweat and slightly shaking. During the interview, Derek presented with a shy and nervous demeanor, characterized by minimal eye contact, frequent gazes toward the floor, low voice volume, foot tapping, and persistent hand fidgeting. At times during the interview, he was timid and seemed unsure about himself when responding to questions. For example, he required about 60 seconds to respond with assuredness that one of his favorite hobbies was collecting baseball cards.

Derek's presentation of affect varied appropriately throughout the intake evaluation and the duration of treatment. When discussing enjoyable activities, he smiled and laughed on several occasions during treatment. After a "warm-up" period of three sessions with the initial female therapist and two sessions with the male therapists, good rapport was established and maintained. Although his attendance was inconsistent at times due to "car problems," Derek generally was on time or a few minutes late to therapy sessions and was moderately enthusiastic and willing to participate in treatment components with the encouragement of his therapists. His family had no knowledge of his attending therapy. He was very specific in telling the therapist that he did not want his family to know he was in therapy.

CHIEF COMPLAINTS

Derek's primary complaints were twofold: He experienced significant problems with "performance anxiety" at work and school settings; he was significantly displeased with the negative effects this anxiety had on his social interactions with friends. Derek described his performance anxiety as fear of "looking foolish in front of others" and "not being able to do anything while others are watching." He indicated that if he began to get nervous, he would shake, sweat, and want to leave any situation in which he believed he was being watched and evaluated by others.

WORK SETTING

At the beginning and throughout the first half of therapy, Derek reported significant problems at work that were related to his persistent fear of negative evaluation by others, particularly his supervisor. Just prior to coming for treatment, Derek worked in a grocery store as a checkout clerk. He was unable to continue working at this position because of the aversiveness of constant performance anxiety in the presence of others. For example, when customers came to the checkout counter, he would "freeze" and forget how to operate the cash register and what he was supposed to do next. His hands shook uncontrollably and his perspiration was excessive. After two weeks of battling these difficulties, Derek quit work at the grocery store and obtained employment as a food preparer in a small restaurant. He specifically requested to work in the kitchen away from customers, despite wanting to make more money as a server, to reduce the likelihood of interactions with restaurant patrons.

SOCIAL SITUATIONS

Derek had extreme levels of performance anxiety and fear of negative evaluation throughout high school. Although his grades were average, he described his participation in classroom activities as minimal. Specifically, he avoided answering questions posed to the class by the teacher and giving oral class presentations; on several occasions, he avoided classes by arriving late or not showing up, or escaped by leaving early. He indicated that his primary fear, although acknowledging it as irrational, was that he would say something foolish in class and his classmates would laugh at him.

In situations with his friends, Derek expressed extreme difficulty when approaching groups of more than two people. In this circumstance, he avoided the interaction by walking down another hallway at school or turning in another direction when outside of school, even if he needed to speak with one of his friends. Also, one of Derek's romantic relationships with a young woman during high school ended because she was unhappy that he could attend parties and other social activities only with extreme difficulty. The few additional romantic relationships Derek had in high school ended within two or three months for similar reasons.

Another area of dissatisfaction that resulted from social anxiety was in regard to playing sports. Derek had always enjoyed playing basketball and football with friends who lived in his neighborhood. Soon after he developed his social fears, however, he discontinued playing sports with his friends and said that he did not want to look foolish or have them criticize his performance on the playing field.

HISTORY

Various theoretical accounts have conceptualized the initiation, maintenance, and treatment of Social Phobia. Although several cognitive-behavioral (e.g., Hope, Heimberg, Juster, & Tork, 2000; Rapee, 1998) or behavioral (e.g., Turner, Beidel, & Cooley-Quille, 1997) empirically-supported, manualized treatments are available for the treatment of Social Phobia, the present case was treated using an idiographic behavioral focus. The strength of the concerns about being observed, and other performance components of Derek's Social Phobia, were somewhat unique, arguing for an individualized approach (Eifert, 1996). Thus, a brief description of the onset, maintenance, and treatment of Social Phobia from a behavioral perspective is provided (see Beidel & Turner, 1998; McNeil, Lejuez, & Sorrell, 2000).

Although there are various routes of acquisition (Beidel & Turner, 1998), onset of Social Phobia can be initiated by traumatic conditioning in which behavior in a social situation is followed by an aversive consequence(s). The aversive consequence is often humiliation, social ridicule, fear, and/or panic-like physiological responses (e.g., increased heart rate, perspiration, fight-or-flight response). In fact, individuals diagnosed with Social Phobia often panic in social situations (Barlow, 2002), and the panic attack itself is the aversive consequence. Subsequent exposure to similar social situations, though in the absence of the actual aversive consequence, elicits the same or similar fear response. For example, Derek recounted his childhood as normal and free of difficulty in social situations. He recalled that when he was approximately 16 years old, however, his social anxiety emerged following a "traumatic incident at church." He was called on by the minister to read aloud a passage from the Bible and suddenly "froze" on the altar in front of everyone in attendance. He trembled, could not speak, and felt terribly humiliated. As a result, he did not return to church again. Although he was able to identify a precipitating event to his social concerns, many individuals with Social Phobia are not able to recall a traumatic conditioning event (McNeil et al., 2000).

The case example of Derek shows in part how a behavioral approach accounts for the etiology of Social Phobia (see McNeil et al., 2000, for a review of behavioral theories of Social Phobia). Social Phobia, however, may continue for other reasons. For example, avoidance and escape behaviors involve removal, reduction, postponement, or prevention of aversive stimulation (Hineline, 1977); thus, through negative reinforcement, behaviors that decrease contact with negative social situations are increased. By not attending church, Derek learned that he could avoid the aversiveness of "freezing" and feeling humiliated by staying home and not engaging in social activities. Avoidance of these negative consequences helped maintain his behavior of not going to church with the rest of his family.

Derek's fear of negative social evaluation did not remain isolated to the context of reading in front of others at church because other social situations, such as giving a presentation at school, were similar enough to the initial conditioning event to elicit the same fear response. Thus, subsequent avoidance behavior of these social situations was negatively reinforced, as with church avoidance, because of the removal, reduction, and postponement of the feared social consequence.

BEHAVIORAL ASSESSMENT

Multimethod approaches to the assessment of patients with Social Phobia have been established for a more comprehensive evaluation than those that rely on one dimension of assessment (Barlow, 2002). Specifically, a multimethod approach to Social Phobia assessment includes the use of self-report questionnaires, behavioral measures, and physiological responses to more broadly understand how persons with Social Phobia are affected by social situations. As such, a multimethod assessment was initiated with Derek. In addition to a semistructured clinical interview, Derek completed standardized self-report questionnaires, an individualized behavior test, and verbally reported specific physiological responses to social situations.

SELF-REPORT QUESTIONNAIRES

Pretreatment scores on theoretically and clinically relevant self-report assessment questionnaires are presented in Table 5.1. Derek showed social impairment and social avoidance consistent with Social Phobia populations (McNeil, Ries, & Turk, 1995) on the Social Phobia Anxiety Inventory (SPAI; Turner, Beidel, Dancu, & Stanley, 1989). The State-Trait Anxiety Inventory, Trait Form (STAI-T; Spielberger, Gorsuch, & Luschene, 1970) also showed heightened general anxiety. Although depression is found to be highly comorbid with anxiety disorders (Barlow, 1991), Derek did not evince depressive symptoms on the Beck Depression Inventory-II (BDI-II; Beck, Steer, & Brown, 1996) beyond the normal range.

Table 5.1
Pre- and Post-treatment Scores on Self-Report
Questionnaires for Derek

Assessment Questionnaire	Pre	Post	Possible Range of Scores
Social Phobia Anxiety Inventory (total or difference score)	121.45	27.3	−78–192
State-Trait Anxiety Inventory (trait score)	54	34	20–80
Beck Depression Inventory-II	7	0	0–63

BEHAVIORAL TEST

During the assessment of Derek's social problems, a brief behavioral test was initiated to qualitatively determine which specific aspects of social situations were difficult for him. He had indicated that starting conversation with others in class at school was particularly difficult. Therefore, a five-minute enactment of this feared social situation was conducted to observe his approach style and skill level to this encounter, consistent with research methodologies in this area (Boone et al., 1999).

In this enactment, Derek pretended that he was sitting in class waiting for the teacher to begin lecturing. While waiting, he was to start a conversation with a neighboring student about "anything that comes to mind." Such role play (with one of the therapists) allowed the opportunity to assess Derek's social skills level, self-report of comfort, and nonverbal behavior during casual conversation. Therapist and client impressions from the behavior test revealed that he reported feeling very uncomfortable throughout the procedure and Derek likely would benefit from social skills training. For example, several times at the beginning of the role play, Derek stopped and expressed concern that he did not know what to say. When he engaged the other "student," he behaved similarly to the way he presented to the therapist: soft-spoken, averted gaze, trembling voice, and fidgeting hands.

Throughout the course of therapy, several additional behavior tests were used to reevaluate Derek's level of social skills and reported comfort. Specific details and comfort ratings are discussed in the Course of Treatment section that follows.

PHYSIOLOGICAL INFORMATION

Although actual physiological data (e.g., heart rate and skin conductance) were not collected in the assessment of Derek's condition, his self-report of physiological arousal was obtained. As noted previously, he often experienced heightened heart rate levels during social interactions. He reported that he felt his heart would "pound through" his chest when he was in an aversive social encounter. In addition, he was concerned about his excessive perspiration when in class, with groups of people, and while working. He felt that these symptoms made everything worse and that when he noticed them, he could tell that the situation would turn bad. Other physiological symptoms he experienced and expressed concern over were increased muscle tension, shaky voice, and psychomotor activity with his hands and feet.

MEDICAL CONSULTATION

As with all psychological evaluations, potential medical reasons for problem behaviors were considered. With anxiety disorders in general and Social Phobia in
particular, possible medical conditions that might induce, or contribute to, such
behavior include substance use/dependence, central nervous system tumors,
cerebrovascular disease, deficiencies in electrolytes, glucose, calcium, and problems with liver or thyroid functioning, among others (Kaplan & Sadock, 1998).
Derek reported that his most recent medical exam was within the year prior to
intake and did not reveal any abnormalities. Given Derek's reported normal developmental history and no medical problems, additional medical consultation
was not pursued.

CASE CONCEPTUALIZATION

Although cognitive-behavioral conceptualizations for treatment of Social Phobia
are prominent (Hofmann, 2000) and have been shown to be helpful in establishing effective treatment plans (Heimberg, 1990), a primarily behavioral approach
to Derek's case conceptualization was taken. Figure 5.1 represents the behavioral
conceptualization used to lead the subsequent treatment implemented. A behavioral approach was determined to be more relevant to Derek due to absence of evidence suggesting negative cognitive appraisals influencing his social fears and
concerns. Furthermore, although research has clearly shown cognitive-behavioral
therapy to be effective (e.g., Heimberg & Juster, 1995), other studies have demonstrated that cognitive-behavioral treatment is no more effective than behavior-
based therapy alone (e.g., Taylor, 1996).

As Figure 5.1 illustrates, onset of Social Phobia often is initiated in the context
of a biological predisposition, or sensitivity, for social anxiety. Barlow (2002) discusses anxiety in terms of a diathesis-stress model, in which one has a biological
predisposition or genetic vulnerability to develop an anxiety disorder. Although
in some individuals an anxiety disorder may develop in the absence of an environmental stressor, according to this model it is not until that individual encounters a significantly stressful life event that the disorder emerges. In this model,
the environmental stressor (e.g., a traumatic social event) is found in the second
level of the behavioral conceptualization. At this level, one is engaging in a social
activity (e.g., reading aloud at church) and suddenly, either expected or not, one
"freezes" or becomes unable to perform. The aversive consequence of this response then is contacted (e.g., humiliation, panic, fear) and stimuli in the environment acquire conditioned aversive properties (see the Rescorla-Wagner model
of conditioning for a review of this process; Rescorla & Wagner, 1972).

Following the traumatic social event, stimuli that have acquired aversive conditioning properties will come to elicit responses similar to those experienced in
the actual traumatic event (e.g., panic). With repeated experiences of these environmental variables, they come to function as discriminant stimuli (S^{D+};
Dinsmoor, 1995). That is, a particular response is stronger and more likely to
occur in the presence of that stimulus compared to behavior emitted in its absence. The stimulus operating as an S^{D+} does so as a function of the organism's
behavioral history with that stimulus and the stimulus's relation to reinforcement and punishment contingencies. Therefore, in a social situation, for example,

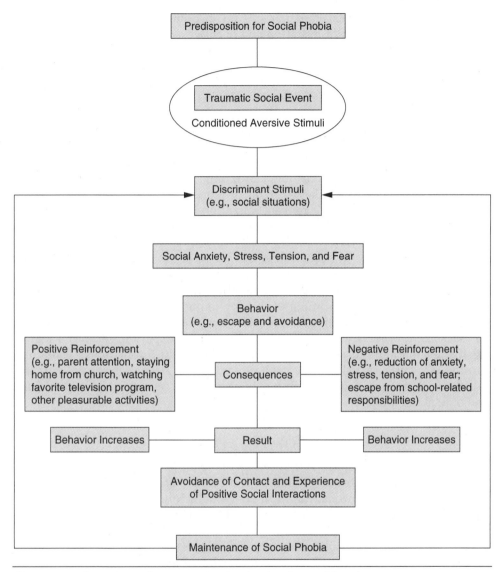

Figure 5.1 Behavioral Conceptualization for the Case of Derek

an anxiety or fear response is more likely for a person with Social Phobia than in the absence of that socially related stimulus.

Eventually, other responses are made by the socially phobic individual to reduce contact with these conditioned aversive stimuli. The most notable responses are avoidance and escape behaviors, although freezing or social camoflauge (e.g., dressing or acting in ways to remain inconspicuous) also serve the same function. These behaviors function to remove, reduce, postpone, or prevent aversive stimulation (Hineline, 1977) and are consequently maintained by negative reinforcement. In the case of Derek, by removing himself from social situations such as going to church and conversing with groups of friends, he was able to maintain lower levels of anxiety, fear, and panic. And in doing so, he was successful at avoiding the possibility of humiliation and negative evaluation by others.

A second consequence of escaping and avoiding social interactions is increased time and opportunity to engage in behaviors that are enjoyable. Positive reinforcement is a principle in which a stimulus or event (i.e., a positive reinforcer) is presented contingent on a behavior and results in the increased frequency or likelihood of occurrence of that behavior (Gleeson, 1991). Behaviors that are followed by positive consequences or "rewards" tend to increase in frequency, duration, magnitude, and/or intensity. Therefore, if behaviors such as watching television and withdrawing from social events are followed by reinforcing consequences (e.g., laughing at a favorite television program or increased attention/contact with family members), they likely will occur more often in the future.

The final component in the conceptualization of Derek's social problems regards social skills. If individuals with Social Phobia are crippled by fear of negative social evaluation, have a skills deficit problem that prevents them from behaving appropriately in social situations, or have a combination of both (see Stravynski & Amado, 2000, for a review), social skills training is an important facet at the beginning of treatment. As mentioned previously, a brief behavioral test was initiated at the beginning of therapy to qualitatively determine specific aspects of Derek's skill level and approach style to social encounters. Following the assessment process, it was concluded that Derek experienced both a fear of negative evaluation and a deficit in skill during social interactions. Therefore, learning more effective skills in social arenas, coping strategies to deal with social fear and anxiety, and practicing new social skills while experiencing some level of fear and anxiety, would address these problems.

RATIONALE FOR TREATMENT CHOICE

During the assessment phase of therapy, Derek and his therapist identified three primary goals to work toward. First, he indicated that he wanted to physically feel more comfortable interacting in his personal friendships and with coworkers. Second, he desired to feel more comfortable during social interactions and to have such encounters go more smoothly. Third, he ultimately wanted to advance in his job to a position with higher pay (e.g., food server) and to increase his performance in academic areas affected by his social discomfort.

Given Derek's stated goals, the first phase of treatment addressed his reported physiological discomfort (e.g., increased heart rate, perspiration, and muscle tension) associated with social situations. Progressive muscle relaxation (PMR) training was initiated to serve three main purposes. First, it likely would help him learn to differentiate the sensations of tension in different muscles throughout his body. Second, PMR would expose him to these physiological sensations, and through experience, he would learn that these sensations are normal and not necessarily threatening. Exposure to physiological discomforts also likely would decrease their overall aversiveness. Third, training in PMR would help decrease his general level of stress and muscle tension, thus helping him more effectively cope with acute life and social stressors.

The second phase of therapy involved simultaneous exposure to social situations and skills training exercises. Exposure to social situations and interactions were intended to allow Derek to experience the aversiveness of these situations without the same reinforcing consequences that he experienced in his natural environment prior to therapy (e.g., escape and avoidance). Repeated trials of exposure exercises would eventually result in decreased arousal and aversiveness of the situation (i.e., habituation).

Social skills training also occurred during the exposure exercises. To assist Derek in improving his general social skills, immediate feedback about his performance was provided by the therapists. Using the method of successive approximations and positive verbal praise as reinforcement, Derek's social skill behavior was shaped to a higher level of functioning. For example, feedback was given on specific nonverbal behaviors (e.g., body posture, gestures, tone of voice) so that Derek could be more aware of these behaviors on the next exposure trial. Also, a more specific area of performance (i.e., public speaking) was eventually targeted during therapy to help him prepare for taking college courses that required giving presentations in class.

COURSE OF TREATMENT

Following the intake session, Derek requested that he meet with the initial therapist on a bimonthly basis, rather than weekly, because of his work schedule. He indicated that he would not be able to request an afternoon off from work every week and that paying for gasoline to drive 40 minutes to and from the clinic would be too expensive. The two sessions after the intake included a focus on exploring anxiety-provoking social activities. As homework, Derek recorded the social activities that were difficult for him to endure and recorded how they made him feel. Activities that he avoided during the week also were discussed. After the therapist had a fairly representative sample of the social activities that Derek avoided or endured with difficulty, a hierarchy was established to be used for exposure exercises at a later date.

After the activities hierarchy was developed, PMR training was introduced during sessions 3 and 4 to help him deal with aversive physiological arousal associated with being in social situations. Derek was taught to separately tense and relax eight different muscle groups throughout his legs, arms, shoulders, neck and face. During the PMR, he was asked to focus his attention on the sensations of tension only in the muscle group that he was working on at a given time. Then, as he released this tension, he was to concentrate on the relaxed state that returned to his muscles. He was instructed to practice once a day for approximately 20 to 30 minutes. On a behavior record sheet, Derek recorded his tension and anxiety levels before and after each practice session.

After Derek reported feeling comfortable doing the PMR on his own, therapy began to focus on role-play exercises to more formally assess his social skills and to begin exposure to the discomforts of social situations. The fifth therapy session involved an elaborate role play that included the therapist, Derek, and a female and a male confederate. The two confederates were therapist trainees from the clinic whom Derek agreed to have participate in the session. Because one of Derek's most significant concerns at this point in therapy involved feeling uncomfortable initiating and maintaining conversations with small groups of peers, this type of situation was simulated with the two confederates and the therapist. The therapy room was arranged as if it were a high school classroom with rows of chairs, in which the therapist sat to the immediate left of Derek, a confederate sat behind the therapist, and the other confederate sat immediately behind Derek. Before and after each of the 3 to 5-minute role plays that were conducted during this session, subjective units of distress ratings (SUDs) were obtained from Derek. The SUDs were based on a 0 to 10 scale, with lower numbers equivalent to "little or no distress" and higher number ratings equivalent to "a lot of distress."

To start the role-play exercise, Derek was required to turn to one of the confederates and start any type of conversation. At some point during the role play, the other confederate and the therapist joined the conversation. Topics of conversation included: What is your favorite part of this class? What did you think of the last test? and What classes are you taking next year? When each role play was over, Derek was asked what went well and what he could improve during the next exercise. Also, feedback was given to him by each of the confederates and the therapist. In general, his SUDs ratings decreased over the course of the session and it was noted that he made efforts to improve gaze aversion and fidgeting with his hands during the conversation.

During sessions 6, 7, and 8, a different exposure activity was conducted in which Derek went to West Virginia University's Student Union and initiated conversations with strangers in line at a convenience store and a fast food restaurant and sitting at tables throughout the student union. To help ensure patient confidentiality, the therapist remained removed from Derek (e.g., was seated at another table) and did not provide feedback until they were back in the clinic. During these activities, as with the initial role-play exercises, SUDs were obtained before and after each social encounter. SUDs ratings decreased from 10 in the sixth session to 3 in the eighth session.

Also during sessions 6, 7, and 8, Derek reported that he was beginning to engage in more conversations with coworkers and was more often being involved in group interactions of two to five people at work. He indicated he was doing well at work and interacting with people one-on-one and in small groups. He also mentioned that he was planning on taking college courses at a state college in the upcoming semester and that he would like to focus more on public speaking (e.g., giving a prepared speech). Derek reasoned that it would be important academically for him to be comfortable giving class presentations. He expressed concern that his grades in high school suffered because of difficulty in this area and he did not want this to occur in college. Thus, at Derek's request, the focus of therapy was redirected to address his public speaking concern. Note that given his presenting complaints, no formal assessment of public speaking anxiety initially was conducted.

New exposure and skills training exercises involved going to different classrooms and having Derek read segments of magazine articles and giving prepared speeches. During session 7, Derek stood at the head of a classroom empty except for the therapist, and read the same magazine article several times until his SUDs ratings decreased to 2. The same procedure was conducted in session 8, in a different classroom for generalization. Over the next two sessions (i.e., 9 and 10), he prepared short (i.e., less than two minute) speeches and practiced delivering them to the therapist.

After session 10, however, the first therapist was no longer able to provide treatment, so Derek was transferred to two male therapists. Therefore, during session 11, the new therapists took the time to acquaint themselves with Derek and review what he had accomplished thus far in therapy. At the end of this session, Derek was asked to prepare a short two to three-minute speech for homework on his baseball card collection; to be presented during the subsequent exposure and skills training sessions.

Sessions 12 to 14 involved Derek standing at a podium in front of the two therapists in an otherwise empty classroom. He gave his prepared, two to three minute speech, several times throughout the session. Following each trial, both therapists commented on things Derek did well and things to work on during the next trial. Pre- and post-SUDs ratings also were recorded. During session 15, he repeatedly gave the speech in the presence of the therapists and two confederates.

After the fifteenth session, Derek was asked to give several impromptu speeches, rather than prepared ones. This increase in social demand was calculated by the therapists, based on his increased progress, to likely be beneficial to Derek's treatment because it required him to further develop his public speaking skills to another level. Prior to his first impromptu speech, both therapists modeled speeches for Derek. Following their brief impromptu speeches, Derek gave them feedback and then initiated his own speech. Again, pre- and post-SUDs ratings were obtained for each trial.

Derek continued to make positive gains with public speaking skills and he reported feeling more comfortable with each exposure exercise. Therefore, after session 17, Derek requested that exposure exercises also include the student union so he could practice interacting with people in line at the fast food restaurants and convenient store. With this environmental change in focus for social interactions, he continued to do well with social skills and managing his level of distress.

For the final two sessions of therapy, the therapists monitored Derek's activities at home, work, and the beginning of taking college courses. Derek reported that things were going well at home and work and that he was excited and confident about attending classes. After the final session, the SPAI, STAI, SIAS, and BDI-II were readministered.

THERAPIST-CLIENT FACTORS

Therapist-client factors have been shown to account for as much as 50% of the outcome variance of exposure treatments and therefore should be considered by therapists before and during treatment (Schulte & Eifert, 2001). Among some of the variables that have been shown to affect treatment success are patients seeking treatment versus dropping out, cooperation (high versus low), and exploring and testing out new behaviors. A factor that certainly may affect these variables is the level of rapport that the therapist has established with the client. Factors in the present case that could compromise rapport include ethnicity (i.e., all therapists were Caucasian and the client was African American) and gender differences (i.e., the initial therapist was female and the client was male), as well as change of therapists midway through treatment. Although each of these factors could have affected rapport with Derek, none seemed to be an issue. With all three therapists, rapport was established relatively quickly, despite gender and ethnicity differences and switching from one to two therapists halfway through therapy.

COURSE OF TERMINATION

As of session 19, treatment was mutually terminated. The decision to end therapy was based on several factors. First, pre- and post-differences on theoretically relevant assessment measures showed clinically meaningful improvements. Second, from Derek's report, he was feeling better during exposure exercises and social interactions in his daily life. Third, his reported and observed improvement in social skills level illustrated the gains he had made throughout the course of therapy. Fourth, he had returned to attending church, where he had a traumatic social event that initiated, at least in part, his problems.

DISTRESS RATINGS DURING BEHAVIORAL EXPOSURE

Figure 5.2 shows Derek's average distress levels across exposure sessions. This figure shows a progressive decrease in distress levels as therapy continued. This decreasing trend suggests that Derek was becoming more comfortable with his ability to present in public speaking situations.

POSTMEASURES

Post-treatment assessment using the same questionnaires administered prior to treatment revealed change scores on the SPAI, STAI, and BDI-II to be –95.15, –20, and –7, respectively. In general, these results show a decrease in levels of social fear and anxiety, avoidance, and anxiety during social encounters.

SOCIAL SKILLS

As Derek's ability to cope with social anxiety improved, so did his skill level in social interactions and related situations. It is difficult to know exactly how much improvement was a function of coping with social anxiety and how much was due to increased social skills; nonetheless, the reported and observed improvement in social skills was quite noticeable. For example, in the beginning of

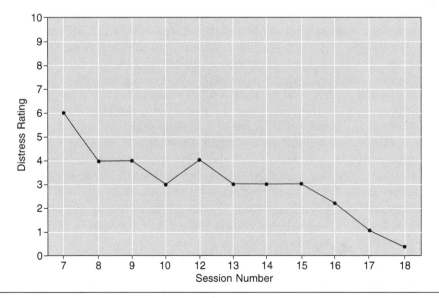

Figure 5.2   Average Distress Ratings for Derek across Public Speaking Exposure Exercises

therapy, specifically during the first few role-play exercises, Derek did not seem to know how to initiate a conversation with a "classmate" without the help of the therapist. As he progressed through therapy, however, he was able to initiate conversations with complete strangers while waiting in line at a convenience store.

OVERALL PROGRESS

Although Derek began therapy with serious social anxiety concerns, he reported having learned to overcome many of his social fears. Since the start of treatment, Derek began taking courses in college, achieving one of his major short-term goals set at the beginning of therapy. He reported adjusting well to the rigors of academic demands and maintaining low levels of anxiety in various social situations. He additionally reported feeling confident that he would do well in his academic endeavors and would continue to apply the skills he learned in therapy to his everyday life.

FOLLOW-UP

There was no formal follow-up session conducted with Derek after therapy was terminated. He was encouraged, however, to contact the QCC anytime he believed it was necessary to reinitiate treatment. Derek did not contact the clinic for at least two years. Also, because he did not inform his family or any friends that he was seeking treatment, he was not contacted for follow-up assessment to ensure confidentiality.

MANAGED CARE CONSIDERATIONS

Derek did not have health insurance that included mental health benefits, so he paid out-of-pocket. Because he did not want his family to know he was in therapy, they did not provide him with financial assistance to attend. Although he discontinued working at the grocery store prior to the start of therapy, he did maintain a position in a small restaurant as a food preparer. By working full-time at the restaurant, he was able to secure the funds necessary to pay for gasoline for his car and the fee for treatment.

OVERALL EFFECTIVENESS

By the end of therapy, Derek had made clinically significant gains in so many areas targeted that the overall level of treatment was considered successful. As mentioned previously, he made clinically meaningful improvements in psychological factors related to Social Phobia as determined by standardized assessment measures (e.g., SPAI). He also made several noteworthy behavioral improvements during the treatment. He successfully learned PMR training and reported practicing this exercise regularly. Second, Derek exhibited marked decreases in distress levels over the course of therapy during exposure activities, and he was able to show increases in social skills during various social situations.

Possibly the most significant gain that Derek was able to achieve, however, was his ability to extend treatment improvements to his natural environment. He displayed this ability in work-, social-, and school-related areas of his life. At work, for example, Derek received an outstanding employee of the month award during a staff meeting toward the end of therapy. As his supervisor gave him the award, his coworkers asked for a brief acceptance speech. At the following therapy session, Derek proudly told the therapists that he was able to give the short speech without getting so nervous and anxious that it crippled his delivery. In social areas of his life, Derek reported feeling more comfortable approaching friends in small groups and that he was having more social contact with friends outside of school (e.g., playing basketball after school). Just prior to treatment termination, he indicated that he had begun dating again and was starting a romantic relationship with a woman with whom he had attended high school. With regard to school-related functioning, he had started taking courses at a state college, while still living at home. At the final therapy session, he said that classes had started off well and that he was able to attend class with lower levels of anxiety compared to high school. He was looking forward to the next semester when he planned to attend a larger educational institution.

As the results of this case indicate, Derek was able to learn new social skills and coping strategies to manage his severe social anxieties. Although he was not completely "cured" of his social fears and concerns, he was able to use therapy as a way to decrease how many of those problems affected his daily life.

REFERENCES

American Psychiatric Association. (2000). *Diagnostic and statistical manual of mental disorders* (4th ed., text rev.). Washington, DC: Author.

Barlow, D. H. (1991). Disorders of emotion. *Psychological Inquiry, 2,* 58–71.

Barlow, D. H. (2002). *Anxiety and its disorders: The nature and treatment of anxiety and panic* (2nd ed.). New York: Guilford Press.

Beck, A. T., Steer, R. A., & Brown, G. K. (1996). *Manual for the Beck Depression Inventory–II.* San Antonio, TX: Psychological Corporation.

Beidel, D. C., & Turner, S. M. (1998). *Shy children, phobic adults: Nature and treatment of Social Phobia.* Washington, DC: American Psychological Association.

Boone, M. L., McNeil, D. W., Masia, C. L., Turk, C. L., Carter, L. E., Ries, B. J., et al. (1999). Multimodal comparisons of Social Phobia subtypes and Avoidant Personality Disorder. *Journal of Anxiety Disorders, 13,* 271–292.

Dinsmoor, J. A. (1995). Stimulus control: Part, I. *Behavior Analyst, 18,* 51–68.

Eifert, G. H. (1996). More theory-driven and less diagnosis-based behavior therapy. *Journal of Behavior Therapy and Experimental Psychiatry, 27,* 75–86.

Gleeson, S. (1991). Response acquisition. In I. Iversen & K. A. Lattal (Eds.), *Research methods in the behavioral and neural sciences: Experimental analysis of behavior.* Amsterdam: Elsevier.

Heimberg, R. G. (1990). Cognitive behavior therapy for Social Phobia. In A. S. Bellack & M. Hersen (Eds.), *Comparative handbook of treatments for adult disorders* (pp. 203–218). New York: Wiley.

Heimberg, R. G., & Juster, H. R. (1995). Cognitive-behavioral treatments: Literature review. In R. G. Heimberg, M. R. Liebowitz, D. A. Hope, & F. R. Schneier (Eds.), *Social Phobia: Diagnosis, assessment, and treatment* (pp. 261–309). New York: Guilford Press.

Hineline, P. N. (1977). The several roles of stimuli in negative reinforcement. In P. Harzem & M. D. Zeiler (Eds.), *Predictability, correlation, and contiguity.* New York: Wiley.

Hofmann, S. G. (2000). Treatment of Social Phobia: Potential mediators and moderators. *Clinical Psychology: Science and Practice, 7,* 3–16.

Hope, D. A., Heimberg, R. G., Juster, H. R., & Turk, C. L. (2000). *Managing social anxiety: A cognitive-behavioral therapy approach.* San Antonio, TX: Psychological Corporation.

Kaplan, H., & Sadock, B. (1998). *Synopsis of psychiatry: Behavioral sciences/clinical psychiatry* (8th ed.). Baltimore: Williams & Wilkins.

Kleinknecht, R. A., Dinnel, D. L., Kleinknecht, E. E., Hiruma, N., & Harada, N. (1997). Cultural factors in social anxiety: A comparison of Social Phobia symptoms and *Taijin Kyofusho. Journal of Anxiety Disorders, 11,* 157–177.

Lang, P. J. (1979). A bio-informational theory of emotional imagery. *Psychophysiology, 16,* 495–512.

McNeil, D. W. (2000). Terminology and evolution of constructs in social anxiety and Social Phobia. In S. G. Hofmann & P. M. DiBartolo (Eds.), *Social Phobia and social anxiety: An integration* (pp. 8–19). Needham Heights, MA: Allyn & Bacon.

McNeil, D. W., Lejuez, C. W., & Sorrell, J. T. (2000). Behavioral theories of Social Phobia: Contributions of basic behavioral principles. In S. G. Hofmann & P. M. DiBartolo (Eds.), *Social Phobia and social anxiety: An integration* (pp. 235–253). Needham Heights, MA: Allyn & Bacon.

McNeil, D. W., Ries, B. J., Taylor, L. J., Boone, M. L., Carter, L. E., Turk, C. L., et al. (1995). Comparison of Social Phobia subtypes using Stroop tests. *Journal of Anxiety Disorders, 9,* 47–57.

McNeil, D. W., Ries, B. J., & Turk, C. L. (1995). Behavioral assessment: Self-report, physiology, and overt behavior. In R. G. Heimberg, M. R. Liebowitz, D. A. Hope, & F. R. Schneier (Eds.), *Social Phobia: Diagnosis, assessment, and treatment* (pp. 202–231). New York: Guilford Press.

Rapee, R. M. (1998). *Overcoming shyness and Social Phobia: A step-by-step guide.* Northvale, NJ: Aronson.

Reich, J. (2000). The relationship of Social Phobia to Avoidant Personality Disorder. In S. G. Hofmann & P. M. DiBartolo (Eds.), *Social Phobia and social anxiety: An integration* (pp. 148–161). Needham Heights, MA: Allyn & Bacon.

Rescorla, R. A., & Wagner, A. R. (1972). A theory of Pavlovian conditioning: Variations in the effectiveness of reinforcement and nonreinforcement. In A. H. Black & W. F. Prokasy (Eds.), *Classical conditioning II: Current research and theory* (pp. 64–69). New York: Appleton-Century-Crofts.

Schulte, D., & Eifert, G. (2001). *What to do when manuals fail: The dual model of psychotherapy.* Manuscript submitted for publication.

Spielberger, C. D., Gorsuch, R. L., & Luschene, R. E. (1970). *State-Trait Anxiety Inventory.* Palo Alto, CA: Consulting Psychologists Press.

Stravynski, A., & Amado, D. (2000). Social Phobia as a deficit in social skills. In S. G. Hofmann & P. M. DiBartolo (Eds.), *Social Phobia and social anxiety: An integration.* Needham Heights, MA: Allyn & Bacon.

Taylor, S. (1996). Meta-analysis of cognitive-behavioral treatments for Social Phobia. *Journal of Behavior Therapy and Experimental Psychiatry, 27,* 1–9.

Turner, S. M., Beidel, D. C., & Cooley-Quille, M. R. (1997). *Social effectiveness therapy: A program for overcoming social anxiety and Social Phobia.* North Tonawanda, NY: Multi-Health Systems.

Turner, S. M., Beidel, D. C., Dancu, C. V., & Stanley, M. A. (1989). An empirically derived inventory to measure social fears and anxiety: The Social Phobia and Anxiety Inventory. *Psychological Assessment, 1,* 35–40.

CHAPTER 6

Posttraumatic Stress Disorder

MATT J. GRAY and RON ACIERNO

DESCRIPTION OF THE DISORDER

ALTHOUGH PSYCHOLOGISTS AND other mental health professionals have long appreciated the potential for life-threatening or other inordinately distressing life events to result in profound emotional and behavioral disturbances, inception of Posttraumatic Stress Disorder (PTSD) into the professional nomenclature is a fairly recent development. Prior to the third edition of the *Diagnostic and Statistical Manual of Mental Disorders* (*DSM-III*; American Psychiatric Association [APA], 1980), trauma-related sequelae were identified by a number of different labels corresponding to the specific traumatic event experienced (e.g., shell shock or combat fatigue, rape trauma syndrome; Foa & Meadows, 1997). It was only when researchers and clinicians began to note similarities in symptom course and treatment implications among these syndromes that they were classified together under the rubric of Posttraumatic Stress Disorder.

PTSD, an anxiety disorder, is necessarily secondary to particularly distressing events. Events that most frequently precipitate PTSD involve real or perceived life threat (such as combat, natural disasters, or violent crime), witnessing or experiencing significant accidents or injuries, or sexual assault. To meet *DSM-IV* diagnostic criteria, the individual must have experienced (or witnessed) such an event and exposure to this event must have elicited intense fear, helplessness, or horror (APA, 1994). The original criteria for PTSD held that for the diagnosis to be given, the person must have experienced a traumatic event that was "outside the realm of normal human experience" (APA, 1980). Subsequent epidemiological studies clearly demonstrated that experience of events known to elicit PTSD is far from atypical. For instance, a large-scale epidemiological study of a representative national sample of nearly 6,000 U.S. citizens estimated that approximately 61% of men and 51% of women have experienced at least one traumatic event at some point in their lives (Kessler,

Sonnega, Bromet, Hughes, & Nelson, 1995). Because incidence of traumatic events is unfortunately common, we no longer deem traumatic events to be outside the realm of normal human experience.

In addition to experiencing a traumatic event, diagnosis of PTSD also requires (1) at least one symptom of persistent reexperiencing of the event as evidenced by intrusive memories of the event, nightmares, flashbacks, or psychological or physiological reactivity to reminders of the trauma; (2) three or more symptoms of pervasive avoidance of stimuli or thoughts associated with the traumatic event, and/or emotional numbing; and (3) two or more persistent symptoms of increased arousal, such as hypervigilance, sleep difficulties, irritability, or exaggerated startle responses (APA; 1994). Moreover, these symptoms must persist for more than one month following the trauma and must be significantly debilitating so as to impair social, educational, or occupational functioning.

The rationale for the requirement that symptoms persist for more than a month rests on a finding that a majority of individuals who encounter a traumatic event will experience these symptoms in the immediate aftermath of the trauma. Accordingly, symptoms are not considered pathological shortly after the traumatic event, but instead are considered a normal reaction to inordinately distressing events. Although the one-month cutoff point is arguably arbitrary, there is accumulating evidence that individuals who are still markedly distressed one month after the traumatic event are significantly more likely to develop chronic symptoms of PTSD and are more likely to require treatment to ameliorate those symptoms (e.g., Brewin, Andrews, Rose, & Kirk, 1999).

Although exposure to events that can result in PTSD is not rare, the majority of individuals who experience such events do not ultimately develop chronic psychopathology. Lifetime estimates of PTSD following trauma depend on the nature of the traumatic event experienced, with some events resulting in higher incidence of PTSD than others. For instance, Breslau et al. (1998) estimated that approximately 49% of rape victims developed PTSD compared to 4% of natural disaster survivors. Lifetime prevalence of PTSD in the population at large is estimated at between 5% and 10%, making it one of the most common anxiety disorders (Ballenger et al., 2000).

PTSD can be very debilitating, and secondary clinical problems or difficulties are very common. Because of the persistent and sometimes extreme efforts to avoid cues, conversations, or places that serve as reminders of the traumatic events, individuals with PTSD often abuse substances and may withdraw from social situations, thereby increasing the likelihood of substance dependence disorders and secondary depression, among other complications (Kilpatrick, Acierno, Resnick, Saunders, & Best, 1997; Kessler et al., 1995).

In addition to the overwhelming burden that this disorder places on the individual trauma victim, it also is associated with significant costs to society. As a point of fact, it can significantly impair occupational functioning (based on work days lost or reduced productivity), resulting in a conservatively estimated financial loss of over $3 billion in the United States (Ballenger et al., 2000). In sum, PTSD is unfortunately prevalent, is significantly debilitating to the individual trauma victim, is often accompanied by complicating secondary disorders or clinically significant problems, and exacts a substantial toll on the society as a whole. Fortunately, empirically validated treatments capable of greatly alleviating these difficulties have been developed, as illustrated in the following.

CASE DESCRIPTION

Mr. S. is a 34-year-old White male who was referred for assessment and treatment of symptoms secondary to being kidnapped and repeatedly physically assaulted during a cocaine purchase. At the time of his presentation for treatment, he had been married for five years and had a 4-year-old daughter. Initially, his marriage was very fulfilling, but his wife had an affair with one of his coworkers approximately two years into the marriage. Since that time, he and his wife have had somewhat frequent arguments and are more emotionally distant.

Mr. S. began using cocaine when he was approximately 31 years of age. He attributes onset of his cocaine usage to his wife's affair. He estimated that he used cocaine approximately two to three times per week until voluntarily seeking treatment approximately one year prior to the kidnapping and assault. He realized that his usage was interfering with his job performance, and he was concerned about his ability to parent while abusing cocaine. He also smoked marijuana regularly since the age of 18, but had not used any substances in the year preceding the assault, according to his report. He did relapse on the night he was kidnapped and assaulted, however.

According to Mr. S., he was particularly upset about an argument that he and his wife had earlier in the evening, so he left the home and went to the apartment of his former dealer to buy cocaine. After Mr. S. used some of the cocaine, the dealer pointed a pistol at him and robbed him. Not satisfied with the amount of money that Mr. S. was able to provide, the dealer forced him into a car and drove to several ATMs during the night, demanding that he withdraw more money from his accounts. The dealer was never satisfied, believing there to be more money in Mr. S.'s checking and savings accounts than he withdrew. The following morning, the dealer picked up two friends and they drove to Mr. S.'s wife's place of employment. They called her from their cellular phone and instructed her to meet them in the parking lot, where they demanded money and threatened to kill Mr. S. if she did not cooperate. She stated that she would try to call friends and relatives to get more money by the end of the day. In the meantime, the perpetrators drove Mr. S. to a secluded field, where they proceeded to beat him severely with their fists and tree limbs. They were alternately assaulting him and stopping to smoke marijuana. Mr. S. remembers hearing them laughing while beating him. At one point, he was forced into the trunk of the car for approximately 30 minutes while they continued to smoke marijuana. They called his wife and demanded that she meet them at a specified location with ransom money. At this point, they opened the trunk and beat Mr. S. while holding the phone to his head so that she could hear him scream.

They drove Mr. S. to the location where they were to meet his wife. She had not arrived yet, so one of the perpetrators stabbed Mr. S. in the stomach with a box cutter. Immediately after this, several policemen arrived and apprehended the perpetrators, as Mr. S.'s wife had notified the police of the situation and the meeting place. In addition to the stab wound, Mr. S. sustained numerous bruises and abrasions, as well as a concussion from being hit on the head with tree limbs. He was taken to the hospital, treated, monitored overnight, and discharged the next day.

CHIEF COMPLAINTS

Mr. S. presented for treatment approximately four weeks after this incident. He reported that he was experiencing frequent nightmares of the event, significantly diminished sleep, overwhelming anxiety, and that he was constantly "on edge," fearing reprisal from the perpetrators. Although he knew that they were all in jail, he was concerned that they would be released on bail prior to their trial, or that their friends or family members would exact revenge against him for their imprisonment. He resumed working approximately one week after the assault, but reported that his concentration was significantly impaired and that he was unable to perform his job as well as he had previously. Although his supervisors were unaware of difficulties he was having, he stated that he was making numerous mistakes that his supervisors would eventually notice. In addition to the recurrent nightmares, he reported that he had vivid memories of the assault repeatedly throughout the day, and that these memories were accompanied by intense anxiety and strong physiological arousal, including an accelerated heart rate and rapid breathing. Although he went to great lengths to suppress such thoughts and to avoid all reminders of the trauma, he could not prevent the frequent, distressing memories of the event.

In addition to pronounced symptoms of PTSD, Mr. S. reported experiencing a very depressed mood. He attributed this depression to feelings of guilt about his relapse and about not being an adequate father to his daughter. Moreover, his wife was generally unsupportive as she continued to assert that the abduction and assault would have never happened had he remained clean and sober. Although he denied any previous history of alcohol abuse or dependence, he reported that he had been drinking two to three beers per night since the assault in an effort to relieve his anxiety and to facilitate falling asleep. Finally, he stated that he had been experiencing frequent headaches since the assault.

HISTORY

PTSD differs from other disorders by virtue of the fact that it develops in response to an objective, readily identifiable event (i.e., the traumatic event). Clearly, occurrence of a traumatic experience is a necessary precondition that must be met for the diagnosis to be given. In one sense, then, we could discuss the history of Mr. S.'s disorder only in terms of the traumatic event and the development of symptoms in response to that event. Although a trauma is necessary for PTSD to occur, it is certainly not sufficient, as evidenced by the fact that the majority of people who experience a traumatic event do not develop chronic psychopathology.

Accordingly, to fully consider the history of the disorder, attention must be paid to preexisting factors that have been identified as sources of vulnerability to developing PTSD following trauma. Notably, prior exposure to trauma, personal history of psychiatric disorder, and family history of psychiatric disorder all predict chronic PTSD following traumatic exposure (Marshall, Spitzer, & Liebowitz, 1999). Mr. S. reported that his childhood was quite difficult, as his father was an alcoholic and often abused his mother. In addition to witnessing violence in his home, he also witnessed a great deal of violence in his neighborhood and school. His parents divorced when he was 9 years of age. Despite these difficulties, he described his childhood relationships with peers as quite good and noted that he performed well academically. He ultimately earned a bachelor's degree in biology and obtained a position as a laboratory technician. From such minimal information pertaining to personal and family history, it is apparent that all of these factors might be relevant. Although he denied being physically abused by his parents, he witnessed considerable violence both at home and at school. Some of these instances may have been severe enough to meet *DSM-IV* diagnostic criteria for a PTSD-eliciting traumatic event. He denied currently experiencing significant distress related to those events, but some have argued that the effects of trauma are cumulative, such that exposure to multiple traumas may exacerbate one's response to subsequent traumatic events (Dougall, Herberman, Delahanty, Inslicht, & Baum, 2000). With respect to family history of psychiatric disorder, at a minimum we know that his father abused alcohol. Finally, Mr. S. acknowledged a preexisting substance dependence problem of his own. Although none of these events may have contributed to his current PTSD, they were risk factors that should be considered.

In addition to previous stress events, peritraumatic and posttraumatic environment factors also can affect the likelihood of developing PTSD following trauma. With respect to his specific traumatic experience, kidnapping and prolonged assaults are associated with a very high incidence of subsequent PTSD diagnoses (Breslau et al., 1998). As for the posttrauma recovery environment, there is considerable evidence that social support in the aftermath of trauma is associated with positive posttraumatic adjustment (e.g., Taft, Stern, King, & King, 1999). Unfortunately, Mr. S.'s spouse was not very supportive following his trauma, which may have adversely impacted his symptom course and recovery. Enhancing his support system will likely be a very useful adjunct to trauma-focused therapy.

BEHAVIORAL ASSESSMENT

In 1988, researchers noted that despite the considerable need for measures of posttraumatic symptomatology, very few instruments with adequate psychometric properties were available (Keane, Caddell, & Taylor, 1988). However, since that time, trauma researchers and clinicians have witnessed a proliferation of structured interviews and self-report measures designed to assess exposure to potentially traumatic events (PTEs) and symptoms of PTSD. Although most of these measures are reasonably reliable and valid, they often are not directly compared with alternative, established measures. This has resulted in an array of duplicated measures that generally lack data demonstrating incremental utility or accuracy (Litz, Miller, Ruef, & McTeague, in press). Consequently, practitioners and investigators often have little basis for selecting a particular measure over others that are available. Excellent reviews of measures for PTSD are available (Litz et al., in press; Weathers & Keane, 1999). Here, we briefly describe a structured interview and a paper-and-pencil measure that are characterized by sound psychometric properties. These appear to offer great promise in overcoming the limitations of existing measures.

Perhaps the greatest advance in assessing PTSD is represented by the Clinician-Administered PTSD Scale (CAPS-1; Blake et al., 1990). The CAPS-1 items provide point-to-point correspondence with the 17 symptoms that constitute *DSM-IV* criteria for the disorder. Unlike other interviews for PTSD, frequency and intensity of symptoms are not conflated, as both dimensions are rated separately for each symptom on a 5-point Likert-type scale. The CAPS-1 provides standard prompt questions, suggested follow-up queries, and behaviorally specific anchors to facilitate clinician ratings. Importantly, it evaluates dichotomous diagnostic status (i.e., caseness) as well as continuous scaling of PTSD severity. Given the care that went into its construction, it is not surprising that the CAPS-1 has excellent test-retest reliability, internal consistency, sensitivity, and specificity (Blake et al., 1995). The primary limitations of the CAPS-1 are that it does not elicit an exhaustive trauma history and that it requires an average of 45 minutes or more to administer. These limitations are shared by all other structured PTSD diagnostic interviews, however. Other promising structured interviews have been developed to assess PTSD, but more extensive validation efforts will be necessary to evaluate their utility relative to the CAPS-1.

Although structured clinical interviews may provide the most accurate diagnostic information (Norris & Riad, 1997), there are many purposes for which intensive interviews are not feasible. Paper-and-pencil measures of PTSD symptomatology are a much more efficient use of resources for many clinical purposes such as tracking symptom change over the course of treatment. A structured interview such as the CAPS-1 should be administered for formal diagnostic purposes, but paper-and-pencil PTSD symptom measures can be administered periodically thereafter to monitor therapeutic progress.

Although there are many psychometrically sound paper-and-pencil PTSD measures available, the only one that provides separate ratings of symptom frequency and intensity is the Modified PTSD Symptom Scale (MPSS; Falsetti, Resnick, Resick, & Kilpatrick, 1993). The MPSS can be scored dichotomously for informal diagnostic purposes, but can also be scored as a continuous measure. Frequency of each symptom is rated by respondents on a 4-point scale ranging from "not at all" to "almost always," and severity is rated on a 5-point scale from "not at all distressing" to "extremely distressing." It has demonstrated very good internal consistency and appears to be quite valid, as evidenced by its strong convergence with structured clinical interviews for PTSD (Falsetti et al., 1993). The MPSS is the self-report measure that is most analogous to the CAPS because it provides dichotomous and continuous scaling of PTSD severity and separate frequency and intensity ratings for symptoms.

Mr. S. clearly met diagnostic criteria for PTSD using the CAPS-1. Although the diagnosis only requires one reexperiencing symptom, three avoidance and numbing symptoms, and two hyperarousal symptoms, Mr. S. endorsed several symptoms in each category. The average symptom endorsed by him was experienced several times per week and was rated as being at moderately to severely distressing. The MPSS was administered every two weeks to evaluate therapeutic progress such that treatment could be revised if needed.

It is rarely the case that a trauma victim develops severe symptoms of PTSD without incurring other psychological symptoms or emotional difficulties. Thus, even if PTSD is strongly suspected or the most readily identifiable clinical problem, one should assess for other emotional or behavioral difficulties. Accordingly, Mr. S. also completed the Symptom Checklist-90-Revised (SCL-90-R; Derogatis, 1983), which is a relatively brief paper-and-pencil measure of wide-ranging psychological symptoms. Pronounced symptom scales on the SCL-90-R may indicate a need for further structured interviews or more in-depth assessment. His scores on scales assessing depression, anxiety, paranoid ideation, and somatic complaints were quite elevated. When later asked about somatic symptoms that he endorsed, he reported that his primary somatic complaints pertained to the aforementioned frequent headaches that he experienced following the assault. Finally, Mr. S. completed the Beck Depression Inventory-II (BDI-II; Beck, 1996). His responses were indicative of a moderate-to-severe level of depression. Further interviewing confirmed that he met *DSM-IV* diagnostic criteria for a Major Depressive Episode. He denied experiencing any similar symptoms or prolonged periods of depressed mood prior to his kidnapping and assault.

MEDICAL CONSULTATION

Clearly, the most pressing physical complaints that required a referral to a physician for further evaluation and possible treatment were the frequent headaches he had been experiencing secondary to his physical assault. Although he received medical attention following his trauma, it should not simply be assumed that he was receiving follow-up medical care. Even if physicians who treated him strongly encouraged him to return for future appointments or to report any chronic pain or other difficulties following the assault, the sustained head injuries could conceivably have prevented consolidation or retrieval of this information. The concentration difficulties that he reported could simply be a symptom of PTSD that is not related to any structural damage or neurological deficit. But it is entirely possible that he could have sustained neurological damage as a result of the brutal assault. Not only is this important to evaluate and treat in its own right, but any cognitive deficits stemming from the trauma could have implications for psychotherapy. For instance, severe concentration deficits could interfere with his ability to engage in therapeutic exercises in session, and memory deficits could prevent him from engaging in therapeutic work between sessions.

In the case of Mr. S., subsequent neuropsychological testing revealed no significant cognitive functioning impairments that would adversely impact treatment. Moreover, neuroimaging techniques did not reveal any structural damage. His headaches were monitored by his physician and gradually remitted over time. The psychiatrist on staff also evaluated Mr. S. and prescribed an SSRI (selective serotonin reuptake inhibitor) to address his depressive symptoms, but SSRIs can also facilitate the treatment of PTSD (Friedman, Davidson, Mellman, & Southwick, 2000).

CASE CONCEPTUALIZATION

Diagnoses of PTSD are often overlooked because trauma victims may attempt to deal with or suppress trauma-related sequelae for months or years before presenting for treatment. In such instances, they may complain of general symptoms of anxiety and depression without referencing a specific traumatic event. Unfortunately, primary care physicians, as well as mental health professionals who are relatively unfamiliar with trauma, typically do not routinely screen for exposure to traumatic events. Clients who struggle with these difficulties for long periods of time may be so focused on describing their emotional experiences and symptoms when they finally do present for treatment that they may not mention that the symptoms ensued following some traumatic event. If the clinician does not explicitly ask about this possibility, the diagnosis of PTSD can easily be overlooked.

In Mr. S.'s case, the diagnosis was really quite simple because he sought treatment very soon after the traumatic event and noted that his emotional difficulties began immediately following his kidnapping and assault. Furthermore, he denied experiencing any significant distress prior to the assault, reducing the likelihood that his difficulties may have been owing to an exacerbation of a pre-existing condition. Not only did his early presentation simplify the diagnostic picture, it also likely facilitated the course of treatment because prognosis tends to be better for patients who seek treatment relatively soon after trauma (Shalev, Bonne, & Eth, 1996).

In any case, Mr. S. exceeded the minimal criteria for the diagnosis of PTSD. His harrowing experience would be considered traumatic by any reasonable diagnostician. Although the diagnosis requires only one reexperiencing symptom, Mr. S. reported several, including nightmares, intrusive and distressing memories of the assault during waking hours, and significant psychological and emotional reactivity to reminders of the event. Similarly, he clearly exhibited avoidance and emotional numbing symptoms that characterize the disorder. This is evident by the fact that he often would go to great lengths to avoid any cues or conversations that would remind him of his traumatic experience. To cite one of many examples, he stopped watching television altogether because of the numerous legal, medical, and law enforcement dramas that often depict violent crime or its aftermath. He also reported feeling detached from others and having a sense of a foreshortened future. Finally, with respect to the symptom category of increased arousal, he reported sleep difficulties, difficulty concentrating, hypervigilance, and an exaggerated startle response.

Although the three symptom categories (reexperiencing, avoidance/numbing, and hyperarousal) are presented and discussed in isolation, it is important to note that they are intimately interconnected. Etiological models of PTSD that have garnered the most empirical support have discussed the interplay between intrusive (i.e., reexperiencing) symptoms and avoidance symptoms in maintaining the disorder. Specifically, conditioning models (e.g., Keane, Zimering, & Caddell, 1985) hold that during an assault (or other type of traumatic event), intense fear is an unconditioned response to the traumatic event (the unconditioned stimulus). This emotional response (fear) is paired with stimuli that are present during the assault. Accordingly, a conditioned fear response is elicited by cues that have been paired with the traumatic event (i.e., conditioned stimuli), such that those stimuli are later capable of producing significant fear, anxiety, and distress when they are encountered following the trauma. A simple classical conditioning model cannot fully account for PTSD, however, because repeated experience with those cues or conditioned stimuli in the absence of actual trauma should result in extinction of the fear response.

This is precisely why the avoidance symptoms are relevant to the maintenance of the disorder. As applied to PTSD, Mowrer's (1960) two-factor model posits that this initial classical conditioning process is followed by operant conditioning (Keane et al., 1985; Shalev et al., 1996). Specifically, a trauma victim will subsequently avoid trauma-relevant cues or reminders, and this avoidance is negatively reinforcing in that it reduces aversive emotional states of fear and anxiety. Avoidance is immediately rewarded by a reduction in negative affect, but extinction of the classically conditioned fear and anxiety response never occurs because exposure to trauma cues (including thoughts and memories about the trauma) does not occur frequently enough or for a long enough duration. More recent etiological models of PTSD have retained a primary emphasis on these classical and operant conditioning processes, but have also incorporated cognitive factors such as perceptions of predictability and control as being influential in the development and expression of posttraumatic psychopathology (e.g., Foa & Kozak, 1986).

In the case of Mr. S., he experienced extreme fear, helplessness, and anxiety during the attack. These emotional responses were easily elicited (i.e., a conditioned emotional response occurred) whenever he encountered internal or external cues that reminded him of the assault. Quite understandably, he attempted to avoid all thoughts, people, places, and conversations that reminded him of the trauma in an effort to prevent or minimize severe anxiety and distress that would inevitably follow. Unfortunately, trauma cues and memories are ubiquitous and, like virtually all trauma victims, Mr. S. was unable to avoid all such reminders. He continued to experience overwhelming distress secondary to his traumatic experience and, paradoxically, his extreme attempts to avoid trauma cues and keep this distress at bay only served to maintain the disorder. Accordingly, treatment necessarily involved intentional exposure to (objectively safe) trauma memories and cues (discussed in greater detail later in this chapter).

Given Mr. S.'s previous substance dependence problem, it was necessary to continually monitor his substance abuse. Significant abuse or dependence would likely interfere with therapy commitment and compliance and would need to be resolved first. Fortunately, Mr. S. did not resume cocaine abuse following his traumatic experience. Although he did not have a history of alcohol dependence, he was very forthright in acknowledging that he had been consuming more alcohol in an effort to address his sleep deficits. Although this is quite common for trauma victims with a history of substance abuse or dependence, it bears mentioning that even those without such a history have an increased incidence of substance abuse following trauma (Kilpatrick et al., 1998). Given the many ways that trauma victims attempt to avoid thoughts and feelings related to the trauma, it is not at all surprising that substances are often abused by victims in a futile attempt to cope with the aftermath of trauma.

Mr. S. also met *DSM-IV* diagnostic criteria for a Major Depressive Episode. Because these symptoms began immediately after his traumatic experience and because he did not have a history of mood disturbance, his depressive symptoms were viewed as secondary to trauma and a restricted lifestyle that is often attendant with PTSD. Major Depressive Disorder is the most prevalent comorbid disorder with PTSD (Kessler et al., 1995). Accordingly, trauma-focused therapy was recommended, as this typically results in an alleviation of both PTSD and depressive symptoms when, in fact, the depression is not a chronic pretraumatic condition. Obviously, the SSRI he was prescribed would also likely be helpful in alleviating his depressive symptoms.

Prior to beginning trauma-focused treatment, it is necessary to evaluate the recovery environment and factors that may hinder therapeutic progress. In particular, safety planning is of the utmost importance. It is inadvisable to expose trauma victims to thoughts, cues, and reminders of the traumatic event in an effort to extinguish the conditioned emotional response, if the individual is not objectively safe or is realistically concerned about a recurrence of the trauma.

Mr. S. endorsed significant symptoms of paranoid ideation on the SCL-90-R. Such pronounced suspiciousness can be delusional and is often indicative of a psychotic disorder. It should be acknowledged, however, that this type of concern is quite reasonable and not necessarily pathological given his very recent assault history. Upon further interviewing, he noted that he had never previously been suspicious of others, but that his primary concern regarding others' intentions was possible retaliation by friends or family members of the perpetrators. Although his concerns are arguably not unfounded given the recency of his assault and the realistic possibility that friends of the perpetrators could seek to harm him, it is still necessary to allay these fears as much as possible before beginning therapy.

Finally, social support is associated with greater posttraumatic adjustment. Increasing victims' interaction with friends and family members is often an essential adjunct to treatment. More important, encouraging emotional disclosure to one or two very intimate and supportive friends or family members can be very helpful in promoting recovery.

RATIONALE FOR TREATMENT CHOICE

The rationale for exposure therapy derives logically from empirically validated etiological models of posttraumatic stress, described earlier. If in fact avoidance of thoughts, people, places, or other cues that remind victims of their traumatic experiences prevents extinction of the conditioned emotional response, it stands to reason that systematic exposure to such (objectively benign) cues will allow reduction of the fear response to occur. With repeated exposure to traumatic memories and trauma-relevant cues, their association to actual trauma and their capacity to elicit significant emotional and psychological distress are greatly attenuated.

Exposure therapy can be imaginal in nature or in vivo, although most treatment protocols use both procedures. In the former, trauma victims are asked to close their eyes and vividly imagine their traumatic event. They are asked to describe it aloud in the present tense, and to provide as much detail (sensory as well as attendant thoughts and feelings) as they can. This account is tape-recorded and the client is usually asked to listen to the tape at least once per day between sessions. This procedure is repeated in and across sessions until there is a significant reduction in anxiety and distress, as described below. During in vivo exposure, clients are asked to purposely expose themselves to activities, places, or other cues that are realistically safe and that they have been avoiding since the trauma. For instance, motor vehicle accident survivors who have been avoiding driving since their accident would be asked to begin going on short drives around their neighborhood. In vivo exposure is conducted only with stimuli that are objectively safe. Quite obviously, assault victims would not be encouraged to have contact the perpetrators.

Two comprehensive, critical reviews of psychosocial treatments for PTSD have concluded that cognitive-behavioral treatments generally, and exposure therapy specifically, have been the most rigorously tested and validated treatment methods for PTSD (Foa & Meadows, 1997; Rothbaum, Meadows, Resick, & Foy, 2000). The authors of both reviews identify multiple studies that converged to document the efficacy of exposure procedures in effectively reducing symptoms of PTSD. They commend exposure therapy as the "treatment of choice for PTSD" because of its demonstrated efficacy in varied trauma populations and its relative ease of implementation. Similarly, a recent meta-analysis of 61 treatment-outcome trials of psychological treatments for PTSD revealed that among treatments demonstrating positive therapeutic outcomes, exposure therapy was associated with the largest effect size from an independent evaluator (see Foa, 2000).

A common misconception about exposure therapy is that it only targets symptoms of anxiety and does not address other posttraumatic difficulties (e.g., depression), or that extinction of the fear response is its only benefit. Studies that have included other outcome measures have consistently documented global and diverse treatment gains (Marks, Lovell, Noshirvani, Livanou, & Thrasher, 1998; Tarrier, Pilgrim, et al., 1999; Tarrier, Sommerfield, Pilgrim, & Humphreys, 1999).

As mentioned previously, recent etiological models of PTSD have implicated cognitive variables such as predictability and control as being important in the development of the disorder following trauma. Interestingly, treatments that have been developed to specifically target these cognitive variables, whether administered alone or in conjunction with traditional exposure methods, have not outperformed exposure therapy alone (Marks et al., 1998; Tarrier, Pilgrim, et al., 1999; Tarrier, Sommerfield, et al., 1999). It is arguably not the case that these cognitive factors are unimportant, but rather, that they can be modified by exposure as well as cognitive interventions (e.g., Socratic questioning) that are specifically designed to target them. Foa and Meadows (1997) assert:

> Exposure promotes symptom reduction by allowing patients to realize that contrary to their mistaken ideas: (a) being in objectively safe situations that remind one of the trauma is not dangerous; (b) remembering the trauma is not equivalent to experiencing it again; (c) anxiety does not remain indefinitely in the presence of feared situations or memories, but rather it decreases even without avoidance or escape; and (d) experiencing anxiety/PTSD symptoms does not lead to loss of control. (p. 462)

Over the course of exposure therapy, clients confront their fears that lead to avoidance, and consequently, maladaptive or erroneous cognitions that developed following trauma are disconfirmed. In short, exposure does not simply lead to reductions in aversive affective states. Reductions in conditioned fear and anxiety are accompanied by cognitive changes, including enhanced perceptions of control.

A final misconception about exposure therapy is that it is associated with greater therapy attrition rates or that it can exacerbate the disorder. Comprehensive reviews conclude that cognitive-behavioral treatments for PTSD (including exposure therapy) have lower dropout rates than pharmacological treatments (Foa, 2000), and the dropout rate for PTSD is not different than the rate for other anxiety disorders (Ballenger et al., 2000). Moreover, some studies (e.g., Foa, Dancu, Hembree, Jaycox, Meadows, & Street, 1999) show lower attrition in exposure conditions relative to other psychosocial interventions for PTSD.

It should be noted at the outset that any trauma-focused treatment is likely to produce immediate but transient symptom exacerbation in some patients. After all, most patients have expended considerable physical and cognitive resources trying to refrain from talking about or otherwise being reminded about their traumatic experiences. When they finally present for therapy to address symptoms secondary to trauma, they are being asked to do something (i.e., talk about their traumas) that they are strongly motivated not to do because avoidance is part and parcel of the disorder. It stands to reason, then, that beginning to talk about their trauma and the symptoms resulting from trauma will be accompanied by heightened anxiety as patients confront that which they would most like to avoid. But this is equally true for all interventions that seek to address trauma and its sequelae. Contrary to ubiquitous myths about exposure therapy, enduring adverse reactions are uncommon and are no more prevalent or severe than difficulties that arise in other treatments (Foy et al., 1996).

COURSE OF TREATMENT

As mentioned previously, it is of the utmost importance to ensure that the client's safety needs are met. Beginning exposure therapy while Mr. S. was still justifiably concerned about retaliation from the perpetrators' friends and family members could well have heightened his anxiety rather than alleviating it. Many states have passed victim advocacy legislation, including victim notification programs. Mr. S. registered for such a program that would notify him if and when any of the perpetrators were released from jail. He could also call a toll-free number to learn the status of their legal cases and incarceration. He purchased a home alarm system that allayed his concerns somewhat, although he was still worried about the possibility of a home invasion. This specific concern was relatively mild because it had been over a month since the perpetrators were imprisoned and he had not received any threats or harrassment. The alarm system and his enrollment in the victim notification program helped to alleviate his suspiciousness and fear of reprisal enough to allow us to proceed with trauma-focused therapy. He became increasingly confident that no reprisals would be forthcoming as his trauma became more distant. If his fear of a home invasion were more pronounced and persistent or if he had received threats, it may have been necessary for him to reside temporarily with friends or relatives.

In addition to safety planning, the first three sessions consisted of psychoeducation about PTSD and the role that avoidance plays in maintaining the disorder. During this time, Mr. S. was allowed to discuss the event at his own pace and at a level of detail with which he was comfortable. This process facilitates rapport and allows people to disconfirm fears they may have about discussing their traumas. During this initial phase of therapy, Mr. S. was also encouraged to use existing social supports. Unfortunately, his wife was so angry about his relapse that she was not able to be very supportive. We then took a twofold approach. First, Mr. S. had a very close relationship with his brother. He was encouraged to discuss with his brother difficulties he was having and to use this valuable source of support. Second, his wife was encouraged to come to one of his first sessions, during which she was allowed to express her frustrations and was educated about PTSD and the process of recovery as well as the importance of social support for trauma victims generally. Mr. and Mrs. S. were also given the contact information for a couple's therapist, who began working with them on issues of trust and communication. Mrs. S.'s anger about her husband's relapse waned over time, and although she was never as supportive as other figures in Mr. S.'s life during trauma-focused treatment, she was less critical of him and committed to continuing to work on their relationship.

The success of exposure therapy for PTSD hinges on the degree to which patients understand the role that avoidance plays in maintaining the disorder, as well as their understanding of the rationale for this approach. Clear presentation of the rationale, followed by evaluation of the patient's understanding of it, may be the single most important aspect of trauma-focused therapy for PTSD. This is because clients are being asked to engage in activities that they would very much like to avoid, and because transient symptom exacerbation can precede significant treatment gains. As such, their understanding of the rationale and course of exposure therapy may dictate their level of treatment compliance and adherence. Although attrition is not higher in exposure therapy than in other forms of treatment for PTSD, those who do not benefit from treatment (exposure or other types of psychotherapy) rate therapy as less credible and miss more sessions than those who improve (i.e., they do not "buy into" the rationale; e.g., Tarrier, Pilgrim, et al., 1999). Thus, a client's understanding of the premise of exposure therapy coupled with regular attendance will allow him or her to benefit maximally from treatment. Moreover, informing patients that minor but transient symptom exacerbation often occurs can be very reassuring and can facilitate compliance and commitment to therapy in the event that initial increases in intrusive symptoms occur.

We advise therapists to ask patients to describe the rationale for exposure therapy in their own words prior to beginning exposure activities, to ensure that patients do not have misconceptions about the procedure or course of therapy. Mr. S. was able to articulate the reasons for imagining the assault and engaging in previously avoided activities despite the fact that this would be difficult. Like most victims' experiences, when he actually began to engage in these feared activities, he found them much more tolerable than he had anticipated.

EXPOSURE THERAPY (9 SESSIONS)

Most treatment-outcome studies of exposure therapy use the same frequency and duration of exposure sessions for all participants to render more readily interpretable experimental results. In practice, however, it is most advantageous to tailor both the duration and number of sessions to the needs of the particular individual. Because trauma victims present with widely varying traumatic experiences, symptom levels, recovery environments, and individual differences, a one-size-fits-all approach to treatment is ill-advised. Each session of exposure therapy should not end until the patient has experienced a significant reduction in anxiety (e.g., 50%), because stopping a session while the client is still experiencing maximal levels of anxiety can result in sensitization rather than extinction (Frueh, Turner, Beidel, & Mirabella, 1996). Moreover, exposure therapy cannot simply be doled out in weekly, 50-minute doses as therapy is traditionally practiced. Although criterion anxiety-reductions are achieved much more quickly in later sessions, initial therapy sessions can average approximately 90 minutes (Frueh et al., 1996) and occur more than once per week. If one of the primary benefits of exposure is that it disconfirms victims' fears about consequences of thinking about trauma and demonstrates that thinking about it is not nearly as bad as experiencing it, then discontinuing a session prior to a reduction in anxiety would be countertherapeutic.

In terms of number of sessions, this too depends on several factors, including the chronicity of the disorder, the severity of symptoms, and the degree of exposure the client is able to engage in between sessions. Generally, exposure therapy continues until a client can, at the beginning of a session, relay his or her traumatic event with fairly minimal distress. Most published investigations that have employed exposure techniques have ranged from 10 to 20 sessions (Rothbaum et al., 2000), although positive outcomes have been observed in as few as 4 sessions (Foa, Hearst-Ikeda, & Perry, 1995). Although Mr. S. had relatively severe PTSD symptoms, the recency of the trauma coupled with his diligence between sessions predicted a shorter course of therapy.

Imaginal exposure involves imagining the traumatic event as vividly as possible; in most cases, the entire event can be described in vivid detail because most traumas are discrete events that rarely last more than several minutes. Because his trauma occurred over the course of a 24-hour period, it was first necessary to determine which specific aspect(s) of the kidnapping and assault were most distressing. From a practical standpoint, if the victim describes in detail a series of events that took place over the course of 24 hours, it will be difficult to repeat this process a number of times within a session to the point that anxiety reduction occurs. From a theoretical standpoint, focusing on the most distressing aspect of a traumatic event in exposure therapy will likely produce greatest change in the shortest time. Moreover, because avoidance is such an integral part of the disorder, clients may be inclined to imagine/describe less distressing aspects of the trauma in much greater detail than more distressing aspects, which would not be especially therapeutic.

If the clinician is not certain which aspects are genuinely most distressing, he or she will be unable to encourage more vivid, detailed accounts of those aspects. Accordingly, it is important to ask the victim to identify the particular memories that cause the most distress. Commonly, victims will not be able to provide this information when directly asked because they rightfully regard the entire event as a harrowing ordeal. Although this is certainly true, it is invariably the case that some aspects of a prolonged ordeal are more distressing than are others. If a client reports that he or she cannot discern the most distressing part of a prolonged trauma, this can be easily ascertained by having him or her vividly imagine and describe the entire series of events in as much detail as possible. At key points throughout this narrative, the therapist can stop the client and ask him or her to provide an anxiety rating on a 0 to 10 scale, with 0 representing absolutely no distress and 10 representing the most distress the person has ever experienced. In Mr. S.'s case, he had no difficulty nominating the most distressing aspects of his kidnapping and assault. Although the entire series of events was traumatic, the memories that caused him the most anxiety for several weeks after the trauma involved being locked in the trunk of a car and repeatedly beaten when the perpetrators drove him to the secluded area.

Mr. S. was asked to close his eyes and describe in vivid detail, aloud, and in present tense this portion of the kidnapping and assault. As he proceeded, the therapist interjected with prompts and queries about sights, sounds, smells, and so forth to ensure that he was creating as vivid an image as possible and not avoiding important aspects. He was asked to recall and describe his thoughts, feelings, and bodily sensations during the assault, all the while using the present tense (e.g., "I am walking down the hall" versus "I walked down the hall"). At the end of this narrative, he was asked to rate his distress on the 0 to 10 scale; this served as the baseline anxiety level for the session. This process of imaginal exposure followed by an anxiety rating was repeated until a 50% reduction in baseline had been achieved, at which point the session was terminated. During his first session of imaginal exposure, Mr. S.'s initial anxiety rating was 9. After 10 accounts of the event (which lasted for a total of 75 minutes), his anxiety rating was 4 and the session was terminated following a few minutes of progressive muscle relaxation. Each session was recorded, the tape was given to him at the end of the session, and he was asked to listen to it at least once per day before the next session.

When he returned the following week and described the event in detail, his initial anxiety rating was 7, and it required nine iterations for his anxiety rating to reduce to a rating of 3. Typically, over the course of exposure therapy sessions, clients will report initial anxiety ratings that are somewhat lower than the initial rating given in the previous session, but higher than the rating they provided at the end of the last session. This treatment usually requires successively fewer exposure repetitions during each session to produce a 50% decrement in anxiety ratings. A benefit of this is that remaining time in session can be used to review compliance with imaginal in vivo exposure homework, to identify additional situations or trauma cues that the victim is avoiding, to plan in vivo exposure assignments accordingly, and to address obstacles that may interfere with these assignments.

By the ninth session, Mr. S. was able to imagine the assault in session without significant anxiety from the outset. Specifically, after his first imaginal exposure, he reported an anxiety rating of 2 and, unlike in earlier sessions, did not exhibit any visible signs of anxiety or distress. When victims can discuss their traumatic event without experiencing great distress, and when they can encounter unanticipated reminders of the event in the absence of significant distress, trauma-focused exposure therapy may be discontinued. It is important to note (and to inform clients explicitly) that treatment is not capable of eradicating all memories of the traumatic event, nor is it capable of rendering those memories neutral. After all, people who experience traumatic events but do not develop PTSD still have unpleasant thoughts and occasional memories about their traumas. The difference is that they are not incapacitated or overwhelmed with anxiety when these thoughts occur. The thoughts and memories of trauma after successful therapy are still unpleasant, but they are relatively infrequent and they are manageable.

THERAPIST-CLIENT FACTORS

Exposure therapy is widely regarded as the standard of care for PTSD (Rothbaum et al., 2000) because it is effective, but also because it is readily administered and requires relatively less training to be effectively implemented (Foa & Meadows, 1997; Marks et al., 1998; Tarrier & Humphreys, 2000). Because much of the "active ingredient" in exposure therapy is supplied by the client in the form of his or her ability to vividly imagine the trauma as well as his or her compliance with imaginal and in vivo exposure assignments, this treatment relies relatively less on the interplay between therapist and client.

It would be a mistake however, to assume that therapist-client factors are unimportant when conducting exposure therapy. As mentioned previously, successful outcomes depend almost fully on the extent to which the rationale for exposure therapy is effectively communicated to the client. Clear descriptions at the beginning of therapy of the process and typical course of exposure therapy, including difficulties that may be encountered along the way (e.g., temporary symptom exacerbation), can facilitate rapport, alleviate unnecessary anxiety about trauma-focused therapy, and enhance treatment compliance.

It is often mistakenly assumed that exposure therapy is "cold," unempathic, and mechanistic in its delivery. This is a misconception. In fact, therapists who would attempt to provide exposure therapy in such a fashion would soon find themselves without clients. Trauma-focused therapy, regardless of its form, is a most difficult undertaking for trauma victims and requires a safe, supportive environment. To the extent that the therapist is perceived by patients as caring and empathic, they will be more forthcoming in therapy and will be more apt to trust the therapist enough to discuss their trauma. The very nature of PTSD motivates clients to refrain from discussing their trauma. Only a caring, supportive, emotionally responsive therapist will allow the client to risk discussing the trauma and to experience the emotional vulnerability that inevitably ensues. Only when the client feels safe and is willing to take this risk can exposure therapy begin.

COURSE OF TERMINATION AND FOLLOW-UP

Therapy does not simply end when the trauma victim is able to engage in imaginal exposure in the absence of significant distress. Although this marks the end of exposure therapy proper, it is necessary to meet with clients two or three more times to monitor symptoms and to again provide psychoeducation concerning urges that they may have to avoid thoughts or reminders of the trauma and the importance of resisting such urges.

After successful therapy, clients do not need to go out of their way to encounter trauma reminders. It will be important, however, for clients to refrain from making efforts to avoid reminders during the course of their normal activities. Victims should be informed that they might experience distressing traumatic memories or other intrusive symptoms from time to time, but that these are usually transient and manageable. In fact, they should allow these experiences to occur, as consistent efforts to prevent or avoid them can result in a worsening symptom course. In the event that the intrusive symptoms they experience in the future are enduring or pronounced, they should be encouraged to contact the clinician for "booster sessions," although this typically is not necessary.

If additional problems remain that are not specifically trauma-related, additional sessions or referrals to appropriate treatment providers will, of course, be necessary. For instance, following trauma-focused therapy, Mr. S. continued outpatient relapse-prevention therapy to target substance abuse behaviors, and he and his wife continued working on their marital relationship through couples therapy. Although many difficulties that do not fall under the rubric of PTSD will be alleviated with successful trauma-focused treatment, a thorough assessment of residual symptoms and difficulties will need to be conducted to ensure that the victim receives appropriate follow-up care when needed. This may consist of continued weekly therapy targeting these other problems (as in the case of Mr. S.), or it may simply consist of a single follow-up session a few weeks after termination to ensure that the patient is doing well and not in need of further treatment.

MANAGED CARE CONSIDERATIONS

Treatment for PTSD is generally reimbursed by most major insurance companies, Medicare, and Medicaid. Because exposure-based treatment techniques are brief and focused, insurance may pay for most or all of therapy. Because relatively few sessions are required for treatment gains to occur, any fees that the client will need to pay out-of-pocket will be kept to a minimum relative to other PTSD treatments. In some instances, insurance payments may not even be an issue for victims. This is because some states have victim compensation programs that pay for medical and psychological needs of crime victims. These programs are commendable, as victims are not further burdened with financial difficulties incurred as a result of seeking help.

OVERALL EFFECTIVENESS

Mr. S. demonstrated significant and meaningful improvement by any reasonable standard. Subjectively, he was able to recall and discuss his trauma and encounter reminders of it without experiencing the overwhelming anxiety with which he originally presented. Objectively, the moderate-to-severe symptom levels that he reported on assessment measures at the beginning of therapy declined to very mild levels by the last session. For instance, his total symptom score on the CAPS (Blake et al., 1990), which is derived by summing frequency and intensity ratings on all symptoms, decreased from 79 to 23. Although a score of 23 is well below his initial symptom level and well below the level endorsed by those with PTSD, it indicates that by the end of therapy, he was still experiencing some mild and relatively infrequent symptoms of PTSD. This is quite common among treatment responders or "successes" in that the majority will continue to experience mild symptoms (Ballenger et al., 2000). Patients and family members should be made aware of this fact from the outset.

In summation, exposure therapy is the most frequently studied and validated treatment for PTSD. Despite the fact that more complex etiological models have supplanted the simple conditioning models that gave rise to exposure therapy, novel treatments that incorporate other components (e.g., cognitive restructuring) have not outperformed exposure-based techniques in the treatment of PTSD. Short-term symptom exacerbation can occur when using exposure-based techniques, but this is no less true of other trauma-focused interventions. Contrary to clinical lore, complications that arise during the course of exposure therapy are no more common than when using other forms of treatment for PTSD. By contrast, ample empirical evidence supports the notion that exposure therapy is efficient, cost-effective, and readily implemented. Based on the preponderance of evidence attesting to its efficacy, we concur with others (Foa & Meadows, 1997; Rothbaum et al., 2000) in recommending exposure therapy as the intervention of choice when treating PTSD.

REFERENCES

American Psychiatric Association. (1980). *Diagnostic and statistical manual of mental disorders* (3rd ed.). Washington, DC: Author.

American Psychiatric Association. (1994). *Diagnostic and statistical manual of mental disorders* (4th ed.). Washington, DC: Author.

Ballenger, J. C., Davidson, J. R., Lecrubier, Y., Nutt, D., Foa, E., Kessler, R., et al. (2000). Consensus statement on Posttraumatic Stress Disorder from the International Consensus Group on Depression and Anxiety. *Journal of Clinical Psychiatry, 61*(Suppl. 5), 60–66.

Beck, A. T. (1996). *The Beck Depression Inventory* (2nd ed.). San Antonio, TX: Psychological Corporation.

Blake, D. D., Weathers, F. W., Nagy, L. M., Kaloupek, D. G., Gusman, F. D., Charney, D. S., et al. (1995). The development of a clinician-administered PTSD scale. *Journal of Traumatic Stress, 8*, 75–90.

Blake, D. D., Weathers, F. W., Nagy, L. M., Kaloupek, D. G., Klauminzer, G., Charney, D. S., et al. (1990). A clinician rating scale for assessing current and lifetime PTSD: The CAPS-1. *Behavior Therapist, 13*, 187–188.

Breslau, N., Kessler, R., Chilcoat, H., Schultz, L., Davis, G., & Andreski, P. (1998). Trauma and Posttraumatic Stress Disorder in the community. *Archives of General Psychiatry, 55,* 626–632.

Brewin, C., Andrews, B., Rose, S., & Kirk, M. (1999). Acute Stress Disorder and Posttraumatic Stress Disorder in victims of violent crime. *American Journal of Psychiatry, 156,* 360–365.

Derogatis, L. R. (1983). *SCL-90-R: Administration, scoring, and procedures manual: II.* Towson, MD: Clinical Psychometric Research.

Dougall, A., Herberman, H., Delahanty, D., Inslicht, S., & Baum, A. (2000). Similarity of prior trauma exposure as a determinant of chronic stress responding to an airline disaster. *Journal of Consulting and Clinical Psychology, 68,* 290–295.

Falsetti, S., Resnick, H., Resick, P., & Kilpatrick, D. (1993). The Modified PTSD Symptom Scale: A brief self-report measure of Posttraumatic Stress Disorder. *Behavior Therapist, 16,* 161–162.

Foa, E. (2000). Psychosocial treatment of Posttraumatic Stress Disorder. *Journal of Clinical Psychiatry, 61*(Suppl. 5), 43–51.

Foa, E., Dancu, C., Hembree, E., Jaycox, L., Meadows, E., & Street, G. (1999). A comparison of exposure therapy, stress inoculation training, and their combination for reducing Posttraumatic Stress Disorder in female assault victims. *Journal of Consulting and Clinical Psychology, 67,* 194–200.

Foa, E., Hearst-Ikeda, D., & Perry, K. J. (1995). Evaluation of a brief cognitive-behavioral program for the prevention of chronic PTSD in recent assault victims. *Journal of Consulting and Clinical Psychology, 63,* 948–955.

Foa, E., & Kozak, M. (1986). Emotional processing of fear: Exposure to corrective information. *Psychological Bulletin, 99,* 20–35.

Foa, E., & Meadows, E. (1997). Psychosocial treatments for Posttraumatic Stress Disorder: A critical review. *Annual Review of Psychology, 48,* 449–480.

Foy, D., Kagan, B., McDermott, C., Leskin, G., Sipprelle, R., & Paz, G. (1996). Practical parameters in the use of flooding for treating chronic PTSD. *Clinical Psychology and Psychotherapy, 3,* 169–175.

Friedman, M., Davidson, J., Mellman, T., & Southwick, S. (2000). Pharmacotherapy. In E. Foa, T. Keane, & M. Friedman (Eds.), *Effective treatments for PTSD* (pp. 84–105). New York: Guilford Press.

Frueh, C., Turner, S., Beidel, D., & Mirabella, R. (1996). Trauma management therapy: A preliminary evaluation of a multicomponent behavioral treatment for chronic combat-related PTSD. *Behaviour Research and Therapy, 34,* 533–543.

Keane, T. M., Caddell, J. M., & Taylor, K. L. (1988). Mississippi Scale for Combat-Related Posttraumatic Stress Disorder: Three studies in reliability and validity. *Journal of Consulting and Clinical Psychology, 56,* 85–90.

Keane, T. M., Zimering, R. T., & Caddell, J. M. (1985). A behavioral formulation of Posttraumatic Stress Disorder in Vietnam veterans. *Behavior Therapist, 8,* 9–12.

Kessler, R., Sonnega, A., Bromet, E., Hughes, M., & Nelson, C. (1995). Posttraumatic Stress Disorder in the National Comorbidity Survey. *Archives of General Psychiatry, 52,* 1048–1060.

Kilpatrick, D., Acierno, R., Resnick, H., Saunders, B., & Best, C. (1997). A 2-year longitudinal analysis of the relationships between violent assault and substance use in women. *Journal of Consulting and Clinical Psychology, 65,* 834–847.

Litz, B., Miller, M., Ruef, A., & McTeague, L. (in press). Assessment of adults exposed to trauma. In M. Antony & D. Barlow (Eds.), *Handbook of assessment, treatment planning, and outcome evaluation: Empirically-supported strategies for psychological disorders.* New York: Guilford Press.

Marks, I., Lovell, K., Noshirvani, H., Livanou, M., & Thrasher, S. (1998). Treatment of Posttraumatic Stress Disorder by exposure and/or cognitive restructuring. *Archives of General Psychiatry, 55,* 317–325.

Marshall, R., Spitzer, R., & Liebowitz, M. (1999). Review and critique of the new *DSM-IV* diagnosis of Acute Stress Disorder. *American Journal of Psychiatry, 156,* 1677–1685.

Norris, F., & Riad, J. (1997). Standardized self-report measures of civilian trauma and Posttraumatic Stress Disorder. In J. Wilson & T. Keane (Eds.), *Assessing psychological trauma and PTSD* (pp. 7–42). New York: Guilford Press.

Rothbaum, B., Meadows, E., Resick, P., & Foy, D. (2000). Cognitive-behavioral therapy. In E. Foa, T. Keane, & M. Friedman (Eds.), *Effective treatments for PTSD* (pp. 60–83). New York: Guilford Press.

Shalev, A., Bonne, O., & Eth, S. (1996). Treatment of Posttraumatic Stress Disorder: A review. *Psychosomatic Medicine, 58,* 165–182.

Taft, C., Stern, A., King, L., & King, D. (1999). Modeling physical health and functional health status: The role of combat exposure, Posttraumatic Stress Disorder, and personal resource attributes. *Journal of Traumatic Stress, 12,* 3–24.

Tarrier, N., & Humphreys, L. (2000). Subjective improvement in PTSD patients with treatment by imaginal exposure or cognitive therapy: Session by session changes. *British Journal of Clinical Psychiatry, 39,* 27–34.

Tarrier, N., Pilgrim, H., Sommerfield, C., Faragher, B., Reynolds, M., Graham, E., et al. (1999). A randomized trial of cognitive therapy and imaginal exposure in the treatment of chronic Posttraumatic Stress Disorder. *Journal of Consulting and Clinical Psychology, 67,* 13–18.

Tarrier, N., Sommerfield, C., Pilgrim, H., & Humphreys, L. (1999). Cognitive therapy or imaginal exposure in the treatment of Posttraumatic Stress Disorder: Twelve-month follow-up. *British Journal of Psychiatry, 175,* 571–575.

Weathers, F. W., & Keane, T. M. (1999). Psychological assessment of traumatized adults. In P. Saigh & J. D. Bremner (Eds.), *Posttraumatic Stress Disorder: A comprehensive approach to research and treatment* (pp. 219–247). Needham Heights, MA: Allyn & Bacon.

CHAPTER 7

Generalized Anxiety Disorder

MICHEL J. DUGAS

DESCRIPTION OF THE DISORDER

APPROXIMATELY 5% OF the general population will suffer from Generalized Anxiety Disorder (GAD) at some time in their life (Kessler et al., 1994). Although GAD is a highly prevalent disorder that leads to considerable distress, specific treatments for GAD have only recently begun to appear in the literature (e.g., Borkovec & Costello, 1993; Dugas & Ladouceur, 2000). This chapter illustrates the application of such a treatment to a specific case. The first section outlines the diagnostic criteria and clinical presentation of GAD, and subsequent sections provide a detailed description of the treatment of a GAD client.

According to the fourth edition of the *Diagnostic and Statistical Manual of Mental Disorders* (*DSM-IV*; American Psychiatric Association [APA], 1994), the main feature of GAD is excessive, uncontrollable worry and anxiety about a number of events or activities. *DSM-IV* also states that much worry and anxiety must be associated with at least three of the following six somatic symptoms: restlessness or feeling keyed up or on edge, being easily fatigued, difficulty concentrating or mind going blank, irritability, muscle tension, and sleep disturbance. Furthermore, the focus of the worry and anxiety must not be confined to features of another Axis I disorder. For example, a GAD diagnosis would not be assigned to someone who worries only about the possibility of having a panic attack (as in Panic Disorder) or about being embarrassed in public (as in social phobia). As is the case with other Axis I disorders, symptoms must lead to clinically significant distress or impairment in important areas of functioning (APA, 1994, pp. 435–436).

Although the *DSM-IV* nicely encapsulates symptoms of GAD, it is sometimes difficult for therapists to identify GAD solely on the basis of *DSM-IV* diagnostic criteria. Additional information about the typical clinical presentation of GAD clients can be useful when making difficult diagnostic decisions. For example, do GAD clients typically consult for their worries, their anxiety, or their somatic symptoms? Although excessive and uncontrollable worry is the cardinal feature

125

of GAD, these clients most often seek professional help for their feelings of anxiety and their somatic symptoms. They may believe that they are "born worriers," that worry represents an immutable personality trait, and that there is therefore no reason to discuss their worries with their therapist. Thus, GAD clients typically do not mention their worries unless their therapist asks about them. "Have you recently been worrying more than usual?" is a simple question that is often neglected by therapists when clients report symptoms such as anxiety, fatigue, muscle tension, and problems with sleep.

Information about the typical worry themes of GAD clients also can be useful when making complex diagnostic decisions. For the most part, the worry themes of GAD clients are similar to those of individuals from the general population. For example, GAD clients commonly worry about interpersonal relationships, family, home, finances, work, and illness (Sanderson & Barlow, 1990; Shadick, Roemer, Hopkins, & Borkovec, 1991). It does appear, however, that GAD clients tend to worry more about minor matters (Craske, Rapee, Jackel, & Barlow, 1989) and about unlikely future events (Dugas et al., 1998). Thus, although worry themes of GAD clients are similar to those of nonclinical individuals, there seem to be subtle differences between the worries of these two populations. Excessive worries about everyday, minor matters (e.g., "Will I get caught in traffic on my way to work?") and highly unlikely future events (e.g., "Will I someday go bankrupt?") may be relatively specific to GAD and may help therapists to recognize this anxiety disorder. This does not imply that all GAD clients worry about minor matters or improbable future events, but that very few individuals without GAD report these worries.

A final feature of the clinical presentation of GAD clients discussed here is their tendency to "live in the future." Given that worry is mainly future-oriented, this feature of the clinical presentation is not surprising. However, this tendency to live in the future often creates subtle forms of distress and interference with daily living for clients with GAD. For example, these individuals may have considerable difficulty unwinding over the weekend because they are worried about what will happen at work on Monday morning. At work, they may have difficulty concentrating on the task at hand because they are worried about what others will think of their performance. This difficulty with living in the present thus represents another important feature of the clinical presentation of GAD clients.

CASE DESCRIPTION

The client, who will be referred to as Anne, was a 22-year-old undergraduate nursing student. She lived alone in a small apartment on campus and seemed to enjoy living on her own. Her parents, who lived in a small town 120 miles away, had helped her get started when she left to go to university by buying her the "essentials" for her apartment. Anne was involved in a steady relationship and had been with her boyfriend for just over two years. Although their relationship had its ups and downs, she truly cared for her boyfriend and hoped they would someday be married. Anne also had many friends and was quite active socially. She often had friends over for dinner on the weekend and was generally well liked by other students.

Anne was the eldest of three children. During her childhood, she often had to "take care" of her brothers, who were two and three years younger than she.

When she was between the ages of 5 and 10, her father and mother experienced some marital difficulties, and her mother often confided in her. Although Anne was only a child, she often felt that she needed to take care of her mother, who seemed to feel vulnerable in the midst of these marital problems. Anne reported that she not only felt that she had to watch over her younger brothers, but also, to some extent, over her mother. Although she believed that her parents had a sound relationship and she certainly felt loved by both of them, she also felt a large degree of responsibility for the happiness of her brothers and mother. She reported that she was often on the lookout for problems and always tried to detect the first signs of difficulties between her parents.

Anne had always done very well in school, and was a self-proclaimed perfectionist who always tried to earn the top grade. In high school, she had managed to get straight As while being very active in extracurricular activities. She was a member of the school's student association, was president of her class in grades 11 and 12, and was on the school basketball team every year. High school had been a wonderful time for Anne and she had many fond memories of those years.

After finishing high school, Anne became unsure about pursuing a career in nursing and decided to take a year off to work before beginning her university education. During that year, she worked in a department store. Although she generally enjoyed her job, she continued to worry about her choice of career. At this time, her worries were not excessive, but she felt it was important not to delay her university education for more than a year. She eventually chose to enter a nursing program at a large university two hours away from her parents' home. During her first year in the nursing program, she was very successful. She enjoyed her courses, earned grades that were comparable to those she got in high school, and felt she had made the right choice by entering the nursing program. However, she began to experience anxiety problems during her second year at the university, which quickly escalated and became difficult to control. By the time Anne was in her third year, she could no longer cope with her problems and decided to consult our clinic.

CHIEF COMPLAINTS

As is often the case with GAD clients, Anne's chief presenting complaint was her somatic symptoms. Specifically, she was concerned that these symptoms were interfering with her schoolwork. For example, because of her difficulties concentrating, Anne had great difficulty understanding the required readings for her courses. Given her sleep difficulties, she often felt tired, and this also interfered with her schoolwork. Furthermore, the constant tension in her muscles made attending class very unpleasant. By seeking help from a specialist, Anne hoped to rid herself of these symptoms and return to her previous level of academic success and enjoyment. She had not thought of mentioning her worries to the therapist because it did not seem to her that they were part of the problem, much less the key element of the problem.

When the therapist asked Anne if she had been particularly worried over the past few months, she burst into tears. She explained that over the past year, she was "always" worrying about her parents. Ever since her best friend's mother had died of cancer the previous year, she had begun to worry that her own mother, who was in excellent health, would also develop breast cancer. She soon began to worry about her father's health and wondered if he might not develop some form of cancer as well. These worries about her parents' health had steadily gotten worse over the past year, and she now spent about five hours every day worrying that her parents would develop cancer. When the therapist asked Anne if she had any other worries, she responded by saying that she had begun to worry "about everything." For example, she worried about her schoolwork, her relationship with her boyfriend, and "all sorts of little things" such as being late for class and having enough time to get everything done each week. Clearly, although Anne's initial presenting complaint was not excessive and uncontrollable worry, she suffered from GAD.

HISTORY

As mentioned previously, Anne had always been a highly successful student, earning straight As all through high school and in her first year at university. However, she had begun to experience difficulties in school over the past year. Anne was now in the third year of her nursing program, her marks had dropped considerably, and she felt overwhelmed by her schoolwork. Her problems began when her best friend's mother passed away. This friend's mother had initially been diagnosed with breast cancer, which had spread to her entire body, and within six months her friend's mother had passed away. Anne suddenly realized that this could happen to her own mother and she began to worry about her mother's health. Anne's worries quickly grew and she began to worry about her father's health. When these worries first began, in the second year of Anne's nursing program, they did not interfere extensively with her schoolwork. All too soon, however, her worries became more frequent and uncontrollable, and she began to have difficulty falling asleep at night because of them. By the end of her second year, her worries were taking up much of her waking time and she had developed other somatic symptoms. In addition to her problems falling asleep, she now had difficulty concentrating (reading had become very difficult), she always felt tired, and she suffered from severe muscle tension, especially in her neck and shoulders.

As Anne's worries about her parents became more difficult to control, she started to telephone them more often. By the end of her second year, Anne was calling her parents three or four times a week. Typically, the reassurances of her parents were helpful in the short term, but Anne's worry and anxiety soon returned. By the third year of her program, she was calling her parents every day, "just to make sure that everything was okay." At this point, reassurances from her parents were no longer useful, even in the short term.

The first half of Anne's third year of university marked the period when she truly began to worry about a number of different things. By this time, her worry, anxiety, and somatic symptoms were quite severe and interfered considerably with her schoolwork. She became very worried about her school performance and grades. To make things worse, she began to put off studying because she did not want to be confronted with her concentration problems. It was also at this time that Anne started to worry about her relationship with her boyfriend. In an attempt to cope with these worries, she began to ask her boyfriend for reassurance that he still cared for her and had not found anyone else more "interesting." Despite his reassurance, she became convinced that it was just a matter of time before her boyfriend would leave her for someone else.

What Anne found most difficult to understand was that she had also begun to worry about all sorts of minor things that had never worried her before. She now worried about every new situation if there was uncertainty involved. Even going out with friends over the weekend had become a source of worry and anxiety. By the time she consulted our clinic, Anne felt overwhelmed by her symptoms and was very discouraged by what she termed "going downhill."

ASSESSMENT

DIAGNOSTIC

Anne received a diagnosis of GAD, with a severity of 7/8 on the Anxiety Disorders Interview Schedule for *DSM-IV* (ADIS-IV; Brown, Di Nardo, & Barlow, 1994). The ADIS-IV was administered at the second assessment session given the low diagnostic reliability and high comorbidity rate of GAD. In this case, however, no other disorder was identified, so Anne received a diagnosis of "pure" GAD. Although pure GAD is uncommon, in Anne's case there were clearly no comorbid disorders. Unstructured clinical interviewing, however, did uncover the presence of avoidant and dependent personality traits. Although Anne did not appear to meet diagnostic criteria for Avoidant or Dependent Personality Disorder, these traits were taken into consideration during the course of treatment.

BEHAVIORAL

Because Anne's main reaction to her worry and anxiety was to seek reassurance, the therapist initially asked her to monitor her reassurance-seeking behaviors. This monitoring exercise was very useful because it helped Anne realize the extent to which she sought reassurance from her family, boyfriend, and friends. For example, Anne noted that when she called her parents, she would repeatedly ask them about their health and wonder if they were "concealing" health problems from her so as not to worry her. She also noted that she repeatedly sought reassurance from her boyfriend about their future together. She also sought reassurance from her friends, casually asking them how long it took them to carry out their homework assignments, to be sure that she was not taking "too long" to complete the same assignment. In addition to helping Anne become more fully aware of her reassurance-seeking behaviors, this monitoring exercise also allowed the therapist to identify targets for subsequent treatment interventions.

SELF-REPORT

Self-report assessment included four questionnaires and a daily self-monitoring booklet. Anne completed the Worry and Anxiety Questionnaire (WAQ; Dugas et al., 2001), the Penn State Worry Questionnaire (PSWQ; Meyer, Miller, Metzger, & Borkovec, 1990), the Intolerance of Uncertainty Scale (IUS; Freeston, Rhéaume, Letarte, Dugas, & Ladouceur, 1994), and the Beck Depression Inventory-II (BDI-II; Beck, Steer, & Brown, 1996). Anne's responses on the WAQ, which assesses GAD diagnostic criteria, confirmed that she suffered from GAD. Her score of 67 on the PSWQ, a measure of the tendency to worry, indicated that she was well within the range of expected scores for someone with GAD; data from our clinic indicate that the mean PSWQ score for GAD clients is 63, with a standard deviation of 10 (see Dugas, Gagnon, Ladouceur, & Freeston, 1998). Anne's score of 95 on the IUS indicated that she had a very low tolerance for uncertainty. In other words, she had great difficulty accepting the possibility that a negative event could occur, even when the probability of its occurrence was very low. Our research has repeatedly shown that GAD clients are highly intolerant of uncertainty, and the IUS has now become a standard measure of GAD processes at our clinic. Finally, Anne's BDI-II score of 10 suggested that she was having some problems with her mood. Clinical experience with GAD clients suggests that they are often demoralized from the worry and anxiety they experience, but that clinical depression does not necessarily result from GAD.

Anne was asked to assess her level of worry, anxiety, and depression on a daily basis using a self-monitoring booklet (see Dugas & Ladouceur, 2000). The therapist suggested that she leave the booklet on her pillow and fill it out every night before she went to bed. The self-monitoring of worry, anxiety, and depression is extremely important for GAD clients because it allows not only for the assessment of treatment gains, but also for the evaluation of symptom fluctuations during the entire course of treatment.

PHYSIOLOGICAL

Although Anne was diagnosed with severe GAD, she did not have any striking physiological symptoms. For example, she did not report heart palpitations, sweating palms, shaky knees, or hyperventilation. Her somatic profile was typical of GAD patients who do not also suffer from another anxiety disorder such as Panic Disorder or social phobia. In fact, Anne reported that when she worried about her parents, boyfriend, or grades, she usually felt numb and "disconnected." Therefore, physiological assessment was not a major component of the overall assessment strategy.

MEDICAL CONSULTATION

Five months before our intake interview, Anne had her annual physical checkup with her family doctor. Although all of her vital signs were within the normal range, the visit was a lengthy one because Anne had discussed her sleep problems with her physician. She had received a prescription for minor tranquilizers, but had never had the prescription filled because she feared that she might be "the type of person" who could become dependent on sleep medication. During her examination, she had talked at length about her other somatic symptoms (i.e., problems concentrating, fatigue, and muscle tension), but had not mentioned that she was worried about her parents, boyfriend, and grades. Unfortunately, because worry had not been discussed during the examination, GAD had gone undetected, which may have delayed Anne's visit to our clinic.

CASE CONCEPTUALIZATION

As mentioned above, Anne had great difficulty tolerating the uncertainty involved in various aspects of her life. It appeared that she had developed a low threshold of tolerance for uncertainty at a very young age, in part because of her parents' marital difficulties. For example, she had learned to be vigilant about problems between her parents and to any signs that her mother might need her help. Currently, her intolerance of uncertainty manifested itself in various ways. Although there was no evidence that her parents' health was deteriorating, she constantly wondered how long they would remain healthy and called them every day "just to make sure" they were well. Furthermore, her intolerance of uncertainty led to daily reassurance seeking. Like many GAD clients, Anne tried to eliminate uncertainty through reassurance-seeking behaviors, rather than accepting life's uncertainty (such as the uncertainty involved in the continued good health of loved ones). Although her daily phone calls to her parents did initially reassure her, she had to go through the same process every day, and eventually her parents' reassurances failed to have any impact on her worry.

Anne's low threshold of tolerance for uncertainty also contributed to her other worries. Although her relationship with her boyfriend seemed to be going relatively well, she worried that "something might happen" or that he might meet someone else. She and her boyfriend had not encountered insurmountable problems in their relationship, but she felt she couldn't be sure that none would arise. She also had difficulty tolerating the uncertainty involved in her course work. As mentioned above, Anne's concentration problems were interfering with her studying. Although her grades had not dropped dramatically, longer study hours and slightly lower grades had made her realize that she may receive a low grade in one of her courses. From Anne's point of view, it was very difficult not to worry about something as important as school, if a good outcome could not be guaranteed. It seemed, therefore, that Anne's low tolerance for uncertainty was a key cognitive process involved in the maintenance of her excessive worries. In fact, instead of recognizing and trying to accept the inevitable uncertainty in her life, she tried to eliminate all uncertainty from various situations. She admitted, very early in therapy, that she hoped the therapist would help her to attain a greater level of certainty about the situations that worried her . Her quest for certainty, however, did not seem to be helping her to worry less, feel less anxious, or experience more enjoyment in life.

Anne's intolerance of uncertainty also led her to overestimating the usefulness of worrying. Like many GAD clients, Anne believed that worrying was useful for a number of reasons. For example, she believed that worrying about her parents was very useful because her worry might in some way protect them from becoming seriously ill. In a sense, she believed that her worries about their health were "magically" protecting them from developing a serious illness such as cancer. She also felt that worrying about her relationship with her boyfriend was useful, albeit for a different reason: She believed that these worries helped her to be more vigilant about any problems that might arise in their relationship. Because of her worries, Anne felt she would be able to see problems quickly and resolve them before they became too serious. Finally, she felt that her worries about her schoolwork were useful because they motivated her to get things done. She felt that if she did not worry, she would not prepare adequately for her exams and would fail her courses. In summary, Anne seemed to overestimate the usefulness of worrying, and this contributed to maintaining her excessive level of worry. She did, however, believe her various worries were useful for different reasons.

Another important aspect of this case is that Anne reported two types of worries. When she worried about her parents, she was essentially worrying about a situation that did not yet exist (i.e., her parents being seriously ill). In other words, this worry concerned a *potential problem*. When she worried about her boyfriend or her schoolwork, however, she was primarily worrying about situations that already existed (i.e., relationship problems and difficulties staying focused on schoolwork). In other words, these worries concerned *current problems*. The distinction between worries about potential problems and worries about current problems is a key one for case conceptualization, because worry type has implications for the course of treatment. Although this issue will be dealt with in the Course of Treatment section, suffice it to say that instrumental problem solving cannot be used for problems that do not yet exist!

One of the striking features of this case was that, although she spent much of her waking time worrying about her parents, boyfriend, or schoolwork, Anne had considerable difficulty describing her worries in detail. For example, when asked about what might happen to her parents, she would first say that she disliked thinking about what might happen, then she would proceed to describe what might happen in a vague, general way. When asked to describe her worry in greater detail, she would typically respond that she "did not want to go there." It seemed that Anne was avoiding thinking about the worrisome situations in specific or salient ways. In particular, she appeared to be avoiding concrete mental images of what might happen to her parents (see Stöber, 2000). Her worries, particularly about her parents, had a very vague quality to them that may have interfered with the emotional processing of the worrisome situation (see Borkovec & Lyonfields, 1993). It appeared, therefore, that Anne was avoiding specific thoughts about what might happen to her parents, and that this avoidance led to the maintenance of the worry because of incomplete emotional processing.

As for her worries about her boyfriend and her schoolwork, Anne reported that she was experiencing current problems. Like most individuals with GAD, Anne appeared to have a negative problem orientation (see Ladouceur et al., 1999). This is a dysfunctional cognitive set involving the tendency to appraise problems as threats, to view problems as unsolvable, to doubt that one has the ability to solve problems, and to become frustrated and upset when problems arise. Anne tended to view her problems as major threats to her well-being and believed that she could do nothing to solve them. With regard to her relationship with her boyfriend, she believed that she was unable to deal with the problems that came up from time to time. In addition, she felt that she could not handle her other problems if she could not rely on her boyfriend for unconditional support. Anne also believed that her boyfriend was the only person capable of resolving their problems and that she herself had little to contribute to the problem-solving process. Furthermore, when she worried about her schoolwork, she believed that she absolutely must continue to get straight As but that there was nothing she could do to improve her grades because her problems concentrating were "beyond her control."

In summary, Anne's intolerance of uncertainty, her tendency to overestimate the usefulness of worrying, her tendency to avoid specific and concrete thoughts about what she feared might happen, and her negative problem orientation all contributed to her GAD symptoms. It was concluded that treatment should target these cognitive processes.

RATIONALE FOR TREATMENT CHOICE

Anne was offered a cognitive-behavioral treatment that aims to increase tolerance for uncertainty by targeting beliefs about the usefulness of worrying, the avoidance of threatening mental images, and negative problem orientation. Many considerations led to this decision. First, clinical observations and Anne's score on the IUS indicated that she was highly intolerant of uncertainty. Given the key role of intolerance of uncertainty in her tendency to worry about her parents, her boyfriend, and her schoolwork, it was felt that increasing her tolerance for uncertainty should be a central theme of therapy. Anne certainly acknowledged that she had great difficulty tolerating uncertainty and realized that this contributed to her worries and anxiety. Second, two recent clinical trials indicate that this cognitive-behavioral treatment is effective for individuals with GAD (see Dugas & Ladouceur, 2000; Ladouceur et al., 2000). In particular, Ladouceur and colleagues showed that this treatment led to a 77% remission rate at posttreatment. Furthermore, treatment gains were fully maintained at one-year follow-up. Given these considerations, the cognitive-behavioral treatment appeared to be a good choice for Anne.

It may be surprising to some readers that the chosen treatment did not include an anxiety reduction strategy such as applied relaxation or anxiety management training, given that these strategies have been shown to be useful in the treatment of GAD (see, e.g., Barlow, Rapee, & Brown, 1992; Borkovec & Costello, 1993). However, Anne's case conceptualization suggested that her worries were leading to her anxiety and somatic symptoms. In other words, the clinical working hypothesis was that a decrease in worry would lead to a decrease in anxiety and somatic symptoms, given the bidirectional interaction among the three (see Borkovec & Newman, 1999). In the clinical trial mentioned above (i.e., Ladouceur et al., 2000), a variant of the treatment chosen for Anne, which did not include an anxiety reduction component, led to a marked decrease in the severity of GAD somatic symptoms. Specifically, a treatment effect size of 1.58 (Cohen's d) was obtained for the measure of GAD somatic symptoms. These findings led our group to conclude that although anxiety reduction techniques are effective for the treatment of GAD, they do not appear to be an essential treatment component for most GAD clients.

COURSE OF TREATMENT

The treatment was administered during 14 one-hour therapy sessions conducted over 16 weeks. It consisted of the following components: (1) presentation of treatment rationale, (2) awareness training, (3) reevaluation of the usefulness of worrying, (4) cognitive exposure, (5) problem-solving training, and (6) relapse prevention.

Session 1: Presentation of Treatment Rationale

Following the two assessment sessions, the first treatment session was devoted to the presentation of treatment rationale. The therapist explained that Anne's perception and interpretation of uncertainty were an important source of her worry and anxiety. The therapist stressed that because uncertainty is pervasive in everyday life, the treatment's goal would not be to help Anne eliminate uncertainty, but rather to help her recognize uncertainty and develop coping strategies when faced with it. Anne was initially disappointed with the treatment rationale because she had secretly hoped that the therapist would reassure her about her parents, her boyfriend, and her schoolwork. In a sense, she had hoped that the therapist would help her to become "certain" that everything would turn out okay. The presentation of treatment rationale thus was very important for Anne because it changed her perception of what the therapist had to offer. The therapist could not help Anne to become certain that bad things would not happen, but he could help her to become more tolerant of the uncertainty she was faced with.

SESSIONS 2 AND 3: AWARENESS TRAINING

Following presentation of treatment rationale, awareness training was introduced. The therapist explained that the main purpose of awareness training was to become better acquainted with the two types of worry (i.e., worry about potential problems and worry about current problems). Examples of Anne's worries were used to depict both types. During the two weeks of awareness training, Anne was asked to stop what she was doing at three predetermined times of the day and record her worries in a notepad. She also noted whether each worry concerned a potential problem or a current problem. Anne recorded a great variety of worries during awareness training, but her worries about her parents' health (potential problem), her relationship with her boyfriend (current problem), and her schoolwork (current problem) were clearly her most frequent and disturbing worries. Anne also began to notice, due to Socratic questioning on the part of the therapist, that intolerance of uncertainty was closely tied to her worry themes.

SESSIONS 4 AND 5: REEVALUATION OF THE USEFULNESS OF WORRYING

The next treatment phase dealt with Anne's beliefs about the usefulness of worrying. To help identify her beliefs, the therapist asked Anne to role-play a lawyer who had to convince a jury that her worries were useful. In other words, Anne was asked to make a convincing argument that there were advantages to her various worries. The therapist stressed that different worries might have different advantages, so that Anne should address the advantages of each worry individually. In carrying out this exercise, Anne identified several advantages to her worries. For example, not only did her worries about her parents' health "magically" protect them from becoming ill, they also motivated her to call them every day, which "proved" that she truly cared for them. She also felt that worrying about her relationship with her boyfriend was useful. She believed it made her more vigilant about any problems that might arise, and that by worrying, she would notice problems more quickly and avoid the worst. Anne also felt that by worrying about her relationship, she would be able to find better solutions to some of the problems she and her boyfriend were already experiencing. Finally, she felt that her worry about her schoolwork was useful in that it motivated her to get things done. She felt that if she did not worry, she would not prepare adequately and would end up failing in school.

The therapist then asked Anne to play the role of a prosecutor and try to convince the jury that there was no proof that worrying was useful. Although she did find this role play more difficult, Anne was able to come up with various arguments suggesting that her worries were not as useful as she had thought. For example, she doubted that she would stop calling her parents if she stopped worrying about them. She also questioned the idea that caring about someone necessarily meant worrying about him or her. With regard to her relationship worries, she acknowledged that her vigilance had not been very useful so far and had actually created some difficulties, as her worrying sometimes led her to perceive a problem where none existed. Finally, she argued that she had always done well in school, even before she began to worry excessively.

Following this exercise, Anne admitted that she felt confused: Was worrying useful or not? She could now see both points of view. The therapist explained that it was perfectly normal to have beliefs that appeared to contradict each other. He also asked Anne about the possibility that her beliefs about the usefulness of worrying shifted according to her level of anxiety. Specifically, the therapist questioned whether Anne might feel that worrying was not useful when she was calm, but that she might believe worrying was very useful when she was anxious. Using everyday language, the therapist thus began to help Anne see the difference between "hot" and "cold" cognition. The goal of this phase of therapy was to introduce greater flexibility in Anne's thinking and help her see the possibility that she was overestimating the usefulness of worrying. The therapist also pointed out how some of these beliefs were related to Anne's intolerance of uncertainty. For example, if Anne wanted to make sure that her parents were well, she believed that all she had to do was worry about them to be "certain" that they were fine.

SESSIONS 6 THROUGH 10: COGNITIVE EXPOSURE

Sessions 6 through 10 were devoted to cognitive exposure. The therapist first presented the rationale for cognitive exposure and explained that Anne's worries about her parents' health could be addressed with this treatment strategy. Because her parents were not currently ill, Anne agreed that it did not make sense to use a problem-solving strategy, as the problem did not yet exist. The therapist then explained that excessive worries often are maintained by cognitive avoidance. Specifically, when Anne worried about her parents' health, her thoughts often took the form of an internal monologue (see Borkovec & Inz, 1990) rather than mental images of her parents being ill. Stated differently, Anne would mentally "verbalize" her fears and avoid "seeing" what might happen to her parents. In this way, she could avoid vivid and concrete thoughts about her parents becoming ill, which often took the form of mental images (see Stöber, 2000). Anne agreed that she did not like to think about what might happen to her parents and certainly did not want to vividly imagine them being ill.

The therapist and Anne also discussed how the avoidance of vivid mental images might interfere with the "digestion" (i.e., emotional processing) of her fears about her parents. The therapist explained that by avoiding vivid mental images of what she feared, Anne was to some extent also able to avoid feelings of anxiety and the unpleasant physiological sensations associated with those fears. Using nontechnical language, the therapist then helped Anne to understand the principles of emotional processing (see Foa & Kozak, 1986). Specifically, the therapist explained that Anne could "digest" or emotionally process her fear about her parents' health only if she allowed herself to fully experience her fear. If she could learn to stay focused on a vivid mental image of what she feared, and experience the subjective feelings of anxiety and the unpleasant physiological sensations accompanying the image, she would eventually be able to process her fear, thereby reducing or even eliminating it. Through examples and simple analogies, Anne came to understand the importance of full network activation for emotionally processing her fear. At this point, she began to see that avoidance of vivid mental images played a role in her worries about her parents' health. Finally, the therapist explained that if Anne could vividly imagine what she feared for a prolonged period of time (30 to 60 minutes) every day over a two- to four-week period, her fear would decrease.

Once Anne understood the basic principles of exposure, she was asked to draft a scenario of what might happen to her parents. The therapist explained that the scenario should be frightening but realistic. He further explained that the text should include everything she found "scary" about this situation, and that she should try to use her five senses in the description to create the most vivid image possible (colors, sounds, smells, etc.). Moreover, the therapist emphasized that the text should not include reassuring or minimizing elements that would "neutralize" the exposure and interfere with Anne's full experience of her fear. The therapist explained that neutralization is a voluntary attempt to reduce discomfort when confronted with fear. Like many GAD clients, Anne had written a scenario that related to her fear but that also contained many elements of neutralization. The therapist explained that the scenario was an excellent beginning, but reminded Anne that the scenario should represent her worst fear about her parents' health and should not contain any elements that would make it less frightening. After discussing this at some length, Anne agreed that she had included some neutralizing elements in the scenario. With the help of the therapist, Anne reworked her scenario to make it more representative of her actual core fear. Her final exposure scenario was as follows:

> My mother has cancer. It started out as breast cancer but has now spread to her entire body. I am standing beside her hospital bed. She is hooked up to all these machines with blinking lights and there's that awful hospital smell. I can't believe how ill she looks. She has lost 45 pounds and now weighs less than 100 pounds. She is unconscious and only has a few days to live. I wish I could talk to her one last time but I know it is too late. We will never talk again. As I realize this, I begin to cry uncontrollably. I feel sick to my stomach.

Once the exposure scenario was finalized, Anne recorded it on the looped tape that she brought to the session. The therapist explained that she should read the scenario slowly, with a lot of emotional expression in her voice, so that she would be able to form a clear mental image. The session ended with the scenario being recorded.

During the following session, Anne experienced functional cognitive exposure for the first time. She sat comfortably in a reclining chair in the therapist's office and put on the headset to the portable cassette player. The lights in the office were turned down to avoid any distraction. Anne turned on the cassette player and listened to her scenario. Every time the scenario ended (one minute's duration), Anne would state her anxiety level on a scale of 1 to 10; and the therapist plotted the rating on a simple graph. The exposure exercise, which lasted 40 minutes, was terminated when Anne experienced habituation (see the therapist's instructions in the next paragraph).

Following exposure, the therapist showed Anne the graph depicting her anxiety so that she could see how staying focused on her fear had led to a decrease in anxiety. Between sessions, Anne carried out exposure at home on a daily basis.

The therapist gave Anne the following instructions to help her carry out cognitive exposure at home:

> For cognitive exposure to be effective it should be done every day and for a prolonged period of time, approximately 30 to 60 minutes. You should stay fixed on the scenario for as long as it takes to experience an exposure curve; that is, the anxiety should have time to rise, stay elevated for several minutes, and descend gradually until the level is as low as before the exposure. In this way, you will learn, through your own experience, that anxiety decreases on its own if you remain exposed to your fear without neutralizing (for example, thinking "It's just an invented scenario, it's not real"). Remember that the first exposure session is a learning experience. For instance, you will find it difficult to stay concentrated on a vivid image you have often avoided in the past. Every time you catch yourself not thinking about the scenario during the exposure session, gently return to the scenario and continue with exposure. In time, you will develop your ability to carry out cognitive exposure on your own.

After three weeks of daily exposure sessions, the scenario no longer elicited an anxiety response from Anne. More important, however, Anne was no longer excessively worried about her mother developing cancer. Furthermore, the treatment gains had generalized to her father's health and Anne was no longer excessively worried about the health of either of her parents. Given the progress made with Anne's worries about her parents' health, the focus of therapy shifted to her worries about her current problems.

SESSIONS 11 THROUGH 13: PROBLEM-SOLVING TRAINING

Problem-solving training was used to address Anne's current problems: her relationship with her boyfriend and her schoolwork. The therapist first presented and discussed the importance of having a positive problem orientation when dealing with problems. For example, Anne felt that it was unfair that she had to deal with her academic difficulties, and that she should be able to solve this problem instantly and entirely. In other words, she did not seem to believe that it was normal to have problems, particularly problems requiring a lot of time and effort to solve. The therapist explained that this could not be farther from the truth, as some problems are very complex and require considerable effort before they can be resolved. In fact, many problems cannot be solved right away. Anne was reminded that her GAD symptoms were interfering with her schoolwork, and that it was unreasonable to expect her academic difficulties to vanish unless she could get her GAD symptoms under control. This was helpful because Anne realized that compared to the beginning of therapy, she was having fewer concentration problems because she had begun to worry less about her parents. Thanks to the therapist's Socratic questioning, Anne concluded that if her GAD symptoms continued to decrease, her academic problems would take care of themselves. It was thus decided that Anne would work on solving her relationship problems in the hope that this would lead to further improvement in her academic performance.

The main problem Anne appeared to have with her relationship was that she became excessively upset if she encountered any difficulty with her boyfriend. The therapist and Anne discussed how her "negative" emotions could actually be helpful because she could use them as cues to enter her "problem-solving mode." In other words, her negative emotions could help her to identify a problem before it got out of hand. This intervention had two positive impacts on Anne: First, she was able to use her emotions as a cue to identify problems at an early stage; second, she was able to view her negative emotions in a slightly less "negative" way.

The therapist asked Anne to define the problem she was having with her boyfriend. Initially, Anne stated that her boyfriend didn't always understand her. The therapist pointed out that this way of defining the problem was very vague and would interfere with Anne's ability to solve the problem. After much discussion, Anne stated that she had a problem setting appropriate limits in her relationship. Essentially, her boyfriend did not understand why she did not want to spend more time with him during the week. Her perspective, however, was that she needed to fully concentrate on her schoolwork during the week so she could have more free time over the weekend. Once the problem was properly defined, Anne was able to sit down with her boyfriend and discuss potential solutions to their problem. She and her boyfriend then agreed that they would see each other on Wednesday evenings as well as on the weekend, which seemed to be an acceptable compromise for both. What was striking about this simple solution was that it led to considerable improvement in other areas of the relationship, as the fundamental issue of limit setting had been directly addressed. Although the relationship was not perfect, Anne worried much less about her boyfriend, both because the relationship had already improved and because she felt empowered by having dealt with the problem of limit setting.

SESSION 14: RELAPSE PREVENTION

The final session was devoted to relapse prevention. The therapist pointed out that Anne now had the tools she needed to be her own therapist. As such, it was important that she regularly evaluate the success of her strategies, encourage herself to persevere even when things became difficult, and congratulate herself for her successes. The therapist reminded Anne that she would inevitably experience times when her worry and anxiety would increase, because these are normal reactions to stressful situations. Given that difficult life events are unavoidable, it was important that she expect these increases in worry and anxiety and understand how to deal with them. The therapist stressed that the key to dealing with fluctuations in worry and anxiety is to recognize that there is a crucial difference between a lapse (normal fluctuation in worry and anxiety levels) and a relapse (a return to pretherapy state). The therapist also underscored that everyone worries and feels anxious from time to time, and that the goal of Anne's therapy had not been to prevent her from worrying, but to help her change the thoughts, behaviors, and emotions that had made her worries excessive and uncontrollable. Anne felt that this was already the case, and the therapist agreed, pointing out that she had made wonderful progress.

THERAPIST-CLIENT FACTORS

From the very beginning of therapy, therapist-client factors played an extremely important role in the therapeutic process. The assessment, which was carried out with state-of-the-art measures, was important in establishing the therapist's credibility. Furthermore, use of the ADIS-IV in the second assessment session was instrumental in establishing a good therapeutic alliance. Although rigid adherence to the form of a structured interview may interfere with therapist-client rapport, a structured interview used in a flexible and open manner can actually help to establish a strong working alliance. Anne reported that the structured interview had been very useful and that she clearly understood its importance; furthermore, she mentioned that the thorough diagnostic assessment had left her feeling confident about therapy.

As is often the case, the therapeutic alliance was tested when the therapist asked Anne to engage in cognitive exposure. Anne had a long history of avoidance, and the thought of exposing herself to threatening mental images was very frightening. The session spent discussing the principles of emotional processing (referred to as "digestion") helped Anne to become engaged in truly functional exposure. The sound therapeutic alliance was essential, however, as it allowed Anne to trust the therapist enough to actually attempt her first session of cognitive exposure. Seeing that the therapist truly believed in the merits of exposure and that he suggested she directly tackle her worst-case scenario, Anne was left feeling that exposure was frightening but not dangerous. She trusted her therapist and felt sure he would not suggest anything that would put her in danger.

COURSE OF TERMINATION

Many important issues arose in the course of termination. For example, given Anne's dependent and avoidant personality traits, she was not sure that she was capable of being "her own therapist," and doubted whether she would be able to solve her problems without her therapist's help. The therapist used a number of strategies to help her deal with the uncertainty she felt about termination. First, the therapist instituted a brief fade-out period: The first 12 sessions were held weekly, but the last 2 sessions were separated by a two-week time interval. This brief fade-out period helped Anne to develop greater confidence in her ability to face her problems alone, without relying on her weekly session with the therapist.

The therapist also prescribed various problem-solving assignments during the last few weeks of therapy. By problem-solving between therapy sessions, without the help of the therapist, Anne was able to develop further confidence in her ability to be her own therapist. For example, following session 12, Anne and her boyfriend got into a serious argument about her friends. Rather than breaking down, as she would have done previously, Anne was able to generate a number of alternative solutions and suggest a compromise. After some discussion, Anne's boyfriend agreed that her solution was reasonable, and the problem was effectively solved. Although she and her boyfriend usually managed to solve their problems, this was virtually the first time that Anne had been the one to suggest a solution.

During the last session, the therapist explained that it was very important that Anne try to handle her worries and anxiety on her own. In a sense, Anne now had to prove to herself that she could continue to successfully use the treatment strategies independently, without the therapist's guidance. The therapist did explain, however, that if, after she tried applying the strategies on her own for at least one week, her worry and anxiety still were spinning out of control, she could call the therapist for advice. Anne never did resort to calling the therapist because she was able, for the most part, to keep her worry and anxiety under control by applying the principles she had learned in therapy.

FOLLOW-UP

Follow-up sessions were held at 3, 6, and 12 months. The 3-month follow-up was instrumental in helping Anne to accept therapy termination. Knowing that her next session was "only" three months away helped her to have positive expectations at the last therapy session. As is often the case following cognitive-behavior therapy for GAD, Anne had lower symptom scores on the self-report questionnaires at 6- and 12-month follow-up than she had at the 3-month follow-up. It seemed that as time passed, she became more and more confident that she was truly capable of being her own therapist.

The goals of the follow-up sessions were to assess Anne's evolution, target any problems, and review the main principles of therapy. In Anne's case, one of the main issues discussed during her follow-up sessions was the fact that some worry is normal. In the process of actively trying to decrease her worries and anxiety, she had begun to expect that she could eliminate her worry, rather than simply controlling it. During the follow-up sessions, the therapist reminded Anne that the goal of therapy was not to help her eliminate all her worry, but to help her eliminate her excessive worry. In a sense, the follow-up sessions allowed Anne to appreciate the work she had done and reminded her not to attempt unrealistic goals. Ironically, the therapist had to stress that a moderate amount of worry was not only normal, it could even be useful. Anne thought this was quite funny: After everything she had learned, her therapist was now telling her that worry could sometimes be useful! The therapist did remind her, however, that it was important not to overestimate the usefulness of worrying.

MANAGED CARE CONSIDERATIONS

The treatment presented here was administered over 14 sessions. Given the multiple treatment components (presentation of treatment rationale, awareness training, reevaluation of the usefulness of worrying, cognitive exposure, problem-solving training, and relapse prevention), 14 sessions appeared to be the minimum amount of time required to adequately cover all treatment components. In our managed care context, where fewer than 10 treatment sessions are typically covered by insurance companies, this creates an interesting dilemma. Should each treatment component be covered briefly, or should some components be eliminated from the treatment to maintain the full duration of the remaining components? Although a case could be made either way, a recent study has produced some data that may help to address this question.

Using a case formulation approach, it may be possible to identify GAD clients' main type of worry (i.e., worry about potential problems or worry about current problems). A cognitive exposure approach could then be used for those who worry mainly about potential problems, and a problem-solving approach applied for clients who have worries mostly about current problems. Although this scaled-down approach to the treatment of GAD does not appear to be as effective as the full treatment described in this chapter, research suggests that it remains a relatively effective way of treating GAD (see Provencher & Ladouceur, 1999). Specifically, data show that both approaches (cognitive exposure and problem-solving training) were equally effective, and that overall, 11 of 15 GAD participants reached a clinically significant level of improvement. Thus, this treatment approach appears to represent a promising alternative when managed care considerations seriously limit the number of therapy sessions.

OVERALL EFFECTIVENESS

Treatment effectiveness was assessed with the structured diagnostic interview (ADIS-IV), self-report questionnaires, and the daily self-monitoring booklet. On the ADIS-IV and the WAQ, although Anne reported some residual symptoms, she clearly no longer met diagnostic criteria for GAD. Her scores on the other self-report measures were now all in the nonclinical range: 47 on the PSWQ, 58 on the IUS, and 5 on the BDI-II. Finally, visual inspection of the daily self-monitoring data indicated that time spent worrying, feelings of anxiety, and depression had decreased over the course of treatment. Although worry, anxiety, and depression had temporarily increased when cognitive exposure was introduced, all three had continued to decrease soon thereafter. The self-report questionnaires were also administered at 3-, 6-, and 12-month follow-ups. As mentioned previously, although Anne's symptoms had increased somewhat at 3-month follow-up, her questionnaire scores at 6- and 12-month follow-ups were similar to her posttreatment scores. Thus, both posttreatment and follow-up assessments indicated that this treatment was effective in helping her eliminate her GAD.

One additional point merits specific attention. Although this treatment did not include an anxiety reduction technique such as applied relaxation or anxiety management training, it led to clinically significant change in GAD somatic symptoms as evidenced by scores on the Somatic Subscale of the WAQ. This is consistent with our previous clinical trials with GAD, which have shown that cognitive-behavioral treatment targeting worry also leads to a decrease in GAD somatic symptoms (Dugas & Ladouceur, 2000; Ladouceur et al., 2000). Borkovec and his collaborators have convincingly argued that anxiety involves a process of interacting subsystems: cognitive, affective, behavioral, and physiological (see Borkovec & Costello, 1993; Borkovec & Newman, 1999). This implies that changes in one of these subsystems may lead to changes in the others. Thus, if GAD clients decrease their level of worry, they also should experience changes in their subjective level of affect, their worry-related behaviors, and their physiological responding. In Anne's case, for example, the treatment focus of decreasing worry also resulted in decreased feelings of anxiety and depression, reassurance-seeking behaviors, and GAD somatic symptoms.

REFERENCES

American Psychiatric Association. (1994). *Diagnostic and statistical manual of mental disorders* (4th ed.). Washington, DC: Author.

Barlow, D. H., Rapee, R. M., & Brown, T. A. (1992). Behavioral treatment of Generalized Anxiety Disorder. *Behavior Therapy, 23,* 551–570.

Beck, A. T., Steer, R. A., & Brown, G. K. (1996). *The Beck Depression Inventory* (2nd ed.). San Antonio, TX: Psychological Corporation.

Borkovec, T. D., & Costello, E. (1993). Efficacy of applied relaxation and cognitive-behavioral therapy in the treatment of generalized anxiety disorder. *Journal of Consulting and Clinical Psychology, 61,* 611–619.

Borkovec, T. D., & Inz, J. (1990). The nature of worry in generalized anxiety disorder: A predominance of thought activity. *Behaviour Research and Therapy, 28,* 153–158.

Borkovec, T. D., & Lyonfields, J. D. (1993). Worry: Thought suppression of emotional processing. In H. W. Krohne (Ed.), *Attention and avoidance* (pp. 101–118). Seattle: Hogrefe & Huber.

Borkovec, T. D., & Newman, M. G. (1999). Worry and generalized anxiety disorder. In A. S. Bellack & M. Hersen (Series Eds.) & P. Salkovskis (Vol. Ed.), *Comprehensive clinical psychology: Vol. 4. Adults: Clinical formulation and treatment* (pp. 439–459). Oxford, England: Elsevier Science.

Brown, T. A., Di Nardo, P. A., & Barlow, D. H. (1994). *Anxiety Disorders Interview Schedule for DSM-IV.* San Antonio, TX: Psychological Corporation.

Craske, M. G., Rapee, R. M., Jackel, L., & Barlow, D. H. (1989). Qualitative dimensions of worry in *DSM-III-R* generalized anxiety disorder subjects and nonanxious controls. *Behaviour Research and Therapy, 27,* 397–402.

Dugas, M. J., Freeston, M. H., Ladouceur, R., Rheaume, J., Provencher, M., & Boisvert, J.-M. (1998). Worry themes in primary GAD, secondary GAD, and other anxiety disorders. *Journal of Anxiety Disorders, 12,* 253–261.

Dugas, M. J., Freeston, M. H., Provencher, M. D., Lachance, S., Ladouceur, R., & Gosselin, P. (2001). Le Questionnaire sur l'inquiétude et l'anxiété: Validation dans des échantillons non cliniques et cliniques [The Worry and Anxiety Questionnaire: Validation in nonclinical and clinical samples]. *Journal de Thérapie Comportementale et Cognitive, 11,* 31–36.

Dugas, M. J., Gagnon, F., Ladouceur, R., & Freeston, H. (1998). Generalized anxiety disorder: A preliminary test of a conceptual model. *Behaviour Research and Therapy, 36,* 215–226.

Dugas, M. J., & Ladouceur, R. (2000). Treatment of GAD: Targeting intolerance of uncertainty in two types of worry. *Behavior Modification, 24,* 635–657.

Foa, E. B., & Kozak, M. J. (1986). Emotional processing of fear: Exposure to corrective information. *Psychological Bulletin, 1,* 20–35.

Freeston, M. H., Rhéaume, J., Letarte, H., Dugas, M. J., & Ladouceur, R. (1994). Why do people worry? *Personality and Individual Differences, 17,* 791–802.

Kessler, R. C., McGonagle, K. A., Zhao, S., Nelson, C. B., Hughes, M., Eshleman, S., et al. (1994). Lifetime and 12-month prevalence of *DSM-III-R* psychiatric disorders in the United States: Results from the National Comorbidity Survey. *Archives of General Psychiatry, 51,* 8–19.

Ladouceur, R., Dugas, M. J., Freeston, M. H., Léger, E., Gagnon, F., & Thibodeau, N. (2000). Efficacy of a cognitive-behavioral treatment for generalized anxiety disorder: Evaluation in a controlled clinical trial. *Journal of Consulting and Clinical Psychology, 68,* 957–964.

Ladouceur, R., Dugas, M. J., Freeston, M. H., Rhéaume, J., Blais, F., Boisvert, J.-M., et al. (1999). Specificity of generalized anxiety disorder symptoms and processes. *Behavior Therapy, 30,* 191–207.

Meyer, T. J., Miller, M., Metzger, R. L., & Borkovec, T. D. (1990). Development and validation of the Penn State Worry Questionnaire. *Behaviour Research and Therapy, 28,* 487–496.

Provencher, M. D., & Ladouceur, R. (1999, May). *Efficacy of a treatment for generalized anxiety disorder based on a case formulation approach.* Poster session presented at the annual meeting of the Canadian Psychological Association, Halifax, Nova Scotia, Canada.

Sanderson, W. C., & Barlow, D. H. (1990). A description of patients diagnosed with *DSM-III-R* generalized anxiety disorder. *Journal of Nervous and Mental Disease, 178,* 588–591.

Shadick, R. N., Roemer, L., Hopkins, M. B., & Borkovec, T. D. (1991, November). *The nature of worrisome thoughts.* Poster session presented at the annual meeting of the Association for Advancement of Behavior Therapy, New York.

Stöber, J. (2000). Worry, thoughts, and images: A new conceptualization. In U. von Hecker, S. Hecker, S. Dutke, & G. Sedek (Eds.), *Generative mental processes and cognitive resources: Integrative research on adaptation and control* (pp. 223–244). Dordrecht, The Netherlands: Kluwer Press.

CHAPTER 8

Bulimia Nervosa

J. SCOTT MIZES and DEANNE ZOTTER BONIFAZI

DESCRIPTION OF THE DISORDER

ULIMIA NERVOSA IS an eating disorder characterized by recurrent episodes of binge eating, followed by some type of compensatory behavior aimed at preventing weight gain. According to the *Diagnostic and Statistical Manual of Mental Disorders* (*DSM-IV*; American Psychiatric Association [APA], 1994), a binge episode is defined as the consumption of a large amount of food in a discrete period of time and a feeling of lack of control over eating during the binge. This definition is somewhat subjective. In reality, there is extreme variability among bulimics in the amount of food consumed during a binge episode. For many, it is the quality of the binge (i.e., eating something "forbidden") and not the quantity of food eaten that characterizes a binge episode (Garner, Shafer, & Rosen, 1992). Binge episodes typically consist of foods that the bulimic restricts from his or her diet, often including high-carbohydrate desserts or "junk foods." Negative mood states have been found to trigger binge episodes, with guilt and self-reproach occurring following a binge.

The *DSM-IV* categorizes individuals with bulimia into two groups, purging and nonpurging, based on the particular compensatory behaviors used. Purging behaviors include self-induced vomiting and the use of laxatives, diuretics, and enemas. Nonpurging behaviors include excessive exercise and fasting. The majority of individuals who present for treatment are the purging type, most commonly compensating for their binges by self-induced vomiting. Research shows that individuals of the purging type exhibit more psychopathology than nonpurgers. The diagnosis of bulimia nervosa requires that binge episodes and compensatory behaviors occur, on average, at least twice a week for a period of three months (APA, 1994).

An additional symptom of bulimia nervosa is excessive body concern; as defined by the *DSM-IV*, "Self-evaluation is unduly influenced by body shape and weight" (APA, 1994, p. 550). Individuals with bulimia often link their self-esteem to their appearance. Unlike individuals with anorexia nervosa, who are

144

underweight, individuals with bulimia tend to be within the normal weight range. Nevertheless, they experience extreme body dissatisfaction and fear of weight gain. In fact, most bulimics tend to restrict their intake at nonbinge times in an attempt to reduce their weight. Research has shown that bulimics focus a great deal on their body and report that a high percentage of their daily thoughts relate to body image and weight (Bonifazi & Crowther, 1996).

Bulimia is frequently associated with additional psychopathology, including depression, anxiety, substance abuse, and personality disorders. In addition to these psychological complications, physical complications can result from the disorder (see physiological assessment section). Bulimia nervosa affects more women than men, with the majority of bulimic patients being in the late adolescent to young adult period. Prevalence rates for females in this age range are estimated to be 1% to 3%, with some reporting especially high prevalence rates among college populations (e.g., 12.5% to 18.5%; Pope, Hudson, Yurgelun-Todd, & Hudson, 1984).

Bulimia nervosa is a complex disorder, caused by a multitude of factors, including genetic/biological, social/environmental, familial, and individual/psychological factors. There is no one pathway to the development of bulimia nervosa, yet many of those afflicted experience a somewhat similar course. Most begin bingeing following a period of restrictive dieting. Compensatory behaviors soon follow and often lead to an increase in the severity of binge eating episodes. Most bulimics tend to be secretive about their disorder and may not seek treatment until the behaviors become chronic.

CASE DESCRIPTION

Cindy was a 25-year-old, single, Caucasian female from an intact, upper-class family. She had one older sister. Both her mother and father were moderately overweight. Her sister was of normal weight, but watched her weight carefully. Cindy stated that the family had been preoccupied with "fatness" and dieting for as long as she could remember.

Cindy described her father, a corporate lawyer, as "intimidating and critical." Thinking back on her childhood, she recalled his being very critical of her older sister and remembered always trying to be "perfect" to avoid having him directing his criticisms at her. She described her mother as "overinvolved and controlling." Cindy found it difficult to talk to her mother. She believed that her own difficulty handling negative emotions came from her mother, who denied and avoided negative emotions at all costs. She described a good relationship with her sister, but stated that she would like to be closer. Cindy felt that she and her sister had been somewhat competitive with each other over the years. She described her role in the family as that of "peacemaker" and "caregiver." She often would intervene when problems arose between her parents or between her parents and her sister.

Cindy was of above-average intelligence. She performed well academically during her school years and maintained a network of friends. Most who knew her likely would have described her as well adjusted and confident. However, she frequently struggled with insecurities and low self-esteem, particularly where her appearance was concerned, although she was actually very attractive. Her eating disorder symptoms began during her sophomore year of high school, in part, from these insecurities.

Cindy began dating during her junior year of high school and had one long-term relationship prior to high school graduation. Following graduation, she went to a private college to study political science. There too she did well academically, frequently making the Dean's List. In addition, she had an active social life and joined a campus sorority. She dated regularly and maintained one long-term romantic relationship. In spite of her successful college career, her eating disorder worsened throughout college. Remarkably, though, it did not interfere with her schoolwork and only minimally interfered with her social activities.

Following college graduation, Cindy returned home and took a job with an insurance company. She began dating an attorney and contemplated going to law school. She realized, however, that her motivation for law school was primarily to please her father. Instead, she enrolled in a graduate program in social work, with the goal of helping children and families. Prior to leaving home for graduate school, her grandfather passed away. This was very difficult for Cindy, as they had been very close. The stress of graduate school and her grandfather's death contributed to an increase in her eating disorder symptoms. During her first year of graduate school, Cindy received treatment at the university's counseling center.

CHIEF COMPLAINTS

At the end of the first year of graduate school, Cindy returned home for the summer. Her therapist from the university counseling center encouraged her to continue her treatment at home. She recommended family therapy for Cindy. Although her family had become increasingly supportive of Cindy's struggle with her eating disorder, family issues remained, particularly with her mother, who continued to have difficulty understanding and supporting Cindy. Not feeling comfortable with the idea of family therapy, Cindy instead sought out for individual therapy a psychologist who specialized in eating disorders.

At the time of the initial evaluation, she was bingeing and vomiting approximately three times per day, with binge-purge episodes often lasting as long as 90 minutes. She stated that two or three days a week she would eat three meals, but her usual pattern was to skip breakfast and dinner and eat only lunch. Her typical eating routine was to miss breakfast, have a small lunch, and then binge and purge in the late afternoon and evening. A typical binge consisted of salad, a box of cereal, a box of cookies, and occasionally included ice cream, fried chicken, or pasta. She denied use of laxatives or diuretics, but acknowledged that she would take one Dexatrim pill per day.

At the time of the initial evaluation, Cindy reported being 5'4" tall and 118 pounds. She viewed her ideal weight as 110 pounds. The U.S. Department of Health, Education and Welfare projected ideal weight for her height is 131 pounds, with the cutoff for anorexia nervosa being 111 pounds. She denied any symptoms of depression or substance abuse, but reported significant anxiety associated with her fears of weight gain.

HISTORY

Cindy's eating disorder symptoms began during her sophomore year in high school, when she became increasingly interested in boys and witnessed her father's negative comments to her mother and older sister about their weight. She began restrictive dieting and increased her level of exercise. By her junior year, her eating was erratic and she had begun bingeing and purging (via self-induced vomiting). Cindy's mother began suspecting bulimia and confronted her, telling her she should not tell anyone about her problem or she may jeopardize her chances of getting into a good college. Her mother ordered her to "stop it" on her own. In an attempt to stop the vomiting, Cindy briefly switched to laxatives, but quickly returned to vomiting. Although she was not able to stop on her own, she did heed her mother's advice and kept her bulimia a secret.

Following high school graduation, Cindy left home for college. She immediately joined a sorority, where she found friends who were as appearance-conscious as she. She found herself becoming very competitive with her sorority sisters, wanting to be thinner and prettier than they. This led to a decrease in her bingeing behaviors, but she increased her restrictive dieting, increased her exercise, and began abusing diet pills. She also continued her purging behaviors whenever she felt she had overeaten. By her sophomore year in college, she weighed only 105 pounds. She lost her menses for a period of six months and would have been diagnosed with anorexia nervosa had she sought professional attention at this time.

At the end of her sophomore year, Cindy began dating a popular man on campus. Her confidence level escalated and she found herself less focused on losing weight. Over the summer, her menses returned as she began gaining weight. The return to school in the fall brought with it some relationship problems between Cindy and her boyfriend. He no longer seemed as attentive and began spending more time with his friends than with Cindy. Her insecurities returned and she began restrictive dieting again. Episodes of binge eating quickly followed, as her relationship with her boyfriend deteriorated. During much of her junior year, Cindy was consuming no regular meals and was bingeing and purging as often as 4 to 5 times per day. By her senior year, she felt out of control with her eating. She began thinking about seeking professional help, but did not feel she could disclose her problem. In fact, one of her sorority sisters revealed her own bulimia to Cindy, looking for advice and support, but Cindy was unable to disclose her eating disorder in return.

Following college graduation, Cindy moved home. She took a job with an insurance company and began dating an attorney. Over the next year, her weight climbed to 140 pounds. Although this weight is in the normal weight range for her height, it greatly distressed her. Her mother began monitoring her eating behaviors, and her father made subtle comments about her weight. Cindy returned to her restrictive eating practices and decided to leave home and return to school. She entered a graduate program in social work. During her first semester, she was bingeing and purging approximately once per day. She finally decided to disclose her disorder and seek help at the university's counseling center, where she received individual therapy. She made progress in identifying her negative emotions and was able to identify her core belief: "Being thin means being happy, worthwhile, lovable, and in control." However, little progress was made in reducing her bingeing and purging behaviors.

BEHAVIORAL ASSESSMENT

Behavioral

A major component of assessment for bulimia nervosa involves self-monitoring of food intake and binge-purge episodes. Self-monitoring was introduced during the initial session with Cindy. She was instructed to record the amounts and types of foods consumed, the time and location of the eating episode, whether she felt the episode was a binge, whether she induced vomiting, and the context in which the eating episode took place (including thoughts and feelings associated with eating). Initial self-monitoring sheets confirmed the presence of restrictive dieting early in the day with binge-purge episodes occurring in the evenings. They also revealed an increase in binge-purge episodes on days when she was overly restrictive with her eating. Self-monitoring also revealed a good deal of anxiety following binge episodes that was somewhat relieved following self-induced vomiting. Self-monitoring was continued throughout Cindy's treatment and was used to continually assess problem areas, as well as measure progress.

SELF-REPORT

Several self-report inventories were administered to Cindy during her initial evaluation. The Minnesota Multiphasic Personality Inventory (MMPI) was used as a measure of general psychopathology and personality functioning. The validity scales indicated some tendency for Cindy to underestimate her degree of psychological distress. While her F scale score (T = 60) suggests difficulties in some problem area, her K scale score (T = 66) suggests that she tries to downplay these difficulties, preferring to give an appearance of adequacy and control. Nonetheless, she responded in a valid manner and the pattern of scores indicated modest physical and psychological distress, likely directly attributable to her eating disorder. There was no evidence of depression (Scale 2, Depression, T = 59). MMPI results did suggest that Cindy endorses traditional female gender roles (Scale 5, Male/Female, T = 39), which is consistent with her sensitivity to what others' think of her, her sensitivity to criticism, and her focus on physical appearance. Results also revealed a high energy level (Scale 9, Mania, T = 73), which, although it may be positive, could lead to a tendency to become involved in too many activities such that she cannot see them all through to completion. MMPI results supported her obvious extroverted personality style (Scale 0, Social Isolation, T = 40), but suggested that some of this may be due to her high needs for attention and approval (Harris and Lingos Hysteria Subscale 2, T = 73).

Cindy also responded to the Mizes Anorectic Cognitions questionnaire (MAC; Mizes & Klesges, 1989) during the initial evaluation as well as at the conclusion of treatment. The MAC was used to assess her eating and body-image related thoughts, as well as serve as a baseline to assess progress. Cindy scored one standard deviation above the mean on the Total Score (T = 60). She also scored one standard deviation above the mean on the Rigid Weight Regulation and Fear of Weight Gain Scale (T = 61) and the Self-Control and Self-Esteem Scale (T = 63). These scores were somewhat lower than typical eating disorder patients presenting for treatment. Usually, the total and subscale scores are approximately two standard deviations above the normative sample mean. Interestingly, Cindy scored at normal levels on the Weight and Approval Subscale (T = 46).

Finally, Cindy was administered the Eating Disorders Inventory. This was used as another measure of the cognitive and behavioral aspects of her eating disorder. She showed significant elevations on the three main eating disorder subscales: Drive for Thinness, which measures concern with dieting, preoccupation with weight, and fear of weight gain; Bulimia, which measures tendencies to think about and engage in binge eating; and Body Dissatisfaction, which measures dissatisfaction with one's body size and shape. On the secondary psychopathological scales, she showed modest elevations on the Perfectionism subscale, which measures beliefs that only the highest standards of personal performance are acceptable, and the Interoceptive Awareness subscale, which measures a disturbance in recognizing and responding to internal states, including emotions and physical sensations such as hunger and satiety.

Overall, Cindy's pattern of scores was consistent with a diagnosis of bulimia nervosa. In addition, her results suggest no other major psychopathology other than her primary eating disorder diagnosis.

PHYSIOLOGICAL

Weight should be monitored regularly, preferably during therapy sessions. This provides the therapist with useful information regarding clients' reactions to changes in their weight. As treatment progresses, regular weighing also helps clients see that their weight changes very little, despite reductions in purging. As with many bulimic patients, this was critical with Cindy, given her intense fear of weight gain.

Given the numerous potential physical complications associated with bulimia nervosa, all clients should be seen for a medical evaluation. Because many bulimic clients have normal physical examinations, it is essential that the client see a physician who is familiar with eating disorders for a thorough evaluation. A thorough cardiac, pulmonary, abdominal, musculoskeletal, neurologic, and (in women) gynecologic examination is important (Pomeroy, 1996). Special attention should be given to possible electrolyte abnormalities (especially low serum levels of potassium) resulting from purging and diuretic or laxative abuse that can lead to cardiac arrhythmias and even death. Other physical problems also should be assessed. Dehydration resulting from purging or diuretic abuse may lead to low blood pressure and orthostatic changes. Any client who has used Ipecac for inducing vomiting should be assessed for cardiomyopathy. Abdominal pain and bloating, likely associated with delayed gastric emptying, is common. Recurrent vomiting can lead to esophageal irritation, heartburn symptoms, and dental erosion. Severe vomiting can lead to esophageal perforation. Long-term use of laxatives may result in constipation and laxative dependence. Menstrual irregularities are also common.

MEDICAL CONSULTATION

Cindy was medically evaluated prior to presenting for treatment. Her evaluation indicated potassium levels within normal limits, although she was somewhat anemic. Physical symptoms reported included swollen parotid glands, occasional edema, occasional orthostatic hypertension, and coldness in extremities. She reported regular periods (she was not on the birth control pill). Given the relatively normal findings from her medical evaluation, Cindy did not need regular medical monitoring during the course of treatment.

A medical consultation for psychotropic medications may be warranted with some bulimic clients. Antidepressants often have been used in the treatment of bulimia. Cindy, however, did not report depressive symptoms, nor did she appear depressed based on the MMPI results; therefore, no such consultation was sought.

CASE CONCEPTUALIZATION

Cindy's eating disorder began during her adolescence, a common time for the development of bulimia nervosa. For most girls, puberty brings with it unwanted weight gain. At a time when peer acceptance is critical and interest in the opposite sex is heightened, appearance becomes all-important. In many industrialized societies, a slender body becomes the ideal for most young women and body dissatisfaction can easily develop. It is likely that Cindy's perfectionistic tendencies, focus on appearance, and need for approval all contributed to her insecurities and problems with self-esteem during adolescence. Being raised in a family where fatness was a clear concern and dieting was frequent, against the backdrop of a society that condemns fatness and extols the virtues of weight loss, it is not surprising that she began restrictive dieting when she became dissatisfied with her social life.

Much research supports the idea that restrictive dieting can lead to binge eating, particularly when rigid dieting rules are established (i.e., dietary restraint). Again, given Cindy's perfectionism, it is likely that her dieting rules were very strict. Dichotomous (i.e., all-or-nothing) thinking results from rigid dietary rules and leads to the establishment of "good" (i.e., safe) foods and "bad" (i.e., forbidden) foods. Restrictive dieting leads to physical and psychological depravation, which can heighten one's responsiveness to external food cues. In times of stress, when the rigid dietary rules are broken, dichotomous thinking can lead to a binge-eating episode. For example, when Cindy "slipped" and ate one of her forbidden foods (e.g., a cookie), she would say to herself, "Well, I've blown my diet now, I may as well just eat the whole box!" Following a binge episode, intense anxiety begins to mount. Given Cindy's desire for a slender body, it is not surprising that she would feel self-disgust, guilt, and increased anxiety following a binge. For many, this anxiety leads them to resolve to be more disciplined in their eating and they resume restrictive dieting practices. For others, like Cindy, this anxiety is so great that a sense of urgency arises that something must be done to rid the body of the unwanted calories. For Cindy, the answer was to induce vomiting. Purging leads to an immediate reduction in anxiety. For many individuals with bulimia, purging serves as a negative reinforcer, removing the anxiety over potential weight gain. In fact, purging reduces anxiety so well that for many, once purging begins, binge episodes become more frequent with larger quantities of food consumed. Some clients report that, over time, purging has become the primary goal. That is, they binge so that they can purge and even select binge foods that will be easy to vomit.

It follows, then, that if Cindy can stop the purging behavior, her binge episodes should become less severe and less frequent. The decision to use Exposure and Response Prevention (ERP) with Cindy was based on this thinking. ERP can be looked at as serving two functions. First, ERP is a means of extinguishing the association between anxiety and vomiting. Over the years, purging had become habitual for Cindy whenever she felt anxiety over what she had eaten. By interrupting the association between anxiety and vomiting, she can learn that the anxiety will dissipate without purging. Second, ERP can be viewed as a means of enhancing self-efficacy for coping with the triggers for vomiting. As Cindy learns to deal with the anxiety in a healthy way instead of purging, her sense of self-efficacy will increase. Using cognitive strategies to help deal with anxiety can lead also to an examination of her rigid dietary rules and dichotomous thinking style. In addition, her focus on weight and appearance as a measure of self-worth can be examined.

RATIONALE FOR TREATMENT CHOICE

Treatment of this patient presented numerous challenges that are relatively common among bulimia nervosa patients. First, as is a common referral, Cindy was home from college, and thus the time frame for treatment was short. Second, the severity of her eating disorder was quite high, given the high frequency of binge eating and purging as well as a history of previously probably meeting criteria for anorexia nervosa. Third, a previous trial of outpatient psychotherapy at the counseling center at her college had resulted in only modest improvement in her eating disorder symptoms, as evidenced by the high rate of binge eating and purging at the time of our initial interview.

Given the above factors, it was mutually decided with Cindy to use explicit ERP for forbidden foods as a main component of her treatment. It was also decided to schedule sessions on a twice-weekly basis. There were several reasons for the decision to approach treatment in this manner. First, her probable prior history of anorexia nervosa would suggest a more difficult treatment course, as would her high level of binge eating and purging. Additionally, her level of food restriction was very high, even after some modest improvement in the prior treatment. At the time of our initial evaluation, she indicated that there were only two or three days a week when she could eat three meals a day. On the other days, the only meal she would eat was lunch. These clinical observations suggested that her fear of eating forbidden foods and associated fear of weight gain was very strong. Thus, more aggressive treatment was needed, directly targeted to reduce her fear of eating forbidden foods so as to allow her to normalize eating and to reduce her significant dietary restraint. Last, a more aggressive approach was selected given the short time frame for treatment over the summer.

There has been some debate about whether formal ERP for forbidden foods is a necessary part of treatment, or if formal ERP adds to treatment outcome as an addition to the standard cognitive-behavioral therapy (CBT) for bulimia. Agras and colleagues (1989) argued that formal ERP does not add to overall effectiveness. They found that addition of ERP did not add to efficacy of CBT as compared to CBT alone. Others have differed in their interpretation of the results of this research (Leitenberg & Rosen, 1989). Moreover, substantial research has supported use of formal ERP in the treatment of bulimia nervosa as part of a comprehensive treatment package for this disorder (Wilson, Fairburn, & Agras, 1997).

In considering this issue, we distinguish between formal and informal ERP. Effective CBT consistently includes a treatment component where patients are gradually asked to progressively add forbidden foods to the range of foods they eat. Certainly, this can be conceptualized as "informal" exposure to forbidden foods, and patients tend to report greater comfort in including these foods in their diets over time. The formal ERP procedure involves explicit exposure to forbidden foods in the office, as well as explicit exposure sessions at home, separate from regular planned eating. Formal ERP is not viewed as a stand-alone treatment, as many of the elements of the traditional CBT treatment package are included. Clinically, we avoid debating relative efficacy of CBT and ERP as if they are two completely different treatments. Rather, in our view, it is a matter of relative emphasis on the exposure versus other CBT treatment components shown to be effective for bulimia. Moreover, it is a matter of clinical judgment on which balance of treatment procedures will most likely benefit the individual patient.

The decision to utilize formal ERP in the current case was based on the high level of binge eating and purging behavior and the short time for treatment. Additionally, this decision was guided by the axiom that the more severely entrenched the problem behavior, the more behavioral the treatment needs to be rather than relying on cognitive or other verbal interventions.

It was decided not to use antidepressant medication with Cindy. First, in general, antidepressant medications are not viewed as the first line of treatment due to side effects and high rates of relapse after withdrawal of the drug. Second, she did not report current depressive symptoms at the time of initial evaluation. In general, based on clinical grounds, we reserve the use of antidepressant medications for those patients with marked comorbid Major Depression and those patients with extremely high binge-purge rates who are unsuccessful in making any reductions in binge-purge frequency early in treatment. Cindy met neither of these criteria.

COURSE OF TREATMENT

After her initial intake interview, Cindy was seen twice a week (as scheduling would allow) for approximately two months, until her return to college. At the intake interview, she was started on self-monitoring of binge-purge episodes, as described previously. At her first treatment session, her food diary showed that she was having 1 to 2 binge-purge episodes per day, and that interpersonal interactions in which she felt disapproval were frequent binge triggers. This theme recurred frequently throughout therapy. Additionally, she often skipped breakfast and would wait as long as she could until eating for the first time in the afternoon.

In this first session, there was discussion of possible collateral therapy visits with her mother or both parents. It is often useful for the patient to reveal her eating disorder to significant others to reduce the secrecy surrounding their binge eating and purging, as well as to enlist adaptive support of others. Often, this involves addressing the anxieties of significant others regarding feared dire consequences of the bulimia, as well as encouraging them to not be a "watch dog" or to take responsibility for monitoring and controlling the patient's eating or binge-purge behavior. In this case, her mother had confronted Cindy about possibly having an eating disorder in high school. Her mother was very anxious about her daughter's eating disorder, as well as embarrassed that there was a problem in the family. In contrast, even though Cindy previously perceived her father as intimidating and critical, she felt that he had become supportive after learning of her bulimia nervosa. Due to the strained relationship with her mother, Cindy did not want to have any joint sessions with her, nor have her mother participate in individual sessions to assist in adjusting to this disorder. Interestingly, she did allow her father to attend the first several minutes of her third treatment session, during which it was discussed how he could be most helpful to her.

In the second session, Cindy's food diary records showed additional triggers for binges, including boredom and having unstructured time, eating a forbidden food at a meal, and feeling "fat" when getting dressed and going to a social outing. She was assigned the homework of getting feedback from others at social situations on whether or not she looked fat (to gather objective data in this regard). After explaining the rationale for ERP, Cindy decided initially to work on eating two cookies in the office with a clear understanding that purging was not allowed. Exposure to two cookies was selected because they were less threatening in terms of the urge to purge. It was understood that she would progressively move up to more threatening forbidden foods.

In the third session, formal ERP began. Cindy ate the cookies slowly and with clear anxiety. Previously, the therapist had explained that he would not engage in conversation with her during the first half of the exposure session so that she would not distract herself from what she was eating or the eating-disordered thoughts that were being triggered. Later in the session, the therapist asked her to describe her thoughts, partly to heighten their salience, but also to understand the unique eating-disordered thoughts she experienced. Only toward the end of the session did the therapist provide possible rational alternatives to the thoughts she reported.

Throughout each exposure session, Cindy was asked to rate every five minutes the combined intensity of her anxiety, discomfort, and urge to purge on a 0 to 10 scale (10 = high). After five minutes, her rating increased to 8.5, and stayed in the 8.5 to 9 range for the next 30 minutes. Her discomfort gradually lessened, and after another 30 minutes, her rating was down to 4. To help her successfully avoid purging after an hour-long session, she was permitted to stay in the waiting room, continuing to rate her discomfort until it had decreased significantly for her to feel confident that she would not purge.

The next two sessions continued with exposure to two cookies. Expectedly, her discomfort decreased during and across sessions. In the second exposure session, her discomfort rating briefly peaked at 8, but was down to 4 within 30 minutes. In the third exposure session, her starting discomfort rating was the lowest to date (2), briefly peaked at 6, and was down to 2 after 15 minutes. Given her success on her first food exposure item, several key points were made by the therapist. First, it was noted that marked discomfort after eating a forbidden food could and would go away *without purging*. Second, it was noted that her discomfort was in fact tolerable, although clearly unpleasant. Moreover, the therapist underscored that the ability to tolerate discomfort was aided considerably by the firsthand experience of knowing that the discomfort would not last forever. Third, the therapist pointed out that this previously forbidden food had shifted "status" and was now in the "safe" food category. The idea that a forbidden food could in fact become comfortable for her to eat was something Cindy could not have imagined. Moreover, if this could happen with one food, then it could happen with other currently "forbidden" foods as well. Finally, it was noted that the pattern of decreasing discomfort was entirely consistent with the process of extinction that had been described to her prior to starting exposure treatment. Thus, Cindy could "trust" the treatment.

In the sixth treatment session, exposure was temporarily interrupted. Cindy had visited an older, out-of-town relative and had experienced a significant increase in her purging, approximately three per day during the trip. Due to her distress about the trip and increase in her purging behavior, the decision was made to defer exposure until the next session. The relative had arranged for them to go to restaurants to eat three times per day, as well as arranged parties where food was present. Perhaps more important, this relative was quite weight-preoccupied herself, which made it difficult for Cindy to cope effectively with her own eating-disordered thinking. Additionally, she felt insecure about this relative's esteem for her, as the relative was critical about her weight and very focused on social appearances. In session, Cindy began expressing her growing dissatisfaction with the family's high expectations with regard to weight and appearance, professional achievement, and status. The therapist discussed this with her in terms of her own perfectionistic expectations of herself, both as these related to appearance and body image but also to "external" accomplishments. The alternative of basing self-esteem on "internal" characteristics was discussed.

In the seventh session, Cindy reported that she had a long talk with her mother, clarifying many issues and concerns about their relationship. One of the most important of these was that her mother did not have the extreme expectations for Cindy to be thin as she had feared. Review of her food diary (which occurred each session) showed that she was continuing to skip meals (mainly breakfast), that the amount of food eaten during meals was low, and that the range of foods she would eat was still restricted. She agreed to start eating three meals a day and to increase her calorie intake at meals to normal levels. ERP was continued. However, the amount was increased to four cookies. As expected, she had more discomfort than in her previous exposure session on two cookies, but her overall discomfort was less than it was the first time she did exposure for two cookies. Her discomfort peaked briefly for 5 minutes at a rating of 8, stayed at 6 for about 20 minutes, and was down to 4 45 minutes after exposure had started.

By the eight session, Cindy reported her first two purge-free days during treatment, and presumably, for several years. Exposure was increased to six cookies, and although her discomfort peaked briefly, it also dissipated quickly and was at low levels after approximately 35 minutes. She reported trying to eat regular meals for a total of 2,000 calories per day, but initially had inconsistent results in achieving this goal. In terms of her rational self statements in session and at home, it was noted that she tended to address nutritional misinformation that led her to believe that she would gain weight quickly (i.e., rigid weight regulation beliefs). It was suggested that she needed to work on addressing approval concerns about weight, as well as her own self-esteem issues regarding weight. In the next session, exposure was increased to eight cookies. She experienced somewhat more distress than in the previous session, but again the discomfort reduced notably after 30 to 40 minutes.

In the tenth session, Cindy reported having three binge-purge episodes in the previous five days, but also some binge-purge-free days. This represented improvement in her starting frequency of one to two binge-purge episodes per day. Her self-monitoring records showed a significant expansion in the range and amount of foods consumed. For example, she had eaten pasta and cake, which she previously would have avoided, and did not purge. Exposure to a Reuben sandwich was planned, partly because it represented a highly forbidden food (greasy, etc.) and also because it triggered a feeling of fullness, which she tried to avoid. A full stomach was something that resulted in her feeling fat, and she preferred feeling that her stomach was "empty." During exposure, she experienced moderate levels of discomfort (ratings 6 to 7), with a brief peak at 8. However, due to the difficulty of this food, her discomfort continued past the end of the session.

In the eleventh session, she reported having no binge-purge episodes since the previous session, although she did report reducing the amount she ate in her three meals after the prior exposure session. Her discomfort during exposure to the Reuben sandwich was modestly high (ratings 7 to 8), and had not yet decreased because exposure was started late in the session. Of note, Cindy was weighed this session, and her weight had remained essentially stable despite overall significant reduction in her purging behavior. Thus, she was provided with behavioral evidence that purging was not necessary to control weight. Also, in this session, we began more extensive work on developing rational counterstatements to eating-disordered thoughts that she could use at home.

In the twelfth session, she reported four binge-purge-free days and one day with two binge-purge episodes. She showed modest reduction in her distress during exposure to the Reuben sandwich. Moreover, she had made significant progress on developing rational counterstatements for eating-disordered thoughts. In the thirteenth session, she reported two difficult days during which she had three binge-purge episodes. She felt this was due to anxiety about the wider range of foods she was eating possibly leading to weight gain. This was addressed by noting the behavioral evidence that her weight (measured at most sessions) had remained stable even though she was eating a variety of forbidden foods in session and at home. Additionally, basic nutritional concepts were rereviewed, such as "There are no forbidden foods because no food is inherently fat-producing." Exposure to the sandwich resulted in approximately equal levels of discomfort as in the previous session. During session 14, she reported one binge-purge-free day and one day with two binge-purge episodes in the previous two days. We identified her continued desire to weigh less than her current weight as a barrier to further improvement. This was discussed extensively, emphasizing that accepting herself at her current weight (or a few pounds more) and ending her efforts to control or lose weight were necessary for complete remission of her eating disorder. Exposure to the sandwich again resulted in a modest decrease in her discomfort.

In session 15, Cindy continued to report some binge-purge-free days and some in which episodes occurred. Exposure to the sandwich resulted in minimal decrease in discomfort from the previous session. A major focus of this session was continued discussion of self-acceptance of her current body weight and shape. She agreed to a homework assignment of developing a variety of activities and ways of thinking that would facilitate this self-acceptance. Possible activities included wearing clothes that fit rather than loose clothing that would conceal her shape and weight, and looking at her shape in a mirror. In terms of thinking, Cindy developed specific self-statements providing herself evidence of her worth independent of her shape and weight, relating to her talents and accomplishments as well as her desirable personal (rather than physical) qualities. In session 16, her last treatment session, she reported only one purge episode. That purge was prompted by eating steak, which she still viewed as an "unhealthy food." Nonetheless, she continued to show improvement in the range of foods eaten, as she was including many previously forbidden foods in her diet. This session included her last exposure to the Reuben sandwich, and she reported substantially lower discomfort. Thus, it had required seven exposure sessions to the sandwich to substantially reduce her discomfort and urge to purge. Given that the Reuben sandwich was very high on her list of forbidden foods, it is not surprising that several exposure sessions were needed to reduce her discomfort.

THERAPIST-CLIENT FACTORS

Good rapport between patient and therapist is always a positive factor in treatment. However, it is likely even more necessary in the treatment of eating-disordered patients. It is very important that patients have a deep sense of trust in their therapist, not only for the therapist's clinical knowledge and skill in treating eating-disordered patients, but also trust in the therapist's acceptance of the patient and genuine interest in his or her welfare. This is likely due to at least two factors. First, more than other clinical disorders, eating disorders are characterized by low self-esteem and faulty self-schema. Thus, it is not uncommon for eating-disordered patients to fear rejection and criticism from the therapist due to their core feelings of worthlessness. Therefore, it is important for the therapist to not be perceived as rejecting or critical, particularly when the patient has experienced problems in treatment, such as returning to use of laxatives or purging, a bad week in terms of binge eating, or not following planned coping strategies. In fact, it is useful for the therapist to explicitly model examining these difficulties with a problem-solving approach rather than the self-criticism that patients already likely inflict on themselves.

Second, eating-disordered patients are quite fearful because their self-esteem is dependent almost exclusively on their body weight and shape as well as regulation of their eating behavior. Thus, changes that eating-disordered patients are asked to make in their eating and beliefs about the significance of shape and weight are extremely frightening, as these changes feel like the loss of their self-identity. It requires a very high level of trust in the therapist to do something he or she suggests that feels like a direct threat to the client's physical or emotional safety.

In Cindy's case, there was strong rapport and trust in the patient-therapist relationship. Some of this was derived from Cindy's awareness of the therapist's years of experience with eating disorders. More important was development of a collaborative relationship, facilitated by the therapist's validating her emotions (such as fear of weight gain), clearly explaining the rationale for treatment procedures, and suggesting hypotheses to her (such as that stopping purging will not result in substantial weight gain) that were eventually shown to be accurate. The net result was that the positive patient-therapist relationship in this case was sufficient to allow Cindy to try many behaviors she had previously avoided, such as increasing the amount and range of foods eaten, stopping her purging, and undergoing the exposure treatment.

COURSE OF TERMINATION

The process of termination was different in this case, because it was known from the outset that treatment with this therapist would be time-limited due to Cindy's going back to college. However, it is useful to note that some approaches to treatment of bulimia, including CBT strategies, specifically use time-limited therapy for all patients from the outset (Miller & Mizes, 2000). Many adherents of this view argue that time-limited therapy encourages both patient and therapist to work harder on specific changes needed to achieve identified goals. Additionally, because there is evidence that clinical improvement can eventuate after the end of formal CBT treatment, continuing treatment until being completely symptom-free may not be necessary. Having a time limit for treatment also may ease the termination of the patient-therapist relationship. From the beginning, it is understood the relationship is a professional one, designed to achieve certain goals. Once the goals are achieved, the relationship ends. This is in contrast to long-term therapy, which encourages a stronger interpersonal attachment of the patient to the therapist. Under these circumstances, termination of the therapeutic relationship may be more difficult for the patient.

For Cindy, the time limit on therapy may have been a significant factor in her making numerous behavioral and cognitive changes in a short period of time. It also was likely a factor in her willingness to undertake the rigors of the ERP procedure. It was clear that she felt she was working with a therapist with specific expertise in eating disorders (unlike her previous therapists), and she wanted to take full advantage of this in the time available. Also, the termination process itself was rather straightforward and discussed explicitly only in the last two sessions. This consisted of reviewing her progress, developing plans for possible high-risk situations on return to college, and assisting her in finding an eating disorder therapist near her college.

In terms of ending the therapeutic relationship, no problems were encountered. Rather, the tone was one of "a job well done" by collaborators who had made substantial progress toward Cindy's goals, and now it was time for the relationship to end. However, the therapist did receive a follow-up letter several months later, which indicated that Cindy's relationship with the therapist was significant to her.

FOLLOW-UP

Due to the fact that Cindy returned to college, no formal follow-up was scheduled. Had she remained in the area, treatment would have continued until she had a more established pattern of binge-purge-free weeks. After that time, it would be typical for the treatment sessions to gradually fade in their frequency, perhaps every other week at first, and then monthly. The focus of these sessions would be on relapse-prevention training. Also, scheduled sessions to have her "check in" would provide some external accountability, which might enhance the continued application of the procedures and skills learned in treatment.

Although no formal follow-up was scheduled, as noted previously, the therapist did receive a letter three months after treatment ended. Cindy indicated that treatment had been very helpful to her. She also wrote that she had been "doing really well for the past month and a half and I feel very good about it." Significantly, she used the past tense to say that she *was* bulimic, which would suggest substantial periods of being binge-purge-free, perhaps over the past month and a half. Finally, she wrote, "In some ways, I feel healthier than some of my friends." Overall, her letter conveyed the message that she had substantially benefited from the treatment.

MANAGED CARE CONSIDERATIONS

Fortunately, Cindy's insurance did not have a managed care mental health carve-out with highly restrictive policies. Thus, no barriers were encountered in this regard. Had she had such an insurance policy, several characteristics of the CBT approach are compatible with managed care. The treatment is relatively short, has specific treatment procedures and concrete goals, and each session monitors progress toward those goals. These characteristics make completing managed care treatment plans and reauthorizations relatively straightforward. Also, talking with managed care reviewers is facilitated because the CBT therapist can talk the reviewer's "language," which emphasizes concrete goals and objectives. Also, unlike treatment of anorexia nervosa, persons with bulimia nervosa rarely need to be treated on an inpatient basis for their eating disorder. Thus, the formidable barriers to hospitalization for anorectics rarely become an issue for bulimia nervosa patients.

One of the main barriers to effective treatment involves the limitations on a particular managed care company's provider panel. Treatment of eating disorders is still a highly specialized area. Training in the treatment of eating disorders is still not routine in graduate programs, internships, and residencies. Thus, it is not at all uncommon for a particular panel to have few, if any, highly skilled eating disorder specialists. In those cases, we strongly encourage patients to assertively advocate for approval to see an eating disorder specialist out-of-network.

The limitations of managed care are a greater problem for bulimia nervosa patients with significant comorbid conditions, such as Borderline Personality Disorder, chemical dependency, or histories of abuse and associated Posttraumatic Stress Disorder. The main barrier is in terms of number of sessions allowed by the particular insurance policy, which is often inadequate for patients with complex clinical conditions requiring longer, multifaceted care.

OVERALL EFFECTIVENESS

At the end of treatment, Cindy showed a substantial improvement in the frequency of binge-purge episodes, with a reduction of over 70%. Initially, she was having two to three binge-purge episodes per day; at the end of treatment, she was averaging two to three episodes per week. Although this improvement was significant, it is also important to note that the end-of-treatment levels of binge-purge episodes still met minimal criteria for the bulimia nervosa diagnosis. However, evidence of improvement was that she was eating three meals a day much more consistently. As well, she was eating a much wider range of foods, particularly previously "forbidden" foods. She also showed improvement in her eating-disordered cognitions, as evidenced by her end-of-treatment MAC scores. For the Total MAC, her T-score was 46; Rigid Weight Regulation and Fear of Weight Gain subscale, T = 50; Self-Control and Self-Esteem subscale, T = 50, and Weight and Approval subscale, T = 42. These scores suggest that Cindy's eating-disordered cognitions were in the normal range when compared with normal young adult women.

Treatment outcome for Cindy is consistent with the outcome found in studies of CBT treatment for bulimia nervosa. Overall, CBT treatment results, on average, in a reduction of 70% in the frequency of binge-purge episodes (Fairburn, 1995). Approximately one third to one half of patients are free of binge-purge episodes at the end of treatment; another third experience a substantial decrease in binge-purge episodes, as did Cindy. Thus, although CBT for bulimia does result in substantial improvements for many patients, it certainly is not a "cure" for all patients.

Normalization of Cindy's eating-disordered cognitions is important, in that it indicates potential for a favorable treatment outcome over the long term. It appears that the chances of relapse are more likely if there are high levels of concern about shape and weight, as well as eating-disordered cognitions at the end of treatment.

REFERENCES

Agras, W. S., Schneider, J. A., Arnow, B., Raeburn, S. D., & Telch, C. F. (1989). Cognitive-behavioral and response-prevention treatments for bulimia nervosa. *Journal of Consulting and Clinical Psychology, 57,* 215–221.

American Psychiatric Association. (1994). *Diagnostic and statistical manual of mental disorders* (4th ed.). Washington, DC: Author.

Bonifazi, D. Z., & Crowther, J. H. (1996). In vivo cognitive assessment in bulimia nervosa and restrained eating. *Behavior Therapy, 27,* 139–158.

Fairburn, C. G. (1995). Short-term psychological treatments for bulimia nervosa. In K. D. Brownell & C. G. Fairburn (Eds.), *Eating disorders and obesity: A comprehensive handbook* (pp. 344–348). New York: Guilford Press.

Garner, D. M., Shafer, C. L., & Rosen, L. W. (1992). Critical appraisal of the *DSM-III-R* diagnostic criteria for eating disorders. In S. R. Hopper, G. W. Hynd, & R. E. Mattison (Eds.), *Child psychopathology: Diagnostic criteria and clinical assessment* (pp. 115–128). Hillsdale, NJ: Erlbaum.

Leitenberg, H., & Rosen, J. C. (1989). Cognitive-behavioral therapy with and without exposure plus response prevention in treatment of bulimia nervosa: Comment on Agras, Schneider, Arnow, Raeburn, and Telch. *Journal of Consulting and Clinical Psychology, 57,* 776–777.

Miller, K. J., & Mizes, J. S. (Eds.). (2000). *Comparative treatments of eating disorders.* New York: Springer.

Mizes, J. S., & Klesges, R. C. (1989). Validity, reliability, and factor structure of the Anorectic Cognitions Questionnaire. *Addictive Behaviors, 14,* 589–594.

Pomeroy, C. (1996). Anorexia nervosa, bulimia nervosa and binge eating disorder: Assessment of physical status. In J. K. Thompson (Ed.), *Body image, eating disorders, and obesity: An integrative guide for assessment and treatment* (pp. 117–204). Washington, DC: American Psychological Association.

Pope, H. G., Hudson, J. L., Yurgelun-Todd, D., & Hudson, M. (1984). Prevalence of anorexia nervosa and bulimia in three student populations. *International Journal of Eating Disorders, 3,* 45–54.

Wilson, G. T., Fairburn, C. G., & Agras, W. S. (1997). Cognitive behavioral therapy for bulimia nervosa. In D. M. Garner & P. E. Garfinkel (Eds.), *Handbook of treatment of eating disorders* (2nd ed., pp. 67–93). New York: Guilford Press.

CHAPTER 9

Borderline Personality Disorder

SOONIE A. KIM and BRIAN C. GOFF

DESCRIPTION OF THE DISORDER

THE *DIAGNOSTIC AND Statistical Manual of Mental Disorders* (*DSM-IV*; American Psychiatric Association, 1994) characterizes Borderline Personality Disorder (BPD) as "A pervasive pattern of instability of interpersonal relationships, self-image, and affects, and marked impulsivity beginning by early adulthood and present in a variety of contexts" (p. 654). Five out of nine diagnostic criteria must be met for a client to be diagnosed with BPD: (1) frantic attempts to avoid abandonment, whether real or imagined; (2) unstable relationships, alternating between idealization and devaluation; (3) severely unstable self-image or sense of self; (4) potentially self-damaging impulsive behavior in at least two areas, such as binge eating, drinking, or spending; (5) suicidal or self-mutilating behavior; (6) severe reactivity of mood lasting a few hours to a few days; (7) chronic feelings of emptiness; (8) uncontrollable anger (subjectively experienced or outbursts); and (9) brief paranoid ideas or dissociative symptoms when under stress.

Linehan (1993a) reorganizes the diagnostic criteria of the *DSM-IV* into five areas of dysregulation. The first area, *emotion dysregulation*, is described as the tendency to be emotionally sensitive and reactive, including difficulties with episodic depression, anxiety, irritability, and anger and anger expression. The onset of these emotions is typically quick, the intensity high, and the return to normal mood slow. The second category, *behavioral dysregulation*, includes extreme and problematic impulsive behaviors as well as suicidal and parasuicidal behavior (i.e., self-harming behavior without the intent to die). The third category is *interpersonal dysregulation*, which encompasses a number of dysfunctional relationship patterns such as frantic efforts to avoid rejection or loss and highly chaotic and conflictual relationships. The fourth category, *cognitive dysregulation*, is marked by dichotomous thinking (i.e., all-or-nothing thinking) and cognitive rigidity. Paranoid ideation and dissociative behavior are additional varieties of the experience of cognitive dysregulation. The fifth category, *self dysregulation*, includes instability in identity and feelings of emptiness.

BPD is a diagnosis of increasing concern in the psychiatric community, as the high prevalence of the disorder, coupled with its severe nature and chronic course, make it a significant public health problem. Although prevalence estimates of BPD range from approximately .5% to 2% of the general population, rates within the psychiatric population are as high as 10% among outpatients and 20% among inpatients. When a subgroup of "high-utilizing" inpatients is considered, the prevalence rate doubles (Linehan, Kanter, & Comtois, 1999).

Studies suggest that individuals with BPD continue to meet diagnostic criteria for years, experience little change over time in their level of functioning, and evidence consistently high rates of psychiatric hospitalization. In addition, a comorbid diagnosis of BPD is often associated with worse outcomes across several Axis I diagnoses, including several mood and anxiety disorders. Finally, approximately 10% of individuals diagnosed with BPD will eventually die by suicide, with the rate doubling for BPD individuals who have made a suicide attempt or engaged in self-injurious behavior at least once in the past (Linehan, Kanter, et al., 1999).

CASE DESCRIPTION

Claudia P.[1] is a single, 25-year-old Caucasian female employed as a nurse in a hospital emergency department. She was referred to the Portland Dialectical Behavior Therapy (DBT) Program[2] by an inpatient psychiatric unit after a suicide attempt by ingestion of 20 sleeping pills and a half-bottle of wine following a fight with her boyfriend. This was Claudia's fourth suicide attempt in the past five years. She reports chronic depression and suicidal ideation dating back to her teens, but no attempts until the age of 20. Each of her attempts has been precipitated by relationship problems; methods have been overdosing on pills or cutting her wrists. She has been admitted to psychiatric inpatient units following each attempt, with stays ranging from overnight to one week.

Claudia has been in an intimate relationship for about a year (her longest yet) that she describes as "hot and cold." She is aware that she "flip-flops" between fawning over her boyfriend and hating him. Although they are together frequently, she feels he does not value the relationship as she does, as evidenced by his other interests and friends. Claudia states that her boyfriend tells her he feels pressured by her demands for constant attention. Her response to this complaint has ranged from being overly apologetic and repentant, to caustic and enraged. She reports often thinking that he finds her unappealing and is likely to leave her because she isn't "smart or pretty enough." She is terrified at this possibility and fantasizes about leaving him before he can leave her (as she has done with other boyfriends in the past). She aborts her plan when she "comes to her senses," realizing that "he is a good man who loves me, and my urge to get out of the relationship is all about my own insecurity."

---

[1] The case of Claudia is fictional. She is a composite of various clients who have been seen at the Portland DBT Program.
[2] Portland DBT Program (Portland, Oregon) contact information: email—mail@portlanddbt.com, Web site—www.portlanddbt.com, phone—503-231-7854.

CHIEF COMPLAINTS

Claudia indicates that her problems began when she was a teenager and have steadily gotten worse over the years. She states that family and friends accuse her of being overly reactive and sensitive and expect that she should be able to "just pull herself together." She indicates that her anger outbursts and unpredictable moods have been a strain on her relationships, both in the past and currently. She reports that she is frequently "hijacked" by her emotions, saying and doing things she later regrets. She also complains of feeling chronically depressed, frequently loathes and doubts herself, and feels lethargic and listless most of the time. She states that she has forced herself to work despite her poor mood and fatigue, primarily because feelings of worthlessness temporarily remit when she is performing well at work. Even at work, however, she often feels like a fraud, thinking that if people knew about her various difficulties, they would fire her.

Claudia reports having "horrible coping skills." She indicates that she binge eats in response to stress, then purges to undo the potential effect (weight gain) as a result of the binge. She says that, as a nurse, she is well aware of the harmful physical effects of purging, but that after eating too much, the purge feels inevitable. She reports that such binge-purge behavior occurs weekly, usually in the evening and after a long, especially tiring day at work. In addition, she states that at times, she drinks to excess in the context of feeling anxious or angry and wants to "calm down." She has driven her car in this state, although she has never been in an accident or been arrested for driving under the influence.

Finally, Claudia reports that cutting, typically with razor blades and occasionally with a knife, also helps her to relieve stress. Self-harm behavior is usually preceded by intense agitation and self-loathing and followed by a sense of relief. More often than not, her wounds require nothing more than Band-Aids or gauze and tape; however, occasionally she has cut deeper because "the superficial cuts weren't enough" and has needed stitches.

HISTORY

Claudia's family consists of her biological parents and two younger brothers. She states that she has some contact with her family at the major holidays but otherwise has little to do with them. She recalls her childhood as "unhappy" and her years in high school as "miserable." She attributes feeling worse as a teenager to her growing awareness of her father's perfectionist demands and expectations and the knowledge that no matter how hard she tried, she was never going to get his love and approval.

According to Claudia, her father was disappointed when she was born because he had wanted a son. Consequently, she always felt that her father favored her younger brothers. Growing up, she felt "disapproved of" by her father, particularly around displays of weakness or emotion. One such instance involved falling out of a tree as a little girl and spraining her ankle. In response to her crying, her father called her a "crybaby" and said that she wasn't really hurt, later commenting that the incident had "ruined a perfectly good Sunday afternoon." Although he was never physically abusive, Claudia reports that her father was verbally explosive: easily "set off" and "slow to cool down." She describes her mother as a docile woman who played the role of "peacekeeper" in the home, frequently intervening to assuage her father's irritability. She often tried to excuse his behavior by explaining that he was under a lot of stress and urged Claudia to stay out of his way "so as not to upset him."

Throughout primary and middle school, Claudia was an honor roll student and involved in a number of extracurricular activities. During high school, although her academic performance remained above average, she became less involved socially and in activities. She reports feeling lonely and isolated during most of her teenage years, not "fitting in" with any particular crowd. She described friendships, as well as relationships with boyfriends, as "short-lived and intense"; making friends was easy for her, but over time, she felt misunderstood and taken advantage of, eventually leading to a confrontation and breakup of the relationship.

Claudia first entered therapy during her senior year of high school, when her mother noticed a scar from self-injury. She was diagnosed with "clinical depression" and prescribed an SSRI antidepressant. The therapist recommended family therapy, but her father refused to participate, saying that this was Claudia's problem to solve. She continued in individual therapy for a short time but did not find it very helpful and eventually quit, stating that her therapist "just didn't understand." She continued on the antidepressant for about a year with some improvement in her depressive symptoms, but discontinued the medication when she felt it stopped working.

Midway through her sophomore year of college, and involved in what she considered her first serious relationship, Claudia's mood markedly deteriorated and she sought counseling at her college's counseling center. At that time, she started work with a therapist who diagnosed her with depression, Generalized Anxiety Disorder, and bulimia. She was also referred to a psychiatrist who prescribed an SSRI and anxiolytic medication. Following a breakup with her boyfriend, Claudia made her first suicide attempt by cutting her wrists and was subsequently admitted to a psychiatric unit. Her therapist terminated therapy with her, stating that she was not prepared to work with such a high-risk client. Between that time and her referral to our program, Claudia has seen another three therapists. The first two she prematurely terminated with because, according to Claudia, they did not "click," and the third because of "scheduling problems."

BEHAVIORAL ASSESSMENT

Research supports the use of self-report inventories as diagnostic screening devices for BPD (e.g., Patrick, Links, van Reekum, & Mitton, 1995). Thorough diagnostic assessment of BPD can be accomplished using one of a number of semistructured interviews developed to assess personality disorders (e.g., DIB-R, Zanarini, Gunderson, Frankenburg, & Chauncey, 1989; SCID-II, First, Spitzer, Gibbons, Williams, & Benjamin, 1996). The relationship of comorbid Axis I disorders to BPD is varied, ranging from consequence, to affect-regulation behavior (e.g., alcohol abuse), to overlap of criterion sets (e.g., dysthymia). It is thus important to assess both the presence and, more important, the possible function of the behaviors that constitute comorbid conditions.

The number of *DSM-IV* criteria for BPD is nearly double the minimum number required for the diagnosis (American Psychiatric Association, 1994), allowing numerous behavioral presentations of the disorder; therefore, a diagnostically homogeneous group of individuals could be quite behaviorally heterogeneous (Comtois, Levensky, & Linehan, 1999). Assessment should be behaviorally focused rather than categorically focused and occur at treatment onset and throughout.

BEHAVIORAL

Early in treatment, a thorough history of all prior suicidal and parasuicidal behaviors, including detailed contextual information, is obtained for the assessment of short- and long-term risk. Other suicide-related behavior is examined, including suicidal ideation and communications, expectancies and beliefs regarding suicide, and suicide-related affect. A frequency rate of problematic behaviors (e.g., suicidal and parasuicidal behaviors, binge-purge episodes), as well as use of crisis services (e.g., visits to the ER or crisis center, hospital stays) can be obtained at treatment onset as a baseline measure for assessing progress. Throughout treatment, the process of analyzing problematic behaviors, including assessing the factors that initiate and maintain the behaviors and identifying deficiencies and excesses that interfere with desired behaviors, is conducted.

SELF-REPORT

Individuals with BPD may experience greater psychiatric disturbances than is evident in their behavioral presentation (Edell, Joy, & Yehuda, 1990) or suggested by the absence of comorbid disorders (Comtois, Cowley, Dunner, & Roy-Byrne, 1999). It is thus useful to assess beyond clinical observation and diagnostic assessment.

Data regarding disruptive affective states, maladaptive cognitive patterns, dissociative behavior, and interpersonal problems can be obtained using various self-report instruments. Brief instruments of affect states (e.g., Brief Symptom Inventory [BSI]; Derogatis & Spencer, 1982) and functioning (Outcome Questionnaire-45 [OQ-45]; Lambert & Hill, 1994) can provide objective measures of client status and assist in tracking clinical progress. Specific measures of other relevant variables (e.g., dissociative behavior, interpersonal sensitivity) are used when appropriate. It is also important to take a detailed relationship history and assess for instability in sense of identity.

PHYSIOLOGICAL

In-session chain analyses of suicidal and parasuicidal behaviors include client reports of physiological events. At times, psychophysiological arousal proceeds self-harm, either as an affective state to be relieved or as anticipatory excitement. Other times, individuals experience a reduction in physiological arousal following self-harm, which serves to negatively reinforce the self-harm behavior. There is also evidence of analgesia/numbing during self-harm for some BPD individuals, whereas these same individuals report normal pain from accidental injury (Haines, Williams, Brain, & Wilson, 1995).

Claudia was interviewed using the Structured Clinical Interview for the *DSM-IV* (SCID-I; First, Spitzer, Gibbon, & Williams, 1995) and SCID-II. She was given Axis I diagnoses of Dysthymia, Eating Disorder Not Otherwise Specified, and Alcohol Abuse, and an Axis II diagnosis of Borderline Personality Disorder. Baseline rates of suicidal and parasuicidal behavior, as with binge-purge episodes and drinking, were established at onset. Claudia's binge-purge episodes were occurring approximately weekly, as were her self-harm episodes. She was drinking about three drinks four times a week, with drinking to the point of intoxication occurring weekly. Ongoing functional assessment of Claudia's self-harm, binge-purge, and drinking behaviors clarified the function of all of these as emotion-regulation behaviors.

Claudia completed the BSI and OQ-45. BSI results showed general elevations across most subscales, with pronounced elevations on measures of depression, anxiety, hostility, and interpersonal sensitivity. OQ-45 results revealed impairment in interpersonal functioning but only slight distress with occupational functioning.

MEDICAL CONSULTATION

A medical consultation after intake is recommended for clients who are not on medication but whose symptom profile indicates possible benefit, as well as for clients whose current medication regimen is potentially problematic. However, a number of problems arise in the area of pharmacotherapy for BPD.

Because of diverse and complicated symptom presentation, clients often are prescribed multiple medications targeting an array of symptoms. As a result, they are more likely to be overmedicated and to suffer drug interactions and side effects that interfere with treatment, particularly lethargy, cognitive dulling, and agitation. Even when a medication regimen is comfortable for them, clients may fail to take medications long enough, consistently enough, or at the prescribed dosages. Overdosing is a common occurrence, making many prescribers hesitant to take these clients into their practice (Dimeff, McDavid, & Linehan, 1999).

In addition, clients in search of the "magic bullet" frequently blame recurring symptoms and problems on inadequate or inappropriate medications and demand changes. When medication changes result in only temporary satisfaction, as is often the case, the cycle begins again. This process can distract clients from focusing on what they need to in treatment and may become a major point of contention between client and therapist.

Finally, certain psychotropic medications are potentially dangerous for individuals with BPD. For example, the disinhibiting effects of anxiolytics, particularly when taken with alcohol, presents a serious problem for those whose impulse control is already impaired at baseline. Drugs that can cause irreversible damage or death if taken in large quantities, such as tricyclic antidepressants, are extremely risky in the hands of someone who is chronically suicidal or parasuicidal (Dimeff et al., 1999).

To prevent and correct for these problems, Dimeff and colleagues (1999) offer the following recommendations: (1) Combine pharmacotherapy with active psychosocial treatment; (2) do not give lethal drugs to lethal people; (3) consult with the client about how to interact effectively with his or her pharmacotherapist, versus intervening on the client's behalf; (4) treat medication noncompliance as therapy-interfering behavior; and (5) focus on safety and effectiveness when prescribing medications. In keeping with this final recommendation, the following "Five Ss" guide the selection of psychotropic medications:

Safe: Use safe, nonlethal drugs.

Simple: Simple psychotropic medications regimens are preferred.

Specific: Specific symptoms are targeted first.

Scientific: Start with efficacious drugs for BPD populations.

Swift: Move the client as quickly as possible to the intended maintenance level.

Claudia came to our program on an SSRI for her depressive symptoms, as well as anxiolytic medication for chronic low-grade anxiety. Because of her occasional alcohol abuse and poor impulse control, we coached Claudia to talk with her psychiatrist about taking her off the anxiety medication. She was advised to ask her prescriber for a medication that was nonaddictive and without the potential for serious damage or death if taken with alcohol or in an overdose. She was also referred to her primary care physician for a thorough physical exam prior to starting treatment. She was coached in how to talk with him about her psychiatric problems, particularly her problem with binging and purging. From there, she was referred to a nutritionist, who helped her develop a balanced diet and exercise plan that fit her lifestyle and habits.

CASE CONCEPTUALIZATION

Due to the number and nature of problems with which borderline clients present, theory-driven case conceptualization is essential to cogently think about and treat these clients. First and foremost, behavioral theory for BPD views the enduring behaviors of the borderline individual as resulting from capability deficits (e.g., self-regulation skills) and problems with motivation (i.e., personal and environmental factors that inhibit skillful behavior and reinforce dysfunctional behavior). Causes of behavior are not *assumed* based on personality traits, drive states, or self-object structures; they are *hypothesized* according to respondent, operant, and observational learning models.

In response to the limitations of standard cognitive and behavior therapy protocols, modifications were made to standard CBT that formed the basis of dialectical behavior therapy (DBT).[3] At an introductory level, three basic sets of theoretical concepts are important in DBT case formulation beyond standard learning principles: (1) the biosocial theory of BPD, (2) dialectics, and (3) dialectical dilemmas derived from common behavioral patterns of BPD (Koerner & Linehan, 1997).

BIOSOCIAL THEORY

DBT case conceptualization is guided by the biosocial theory, which posits that the transaction of a biological vulnerability to emotional dysregulation with an invalidating environment, over time, creates and maintains BPD. The model is *transactive* rather than *interactive:* The two factors operate together and influence each other.

Biologically, borderline individuals are thought to be predisposed to heightened emotional sensitivity, heightened reactivity, and delayed return to baseline mood.

---

[3] The information presented in this chapter is based primarily on Marsha M. Linehan's (1993a, 1993b) extensive writing on DBT. This is a complex treatment requiring serious study and training to conduct effectively. Readers are advised to consult her text on the subject and the companion skills training manual for a more thorough understanding of the model. For more information on training in DBT, contact the Behavioral Technology Transfer Group at 206-675-8588.

Borderline individuals also lack the ability to regulate strong emotions, which involves (1) adjusting physiological arousal associated with emotion, (2) reorienting attention when emotional, (3) inhibiting mood-dependent actions, (4) experiencing emotions without escalating or blunting, and (5) organizing behavior in the service of non-mood-dependent goals (Gottman & Katz, 1990). It is the combination of emotional vulnerability and inability to modulate the resulting intense emotions that constitutes the emotional dysregulation in borderline individuals.

Over time, such biological vulnerability transacts with an invalidating environment. The invalidating environment inconsistently responds to the individual's emotional responses in ways that communicate that the responses are incorrect, inappropriate, unimportant, or pathological. By oversimplifying problem-solving ease, the environment fails to teach the individual to form realistic goals and tolerate distress. By punishing communication of negative experiences and responding only to negative emotional displays when they are escalated, the environment teaches the individual to oscillate between inhibiting emotions and communicating emotions in an extreme manner. Individuals eventually learn to invalidate their own thoughts and feelings and instead search the environment for cues about how to think and feel. Ultimately, free-operant behaviors are blocked and behavior is primarily that under the direct control of social consequences or immediate external reinforcement (Koerner & Linehan, 1997).

The biosocial model is compensatory: An extremely invalidating environment can result in borderline behavior patterns in individuals with only moderate biological vulnerability. Conversely, an individual with high vulnerability may develop borderline behaviors after transacting with moderate invalidation from the environment. Either way, emotional dysregulation and an invalidating environment are central to the etiology and maintenance of the disorder.

DIALECTICS

Dialectical philosophy holds that nothing is isolated and independent; everything is connected. Thus, formulations about the client in isolation are distorted because parts are meaningful only in their relations to the whole. Dialectical case conceptualization gives equal attention to client and context, as their distinction is somewhat artificial. Client and context are parts of a larger whole, and the interrelation between the two is dynamic and mutually influencing. The therapist considers the effects of systems (including the therapy system) on clients and clients' reciprocal effects on systems.

Dialectics maintains that reality is full of contradictions. These opposing forces create dialectical tensions: actively harmonious and mutually controlling relationships between thesis and antithesis. Reality is thought to be a process rather than a state. This constant flux implies that the synthesis of thesis and antithesis forms a new thesis for which there is a complementing opposite. Understanding truth is not a destination because truth is change. Applied to thought, the question "What is being left out?" acknowledges that the current perspective has truth, but only part of it. Applied to behavior, problematic behavior is at once valid and invalid, understandable and ineffective. Applied to emotions, dialectics seeks a synthesis of regulating emotions and accepting them. Indeed, the central dialectic in case conceptualization is the focus on changing the behavior of clients while radically accepting them as they are.

DIALECTICAL DILEMMAS

Resulting from the biological and social influences detailed in the biosocial model, borderline individuals frequently show behavioral patterns of either underregulating emotions (primarily biologically influenced) or overregulating emotions (primarily socially influenced). Borderline individuals oscillate between these behavioral poles, with each pole reinforcing the opposing pole and forming what Linehan (1993a) calls dialectical dilemmas. Dialectical behavior patterns are referred to as "secondary targets," as they often drive primary targets (e.g., suicidal and parasuicidal behavior) and can destroy therapy if not directly addressed.

The central dialectical tension, emotion vulnerability and self-invalidation, is between clients' intensely painful experience of emotion dysregulation ("I can't stand it") and their experience of emotions as invalid ("I shouldn't feel this way"). The second dialectical tension is between active-passivity and apparent competence. Active-passivity is the tendency to approach problems passively and, at the same time, demand that the environment solve the problem. Conversely, apparent competence is the tendency to underutilize resources in the environment and act in ways that lead others to expect more than can be done. The final dialectical tension is between unrelenting crisis and inhibited grieving. Unrelenting crisis refers to a behavioral pattern that creates and responds to unremitting aversive events. Inhibited grieving, on the other hand, is a learned but involuntary inhibition of the natural experience of painful emotions (see Linehan, 1993a, for detailed description of dialectical tensions and the dilemmas they create for both client and therapist).

In summary, the biosocial model defines the central variables at issue in borderline behavior patterns. Dialectics keeps the conceptual lens focused on both client and context and minimizes the polarization of opposites within and between therapist and client. Dialectical dilemmas organize behaviors into sets that are functionally linked to problem behaviors and that interfere with changing those behaviors.

The initiation and maintenance of Claudia's difficulties, as viewed through biosocial theory, are explained through the transaction of her emotional vulnerability and her experience of invalidation in her environment. Her experience of intense and reactive emotions and her subsequent difficulty regulating these emotions and engaging in mood-dependent behaviors (e.g., parasuicidal behavior, outbursts of anger) are evidence of her emotional vulnerability. Invalidation in her environment is evidenced by her parents' dismissals and minimizing of her emotional experiences when younger, and more recently, the pejorative labeling (e.g., "overly reactive and sensitive") and oversimplifying responses (e.g., "Just pull yourself together") from family and friends alike. Over time, Claudia has developed a pattern of oscillating between self-invalidation of her emotions (e.g., "I shouldn't feel like this") and feeling overwhelmed by her emotions, further escalating her communication of emotional experiences so that they will be taken seriously (by others and herself).

Dialectically conceptualizing Claudia's problematic behaviors entails consideration of Claudia, her environment, the environment's tendency to generate certain behaviors from her, and the behaviors of Claudia that reciprocally generate certain responses in the environment. The focus of intervention is balanced between client and environment. The goal is balanced between behavior change and behavior acceptance.

RATIONALE FOR TREATMENT CHOICE

DBT is an empirically validated treatment for BPD. Numerous studies have demonstrated the association between DBT and decreases in parasuicidal behavior, psychiatric hospitalization, anger, suicidal ideation, depression, hopelessness, and dissociation and with increases in client retention, overall level of functioning, and overall social adjustment (see Koerner & Dimeff, 2000, for a review). Although critical reviews of the empirical literature suggest that the support for DBT is limited, the "research generated for DBT represents the most thorough empirical exploration to date of any one psychotherapeutic treatment for BPD" and DBT "meets and probably exceeds" established criteria to judge treatment efficacy (Scheel, 2000, p. 83).

There are numerous challenges in treating borderline individuals. Myriad problematic and crisis-related behaviors frequently disrupt both client and therapist such that with each session there is a new and pressing problem. Client retention is typically low and treatment outcomes are often poor (see Linehan & Heard, 1999, for a review). High hospitalization rates and serious suicide risk invariably increase therapist stress. Finally, nearly every criterion of BPD has a potentially negative impact on the therapeutic relationship, contributing to the generation of pejorative, and thus empathy-reducing, labels for borderline behaviors (e.g., "manipulation") and therapist burnout (Linehan, Cochran, Mar, Levensky, & Comtois, 2000). DBT addresses these and other treatment-interfering challenges through a hierarchical ordering of treatment targets, maintaining a dialectical frame, use of a treatment team, and adherence to assumptions regarding clients and their therapy.

As an overall map for therapy and to minimize fragmentation from one session to the next, DBT organizes treatment into stages and targets what to treat in each stage hierarchically. It is this hierarchy that guides the therapy agenda more than what the client (or therapist) would like to talk about in a given session.

Dialectics addresses the tendency of polarization in the treatment of borderline individuals: polarization within the client, polarization within the therapist, and polarization between client and therapist. Dialectics advocates a "yes/and" response to tensions (whatever the struggle) in that both positions contain an element of truth and are actually in harmony. For instance, the tension between a client insisting "I can't" and a therapist insisting "You must" is resolved in the synthesis "You are doing the best you can, and we must find a way for you to do better to reach your goals."

Linehan (1993a) insists that therapists need support in treating borderline clients. Without a treatment team, therapists may (1) drift in treatment adherence to DBT, (2) engage in client-reinforced behaviors that are iatrogenic, (3) become polarized in their conceptualization or intervention with a particular client, or (4) burn out due to lack of reinforcement for their work. The treatment team and consultation meetings in DBT are designed to avoid these pitfalls. Team members help each other to adhere to the treatment model, point out polarization and bring each other back into a dialectical synthesis, and at times, simply cheer one another on. Just as clients work to increase capabilities and motivation to be a DBT client, the consultation team increases the therapist's capabilities and motivation to be a DBT therapist.

Finally, DBT contains basic assumptions about borderline clients and their therapy (Linehan, 1993a). DBT's client and therapy tenets counter therapists' pejorative interpretations of client behaviors and tendency to "blame the victim." For example, it is assumed that clients are doing the best they can. Believing the opposite would likely decrease the motivation of the therapist to work hard. Furthermore, communicating to clients that they are not trying or simply need to try harder invalidates their efforts and serves only to discourage the client. The client and therapy assumptions are, in essence, cognitive therapy for the therapist.

COURSE OF TREATMENT

TREATMENT STRUCTURE

When multiproblem clients present for treatment, it is necessary to "put first things first." Thus, DBT is structured into stages, with specific goals at each stage. The time a client spends in any one stage is variable and depends on goal attainment and stabilization. Two overarching goals, however, are addressed regardless of the current stage of treatment. The first is to increase dialectical behavior patterns, that is, patterns in thinking and responding that are balanced, rather than dichotomous and extreme. The second is to build adaptive skills in living and relating to others. For individuals prone to emotion dysregulation, this means responding effectively in the most difficult situations, even when their emotional state or mood may dictate otherwise (Comtois, Levensky, et al., 1999).

In the pretreatment stage of DBT, "getting ready" targets are addressed. These include assessment, orientation to treatment, and establishing some level of initial commitment to participate in therapy. Pretreatment is followed by Stage 1, where treatment focuses on reducing behaviors arranged hierarchically as follows: (1) suicidal and parasuicidal behaviors, (2) behaviors that interfere with the conduct of therapy, and (3) behaviors that severely interfere with a reasonable quality of life (e.g., impulsive behaviors that are not life-threatening, severely dysfunctional relationship behaviors). Stage 2 of treatment addresses behaviors related to Posttraumatic Stress Disorder (PTSD), as many (but not all) BPD clients present with this concurrent diagnosis. Treatment in this stage typically involves exposure techniques designed to change clients' emotional responses to trauma-related cues, and cognitive strategies to modify clients' perceptions and beliefs regarding the trauma or its sequelae. This stage is begun only when primary targets are under adequate control, ensuring that the client has the necessary capabilities and supports to explore and resolve the trauma successfully. Ameliorating PTSD is often a process that is started, stopped, and restarted throughout the course of treatment. The third and final stage of treatment targets increasing self-respect, as well as working on other issues and problems the client may want help with. These may include developing more rewarding relationships or resolving work- or career-related problems (Linehan, 1993a).

TREATMENT FUNCTIONS

The five basic functions of DBT are to (1) enhance client motivation, (2) enhance client capabilities, (3) promote generalization of capabilities to all relevant contexts, (4) structure the environment to support capabilities, and (5) enhance therapist capabilities and motivation to conduct effective therapy (Linehan, 1993a).

Depending on the treatment setting, different treatment modalities are implemented to address these five functions. The four primary modes of outpatient DBT are individual therapy, skills training, telephone consultation, and therapist consultation group.

TREATMENT MODALITIES

Individual Therapy Of the four modalities, individual therapy is the "main course" of DBT, as it serves the primary function of enhancing clients' motivation both to participate effectively in treatment and to apply the behavioral skills they are learning to their outside lives. Behaviorally, enhancing motivation requires recognizing and manipulating contingencies operating in the client's environment so that adaptive behaviors are reinforced and maladaptive behaviors are not (Comtois, Levensky, et al., 1999). This is not a process imposed on clients without their knowledge, but a collaborative effort that involves teaching clients about learning theory and its methods in a personally relevant way.

Individual therapy sessions are structured around balancing problem-solving and validation strategies. Content for any given session is provided by diary cards (a self-monitoring device) on which clients record occurrences of their target behaviors as well as skills used throughout the week. The first step in problem solving involves acknowledging and accepting the problem at hand. Although an obvious starting point, this can be a time-consuming and difficult task, as clients often view the behavior targeted for change (the problem, in the therapist's eyes) as a viable and effective solution (at least in the short term). Once agreement is obtained, a behavioral analysis of the target behavior is conducted. This involves gathering detailed information on the behavior itself, as well as internal and external variables that precede and follow the behavior.

Based on data generated in the behavior analysis, hypotheses as to what might be influencing the target behavior are explored and more adaptive solutions generated. Solutions usually fall into one of four categories: (1) behavioral skill acquisition or strengthening (to ameliorate behavioral skill deficits); (2) manipulating contingency arrangements (to change antecedents and consequences that promote dysfunctional over functional behavior); (3) exposure strategies (to reduce problematic emotions and avoidant behaviors that prevent effective action); and (4) cognitive modification techniques (to change distorted, rigid, or extreme thinking that inhibits functional behavior; Comtois, Levensky, et al., 1999).

However, interventions focused solely on change risk recapitulating the invalidating environment, causing the client to become more dysregulated and the client-therapist relationship to become more polarized. To prevent this from happening, validation strategies are skillfully woven throughout problem and solution analyses. Linehan (1993a) outlines many levels of validation, but the essence of these strategies is to communicate to the client that his or her experience (or some aspect of it) makes sense (is real or valid) given his or her life context or the situation at hand. The purpose of validation is threefold: to balance the push for change, to reinforce client progress, and to strengthen the therapeutic relationship. It also serves as modeling to clients in how they might self-validate and is a set of skills taught to significant others as part of treating the environment (see Linehan, 1993a, for a detailed description of individual therapy strategies, including problem-solving and validation strategies).

Another important function of individual therapy is termed "structuring the environment" (Linehan, 1993a). Here, the therapist teaches clients how to communicate to others in a way that will best serve their interests and help facilitate progress toward their goals. Change in the client's environment comes primarily through the therapist's acting as a "consultant to the client" rather than through direct intervention. Consultation may also involve teaching clients how to secure resources for themselves or coaching them in how to effectively coordinate care among therapists, prescribers, hospitals, and crisis centers. In our program, we offer ancillary treatment modalities related to structuring the environment: a one-time orientation workshop on BPD and DBT for family members and friends of program clients; two separate 10-week groups (one for parents of program clients and another for partners); and DBT-based couples or family therapy (Hoffman, Fruzzetti, & Swenson, 1999).

Skills Training   Skills training focuses on increasing client capabilities through skills acquisition and strengthening. Skills training may be delivered individually but preferably is conducted in a group setting to help the therapist stay on task and to take advantage of group dynamics that can facilitate learning. Training occurs in four primary skill sets: mindfulness (nonjudgmental awareness of the here and now), emotion regulation, distress tolerance, and interpersonal effectiveness (Linehan, 1993b). Skills training is accomplished primarily through didactic strategies: lecture, discussion, in-group practice, and homework assignments. In standard DBT as proposed by Linehan (1993a, 1993b), a skills training group lasts one year, with clients cycling through all four skill modules twice in two six-month blocks. In our program, initial skills training lasts six months, with options to continue based on client need and circumstance.

Telephone Consultation   Newly acquired skills do not automatically generalize to all relevant contexts, particularly in crisis situations, where intense affect can inhibit skillful behavior. In such instances, direct intervention often is needed to promote generalization. Telephone consultation is conducted by the client's individual therapist, someone who knows the client well and has a strong relationship with the client. Through this relationship, the individual therapist can sometimes get the client to do (or not do) things that an unknown crisis line or hospital worker cannot. It should be emphasized that telephone consultation is not supportive therapy over the phone. Clients are clearly instructed that the purposes of telephone consultation are to teach them how and when to appropriately ask for help, and for skills coaching, relationship repair, and crisis intervention. For clients who call in crisis, DBT offers special strategies that address suicidal and parasuicidal behavior. The suggested protocol is to conduct a risk assessment, explore the problem at hand, validate the problem and the associated emotional pain, develop a solution, and obtain commitment to a plan of action. To avoid reinforcing self-injury, clients are not allowed to call their therapist for 24 hours after engaging in self-harm behavior, except to ensure their safety (Kim & Goff, 2000).

Therapist Consultation Group   This mode of treatment is designed to enhance therapist capabilities and motivation. Therapist consultation group meets weekly, with all individual and skills training therapists present. The group can be seen as "treatment for the treater," where team members provide one another consultation and support in their attempts to apply DBT. Particularly difficult therapist-client situations are reviewed that focus on finding nonpejorative, phenomenological, empathic interpretations of behavior, while simultaneously looking for what may be missing in any given analysis or hypothesis. Practice exercises (e.g., role plays), feedback, and cheerleading are an integral part of this process.

Claudia's pretreatment stage occurred over two sessions. She stated that her overall goals for therapy were to have a good relationship with her boyfriend, feel less depressed, and generally feel better about herself. As she elaborated on these problem areas, her therapist validated her pain and the conditions under which it occurred. This was the first attempt on the therapist's part to build a strong relationship. In the process of exploring Claudia's history, her therapist oriented her to the biosocial model, weaving formal teaching points into their conversation and strengthening them by pointing out many examples from Claudia's life. He also oriented her to the DBT model and attempted to connect Stage 1 targets (decreasing suicidal and parasuicidal behaviors and increasing adaptive coping and communication skills) to her stated goals (to improve her relationship and feel better). In providing a rationale for working on Stage 1 targets that was consistent with Claudia's goals, commitment and motivation were strengthened.

Claudia then began the first stage of DBT, attending individual and group therapy weekly. She found the group very reinforcing, stating, "I can relate to the struggles of other members. It's comforting to know I'm not alone. During check in, I like hearing about how people used skills to help themselves. It gives me ideas about what I can do for myself and hope that maybe things can get better." Individual therapy was another matter, however, as right from the start, Claudia had difficulty keeping a diary card (a therapy-interfering behavior). Her therapist noted this, explained the usefulness of the cards, and while validating what he could regarding why she did not complete them, problem-solved with Claudia about how she might get them done. In addition, when Claudia did not bring in a diary card, she and her therapist did one together at the start of their session. This took up half the session and was quite aversive to Claudia, who had more pressing things she wanted to discuss (a form of contingency management on the therapist's part).

Several behavior analyses of Claudia's suicidal and parasuicidal behavior were conducted in Stage 1, and eventually a typical pattern emerged: Boyfriend is emotionally and behaviorally distant (invalidating environment). She "picks a fight" (gets boyfriend to engage and, thus, is positively reinforced). He leaves, which prompts intense emotional arousal, primarily anxiety (emotion dysregulation). Claudia feels "helpless and out of control," oscillating between attacking or blaming her boyfriend for his lack of caring and support, and attacking or blaming herself for being so "mean" to him (secondary targets of emotional vulnerability and self-invalidation). Self-invalidation leads to increased guilt and shame accompanied by thoughts of "Nothing I do makes a difference, life will never change" (cognitive dysregulation, extreme, black-or-white thinking), which then lead to increased hopelessness and despair. At this point, Claudia begins to think about killing herself or cutting. If she has been drinking, and especially if drinking occurs after taking anxiolytic medication, a suicide attempt or self-harm is likely (behavioral dysregulation exacerbated by substance abuse). Life-threatening behavior (both ideation and overt behavior) serves to distance Claudia from what seem like overwhelming and unsolvable problems and to decrease emotional arousal (avoidant behavior that is negatively reinforced). It may also validate her sense of vulnerability or perception of herself as inherently "bad." Later in the sequence, when her boyfriend returns, she apologizes, blaming herself and her "condition," thereby eliciting her boyfriend's sympathy, concern, and other affiliative behaviors (positive reinforcement).

As is evident from this analysis, there are many places to intervene depending on where one finds oneself in the chain of events. First among interventions are mindfulness skills, used to place clients on a path and recognize landmarks that prompt a course of action. A possible solution late in the chain (when Claudia is highly dysregulated) is using phone consultation for coaching in distress-tolerance skills to deter life-threatening behavior. In addition, alcohol combined with anxiolytic medication use must be addressed immediately, as this is a potentially life-threatening behavior in and of itself, as well as a critical link between self-harm ideation and action.

Moving back in the chain, Claudia might use emotion regulation skills to decrease arousal after her boyfriend leaves, as well as cognitive modification and dialectical strategies to address extreme thinking. Even farther back, she might try interpersonal effectiveness skills to communicate what she feels and needs from her boyfriend in response to his distancing. Additional interventions include structuring the environment to decrease invalidation and extinguish reinforcement of maladaptive behavior; using exposure techniques to desensitize her to cues related to being left or alone; and treating secondary targets of emotion vulnerability and self-invalidation. Throughout the process of addressing Stage 1 targets, Claudia's therapist validated what he could and encouraged her to think in terms of learning models as a "less judgmental" (and more precise) way of conceptualizing and solving problems.

About five months into treatment, Claudia's boyfriend began attending a DBT partners group. Through his participation in the group, he got better at validating Claudia as well as at reinforcing adaptive behavior and extinguishing maladaptive behavior. It took some convincing to get him into the group, as his experiences with Claudia had left him hopeless, bitter, and unwilling. Acting as a consultant to the client, Claudia's therapist coached her in how to use interpersonal effectiveness skills to get her boyfriend to reinvest in the relationship, initially by taking a more active role in her treatment.

In the first year of treatment, Claudia's life-threatening behaviors were significantly reduced and eventually eliminated. In her second year, her targets fell into the quality-of-life interfering category, as she worked on reducing her binge-purge episodes and alcohol abuse. Treatment involved using basic exposure with response prevention strategies and skills training (e.g., mindfulness and emotion regulation skills), as these behaviors were determined to function primarily as emotion regulators. Secondary targets of emotion vulnerability and self-invalidation continued to be a focus of treatment throughout the second year.

THERAPIST-CLIENT FACTORS

In individual DBT, the relationship between client and therapist is the primary contingency the therapist uses to influence behavior during the course of treatment. Through the relationship, the therapist gets firsthand experience with problematic client behaviors, thus being provided the opportunity to treat dysfunctional behavior in vivo. Qualities of the therapeutic relationship include:

Radical genuineness: The therapist is a real person (as opposed to transferential object), fully engaged in an authentic relationship with the client.

Effective compassion: The therapist attempts to do what works to facilitate client progress over the long run, versus giving the client what he or she might want or what feels good in the moment.

Balanced communication: The therapist balances a responsive, warm, and genuine communication style with one that is irreverent, unorthodox, and matter-of-fact (but not mean-spirited).

However, establishing and maintaining a relationship with a BPD client is often difficult. To begin with, these clients are notorious for interrupting therapy, and the therapeutic relationship, as a result of "mood-dependent behavior": engaging in behavior based on how they are feeling in any given moment. A common example is not attending therapy when a crisis or problem arises or, conversely, when they begin to feel better after an immediate crisis or problem is resolved. Even when contact is maintained more consistently, other dynamics can tax the relationship. Heightened emotion sensitivity and reactivity coupled with poor regulation skills can result in intense anger and attacking of the therapist or frequent crisis calls to the therapist when experiencing extreme distress. Although these behaviors may achieve the client's aims in the short term, in the long run they can lead to therapist burnout, create negative feelings toward the client, and lead to avoidance and escape behaviors on the therapist's part (Linehan, Cochran, Mar, Levensky, & Comtois, 2000).

DBT incorporates many interventions to establish and maintain a relationship in the face of these difficulties. In the pretreatment stage, clients are informed as to what is expected of both client and therapist to maintain a good, working relationship. Behaviors that promote "liking" of one another are described and explored, as are behaviors that may negatively impact the relationship. When problems do occur in the relationship, as they often do, they are addressed directly and in a descriptive, nonjudgmental manner. Problems are analyzed as to internal and external influences, and this information is used to generate hypotheses and devise solutions. Central to maintaining a productive relationship with the client is the therapist's relationship with his or her team. Therapists must be as open and willing to engage in treatment with the team as they expect clients to be with them.

There were many times in therapy when Claudia had difficulty applying skills in her outside life, stating, "It's too overwhelming. I try these skills, but they just don't work." When her therapist pushed her to try harder ("Although it's difficult, you can do it"), Claudia would become tearful and angry and respond with "You're just not getting it, are you? I'm trying as hard as I can, and yet you make me feel like a failure!" Following this, her therapist would become more frustrated, colder in his response, and more grounded in his position. The therapist took the problem to his consultation team. The team validated the therapist's frustration and at the same time pointed out that the way the therapist was responding in the situation was, in fact, making things worse. They identified the problem as invalidation on the therapist's part (oversimplifying the ease of problem solving) and emotional vulnerability on the client's part, suggesting possible solutions to resolve the impasse and using role play to practice them. Although the problem continued to arise at various points in Claudia's treatment, she and her therapist were able to recognize and address it more quickly and effectively.

COURSE OF TERMINATION

The recommended minimum length of Stage 1 treatment in DBT is one year. Although one year is sufficient time for gains to be realized, clients with the severe problems associated with a diagnosis of BPD are far from being "cured." Within the first year, serious behavioral dyscontrol (e.g., suicide attempts and other self-harm behavior) is often significantly reduced, sometimes even eliminated, and behavioral skills are implemented on a more regular basis. However, complaints related to mood, self-image, and relationships generally continue. Therefore, therapy is often necessary beyond the first year, both to continue work on abiding Stage 1 problems and to refine and strengthen newly acquired skills.

To ensure that treatment gains are generalized and maintained over time, DBT uses a self-management model. Self-management, a subarea within the larger arena of applied behavior analysis, teaches clients a new way of conceptualizing and solving problems. Clients learn to define problems behaviorally, monitor and collect data on these behaviors in context, analyze this information according to models of learning, and develop solutions to change behavior based on their analyses. In a sense, DBT teaches clients how to be their own behavior therapist. In our program, we have added a fifth skills set on relapse prevention, borrowed from Marlatt and Gordon's (1985) work in substance abuse treatment. Information conveyed in this unit includes normalizing the occurrence of relapse as part of the process of change, forewarning clients of the "abstinence violation effect," and increasing awareness of relapse triggers. Developing a personalized relapse prevention plan is the "final student project" in this unit.

Even with self-management and relapse-prevention skills in place, the end of formal treatment is often difficult for clients with BPD. Their reactive and sensitive nature, coupled with an elevated dependence on the environment for help, put them at risk for additional problems as treatment concludes. For this reason, it is recommended that services be reduced slowly over time. In this way, problems and issues that arise as therapy services are decreased can be directly addressed while clients are still active in therapy. In our experience, we have found that clients have an easier time reducing individual therapy if they remain in a skills training group during the process. Telephone consultation with the individual therapist is also helpful, although this too is gradually reduced. While the process of termination is occurring, it is important to remember that receiving less service as one gets better is generally not a motivating contingency for clients who are sensitive to rejection, fear abandonment, and live in environments that provide little reinforcement for their new behaviors. Therefore, from the very start of treatment, it is imperative that therapists help clients structure their environment to increase reinforcing activities and relationships outside of a treatment context.

Claudia was in our program for two years. In her second year of treatment, sessions with her individual therapist were cut back to twice a month. The anxiety she felt as contact with her therapist was reduced was minimized by her continued participation in a "graduate" skills training group and through collaborative work with her individual therapist directly targeting her anxiety and the cues that initiated it.

A central task in terminating therapy with Claudia was making activities and relationships outside of treatment more reinforcing than those experienced within. Although her relationship with her boyfriend was a potential source of reinforcement in her life, the relationship was quite troubled. During her second year of treatment, Claudia and her boyfriend were referred to a DBT couples therapist in the clinic. The purpose of couples therapy was to help stabilize the relationship and improve its reinforcing value. Because her boyfriend had participated in a partners group, the couple was able to start therapy with a common language and model by which to talk about and understand their problems. Claudia and her boyfriend remained in couples therapy for about six months, with treatment ending around the time they became engaged.

FOLLOW-UP

It is suggested that termination of therapy not occur until after clients complete Stage 2 of therapy: resolution of behaviors associated with PTSD. DBT is most unique from other behavioral therapies at Stage 1 but becomes much like other behavioral treatments at Stage 2 (although not entirely; e.g., Zayfert & Becker, 2000). When clients do terminate from DBT after Stage 1, they typically are referred for additional therapy elsewhere. It is recommended that in such cases, even after formal DBT is complete, booster sessions be scheduled to address maintenance issues and for help with problem-solving and skills review.

After two years of treatment, although no longer in group or couples therapy, Claudia received booster sessions every few months from her individual therapist. The purpose of these sessions was to review typical patterns and rehearse skills application. Sessions were scheduled on a fixed-interval basis, not granted as needed, to avoid reinforcing crisis behavior with attention from her therapist. It was also during this time that Claudia joined a community-based women's support and discussion group. There she was able to continue her work on self and interpersonal issues and develop a few meaningful friendships. She also joined an Internet discussion listserve for DBT clients and graduates, the purpose of which was to provide a forum for DBT skills review and discussion.

MANAGED CARE CONSIDERATIONS

The primary goals of managed care are to ensure (1) medical necessity: that services delivered are necessary and appropriate to the presenting health problem; and (2) cost effectiveness: that services rendered provide adequate relief of the problem in the most economically efficient way. Many aspects of DBT are consistent with these goals. DBT is one of the few empirically validated treatments for BPD currently available, with research demonstrating improvement in multiple problem areas (see Koerner & Dimeff, 2000, for a review) and cost savings for high utilizers of psychiatric services (Linehan et al., 1999). The treatment team approach assures adherence to the model and promotes quality control. Team members support each other as built-in consultants and therapists available for backup coverage (an important safeguard in managing high-risk clients). Treatment goals are stated in terms of measurable behaviors that are formally monitored and recorded on a weekly basis. Finally, individual therapists are available around the clock to clients for telephone consultation, promoting generalization of treatment gains to natural contexts and reducing inappropriate (and potentially reinforcing) after-hours use of crisis, respite, and inpatient services.

Nonetheless, certain aspects of DBT become problematic in a managed care system. Whereas commercial insurance plans typically allow from 24 to 40 visits in a one- to two-year period, DBT requires approximately 50 visits in the first six months of treatment. Managed care demands that treatment plans be tailored to individual client need, but DBT is a structured program with a predetermined and standard set of services delivered across a specific period of time. Many managed care organizations require that treating therapists be members of their provider panel, but team therapists are unlikely to be paneled on every insurance plan to which presenting clients may subscribe, and provider panels are frequently closed to new members. Finally, BPD (for which DBT is designed) is not a covered condition under many managed care plans, either because of the belief that BPD is an untreatable disorder or that treatment requires long-term work that is too costly to provide (Comtois, Levensky, et al., 1999).

Claudia's case illustrates some of the accommodations that may have to be made for DBT to be delivered under managed care. When she arrived at the program, she already had used most of her allotted outpatient visits for the year. Further sessions required during Claudia's first year of treatment were made possible when her therapist was able to negotiate an in-patient to out-patient benefit transfer with her insurance company. Additionally, because the group therapist was not a provider under her managed care plan, it was necessary that she pay for this service out-of-pocket. Limited financial resources made it impossible for Claudia to afford her individual therapy copay and the full group fee, so her group fee was reduced. After the first year of skills training group, Claudia signed up for a second year and also began couples therapy. She had to pay out-of-pocket for both services, as they were not covered under her managed care plan. To ease her financial burden during this time, individual therapy was cut back to twice a month. This service was fully covered by her insurance with the renewal of her yearly benefit.

OVERALL EFFECTIVENESS

DBT is an empirically validated cognitive-behavioral therapy for individuals with BPD. Its driving theoretical concepts combine theory and methods of standard CBT with principles and practices drawn from Eastern meditative traditions. This apparent paradox is instead a dialectical synthesis of a technology of change with a position of radical acceptance.

DBT is multimodal and multifunctional, with each modality designed to address specific therapeutic functions. Its team approach functions to increase therapists' motivation and skills while therapists strive to increase their clients' motivations and skills. It is a community of therapists in a therapeutic but genuine relationship with a community of clients.

Claudia successfully completed Stage 1 of DBT. Her scores on outcome measures showed significant improvements, particularly in depression, hostility, and interpersonal sensitivity on the BSI. By observation and her own report, she became more dialectical and less judgmental in her evaluation of herself and others. She also became more self-validating of her emotions and subjectively less overwhelmed and more grounded when upset ("I can have the emotion without the emotion having me").

During her two years in active treatment, Claudia did not make a suicide attempt and was not hospitalized. After three months of treatment, the frequency of her self-harm behavior began to decrease, and by month 8, she had eliminated self-harm behavior, with the exception of one incident at month 12. Her suicidal ideation decreased along a similar pattern and was extinguished by month 14. Claudia's binge-purge behaviors and alcohol abuse were significantly reduced from pretreatment levels. All of these gains were maintained throughout the follow-up period.

REFERENCES

American Psychiatric Association. (1994). *Diagnostic and statistical manual of mental disorders* (4th ed.). Washington, DC: Author.

Comtois, K. A., Cowley, D. S., Dunner, D. L., & Roy-Byrne, P. P. (1999). Relationship between Borderline Personality Disorder and Axis I diagnosis in severity of depression and anxiety. *Journal of Clinical Psychiatry, 60,* 752–758.

Comtois, K. A., Levensky, E. R., & Linehan, M. M. (1999). Behavior therapy. In M. Hersen & A. S. Bellack (Eds.), *Handbook of comparative interventions for adult disorders* (2nd ed., pp. 555–583). New York: Wiley.

Derogatis, L. R., & Spencer, P. M. (1982). *Brief Symptom Inventory: Administration, scoring, and procedures manual.* Baltimore: Clinical Psychometric Research.

Dimeff, L. A., McDavid, J., & Linehan, M. M. (1999). Pharmacotherapy for Borderline Personality Disorder: A review of the literature and recommendations for treatment. *Journal of Clinical Psychology in Medical Settings, 6,* 113–138.

Edell, W. S., Joy, S. P., & Yehuda, R. (1990). Discordance between self-report and observed psychopathology in borderline patients. *Journal of Personality Disorders, 4,* 381–390.

First, M. B., Spitzer, R. L., Gibbons, M., & Williams, J. B. W. (1995). *Structured Clinical Interview for Axis-I DSM-IV Disorders: Patient edition (SCID-I/P).* New York: New York State Psychiatric Institute, Biometrics Research Department.

First, M. B., Spitzer, R. L., Gibbons, M., Williams, J. B. W., & Benjamin, L. (1996). *User's guide for the Structured Clinical Interview for DSM-IV Axis II Personality Disorders (SCID-II).* New York: New York State Psychiatric Institute, Biometrics Research Department.

Gottman, J., & Katz, L. F. (1990). Effects of marital discord on young children's peer interaction and health. *Developmental Psychology, 25,* 373–381.

Haines, J., Williams, C. L., Brain, K. L., & Wilson, G. V. (1995). The psychophysiology of self-mutilation. *Journal of Abnormal Psychology, 104,* 471–489.

Hoffman, P. D., Fruzzetti, A. E., & Swenson, C. R. (1999). Dialectical behavior therapy: Family skills training. *Family Process, 38,* 399–414.

Kim, S. A., & Goff, B. C. (2000). Borderline Personality Disorder. In M. Hersen & M. Biaggio (Eds.), *Effective brief therapies: A clinician's guide* (pp. 335–354). San Diego, CA: Academic Press.

Koerner, K., & Dimeff, L. A. (2000). Further data on dialectical behavior therapy. *Clinical Psychology: Science and Practice, 7*, 104–112.

Koerner, K., & Linehan, M. M. (1997). Case formulation in dialectical behavior therapy for borderline personality disorder. In T. D. Eells (Ed.), *Handbook of psychotherapy case formulation* (pp. 340–367). New York: Guilford Press.

Lambert, M. J., & Hill, C. (1994). Assessing psychotherapy outcomes and processes. In A. E. Bergin & S. L. Garfield (Eds.), *Handbook of psychotherapy and behavior change* (4th ed., pp. 72–113). New York: Wiley.

Linehan, M. M. (1993a). *Cognitive-behavioral treatment of Borderline Personality Disorder.* New York: Guilford Press.

Linehan, M. M. (1993b). *Skills training manual for treating Borderline Personality Disorder.* New York: Guilford Press.

Linehan, M. M., Cochran, B. N., Mar, C. M., Levensky, E. R., & Comtois, K. A. (2000). Therapeutic burnout among borderline personality disordered clients and their therapists: Development and evaluation of two adaptations of the Maslach Burnout Inventory. *Cognitive and Behavioral Practice, 7*, 329–337.

Linehan, M. M., & Heard, H. (1999). Borderline Personality Disorder: Costs, course, and treatment outcomes. In N. Miller & K. Magruder (Eds.), *The cost-effectiveness of psychotherapy: A guide for practitioners, researchers and policy makers* (pp. 291–305). New York: Oxford University Press.

Linehan, M. M., Kanter, J. W., & Comtois, K. A. (1999). Dialectical behavior therapy for Borderline Personality Disorder: Efficacy, specificity, and cost effectiveness. In D. S. Janowsky (Ed.), *Psychotherapy: Indications and outcomes* (pp. 93–118). Washington, DC: American Psychiatric Press.

Marlatt, G. A., & Gordon, J. R. (Eds.). (1985). *Relapse prevention: Maintenance strategies in the treatment of addictive behaviors.* New York: Guilford Press.

Patrick, J., Links, P., van Reekum, R., & Mitton, J. E. (1995). Using the PDQ-R scale as a brief screening measure in the differential diagnosis of personality disorder. *Journal of Personality Disorders, 9*, 266–274.

Scheel, K. R. (2000). The empirical basis of dialectical behavior therapy: Summary, critique, and implications. *Clinical Psychology: Science and Practice, 7*, 68–86.

Zanarini, M. C., Gunderson, J. G., Frankenburg, F. R., & Chauncey, D. L. (1989). The revised diagnostic interview for borderlines: Discriminating Borderline Personality Disorder from other Axis II disorders. *Journal of Personality Disorders, 3*, 10–18.

Zayfert, C., & Becker, C. B. (2000). Implementation of empirically supported treatment for PTSD: Obstacles and innovations. *Behavior Therapist, 23*, 161–168.

CHAPTER 10

Alcohol Abuse

PAUL R. STASIEWICZ and CLARA M. BRADIZZA

DESCRIPTION OF THE DISORDER

ACCORDING TO THE *Diagnostic and Statistical Manual of Mental Disorders,* fourth edition (*DSM-IV;* American Psychiatric Association, 1994), alcohol-use disorders can be classified as either alcohol abuse or alcohol dependence. Alcohol abuse is defined primarily by occurrence of negative consequences that are the result of the misuse of alcohol. These alcohol-related problems include recurrent difficulties fulfilling responsibilities at work, school, or home, using substances in situations that may result in physical harm (e.g., driving a car or operating large machinery), legal difficulties, and conflicts with other people. These problems must occur within the same 12-month period. This diagnosis is usually met by individuals with relatively brief histories of substance use. Alcohol dependence is usually considered a more severe disorder than alcohol abuse and reflects the continued use of alcohol despite the occurrence of cognitive, behavioral, and physiological problems. According to *DSM-IV* criteria, an individual must experience three or more of the following symptoms in the same 12-month period to be diagnosed with alcohol dependence: tolerance; withdrawal; drinking alcohol in larger quantities or over a longer period of time than intended; persistent desire or unsuccessful attempts to cut down or control alcohol use; spending a great deal of time in activities necessary to obtain, use, or recover from the effects of alcohol; giving up or limiting important social, occupational, or recreational activities because of alcohol use; and continued drinking despite knowledge that it is causing or exacerbating a psychological or physical problem.

With regard to symptoms of alcohol dependence, tolerance is the need for increased amounts of alcohol to achieve intoxication (or the desired effect) or a greatly reduced effect with continued use of the same amount of alcohol. Alcohol withdrawal occurs when an individual stops drinking or greatly reduces alcohol intake following consumption of large amounts of alcohol over an extended period of time. Alcohol withdrawal can include the following symptoms: autonomic

181

hyperactivity (e.g., sweating, racing pulse); hand tremor; insomnia; nausea/vomiting; visual, tactile, or auditory hallucinations; psychomotor agitation; anxiety; and grand mal seizures. These symptoms are the result of a drop in blood or tissue concentrations of alcohol in an individual who has been drinking steadily for an extended period of time. Withdrawal usually begins fairly rapidly, within 4 to 12 hours after stopping alcohol consumption; however, it can start as late as 60 hours following abrupt cessation or reduction in alcohol use. Symptoms usually peak during the second day of abstinence. If a delirium develops, in which the individual experiences significant memory deficits, disorientation, or language disturbance, it is likely that a serious medical condition may exist, such as liver failure, pneumonia, or gastrointestinal bleeding, and a medical evaluation is necessary.

Although most clinicians determine diagnosis based on a clinical interview, the most reliable and valid means of assessing whether an individual has an alcohol abuse or dependence diagnosis is by means of a structured diagnostic interview. The most frequently used instrument in clinical practice is the Structured Clinical Interview for *DSM-IV* (SCID-IV; First, Spitzer, Gibbon, & Williams, 1996). The patient version of this instrument (SCID-P) is reasonably brief and is intended to gather only information directly relevant to making a diagnosis. The substance use disorders section of the SCID-P includes a separate diagnostic evaluation of alcohol abuse and alcohol dependence. In instances where SCID-P administration is not feasible (e.g., primary health care settings), a brief screening instrument may be useful. For example, the Alcohol Use Disorders Identification Test (AUDIT; Saunders, Aasland, Babor, De La Fuente, & Grant, 1993) is a 10-item measure that is useful for early detection of harmful alcohol use.

Individuals with alcohol problems are a heterogeneous group. Problem drinkers may differ in terms of current life problems, severity of alcohol abuse or dependence, and motivation to change. With regard to the latter, individuals may present to treatment for a variety of reasons. They may be court-mandated or court-referred, in which case they may face legal consequences if they continue to use alcohol or if they leave treatment prematurely. Even those individuals who are not legally mandated to treatment may be experiencing pressure from family members, employers, or friends. These individuals may appear reluctant to acknowledge the extent of drinking and drinking-related negative consequences and may demonstrate little enthusiasm for participation in the treatment. These behaviors are often termed "denial" by alcoholism treatment providers. Alternatively, similar behaviors may be viewed as the client's ambivalence regarding change. More recently, motivational interventions have been developed to address these cognitive and behavioral barriers to change.

CASE DESCRIPTION

Gayle is a 36-year-old, never married, African American woman who called the therapist requesting help for a drinking problem. She is a professional with a master's degree in business administration and computer science. She resides in a large Midwestern city where she has been living for the past six years. She is employed in upper-level management at a fast-growing computer company where she works 60 to 70 hours per week. To ensure the confidentiality of her treatment, the client requested private payment for her treatment sessions with no health insurance company involvement.

CHIEF COMPLAINTS

Gayle reported concern about her drinking and described several recent alcohol-related incidents. She has business dinners with company clients a few times per week and stated that there have been an increasing number of incidents when she has had too much to drink. During these evenings, she finds herself saying and doing things that she later regrets. For example, she recently had dinner with clients while out of town on business and had six drinks over the course of about four hours. She began talking about personal issues that were not appropriate for a business dinner and had made several inappropriate comments to her attractive waiter. The next day, she felt very embarrassed when having to face her clients at all-day meetings. In addition, she stated that once a week, she goes out for drinks with colleagues from work and finds herself having four to five drinks over the course of several hours. She recently had to be driven home by a coworker because she was too intoxicated to drive. Following several of these heavy drinking episodes, she has arrived late for work the next day and has had to reschedule several meetings with her staff. She fears she is leaving a bad impression with both her clients and her office staff. She recognizes that drinking has begun to interfere with her work performance and is concerned that she may have an alcohol problem. She also is concerned about a 10 lb. weight gain over the past year, most likely the result of an increase in alcohol consumption and a decrease in exercise.

HISTORY

IMMEDIATE PRECIPITANTS

When asked about recent stressors, Gayle reported that her work stress has increased as the demands and expectations of her job have risen. She has changed jobs six times in the past five years, with each job change resulting in a promotion. She is pleased with her career advancement but feels she has given up a lot in exchange for her achievements. For example, she has not had a stable romantic relationship in several years. She has little in common with her married friends and has begun to feel isolated and alone. Gayle reported that her social difficulties are not new and that she has always felt uncomfortable meeting new people.

FAMILY HISTORY

Both of her parents are professionals with college degrees who reside on the East Coast, where she was raised. She speaks to her parents every couple of weeks and visits with them approximately twice per year. There is no family history of alcohol or drug problems. She has an older brother who is married with three children and lives on the West Coast. She speaks to him about once a month and sees him once or twice a year when she is out on business or visiting her parents. She reported having a good relationship with both her parents and her brother, stating that they have few conflicts. When asked more specifically about conflicts, Gayle stated that she does not share very personal events and thoughts with her family, as this tends to increase the tension between them. As a result, there is little friction but also little closeness.

PERSONAL HISTORY

Gayle stated that she was quite shy as a child and preferred to read novels, watch movies, and listen to music. She did not socialize much in high school, as she felt uncomfortable and anxious around others. Despite her discomfort, she began socializing in college, where she also began dating men. It was during this time that she began to drink alcohol. She dated occasionally up until her late 20s, when her life became focused on her career. She has dated infrequently since then, with only three dates in the prior 12 months. She has friendships with several female friends but has felt herself drifting away from these relationships as her friends marry and have children. She was raised in a predominantly White neighborhood and as a result feels comfortable interacting in White settings. However, many Whites are noticeably less comfortable around her. This is something that she is acutely aware of and that causes her to feel isolated both at work and in her personal life. She feels that being a minority woman has created difficulties in her interactions with both clients and coworkers. At times, clients seem surprised or even put off when she shows up for a first meeting. She feels she has had to work harder than others to earn the respect of her colleagues.

SUBSTANCE USE HISTORY

Gayle did not use any alcohol or drugs until college. During her college years, she was consuming three to four drinks per occasion, three to four times per month. She occasionally used marijuana socially and had used amphetamines several times to stay up late to complete school assignments. There has been no use of either marijuana or amphetamines since college, and she denied any other drug use. She reported being an occasional social drinker in her 20s. She would usually have one to two drinks, two to three times per month. Gayle's drinking increased in her late 20s as her job became more demanding and she was expected to handle increasingly more complex social situations at work. Anticipating these situations caused her anxiety, and she drank to cope with the anxiety. Up until a year earlier she was drinking three drinks two to three times per week. She now finds herself having five drinks two to three times per week when she is out in the evening, and two drinks on both Saturday and Sunday when she is home alone. She often feels lonely on the weekend and reported that a couple of drinks in the evening relaxes her and helps her to fall asleep.

BEHAVIORAL ASSESSMENT

Behavioral assessments of alcohol use are important for several reasons: (1) They provide information about problem severity that can be used to develop an individualized treatment plan; (2) objective feedback of assessment information can be used to increase the client's motivation to change; (3) ongoing assessment information can be used to modify the treatment plan; and (4) treatment outcome can be assessed. A behavioral assessment of Gayle's alcohol use was conducted one week after the initial visit with the therapist. The assessment consisted of a structured clinical interview to determine diagnosis, self-report questionnaires, and a computer-assisted interview of recent drinking patterns. The general approach to assessment involved a nonconfrontational style with the goal of increasing Gayle's motivation to change her drinking behavior.

BEHAVIORAL

An important component of behavioral assessment is a functional analysis.[1] In the case of problem drinkers, the consumption of alcohol constitutes the target behavior. A functional analysis of drinking specifies the relevant events associated with both increases and decreases in alcohol use (L. C. Sobell, Toneatto, & Sobell, 1994). The information gathered from the client can be useful in forming hypotheses about the nature of the relationships among variables. Therefore, once the alcohol-use patterns are thoroughly described, attention can be devoted to the types of cognitive, emotional, interpersonal, and environmental events that increase or decrease alcohol use. Positive and negative mood states can easily be conceptualized as antecedents for alcohol use. Similarly, the consequences of alcohol use are examined to determine the potential sources of reinforcement maintaining the alcohol use. An analysis of antecedents and consequences assumes an idiographic approach to understanding alcohol-use behavior, and the information gathered during this assessment is used in developing the individual's treatment plan.

At the end of the assessment session, Gayle was given a reading assignment that provided information about identifying the antecedents and consequences of drinking. She was asked to identify the antecedents and consequences for three high-risk drinking situations. The results of Gayle's functional analysis are presented below in the section titled "Course of Treatment."

SELF-REPORT

The alcohol-use disorders section of the SCID-P was used to determine diagnosis. Gayle reported little tolerance to the effects of alcohol and no history of withdrawal symptoms. She acknowledged drinking larger amounts of alcohol than she intended on many occasions during the prior year. She denied spending a great deal of time obtaining, using, or recovering from the effects of alcohol use and had not given up social, occupational, or recreational activities because of her alcohol use. She denied any persistent physical or psychological problems exacerbated by alcohol use. She recognized that she has failed to meet her work expectations on a number of occasions due to her drinking behavior. This information indicates that Gayle meets *DSM-IV* criteria for Alcohol Abuse but not for Alcohol Dependence.

Verbal self-report continues to be the primary method by which clinicians and researchers obtain measurements of a person's past drinking. The Timeline Followback (TLFB; L. C. Sobell & Sobell, 1992) procedure was used to assess quantity and frequency of alcohol use during the six-month period prior to treatment. On the TLFB, Gayle drank four to five days per week and consumed approximately 20 drinks per week. Heavier drinking occurred during weekday evenings, and lighter drinking occurred on the weekend. The Short-form Alcohol Dependence Data Questionnaire (Raistrick, Dunbar, & Davidson, 1983) was administered to

---

[1] Technically, a functional analysis is an active manipulation that is used to demonstrate that changes in one behavior result in unambiguous changes in another. The term, however, is often extended to include the client's self-report of factors associated with the target behavior. In this chapter, the use of term "functional analysis" refers to a client's self-report of the antecedents and consequences of drinking.

assess her current level of alcohol dependence. She obtained a score of 2, suggesting a low level of alcohol dependence.

The Drinker Inventory of Consequences (DRINC; Miller, Tonigan, & Longabaugh, 1995) was administered to assess possible negative consequences of alcohol use. These items sample several domains of possible negative consequences, including physical (e.g., trouble sleeping, physical health), intrapersonal (e.g., guilt, negative personality changes), social responsibility (e.g., missed work, failure to meet expectations), interpersonal (e.g., problems with family or friends, damaged social life), and impulse control (e.g., drinking and driving, physical fights). Gayle's responses suggested that she is experiencing moderate levels of social responsibility and intrapersonal negative consequences (e.g., late for work, embarrassment over becoming intoxicated). She obtained low scores on all other subscales of the DRINC.

To assess current level of motivation to change her alcohol-use behavior, the Stages of Change Readiness and Treatment Eagerness Scale (Miller & Tonigan, 1996) was administered. This instrument assesses motivation on three distinct factors: Ambivalence, Recognition, and Taking Steps. Gayle scored high on the Recognition subscale, indicating recognition of an alcohol problem. Her responses to the Taking Steps items indicated that despite her recognition of a problem, she had made few recent changes to her drinking behavior.

High-risk alcohol-use situations were assessed using the Alcohol version of the Inventory of Drug-Taking Situations (Annis & Martin, 1985). This instrument consists of 50 questions assessing the risk of heavy drinking in a variety of situations, classified into one of eight categories: Unpleasant Emotions, Physical Discomfort, Pleasant Emotions, Testing Personal Control, Urges/Temptations to Use, Conflict with Others, Social Pressure to Use, and Pleasant Times with Others. Gayle's responses indicated that her highest-risk situations were those involving social pressure to use, pleasant times with others, and negative affect. She indicated that she drank when in the presence of others who were drinking, when she wanted to increase her enjoyment while in the company of others, when she was feeling anxious in the presence of other people, and when she was lonely, sad, or overwhelmed.

Finally, Gayle was asked to complete a Goal Statement. This is used to assess the client's drinking goals involving either abstinence or nonabstinence. If nonabstinence is the goal, the terms and amount of drinking are made explicit, the importance of the goal is determined, and the confidence in achieving the goal is assessed. Gayle indicated that she would like to reduce her drinking such that she is consuming no more than two drinks per day and drinks no more than three days per week. Pending the results of a medical evaluation, these were determined to be safe, reasonable goals. Gayle indicated that reaching her goal was very important to her at this time and she was confident that she could achieve it.

Psychiatric Comorbidity

Individuals with psychiatric disorders have higher rates of substance use disorders compared to individuals with no co-occurring mental illness (Regier et al., 1990). For example, the lifetime prevalence of a substance use disorder for persons with anxiety disorder is approximately twice that of individuals with no comorbid anxiety disorder. Presence of a comorbid mental disorder is associated with poorer outcome for substance abuse treatment. Among persons with an alcohol disorder, those with psychiatric symptoms (anxiety, depression) generally have higher rates of relapse. Until recently, persons with co-occurring disorders were treated through separate mental health and substance-abuse service systems. Treatment has moved away from this model toward integrating substance abuse and mental health treatment into comprehensive programs. Behavioral assessment fits well into an integrated treatment model because it aims to identify the interdependence of substance use and psychiatric symptoms.

Long-standing problems with social anxiety, and more recent concerns about social isolation, prompted the therapist to assess Gayle for Social Phobia, an anxiety disorder characterized by a persistent fear of one or more social or performance situations. Although the results of the SCID-P diagnostic interview were negative for Social Phobia, Gayle did express fear of negative evaluation by others. She indicated that difficulties initiating and maintaining conversations resulted in anxiety when meeting new people. She tended to avoid meeting new people, but her recent promotion included more frequent meetings with coworkers and business clients. Thus, her new job made it difficult for her to avoid anxiety-provoking situations. When meeting with business clients, she drank to put herself at ease, and she found it easier to engage in conversation after drinking.

MEDICAL CONSULTATION

Gayle was referred to her physician for a physical examination. It was important to determine whether Gayle had any medical conditions that could be exacerbated by continued, moderate use of alcohol. For example, if Gayle was found to suffer from certain medical problems (e.g., diabetes, high blood pressure), then a drinking reduction program would not be advisable because even limited drinking could worsen such a condition. Results of her physical examination indicated normal levels of gamma-glutamyl transpeptidase (GGTP, a liver enzyme) and red blood cell size (mean corpuscular volume; MCV). Both GGTP and MCV are markers of recent, heavy drinking. Other than a 10-lb. increase in weight during the prior year, the results of the medical evaluation revealed that Gayle was in good health.

Prior to seeing her physician, Gayle's therapist discussed several medications that have shown promise in the treatment of alcohol problems. Medications often are used as adjuncts to behavioral treatment. Disulfiram (Antabuse) has a long history of use as a deterrent medication. When taken with alcohol it can produce nausea, vomiting, dizziness, difficulty breathing, headache, flushing, and rapid heartbeat. Disulfiram is administered orally on a daily basis, and the client cannot drink for four to seven days following discontinuation of the medication. This delay often provides the individual with time to reconsider the decision to begin drinking. Naltrexone (Revia) is an orally administered opioid antagonist that recently has been found to be effective for the treatment of alcohol problems. It has been found to decrease craving for alcohol and to produce lower relapse rates when added to psychosocial treatment for alcoholism.

The option to add these medications to Gayle's current behavioral treatment was discussed; she declined, stating that she would reconsider use of medication if she was having difficulty achieving her reduced drinking goal. In this case, she would switch to a goal of abstinence and consider taking medication either as a deterrent to drinking or to decrease her alcohol cravings.

CASE CONCEPTUALIZATION

Several factors were determined to be contributing to Gayle's pattern of problem drinking. First, she has a history of social anxiety combined with several social skills deficits. Second, job-related stressors have increased since her recent promotion and have taxed her ability to cope effectively. Third, she lacks a social support network outside of work and is often isolated and alone. These problems are discussed in more detail below.

SOCIAL ANXIETY AND SOCIAL SKILLS DEFICITS

Gayle has a history of social anxiety leading back to childhood. As a child, she coped by focusing on her schoolwork, isolating herself from others, and avoiding social situations. She began drinking regularly in college after discovering that alcohol helped her cope with social anxiety. When she was drinking, she felt less self-conscious around others and enjoyed herself more. Drinking was an accepted behavior in her peer group. Because of alcohol's availability and its short-term reinforcing effects, drinking became the primary coping strategy for Gayle in new social situations.

WORK-RELATED STRESS AND SOCIAL ISOLATION

Gayle experiences significant day-to-day pressure due to the demands of her job and the absence of a strong social support system. Her work is stressful, and she has devoted an increasing amount of time over the past 10 years to her career. Her career advancement has seen a concomitant rise in job expectations. As a result, she has had to make compromises in her personal life. At a time when most of her friends are in long-term relationships and many have children, she has no partner and has not had a stable romantic relationship in several years. Her life has diverged from those of her long-time friends, and she feels she has little in common with them. As a result, she feels increasingly lonely and sad. She states that often she is so tired at the end of her long work week that she does not have the energy to socialize or go on a date but finds watching television or movies at home with a few glasses of wine relaxing.

Although the development of addictive behaviors is often multiply determined and maintained, similar factors appear to be involved in the development and maintenance of Gayle's drinking problem. First, her drinking was primarily driven by alcohol's short-term reinforcing effects. Second, alcohol provided her with some relief in interpersonal situations and in situations involving unpleasant emotions. Third, a perceived lack of alternative coping strategies combined with a lack of social support served to maintain her maladaptive pattern of alcohol use.

RATIONALE FOR TREATMENT CHOICE

Guided self-change (M. B. Sobell & Sobell, 1993) was the recommended treatment for Gayle's alcohol problem. This treatment is based on the idea that many problem drinkers can reduce the harmful consequences of drinking if they are sufficiently motivated and are given some guidance and support. In this treatment program, an individual may learn to identify the determinants of his or her own problem drinking and to develop effective behavior change strategies. Guided self-change is recommended for problem drinkers who are not severely dependent on alcohol. Problem drinkers are generally younger, have shorter problem drinking histories, are better educated, and have greater personal, social, and economic resources to draw on when in treatment. In this case, Gayle was an ideal candidate for guided self-change because she did not have a severe alcohol problem, was motivated to change, and had the personal and economic resources necessary to initiate a self-management treatment approach.

Guided self-change is one of several brief interventions available for use with problem drinkers. There is considerable evidence that brief interventions are as effective as longer-term treatments for individuals who are not alcohol-dependent (Zweben & Fleming, 1999). In addition, more traditional methods of treatment are often less flexible in terms of goal choice (i.e., abstinence versus nonabstinence) and very demanding in terms of time commitment (e.g., 28-day inpatient stay), and therefore may compete with a person's personal and professional life. If the demands of treatment become too great, noncompliance with treatment may increase. Moreover, when the goal is drinking reduction, brief interventions for problem drinking have been shown to be more effective among women than among men.

In addition to treatment for Gayle's alcohol problem, problems with social anxiety and social skills also required attention. These problems were associated with her alcohol use and therefore may have put her at risk for relapse. Information derived from the behavioral assessment of Gayle's high-risk drinking situations indicated that she could benefit from several social skills training exercises (see Monti, Abrams, Kadden, & Cooney, 1989). In this regard, exercises involving drink refusal skills, starting conversations, and enhancing social support networks were added to the treatment plan.

COURSE OF TREATMENT

The guided self-change approach used with this client followed the format laid out by M. B. Sobell and Sobell (1993). The treatment program included an initial assessment session, four individual treatment sessions, and two follow-up sessions. The first two treatment sessions were spaced one week apart and the last two sessions were spaced two weeks apart. This allowed both therapist and client more time in which to evaluate the client's progress. The total duration of treatment was six weeks, not including the two follow-up appointments.

Each treatment session followed a standard outline: (1) collect homework and self-monitoring forms, (2) review self-monitoring, (3) review homework and reading assignments, (4) hand out any new reading and/or homework assignments, (5) encourage client to continue self-monitoring, and (6) close session by reinforcing client's progress toward goals (e.g., completion of self-monitoring, achieving weekly drinking goals). Role plays were included in several sessions to rehearse specific social skills. The therapist played the role of other people in Gayle's life and Gayle played herself. On occasion, the therapist would model the skill first and then involve Gayle in the role-play exercise.

At the end of the assessment session, Gayle was provided with a weekly log and instructions for monitoring her daily drinking behavior. Self-monitoring is one of the most effective ways to increase awareness of alcohol use, and Gayle was informed that she would be monitoring her drinking behavior for the next six weeks. For each drinking occasion, she was instructed to record the date and time of day, the type of alcohol consumed (i.e., beer, wine, or liquor), the number of standard drinks consumed, the drinking context (e.g., bar, home), and her mood just prior to drinking. Gayle also was given the first of several reading and homework assignments.[2] The reading material, "Understanding Your Drinking Problem," explains that the client is responsible for change and that the purpose of treatment is to help people to help themselves. It provides information about identifying antecedents and consequences of drinking and ends with an introduction to the companion homework assignment. The homework assignment asks clients to identify the antecedents and consequences of drinking for three high-risk drinking situations. A high-risk drinking situation was defined for Gayle as one that increased her risk of exceeding her drinking goal or increased her risk of experiencing alcohol-related negative consequences. For example, during a typical Friday evening, Gayle consumed five drinks in approximately three hours and then drove home. Given her height and weight (5'5" tall and 130 lbs.), it is estimated that her blood alcohol level (BAL) would be 0.12, which exceeds the criterion for legal intoxication in all states. At this BAL, Gayle greatly increases the risk of arrest or an automobile accident. She was asked to bring her completed self-monitoring log and homework assignment to the next session.

TREATMENT SESSION 1

The weekly self-monitoring log was reviewed first. Gayle stated that she was uncomfortable recording her drinks when other people were present. This occurred once during the previous week, and she recorded the information when she returned home later that evening. Although it is preferable to record the information prior to the first sip, if clients fail to record the information immediately, they are encouraged to do it later. In this case, the therapist worked collaboratively with Gayle to resolve the problem. Gayle was comfortable with the idea of telling people (if they asked), "I'm trying to lose weight and I'm keeping track of everything I eat or drink."

Gayle's self-monitoring log revealed that she consumed alcohol on three days during the prior week. She consumed a total of seven drinks for the week. On Friday, her heaviest drinking day, she consumed three drinks. On this day, she met several coworkers for dinner and drinks after work. Although she had significantly reduced her weekly consumption of alcohol, it was difficult to limit her Friday evening drinking. Further discussion of this situation revealed that Gayle had consumed the first two drinks within an hour of arriving at the restaurant, and then had difficulty abstaining from further drinking during dinner. When asked what caused her to stop at three drinks, she said that recording her drinks helped remind her of her drinking goal. She also began thinking about the potential negative consequences of heavy drinking, such as driving while intoxicated. In this situation, self-monitoring led to increased awareness of her drinking goal, and her desire to reduce the harmful consequences of drinking served as a deterrent to further drinking.

---

[2] The guided self-change homework and reading assignments can be found in M. B. and L. C. Sobell *Problem Drinkers: Guided Self-Change Treatment* (1993).

After reviewing her self-monitoring log, the first homework assignment was reviewed. Gayle stated that she was more aware of the antecedents and consequences of her drinking after completing the homework assignment. In Part 1 of this assignment, Gayle was asked to conduct a functional analysis of three high-risk drinking situations. The antecedents and consequences for the high-risk situations are presented in Table 10.1. She identified these situations as posing the greatest risk for heavy drinking. With regard to the first situation, she reported that she drinks heavily when entertaining business clients. The second high-risk situation involves socializing with coworkers, and the third situation involves being home alone on the weekend. In all three situations, Gayle often drank more than she intended and lacked confidence in her ability to reduce her drinking.

A functional analysis can be used to assess both immediate and delayed positive and negative consequences of alcohol use. As the table illustrates, Gayle reported experiencing several short-term positive consequences following alcohol consumption. She was able to identify the delayed negative consequences of drinking, which included a hangover, being late for work, feelings of embarrassment, weight gain, and a loss of self-esteem. However, the short-term consequences of alcohol use (e.g., tension reduction) are often more salient than the long-term consequences (e.g., hangover, expense); therefore, they can exert a stronger influence on behavior. When in a high-risk drinking situation, Gayle reported thinking only about the short-term, positive effects. During subsequent treatment sessions, the information gathered from the functional analysis was used to help develop Gayle's initial treatment plan.

After briefly discussing her high-risk drinking situations, Gayle was given a second homework assignment. The Lifestyle Assessment (M. B. Sobell & Sobell, 1993) inquires about several broad areas of client functioning that may indicate either barriers to change or client strengths that can be used to facilitate change. Social relationships, recreational activities, and availability of alcohol are several of the major areas assessed with this instrument. Gayle was instructed to bring the completed form to the next session. She also was told to continue the self-monitoring exercise.

Session 2

Gayle's weekly self-monitoring log revealed that she consumed a total of seven drinks for the week. She had two drinks during the course of a business dinner, three drinks on Friday when out with coworkers, and two drinks on Saturday evening when home alone. Gayle was aware that she had again exceeded her daily drink limit on Friday. According to her, she had been drinking wine and had purchased the first two drinks herself. The third drink was purchased for her by a coworker and she found it difficult to refuse his offer. Several strategies for dealing with this situation were discussed. First, Gayle could decide how many drinks she was going to have *before* entering a situation. This would help in asserting her commitment to stay within her prescribed drink limit. Second, she could benefit from learning drink refusal skills. Being prepared to deal with offers and even outright pressure to drink would help her *not to drink* when she decides that she doesn't want to. In the situation described above, Gayle felt "on the spot" when the drink was offered.

Table 10.1
Functional Analysis of Selected High-Risk Drinking Situations

| Trigger | Thought | Feeling | Old Behavior | | New Behavior | |
			Behavior	Consequence	Behavior	Consequence
Business dinner	"A drink will help me relax."	Anxious	Drink	Reduce anxiety	Utilize conversation skills	Reduce anxiety
	"If I don't order a drink, I'll have to explain myself."	Worried	Drink	Reduce worry	Order one glass of wine with dinner only	Reduce worry
An evening out with coworkers	"I can't wait to feel the warm glow."	Anticipation	Drink	Increase pleasure	Alternate alcoholic and nonalcoholic drinks	Increase pleasure
	"It's been a stressful week and I need to unwind."	Stress/Tension	Drink	Decrease stress	Limit number of drinks; exercise	Decrease stress
Home alone	"I wish I had someone in my life.	Lonely	Drink	Decrease loneliness	Call a friend; join dating service	Increase social contacts

The situation described above was difficult for Gayle because her coworkers did not know about her decision to reduce her drinking, and she wasn't comfortable telling them that she had a drinking problem. She was concerned that she would lose their respect and that such information could jeopardize opportunities for promotion. Sometimes, telling others about one's drinking problem is useful in eliciting their support; however, Gayle and her therapist determined that it would be unnecessary to share this information with her coworkers. After reviewing the available options, Gayle felt better prepared to deal more effectively with this situation in the future. She decided that she would first say "No, thank you" and then suggest an alternative. Alternatives included having something else to drink or eat. For example, she could say "No, thanks, but I'll have a Coke" or "No, thanks. I'd really like to order something to eat instead. How about sharing an appetizer with me?"

The therapist then arranged a role-play exercise to demonstrate the alternative responses. Gayle was encouraged to anticipate potential difficulties that could arise and to use the skill guidelines she had learned to develop effective alternatives. To assist with this process, Gayle was given a Drink Refusal Skills worksheet (Monti et al., 1989) that included several practice exercises. She was asked to consider how she would respond to the different situations listed on the worksheet.

Gayle's answers to the Lifestyle Assessment revealed that she often drinks in the company of others and that there are some people in whose company she would find it difficult not to drink. She also reported having few friends whom she could count on to support her efforts to reduce drinking. Drink refusal skills could help Gayle address the first situation; the second one was addressed by completing a practice exercise aimed at enhancing her social support network (Monti et al., 1989). Gayle spent time each week engaged in activities that did not involve drinking. This demonstrated that she exercised control of her drinking in other contexts and with other people. For example, she met once a month with members of a book club that read contemporary American literature. There were several older women in the group, and Gayle viewed this as an opportunity to invite one or more of them out for coffee after the discussion group ended to continue their conversations.

After discussing drink refusal skills and completing the practice exercise, Gayle was given a second reading and a companion homework assignment. The reading presents information about how to develop and implement plans to avoid problem drinking in specific high-risk situations. The accompanying homework assignment uses a problem-solving approach to help individuals develop a specific plan of action for coping with a given high-risk situation. Gayle was asked to complete an action plan for each of her three high-risk drinking situations and to bring the completed worksheet to the next session in two weeks.

SESSION 3

The self-monitoring logs were reviewed and revealed that Gayle had been successful in achieving her drinking goals during the preceding two weeks. However, she reported that her newly acquired drink refusal skills had been put to the test. The same coworker had offered to buy her a drink and she refused, saying that she would prefer a bottle of sparkling water instead. The therapist praised Gayle for her success and inquired about her thoughts and feelings about the situation.

Gayle stated that she felt she needed to explain her choice to her coworker, even though she knew it wasn't necessary. The need to explain was viewed as an attempt to head off being pressured by her coworker. Although the coworker accepted her explanation, the therapist asked Gayle to develop several alternative responses for situations in which she felt someone was pressuring her to drink. Next, the homework assignment was reviewed. Gayle's high-risk situations included business dinners, Friday evenings out with coworkers, and being home alone on the weekend. For the first two situations, Gayle decided to drink but not to exceed her two-drink limit. To accomplish this goal, her action plan was to eliminate the before-dinner drink and to have a drink only with her food. To manage her social anxiety, she prepared a list of several open-ended questions that she could use to promote conversation. Her action plan for Friday evenings with coworkers included arriving 30 minutes later, ordering an appetizer, alternating alcoholic with nonalcoholic beverages, and leaving 30 minutes earlier. She decided also to begin work slightly later on Friday mornings to accommodate an early morning exercise class (see below). This would help decrease her stress toward the end of the week, making it easier to maintain her drinking goals on Friday evenings.

The final situation involved being home alone on weekends. On occasion, Gayle drank heavily in this situation to cope with feeling lonely and as an aid to sleep. Her plan involved becoming more active on the weekends. She stated that she was looking into joining a dating service for professionals. Her plan involved having a "coffee date" at least two weekends per month. Her book club met the first Sunday of every month and to "fill up" the other weekend evenings, she enrolled in a Tae Kwon Do class that offered early morning, weekend, and evening classes. Finally, to reduce the risk of "unplanned" drinking, she decided not to keep alcohol in her home.

SESSION 4

During the previous two weeks, Gayle successfully met her drinking goals. She reported that her desire to drink had decreased since beginning treatment, and she identified some benefits of having reduced her drinking. She indicated that she slept better on Friday evenings and woke Saturday mornings feeling more rested. She also described feeling more energetic on evenings when she had a business dinner. She realized that alcohol made her feel tired and had been disrupting her sleep. She also felt good about herself for reaching her goals. She described having greater skill in social situations and reported feeling more at ease when conversing with others. She was also rewarded for her efforts to increase her social/recreational activity. She had been on several fun "coffee dates," had established friendships with two members of her book group, and had lost four pounds. The weight loss was most likely a consequence of her reduced drinking and increased exercise. A follow-up appointment was made for three and six months posttreatment.

THERAPIST-CLIENT FACTORS

One factor to consider is differences in lifestyle, values, and background between therapist and client. In the present case, Gayle, an African American woman, was treated by a White female therapist who had experience working with a diverse clientele. Before beginning treatment, the therapist talked with Gayle about how she felt working with a therapist from a different cultural background. The therapist also sought to identify and address any cultural issues that could affect Gayle's treatment. Although Gayle indicated that she would be comfortable working with the therapist, she did mention that her race might be a factor with some business clients who seemed less open when learning that she was a Black female. As Gayle noted, however, it wasn't clear whether it was because she was Black, female, or both. This issue was addressed in treatment when discussing her fear of negative evaluation by others and the impact of her anxiety on her drinking. In general, much of what the therapist did to be culturally sensitive was to follow good clinical practice, for example, not making assumptions about the meaning of Gayle's thoughts, feelings, or behaviors.

The therapeutic alliance, or working relationship, between therapist and client is another important factor. Defined as a collaborative relationship between therapist and client, it is characterized by a shared view of the tasks and goals of treatment. Among outpatient problem drinkers, the therapeutic alliance has been demonstrated to impact on treatment participation and outcome (Connors, Carroll, DiClemente, Longabaugh, & Donovan, 1997). The guided self-change program facilitates therapist-client collaboration by offering clients the opportunity to select their own treatment goals (with some guidance from the therapist). Self-selection of treatment goals is thought to increase treatment compliance and outcome, presumably because people feel an increased commitment to fulfill their own goals. Although many problem drinkers would prefer to select their own treatment goals (M. B. Sobell, Sobell, Bogardis, Leo, & Skinner, 1992), clients should be advised against a reduced drinking goal if there are contraindications to drinking (e.g., medical reasons).

COURSE OF TERMINATION

As with other structured treatment approaches, the guided self-change program offers a set number of treatment sessions. In this way, the date of termination was known both by Gayle and her therapist at the onset of treatment. At the end of the last formal treatment session, the therapist reviewed Gayle's progress. She reviewed Gayle's goal statement and summarized the many changes she had made to support her reduced drinking goal. The therapist reinforced Gayle's commitment to treatment and supported her sense of self-efficacy by emphasizing that she had the ability to make changes in her life. Gayle was then reminded of the three- and six-month follow-up sessions and that these appointments were important in maintaining the changes she had made. The therapist provided Gayle with a small calendar on which the dates of the two follow-up sessions were circled. The therapist informed Gayle that she could use the calendar to monitor and record her daily drinking during the follow-up period. Any drinking days that exceeded her goals could be circled and discussed during the first follow-up appointment.

FOLLOW-UP

At the three- and six-month follow-up, Gayle completed a Timeline Followback calendar of her drinking behavior for the preceding 90-day period. At the three-month appointment, she reported that she exceeded her daily drinking goal on one occasion. She was on a business trip and had met a friend from college; they had dinner together and Gayle consumed four drinks as the two of them shared stories from their college days. She reported drinking more in an attempt to increase the "pleasure of the moment." When asked if drinking had increased her pleasure, Gayle said that it had not; she said that she was drinking to avoid feelings of sadness. According to Gayle, talking to her friend reminded her of how out of touch she has been with people she once cared about. She also said that her level of intoxication had actually impaired communication with her friend (e.g., slurred speech, difficulty forming her thoughts) and that she woke the next day feeling tired and somewhat embarrassed about her behavior the night before. After thinking about the negative consequences that resulted from her drinking, she stated that she was motivated to resume her goal plan. In this regard, reviewing the negative consequences of drinking served as a deterrent to continued heavy drinking.

At the six-month follow-up, Gayle showed distinct improvement since completing treatment. She increased her abstinent days from 20% to 64%, and the proportion of her total drinking days that were light drinking days ($\leq$ 3 drinks) increased from 54% to 100%. She also reported having more confidence in social situations. From her perspective, she felt less need to drink in these situations because she felt more in control and less anxious.

MANAGED CARE CONSIDERATIONS

As mentioned earlier, Gayle was concerned about her confidentiality and chose to pay for her treatment out-of-pocket. She could afford to do so because she made a good salary and the duration of treatment was relatively brief.

OVERALL EFFECTIVENESS

This case illustrates how behavioral assessment can provide a framework for the treatment of alcohol problems. In addition, the behavioral assessment approach used in this case identified a functional relationship between the client's social skills deficits and her pattern of problem drinking. Social skills deficits were viewed as contributing to both the development and maintenance of the client's alcohol problem. For this reason, the therapist decided to incorporate several social skills training modules into the guided self-change program for the treatment of problem drinkers. In this case, the overall outcome was positive for reducing the client's alcohol consumption. As discussed earlier, individuals with less severe alcohol problems who also have good personal, social, and economic resources often respond well to brief interventions (Bien, Miller, & Tonigan, 1993). Individuals who fail to respond to brief interventions may require a more intensive program of treatment. For these individuals, a "stepped care" approach may be used (M. B. Sobell & Sobell, 1999). Stepped care is relevant to both behavioral assessment and treatment as ongoing assessment information is used to make decisions regarding the most appropriate next level of care. Such an approach is also consistent with general health care practice and would appeal to health care managers seeking empirically based, cost-effective treatment approaches for individuals with alcohol problems.

REFERENCES

American Psychiatric Association. (1994). *Diagnostic and statistical manual of mental disorders* (4th ed.). Washington, DC: Author.

Annis, H. M., & Martin, G. (1985). *Inventory of drug-taking situations.* Toronto, Canada: Addiction Research Foundation of Ontario.

Bien, T. H., Miller, W. R., & Tonigan, J. S. (1993). Brief interventions for alcohol problems: A review. *Addiction, 88,* 315–336.

Connors, G. J., Carroll, K. M., DiClemente, C. C., Longabaugh, R., & Donovan, D. M. (1997). The therapeutic alliance and its relationship to alcoholism treatment participation and outcome. *Journal of Clinical and Consulting Psychology, 65,* 588–598.

First, M. B., Spitzer, R. L., Gibbon, M., & Williams, J. B. W. (1996). *Structured clinical interview for DSM-IV.* Washington, DC: American Psychiatric Press.

Miller, W. R., & Tonigan, S. (1996). Assessing drinkers' motivation for change: The Stages of Change Readiness and Treatment Eagerness Scale (SOCRATES). *Psychology of Addictive Behaviors, 10,* 81–89.

Miller, W. R., Tonigan, S., & Longabaugh, R. (1995). *The Drinker Inventory of Consequences (DrinC): An instrument for assessing adverse consequences of alcohol abuse.* NIAAA Project MATCH monograph series. Washington, DC: Government Printing Office.

Monti, P. M., Abrams, D. B., Kadden, R. M., & Cooney, N. L. (1989). *Treating alcohol dependence.* New York: Guilford Press.

Raistrick, D., Dunbar, G., & Davidson, R. (1983). Development of a questionnaire to measure alcohol dependence. *British Journal of Addiction, 78,* 89–95.

Regier, D. A., Farmer, M. E., Rae, D. S., Locke, B. Z., Keith, S. J., Judd, L. L., et al. (1990). Comorbidity of mental disorders with alcohol and other drug abuse. *Journal of the American Medical Association, 264,* 2511–2518.

Saunders, J. B., Aasland, O. G., Babor, T. F., De La Fuente, J. R., & Grant, M. (1993). Development of the Alcohol Use Disorders Identification Test (AUDIT): WHO collaborative project on early detection of persons with harmful alcohol consumption: II. *Addiction, 88,* 791–804.

Sobell, L. C., & Sobell, M. B. (1992). Timeline Followback: A technique for assessing self-reported ethanol consumption. In J. Allen & R. Z. Litten (Eds.), *Measuring alcohol consumption: Psychosocial and biological methods* (pp. 41–72). Totowa, NJ: Humana Press.

Sobell, L. C., Toneatto, T., & Sobell, M. B. (1994). Behavioral assessment and treatment planning for alcohol, tobacco, and other drug problems: Current status with an emphasis on clinical applications. *Behavior Therapy, 25,* 533–580.

Sobell, M. B., & Sobell, L. C. (1993). *Problem drinkers: Guided self-change treatment.* New York: Guilford Press.

Sobell, M. B., & Sobell, L. C. (1999). Stepped care for alcohol problems: An efficient method for planning and delivering clinical services. In J. A. Tucker, D. M. Donovan, & G. A. Marlatt (Eds.), *Changing addictive behavior: Bridging clinical and public health strategies* (pp. 331–343). New York: Guilford Press.

Sobell, M. B., Sobell, L. C., Bogardis, J., Leo, G. I., & Skinner, W. (1992). Problem drinkers' perceptions of whether treatment goals should be self-selected or therapist-selected. *Behavior Therapy, 23,* 43–52.

Zweben, A., & Fleming, M. F. (1999). Brief interventions for alcohol and drug problems. In J. A. Tucker, D. M. Donovan, & G. A. Marlatt (Eds.), *Changing addictive behavior: Bridging clinical and public health strategies* (pp. 331–343). New York: Guilford Press.

CHAPTER 11

Sexual Dysfunction

BARRY W. McCARTHY

DESCRIPTION OF THE DISORDER

SEXUAL DYSFUNCTION IS a common problem for married couples, nonmarried couples, and single adults, whether straight or gay. A healthy sexually functioning person is capable of desire, arousal, orgasm, and satisfaction. The positive functions of couple sexuality are a shared pleasure, a means to reinforce and deepen intimacy, and a tension reducer to deal with the stresses of life and the relationship.

Dysfunction is divided into primary problems (e.g., primary early ejaculation means the man has always ejaculated rapidly) and secondary problems (e.g., secondary nonorgasmic response means the woman had been orgasmic but is now nonorgasmic). Rates of sexual dysfunction and dissatisfaction remain high (Laumann, Rosen, & Paik, 1999). What has changed since the groundbreaking work of Masters and Johnson (1970) is the reduction in primary dysfunction and the increase in secondary dysfunction. The most common sexual dysfunction, especially among women, is inhibited sexual desire. Kaplan (1974) introduced the concept of desire problems in her triphasic model of sexual function and dysfunction: desire, arousal, and orgasm. The most common secondary dysfunction for males, especially with aging, is erectile problems. Introduction of Viagra in 1998 (Goldstein et al., 1998) has revolutionized both the medical community's and the public's approach to male sexual problems. Viagra is the first user-friendly medical intervention for this problem and can be a valuable therapeutic resource when integrated into a comprehensive assessment and treatment protocol, but it is subject to misuse and can have iatrogenic outcomes (McCarthy, 1999a).

The most common female sexual dysfunctions are (1) inhibited sexual desire; (2) nonorgasmic response during partner sex; (3) painful intercourse (dyspareunia); (4) female arousal dysfunction; (5) primary nonorgasmic response; and (6) vaginismus. The most common male sexual dysfunctions are (1) early ejaculation; (2) erectile dysfunction; (3) inhibited sexual desire; and (4) ejaculatory inhibition.

There have been major advances in the conceptualization, assessment, and treatment of sexual dysfunction in the past 30 years (Leiblum & Rosen, 2000; McCarthy, in press; Wincze & Carey, 2001). Although rates of dysfunction and dissatisfaction remain high, the sex therapy profession is actually shrinking. Reasons for this include lack of licensing for sex therapists, insurance companies not reimbursing for sex therapy, few sex therapy training programs, and little financial support for sex therapy research (with the exception of drug company funding for medical interventions). The controversy over sexual trauma (especially recovered memories of child sexual abuse) has made the field professionally suspect and has resulted in lower status.

Sex therapy is best understood as a subspecialty field. The great majority of sex therapists are trained and licensed in another mental health discipline (clinical or counseling psychology, social work, marriage therapy, psychiatry, pastoral counseling, psychiatric nursing). Sex therapy requires competence in individual therapy, couple therapy, sexual function and dysfunction, and the ability to design and process sexual exercises. Sexual exercises have greatly expanded from the Masters and Johnson sensate focus format to include erotic scenarios and techniques as well as specific exercises for each sexual dysfunction (McCarthy & McCarthy, in press; Wincze & Barlow, 1996).

People presenting for couple sex therapy in the twenty-first century are quite different from those in 1970. Lack of information, primary dysfunction, and rigid, antisexual values are now less common. Dysfunctions now are more likely to be secondary, based on performance and anticipatory anxiety, disappointment and frustration with the spouse, and a conflictual relationship characterized by blame and counterblame. The couple usually has been unsuccessful in previous attempts to resolve the sexual issue. The problem is chronic, with layers of frustration, blame, and a devitalized marriage. Sexual problems do not remain at a plateau; if not resolved, they become more severe and chronic. Couples presenting for sex therapy have complex, chronic problems and low or ambivalent motivation. It is unusual for a sex therapist to be the first health professional consulted; more typically, the person has consulted a physician and might have consulted an individual therapist. Often, the couple has consulted a pastoral counselor or marriage therapist. Unsuccessful attempts to understand and change the problem negatively impact the relationship and expectations for change. This is unfortunate because couple sex therapy is highly successful with motivated couples where the problem is acute.

CASE DESCRIPTION

This case involves 46-year-old Robert, who is in a second marriage with 38-year-old Terri, for whom this is a first marriage. They have been married five years. Sexual problems have existed throughout the marriage. At this point, Robert and Terri avoid trying to be sexual. Using the criterion of being sexual fewer than 10 times a year, they have a nonsexual marriage. A nonsexual relationship affects one in five married couples and one in three nonmarried couples who have been together more than two years (Laumann, Gagnon, Michael, & Michaels, 1994).

When Robert and Terri presented for sex therapy, they were a demoralized couple caught in the cycle of avoidance and a nonsexual marriage. The precipitant for sex therapy was recommendation of a previous marital therapist who saw them once after Terri called saying she felt "hopeless about sex" and their ability to conceive. The therapist worried that the gains made in marital therapy were eroding because of the sexual problems. Robert was reluctant to participate in therapy again, especially with a focus on erection and desire. Typically, males are eager for sex therapy if the focus is on female dysfunction, but embarrassed if the focus is on the man. Their sexual problems were chronic, and neither party felt hopeful. Terri was more aware than Robert of the corrosive effect of the nonsexual state of the marriage. Robert was afraid of the stigma of a second divorce. A prime motivator for Terri was the desire to become pregnant. She experienced the double pressure of wanting a sexual life and a baby, and felt stymied on both fronts. She resented Robert's avoidance and her anger was growing.

CHIEF COMPLAINTS

Robert and Terri had "his, her, and our sexual dysfunctions." They were stuck in the cycle of anticipatory anxiety, tense and faked intercourse attempts, and sexual avoidance. The sexual problems dominated the marriage, draining intimacy and vitality. Robert was experiencing secondary erectile dysfunction and secondary inhibited sexual desire. Terri was experiencing secondary arousal dysfunction and secondary inhibited sexual desire. The sexual dysfunctions were the cause of the infertility problem and were threatening marital viability.

HISTORY

As is often the pattern, Robert and Terri reported that their best sexual experiences were in the first six months of their marriage. Robert especially remembered this as an energetic, erotic period. He had been divorced less than three months but separated over a year when he met Terri. It was a difficult divorce, precipitated by discovery that his wife was engaged in an extramarital affair with someone from work. There had been attempts at reconciliation, but lack of trust and bitterness torpedoed these efforts. Attempts to save the relationship were further stymied by Robert's intermittent erectile problems. Erectile problems had occurred three times before the crisis precipitated by the affair, associated with drinking. Erectile problems now occurred on a regular basis, and Robert blamed this on the affair. When erectile functioning returned strongly with Terri, Robert felt vindicated.

As Robert and Terri began making marriage plans, erectile problems reoccurred on an intermittent basis. This was the first time Terri had encountered erectile dysfunction. She attributed it to "wedding jitters" and was confident it would soon disappear. Instead, Robert and Terri fell into the pattern of anticipatory anxiety, tense and failed intercourse, and increasing sexual avoidance.

Robert consulted a urologist (without Terri's knowledge), who prescribed penile injections. At first they worked and Robert was very pleased. Terri did not understand how suddenly he had such strong erections that did not dissipate after ejaculation. When Terri stimulated the penis she felt a cold sensation, which decreased her erotic response. Robert discouraged her stimulation, wanting to quickly proceed to intercourse. Robert would surreptitiously go into the bathroom, self-inject (he found the injections more painful over time), rush fore-play, and move to intercourse as soon as possible.

Terri thought of herself as prosexual, experiencing no problems with arousal or orgasm. Her pattern was to be orgasmic with manual or oral stimulation, al-though she could be orgasmic during intercourse. However, with this awkward, rushed sexual scenario, she had difficulty feeling turned on and lubricating. Terri was becoming an uninvolved spectator. Once, when the injection was not work-ing well, Terri tried to stimulate Robert. He reacted with frustration and pushed her away. In the emotional heat of this failed sexual experience, the four-month secret of Robert's injections came out. Terri felt she had been "played for a fool," resenting Robert's secrecy. Although they tried injections four more times, it was awkward and self-conscious for both, and no longer effective. Psychological and relational factors can and do subvert medical interventions.

Sex between Robert and Terri became infrequent and unsatisfying. Three years later, Robert (this time with Terri's knowledge) went to the internist to get a prescription for Viagra. The physician did not explore psychological, relational, or sexual factors, but just made sure there were no medical counterindications and wished Robert good luck. Viagra requires sexual desire as well as erotic stim-ulation to facilitate an erection. Robert tried it five times, resulting in intercourse three times, but it was *not* the miracle drug he had anticipated. Erections did not return to the easy, predictable, autonomous pattern of his 20s. Terri found it strange to wait an hour, and there was a tentativeness and self-consciousness about sexual touching, which she experienced as antierotic. She found Robert's preoccupation with the state of his penis off-putting. Sexuality was not inviting, arousal problems worsened, and she no longer felt desire. Robert and Terri were caught in a self-conscious, performance-oriented cycle. Although neither verbal-ized that sex had become more of a struggle than a pleasure, they nonverbally col-luded in sexual avoidance.

Terri suggested they seek marital therapy with a social worker recommended by a friend. Robert was a reluctant participant, but did not want to antagonize Terri. Marriage therapy focused on improving communication and commitment. They liked the therapist and at the beginning felt the intervention was helpful. The assumption was that, with increased closeness, caring, and commitment, sex would improve. This approach is helpful when there are nonspecific sexual prob-lems. However, when there is a specific sexual dysfunction with anxiety and avoidance, directly addressing sexual concerns is necessary.

BEHAVIORAL ASSESSMENT

The format for sex therapy is to conduct the initial session with the couple. This serves a number of functions: viewing sex as a couple issue, emphasizing a collab-orative approach in contrast to guilt/blaming, exploring motivation to address sexual issues, and understanding what had failed in the past so that it is not re-peated. Each person signs a release of information form to consult with present and past therapists, physicians, ministers, or attorneys. These professionals are contacted by phone to discuss assessment, treatment, and recommendations. It is fascinating to compare professionals' and clients' views of treatment and outcome. The urologist had assumed Robert's erectile functioning had been restored. The marital therapist advised continued emphasis on marital communication and commitment; she had no suggestions about sexual functioning. Another issue to assess is whether there is a need for a medical evaluation, especially to rule out side effects of medications as a cause of sexual dysfunction.

The therapy strategy is for each person to take responsibility for his or her sexuality and to join together as an intimate team to develop a comfortable, functional couple sexual style. At the end of the session, the couple is given bibliotherapy, a chapter on revitalizing sexual desire (McCarthy & McCarthy, 1998). This sets a cognitive framework and positive expectations for the change process.

The individual session focuses on assessing positive and negative aspects of sexual development. This is usually a single session, although in selected cases can be as many as five sessions. The therapist's instruction is: "I want to understand as much as possible about you and your sexual development. I ask that you be as honest and frank as possible. At the end, I will ask if there is sensitive or secret information you do not want shared with the spouse. I will respect this and not share it without your permission. However, I need as much information as possible if I am to help you resolve this problem."

Robert's individual history-taking session was anxiety-provoking and challenging and disclosure was difficult for him. He grew up in a traditional family, the middle child of three, all of whom had divorced. His parents liked Terri more than his first wife. As a marital model, the parents were stable, but not close. Robert had minimal sex education from school, none from his parents, and none from the Methodist Sunday school. His first intercourse occurred at age 17 with a 15-year-old high school girlfriend; he ejaculated before intromission and was embarrassed, fearing she would gossip to friends and he would be humiliated. Throughout high school and college, he saw sex as a performance, specifically fearing early ejaculation. He met the first wife as a junior in college; she was a graduating senior majoring in psychology. She had read about ejaculatory control exercises and with her guidance he learned better control. In retrospect, Robert believes he would not have married her except that he felt an obligation for her sexual help. Even before marriage, there were struggles over jobs, money, and especially her desire to live downtown rather than in the suburban neighborhood of which Robert was fond (where he and Terri live). Robert had envisioned a traditional marriage where they had children early, following his parental model. However, she was career- and travel-oriented, and he reluctantly went along. She was disappointed in Robert's career and sexual performance. Robert felt he was always on trial and failing. His response was passive-aggressive, engaging in a series of short affairs.

When his wife told him she was leaving for another man and was pregnant with this man's child, Robert was devastated. The next six months were the worst of his life. He tried desperately to woo her back. The three times they tried to have sex, he was not able to maintain an erection—a source of great frustration and embarrassment. Before the birth of the child, she filed for divorce and obtained a restraining order against Robert. It took a confrontation with a police officer before he accepted the reality of the end of this marriage.

When Terri met Robert three months later, he was a "wounded person." The tonic of her interest, caring, and sexuality restored his confidence. Terri was his advocate against the ex-spouse. Her sexual enthusiasm reawakened his erectile response. In retrospect, Robert realized how dependent he was on women to provide him sexual confidence.

Robert had two sexual secrets: he did not view Terri as attractive as his first wife and he masturbated once a week when at home and daily when on business travel. With masturbation, he had firm erections. It was anxiety that blocked erectile functioning with Terri.

Terri's sexual history illustrated how important it is to conduct histories individually; otherwise, the picture is tainted by giving socially desirable responses in front of the spouse. Terri experienced a number of abusive incidents growing up: She was molested by an older male cousin for four years, had a date rape experience at 16, had two pregnancies resulting in abortion, and felt badly treated during a three-year affair with a married man 15 years her senior. On the positive side, she saw herself as a survivor with a pro-sexual value system. Her parents had been a good marital model and good sex educators, and she benefited from a college-level human sexuality course. Terri was very enthusiastic about Robert, finding him attractive, smart, and successful. Their early sexual relationship was very satisfying; she had felt optimistic about the marriage and them as a sexual couple. She was motivated to have a planned, wanted pregnancy.

Terri was baffled and demoralized by Robert's erection problem and sexual avoidance. It tore at her desire and arousal, although once involved, Terri was orgasmic with Robert's manual and oral stimulation. Previously, she had enjoyed intercourse, but now found it unpleasant and stress-filled. She was disappointed not so much with his erectile functioning as the fact that he was not engaged emotionally or erotically. He was so focused on his penis that he was not involved in the couple encounter.

CASE CONCEPTUALIZATION

The couple feedback session (often scheduled as a double session) is the core intervention in sex therapy. The goals are to create a new narrative and understanding of the sexual problem, which reduces blame and energizes the couple; present the one-two combination of personal responsibility for sexuality and being an intimate team; and introduce the first set of behavioral exercises.

Robert and Terri found the feedback session of great value. Before the session, the therapist phoned Robert to get his permission to share the masturbation secret. Knowing he could get erections would reassure Terri. The strategy of using all their resources to reduce anxiety and build comfort would be a joint effort. The therapist confronted Robert with the point that comparing Terri with the ex-wife was disrespectful, antierotic, and served no useful purpose; it was his responsibility to restructure cognitions about Terri and marital sexuality.

The feedback format is to talk about each spouse's strengths and vulnerabilities (traps) and then about couple strengths and traps. The session is structured and the therapist's activity level is high. Each person is encouraged to ask questions and clarify issues. Being explicit about traps is particularly valuable in highlighting what needs to be confronted so they do not repeat self-defeating behavior.

Feedback began with Terri (focusing first on the less dysfunctional spouse reinforces that this is a team effort, with each having a role). Organizing themes were that Terri had overcome sexual problems in the past, her interest and arousal were healthy for the relationship, and her enthusiasm was necessary in revitalizing sexual desire and rebuilding positive anticipation. An important side effect was that Robert listened (for the first time) to Terri's abuse history and this increased his respect for her. Terri found such comprehensive feedback enlightening; it reinforced her view of herself as a survivor who deserved a successful marital, sexual life and a planned, wanted baby.

Robert's feedback focused on the themes of performance anxiety, dependence on the woman to rescue him sexually, and fear of a second divorce. So much of Robert's motivation was negative. He did not acknowledge strengths (successful career, attractiveness, a good person, desire for a healthy marriage, would be an excellent father), but was acutely aware of psychological and sexual deficits. He was paralyzed by fear and sexual anxieties and took the easy way out by avoiding. Disclosing that erections were functional during masturbation had a major positive impact on both Robert and Terri. Robert had to confront avoidance and relearn couple sexuality as a shared pleasure, not a fearful performance. He needed to take personal responsibility for changing sexual attitudes, behavior, and emotions. Terri was his intimate friend and supporter, but could not do it for him. Viagra would be used as an additional resource to increase psychological confidence and vasocongestion, not as a "magic pill" to cure him (McCarthy, 1999a). Robert needed to be honest with himself and honest with Terri. The shared goal was to build a couple sexual style that was vital and resilient. The trap was that Robert would not "show up" psychologically or sexually.

This couple shared common goals of wanting a stable and satisfying marriage, children, and a vital sexual life, but felt stymied and demoralized. They were caught in the cycle of self-blame and blaming the spouse; the poison of a nonsexual marriage controlled them. The challenge of personal responsibility for sexuality and being an intimate team in confronting sexual problems was one they were prepared to confront. It would have been easier to address this four years earlier, when the problem was acute. However, the therapist's role was to help Robert and Terri maintain motivation and focus.

Robert and Terri were given two assignments. The first was to process the feedback within 48 hours, clarifying what elements were on target, what was unclear, and what was not helpful. Second involved beginning the behavior change program, with exercises on rebuilding sexual desire. Terri was to initiate the comfort exercise and Robert the attraction exercise (McCarthy & McCarthy, in press). For cases of inhibited sexual desire, it is better to start with these exercises rather than the nongenital pleasuring (sensate focus) exercises.

Some clients may not be able to handle this much material, in which case, the therapist would reduce and individualize the feedback and assignments. Robert and Terri were energized by the feedback and exercises. The prescription for vital marital sexuality is intimacy, pleasuring, and eroticism. In sharing information and processing the feedback, Terri felt more emotionally connected to Robert than in the past four years. This put an extra dimension into the relationship that had not been elicited in marital therapy. Nondemand pleasuring with a focus on comfort and a prohibition on intercourse was inviting: Robert felt turned on. The instruction to be genuine in saying what was attractive about Terri freed Robert to express what was unique about her and reduced comparisons with the ex-wife. His requests of Terri involved nonsexual behaviors. Indeed, she was open to changing: to wear her hair differently, to take a financial planning course with him (after completing sex therapy), and to relate in a compassionate manner toward his physically handicapped brother. Terri's requests of Robert were physical: exercising together to improve muscle tone and attractiveness, washing genitals before sex, looking at and talking to her during the sexual encounter.

RATIONALE FOR CHOICE OF COUPLE SEX THERAPY

Couple sex therapy is a semistructured intervention, with initially high therapist activity and structure, decreasing as therapy progresses. The format of the first session is to process exercises and experiences of the prior week, exploring positive learning, feelings, and skills (5:1 positive:negative is an optimum learning ratio), and then to examine anxieties, inhibitions, and disappointments. This is crucial in designing and individualizing exercises. Exercises serve a dual function. The primary function is to develop sexual comfort and skill and create erotic scenarios and techniques. A secondary function is diagnostic and is part of the ongoing assessment/intervention process: What attitudes, behaviors, and emotions block intimacy and sexuality? Which can be changed, which modified, and which must be accepted and worked around so progress can continue? An example of change was that Terri's arousal served as a cue for Robert's arousal rather than anxiety and intimidation. An example of modification was use of a waterbased lubricant to facilitate Terri's arousal so that intromission was easier. An example of acceptance was that Robert allowed Terri to initiate and guide intromission rather than insisting that was the male's role.

The second part of the session examines psychological and interpersonal factors that facilitate or subvert the sexual process. Examples include refining initiation techniques, offering an alternative way to connect instead of just saying no, building comfort with verbal and nonverbal guidance, making time for sexual experiences, being open to planned and spontaneous sexual dates, returning to themes from the feedback session, examining personal vulnerabilities with the spouse being empathic and supportive, and dealing with external factors (jobs, children, house, financial conflicts).

The last phase involves discussing exercises for the coming week and other assignments (readings, watching videotapes, writing exercises) and ensuring there is a positive focus. Issues of ambivalence, worry, and frustration are addressed. The therapist emphasizes that this is a gradual change process, learning from mistakes and conflicts and establishing positive, realistic expectations.

COURSE OF TREATMENT

The second session consisted of developing a trust position so that, if there were a problem, rather than give up, Robert and Terri would reconnect. Then they could either return to the exercise or end the experience in a positive manner. What is not acceptable is the anxiety-avoidance pattern.

The prime focus was erectile function and dysfunction. They were given the guidelines in Table 11.1 to discuss and refer to throughout therapy; these also served as the basis for relapse prevention.

Between sessions 2 and 3, Robert and Terri began genital pleasuring exercises, with a continued ban on intercourse and orgasm. The following week, they watched a psychoeducational videotape on erectile function (Focus, 1994) and

Table 11.1
Arousal and Erection Guidelines

1. By age 40, 90% of males experience at least one erectile failure. This is a normal occurrence, not a sign of erectile dysfunction.
2. The majority of erectile problems (especially for men under 50) are caused primarily by psychological or relationship factors, not medical or physiological malfunctions. To comprehensively evaluate medical factors, including side effects of medication, consult a urologist with training in erectile function and dysfunction.
3. Erectile problems can be caused by a wide variety of factors, including alcohol use, anxiety, depression, vascular or neurological deficits, distraction, anger, side effects of medication, frustration, hormonal deficiency, fatigue, and not feeling sexual at that time or with that partner. As men age, the hormonal, vascular, and neurological systems become less efficient, so psychological, relational, and erotic factors become more important.
4. Medical interventions, especially the oral medication Viagra, can be a valuable resource to facilitate erectile function, but are not a "magic pill." The couple needs to integrate Viagra (or other medical interventions) into their lovemaking style.
5. Do not believe the myth "The male machine is ready to have intercourse at any time, with any woman, in any situation." You and your penis are human. You are not a performance machine.
6. View the erectile difficulty as a situational problem; do not overreact and label yourself "impotent" or put yourself down as a "failure."
7. It is a pervasive myth that if a man loses his initial erection, it means he is sexually turned off. It is a natural physiological process for erections to wax and wane during prolonged pleasuring.
8. In a 45-minute pleasuring session, erections can wax and wane two to five times. Subsequent erections, intercourse, and orgasm are quite satisfying.
9. You do not need an erect penis to satisfy a woman. Orgasm can be achieved through manual, oral, or rubbing stimulation. If you have difficulty getting or maintaining an erection, do not stop the sexual interaction. Women find it arousing to have the partner's fingers, tongue, or penis (erect or flaccid) used for stimulation.
10. Actively involve yourself in giving and receiving pleasurable and erotic touching. Erection is a natural result of pleasure, feeling turned on, and eroticism.
11. You cannot will or force an erection. Do not be a "passive spectator" who is distracted by the state of his penis. Sex is not a spectator sport; it requires active involvement.
12. Allow the woman to initiate intercourse and guide your penis into her vagina. This reduces performance pressure and, because she is the expert on her vagina, is the most practical procedure.
13. Feel comfortable saying "I want sex to be pleasurable and playful. When I feel pressure to perform, I get uptight and sex is not good. We can make sexuality enjoyable by taking it at a comfortable pace, enjoy playing and pleasuring, and being an intimate team."
14. Erectile problems do not affect the ability to ejaculate (men can ejaculate with a flaccid penis). The man relearns ejaculation to the cue of an erect penis.
15. One way to regain confidence is through masturbation. During masturbation, you can practice gaining and losing erections, relearn ejaculation with an erection, and focus on fantasies and stimulation that transfer to partner sex.
16. Do not try to use a waking erection for quick intercourse. This erection is associated with REM sleep and results from dreaming and being close to the partner. Men try vainly to have intercourse with the morning erection before losing it. Remember: Arousal and erection are regainable. Morning is a good time to be sexual.

Table 11.1 *(Continued)*

17. When sleeping, you have an erection every 90 minutes, three to five erections a night. Sex is a natural physiological function. Do not block it by anticipatory anxiety, performance anxiety, distraction, or putting yourself down. Give yourself (and your partner) permission to enjoy the pleasure of sexuality.
18. Make clear, direct, assertive requests (not demands) for stimulation you find erotic. Verbally and nonverbally guide your partner in how to pleasure and arouse you.
19. Stimulating a flaccid penis is counterproductive. The man becomes distracted and obsessed with the state of his penis. Engage in sensuous, playful, nondemand touching. Enjoy giving and receiving stimulation rather than trying to will or force an erection.
20. Attitudes and self-thoughts affect arousal. The key is "sex and pleasure," not "sex and performance."
21. A sexual experience is best measured by pleasure and satisfaction, not whether you had an erection, how hard it was, or whether she was orgasmic. Some sexual experiences will be great for both, some better for one than the other, some mediocre, and others unsuccessful. Do not put your sexual self-esteem on the line at each experience.

practiced the "wax and wane" erection exercise. The prohibition remained on intercourse, but Robert was instructed to take Viagra an hour before the exercise. This allowed him to experience the positive effects of Viagra free from pass-fail intercourse performance.

For Robert, the "window of opportunity" for penile functioning had been very narrow; if he did not have intercourse on his first erection, he panicked. Realizing he could regain an erection and that Terri's arousal and stimulation were synergistic with his feeling turned on was a freeing experience. Prolonged touching and a variety of manual and oral erotic scenarios were highly arousing for Terri. Integrating intimacy, pleasuring, and eroticism is congruent with the woman's sexual response pattern (Basson, 2000). Perhaps this is why women respond better to sex therapy than men. There are specific exercises to enhance female arousal, but these were not needed. Terri's responsiveness to manual and oral erotic scenarios enhanced Robert's arousal and reduced intercourse performance anxiety.

The prohibition was lifted on orgasm, but remained in place for intercourse. Robert was able to maintain an erection and was orgasmic on Terri's manual stimulation, which he preferred to oral stimulation. In the therapy sessions, Terri and Robert processed two themes. The first was that it was normal to engage in self-stimulation during partner sex; Terri felt freer in this regard than Robert, but with time and practice he too accepted this as an erotic technique. The second theme was acceptance of a variable, flexible sexual repertoire. Robert, like most males, believed that "normal sex" is intercourse, you do not need anything from the woman to be aroused, you go to intercourse on the first erection, and sex is totally predictable for the man. This might be true (although not optimal) in one's 20s, but is not true of men in their 40s and older. It is well understood that the traditional double standard damages the sexuality of young women, but double standard learning is even more damaging to the sexuality of middle-age and older men (McCarthy, 2001a). Terri assured Robert that sex was not a competition. At times, he would be more aroused; at other times, she would be more aroused. Sexual variability is normal and healthy.

A major emotional theme was self-acceptance. Robert had an unstable self-esteem, controlled by performance (professionally and sexually) and external approval. The balance between internal and external sources of self-esteem ideally is 60:40; for Robert it was 20:80. He was extremely sensitive and reactive to negative feedback; his response was avoidance or passive-aggression. Terri did not want the role of worst critic or rescuing spouse. Robert needed to respect himself with his strengths and weaknesses. A series of writing and cognitive homework tasks helped him increase respect and self-acceptance. This included seeing sexuality as a positive, integral part of his personality. Terri commented, "You put terrible pressure on your penis." Robert no longer felt he was an unsuccessful intercourse away from being a "failure as a man."

The emotional theme for Terri was that she deserved a healthy marriage, a wanted child, and a satisfying sexual life. She was insightful about past traps and trauma, but found it difficult to integrate this with positive self-esteem and a solid sense of psychological well-being. Terri found Robert's empathy and support of great value, and his respect for her increased.

Intercourse exercises (McCarthy & McCarthy, in press) focus on integrating intercourse as a natural extension of the pleasuring/erotic process. Robert and Terri had developed a sexual style of mutual stimulation, multiple stimulation, and talking as an erotic enhancer. When they returned to intercourse, Robert's instinctive reaction was to revert to the traditional scenario of a single focus on intercourse, no talking, and no additional erotic stimulation. As the intercourse exercises were discussed in therapy, an aware, erotic scenario was proposed. Terri took the initiative in deciding when to transition into intercourse, guide intromission, engage in multiple stimulation before and during intercourse, and continue erotic talk throughout the encounter. Intercourse is not a pass-fail event, but a continuation of the erotic experience. Cognitively, the association is with "pleasure," not "performance." Emotionally, intercourse is involving and mutual. Robert no longer felt "like a deer caught in the headlights." He enjoyed a mutual approach to pleasuring and eroticism, and continued this during intercourse. He experienced intercourse as mutual, intimate, and erotic. This plus use of Viagra for the first three intercourse experiences facilitated successful integration.

For the fourth experience, Robert was instructed to not use Viagra, but practice an erotic, nonintercourse scenario to orgasm. Both Robert and Terri found this arousing. To Robert's surprise, Terri initiated intercourse, which went as well as it had with Viagra. Terri shared with Robert that she found it easier and just as satisfying to be orgasmic during nonintercourse sex; she enjoyed intercourse, but it was not a demand. Robert also enjoyed nonintercourse sex to orgasm, but preferred intercourse. Terri understood this, but insisted they follow the assigned exercise the next time.

In processing experiences at the next therapy session, the clinician emphasized the importance of a comfortable, aware, flexible couple style and acceptance of the normal variability of sexual response. Terri found this easier to accept than Robert. She recounted experiences over the prior six weeks when she enjoyed sensual and erotic feelings even though she did not have an orgasm, experiences when she was highly desiring and orgasmic with oral stimulation, and other times when she felt sensual but not erotic. The clinician validated Robert's preference for predictable arousal and orgasm during intercourse, but cautioned that this not be a perfectionistic demand (which would set him up for failure). They were encouraged to experiment with planned sexual dates when he would use Viagra and spontaneous dates when he did not. He was urged to be open to experiences, sensations, and feelings, and share these with Terri. Robert was aware that Viagra facilitates eroticism and other times eroticism flows on its own.

THERAPIST-CLIENT FACTORS

The major function of the sex therapist is to maintain the couple's motivation and focus. Especially at the beginning of therapy, the clinician takes a very active role in structuring interventions, providing sexuality education and permission, and designing and individualizing sexual exercises. As therapy progresses, the clinician takes a less directive role, encouraging spouses to develop healthy attitudes and skills so they can be their own therapist.

As therapy progresses, the focus is more on emotional and sexual intimacy than sexual dysfunction. Gradually, the focus turns to the couple's agenda. However, the therapist *never* walks in without an agenda and asks "What's up?" The cognitive-behavioral sex therapist has a range of strategies and techniques to help individuals and couples change attitudes, behaviors, and emotional responses. Exercises are individualized depending on progress and feedback.

COURSE OF TERMINATION

One of the worst mistakes clinicians (especially physicians) make is to terminate treatment when sexual functioning resumes. The goal of successful treatment is *not* just to create desire, arousal, and orgasm. It is to *maintain* a comfortable, functional sexual relationship. Positive, realistic expectations means 85% of sexual experiences involve intercourse. The couple is comfortable with two back-up scenarios: The first a comfortable, sensual way to connect and share pleasurable touching, with an understanding that they will be sexual in the next day or two when feeling aware, responsive, and erotic; the second scenario involves erotic techniques using nonintercourse sex (manual, oral, or rubbing stimulation) to orgasm for one or both partners. The couple accept that whether once every 10 times, once a month, or once a year, it is normal for a sexual experience to be negative or a failure. Unless this is understood and acknowledged, they are "only one failure from feeling back at square one."

When therapy sessions are reduced to every other week, the couple is encouraged to continue to preserve the time for themselves. They may take a walk and discuss progress, have a sexual date, process an exercise, or go out for a cup of coffee and focus on problem-solving a nonsexual conflict. Setting aside couple time reinforces the value of the relationship.

The couple is encouraged to engage in "do it yourself" exercises. They are also encouraged to use the exercise structure with communication and problem-solving skills to deal with nonsexual issues.

The best relapse-prevention strategy is high-quality, comprehensive sex therapy (McCarthy, 1993). This was particularly important for Terri and Robert because they wanted to maintain a vital sexual relationship during and after pregnancy. Avoidance of sex subverts the marital relationship. Like any behavior, avoidance feeds on itself; it resensitizes anxiety and dysfunction, and the couple become self-conscious, which interferes with erotic flow. Robert and Terri reached an agreement that if two weeks went by without a sexual interaction, Terri would initiate an intercourse date. If that did not occur within a week, Robert would initiate an erotic, nonintercourse date. If a month went by without a sexual experience, they would call and schedule a "booster session."

A major issue was when to make a concerted effort to become pregnant. For Robert and Terri, sex with the goal of conception was an aphrodisiac. When they did not become pregnant immediately, there was disappointment. In therapy, they explored their different emotional coping styles. Terri was tearful and very upset for two to three days, but after grieving, would be reenergized and ready to try again. Robert minimized his frustration and sadness, but regressed to passivity and avoidance. He depended on Terri to express grief and reenergize sex. He had to learn to be responsible for and express his emotions and sexuality, not be dependent on and reactive to Terri. The next time Terri announced that her period had begun, Robert was to spend 30 minutes alone being aware of his emotions and then initiate a conversation in which he expressed his feelings. For the first time since she knew him, Terri saw Robert cry. (He had cried alone, which she had not known.) Terri mistakenly had labeled Robert a "cold fish." Tears are a powerful emotional expression; like sexuality, tears are an interpersonal phenomenon. Sharing positive and negative emotions increases marital trust and intimacy.

For many couples, the strategy is to separate sexuality and conception. It is easier to become pregnant using insemination with the husband's sperm than intercourse (Elliott, 1998). Conception using medical interventions has the effect of reducing sexual anxiety and allows sex therapy to proceed with a focus on pleasure and eroticism. This was not the right strategy for Robert and Terri, who enjoyed sex during the week of high probability for conception. Robert seldom used Viagra, but would do so if, the night before, he did not have an erection sufficient for intravaginal ejaculation. After five months, they were successful: a cause of great celebration.

They agreed to reduce therapy sessions to once a month. The therapeutic focus was to maintain a close couple connection, both emotionally and sexually, to prepare for the transition to being a family. To their surprise, they were pregnant with twins. Terri reacted with strong emotion and began to mobilize for the challenge. Robert was encouraged to attend prepared childbirth classes and be actively involved as a coach. They used sitting-kneeling and side rear-entry intercourse, the two easiest positions for third trimester intercourse. This required communication and experimentation, and they remained intimately connected throughout the pregnancy. The birth of their daughters was one of the highlights of their life and a strong bonding experience.

FOLLOW-UP

The last two sessions focused on relapse prevention. Jacobson and Addis (1993) note the disturbing trend toward relapse after therapy termination. Relapse prevention is an integral component of couple sex therapy. Different dysfunctions require specific strategies and techniques: Relapse prevention for inhibited sexual desire (McCarthy, 1999b) has different components than relapse prevention for erectile dysfunction (McCarthy, 2001b).

The guidelines in Table 11.2 are given to couples to reinforce a relapse-prevention program for inhibited sexual desire.

Table 11.2
Guidelines for Revitalizing and Maintaining Sexual Desire

1. The keys to sexual desire are positive anticipation and feeling you deserve sexual pleasure.
2. Each person is responsible for his or her desire, with the couple functioning as an intimate team to nurture and enhance desire. Revitalizing sexual desire is a couple task. Guilt and blame subvert the change process.
3. Inhibited desire is the most common sexual dysfunction, affecting one in three couples. Sexual avoidance drains intimacy and vitality from the marital bond.
4. One in five married couples has a nonsexual relationship (being sexual fewer than 10 times a year). One in three nonmarried couples who have been together longer than two years has a nonsexual relationship.
5. The average frequency of sexual intercourse is between four times a week to once every two weeks. For couples in their 20s, the average sexual frequency is two to three times a week; for couples in their 50s, once a week.
6. The initial romantic love/passionate sex type of desire lasts less than two years and usually less than six months. Desire is facilitated by an intimate, interactive relationship.
7. Contrary to the myth that "horniness" occurs after not being sexual for weeks, desire is facilitated by a regular rhythm of sexual activity. When sex occurs less than twice a month, couples become self-conscious and fall into a cycle of anticipatory anxiety, tense and unsatisfying sex, and avoidance.
8. A key strategy is to develop "her," "his," and "our" bridges to sexual desire. This involves ways of thinking, talking, anticipating, and feeling that invite sexual encounters.
9. The essence of sexuality is giving and receiving pleasure-oriented touching. The prescription to maintain desire is intimacy, pleasuring, and eroticism.
10. Touching occurs both inside and outside the bedroom. Touching is valued for itself. Both the man and woman are comfortable initiating. Both partners feel free to say no and to suggest an alternative way to connect and share pleasure. Touching should not always lead to intercourse.
11. Couples who maintain a vital sexual relationship can use the metaphor of touching involving "five gears." First gear is clothes on, affectionate touch (holding hands, kissing, hugging). Second gear is nongenital, sensual touch, which can be clothed, semiclothed, or nude (body massage, cuddling on the couch, showering together, touching while going to sleep or on awakening). Third gear is playful touch, which intermixes genital and nongenital touching, clothed or unclothed, and may take place in bed, dancing, in the shower, or on the couch. Fourth gear is erotic touch (manual, oral, or rubbing) to arousal and orgasm for one or both partners. Fifth gear integrates pleasurable and erotic touch that flows into intercourse.
12. Personal turn-ons facilitate sexual anticipation and desire. These include the use of fantasy and erotic scenarios, as well sex associated with special celebrations or anniversaries, sex with the goal of conception, sex when feeling caring and close, or even sex to soothe a personal disappointment.
13. External turn-ons (R- or X-rated videos, music, candles, visual feedback from mirrors, locations other than the bedroom, a weekend away without the kids) can elicit sexual desire.
14. Males and females with hormonal deficits may use testosterone injections, patches, or creams to enhance sexual desire, but only under supervision. Medical problems and side effects of medication can interfere with sexual desire and function.

(continued)

211

Table 11.2   (Continued)

15. Sexuality has a number of positive functions: a shared pleasure, a means to reinforce and deepen intimacy, and a tension-reducer to deal with the stresses of life and marriage.
16. "Intimate coercion" is not acceptable. Sexuality is neither a reward nor a punishment. Healthy sexuality is voluntary, mutual, and pleasure-oriented.
17. Realistic expectations are crucial for maintaining a healthy sexual relationship. It is self-defeating to demand equal desire, arousal, orgasm, and satisfaction each time. A positive, realistic expectation is that 50% of experiences are very good for both partners; 20% are very good for one partner (usually the man) and fine for the other; 20% are acceptable but not remarkable. Thus, 5% to 15% of sexual experiences are mediocre or failures. Couples who accept this without guilt or blaming and try again when they are receptive and responsive will have a vital, resilient sexual relationship.
18. If the couple has gone two weeks without any sexual contact, the partner with higher desire takes the initiative to set up a planned or spontaneous sexual date. If that does not occur, the other partner initiates a sensual or play date during the following week. If that does not occur and they have gone a month without sexual contact, they call for a "booster" therapy session.
19. Healthy sexuality plays a positive, integral role (15% to 20%) in a relationship, with the main function to energize the bond and generate special feelings. Bad or nonexistent sex has a more powerful negative role than good sex has a positive role. Desire is the core of sexuality.

Robert and Terri were highly motivated and wrote out their strategy to maintain a vital intimate connection after the twins were born. They discussed specific attitudes and techniques to ensure that the husband-wife bond remained vital. With sleep deprivation and parenting tasks, they would have less time and energy to be a couple, but they were committed to maintaining a sexual connection and not regress to self-consciousness, anxiety, and avoidance.

Robert and Terri agreed to six-month follow-ups for the next two years and to call if there was a problem before it became a crisis. Interestingly, the two sessions they scheduled were to discuss nonsexual issues. The first was that Robert's mother was discovered to have a six-year pattern of embezzlement. On one level, Robert was shocked, but on a basic level, he knew something was drastically wrong with his parents' lives and marriage. He could not save his parents, but did encourage them to use this crisis as a wake-up call to confront chronic problems in their lives and marriage. The second session involved discussing the common struggle of balancing career, parenting, and being a couple. This helped confirm their decision to not have more children, and Robert volunteered to have a vasectomy.

Robert and Terri now had the ability to be their own therapist and deal with issues and problems as they occurred. The majority of crises can be prevented by the couple's being aware, planning, not falling into high-risk situations, and making good decisions. However, even with the best plans, sometimes bad things cannot be prevented. Either way, the couple needs to mobilize to deal with problems, crises, and losses. It is hoped that they now are inoculated against sexual problems. If problems do reoccur, they are addressed as an intimate team while in the acute phase.

Robert and Terri were seen in the active phase of treatment for 21 sessions over a 14-month period. The relapse-prevention component included two additional sessions over a two-year period.

MANAGED CARE CONSIDERATIONS

Sex therapists seldom deal with managed care because insurance companies do not reimburse for sex therapy. This is not reasonable because sex therapy is a clearly spelled-out protocol that is usually of moderate duration (12 to 20 sessions). Successful sex therapy has a number of positive effects for the psychological well-being of both individuals. Although some insurance companies do reimburse for marital therapy, they are extremely resistant to reimbursing for sex therapy.

There are a number of negative effects of this policy. Couples either do not receive treatment or consult a physician and receive a medical remedy for what is primarily a psychological/interpersonal disorder. Medical interventions usually involve only one partner, which negates the interpersonal and intimacy dimensions of sexuality. Unfortunately, it is unlikely that managed care companies will change their policy. An alternative strategy is to bill sex therapy either as individual therapy for an anxiety-based disorder or as marriage therapy. This involves difficult ethical and insurance issues for both the clinician and the couple.

OVERALL EFFECTIVENESS

Although the sex therapy literature is growing in comprehensiveness and sophistication (Leiblum & Rosen, 2000), it has not received the careful empirical consideration it deserves and needs. Heiman and Meston (1997) reviewed sex therapy research with recommendations for further empirical research, especially outcome data.

Sex therapy is most effective with committed, motivated couples, where the dysfunction is acute, anxiety-based, where there is a female dysfunction, and where the couple is receptive to permission giving, behavioral exercises, and a variable, flexible approach to developing a couple sexual style. Conversely, couples with a poor prognosis are alienated and blaming, threatening divorce, have a chronic problem, have a male dysfunction and he is avoidant, and have a major sexual secret. When one or both reject a gradual, semistructured approach to rebuilding sexual comfort and confidence and demand a quick solution and return to romantic love/passionate sex, the sex therapist is in a no-win situation. Another example of a poor prognosis is a couple with a hidden agenda (ongoing affair, plan to leave the marriage but want to become pregnant first, financial manipulation, sexual orientation or paraphilia issues, no motivation to revitalize marital sex). Here, even though there is a sexual dysfunction, sex therapy is not necessarily the treatment of choice.

Sex therapy is applicable for nonmarried couples, gay and lesbian couples, and single people without partners. It is crucial to establish a clear therapeutic contract that is acceptable to each person and has a realistic chance of success. An example is a gay couple, in which one partner had a severe problem of ejaculatory inhibition; he coped by being the giving partner in oral sex, and was orgasmic with self-stimulation during telephone chat sessions. This pattern eroded the frequency and vitality of the sexual relationship. In therapy, they were motivated to view sexuality as a couple issue. Behavioral exercises focused on desire, eroticism, and ejaculatory inhibition were successful in improving functioning and building an involving, erotic couple sexual style.

An example of an inappropriate sex therapy case was an unmarried couple who had been living together for three years. The man had a primary dysfunction of early ejaculation and, in the prior year, impaired erectile function; he would thrust as rapidly as possible so that he ejaculated before the erection dissipated. The woman initiated therapy and was the motivated partner. Her hidden agenda was that if the sex improved, he would be satisfied with the relationship and they would marry. Although resolving a sexual dysfunction enhances a relationship, sex is not a litmus test for marriage. In conducting individual histories, it was apparent that although he valued her and the relationship, he did not see this as a viable marriage nor she as an appropriate marital partner. In the couple feedback session, the therapist clarified the limitations of sex therapy and elucidated each person's motivations. Such confrontation with the reality of the situation caused her to realize that this was a fatally flawed relationship. He was relieved that it was her decision because he was ambivalent about both sex therapy and the relationship. Thus, an inadvertent function of sex therapy is to break up tenuous or fatally flawed couples.

Sex therapy strategies and techniques can be useful for single people without partners. Especially valuable is the sexual history process, bibliotherapy, psychoeducational videotapes, masturbation and fantasy training, and guidelines for choosing a partner. Female sexuality groups, which are semistructured and time-limited, can be valuable, especially in addressing primary orgasmic dysfunction and sexual desire issues. Unfortunately, male sexuality groups have been very difficult to organize because of stigma and reluctance to disclose dysfunction to other men.

SUMMARY

Sex therapy is a subspecialty skill. Intimacy and sexuality play a positive, integral role when functional and satisfying, contributing 15% to 20% to marital vitality. However, when sex is dysfunctional or absent, or involves an extramarital affair or fertility problems, sex plays an inordinately powerful negative role, draining the relationship of vitality. Sexuality is a major force in relationship disintegration and divorce.

Couple sex therapy strategies and techniques address desire, arousal, orgasm, and satisfaction. The prescription for healthy, integrated sexuality is intimacy, pleasuring, and eroticism. Each person is responsible for his or her sexuality and the couple are an intimate team. This concept is core in the assessment, treatment, and prevention of sexual problems.

REFERENCES

Basson, N. (2000). The female sexual response. *Journal of Sex and Marital Therapy, 26,* 51–65.

Elliott, S. (1998). The relationship between fertility issues and sexual problems in men. *Canadian Journal of Human Sexuality, 7,* 295–303.

Focus. (1994). *Erection* [Videotape]. Focus International.

Goldstein, I., Lue, T., Padma-Nathan, H., Rosen, R., Steers, W., & Wicker, P. (1998). Oral sildenafil in the treatment of erectile dysfunction. *New England Journal of Medicine, 338,* 1397–1404.

Heiman, J., & Meston, M. (1997). Empirically validated treatment for sexual dysfunction. *Annual Review of Sex Research, 8,* 148–197.

Jacobson, N., & Addis, M. (1993). Research on couples and couples therapy. *Journal of Consulting and Clinical Psychology, 61,* 85–93.

Kaplan, H. (1974). Hypoactive sexual desire. *Journal of Sex and Martial Therapy, 3,* 3–9.

Laumann, E., Gagnon, J., Michael, R., & Michaels, S. (1994). *The social organization of sexuality.* Chicago: University of Chicago Press.

Laumann, E., Rosen, R., & Paik, A. (1999). Sexual dysfunction in the United States. *Journal of the American Medical Association, 281*(6), 537–544.

Leiblum, S., & Rosen, R. (Eds.). (2000). *Principles and practice of sex therapy* (3rd ed.). New York: Guilford Press.

Masters, W., & Johnson, V. (1970). *Human sexual inadequacy.* Boston: Little, Brown.

McCarthy, B. (1993). Relapse prevention strategies and techniques in sex therapy. *Journal of Sex and Marital Therapy, 19,* 142–146.

McCarthy, B. (1999a). Integrating Viagra into cognitive-behavioral sex therapy. *Journal of Sex Education and Therapy, 23,* 302–308.

McCarthy, B. (1999b). Relapse prevention strategies and techniques for inhibited sexual desire. *Journal of Sex and Marital Therapy, 25,* 297–303.

McCarthy, B. (2001a). Male sexuality after fifty. *Journal of Family Psychotherapy, 12*(1), 29–37.

McCarthy, B. (2001b). Relapse prevention strategies and techniques for erectile dysfunction. *Journal of Sex and Marital Therapy, 27,* 1–8.

McCarthy, B. (in press). Sexuality, sexual dysfunction, and couple therapy. In A. Gurman & N. Jacobson (Eds.), *Clinical handbook of couple therapy* (3rd ed.). New York: Guilford Press.

McCarthy, B., & McCarthy, E. (1998). *Couple sexual awareness.* New York: Carroll and Graf.

McCarthy, B., & McCarthy, E. (in press). *Sexual awareness: Couples sexuality for the 21st century.* New York: Carroll and Graf.

Rosen, R., & Leiblum, S. (1995). *Case studies in sex therapy.* New York: Guilford Press.

Wincze, J., & Barlow, D. (1996). *Enhancing sexuality: Client workbook.* New York: Graywind.

Wincze, J., & Carey, M. (2001). *Sexual dysfunction.* New York: Guilford Press.

CHAPTER 12

Marital Dysfunction

GARY R. BIRCHLER and WILLIAM S. FALS-STEWART

DESCRIPTION OF THE DISORDER

MARITAL SEPARATION AND divorce have increased dramatically during the past several decades and have significantly affected a vast majority of individuals, couples, and families in our country. It is estimated that nearly half of all couples are expected to divorce in the foreseeable future (Bray & Hetherington, 1993). Approximately 66% of women and 75% of men remarry within five years; more than half of these second marriages also end in divorce (Glick & Lin, 1986; Hennon, 1983). Given these social trends and the associated consequences of marital conflict, separation, and divorce, marital dysfunction constitutes a major problem in our country. Relational problems are among the most common complaints among adults seeking mental health services.

The *Diagnostic and Statistical Manual for Mental Disorders (DSM-IV)* categories for relational problems, as defined by the American Psychiatric Association (APA, 1994), include V61.1, Partner Relational Problem:

> When the focus of clinical attention is a pattern of interaction between spouses or partners characterized by negative communication (e.g., criticisms), distorted communication (e.g., unrealistic expectations), or noncommunication (e.g., withdrawal) that is associated with clinically significant impairment in individual or family functioning or the development of symptoms in one or both partners. (p. 681)

Typically, individuals displaying these symptoms have an Adjustment Disorder, which, according to *DSM-IV*, is the development of emotional or behavioral symptoms in response to identifiable psychosocial stressor(s) occurring within three months of the onset of the stressors (APA, 1994, p. 623). For couples, the unnamed stressor may be marital conflict. The *DSM-IV* further codifies adjustment disorders according to specific types of symptom expression, for example, Adjustment Disorder with Depressed Mood, Anxiety, Disturbed Emotions or

Conduct. Additionally, certain couples may experience other *DSM-IV*-identified problems related to abuse, for example, physical abuse of adult or sexual abuse of adult. Within marriage, the former is exemplified by spouse beating, the latter by sexual coercion or rape (APA, 1994, p. 682).

Finally, there is no doubt that, in addition to adjustment disorders, marital distress can be either the cause or the result of any number of major psychological disorders experienced by partners or other family members. These problems include, but are not limited to depression, anxiety, substance abuse, personality disorders, and chronic medical problems. Indeed, as research in the area of health and relationship discord becomes more sophisticated, evidence has been increasing that chronic and severe marital dysfunction is related to a number of individual- and family-based mental and physical health problems (Burman & Margolin, 1992; Verbrugge, 1979).

CASE DESCRIPTION

Jackie and Martin are both 55 years old and have been married for over 33 years. They are Caucasian and were brought up in intact middle-class families, raised in the Northwest. Jackie was the oldest of three sisters born to a strict, domineering father (who was an airline pilot) and a passive-submissive mother (who was not occupied outside the home). Jackie's parents were raised in the Midwest during the Depression; consequently, they were quite conservative with finances, in social activities, and in expressions of emotion and displays of affection. Her parents had been married almost 50 years when her father passed away.

Martin was the oldest child and only son of four children. His father worked for 30 years at a beverage company and his mother worked part time for most of his childhood for a fishing tackle manufacturer. Martin's parents had a traditional relationship: Father was in charge of most responsibilities outside the home; mother was decisive inside the home. She handled the family finances and took the lead role in child rearing. Martin's father came from a Germanic immigrant family culture that was not particularly demonstrative of affection, but on many occasions, alcohol consumption served as the basis for boisterous fun and occasional conflicts during extended family gatherings. His mother was born and raised in Texas and was prone stereotypically to giving everyone close to her lots of praise and affection. Martin's parents had been married 41 years when his father passed away.

Jackie and Martin did quite well in school, both academically and socially. For example, in high school, Jackie was a cheerleader and junior class officer; Martin was high school valedictorian and cocaptain of the basketball and baseball teams in his senior year. The couple met during their sophomore year in college. They dated from their mid-sophomore year through college and were married after graduation. They moved to a college town in Oregon, where Martin entered graduate school in psychology and Jackie began teaching in an elementary school. Martin completed his Ph.D. and the couple moved to California, where he started his career in psychology and Jackie worked in a bank. After six years of marriage, they had their first daughter and Jackie stopped working outside the home. Three years later, they had their second daughter. Eventually, Jackie worked full time with an events management company, a job she still had when the couple presented for therapy. Similarly, Martin was maintaining a psychologist position with the federal government for the same period of time. Both daughters had completed college and had been out of the parental home for about two years when the couple entered marital therapy.

CHIEF COMPLAINTS

In most initial sessions of behavioral couple therapy (BCT), the objectives are to (1) introduce the couple to the various policies and procedures of the therapeutic program, (2) establish rapport by therapist demonstration of competence and empathy, (3) determine the partners' chief complaints, and (4) determine whether additional assessment is appropriate and couple therapy is the treatment of choice. Both husband and wife have a right and a responsibility to discuss and to explore their concerns about self, partner, and the relationship. The therapist works to facilitate this discussion by giving both partners equal opportunities to talk, by helping them to articulate and label their issues specifically, and by validating each partner's feelings and perceptions of the problems.

As is typical in couple therapy initial sessions, Jackie (i.e., the wife) was more ready to discuss her concerns. She started by saying that the need for marital therapy was her idea. She said that she had been mildly to moderately depressed in recent years and that part of the reason was the quality of the marriage. She was primarily concerned with Martin's moodiness: a tendency to be negative and critical. She wondered whether Martin also suffered from chronic low-grade depression, due to chronic dissatisfaction with aspects of his job. Over the years, he had become more and more negative, irritable, and, more recently, critical of her. Moreover, it seemed to Jackie that Martin depended more and more on the use of alcohol to lift his mood into a happy emotional space. Basically, Martin drank on a daily basis, usually in moderation. However, he would increase his intake before and during social situations with family or friends. Indeed, on most such occasions, alcohol was used as a drug to enhance his mood; Martin frequently would be "the life of the party." In recent years, from Jackie's perspective, the drinking episodes were resulting too frequently in one of two unsatisfactory outcomes: He would either get intoxicated enough to be in a different "zone" than she (sometimes joining with family or friends in a loud and boisterous party mode) or, and especially if confronted about his drinking and boisterous display, he would get very defensive and become verbally aggressive. Both partners indicated that he came by this dichotomous pattern of emotional liability honestly (i.e., he was just like his father).

Martin's position was that the main purpose and problem with his drinking was social. He loved to drink for effect and to have a good time. He reported that he had never had any DWIs, job attendance or performance problems, or known alcohol-related health problems. He claimed that over the past 10 to 15 years, his wife was the main plaintiff regarding his drinking, although sometimes his daughters or other nondrinking extended family members would have some concerns. Jackie argued that given Martin's sometimes negative attitudes and irritable mood when not drinking, combined with her own difficulty in relating to his boisterous and sometimes defensive behaviors when he was drinking, their level of emotional compatibility and relationship intimacy had fallen below her acceptable standards.

Martin had some reservations in sharing his concerns about the marriage. While acknowledging that alcoholism had affected most of the men in his family, he also said that major depression seemed to run in Jackie's family. Jackie's grandfather committed suicide when her father was 13 years old; her father was clearly depressed, but never diagnosed, and both of her sisters were diagnosed with Major Depression and were being treated with medication. Indeed, Jackie admitted to bouts of depression much of her life, and a few years ago she was diagnosed with Major Depression that was being treated with medication. Martin claimed that, in general, Jackie had a positive outlook on life and was optimistic. However, periodically, a kind of melancholy would affect her outlook and she became more sensitive to employers', coworkers', and family members' behaviors. For example, during these periodic depressions, both Martin and the two daughters would be perceived by Jackie to engage in behaviors that were unloving and inconsiderate. A related personal problem that Jackie had been struggling with over the past several years was a significant weight gain. She became about 50 pounds overweight, and though the weight was lost on two occasions in expensive programs, it was regained each time. This issue was a sensitive one between them (similar to Martin's drinking), and Martin did indicate in his individual session that her weight affected his attraction to her body and thus the frequency of their sexual activity. Interestingly, in Jackie's individual session, she said that Martin's drinking affected her attraction to him sexually. In a conjoint session, they reported that the frequency of sexual intercourse had decreased from weekly to monthly over the past few years.

In summary, the chief complaints obtained during the initial interviews were that, according to Jackie, Martin was not happy with his job and apparently life in general, that often he expressed low-grade depression in the form of a pessimistic and critical attitude, that he seemed to have to drink to relax when he or they were alone or to have a good time with people, and when in this state, much of the time Jackie was not able to relate to him comfortably. Martin thought that Jackie also was vulnerable to depression, manifested by overeating, low self-esteem, sensitivity to family members' or others' unintended or inadvertent "slights," and that she was unable, at times, to tolerate his good moods because he was "drinking too much" or was "too far out there" for her comfort. Interestingly, neither partner denied the basic reality or validity of these mutual complaints.

HISTORY

In the second and third evaluation sessions, there are three objectives: (1) obtain a behavioral sample of marital communication and problem solving, (2) take a developmental history of the couple relationship, and (3) meet with the partners individually to take a personal (i.e., precouple) history and explore any possible hidden agendas, partners' levels of commitment, or any other concerns raised during the previous sessions.

Many of the individual background variables for Jackie and Martin and relevant family-of-origin issues were gathered during the first three meetings and were mentioned in the preceding paragraphs. These two people were successful, high-achieving, first-born siblings raised in relatively large families. They made good grades and consistently operated in the mainstream of social activity all the way through college. Martin was the only son of four children and he learned that academic and sports achievements had high personal and social rewards. He was always a "good son" and was spoiled with attention and affection by his mother. He did not drink alcohol until the middle of his freshman year in college, when he and a fraternity mate celebrated getting the highest semester grades in their fraternity. Thereafter, he quickly grew to enjoy alcohol as a social lubricant and became intoxicated three to four times a year at parties. Other than hangovers, apparently his conduct did not result in any negative consequences. From his junior year in high school until he met his future wife in their sophomore year in college, he dated five women for two to four months each. His standards were set high; all of these brief girlfriends were cheerleaders, class officers, or otherwise highly popular and attractive young women. So-called heavy petting was part of his premarital erotic experience, but his first sexual intercourse was with his wife. Claiming he had had a great childhood, Martin reported that his father began to drink more noticeably several years after Martin left home for college. There were occasional family conflicts, exacerbated by members' alcohol consumption when he and Jackie would return home for various holidays during graduate school.

Jackie also was a high-achiever. The oldest of three sisters, her father favored her, teaching her many skills atypical for a girl. The father built two houses while also flying commercial aircraft for a major airline. However, he often was demanding (of all four women in the nuclear family) and everything had to be done his way, with expediency. No "backtalk" or expression of negative affect was tolerated from his wife or daughters. If his wife or any child did "act up," he would engage in very intimidating behaviors to punish them, ranging from extended silent treatment for several days, to yelling and threatening comments, to throwing things and very occasional physical abuse (i.e., hitting) of his wife. The worst incidents often were exacerbated by her father's alcohol use. Jackie was never encouraged or really allowed to have friends over to her house because her parents were not comfortable having the disruption of routines that outsiders required. Jackie compensated by being very outgoing and popular at school, but more isolated and emotionally reserved within the family. Unfortunately, the sisters were not close and the mother was neither affectionate nor emotionally close to any of the three daughters in this somewhat oppressive family context. It was not until the father passed away that the three sisters began to reminisce and commiserate about their upbringing.

These quite different personal backgrounds and family-of-origin experiences provided a high level of attraction for Jackie and Martin, but they also set the stage for distress in the areas of emotional and communication compatibility, use of and sensitivity to alcohol consumption, and their abilities to cope with biological depression.

BEHAVIORAL ASSESSMENT

BCT features a multimodel assessment approach. As discussed above, semistructured clinical interviews are conducted with the couple conjointly and with each partner individually (Birchler & Schwartz, 1994). Additionally, most practitioners of BCT ask the partners to provide an in vivo sample of couple problem-solving skills while discussing a relationship conflict. Third, partners usually are asked to complete a battery of self-report questionnaires, including standardized indicators of dyadic and individual function.

BEHAVIORAL

In our program, the so-called communication sample is obtained at the beginning of the second evaluation meeting. Typically, the couple have completed and returned the questionnaires (described below) and the therapists are knowledgeable about the presenting complaints reported in the first session. The therapist can easily help the couple to identify a problem to discuss from these two sources of information. The objective is to select a topic about which the couple have current disagreement and that they are willing to discuss on their own for 10 minutes. The topic should be neither too upsetting nor too inconsequential. The couple are told that the therapist would like to observe how they go about resolving a conflict. Depending on the facility arrangements, the therapist may or may not leave the room to observe the interaction via one-way mirror or audio-video equipment. Here is a sample of the interaction provided by Jackie and Martin, who decided to talk about Martin's negative attitude and perceived criticism of Jackie:

JACKIE: I just think you are grouchy all the time and snap at me when I don't deserve it. I don't like to be treated that way and it makes me think you don't really care about me.
MARTIN: You know, sometimes I am grouchy, but mostly I think you are the one who is too sensitive and feel criticism when I don't mean it. Our fights start when you attack or accuse me of being inconsiderate when I'm not ... and that's what makes me mad.
JACKIE: You don't realize how negative your attitude is all the time. You are only in a good mood when you are drinking ...
MARTIN: (Interrupting.) That's B.S.! My attitude is *not* negative all the time. How can you say that? It's like me saying you're depressed all the time! Again, you are so sensitive and take things so personal, when it would be so much better if you could roll with the punches.
JACKIE: (Voice raising.) That's just it. Why should I have to roll with punches from my husband? I just wish you would quit your job and find something to make you happy ... besides drinking. I sure don't seem to make you happy.
MARTIN: You do make me happy. I mean, it's not you that makes me irritable in the first place. But you seem to take my occasional irritability in a personal way, get your feelings hurt, and you either snap back at me or get depressed and withdraw and act like life is not worth living. You even do this with your daughters ...
JACKIE: (Interrupting.) Well, they are inconsiderate of me too. Most of the time I can't seem to do anything right to make anybody happy.
MARTIN: (Interrupting, raising his voice.) See, there you go! Blaming everybody else for how they treat you, then blaming it on yourself and getting all depressed. I really don't know how to help you.
JACKIE: You could start by being in a better mood and figuring out how to get into better moods without drinking.
MARTIN: Oh hell, now it's the drinking again ...

This sample dialogue illustrates how people can get into emotionally laden topics and seem to go around and around in a cross-complaining, lose-lose type of interaction. Getting more and more frustrated, they fail to resolve the problems. This couple did manage to express their frustrations and take turns trying to make their points, and they basically stayed on the assigned topic. Focus, mutual involvement in the discussion, and illumination on the issues important to the couple were positive aspects. Negative aspects included blaming, inability to take responsibility for their own contributions to the problem, escalating negative emotions and statements, and lack of any progress toward resolution.

We always ask couples whether the observed communication sample is representative of such discussions at home, and if not, how they vary. They indicated that the discussion was fairly typical. However, sometimes, especially when one or both had been drinking, more yelling, direct put-downs, and abrupt withdrawal would occur. Jackie might withdraw hurt and mad and sooner or later Martin would approach her to apologize or try to talk about the matter. Employing behavioral observation of couple problem solving, the therapist can learn much about dyadic communication and problem-solving skills and also how the couple recover from typical conflict-based interactions.

SELF-REPORT

Most behaviorally oriented therapists employ standardized individual and relationship-oriented paper-and-pencil questionnaires to help them assess various aspects of dissatisfaction, dysfunction, and the dyad's assets and strengths. The present authors employ a number of such instruments in a package called the Marital Relationship Assessment Battery (Birchler, 1983). Essentially, the partners are asked to complete independently several behaviorally oriented questionnaires, a task that takes them approximately 1.5 to 2 hours. Descriptive and quantifiable information is obtained regarding couple demographics, global marital satisfaction (Dyadic Adjustment Scale [DAS]; Spanier,1976), steps toward separation and divorce (Marital Status Inventory [MSI]; Weiss & Cerreto, 1980) areas of desired relationship change (Areas of Change Questionnaire [ACQ]; Weiss & Birchler, 1975), conflict management (Response to Conflict scale [RTC]; Birchler & Fals-Stewart, 1994), and time allocation to individual and mutually rewarding activities (Inventory of Rewarding Activities [IRA]; Birchler, 1983). Additionally, measures of individual function are included that assess levels of depression, anxiety, and physical symptoms (Self-Description Inventory [SDI]; Wahler, 1968).

Details relating to the specific questionnaires are beyond the scope of this chapter. However, results obtained from the questionnaires were quite useful in conceptualizing this case. The DAS indicated that Jackie was more dissatisfied with the marriage than was Martin; she scored in the moderately dissatisfied range, he scored in the slightly dissatisfied range. Similarly, the MSI scores indicated that Jackie had thought of divorce after their infrequent fights; Martin denied ever entertaining the idea. Compared to most distressed couples, the ACQ scores indicated only a moderate level of desire for change in the area of domestic transactions. As expected, Jackie desired Martin to drink less, to argue less, and to express appreciation and help with household projects more frequently. Interestingly, Martin had no significant desires for change in Jackie's domestic behavior. The RTC suggested a moderate expression of maladaptive responses to marital conflict. Both partners indicated that Martin's conflict style was more active, resulting at times in yelling, sarcasm, and criticism, whereas, except for nagging, Jackie resorted more often to passive behaviors (e.g., sulking, leaving the scene, and crying). Frequency of resorting to these maladaptive behaviors was less than the average distressed couple, but more than for happy couples. The IRA indicated that both partners worked between 40 and 50 hours/week, slept an average of 7 to 8 hours/night, and had a fair balance between rewarding and nonrewarding personal activities during the week. Their time allotted to "socializing with other couples" and Jackie's time with "other adults excluding spouse" were below average. The percentage of "activities with family members" was above average. Finally, on the SDI, Jackie obtained scores suggesting below-average self-esteem, above-average tension and anxiety (this combination indicates moderate depression), and slightly above-average physical symptoms. Martin scored in the average ranges on all three indicators.

MEDICAL CONSULTATION

Whenever either partner presents for couple therapy and is suffering from a significant physical or mental disorder, the therapist should actively consider consultation with the other providers. In particular, if the patient is being treated for mental health problems, it is important that multiple interventions be coordinated so as not to be in conflict. In this case, Jackie had been seeing a psychiatrist at an HMO for several years; her depression was being managed by Prozac antidepressant medication. She was able to articulate the nature of her depression and to articulate actions she needed to take when stresses and symptoms of depression increased (e.g., get more rest, see her doctor, raise the dosage of the medication). A brief phone consultation with her physician confirmed that treatment consisted primarily of medication management visits at the rate of three to four per year and that there should not be any conflicts with the introduction of marital therapy. Even when patients are being treated for major medical problems (e.g., heart problems, diabetes, cancer), unless they can articulate clearly the problems, the prescribed treatments, and how these might interact with couple dynamics, a medical consultation is in order.

CASE CONCEPTUALIZATION

The authors have developed an approach that employs all of the major components of BCT (Birchler, Doumas, & Fals-Stewart, 1999). Used as a framework for assessment and treatment, the heuristic tool is called the 7Cs of long-term intimate relationships. The 7Cs comprise Character features, Cultural and ethnic factors, Contract, Commitment, Caring, Communication, and Conflict resolution.

We will define the 7Cs and note some concepts underlying these domains of personal and interpersonal function as they relate to Jackie and Martin. First and foremost, we are concerned with the (inter)personal abilities and emotional qualities of the two individuals attempting to create the relationship. In our framework, *character features* refer to the aggregate of features and traits that form the individual nature of a person. At one end of the continuum of the potential for interpersonal intimacy is an individual who, by virtue of often complicated biopsychosocial misfortunes, has certain handicaps, personality traits, emotional vulnerabilities, and perhaps limited personal resources or pathological characteristics such that he or she is not a good candidate for maintaining an adult intimate relationship. At the other end of this continuum is the individual who is capable of loving and being loved in the broadest sense of emotional and physical health. This person is responsible and resourceful, can adapt to varying and stressful circumstances, and is able consistently to give and get positive responses. He or she can achieve a healthy and functional balance of independence and interdependence in the relationship. In the domain of character features, theoretical factors relating to individual development, the course of mental illnesses, mate selection, and attachment theory are important considerations for clients with marital dysfunction.

Overall, Jackie and Martin bring to the relationship a number of strong character features: Both are reliable and capable people who financially and structurally have provided for their family; two apparently healthy daughters were put through college and launched successfully in their own lives; the couple has maintained a relationship for over 30 years without any breaks in trust, integrity, or social citizenship. On the other hand, Jackie suffers from Major Depression and poor self-esteem and is relatively sensitive to personal criticism and family conflict. Martin, by virtue of his core personality and predisposition to alcohol abuse, responds to work-related stressors with daily and occasionally excessive drinking. Under stress, he tends to become a negative thinker and his mood is reflected in interactions with family members. These intrapersonal factors represent chief complaints for the couple and will be implicated in any treatment planning.

Cultural and ethnic factors refer to the cultural, ethnic, racial, religious, family-of-origin, socioeconomic, and other societal variables that collectively form the past and present contexts in which individuals and couples exist. Certainly, given these important and diverse developmental and contextual parameters, many adjustments by any couple are required and the potential exists for many types of conflicts to occur, both between the partners and between the couple and their extended families or community. In this domain, cultural diversity, the presence of family-of-origin issues and values (i.e., family systems theory), sex-role preferences, and role strain are relevant considerations.

Jackie and Martin did not report serious conflicts in this area. Both being White, middle-class, Protestant, first-born college graduates from intact families, they shared basic compatibility regarding racial, ethnic, religious, and socioeconomic backgrounds. The one notable difference was the way their parents and extended families expressed emotion: Martin's family displayed more amplitude and tolerance for the expression of both positive and negative affect; Jackie grew up in a family where both positive and negative affectivity was blunted and discouraged. Again, this difference in families of origin will be an important contextual variable when it comes to treatment planning.

As applied in our framework, the notion of *contract* comes from mate selection theory, family systems theory, and social exchange theory. The contract between the partners may refer to *explicit* agreements between the two for the doing or not doing of something specified and expected. However, in close relationships, contract features are more often a complicated set of *implicit* expectations about definition, certain benefits, and the types of interactions expected within the relationship. In or out of awareness, contract problems suggest that individual partners' expectations do not match their experiences. Thus, significant dissatisfaction and intrapersonal and interpersonal conflicts may result. In the present case, contract problems were not primary. The partners, over three decades, were relatively secure in and basically satisfied with their work-related, parent-related, and role-related responsibilities. Their dreams and plans for retirement also seemed to be compatible. Unlike many couples seeking marital therapy, except for mood management and two related behavioral excesses, this pair did not have to renegotiate major relationship features of their contract.

Commitment is thought of as the state of having pledged, devoted, or obligated oneself to another; to be involved, remain loyal, and to maintain the relationship over time. Commitment is a complicated interpersonal variable and can cause much insecurity and distress for a couple. We attempt to simplify the notion by focusing on at least two aspects. First, are partners committed to stability (e.g., no threats or behavioral steps toward separation or divorce; no intention of leaving one another)? Second, are both partners committed to quality; that is, are they willing to invest in an ongoing collaborative process to maintain high relationship quality? In the absence of these aspects of commitment, prognosis is poor regarding the remediation of marital dysfunction.

Jackie and Martin had demonstrated commitment to stability by virtue of their 33-year marriage. Previously, no separations or threats of separation had taken place. However, in the past couple of years, Jackie had considered divorce at times when she became depressed and demoralized with the quality of interaction between them. This suggests that future commitment to relationship *stability* may be jeopardized. Therefore, both partners' commitment to *quality* will be critical because they will need to make some changes to make continued marriage sufficiently satisfying. Commitment is altered through experience, and marital therapy can be helpful in setting the standards for present and future performance.

Caring, obviously an important element of an intimate relationship, is considered from the perspective of social learning theory. We refer to the partners' abilities to express relational behaviors that promote emotional and physical intimacy, including mutual affirmation, support and understanding, demonstrations of affection, and pleasurable sexual activities. Also, partners need to establish an effective balance between partner care and self-care regarding the activities of daily living, the experience of pleasant events, and sources of personal and couple satisfaction.

In the present couple's marriage, caring, in a couple of ways, had been eroded. First, when their moods turned negative and/or depressed, there was evidence of increasing isolation instead of reaching out to one another for understanding and support. Under periodic stress, Martin's drinking and Jackie's hopelessness and vague suicidal thinking had been shouldered alone. They were not taking advantage of their prior history of acting like best friends in these situations. Moreover, their sex life had deteriorated significantly over the past few years, again related to drinking, depression, and weight gain. Although the couple reported that they avoided talking about their sexual relationship openly, it was an important act of intimacy that they had shared successfully in the past. Treatment planning will incorporate improvements in the domain of caring.

For the past 30 years, *communication* effectiveness has been a basic intervention component of BCT. We define effective communication as the open and honest sharing of information between two people: when the messages intended and sent by the speaker are exactly the same as the messages heard or received by the listener. In our approach, the analysis of couple communication and subsequent communication training usually are fundamental to the remediation of marital dysfunction. Jackie and Martin were no exception. Their hectic and sometimes stressful lifestyles contributed to deterioration in their previous ability to communicate support and understanding to one another. Moreover, they allowed other priorities to take the place of connecting with one another on a regular basis. It is difficult to improve interpersonal conflict unless time and setting structures are committed to mutually understand and explore solutions to certain issues. Enhancing communication access and quality will be a treatment priority.

Finally, the last of the 7Cs, *conflict resolution,* refers to the personal skills and interpersonal patterns of interaction that facilitate effective decision making, individual and joint problem solving, the management of anger, and the resolution of marital disputes. Social learning theory and empirical research suggest that people are often deficient in the skills of problem solving, anger management, and conflict resolution, and that, given the proper motivation to improve the relationship, couples usually can be trained to make significant improvements in this important domain of dyadic function. Clearly, poor conflict management was one of the process and skill deficits for this couple. Not only did they have different personal and family-of-origin predispositions for managing interpersonal conflict, but their styles of anger management were incompatible. When confronted with perceived threat, Martin tended to raise his voice and lash out with impulsive, defensive attacks that were soon forgotten by him yet were perceived by Jackie as insensitive and devastating personal criticisms. On the other hand, when Jackie felt anger or negative affect, she tended to withhold information, withdraw, and become very demoralized about her own personal worth. She internalized the process and became depressed and hopeless. The couple needed help to understand the incompatible nature of these styles and help learning better alternatives for identifying and resolving their conflicts.

RATIONALE FOR TREATMENT CHOICE

Marital therapy is indicated whenever one or both partners are complaining about individual problems and/or couple interactions to the extent that they cause problems in the relationship or interfere with either partner's or other family members' quality of life. In some cases, the individual problems are so severe or of such an intrapersonal nature that individual treatment becomes the treatment of choice, either before, concurrent with, or in lieu of couple therapy. This book discusses many such examples in Chapters 2 through 10, such as Major Depressive Disorder, Posttraumatic Stress Disorder, and alcohol abuse.

In the present case, Jackie complained that she was unsatisfied with the marriage, and Martin was at least unhappy with Jackie's perception that the marriage was dysfunctional. Undoubtedly, Jackie felt depressed enough in general to seek individual treatment over several years; this treatment was appropriate concurrently with marital therapy. Her level of depression affected and was affected by interactions in the marriage. Martin's alcohol use and abuse also may have been a problem that requires individualized treatment; however, at this point in the process, he claimed that the only significant negative consequences have been of a social nature. His frequent and occasional excessive drinking had been a problem primarily for his wife. On most occasions, she drank with him and with other family members when he consumed too much and the arguments ensued. Accordingly, the primary problems enumerated by these partners seem to have individual etiological bases, but the dysfunctional interaction within the marriage was definitely an appropriate target for conjoint treatment.

COURSE OF TREATMENT

Currently, many BCT practitioners offer an integrated therapy program that features the combination of traditional BCT components together with interpersonal acceptance strategies. Treatment goals in traditional BCT include improved communication and problem-solving skills applied to the presenting complaints, plus enhanced behavioral exchanges designed to improve caring behaviors and marital satisfaction (Jacobson & Holtzworth-Munroe, 1986). The formal introduction of acceptance strategies has been labeled integrative behavioral couple therapy (IBCT; Jacobson & Christensen, 1996). As yet, there is no consensus as to whether these two basic types of intervention need to be offered sequentially (one or the other before the alternative) or can be integrated fully session by session. The present authors, having practiced BCT for many years, have tended to employ BCT interventions exclusively as long as they are successful. If traditional BCT does not achieve the desired outcomes, acceptance interventions associated with IBCT are then employed. Research is ongoing to determine not only the overall effectiveness of IBCT, but to develop criteria for when to use interventions associated with this model. One idea seems relevant to the present case study: At the outset of treatment, acceptance strategies may be useful when there is little likelihood of behavior change in the presenting complaints. That is, if the couple system is resistant to change, acceptance strategies may promote partners' attitude changes as precursors to or in lieu of desired behavioral changes. In the absence of behavior change, at least the situation may be better tolerated and less distressing. We discuss treatment in the present case in light of this strategy.

Acceptance Strategies

In assisting the couple to establish treatment goals, the therapist initially helped them to reach consensus on several apparent facts. Clearly, the couple's ability to understand and to endorse these fundamental ideas within the first two intervention sessions was a commendation to them and a good prognostic sign for the outcome of therapy. After careful consideration, they came to agreement that (1) for whatever reasons, improved mood management was a goal for each partner; (2) some of their existing "self-medicating" coping strategies were detrimental to the well-being of each person individually and to the relationship in general (i.e., Martin's overdrinking and Jackie's overeating); (3) at their age and length of marriage, certain aspects of their personalities and lifestyle preferences were unlikely to change significantly (i.e., Martin's socially oriented use of alcohol and Jackie's disposition toward becoming depressed under stress, sometimes related to personal anxiety in the same social situations in which Martin enjoyed drinking); and (4) a combination of attitude and behavioral changes would be required to modify both partners' emotional experiences regarding work, family, and couple activities.

Accordingly, as a starting point, realistic treatment goals incorporated the ideas that Martin would continue to drink moderately and to lubricate certain social situations with alcohol; stress at his job also may contribute to alcohol use.

Similarly, Jackie would continue to be vulnerable to high-stress work-related and high-amplitude social situations; coping with these situations might result in symptoms of depression, including social withdrawal and overeating. Given a collaborative acceptance of these basic limitations, opportunities could then be explored to modify some aspects of these behaviors in the interests of personal and couple well-being. Over the course of two months of treatment, the therapist alternated acceptance and behavior-change strategies to achieve maximum attitude and behavior changes.

Two acceptance strategies employed in this case have been labeled *unified detachment* and *empathic joining around the problem* (Jacobson & Christensen, 1996). Unified detachment is a persuasive effort by the therapist to help the couples view *the problem* as a property of the relationship (in contrast to the typical idea that one partner or the other is the problem). Parts of several treatment sessions included the facilitation of intellectualized descriptions of personality styles, typical and persistent conflict themes, and chronic couple interactions that had taken place over many years in this relationship. Neither partner intended to harm or frustrate the other; they just approached coping with internal and external stresses very differently. Indeed, their differences were quite understandable in light of their personal histories. The question for therapy is: What alternatives are available to improve things? The best method is to make some behavioral changes. However, if that is not possible, the next best alternative is to learn to accept things (i.e., their partner) as they are. Finally, the worst alternative is to grow apart further, to continue to cope with these situations ineffectively, and perhaps to lose the relationship completely. Unified detachment is successful when partners understand and accept intellectually the dilemma concerning their relationship. Consequently, they can eliminate or at least reduce the negative emotions associated with the power struggle for change, when change is unlikely to occur.

Empathic joining around the problem also is employed to facilitate intimacy-enhancing acceptance. The idea is to hear out each partner's complaints about the other (couples typically enter therapy blaming one another for the problems), but as soon as possible, to help each partner to convert these complaints into self-revelations about his or her own pain, disappointments, fears of rejection, abandonment, or loss of freedom. Through modeling, eliciting emotions, and exploration of inner feelings, so-called *hard emotions* (e.g., anger, resentment, criticism, blame, put-downs) are revealed to be concealing *soft emotions* (e.g., sadness, insecurity, vulnerability, feelings of inadequacy). This work is not behavior change-oriented. In many cases, when a couple who has retained but momentarily lost a caring base gets in touch with these softer emotions and gain a full understanding of their partner's concerns, the press for behavior change is reduced significantly. At the beginning of treatment, Jackie and Martin were open to these intimacy-oriented acceptance interventions, and within three weeks they were ready to discuss ways to better manage their moods and to enhance couple collaboration and intimacy.

BEHAVIOR CHANGE STRATEGIES

Derived in part from the 7Cs analysis, the behavioral targets for intervention were (1) better mood management for each partner; (2) reductions in drinking for Martin and in eating for Jackie; (3) generally enhanced communication and caring, specifically, improvement in their sex life; and (4) better conflict management regarding expressions of anger.

Mood Management   The interventions for mood management involved a review of their current facilitative activities and a mutual approach to generating and implementing new strategies. Martin indicated that his negative frame of mind was shaped primarily by experiences at work. He admitted that most of his weekday drinking was related to stress reduction. He rarely talked about work with his wife, but undoubtedly he brought work (i.e., negativity) home with him. The new strategy for him was to talk about work at least twice each week during one of the couple's structured "talk times." Jackie was more than willing to listen to his gripes and to help him brainstorm how to avoid negative interactions at work, including cognitive self-instructions to separate work issues from home. Similarly, regarding Jackie's work, she also experienced periodic stress, especially when supervisors criticized her attitude or performance. Previously, under such increased stress, she would come home and withdraw or act depressed without verbalizing her anger and disappointment. Then she would increase her antidepressant medication. For his part, Martin often avoided such discussions when Jackie broached them because they were depressing to him and his solutions did not seem to help her. The new collaborative strategy for mood management also required Jackie to review the work scene at least twice each week with Martin, with goals of briefly sharing the problems perceived. Martin was not responsible for solving Jackie's problems, just to listen to them. Only if Jackie asked specifically would they brainstorm appropriate coping actions. In addition to adding discussions about work to their scheduled talk times, both partners were encouraged to start a modest exercise regimen to facilitate stress reduction; it was suggested strongly that any physical exercise at all would offer significant mind and body benefits. Each agreed to walk for at least one half-hour twice each week individually and to take at least one walk together.

Reducing Behavioral Excesses   Clearly, healthwise, it would be in the best interests of both parties to reduce their excessive intake of alcohol and food. As above, the goal was to begin this reduction modestly and to work at it collaboratively. Previously, any reduced drinking Martin attempted was initiated alone or after a fight with Jackie about drinking. Similarly, Jackie's weight management programs and her battle with symptoms of depression were dealt with by herself. The new strategy was to set up a very modest behavior change plan that was carried out *together*. Accordingly, Martin agreed not to drink alcohol between Monday and Thursday evenings (with the exception of two beers when he had Wednesday night bowling games with his friends). Jackie would support this reduction by making sure that there were some interesting nonalcoholic beverages in the home. For Jackie's part, in addition to taking an exercise class two nights each week (and walking when the class was not in session), she and Martin would plan low-calorie menus for lunches and evening meals Monday through Thursday. If grocery items were available, Martin agreed to help cook two of those four nights. This cooking was in addition to the BBQ activities that were typical for him on the weekends. The difference in this collaborative plan was that they made a dedicated effort to help each other make some needed reductions in negative health behaviors. The previous dysfunctional process featured individual isolation and couple stalemate, where Martin kept drinking and Jackie kept eating and neither one dealt with the problems collaboratively or constructively.

Communication and Conflict Resolution   As is true of so many couples, dysfunctional communication and problem solving are presenting complaints, and they are caused by one or more of the following factors: too little access to one another, skill deficits in communication and conflict resolution, or, over time, the development of conditioned maladaptive patterns of interaction. The work schedules of Jackie and Martin did interfere to some extent with together time during the week, but they did have more than adequate time on the weekends to be together. However, when therapy began, this couple had neither a semistructured tradition of talk time nor a comfortable process. The therapist recognized that there was some avoidance of talk time because of the mutual desire *not* to deal with the stressful and negative aspects of their work and family relationships. However, as conceptualized in this case, it was this very avoidance pattern that kept them from getting a better handle on how to deal with these issues. Each was alone, became somewhat resentful, and tended to store up their negative feelings about life. The homework strategy developed over the course of treatment was to establish a comfortable and secure talk time to gripe about work, share feelings about the marriage, plan home projects and fun activities, and pretty much do the opposite of what they had been doing before therapy began. Indeed, the couple decided to rehabilitate their outside Jacuzzi and get together two or three times each weekend sharing a light snack and glass of wine. Spa time during the late afternoon Happy Hour actually worked very well for this purpose, and by the end of therapy, it was an established ritual. Interestingly, getting into the weekend, out of the house, and into the hot water resulted in an environment and communication process that mitigated against arguments throughout the week. Typically, they would soak and talk for 30 to 45 minutes and then go in to prepare dinner together. Apparently, for this couple, actual skill deficits were less of a problem than was access to one another in a safe, comfortable, and semistructured setting.

Intimacy Enhancement   There were two levels of intimacy enhancement in which these people were interested: general improvement in caring behaviors and companionship activities, and an improved sexual relationship. The former proved to be fairly easily accomplished. First, the acceptance work emphasized during the first three treatment sessions was successful in helping the partners to gain a better understanding of and empathy for each others' developmental upbringing and differing styles of affect management. That work, combined with the progressive and collaborative interventions described above to address mood management and drinking and eating behaviors, prepared them well for additional work on intimacy. By the end of about two months in treatment, they were having talk times at least twice each week, and during these discussions, they planned weekend and vacation activities, with and without their daughters and other relatives, that would be enjoyable for all concerned. For example, with a renewed commitment to travel together, they were able to get their employers to agree to a more extended vacation than was thought possible for many years, such as a three-week vacation to Europe.

General improvement in communication and caring facilitated an honest discussion about the couple's sex life. Throughout most of their marriage, they had been having sex enjoyably about four to six times per month. When they entered therapy, and for the previous couple of years, the frequency had dropped to once a month, at best. Unfortunately, within the present three- to four-month brief therapy experience, this problem was not fully resolved. The couple did learn to discuss the matter much more openly than in the past and they agreed that a certain dilemma existed. On the one hand, Jackie had learned the hard way that she needed to keep taking her antidepressant medication or she became vulnerable to deep depression. However, the medication that was determined to help her depression most effectively also diminished her libido and interest in sex. She really did not think about sex very often. Martin claimed to be interested in sex in general, with a normally operating libido; however, he disclosed that Jackie's moderate obesity simply turned him off to initiating sex with her. When Jackie had lost 40 to 50 pounds on two previous weight-loss occasions, his interest and their frequency increased to at least weekly. So, when Martin does not initiate and Jackie has little drive on her own, nothing happens. Moreover, the couple became aware of the dilemma presented by obesity for some people. On the one hand, people should be loved for who they are, not for the number of pounds they weigh; Jackie disclosed that she did feel rejected by the lack of loving sexual attention because she had enjoyed that type of attention for most of her life. On the other hand, it was fairly difficult for Martin to become aroused by his wife on a physical level because often he found her appearance to be a "turnoff." Of course, on the weekends, when many couples find the time and interest to engage in sexual intimacy, Martin would sometimes drink too much and then Jackie would not be attracted to him even if he were in the mood. So, basically, they experienced a stalemate in this area. During therapy, both partners came to better understand the causal factors and their interactional dynamics, but other than a desire in principle to have sex be a larger part of their relationship, not much was accomplished. The best they could achieve during treatment was to increase the frequency and pleasure of holding each other at night. Previously, the issue of anticipating sex had interfered with touching and hugging one another. To their credit, these two activities were differentiated, and more frequently they were able to fall asleep in one another's arms.

In a total of 15 BCT assessment and treatment sessions, this couple was able to identify increasingly deteriorative and unsatisfactory interaction patterns and to make significant changes in their individual attitudes and moderate changes in certain interpersonal behaviors. They entered therapy moderately distressed and terminated much improved.

THERAPIST-CLIENT FACTORS

In general, the BCT approach features a number of specific therapist skills and characteristics, the combination of which differentiates it from other approaches (Jacobson & Margolin, 1979; Stuart, 1980). These characteristics include the abilities to (1) establish credibility and confidence in self and in the approach, (2) induce and maintain positive expectancies, (3) structure the sessions with a balance of planned agenda and spontaneous response to the needs of the couple, (4) instigate change in the natural environment, (5) be a teacher and consultant regarding healthy relationships, (6) provide emotional support when indicated, (7) identify and modify cognitions that interfere with acceptance and change, and (8) balance alliances across sessions.

In comparison, research has demonstrated that client factors associated with the success of BCT include (1) less severely distressed individuals and couples; (2) younger couples married relatively fewer years; (3) those who are engaged emotionally with one another versus being disengaged or physically or verbally abusive to one another; (4) those who maintain a relatively positive ratio of pleasing versus displeasing behavioral exchanges; (5) those whose communication processes are attentive, respectful, open, and assertive; and (6) those whose problem-solving process includes the ability of partners to negotiate, compromise, and accommodate to one another's desires and needs (Gottman, 1994; Lawrence, Eldridge, Christensen, & Jacobson, 1999).

With respect to these predictive variables, on the whole, Jackie and Martin presented with a fair package of assets and some potential liabilities. Clearly, Jackie's depression and Martin's alcohol abuse represented significant individual variables. However, the couple's level of distress was only moderate. Their age, length of marriage, and periodic withdrawal behaviors, if liabilities, were countered by the following assets: (1) a predominant level of emotional engagement (if sometimes conflicted); (2) evidence of ability to negotiate and compromise regarding a variety of role behaviors (e.g., as workers, parents, and in domestic/household responsibilities); and (3) basic respect in the conduct of their communication, as opposed to verbal or physical abuse of one another.

In the course of therapy, the therapist constantly had to be aware of Jackie's self-esteem issues when offering her constructive criticism and change-related suggestions. Similarly, because Martin is a clinical psychologist, the therapist was mindful of his status and sensitivity to being patronized or talked down to as a "fellow therapist." Providing the couple rationale for attitude- or behavior-change interventions featured a supportive self-care bias for Jackie and a more sophisticated, knowledge-based presentation to Martin. Undoubtedly, the facts that the therapist had many years of experience as a marital therapist and was about the same age as the couple were advantages in this particular case. Sharing anonymous case vignettes of previous successes and citing the literature were helpful in getting cooperation and compliance from Martin. Jackie seemed pleased to have a therapist who could influence her rather stubborn husband.

COURSE OF TERMINATION

Since its inception, BCT has been conceptualized as a brief treatment (Birchler & Fals-Stewart, 2000). After a typical course of 12 to 16 sessions of therapy, the case is terminated and follow-up plans are made. Because the course of therapy is limited, the BCT approach is designed to help couples understand and address their presenting problems expeditiously, but also to teach them analytical, communication, and problem-solving skills so that they can apply these to various problems that may be encountered in the future. Accordingly, planning for termination occurs emphatically in the final month or so of treatment. At this time, the therapist takes a less and less directive role in planning the agenda for the sessions and for the homework assignments. The couple is encouraged to take the executive planning role and to learn how to generalize the application of skills learned and attitudes changed into the future of the relationship.

Jackie and Martin had learned that their options for mood management, despite genetic, family-of-origin, and other intrapersonal predispositions, had important implications for happiness in their marriage and that happiness in their marriage was a primary resource for coping with external stressors. Plans for termination included a commitment to access one another in frequent and semi-structured situations to share their positive and negative feelings and their individual and mutual hopes and fears. They were encouraged to establish this pattern well before termination of therapy and to report about implementation mechanisms, in situ discussions, and emotional experiences.

FOLLOW-UP

Whenever practical, employment of follow-up sessions is recommended. Ideally, after the couple attends 10 to 12 weekly treatment sessions, an additional two sessions can be held two weeks apart to facilitate the generalization of treatment gains to the home environment. Finally, following the protective structure of weekly meetings, it is very effective to invite the couple for a follow-up and final termination session in four to six weeks. Partners seem better able to gain and retain the perspective of adjusted attitudes and behaviors modified when they get the opportunity to come in for a review of progress. Given a planned termination, the couple should be readministered the battery of questionnaires. Comparisons can be made to the original findings and the participants can appreciate where improvements have been made (or not). Finally, graduated termination and follow-up sessions also give the couple a chance to prevent relapse that may be associated with a brief treatment model.

As it so happened in this case, Jackie and Martin had a natural break in regular weekly sessions due to a holiday period. After the ninth treatment session (thirteenth meeting overall), the couple went on vacation for two weeks. On their return, one session was held and a six-week follow-up meeting was planned. Unlike some couples, this couple tended to have a great time on vacations. Being away from daily work pressures, home settings with time-pressured stressors, and family influences worked well for them. Even though Martin and Jackie enjoyed drinking on vacation, the activity level and relaxed setting resulted in no incidents of excessive alcohol consumption. Martin said that he appreciated the opportunities to enjoy Happy Hours with Jackie and he decided to drink in moderation to stay within her comfort level. Moreover, on vacation, the total focus on the relationship in a relaxed setting served to prevent Jackie's experience of any depressive symptoms. Accordingly, the therapist took the opportunity to help the partners to identify and highlight the positive interactions that occurred and the collaborative set of attitudes they had adopted. Moreover, opportunities were highlighted to use these skills and cooperative motives in their everyday home and work environments. At the end of this meeting, the couple were given the marital questionnaires to complete once again. Unfortunately, the meeting at six weeks was not convenient for them; therefore, the therapist arranged to have a 20-minute phone call to offer a review of the original problems, the various gains made in therapy through acceptance or behavior-change mechanisms, a brief review of many improvements suggested by the retest of the marital battery, and the importance of making a positive relationship a first priority in their lives. Finally, the couple was encouraged to call for an appointment should any significant relapse or unmanageable problems occur in the future.

MANAGED CARE CONSIDERATIONS

As mentioned above, the BCT approach to marital dysfunction is well suited to a brief treatment model (i.e., 12 to 20 sessions). If managed care plans cover this amount of work, then marriage treatment can be fairly comprehensive and outcomes usually are positive. Typically, some requirement for meeting a "medical necessity" for care is involved in managed care plans, and this may require that one partner meet criteria for a *DSM-IV* Axis I diagnosis. Although meeting this criterion may open the door for limited couple therapy, it also suggests that at least one of the partners is suffering from a major mental illness or psychiatric disorder; such a condition may complicate and extend the need for couple treatment, while also requiring individual therapy or psychotropic medications. Many practitioners believe that this somewhat restrictive system is workable, as long as 8, 10, 12, or more conjoint sessions are approved. On the other hand, some managed care plans either do not cover conjoint therapy at all, or they cover as few as three sessions. Attempting to evaluate and remediate usually long-standing marital dysfunction in three sessions requires more skill and magic than most therapists possess. Interestingly, Bagarozzi (1996) has proposed a model for providing assessment and treatment for distressed couples in three to six sessions. However, the approach seems to require procedures that focus on a single, most salient problem (i.e., one symptom), and lasting success would require tremendous motivation and readiness to change on the part of the couple. To complete the necessary work, many couples have to pay extra for extended services or seek couple therapy outside the plan.

OVERALL EFFECTIVENESS

BCT, enhanced by certain acceptance strategies included in IBCT, promises to be a very effective treatment program. Generally, using a brief treatment model, BCT is effective posttreatment with about 70% of couples treated, and treatment gains are maintained after one year by about 50% of couples treated. Preliminary results from the IBCT research program suggests that at one year, positive gains are maintained by up to 75% of couples treated (Lawrence et al., 1999). Martin and Jackie were appropriate candidates for BCT/IBCT because their presenting complaints were born of long-standing personality styles and well-conditioned interaction patterns. However, offered the support and structured intervention components described here, they were willing and able to make both attitudinal changes and behavioral changes in their relationship. Indeed, by the end of treatment, they were better able to accept some of the attributes of their long-term marriage that were unlikely to change and to modify certain behaviors that were contributing to their mutual dissatisfaction.

REFERENCES

American Psychiatric Association. (1994). *Diagnostic and statistical manual of mental disorders* (4th ed.). Washington, DC: Author.

Bagarozzi, D. A. (1996). *The couple and family in managed care: Assessment, evaluation, and treatment.* New York: Brunner/Mazel.

Birchler, G. R. (1983). Marital dysfunction. In M. Hersen (Ed.), *Outpatient behavioral therapy: A clinical guide* (pp. 229–269). New York: Grune & Stratton.

Birchler, G. R., Doumas, D. M., & Fals-Stewart, W. (1999). The seven C's: A behavioral-systems framework for evaluating marital distress. *Family Journal, 7,* 253–264.

Birchler, G. R., & Fals-Stewart, W. (1994). The Response to Conflict Scale: Psychometric properties. *Assessment, 1,* 335–344.

Birchler, G. R., & Fals-Stewart, W. (2000). Considerations for clients with marital dysfunction. In M. Hersen, & M. Biaggio (Eds.), *Effective brief therapy: A clinician's guide* (pp. 391–410). San Diego, CA: Academic Press.

Birchler, G. R., & Schwartz, L. (1994). Marital dyads. In M. Hersen & S. M. Turner (Eds.), *Diagnostic interviewing* (2nd ed., pp. 277–304). New York: Plenum Press.

Bray, J., & Hetherington, E. M. (1993). Families in transition: Introduction and overview. *Journal of Family Psychology, 7,* 3–8.

Burman, B., & Margolin, G. (1992). Analysis of the association between marital relationships and health problems: An interactional perspective. *Psychological Bulletin, 112,* 39–63.

Glick, P., & Lin, S. (1986). Recent changes in divorce and remarriage. *Journal of Marriage and the Family, 48,* 433–441.

Gottman, J. M. (1994). *What predicts divorce?* Hillsdale, NJ: Erlbaum.

Hennon, C. B. (1983). Divorce and the elderly: A neglected area of research. In T. Brubaker (Ed.), *Family relationships in later life* (pp. 149–172). Beverly Hills, CA: Sage.

Jacobson, N. S., & Christensen, A. (1996). *Integrative couple therapy: Promoting acceptance and change.* New York: Norton.

Jacobson, N. S., & Holtzworth-Munroe, A. (1986). Marital therapy: A social learning/cognitive perspective. In N. S. Jacobson & A. S. Gurman (Eds.), *Clinical handbook of marital therapy* (pp. 29–70). New York: Guilford Press.

Jacobson, N. S., & Margolin, G. (1979). *Marital therapy: Strategies based on social learning and behavior-exchange principles.* New York: Brunner/Mazel.

Lawrence, E., Eldridge, K., Christensen, A., & Jacobson, N. S. (1999). Integrative couple therapy. In J. M. Donovan (Ed.), *Short-term couple therapy* (pp. 226–264). New York: Guilford Press.

Spanier, G. B. (1976). Measuring dyadic adjustment: New scales for assessing the quality of marriage and similar dyads. *Journal of Marriage and the Family, 38,* 15–28.

Stuart, R. B. (1980). *Helping couples change.* New York: Guilford Press.

Verbrugge, L. M. (1979). Marital status and health. *Journal of Marriage and the Family, 41,* 267–285.

Wahler, H. J. (1968). The Self-Description Inventory: Measuring levels of self-evaluative behavior in terms of favorable and unfavorable personality attributes. *Journal of Clinical Psychology, 24,* 40–45.

Weiss, R. L., & Birchler, G. R. (1975). *Areas of Change Questionnaire.* Unpublished manuscript, University of Oregon, Eugene.

Weiss, R. L., & Cerreto, M. C. (1980). The Marital Status Inventory: Development of a measure of dissolution potential. *American Journal of Family Therapy, 8,* 80–85.

PART II

CHILDREN AND ADOLESCENTS

CHAPTER 13

Behavioral Case Conceptualization for Children and Adolescents

KURT A. FREEMAN and CATHERINE A. MILLER

INTRODUCTION TO CASE CONCEPTUALIZATION

THE PROCESS OF conducting therapy with child and/or adolescent clients involves several major steps (Hawkins, 1986; Hayes & Nelson, 1986; Haynes, 1986). These steps provide a framework for therapists in developing treatment plans collaboratively with clients. The first step in the process involves employing initial assessment procedures to gather information about the client's situation and to identify problem areas. Based on initial assessment findings, target behaviors that will become the focus of treatment are then specified. Next, a case conceptualization or formulation is developed in collaboration with the client. Case conceptualization may be defined as a working hypothesis about the causes, precipitants, and maintaining influences of the client's problems (Eells, 1997). Following development of a case formulation, operationally defined and measurable treatment goals are developed, as well as delineation of specific intervention procedures to attain treatment goals. Continual assessment is employed throughout treatment to evaluate effectiveness of the interventions employed. Finally, once treatment goals have been met in session, programmed generalization is conducted to ensure that in-session treatment gains are exhibited in other settings and with other behaviors. Termination of treatment may result when treatment goals are met, when the gains are exhibited in other settings, and/or when client satisfaction is achieved.

To discuss case conceptualization in this chapter, we address many aspects of the behavior change process. Although the previously discussed steps follow a sequence, it is important to note that the process is circular, requiring constant reevaluation of treatment progress and outcomes. Therapists must consider "assessment, conceptualization, intervention, and analysis of intervention effects [as] both sequential and part of a feedback loop" (Meier, 1999, p. 847). It is imperative that clinicians view a case formulation as a working model of the client's situation, one that is open to revision due to the addition of new data (Persons, 2000). Assessment is the process that is employed throughout treatment to confirm or disconfirm the hypothesis contained in the case conceptualization (Meier, 1999).

CASE CONCEPTUALIZATION DEFINED

As previously stated, case conceptualization or case formulation includes information about the causes and maintaining factors of a client's current problems, including specification of any obstacles to success (Eells, 1997). In addition to this descriptive information, case conceptualization should incorporate prescriptive recommendations or treatment ideas that follow logically from the case information (Eells, 1997). In other words, there are two major layers of case conceptualization (Meier, 1999). The first layer includes information about the etiology or the factors maintaining the client's problems. Based on the first layer, the second layer includes information about the interventions thought to be most helpful for that particular client. A good case conceptualization should integrate assessment information and treatment ideas (Haynes, 1998b). As stated by Bruch (1998), case formulation should "assume a central role as locus of data integration from which all further therapeutic steps should be logically derived; such a formulation is designed to provide a guiding frame for all further therapeutic steps and should enable us to suggest treatment strategies regarding priorities and sequencing and to develop or select appropriate methods" (p. 42). It is clear from these descriptions that development and revision of a case conceptualization incorporates aspects of all of the steps in the sequence of behavior change.

Case conceptualization is a generic and broad term employed by therapists from all orientations; however, several authors have noted that the concept of case conceptualization is especially important to behavior therapists, due to their emphasis on idiographic assessment (Eells, 1997; Haynes, 1998b; Haynes & O'Brien, 1990). As stated by Eells, "A case formulation should embody scientific principles and findings, but also an appreciation of the singularity and humanity of the person in question" (p. 20). In other words, a case conceptualization should "tell a story" about the situational factors controlling the client's symptoms and problems, a story that leads to some intervention ideas (Persons & Tompkins, 1997, p. 319).

There are four basic purposes for developing a case formulation for each client (Bruch, 1998; Clark, 1999; Eells, 1997). First, putting a case formulation in writing may help therapists to organize a large amount of often complex and contradictory information about a client into an integrated and more understandable format (Eells, 1997). In particular, employing a case conceptualization format should help students and beginning therapists to learn "how to collect, organize, and integrate information; how to form and test clinical inferences; and how to plan, implement, and evaluate interventions" (Stevens & Morris, 1995, p. 83). Second, a thorough case formulation, by definition, should help therapists to develop appropriate treatment ideas based on the client's information and needs (Eells, 1997; Persons, 2000). Once developed, a case formulation should be used in every session to guide ongoing treatment decisions (Persons, 2000). Third, a case formulation may assist in establishing a working alliance between therapist and client by helping the therapist to identify issues that are important to the client (Bruch,

1998). Finally, due to the strong working alliance, a thorough case formulation may result in fewer treatment failures and improved client compliance with therapeutic tasks (Clark, 1999).

GENERAL CONSIDERATIONS IN THE DEVELOPMENT OF A CASE FORMULATION

To develop a case formulation, therapists first need to examine their assumptions underlying how psychopathology develops and how people change (Eells, 1997). Clinicians must make "decisions as to what is and what is not 'normal'" (Eells, 1997, p. 8). Each clinician employs criteria against which client behaviors are compared; examples of such criteria include statistical deviations from normative behavior, poor adaptive functioning, and socially constructed diagnostic categories of behavior (Eells, 1997), such as the *Diagnostic and Statistical Manual, 4th edition, Text Revision* (*DSM-IV-TR;* American Psychiatric Association [APA], 2000). Due to the differing criteria employed, clinicians should be on guard against either over-pathologizing client behavior due to "differentness" from the therapist or under-pathologizing client behavior due to "sameness" with the therapist (Eells, 1997).

Second, clinicians must be aware that a good case conceptualization is based on an identified theory (Clark, 1999; Meier, 1999). The clinician's orientation or approach to psychotherapy will greatly influence the resulting case conceptualization (Eells, 1997). Clinicians should strive to clearly articulate their own theoretical orientation and be familiar with the assumptions underlying that particular model.

Third, a case formulation should be considered a hypothesis about a particular client that can be tested (Clark, 1999). Throughout therapy, there must be a continual and ongoing process of developing the case formulation and then testing the hypotheses within the formulation by intervening and monitoring treatment outcome (Tompkins, 1999). If treatment outcome is unsuccessful, many therapists attempt to correct the method of assessment or change the interventions employed (Meier, 1999). However, it is also possible that the original hypotheses are incorrect and that the case formulation must be revised based on the new data obtained from repeated assessment and intervention outcome (Tompkins, 1999).

Fourth, a good case conceptualization should be in written format. Perry, Cooper, and Michels (1987) identified at least two misconceptions about the process of case formulation that may be factors in the resistance of many therapists to writing case formulations. First, many therapists may believe that formal case conceptualizations are useful only for long-term clients. Second, many therapists may believe that written case formulations are academic exercises that are needed only by therapists in training and are not necessary for experienced clinicians. In contrast, Perry and colleagues argue that written case formulations are important for each clinician, regardless of experience, to employ with every client to organize information and determine treatment ideas.

Finally, case conceptualizations should not be rushed. Perry et al. (1987) state that routine use of written case formulations will make such a process less time-consuming and laborious. However, therapists should guard against the cognitive shortcut called "satisficing," which has been defined as "the tendency for individuals facing complex information tasks to expend only the effort necessary for a satisfactory decision" (Meier, 1999, p. 846). In other words, therapists should not cut short the process of integrating complex client information and testing alternative hypotheses once a "satisfactory" working hypothesis is produced. Instead, alternative hypotheses should be considered and tested throughout treatment. Related to the concept of satisficing is the idea of confirmatory bias, which has been defined as "the tendency to pay attention to information that confirms expectancies and to ignore other information" (Meier, 1999, p. 846). It is imperative that therapists be aware of their own biases toward confirming initial beliefs about the client. Clinicians must remain open to new and possibly disconfirming information and should view case formulations as working models rather than validated explanations of client situations.

FOUNDATIONS OF BEHAVIORAL CASE CONCEPTUALIZATION

Clinicians operating from a behavioral perspective rely on the theoretical and empirical foundations of behaviorism when assessing, conceptualizing, and treating children and/or adolescents and their families. To understand the variables relevant to behavioral case conceptualization, it is necessary to be familiar with the foundations of behaviorism. Therefore, in this section, we provide a brief introduction to behavioral theory. We recognize that the term "behaviorism" is applied to various psychological perspectives, such as behavior analysis, neobehaviorism, stimulus-response behaviorism, and cognitive-behaviorism (Iverson, 1994). In the current chapter, we use the term broadly to refer to subdisciplines of psychology that are contextual in nature—those perspectives that espouse that it is the interaction between the person and the environment that best explains current behavior patterns. Readers interested in a more thorough discussion of the different forms of behaviorism are referred to Anderson, Hawkins, Freeman, and Scotti (2000), Iverson (1994), and Schultz and Schultz (1987). Please note that the information presented is in no way intended to be exhaustive. Rather, we intend to inform the reader regarding several general underlying principles that are important for appreciating the behavioral approach to case conceptualization.

Behavioral theory, in particular behavior analytic theory, purports that the best (i.e., most parsimonious and pragmatic) account of human behavior is developed by analyzing the relationship between environmental variables and the organism (Friman, Hayes, & Wilson, 1998; Skinner, 1953). The "cause" of behavior is determined by identifying changes in the independent variables—events or circumstances that can be manipulated *directly* and thus exist in the environment outside of the person—that lead to a change in the dependent variables (e.g., overt behavior, thoughts, feelings). As such, the analysis of clinical phenomena involves assessing the "act-in-context." Use of mentalistic explanations for occurrence of behavior (e.g., the mind, intelligence) are not considered useful by the behavior analyst because relying on such variables to explain overt behavior detracts from the search for variables that can be directly manipulated and thus directly affect behavior (Skinner, 1987).

Behavioral theory also suggests a decidedly idiographic approach to understanding behavioral phenomena. That is, to best understand a client's presenting complaints, it is important to understand the particular variables relevant for the individual. Although there may be similarities observed across clients, behavioral clinicians assume that the most prudent approach to conceptualizing a case is to focus primarily on the individual (Haynes, 1998a). Such an approach shapes the types of assessments used, the reliance on diagnosis, and the process of case conceptualization, as the reader will learn later in the paper.

CASE CONCEPTUALIZATION AS FUNCTIONAL ASSESSMENT

As described earlier, case conceptualization is a process that is shaped by the purpose of conducting the conceptualization, as well as the theoretical perspective of the clinician involved in the activity. Case conceptualization, therefore, does not exist as one "thing" or entity, but rather is a clinical activity that can be accomplished in multiple ways. The theoretical foundations of behaviorism have led to adoption of the functional assessment as the primary method of case conceptualization for behaviorally oriented clinicians. Although the phrase "functional assessment" has different meanings in different contexts (e.g., within geriatric assessment it refers to the client's ability to meet his or her daily needs), the phrase has a particular definition within behavioral psychology. Specifically, functional assessment is defined as the "identification of important, controllable, causal functional relationships to a specified set of target behaviors for an individual client" (Haynes & O'Brien, 1990, p. 654). In other words, conducting a functional assessment involves identifying those variables that increase and decrease the likelihood that a targeted clinical problem will occur. Although various definitions of functional assessment have been provided (e.g., Cone, 1997), we use the term here to refer to all methods available to clinicians that assist in the identification of contextual variables affecting a client's presenting behavior patterns.

Functional assessment is a multistep process that can involve various methods of gathering pertinent information. Methods typically are divided into indirect and direct methods. Indirect methods involve interviews and questionnaires, such as the Functional Analysis Interview Form (O'Neill et al., 1997) and the Motivation Assessment Scale (Durand & Crimmins, 1988). Direct methods include procedures that involve directly observing the individual so as to learn about the relationship between the environment and the problem behavior, and include methods such as the descriptive analysis (Bijou, Peterson, & Ault, 1968), the analog functional analysis (Iwata, Dorsey, Slifer, Bauman, & Richman, 1994/1982), and the structured descriptive assessment (Freeman, Anderson, & Scotti, 2000). A thorough discussion of the different methods of functional assessment for use with children and adolescents is beyond the scope of this chapter. The reader is referred to O'Neill et al. (1997), Sturmey (1996), and McComas and Mace (2000) for more detailed discussions of such methods.

With children and adolescents, as compared to adults, there may be a greater possibility of completing direct methods of functional assessment. Conducting either informal or formal observations in schools, home environment, or the clinic is often standard practice for behaviorally oriented clinicians working with children. Doing so allows the clinician to observe firsthand the associations between presenting complaints and environmental context. In this manner, potential biases in reports given by care providers or the youth themselves is minimized. However, clinicians can and typically do rely primarily on interviewing as a method of gathering relevant information to the behavioral conceptualization. Pragmatic constraints such as distance and time may preclude observation, or clients may resist such "intrusions." Regardless of the method of functional assessment, however, the ultimate goal remains the same: to develop an understanding of the particular environmental conditions that are affecting the client's presenting problem.

COMPONENTS OF BEHAVIORAL CONCEPTUALIZATION WITH CHILDREN AND ADOLESCENTS

To conduct a thorough and complete case formulation, the clinician must gather detailed information regarding the variables that impact the presenting complaint. In this section, we describe the different components of a behavioral conceptualization geared toward the factors relevant to children and adolescents presenting with psychological problems. Specifically, we focus on factors particularly relevant to conducting a thorough functional assessment.

Defining the Problem

For behavioral case conceptualization to occur, the clinician must begin by identifying and defining the particular presenting complaints (Bruch, 1998). Variations in the level of specificity and degree of clarity regarding the definition of the problem exist across different theoretical orientations in psychology. Behaviorally oriented clinicians seek to develop definitions of the problem in descriptive, concrete terms. Thus, clients (or the parents of the clients, with certain children) are asked to avoid interpretations, generalities, and assumptions when describing problematic areas. Further, clients are encouraged to discuss all presenting complaints, even those that do not necessarily appear "psychological" in nature (Persons & Tompkins, 1997). In this manner, the clinician can best appreciate all of the areas of concern, which aids in the formulation process.

The behavioral approach to clinical phenomena is based on the tripartite model of behavior, which asserts that there are three different response modes of interest. There have been various tripartite models put forth, with significant similarities existing across those models. Generally, models suggest that there are three (or four) different interrelated and interacting response modes: verbal-cognitive, physiological-autonomic, and behavioral-motoric (Bruch, 1998; Evans, 1986). The verbal-cognitive mode is typically considered synonymous with such actions as thinking and experiencing visual images/recollections. Physiological behaviors such as heart rate, blood pressure, and pupil dilation are examples of actions consistent with the physiological-autonomic mode. Finally, actions that are potentially observable to others—such as running, walking, hitting another—are classified as members of the behavioral-motoric response mode. Given the assumption that people engage in actions in each of the response modes, behavioral clinicians would assume that problem areas could occur in the form of one or more modes of action. Thus, when defining the client's presenting problem, it is important to adequately assess for and define difficulties in all three modes. All actions of the patient (e.g., overt responses, thoughts, feelings, emotions) are considered worthy subject matter in their own right (Anderson, Hawkins, & Scotti, 1997; Hayes & Wilson, 1995). Actions occurring within the patient are considered private or covert (they are accessible only to the patient) but are analyzed using the same methods applied to overt behavior (behavior observable by others; Dougher, 1993).

Clinical problems presented by children and adolescents can be divided into two categories: behavioral excesses and behavioral deficits. Behavioral excesses are patterns of behavior that occur too often, too intensely, or too severely, such that they cause problems for the individual and/or those around him or her. Examples of behavioral excesses include oppositional behavior, aggression, swearing, substance abuse, excessive crying, and promiscuous behavior. In contrast, behavioral deficits are characterized by the lack of appropriate behavior. Social skills deficits, lack of appropriate food intake, and psychomotor retardation are examples of behavioral deficits. Clinicians must ensure that their assessment and case conceptualization include an analysis of both categories of presenting problems.

Obtaining clear, objective descriptions of presenting complaints facilitates accurate diagnosis. Historically, behaviorists have de-emphasized psychiatric diagnosis as a useful construct (Hayes & Follette, 1992). This has been partly due to the fact that earlier models of diagnoses were based on theoretical perspectives rather than objective criteria. However, most current behavioral clinicians engage in diagnostic classification of their client's presenting complaints (Kratochwill & McGivern, 1996), perhaps for several reasons. First, diagnostic labels facilitate communication across professionals; in other words, they provide a "common language." Second, the primary diagnostic system used by clinicians (APA, 2000) now relies less on classification based on presumed common etiology and more on classification based on likelihood of symptom covariation. Finally, reality in the current climate dictates diagnostic classification as a means of obtaining third-party reimbursement of services, at least when operating within the mental health arena.

However, defining the clinical problem areas goes beyond simple description, which may include diagnosis. Behavioral case conceptualization also involves quantifying the presenting complaints in some form. Thus, determining frequency, duration, intensity, and so forth, of the problem areas occurs when the problems are first defined. For example, take a mother who presents to a clinician because her 4-year-old son tantrums. When asked to do so, the mother defines the tantrums as typically involving crying, dropping to the floor, and throwing objects—an objective and concrete definition obtained through careful interviewing. To complete the definition of the problem, the clinician must determine next how problematic the tantrums are. Thus, assessing frequency of tantrums and the typical duration of a tantrum will help the clinician better understand the severity of the problem. Further, quantification is useful as a means of measuring progress toward treatment goals (Persons & Tomkins, 1997).

Quantification can occur through use of idiographic or nomothetic measures. Given the traditional focus on variables relevant for the individual, behaviorally oriented clinicians have historically focused on the use of idiographic measures. As such, clinicians have devised observation systems, data collection methods, and so forth that meet the needs of individual clients. However, in recent years, there has been increasing recognition among behavioral clinicians of the role of nomothetic devices as part of a comprehensive assessment of the presenting problems (Haynes, 1998b). To this end, it is becoming increasingly more common for behaviorists to rely on the use of standardized, norm-referenced measures during the initial assessment and conceptualization phase, as well as throughout the therapy. Therefore, norm-referenced measures such as the Child Behavior Checklist (Achenbach, 1991), the Fear Survey Schedule for Children-II (Gullone & King, 1992), and the Trauma Symptom Checklist for Children (Briere, 1996) may be used to quantify presenting complaints. Such measures allow the clinician to assess the extent to which a particular child/adolescent's behavior differs from what is expected of individuals of similar demographic characteristics (e.g., age, gender).

By encouraging use of objective description and quantification, the clinician should be able to define the presenting complaints. Further, through use of nomothetic measures, clinicians can determine the extent of the problems. Once these components of the case conceptualization process have been completed, the next step in the process involves developing an adequate understanding of the variables that have resulted in the youth's experiencing the concerns. In the following sections, the relevant issues to consider regarding causal variables are explored.

ASSESSING BACKGROUND OR HISTORICAL VARIABLES

As with all clients, adult or child, a thorough case conceptualization can occur only after assessing for important historical or background variables. There are typically several general areas of information that the therapist should assess regarding background variables. Unlike with adults, it is customary to assess for developmental history when the clinical focus is on children and adolescents. Thus, such factors as prenatal, perinatal, and postnatal development, attainment of major milestones (e.g., sitting, walking, talking), and social/adaptive development should be thoroughly assessed. Developmental history is important from a behavioral point of view because it provides the context for understanding early events that could have provided the foundations for current problems. Let us use as the example a 5-year-old who is socially rejected because he uses aggressive behavior at a very high rate while interacting with peers. Assume that this child had significant delays in speech development, which interfered with his early opportunities to engage in play with same-age peers in a meaningful way. Because of the decreased opportunities for appropriate play, the child does not learn appropriate means of interacting. Thus, he continues to rely on behaviors that work; that is, by hitting others, he gets his peers to react to him (even if it is to tell him to go away).

In addition to developmental history, a thorough understanding of major illnesses, accidents, or hospitalizations that have occurred assists the clinician when conceptualizing current difficulties. Idiosyncratic environments are likely to result for children who experience significant illnesses, accidents, or hospitalizations. For example, parents of an ill child may be overindulgent (i.e., provide noncontingent access to reinforcing stimuli, allow escape from disliked tasks such as chores or homework). Children who reside in hospitals for long periods of time may be deprived of typical social interaction, and thus may be more likely to engage in problematic behaviors to obtain interactions with others. Given the environment that may result when serious illnesses or extended hospitalizations are present, it is not surprising that such experiences may produce greater than expected rates of certain kinds of behavior problems (e.g., self-injury, self-stimulatory behavior).

IDENTIFYING ANTECEDENT EVENTS

As mentioned previously, behaviorally oriented clinicians are interested in understanding the relation between a youth's presenting complaints and environmental variables. Environmental events can be classified based on the effect they have on an individual's behavior. One class of environmental events has been labeled antecedent variables or, more formally, discriminative stimuli. Antecedent events can be defined as those environmental stimuli or conditions that increase the likelihood that a particular behavior will occur (Miltenberger, 2001).

In the context of clinical case conceptualization, antecedents are those events that increase the likelihood of the person's experiencing the presenting complaint. For example, a possible antecedent variable for a child who displays disruptive behavior during class may be some form of teacher or school personnel instruction. Thus, in response to instructions (e.g., "Johnny, it's time to complete your mathematics. Please sit down and pull out your workbook"), the child may commence with the problematic behavior. In this scenario, teacher instructions may serve as antecedents because the child is more likely to be disruptive in their presence as compared to their absence.

Although determining antecedent variables may appear relatively simple to those naïve to the process of behavioral conceptualization, doing so actually requires significant effort. Antecedent variables are not simply those events occurring prior to occurrence of problem behaviors; if that were the case, likely antecedents would be multiple and unwieldy to determine. Continuing the example of the child who is disruptive in school, in addition to teacher instructions, there is also the presence of peers and various physical stimuli (e.g., desks, books, posters on the wall), all of which may be present in the child's environment prior to the occurrence of disruptive behavior. *Functional* antecedents are those events that actually serve to increase the likelihood of problematic behavior. It is unlikely (although perhaps theoretically possible) that variables such as posters on the classroom wall actually serve as the precipitating event for this child's problematic behavior.

To identify functional antecedents, the clinician must determine which variables are temporally and contiguously related to the occurrence of problematic child behavior. Doing so involves identifying those variables for which target behaviors occur in their presence but not in their absence. Thus, if the student from the above example is disruptive when the teacher provides instructions but not when instructions are absent, those instructions are likely operating as functional antecedents.

Given idiosyncratic experiences and learning opportunities, the list of environmental variables that potentially serve as antecedents to clinical problems expressed by children and adolescents is endless. For example, one child who was sexually abused by a male with a beard may response with intense fear every time she sees men with facial hair. However, another child who was sexually abused may display the same fear responses whenever she is told to "be nice" because her abuser used that phrase prior to perpetrating sexual acts against her. Collaboratively with the client (and/or his or her family), the clinician must determine which antecedent variables are relevant for that individual.

DETERMINING RELEVANT ESTABLISHING OPERATIONS

Another class of environmental variables is an establishing operation, which is "an environmental event, operation, or stimulus condition that affects an organism by momentarily altering (a) the reinforcing effectiveness of other events and (b) the frequency of occurrence of that part of the organism's repertoire" (Michael, 1993, p. 192). In other words, establishing operations alter the effect of other environmental variables. To clarify, consider the following scenario. Imagine that you are walking down the street when a vendor offers you a cold soda to drink. You think to yourself that it might be nice to have a drink, so ask how much it costs. "$100," says the vendor. Typically, most of us would not be willing to pay such an exorbitant cost. Now imagine that you have been in the hot desert sun for three days with nothing to drink and you come across the same vendor and the soda is the same cost. In this situation, many of us are likely to spend the money necessary to procure the fluid (given the lack of other methods of obtaining something to drink). In this scenario, the experience of being in the desert is an establishing operation: It changes the function of the presence of the soda and increases the likelihood that we will respond by buying it.

Identifying pertinent establishing operations is necessary when completing a behavioral case conceptualization because doing so helps us understand why the client might act one way at one point in time and a different way in what appears to be the same situation. Children who have improper diets, who do not get enough sleep, who live in chaotic environments, or who experience other distressing situations may not tolerate typical life demands as well as other children who are not exposed to such conditions. In fact, research has demonstrated that variables such as background noise (O'Reilly, Lacey, & Lancioni, 2001), restriction of access to preferred stimuli (Klatt, Sherman, & Sheldon, 2001), structuring routines (Horner, Day, & Day, 1997), and escape from instructional tasks (Piazza, Hanley, Fisher, Ruyter, & Gulotta, 1998) can function as establishing operations that alter whether problem behavior will be present or absent in certain environments.

Establishing operations can be classified into three general categories of variables: physical, social, and medical. Physical establishing operations include factors in the physical environment that impact a child's behavior. Examples of relevant variables include noise level, crowdedness, physical arrangement of the environment (e.g., of desks in a classroom), and the number of people present. Perhaps the child is more likely to act out in response to instructions from a teacher if the noise level in the class is high versus low, or if the desks are in rows versus a circle. Examples of relevant social variables include the amount and quality of interactions and the diversity of interactions. A child with few friends may engage in extreme behavior to obtain interactions with peers compared to a child who has many friends and is frequently involved in social interactions. Or, a child raised in a home in which severe parental conflict is the norm may shy away from interactions with adults. Finally, examples of relevant medical variables include physical anomalies (e.g., deformed appendage), chronic medical conditions (e.g., diabetes, asthma), and medications. Other variables that could be loosely grouped under medical include nutritional health and sleep hygiene.

ANALYZING MAINTAINING CONSEQUENCES

In addition to understanding the variables that increase the likelihood of childhood problems—that is, antecedents and establishing operations—behavioral clinicians are interested in determining those variables in the environment that function to maintain the problems. For behaviorists, this involves determining those events that somehow reinforce the occurrence of a targeted behavior pattern. In behavioral nomenclature, *reinforcement* as a process has a particular definition: a process by which contingent environmental stimulus conditions increase the future probability of a behavior (Miltenberger, 2001). Reinforcement is further divided into positive and negative reinforcement. Positive reinforcement involves the introduction or application of a stimulus contingent on the occurrence of behavior. For example, verbal reprimands given by a parent following (i.e., contingent on) child misbehavior may function as reinforcers, increasing the future probability of misbehavior. Negative reinforcement, an often misunderstood term, also involves strengthening or maintaining a behavior. However, as a process, negative reinforcement involves strengthening a behavior via the contingent removal of a stimulus. Thus, a child who does not like to complete math work may crumple up the paper and throw it at another student because that results in a trip to detention and, more important, escape from having to complete math work.

As with antecedents, the number and type of variables that may function as reinforcing events are limitless. However, environmental events can be divided into those that function as positive or as negative reinforcers. With children and adolescents, several areas are particularly important to assess when attempting to determine maintaining consequences. Social variables of relevance include such factors as the reactions of teachers, parents, siblings, and/or peers to misbehavior, and escape or avoidance of certain people, activities, or tasks. Maintaining consequences might also be tangible reinforcers, such as obtaining access to food, activities, games, and so forth contingent on the exhibition of problem behavior.

The task of the clinician when analyzing consequences is to determine functional consequences—those that are actually involved in maintaining problem behaviors. Many events may occur consequent to problematic behavior. For example, a child might engage in excessive crying, which leads to peer attention, adult attention, and escape or avoidance of a task, such as schoolwork or household chores. The clinician must determine which of those events actually serves to maintain the problem behavior. Perhaps it is the attention from adults, or maybe that from peers; perhaps it is the escape or avoidance that is reinforcing the child's excessive crying; or, perhaps it is some combination of these events depending on the situation and context.

Developing Hypotheses

Once the clinician has done a thorough analysis of the relevant environmental variables, it is time to generate hypotheses regarding the function of the target behavior. In other words, the clinician now needs to synthesize relevant information gathered through the functional assessment process into educated hypotheses about the reasons the target behavior occurs. It is at this point that the clinician transforms obtained data to conceptualization. Although the process by which the hypotheses are developed depends on the method of functional assessment used, the clinician should evaluate available information for patterns of environment-behavior relations. From a behavioral perspective, the process involves grouping information depending on whether it suggests positive reinforcement or negative reinforcement as the process maintaining targeted problem behavior patterns. With this framework at the forefront, the clinician can reorganize the significant amount of information into meaningful hypotheses.

DEVELOPMENTAL CONSIDERATIONS

Assessment and conceptualization of a developing child is a challenging proposition, due to children's rapid and often uneven rate of change over time (Mash & Terdel, 1997). This fact suggests that a case formulation may not reliably predict long-term outcome, especially with young children. In a case conceptualization, a child's "pattern of coping in relation to major developmental tasks, [such as] academic mastery, autonomy, [and] self-control," must be the central consideration (Beck, 2000, p. 190).

It is important to remember that behaviors that are typical or common at a young age may not be considered appropriate at an older age (Mash & Terdel, 1997). For example, tantruming exhibited by a 2-year-old child may not be cause for clinical intervention, whereas the same behavior in a 12-year-old may warrant a referral. Clinicians must stay abreast of accumulating developmental research on age trends for both typical and problematic child behaviors (Mash & Terdel, 1997).

Finally, it is important to remember that childhood diagnostic features change over time. For example, number of fears, nature of feared stimuli, and expression of anxiety change as children age (Barrios & Hartmann, 1997). In addition, expression of disruptive behaviors changes throughout child development (McMahon & Estes, 1997). To develop a case formulation with a child client, clinicians must assess not only behavior, but also the significance of the behavior given the child's age and developmental level.

RESEARCH ON THE USE OF FUNCTIONAL ASSESSMENT WITH CHILDREN AND ADOLESCENTS

Currently, there exists an ever-growing body of research demonstrating the utility of functional assessment as the method of behavioral case conceptualization with children and adolescents. Although a thorough review of this literature is beyond the scope of this chapter, a brief review is provided to familiarize the reader with research on this topic.

Much of the existing research regarding the use of functional assessment has been conducted with youth who display some form of developmental disability. In fact, a quick perusal of any issue of the *Journal of Applied Behavior Analysis* will result in identifying several articles addressing the role of functional assessment in guiding treatment for problematic behaviors. Functional assessment as a guiding process has been used in the treatment of self-injurious behavior (e.g., Anderson, Freeman, & Scotti, 1999), aggression (e.g., Brown et al., 2000), and cigarette pica (e.g., Piazza, Hanley, & Fisher, 1996), for example. In fact, recognition of the utility of functional assessment in guiding treatment for children with developmental disabilities and problem behavior is such that recent federal law (Individuals with Disabilities Education Act, Public Law 105-17) dictates its use for certain children receiving education in public schools.

Research on the role of functional assessment as the process of case conceptualization is not limited to work with people with developmental disabilities, however. There also is an existing literature base regarding the effectiveness of using functional assessment to guide the treatment of target behaviors in youth who are developing typically. For example, Ellingson and colleagues (2000) utilized functional assessment as a method to develop treatment for two children (ages 7 and 10) who engaged in problematic thumb sucking. In their analysis, they determined that the finger sucking of the two participants was maintained by self-stimulation; that is, the reinforcing consequences was the physical stimulation produced by the act of finger sucking. The assessment also revealed that the behavior was very unlikely to occur when the children were engaged in activities or interacting with others. Thus, treatment involved attenuating physical stimulation (via the wearing of a glove) and was implemented only when the children were alone. Results showed significant decreases in finger sucking for both participants, with elimination of the problem occurring with one.

Jones and Friman (1999) relied on functional assessment information to guide the treatment of insect phobia experienced by an adolescent. In their investigation, they analyzed the effects of presence and absence of different insect-related stimuli on the work product of a 14-year-old. The participant was referred for treatment by his school principal because presence of insects in the classroom and taunts by classmates about presence of insects severely disrupted his academic performance. Further, the participant reported difficulties concentrating and working when he thought bugs might be nearby. Thus, the authors conducted a functional assessment to determine the impact of different insect-related stimuli on the participant's academic performance. Use of functional assessment allowed Jones and Friman to determine that it was the presence of an actual insect that interfered with functioning, rather than spuriously informing him of the presence of an insect. Treatment therefore involved graduated exposure to bug-related stimuli plus contingent reward for schoolwork completion, which produced marked increase in completion of that work.

SUMMARY AND CONCLUSIONS

In this chapter, we discussed the development of a behavioral case formulation through the use of functional assessment with child and adolescent clients. Research has supported the utility of functional assessment with child clients, and behaviorally oriented clinicians are encouraged to conduct such assessments with each client. To do so, clinicians should attempt to identify important and causal factors that are related to problem behaviors. Clinicians should assess both antecedent and consequent factors as well as establishing variables. Both nomothetic and idiographic assessment devices should be employed to aid in the functional assessment. When working with children, developmental factors also must be considered. The relevant information must then be synthesized so that the clinician may formulate a hypothesis, or case conceptualization, regarding the particular problem behaviors exhibited by the client.

NEED FOR FUTURE RESEARCH ON CASE CONCEPTUALIZATION

Although research has supported the utility of functional assessment with individual child cases, the process of developing a case formulation per se has received very little research attention. According to Eells (1997), two main questions should be addressed in future research on case formulation. First, researchers should investigate the interrater reliability of case conceptualizations. In other words, we need to know whether clinicians are able to independently construct similar formulations based on the same clinical material. Second, Eells stated that research should focus on the predictive validity of case formulations. In other words, research should evaluate whether predictions contained in case formulations regarding therapy progress and outcome are correct.

Currently, very little research exists to help us answer these two questions. Although an analysis of the second point has been conducted regarding the use of functional assessment as the case conceptualization process with people with developmental disabilities (e.g., Iwata et al., 1994; Scotti, Evans, Meyer, & Walker, 1991), we are unaware of large-scale studies evaluating the predictive validity of the functional assessment as the case conceptualization process with typically developing children. Further, existing research (which focuses primarily on case conceptualization with adults) has not supported either the reliability or validity of the case conceptualization process (Eells, 1997). However, given the different orientations within psychology generally, as well as the different "brands" of behaviorism specifically, it may not be reasonable to expect high reliability across clinicians. In addition, Kanfer (1985) has proposed that reliability of case formulations is not an important subject. Instead, he argued that what is important is that each clinician employ a hypothesis-testing approach to formulation and treatment with each client. The importance of the validity of case conceptualization, however, has not been disputed. It is important for clinicians to assess the validity of each case conceptualization by administering repeated assessment measures and monitoring client progress over time.

REFERENCES

Achenbach, T. M. (1991). *Manual for the Child Behavior Checklist/4–18 and 1991 profile.* Burlington: University of Vermont, Department of Psychiatry.

American Psychiatric Association. (2000). *Diagnostic and statistical manual of mental disorders* (4th ed., text rev.). Washington, DC: Author.

Anderson, C. M., Freeman, K. A., & Scotti, J. R. (1999). Evaluation of the generalizability (reliability and validity) of analog functional assessment methodology. *Behavior Therapy, 30,* 31–50.

Anderson, C. M., Hawkins, R. P., Freeman, K. A., & Scotti, J. R. (2000). Private events: Do they belong in the science of human behavior? *The Behavior Therapist, 23,* 1–10.

Anderson, C. M., Hawkins, R. P., & Scotti, J. R. (1997). Private events in behavior analysis: Conceptual basis and clinical relevance. *Behavior Therapy, 28,* 157–179.

Barrios, B. A., & Hartmann, D. P. (1997). Fears and anxieties. In E. J. Mash & L. G. Terdel (Eds.), *Assessment of childhood disorders* (3rd ed., pp. 230–327). New York: Guilford Press.

Beck, S. J. (2000). Behavioral assessment. In M. Hersen & R. T. Ammerman (Eds.), *Advanced abnormal child psychology* (2nd ed., pp. 177–195). Mahwah, NJ: Erlbaum.

Bijou, S. W., Peterson, R. F., & Ault, M. H. (1968). A method to integrate descriptive and experimental field studies at the level of data and empirical concepts. *Journal of Applied Behavior Analysis, 1,* 175–191.

Briere, J. (1996). *Trauma Symptom Checklist for Children (TSCC): Professional manual.* Odessa, FL: Psychological Assessment Resources.

Brown, K. A., Wacker, D. P., Derby, K. M., Peck, S. M., Richman, D. M., Sasso, G. M., et al. (2000). Evaluation of the effects of functional communication training in the presence and absence of establishing operations. *Journal of Applied Behavior Analysis, 33,* 52–71.

Bruch, M. H. (1998). Cognitive-behavioral case formulation. In E. Sanavio (Ed.), *Behavior and cognitive therapy today: Essays in honor of Hans J. Eysenck* (pp. 31–48). Oxford, England: Elsevier.

Clark, D. A. (1999). Case conceptualization and treatment failure: A commentary. *Journal of Cognitive Psychotherapy: An International Quarterly, 13,* 331–337.

Cone, J. D. (1997). Issues in functional analysis in behavioral assessment. *Behaviour Research and Therapy, 25,* 259–275.

Dougher, M. J. (1993). On the advantages and implications of a radical behavioral treatment of private events. *The Behavior Therapist, 16,* 204–206.

Durand, V. M., & Crimmins, D. B. (1988). Identifying the variables maintaining self-injurious behavior. *Journal of Autism and Developmental Disorders, 18,* 99–117.

Eells, T. D. (1997). *Handbook of psychotherapy case formulation.* New York: Guilford Press.

Ellingson, S. A., Miltenberger, R. G., Stricker, J. M., Garlinghouse, M. A., Roberts, J., & Galensky, T. L. (2000). Analysis and treatment of finger sucking. *Journal of Applied Behavior Analysis, 33,* 41–52.

Evans, I. M. (1986). Response structure and the triple-response-mode concept. In R. O. Nelson & S. C. Hayes (Eds.), *Conceptual foundations of behavioral assessment* (pp. 131–155). New York: Guilford Press.

Freeman, K. A., Anderson, C. M., & Scotti, J. R. (2000). A structured descriptive methodology: Increasing the agreement between descriptive and experimental analyses. *Education and Training in Mental Retardation and Developmental Disabilities, 35,* 55–66.

Friman, P. C., Hayes, S. C., & Wilson, K. G. (1998). Why behavior analysts should study emotion: The example of anxiety. *Journal of Applied Behavior Analysis, 31,* 137–156.

Gullone, E., & King, N. J. (1992). Psychometric evaluation of a revised Fear Survey Schedule for Children and Adolescents. *Journal of Child Psychology and Psychiatry, 33,* 987–998.

Hawkins, R. P. (1986). Selection of target behaviors. In R. O. Nelson & S. C. Hayes (Eds.), *Conceptual foundations of behavioral assessment* (pp. 331–385). New York: Guilford Press.

Hayes, S. C., & Follette, W. C. (1992). Can functional analysis provide a substitute for syndromal classification? *Behavioral Assessment, 14,* 345–365.

Hayes, S. C., & Nelson, R. O. (1986). Assessing the effects of therapeutic interventions. In R. O. Nelson & S. C. Hayes (Eds.), *Conceptual foundations of behavioral assessment* (pp. 430–460). New York: Guilford Press.

Hayes, S. C., & Wilson, K. G. (1995). The role of cognition in complex human behavior: A contextualistic perspective. *Journal of Behavior Therapy and Experimental Psychiatry, 26,* 241–248.

Haynes, S. N. (1986). The design of intervention programs. In R. O. Nelson & S. C. Hayes (Eds.), *Conceptual foundations of behavioral assessment* (pp. 386–429). New York: Guilford Press.

Haynes, S. N. (1998a). The assessment-treatment relationship and functional analysis in behavior therapy. *European Journal of Psychological Assessment, 14,* 26–35.

Haynes, S. N. (1998b). On the changing nature of behavioral assessment. In A. S. Bellack & M. Hersen (Eds.), *Behavioral assessment: A practical handbook* (4th ed., pp. 1–21). Boston: Allyn & Bacon.

Haynes, S. N., & O'Brien, W. H. (1990). Functional analysis in behavior therapy. *Clinical Psychology Review, 10,* 649–668.

Horner, R. H., Day, H. M., & Day, J. R. (1997). Using neutralizing routines to reduce problem behaviors. *Journal of Applied Behavior Analysis, 30,* 601–614.

Individuals with Disabilities Education Act of 1997, Pub. L. No. 105–117, § 615 (1997).

Iverson, G. L. (1994). Will the real behaviorism please stand up? *The Behavior Therapist, 17,* 191–194.

Iwata, B. A., Dorsey, M. F., Slifer, K. J., Bauman, K. E., & Richman, G. S. (1994). Toward a functional analysis of self-injury. *Journal of Applied Behavior Analysis, 27,* 197–209. (Reprinted from *Analysis and Intervention in Developmental Disabilities, 2,* 3–20, 1982)

Iwata, B. A., Pace, G. M., Dorsey, M. F., Zarcone, J. R., Vollmer, T. R., Smith, R. G., et al. (1994). The functions of self-injurious behavior: An experimental-epidemiological analysis. *Journal of Applied Behavior Analysis, 27,* 215–240.

Jones, K. M., & Friman, P. C. (1999). A case study of behavioral assessment and treatment of insect phobia. *Journal of Applied Behavior Analysis, 32,* 95–98.

Kanfer, F. H. (1985). Target selection for clinical change programs. *Behavioral Assessment, 7,* 7–20.

Klatt, K. P., Sherman, J. A., & Sheldon, J. B. (2001). Effects of deprivation on engagement in preferred activities by persons with developmental disabilities. *Journal of Applied Behavior Analysis, 33,* 495–506.

Kratochwill, T. R., & McGivern, J. E. (1996). Clinical diagnosis, behavioral assessment, and functional analysis: Examining the connection between assessment and intervention. *School Psychology Review, 25,* 342–355.

Mash, E. J., & Terdel, L. G. (1997). *Assessment of childhood disorders* (3rd ed.). New York: Guilford Press.

McComas, J. J., & Mace, F. C. (2000). Theory and practice in conducting functional analysis. In E. S. Shapiro & T. R. Kratochwill (Eds.), *Behavioral assessment in schools: Theory, research, and clinical foundations* (2nd ed., pp. 78–106). New York: Guilford Press.

McMahon, R. J., & Estes, A. M. (1997). Conduct problems. In E. J. Mash & L. G. Terdel (Eds.), *Assessment of childhood disorders* (3rd ed., pp. 130–193). New York: Guilford Press.

Meier, S. T. (1999). Training the practitioner-scientist: Bridging case conceptualization, assessment, and intervention. *The Counseling Psychologist, 27,* 846–869.

Michael, J. (1993). Establishing operations. *The Behavior Therapist, 16,* 191–206.

Miltenberger, R. G. (2001). *Behavior modification: Principles and procedures* (2nd ed.). Belmont, CA: Wadsworth.

O'Neill, R. E., Horner, R. H., Albin, R. W., Sprague, J. R., Storey, K., & Newton, J. S. (1997). *Functional assessment and program development for problem behavior: A practical assessment guide* (2nd ed.). Sycamore, IL: Sycamore Press.

O'Reilly, M. F., Lacey, C., & Lancioni, E. (2001). Assessment of the influence of background noise on escape-maintained problem behavior and pain behavior in a child with Williams syndrome. *Journal of Applied Behavior Analysis, 33,* 511–514.

Perry, S., Cooper, A. M., & Michels, R. (1987). The psychodynamic formulation: Its purpose, structure, and clinical application. *American Journal of Psychiatry, 144,* 543–550.

Persons, J. B. (2000, November). *Cognitive-behavioral case formulation and treatment planning.* Paper presented at the annual meeting of the Association for the Advancement of Behavior Therapy, New Orleans, LA.

Persons, J. B., & Tompkins, M. A. (1997). Cognitive-behavioral case formulation. In T. D. Eells (Ed.), *Handbook of psychotherapy case formulation* (pp. 314–339). New York: Guilford Press.

Piazza, C. C., Hanley, G. P., & Fisher, W. W. (1996). Functional analysis and treatment of cigarette pica. *Journal of Applied Behavior Analysis, 29,* 437–449.

Piazza, C. C., Hanley, G. P., Fisher, W. W., Ruyter, J. M., & Gulotta, C. S. (1998). On the establishing and reinforcing effects of termination of demands for destructive behavior maintained by positive and negative reinforcement. *Research in Developmental Disabilities, 19,* 395–407.

Schultz, D. D., & Schultz, S. E. (1987). *A history of modern psychology* (4th ed.). San Diego, CA: Harcourt, Brace Jovanovich.

Scotti, J. R., Evans, I. M., Meyer, L. H., & Walker, P. (1991). A meta-analysis of intervention research with problem behavior: Treatment validity and standards of practice. *American Journal of Mental Retardation, 96,* 233–256.

Skinner, B. F. (1953). *Science and human behavior.* New York: Free Press.

Skinner, B. F. (1987). Whatever happened to psychology as a science of behavior? *American Psychologist, 42,* 780–786.

Stevens, M. J., & Morris, S. J. (1995). A format for case conceptualization. *Counselor Education and Supervision, 35,* 83–94.

Sturmey, P. (1996). *Functional analysis in clinical psychology.* New York: Wiley.

Tompkins, M. A. (1999). Using case formulation to manage treatment nonresponse. *Journal of Cognitive Psychotherapy: An International Quarterly, 13,* 317–331.

CHAPTER 14

Childhood Depression

WILLIAM M. REYNOLDS

DESCRIPTION OF THE DISORDER

EPRESSION IS A significant clinical problem for many children and adolescents (Kovacs, 1989; Poznanski & Mokros, 1994; Reynolds, 1994a, 1996). Research studies suggest that there may be a secular trend in the age of onset of depressive disorders in children and adolescents, with first episodes of depression found in increasingly younger children (Kovacs & Gatsonis, 1994; Lewinsohn, Rohde, Seeley, & Fisher, 1993). Depression is prototypic of internalizing disorders (Reynolds, 1992) in that the recognition of depression in children and adolescents is often a difficult task for parents and teachers, given the internal, covert nature of many of the symptoms. This contributes to an underreferral of affected youth.

To understand the nature of depression in children and adolescents, it is useful to adopt a biopsychosocial perspective that incorporates biological bases (Emslie, Weinberg, Kennard, & Kowatch, 1994), psychological factors (Abramson, Seligman, & Teasdale, 1978; Beck, 1967, 1976; Lewinsohn, 1975; Rehm, 1977), and social-environmental forces (Reynolds, 1998a). This tripartite approach is particularly relevant for understanding depression in children and adolescents, as it integrates significant family dynamics, unique neuroendocrine changes specific to adolescents, and the impact of peers, to name a few factors related to depression in young people. It is important to recognize that reciprocal interactions within and between the three factors may maintain, exacerbate, or moderate depression in this population.

Since 1980, researchers have demonstrated the clinical efficacy of behavioral and cognitive interventions for depression and depressive symptoms in children and adolescents (e.g., Birmaher et al., 2000; Butler, Miezitis, Friedman, & Cole, 1980; Kahn, Kehle, Jenson, & Clark, 1990; Lewinsohn, Clarke, Hops, & Andrews, 1990; Reynolds & Coats, 1986; Stark, Reynolds, & Kaslow, 1987; Vostanis, Feehan, Grattan, & Bickerton, 1996; Wood, Harrington, & Moore, 1996). These empirical studies have shown that psychological interventions are effective in the remediation of depressive symptomatology in children and adolescents.

Depression in children and adolescents presents as a significant perturbation of mood. Depression in young people is typically a distinctly negative psychological state that may be characterized as one of intense subjective misery and despondency, and in some youngsters may also include irritability. Depressed children may be withdrawn from the world around them, experience little pleasure in positive events or settings, and show limited interest in social interactions. Depressed adolescents often feel alone, helpless, and frustrated with friends and family who do not seem to understand them. Many of the symptom domains of depression may be seen in varying degree in youth who are struggling with the biopsychosocial developmental changes associated with adolescence. However, the constellation and severity of symptoms differentiates depression as a clinical disorder from the moodiness that is relatively common during adolescence.

Depressed children and adolescents generally manifest a range of symptoms, some of which may be behavioral and overt in their presentation, such as significant irritability, psychomotor retardation, or distinctly sad appearance. Many other symptoms are covert, as illustrated by feelings of low self-worth, hopelessness, suicidal thoughts, and guilt, or difficult to observe, such as insomnia or difficulty concentrating.

DIAGNOSTIC CATEGORIES

Contemporary approaches and specifications for the diagnosis of depression in children and adolescents date to the early 1970s (Weinberg, Rutman, Sullivan, Penick, & Dietz, 1973), with further delineations in the 1980s (American Psychiatric Association, 1980, 1987; Poznanski, 1982) and little change since then. For a description of the disorder, a reasonable starting point is the primary system used for its diagnosis. Currently, the *Diagnostic and Statistical Manual of Mental Disorders,* fourth edition (*DSM-IV;* American Psychiatric Association, 1994) is the most commonly used set of criteria for depressive disorders in North America, although as applied to children, there have been questions as to the validity of these criteria (Essau, Petermann, & Reynolds, 1999; Nurcombe, 1994).

Depressive disorders in the *DSM-IV* fall under the category of mood disorders and include Major Depression, Bipolar Disorders, Cyclothymic Disorder, and Dysthymic Disorder. Also relevant to children and adolescents is Adjustment Disorder with Depressed Mood. Specific clusters of symptoms, age of onset, and duration of symptoms differentiate disorders. Depressive disorders that are most likely to be found in school-age youngsters are Major Depression and Dysthymic Disorder. Adjustment Disorder with Depressed Mood as a reactive depression is considered diagnostically relevant for some youngsters (Kovacs, 1985). Bipolar Disorders, also less prevalent, may demonstrate onset during adolescence (Carlson, 1994; McGlashan, 1988).

Major Depressive Disorder   Major Depressive Disorder (MDD) according to *DSM-IV* is an acute form of depression that represents a severe level of the disorder. In children and adolescents, MDD is defined by the presence of five of the following symptoms, one of which is either dysphoric/irritable mood or anhedonia (loss of interest or pleasure in all or almost all activities): sleep problems as manifested by insomnia or hypersomnia; complaints or other evidence of diminished ability to think or difficulty concentrating; loss of energy or general fatigue; eating problems as manifested by decreased or increased appetite or significant weight loss or gain (in young children, failure to make expected weight gains is symptomatic); psychomotor retardation or agitation; suicidal or morbid ideation, death wishes, or suicide attempts; and feelings of self-reproach, worthlessness, or excessive or inappropriate guilt (which may be delusional). Symptoms need to be present nearly every day for a period of at least two weeks to meet diagnostic criteria.

MDD may be specified as a single episode or as recurrent. A number of diagnostic features, including melancholic, catatonic, chronic, and atypical, can also be noted in the diagnosis, and criteria are provided to describe the course of the disorder, including rapid cycling and seasonal pattern.

Dysthymic Disorder   Dysthymic Disorder is generally less severe in symptom distress than Major Depression, but usually is of greater duration. Diagnostic criteria for Dysthymic Disorder in children and adolescents include a depressed or irritable mood for most of the day and manifested most of the time over a period of at least one year, although there may be periods of up to two months during which symptoms are not present. In addition to depressed or irritable mood, at least two of the following symptoms must be present when depressed: appetite loss or gain, insomnia or hypersomnia, fatigue or low energy level, low self-esteem, poor concentration or problems making decisions, and feelings of hopelessness. Diagnostic criteria for Dysthymic Disorder in children and adolescents differ from those for adults, for whom symptoms of this disorder must be present for two years for a diagnosis. Children and adolescents with this disorder tend to show lower scores on self-report measures of depression as compared to youngsters with Major Depression, and at a level similar to youngsters with externalizing problems (Fine, Moretti, Haley, & Marriage, 1984).

Beyond the limited number noted above, there are numerous associated symptoms for the diagnosis of either Major Depression or Dysthymic Disorder that are common in depressed children and adolescents. These may include crying, anxiety or worry, social withdrawal, and other symptoms associated with depression but that are not viewed as core symptoms in the *DSM-IV*. Depressive symptoms in children may also include decreased ability to deal effectively with the demands of the classroom or to cope with family problems and an inability to interact effectively with peers (Shaw, 1988). Of clinical importance and an often associated characteristic of depression in children and adolescents is the relatively high proportion of comorbidity with other psychiatric diagnoses (Anderson & McGee, 1994).

TREATING DEPRESSION IN CHILDREN AND ADOLESCENTS

This chapter presents a prototypic case study of the treatment of a 15-year-old adolescent girl. The case study is based on an amalgamation of several cases from therapeutic studies of depression in children and adolescents as well as case reports of contemporary treatments for depression of youngsters seen in an inpatient setting. Although "Alice" as presented here is not an actual case, the history, complaints, assessment, and treatment procedures are drawn from actual clinical cases.

The author's perspective on the treatment of depression in children and adolescents is based on the systematic integration of therapeutic components selected from relevant models of depression (e.g., cognitive, behavioral, interpersonal) buttressed by therapeutic procedures (e.g., relaxation training) that have proven efficacious in the treatment of depressive symptomatology in youth. This broad-based approach to the treatment of depression in young people is also designed to provide a psychoeducational intervention that incorporates life skills and coping strategies targeted at remediating specific underlying behavioral and cognitive deficits and distortions that are associated with depression.

CASE DESCRIPTION

The prototypic case presented here is that of Alice, who is 15 years old and lives with her mother and a sister who is four years older. A brother, who is six years older, does not live at home. Alice is currently a sophomore in high school. She first came to the attention of mental health services when she was 12 years old and was hospitalized for suicide gestures and a previous diagnosis of Posttraumatic Stress Disorder (PTSD).

Alice's mother and father were divorced when Alice was 9 years old, after a very stressful marriage that was characterized by near constant marital discord for much of Alice's childhood. Her father, with whom she has had little contact over the past six years, lives in another state. There was a history of abuse by her father, prior to her parents' divorce.

Alice does well in school, reporting that she usually gets Bs in most classes. Her favorite subject is English and she spends a lot of time writing stories. She anticipates that she will attend college but is unsure of what major would suit her or what job she would like when she is an adult. She reported her height and weight on one of the assessment measures (described below) as 4 ft 11 in. and 155 pounds, which indicates that she is substantially overweight, with a body mass index (BMI) of 31.

Previous mental health reports indicate that Alice has had difficulty with peer relations, although she has little difficulty getting along with adults. She has run away from home several times, the last time over one year earlier, when she felt that no one cared about her. Since that time, her mother has made a concerted effort to understand Alice and her needs and to open up communication between the two of them. At the present time, Alice is open to the idea of psychological treatment for her current mood problem.

CHIEF COMPLAINTS

At the present time, her mother's concerns about Alice's mental health have led to her current evaluation and treatment. Although Alice and her mother have a reasonably good relationship, for the past year her mother has noticed a distinct lowering of her mood, a disengagement from most activities, increasing emotional lability and negative self-statements, difficulty falling asleep, and a general malaise and sloppiness in her appearance and in the home. She is worried that Alice has shown a disregard for her personal hygiene. Alice has stopped bathing on a regular basis and often wears dirty clothes. Her mother is concerned that Alice is heading for a "breakdown" or may revert to previous self-injurious behaviors.

During the clinical interview with the therapist, conducted as a routine assessment component and described in more detail in the following section, Alice indicated that life seems hopeless to her and nothing seems to matter. She reported fatigue and a general disinterest in engaging in school activities or doing things at home, and indicated limited contact with peers. She denied current plans of suicide but did admit to nonspecific suicidal thoughts and did acknowledge that she had previously engaged in suicidal behaviors. Alice said she felt very depressed and that this mood had been going on for some time. She said that she was sad most of the time and could not say or come up with a reason to explain her low mood. She felt that she was a worthless person and had no interest in keeping up her appearance.

HISTORY

Alice has a long history of emotional disturbance, starting when she was 8 years old. Her mother reports frequent periods of moodiness, minor self-mutilation, acting-out behaviors, and running away from home. Once, when she was 13, she stayed away for nearly two weeks. Around the time she began running away from home, there was some evidence that Alice's father sexually abused her, but no formal investigation was undertaken. This incident, along with long-term marital conflict, led to her mother divorcing her father, although Alice was not told the reasons for their divorce. At age 12, Alice was placed in a short-term inpatient facility because of extreme acting-out behavior, self-injurious behavior, and threats of suicide. At this time, she was given a diagnosis of PTSD. She was treated as an inpatient for two months and released. She subsequently saw a therapist for about three months.

BEHAVIORAL ASSESSMENT

Assessment of depression may focus on the evaluation of the severity of depressive symptomatology, be directed at the diagnosis of depression using a set of diagnostic criteria, or both (Reynolds, 1994b). The diagnosis of depression involves the evaluation and comparison of an individual's symptoms and their duration with specified criteria for one or more disorders. This typically requires an individual interview with the adolescent; with children, a parent is present as well. The outcome of this process is often the decision of whether an individual meets the criteria for a specific depressive disorder and possible comorbid disorders. Assessment of severity of depressive symptomatology is typically accomplished by use of self-report paper-and-pencil measures. These measures are useful for their brevity, demonstrate moderate to high levels of reliability with children and adolescents, and distinguish between youngsters with and without depressive disorders (Reynolds, in press).

There were two assessment sessions with Alice prior to the start of therapy. The initial session was designed for the completion of paper-and-pencil measures and an informal interview, when a current life history was obtained. This focused on Alice's current family, school and peer situation, major life events, daily hassles and chronic stressors, and the evaluation of available social supports. In addition to the formal and life history assessments, Alice's cognitive appraisal of events and situations was examined. Evaluation of her perceptions of the cause of her problems, beliefs about her ability to deal with them, and cognitions about responsibility or blame allowed for the evaluation of her self-control skills, her attribution system, and possible cognitive distortions or cognitive deficits. The second session involved the administration of a structured clinical interview along with an informal interview.

SELF-REPORT ASSESSMENT

Alice completed several paper-and-pencil self-report measures, including the Adolescent Psychopathology Scale (APS; Reynolds, 1998b, 1998c) and the Reynolds Adolescent Depression Scale (RADS; Reynolds, 1987, in press), prior to the start of therapy. The APS was administered to provide a comprehensive screening of symptoms associated with 20 *DSM-IV* Axis I clinical disorders and 5 *DSM-IV* Axis II personality disorders, as well as 11 psychosocial problem content and 4 response style scales. The APS includes Major Depression and Dysthymic Disorder subscales. The RADS targets specific depressive symptoms and was used to provide an additional measure of depression as well as a measure for use at the end of therapy and at future follow-up evaluations. It took Alice approximately one hour to complete both the APS and RADS.

On the APS, Alice reported severe clinical symptom ranges (T scores of 80 and above) on the Major Depression, Social Phobia, Separation Anxiety, Sleep Disorder, Bulimia Nervosa, and Panic Disorder Scales. She also scored in this range on the Self-Concept, Introversion, Interpersonal Problems, Alienation-Boredom, and Suicide psychosocial problem scales. Her scores on the Lie (49T) and Consistency (39T) scales suggest that she was providing an honest self-appraisal. She reported subclinical symptom levels on several APS scales of externalizing disorders (e.g., Conduct Disorder) and nonclinical levels on Somatization Disorder and Obsessive-Compulsive Disorder. Mild clinical symptom levels were found on a number of other clinical disorder scales. Her BMI as reported on the APS was 31.

On the RADS, Alice's score of 115 is in the severe clinical symptom range and well above the recommended cutoff score. Using the most recent version of the RADS norms, she obtained a standard score of 87T, in comparison to the re-standardization sample of 3,300 adolescents (Reynolds, in press).

BEHAVIORAL OBSERVATIONS AND CLINICAL INTERVIEW

At the initial assessment session, Alice appeared well groomed, although her clothes appeared to be dirty. She had difficulty maintaining eye contact, with frequent staring at the floor. Her communication was limited to mostly three- and four-word sentences. Her affect was flat, with minimal show of emotion. She was cooperative with directions and was diligent in her completion of the self-report measures. At the end of the session, she seemed comfortable with the clinician and the idea of therapy. She reported that it felt good to fill out the questionnaires and be able to report how she is feeling and the type of problems she was having. It is useful to note that for some adolescents and children, the relatively non-threatening nature of self-report questionnaires and the minimal verbalization demands act as a useful introduction and help to engage the youngster in a collaborative relationship with the clinician.

Alice was interviewed two days later using sections of the Structured Clinical Interview for *DSM-III-R* (SCID; Spitzer, Williams, Gibbon, & First, 1990). The examination of specific symptoms of Major Depressive Disorder suggested a primary diagnosis of this disorder, recurrent type, based on a previous episode at age 12. Alice reported significant dysphoric mood nearly every day, distinct loss of interest in pleasurable activities, social withdrawal, insomnia (both initial and middle), mild psychomotor retardation, excessive feelings of worthlessness and negative self-evaluation, difficulty concentrating, and suicidal tendencies as shown by suicidal ideation. She also demonstrated several symptoms of a hypomanic episode and symptoms of Borderline Personality Disorder, although at a subsyndromal level. She denied hallucinations, thought disorders, and substance use. During the interview, Alice did report a history of suicide attempts, most of which were minor acts of low lethality and always with an adult nearby. She denied any current plans for suicide but did state that she has thoughts about death and frequently wishes that she were dead.

In the interview, Alice described her family life as "dull," although she did talk about how she and her mother got along well. She feels that her mother is supportive, but that other than this, there is not much else going well in her life. She is somewhat distant from her older sister, whom she feels she does not know very well. At school, she has few friends, and feels that no one really cares about her. She does not feel that there is much hope for the future and stated a general despondency about life.

Consultation with Alice's mother lent further support for the diagnosis of recurrent Major Depressive Disorder and the reliability of Alice's symptom report. Her mother was concerned about Alice's mental health and appeared to be a competent observer of her behavior. She reported that Alice spends a lot of time in her room, rarely smiles, and seems remote and disconnected from family activities. Nothing that she does boosts Alice's mood. Her mother reported that she was unaware of Alice's attempting suicide or engaging in suicidal gestures in the past year and that Alice's previous suicidal behavior was considered by professionals at the time to be manipulative.

MEDICAL CONSULTATION

A medical consultation was obtained through Alice's primary care physician, who conducted a physical examination. The physician's report noted that Alice is a moderately obese 15-year-old Caucasian female. An examination of her skin showed numerous scars on her forearms from previous self-harming behavior. All scars appear to be healed, with no evidence of recent skin mutilations. Acne was present on her face, arms, and back. Examination of eyes, ears, and nose were all within normal limits. Abdomen appeared normal and lungs were clear. She denies constipation, diarrhea, or change in bowel functions. A STD panel obtained prior to the examination was negative. Alice has a past history of bronchial infections and allergies; it is thought that these may be exacerbated by stress. She is allergic to dust, cats, and pollens.

Alice did acknowledge that she went through a period three or four months earlier of self-induced vomiting in an attempt to reduce her weight, vomiting nearly every day for about two weeks. This decreased to where she now claims not to have vomited in several weeks. The medical report found no other major current health concerns. Her low mood was noted, and the physician did recommend further evaluation by a psychologist or psychiatrist for possible depression. It was also recommended that Alice see a nutritionist for her weight problem.

CASE CONCEPTUALIZATION AND RATIONALE FOR TREATMENT CHOICE

The treatment approach chosen for Alice is a multimodal procedure that is best viewed as a cognitive-behavioral therapy. Cognitive-behavioral interventions have been used in the treatment of depression in adults and, with modifications, have been shown to be effective with children (Stark, Rouse, & Kurowski, 1994) and adolescents (Lewinsohn, Clarke, & Rohde, 1994). Along with interpersonal psychotherapy (e.g., Mufson, Moreau, Weissman, & Klerman, 1993), they have become the generally accepted contemporary approaches to the treatment of depression in young people. The author and his colleagues have developed structured treatment manuals for the application of these therapeutic procedures with depressed youngsters, although it should be recognized that treatments are often most effective when manuals are used as the basic recipe, with modifications made for specific needs of the child. In the current case, a set of therapeutic procedures relying heavily on behavioral components as well as cognitive restructuring was deemed appropriate for the present case.

Cognitive-behavioral procedures draw from a number of theoretical models of depression, including self-control, cognitive restructuring, social learning, and learned helplessness/hopelessness. Components of therapy are based on these models, by targeting specific deficits, distortions, and maladaptive cognitions and behaviors, and are integrated into a logical sequence of skill-building activities and homework assignments. Additional therapeutic components aimed at stress reduction, social skill acquisition, and, when required, family therapy/ interventions should be considered as needed.

When conducting therapy for depression with children and adolescents, treatment compliance is a major concern. Depressive symptoms of fatigue, withdrawal, feelings of worthlessness, and generalized anhedonia contribute to the difficulty that is often faced by the therapist when engaging depressed children and adolescents in therapy. Many of the depressogenic cognitions of depressed children and adolescents reinforce the belief that nothing they or others do will help them and that the future is hopeless. This seems to be more common in adolescents, and often adds to their alienation from parents and other adults. Without the rapid demonstration that change is possible, these negative and dysfunctional cognitions, such as hopelessness, may become even more entrenched because of an initial expectation for symptom relief. Because of this, brief psychotherapies that have demonstrated effectiveness are highly desirable for treating depression in young people.

The short-term treatment described in the next section is designed to help the youngster to quickly develop and build skills and remediate deficits and, with the guidance of the therapist, apply these skills to real-life situations. The basic tenets of the treatment focus on the training of self-control skills (Rehm, 1977), including self-monitoring, self-evaluation, and self-reinforcement. These skills are introduced within a framework that emphasizes learning and application using a self-change plan, with specific guidance in self-change procedures. Additional therapeutic components focus on attribution retraining, cognitive restructuring, self-instructional training, and problem solving. Relaxation training was also incorporated into Alice's therapy as a general stress-reduction procedure that has shown to be effective in the reduction of depressive symptomatology in adolescents (e.g., Reynolds & Coats, 1986). Because of Alice's reports of past suicidal behaviors and current suicidal ideation, the therapist also monitored her suicidal cognitions during the course of treatment, and more formally at the end of therapy. In addition, another therapist with experience working with depressed and suicidal adolescents was identified and available as a consultant on this case. It is recommended that professional case consultation be available when treating suicidal youth. If Alice's suicidal cognitions or behaviors became an issue during therapy, it would be important for the consultant to review the treatment plan, current progress, and recommendations for further therapy and provide feedback or assistance to the therapist.

The treatment program as presented in this case was relatively structured, a necessity when using time-limited interventions, with added flexibility in the duration of sessions (some sessions may go to 75 minutes or more). When providing therapy for depressed children, it is more desirable to extend the number of sessions, especially for younger children, because it allows for therapeutic components to be presented with greater specification and more examples, as well as providing the child with more opportunities to practice homework and receive and act on therapist-provided feedback.

COURSE OF TREATMENT

The treatment selected may be considered an eclectic cognitive-behavioral intervention. The course of treatment followed a structured short-term psychotherapy presentation designed to be completed in 12 therapy sessions over 10 weeks. The first four sessions were held twice a week, followed by weekly sessions until termination. The short-term treatment was selected with the understanding that Alice would meet on a regular basis with her school counselor to deal with related issues of peer relations and also engage in a weight-loss program under the supervision of her primary care provider.

Although not required in the present case, inclusion of family therapy with a specific focus on the reduction of parent-child conflict is deemed very important in many instances, particularly for the maintenance of treatment gains. Research has shown that parent-child conflict subsequent to the provision of short-term psychotherapy (including cognitive-behavioral therapy) with depressed adolescents is predictive of lack of recovery and reoccurrence of depression (Birmaher et al., 2000).

SESSION 1

The initial session began with a general introduction to both Alice and her mother of the goals of therapy as well as a discussion of some of the characteristics and problems that are experienced and manifested by persons with depressive disorders. It was explained that depression is one of the most common mental health problems of adolescents and is a very treatable problem, and that several treatment modalities, such as psychotherapy and pharmacotherapy, are available. A brief overview of the next 11 sessions was given and it was stressed that therapy would involve homework and also require the cooperation of Alice's mother to monitor homework as well as provide support and assist in scheduling activities as they are required. Her mother was informed that Alice would be taking home a number of workbooks and logbooks to complete as part of the therapy. The therapist encouraged Alice's mother to notify him of family conflicts as well as any problems that emerged during the course of therapy. The remaining sessions were conducted individually with Alice.

SESSION 2

In the second session, a rationale for the cognitive-behavioral therapy and other treatment components was presented to Alice, with examples specific to depression in adolescents. This included a description of behavioral aspects, for example, how mood is related to activity and how, to reduce one's depression, it is important to understand the relationship between mood and activity. Similarly, the therapist related that many people who are depressed tend to focus on unpleasant events and situations to the exclusion of positive events and activities. An example was presented: Alice might do well on a test and receive a compliment from a friend; on the same day, she misses doing things with her friends after school because her mother needs her to do some work at home and she has gained two more pounds. In this example, Alice may be more likely to think of the negative events rather than the compliment or doing well on the test. It was explained how depressed people focus on immediate rather than delayed outcomes, especially delayed rewards. These points were made to help explain how people self-monitor and the importance of making accurate self-observations and how this can effect one's mood. Alice was given a logbook to use for self-monitoring positive activities and recording her mood at the end of each day. The logbook included a list of pleasant activities that had been generated to provide examples for her. She was told to bring the logbook to each session. Her homework assignment was to record her daily mood and positive activities in the self-monitoring logbook.

SESSION 3

In the third session, the relationship between mood and activity was explored further, with an emphasis on how mood can be changed by changing activities. Her self-monitoring logs for the prior several days were examined to see how the number of pleasant activities she engaged in related to her mood of the day. Praise was given for completing the homework assignment, with an emphasis on her effort and a discussion of the aspects that were completed correctly. In this session and all others, very little attention was spent attending to complaints or negative statements.

Using her self-monitoring logs for the past few days, Alice was instructed to graph the number of positive activities along with her mood on a 1 (low) to 10 (positive) scale on a specially prepared graph. She was instructed to look at the one or two days on which her mood was the most positive and note the number of positive activities or pleasant events for those days, and do the same for the days when her mood was the lowest. Further discussion as to the connection between mood and activities was presented, and Alice was encouraged to identify those activities that she found consistently associated with a positive mood. She was told to work at increasing those activities related to positive mood and to continue to self-monitor both positive activities and daily mood.

SESSION 4

Alice was presented with information about cognitive distortions, that depressed people view the world in a negative manner, and how this contributes to maintaining their low affect. It was explained that depressed persons have a tendency to attend to immediate rather than long-term, delayed outcomes of their behavior and events. Alice was given an assignment to select four activities from the prior week as reported in her self-monitoring logbook and describe the effects of each activity in an Intermediate versus Delayed Effect workbook. It was explained that effects can be either positive or negative, and have an immediate or delayed consequence. Alice was provided with an example of the activity of eating a piece of cake during a study break. This activity may be viewed as having the immediate positive effect of tasting good and the delayed positive effect associated with getting more done when you take a break every now and then. Alternatively, it may be viewed as having the immediate negative effect of costing too much money and the delayed negative effect of gaining weight. Alice was told that all of these are potential outcomes and was asked: "Which of these outcomes are easier to think of, immediate or long-term effects? Positive or negative effects? Which effects are you more likely to think of when you are doing something?" She was encouraged to attend to delayed positive outcomes of her behavior and events and to report at least one positive delayed effect of an activity from her self-monitoring logbook.

SESSION 5

The therapy focus in this session was on attribution retraining and the refinement of self-evaluation skills. This session emphasized the need to make accurate self-evaluations for success and failure. Alice was informed that depressed persons often make inaccurate evaluations, especially for their successes and failures. In this manner, depressed persons create faulty beliefs about their responsibility for events. This session examined the assumptions people make in assigning responsibility for events and how accurate self-evaluations of outcomes can help in reducing depression.

A component of this session was on teaching Alice to accurately evaluate the degree to which her own effort, skill, and ability (or lack of these) were responsible for positive and negative events, and the extent to which other people, chance, or luck were responsible. The goal was for Alice to make realistic and adaptive attributions (i.e., attribute failure to more external, unstable, specific factors and success to internal, stable, global factors) for her behavior and events.

Alice was presented with an Attribution of Responsibility exercise to show the assumptions people make in assigning credit, blame, or responsibility for events, and how depressed persons often make faulty assumptions about responsibility for both positive and negative events. Using her self-monitoring logbook to identify several important events, she was shown that she had substantial responsibility for the positive events in her life and that she was able to influence or increase these events. Similarly, examples of unpleasant events were presented to show that she was not solely responsible for their occurrence and that in most instances, these events can be attributed to external factors, such as others or chance. Alice was told to continue to self-monitor and record this in her daily logbook and record as a percentage how much she was responsible for each of the positive activities and events.

Session 6

Relaxation training was introduced as an important skill for dealing with stress as well as an activity that can have a positive effect on one's mental health. Alice was instructed in progressive relaxation techniques with a rationale presented that outlined the relationship between stress-related problems and depression. She was told that one goal of relaxation training was to reduce tension resulting from stress and to enhance her ability to accurately self-monitor her mood, events, and the outcome of behavior. A standard program of progressive muscle relaxation exercises was provided, along with a relaxation logbook for recording homework assignments and documenting the relationship between her relaxation training and mood. Alice was asked to rehearse the relaxation procedures and use imagery to gain a sense of calm and well-being as she achieves a relaxed state. The relaxation procedures were also aimed at reducing Alice's stress response to social situations and panic that she reported on the APS.

This session also provided Alice with social skills training, with an emphasis on giving and receiving compliments, an area that is difficult for her. She also was taught some basic social skills, including making eye contact, reading facial expressions, assertiveness training, and conflict resolution. Because she also was seeing a counselor at her high school and was learning some of these competencies there, this component was presented as a general overview, with role play used to illustrate basic skills.

Session 7

In this session, Alice was provided with the basic skills for developing a self-change plan. The basics for a self-change plan are (1) the belief that one can change; (2) knowing that self-change, similar to self-control, is a skill that can be learned; and (3) the awareness that to change, one has to develop a self-change plan. Alice was instructed on how to specify a problem and decide what to change; how to collect baseline information and track her progress; how to determine antecedents (events or conditions such as social situation, her own feelings and behaviors, physical settings, behavior of other people) related to the problem and how to control these antecedents; how to discover consequences of engaging in specific behaviors, and understand that she should increase behavior that is followed by positive consequences and decrease behavior that is not followed by a positive consequence.

An emphasis was placed on skill building and positive change due to Alice's own actions, effort, and ability. This was also designed to promote a sense of self-efficacy or self-mastery. Alice was told she can take an active role in changing things for the better. Her homework assignment was to select a specific problem to work on and begin to collect baseline information. She also was told to attend to antecedents and consequences of her behavior and events.

SESSION 8

The development of self-change skills were continued in this session, with an emphasis on setting realistic, obtainable goals and subgoals; contracting; and obtaining reinforcement. Alice was told that depressed persons often set unrealistically high goals for themselves, thereby setting themselves up for failure and poor self-evaluations. She was taught to identify a realistic goal that was within her control and to break down this goal into smaller subgoals. She was instructed that goals should be modest and attainable and may be changed. Increasing goals should be done gradually and only when a previous goal has been reached. She was told to make a contract or an agreement to reward herself when she completed a subgoal, and that the reward should be determined in advance and awarded close to the achievement of the goal. The reward (reinforcer) should be one that makes her feel good, is accessible, is consistent with the effort extended in achieving the goal, and is under her control. To assist her, a goal-setting worksheet was provided for her to use to develop a long-range goal and subgoals. She was given a homework assignment to examine her goals and subgoals and make revisions so that they are realistic, in her control, and specific.

SESSION 9

This session focused on teaching self-reinforcement skills, building on the goal-setting skills that Alice had been practicing. She was told that depressed people often do not self-reinforce sufficiently, and may punish themselves too much. She was shown how systematic errors in thinking can lead to negative interpretations and self-evaluation, resulting in self-punishment. The emphasis in this session was instruction on how to self-reward rather than self-punish by learning some basics of self-reinforcement. This was accomplished in part through the development of a reward menu that consisted of a list of enjoyable rewards, ranging in magnitude from large to small, and reasonably obtainable.

Alice was told to develop a self-reward program to assist in increasing her goal-related activities. It was explained that self-reward was a more effective way of producing desired long-range change. She was given a sheet for developing a reward menu and told that the rewards should be enjoyable, vary in magnitude from small to large, and be available. Rewards might be material objects such as clothes and computer games or even activities such as going to a movie or eating out. Each reward on the menu was then assigned a point value from 1 to 10, depending on the perceived magnitude of the reward. Once Alice had done this, she was told to assign points (1 to 10) to the subgoals that she had developed previously. She was then told to use the points earned in achieving the subgoals and spend them on the rewards on the menu. She was instructed to use the self-monitoring logbook to record the points earned and spent and to use the points as soon as possible so that the reward was contingent on performing and attaining the subgoal.

SESSION 10

The previous sessions focused on activities designed to increase overt self-reinforcement and the decrease of overt self-punishment. In this session, Alice was taught procedures for covert self-reinforcement, which are similar to components of self-instructional training. She was told that rewards or punishment may be overt, such as having or denying oneself a piece of cake, or covert, such as praising oneself or thinking about one's failures, and that depressed people often engage in covert self-punishment, frequently to the exclusion of covert self-reward. To deal with this tendency, Alice was given an exercise for increasing her covert self-reinforcement. She was told to make a list of positive self-statements that describe her best qualities, assets, and achievements. She was to repeat this list of positive attributes to herself for one minute. She was instructed to say something positive about herself to herself (covertly) every time she worked on one of her subgoals. For example, she might say to herself, "I finished this just as I planned. I must be doing well," or "I have been doing a good job. I am making progress." She was told to work on using covert self-reinforcement at home and at school and to record her use in her self-monitoring logbook.

Session 11

Session 11 was a review and practice session. It also served as a check of Alice's compliance with the treatment components, homework assignments, and instructions. This involved a check of how well she had monitored and increased her performance of positive activities and engaged in pleasant events, as shown by her self-monitoring logbook. Other ongoing assignments were reviewed and Alice was praised for her efforts. She was told that in addition to overt pleasant activities and events, such as going to a movie or renting a video, pleasant thoughts also are positive activities that are relatively easy to engage in, are covert, and are readily attainable. By this point, Alice could clearly see the relationship between activities and mood, as well as her ability to change the way she is feeling by her own actions.

The therapist examined Alice's selections and revisions of goals and subgoals and discussed with her how well these goals met the criteria of controllability, attainability, and operationalization. The therapist provided feedback and praise for Alice's assignment of points to the subgoals and her development of a reward menu to use for self-reinforcing the attainment of the subgoals, as well as her list of positive self-statements that she uses as covert reinforcers for each subgoal she achieves. The therapist encouraged her to continue to use relaxation exercises as a general mental health procedure and especially when she feels stressed.

Session 12

At the beginning of this session, Alice completed the RADS and the Suicidal Ideation Questionnaire (SIQ; Reynolds, 1988) and was interviewed regarding specific symptoms of depression. She reported few symptoms of depression, and her score on the RADS of 58T, although somewhat elevated, was substantially lower than her initial assessment. On the SIQ, she reported some mild ideation occurring during the prior month, as shown by her raw score of 9, which is at the 55th percentile in comparison to the SIQ standardization sample.

This last session with Alice functioned as a review of the basic principles that were presented for the reduction of depression and the activities directed at instituting change. The therapist provided praise and encouragement for Alice's compliance and the therapeutic gains that she has made. It was critical that she understand what skills she had learned and that these skills be maintained and practiced after the conclusion of therapy. The therapist focused on providing a sense of hopefulness and optimism about her current level of affective functioning and her ability to deal with problems and to reduce her depression if it should reoccur. After completing the RADS and SIQ and reviewing her progress, Alice could see the change that had occurred over the course of therapy. Nearly all of her symptoms of depression were gone. She had no difficulty going to sleep at night, no longer thought about killing herself, enjoyed going out and doing fun activities, and felt much better about herself. She still had problems with peers, but felt that she was capable of dealing this problem.

ADDITIONAL TREATMENT CONSIDERATIONS

The treatment described above was specific to a depressed adolescent. When treating children, it is advisable to increase the number of therapy sessions and incorporate greater parental participation during treatment. This is typically necessary for increasing pleasant events, as well as in the development of a reinforcement schedule, where parents are needed to help carry out activities, provide transportation, and take care of monetary costs. With children, role play and social problem-solving activities typically are added, with extensive use of modeling of therapist-provided examples. In addition, the use of family involvement and family therapy is highly desirable in most cases.

The clinician should recognize that it is not unusual to find affective disorders in parents of children and adolescents who are depressed. The nature of this relationship is complicated by potential biological, psychosocial, environmental, and social learning interactions. In some cases, parental psychopathology may significantly impair parental attachment, nurturing, and the modeling of adaptive responses to stress. For whatever reason, depression or other psychopathology in one or both parents should be considered a potential complicating factor in the treatment of depression in children and adolescents. Depression in parents is sometimes a difficult diagnosis to make if the primary client is the child, although a brief discussion with both parents, individually and together, often provides sufficient opportunity to evaluate the parents' affective status. A depressed parent may reinforce depressive cognitions and behaviors in the youngster, thus compromising therapy until an effective therapeutic relationship can be developed with the parent for the good of the child. In our research, we have found that marital discord is strongly related to depression in youngsters, especially girls (Reynolds & Coats, 1982). A useful tactic is to educate parents who are in conflict that any constructive actions they may take toward resolving their conflicts should assist in their child's treatment and mental health. However, in resistant families, this often does little to stem entrenched conflict behaviors and interactions.

COURSE OF TERMINATION AND FOLLOW-UP

The treatment described above may be considered a brief psychotherapeutic procedure given its time-limited structure. At the beginning of therapy, the treatment program was described to Alice and a contract was drawn up. The contract included reinforcement contingent on attendance and completion of homework assignments throughout the course of treatment and at the end of the program. At the completion of the 12 treatment sessions, Alice was given additional therapeutic exercise forms and told to continue to self-monitor and engage in the therapeutic activities that were used as homework assignments. She was allowed to select a major reward from a list prepared by the therapist with assistance from her mother.

A six-week follow-up evaluation was conducted with the RADS and clinical interview. In addition, the SIQ was administered to check for recurrent suicidal ideation. At this time, Alice reported normative levels of depressive symptomatology and minimal levels of suicidal ideation. She indicated few symptoms of depression and none at a clinical threshold. She had some down days, but these were short-lived, and her typical mood was good. She rarely had problems falling asleep, and felt more relaxed about things going on in her life. She had a few friends and was gaining more acceptance by her peers, although this was a slow process and at times a source of frustration for her. Overall, she was fairly positive about the future.

At the follow-up session, Alice was reminded to continue to use the procedures learned in therapy and to be observant for reoccurrence of depression. It was stressed that she should alert her mother or a mental health professional at school or the therapist if she felt that she needed additional help for depression or any other psychological problem. Alice was scheduled for a reevaluation one year after therapy.

MANAGED CARE CONSIDERATIONS

Managed care has become a consideration in a wide range of health and mental health care settings. Several issues related to the treatment of depression in children and adolescents are of relevance to managed care. Probably the most important issue is that of treatment modality. For many families, their primary care provider, typically a pediatrician, a specialist in family medicine, or sometimes, a specialist in internal medicine, is the most likely to treat children and adolescents who present with depressive disorders. In some cases, the youngster may be referred to a child psychiatrist or psychologist. However, in most instances of managed care, the primary care provider initiates treatment. For this reason, a common intervention modality is pharmacotherapy.

Typically adolescents and some children are treated with selective serotonin reuptake inhibitors (SSRIs; e.g., Prozac, Paxil, Zoloft; Johnston & Fruehling, 1994). The clinical efficacy of these drugs recently has been adjudicated using well-controlled double-blind studies (e.g., Keller et al., 2001) suggesting treatment utility with adolescents. Although the number of research studies showing the effectiveness of pharmacological interventions is small (Emslie & Mayes, 2001), prescribing of SSRIs as well as tricyclic antidepressant medications is relatively common among physicians, with significant increases in their use over the past decade (Zito & Safer, 2001). However, there is little information available regarding the continuation and maintenance of pharmacological interventions with children and adolescents (Emslie, Mayes, & Hughes, 2000).

Utility of brief, time-limited psychotherapy for depression is consistent with most managed care policies. Issues emerge when the number of allowed sessions are too few to complete therapy and realize therapeutic change, or the combination of pharmacotherapy along with psychotherapy is not permitted. Because of these issues, it is beneficial for the psychologist or other mental health provider to work with the primary care physician to ensure that an adequate trial of psychotherapy is provided and that, if indicated, booster sessions be considered part of the child's or adolescent's treatment plan.

OVERALL EFFECTIVENESS

The cognitive-behavioral treatment for depression described previously has proven to be effective in treating children and adolescents. Modifications should be made for younger children. Our knowledge to date on the treatment of depression in children and adolescents is in large part predicated on modifications of treatment approaches for adults and a melding of techniques, such as self-instructional training, that have been developed for use as components in the treatment of other childhood disorders.

In the case of Alice, although she had elevated scores on a number of APS clinical scales, clinical interview results suggested that her primary diagnostic problem was depression. An important consideration in the treatment of depression in adolescents is the potential for comorbidity. Comorbidity of depression and both internalizing and externalizing psychological disorders and problems is relatively common. In particular, conduct disorders, substance abuse, and anxiety disorders have been found to be relatively prevalent disorders coexisting with depression in youngsters (Alessi & Magen, 1988; Anderson & McGee, 1994; Kovacs, 1990; Strauss, Last, Hersen, & Kazdin, 1988). Kovacs (1989) suggests that presence of disorders comorbid with depression in children and adolescents may increase the potential for long-term mental health problems. The treatment of adolescents with depression and comorbid disorders requires additional attention to the other disorder or disorders. For example, Reinecke (1995) has proposed a cognitive-behavioral treatment approach for adolescents with both depression and Conduct Disorder.

A clinical caveat should be made about use of psychotherapy to treat depression in children and adolescents. Psychotherapy in conjunction with pharmacotherapy should be viewed as a recommended procedure for use with some children and adolescents, particularly when there is substantial somatic symptomatology or melancholic features. This combination of therapies also should be considered when presented with a child or adolescent with extreme despondency who may be unresponsive to engagement in therapy due to depressed condition. Similarly, for adolescents with a seasonal pattern depression, phototherapy should be considered a viable therapeutic modality.

REFERENCES

Abramson, L. Y., Seligman, M. E. P., & Teasdale, J. D. (1978). Learned helplessness in humans: Critique and reformulation. *Journal of Abnormal Psychology, 87*, 49–74.

Alessi, N. E., & Magen, J. (1988). Comorbidity of other psychiatric disturbances in depressed psychiatrically hospitalized children. *American Journal of Psychiatry, 145*, 1582–1584.

American Psychiatric Association. (1980). *Diagnostic and statistical manual of mental disorders* (3rd ed.). Washington, DC: Author.

American Psychiatric Association. (1987). *Diagnostic and statistical manual of mental disorders* (3rd ed., rev.). Washington, DC: Author.

American Psychiatric Association. (1994). *Diagnostic and statistical manual of mental disorders* (4th ed.). Washington, DC: Author.

Anderson, J. C., & McGee, R. (1994). Comorbidity of depression in children and adolescents. In W. M. Reynolds & H. F. Johnston (Eds.), *Handbook of depression in children and adolescents* (pp. 581–601). New York: Plenum Press.

Beck, A. T. (1967). *Depression: Causes and treatment.* Philadelphia: University of Pennsylvania Press.

Beck, A. T. (1976). *Cognitive therapy and the emotional disorders.* New York: International Universities Press.

Birmaher, B., Brent, D. A., Kolko, D., Baugher, M., Bridge, J., Holder, D., et al. (2000). Clinical outcome after short-term psychotherapy for adolescents with Major Depressive Disorder. *Archives of General Psychiatry, 57,* 29–36.

Butler, L., Miezitis, S., Friedman, R., & Cole, E. (1980). The effect of two school-based intervention programs on depressive symptoms in preadolescents. *American Educational Research Journal, 17,* 111–119.

Carlson, G. A. (1994). Adolescent Bipolar Disorder: Phenomenology and treatment implications. In W. M. Reynolds & H. F. Johnston (Eds.), *Handbook of depression in children and adolescents* (pp. 41–60). New York: Plenum Press.

Emslie, G. J., & Mayes, T. L. (2001). Mood disorders in children and adolescents: Psychopharmacological treatment. *Biological Psychiatry, 49,* 1082–1090.

Emslie, G. J., Mayes, T. L., & Hughes, C. W. (2000). Updates in the pharmacologic treatment of childhood depression. *Psychiatric Clinics of North America, 23,* 813–835.

Emslie, G. J., Weinberg, W. A., Kennard, B. D., & Kowatch, R. A. (1994). Neurobiological aspects of depression in children and adolescents. In W. M. Reynolds & H. F. Johnston (Eds.), *Handbook of depression in children and adolescents* (pp. 143–165). New York: Plenum Press.

Essau, C. A., Petermann, F., & Reynolds, W. M. (1999). Classification of depressive disorders. In C. A. Essau & F. Petermann (Eds.), *Depressive disorders in children and adolescents: Epidemiology, risk factors and treatment* (pp. 3–25). Northvale, NJ: Aronson.

Fine, S., Moretti, M., Haley, G., & Marriage, K. (1984). Depressive Disorder in children and adolescents: Dysthymic Disorder and the use of self-rating scales in assessment. *Child Psychiatry and Human Development, 14,* 223–229.

Johnston, H. F., & Fruehling, J. J. (1994). Pharmacotherapy for depression in children and adolescents. In W. M. Reynolds & H. F. Johnston (Eds.), *Handbook of depression in children and adolescents* (pp. 365–397). New York: Plenum Press.

Kahn, J. S., Kehle, T. J., Jenson, W. R., & Clark, E. (1990). Comparison of cognitive-behavioral, relaxation, and self-modeling interventions for depression among middle-school students. *School Psychology Review, 19,* 196–211.

Keller, M. B., Ryan, N. D., Strober, M., Klein, R. G., Kutcher, S. P., Birmaher, B., et al. (2001). Efficacy of paroxetine in the treatment of adolescent major depression: A randomized, controlled trial. *Journal of the American Academy of Child and Adolescent Psychiatry, 40,* 762–772.

Kovacs, M. (1985). The natural history and course of depressive disorders in childhood. *Psychiatric Annals, 15,* 387–389.

Kovacs, M. (1989). Affective disorders in children and adolescents. *American Psychologist, 44,* 209–215.

Kovacs, M. (1990). Comorbid anxiety disorders in childhood-onset depressions. In J. D. Maser & C. R. Cloninger (Eds.), *Comorbidity of mood and anxiety disorders* (pp. 271–281). Washington, DC: American Psychiatric Press.

Kovacs, M., & Gatsonis, C. (1994). Secular trends in age at onset of Major Depressive Disorder in a clinical sample of children. *Journal of Psychiatric Research, 28,* 319–329.

Lewinsohn, P. M. (1975). The behavioral study and treatment of depression. In M. Hersen, R. M. Eisler, & P. M. Miller (Eds.), *Progress in behavior modification* (pp. 19–64). New York: Academic Press.

Lewinsohn, P. M., Clarke, G. N., Hops, H., & Andrews, J. (1990). Cognitive-behavioral treatment for depressed adolescents. *Behavior Therapy, 21,* 385–401.

Lewinsohn, P. M., Clarke, G. N., & Rohde, P. (1994). Psychological approaches to the treatment of depression in adolescents. In W. M. Reynolds & H. F. Johnston (Eds.), *Handbook of depression in children and adolescents* (pp. 309–344). New York: Plenum Press.

Lewinsohn, P. M., Rohde, P., Seeley, J. R., & Fisher, S. A. (1993). Age-cohort changes in the lifetime occurrence of depression and other mental disorders. *Journal of Abnormal Psychology, 102,* 110–120.

McGlashan, T. H. (1988). Adolescent versus adult onset of mania. *American Journal of Psychiatry, 145,* 221–223.

Mufson, L., Moreau, D., Weissman, M. M., & Klerman, G. L. (1993). *Interpersonal psychotherapy for depressed adolescents.* New York: Guilford Press.

Nurcombe, B. (1994). The validity of the diagnosis of major depression in childhood and adolescence. In W. M. Reynolds & H. F. Johnston (Eds.), *Handbook of depression in children and adolescents* (pp. 61–77). New York: Plenum Press.

Poznanski, E. O. (1982). The clinical phenomenology of childhood depression. *American Journal of Orthopsychiatry, 52,* 308–313.

Poznanski, E. O., & Mokros, H. B. (1994). Phenomenology and epidemiology of mood disorders in children and adolescents. In W. M. Reynolds & H. F. Johnston (Eds.), *Handbook of depression in children and adolescents* (pp. 19–39). New York: Plenum Press.

Rehm, L. P. (1977). A self-control model of depression. *Behavior Therapy, 8,* 787–804.

Reinecke, M. A. (1995). Comorbidity of Conduct Disorder and depression among adolescents: Implications for assessment and treatment. *Cognitive and Behavioral Practice, 2,* 299–326.

Reynolds, W. M. (1987). *Reynolds Adolescent Depression Scale: Professional manual.* Odessa, FL: Psychological Assessment Resources.

Reynolds, W. M. (1988). *Suicidal Ideation Questionnaire: Professional manual.* Odessa, FL: Psychological Assessment Resources.

Reynolds, W. M. (1992). Introduction to the nature and study of internalizing disorders in children and adolescents. In W. M. Reynolds (Ed.), *Internalizing disorders in children and adolescents* (pp. 1–18). New York: Wiley.

Reynolds, W. M. (1994a). Depression in adolescents: Contemporary issues and perspectives. In T. H. Ollendick & R. J. Prinz (Eds.), *Advances in clinical child psychology* (Vol. 16, pp. 261–316). New York: Plenum Press.

Reynolds, W. M. (1994b). Assessment of depression in children and adolescents by self-report questionnaires. In W. M. Reynolds & H. F. Johnston (Eds.), *Handbook of depression in children and adolescents* (pp. 209–234). New York: Plenum Press.

Reynolds, W. M. (1996). Depression in adolescents. In V. B. Van Hasselt & M. Hersen (Eds.), *Handbook of adolescent psychopathology: A guide to diagnosis and treatment* (pp. 297–348). New York: Lexington Books.

Reynolds, W. M. (1998a). Depression in children and adolescents. In T. H. Ollendick (Ed.), *Comprehensive clinical psychology: Vol. 4. Children and adolescents: Clinical formulations and treatment* (pp. 419–461). New York: Pergamon Press.

Reynolds, W. M. (1998b). *Adolescent Psychopathology Scale: Administration and interpretive manual*. Odessa, FL: Psychological Assessment Resources.

Reynolds, W. M. (1998c). *Adolescent Psychopathology Scale: Psychometric and Technical manual*. Odessa, FL: Psychological Assessment Resources.

Reynolds, W. M. (in press). *Reynolds Adolescent Depression Scale Professional manual* (2nd ed.). Odessa, FL: Psychological Assessment Resources.

Reynolds, W. M., & Coats, K. I. (1982, July). *Depression in adolescents: Incidence, depth and correlates*. Paper presented at the 10th International Congress of the International Association for Child and Adolescent Psychiatry, Dublin, Ireland.

Reynolds, W. M., & Coats, K. I. (1986). A comparison of cognitive-behavioral therapy and relaxation training for the treatment of depression in adolescents. *Journal of Consulting and Clinical Psychology, 54,* 653–660.

Shaw, J. A. (1988). Childhood depression. *Medical Clinics of North America, 72,* 831–845.

Spitzer, R. L., Williams, J. B. W., Gibbon, M., & First, M. B. (1990). *Structured Clinical Interview for DSM-III-R*. Washington, DC: American Psychiatric Press.

Stark, K. D., Reynolds, W. M., & Kaslow, N. J. (1987). A comparison of the relative efficacy of self-control therapy and behavioral problem-solving therapy for depression in children. *Journal of Abnormal Child Psychology, 15,* 91–113.

Stark, K. D., Rouse, L. W., & Kurowski, C. (1994). Psychological treatment approaches for depression in children. In W. M. Reynolds & H. F. Johnston (Eds.), *Handbook of depression in children and adolescents* (pp. 275–307). New York: Plenum Press.

Strauss, C. C., Last, C. G., Hersen, M., & Kazdin, A. E. (1988). Association between anxiety and depression in children and adolescents with anxiety disorders. *Journal of Abnormal Child Psychology, 16,* 57–68.

Vostanis, P., Feehan, C., Grattan, E., & Bickerton, W. L. (1996). A randomized controlled outpatient trial of cognitive-behavioural treatment for children and adolescents with depression: 9-month follow-up. *Journal of Affective Disorders, 40,* 105–116.

Weinberg, W. A., Rutman, J., Sullivan, L., Penick, E. C., & Dietz, S. G. (1973). Depression in children referred to an educational diagnostic center: Diagnosis and treatment. *Journal of Pediatrics, 83,* 1065–1072.

Wood, A., Harrington, R., & Moore, A. (1996). Controlled trial of a brief cognitive-behavioral intervention in adolescent patients with depressive disorders. *Journal of Child Psychology and Psychiatry, 37,* 737–746.

Zito, J. M., & Safer, D. J. (2001). Services and prevention: Pharmacoepidemiology of antidepressant use. *Biological Psychiatry, 49,* 1121–1127.

CHAPTER 15

Obsessive-Compulsive Disorder

MARTIN E. FRANKLIN, MOIRA RYNN, JOHN S. MARCH, and EDNA B. FOA

DESCRIPTION OF THE DISORDER

APPROXIMATELY 1 IN 200 young people suffer from Obsessive-Compulsive Disorder (OCD) (Flament et al., 1988), which can severely disrupt daily functioning (Laidlaw, Falloon, Barnfather, & Coverdale, 1999; Leonard et al., 1993). Unfortunately, pediatric OCD often goes undiagnosed or is inadequately treated, leading to considerable morbidity and comorbidity extending into adulthood. The primary purpose of this chapter is to describe one of the state-of-the-art treatments for pediatric OCD, cognitive-behavior therapy (CBT) involving exposure and ritual prevention (EX/RP), using a case example, in an attempt to help close the gap between the science of treatment development and clinical practice in the real world. Such dissemination efforts are essential, as it is increasingly apparent that only a small minority of anxious children, including those with OCD, likely receive state-of-the-art treatment (Kendall & Southam-Gerow, 1995).

As with adults, children with OCD suffer from anxiety-evoking thoughts and images (obsessions) that prompt behaviors or mental acts (compulsions) intended to reduce obsessional distress and/or to reduce the likelihood of a feared disastrous consequence (e.g., mother perishing in a fiery car accident). The experience of frequent obsessions and the need to perform compulsions can result in significant distress and functional impairment, leaving some youngsters unable to complete schoolwork, pursue their hobbies, or socialize with peers. Passive avoidance is also a common feature of OCD in children and adolescents, such as refusal to enter situations that provoke their obsessional anxiety (e.g., playing ball and being contaminated with dirt). The adult literature suggests that there is a range of insight into the senselessness of symptoms, with approximately 30% of OCD patients reporting very little or no insight (Foa et al., 1995). Poor insight into the senselessness of symptoms is quite common in pediatric OCD; therefore, the *Diagnostic and Statistical Manual of Mental Disorders* (*DSM-IV*) does not require past or present insight for diagnosis of OCD in children and adolescents (American

Psychiatric Association, 1994). Poor insight is a negative predictor of response to CBT in adults. Although no comparable data are available for children, degree of insight should be examined carefully prior to beginning treatment.

Pediatric OCD is formally similar to adult OCD, although the content of obsessions and compulsions is likely to differ depending on the developmental stage of the child. For instance, younger children tend to exhibit more "magical" thinking and are more likely to suffer from superstitious OCD (e.g., "If I don't retrace my steps, something really bad will happen to my little sister"). An adult with contamination fears may be better able to articulate the feared consequence of becoming contaminated (e.g., contracting AIDS) than might a younger person. Generally, because introspection is a challenge in and of itself for younger children, pediatric OCD sufferers may have difficulty articulating obsessions, but may instead refer to their physical reactions ("If I don't do my washing, my tummy will feel really bad"). Additionally, some children who are well aware of their obsessional content may be embarrassed about verbalizing it or fearful that saying their disastrous consequences aloud will magically cause them to occur. We discuss these commonly encountered problems in the assessment section that follows.

As with adults, some pediatric OCD patients are able to identify feared consequences of not ritualizing (e.g., books will be stolen if locker is not checked), whereas others experience anxiety and distress in the absence of articulated consequences. Presence or absence of feared consequences has implications for CBT that are discussed in detail below. Further, whereas the logic of some patients' feared consequences is shared by many in their culture (e.g., contracting some dread disease via direct contact with a public toilet seat), other patients' fears are extremely unusual (e.g., losing their essence by discarding trash that has touched them). It is important to recognize that bizarre content does not preclude a diagnosis of OCD and that patients with such unusual fears may be responsive to CBT procedures (Franklin, Tolin, March, & Foa, 2001). More generally, some pediatric OCD patients present with classic contamination fears and associated washing rituals, but many do not. As we describe subsequently, designing CBT exercises for patients with unusual OCD symptoms (e.g., fears of accidentally causing fires) requires considerable creativity on the part of the therapist.

CASE DESCRIPTION

We have chosen to present the treatment of a child with OCD that allows us to discuss in detail many of the thorny clinical issues that confront mental health professionals when they select and implement treatments for this disorder. We intentionally present a composite case of a patient who presented for CBT after having experienced a partial response to a serotonin reuptake inhibitor (SRI), because many families seek CBT as an augmentation for partial response to SRI in clinical practices that provide CBT. Issues pertaining to concomitant CBT and pharmacotherapy are described, as are the difficult decisions regarding maintenance dosing of SRI versus discontinuation following a robust response to the combined regimen. We also discuss concomitant mood problems that so often occur in the context of OCD, and long-term pharmacotherapy strategy in light of improvements in both OCD and mood symptoms following acute treatment. When presenting specific case information, we have changed key elements to protect the identity of the patients who constitute this composite. Presentation of a composite case allows for comprehensive discussion of more clinically relevant issues than would typically arise if presenting a single case, and serves as a further protection against breaching confidentiality.

Experts often advocate combining medication and CBT when treating OCD (e.g., Greist, 1992), but empirical support for the superiority of combined treatment over monotherapy with CBT is lacking. Several treatment outcome studies have indicated superiority of CBT over SRI monotherapy for adult OCD (e.g., Kozak, Liebowitz, & Foa, 2000), and a recent study indicated that CBT was superior to clomipramine (Anafranil) for pediatric OCD (de Haan, Hoogduin, Buitelaar, & Keijsers, 1998), suggesting that CBT should be considered a first-line treatment for this condition. However, the clinical reality is that often it is quite difficult to find therapists who are knowledgeable in the use of CBT for OCD. Moreover, even when available, an adequate treatment requires a considerable expenditure of time and effort on the part of the patient and the family. Consequently, the first treatment for most OCD patients is typically an SRI. Patients who have had a robust response to SRI alone do not typically present for CBT, and indeed, do not need any augmentation; recommendations regarding maintenance pharmacotherapy for such patients is described elsewhere (e.g., March, Frances, Kahn, & Carpenter, 1997). For patients who do not respond to SRI or who partially respond but still have substantial residual symptoms, augmentation strategies are needed. Given the extensive literature in support of CBT for adult OCD (for a review, see Franklin & Foa, 1998) and the encouraging pilot work on CBT for pediatric OCD (for a review, see March, Franklin, Nelson, & Foa, 2001), CBT is an obvious choice as an augmentation strategy. As we noted earlier, because partial response to SRI is so common, we have decided to present such a situation here and describe the issues that arise in delivering combined treatment.

We also chose to focus our presentation on a case where OCD symptoms were not of the common washing/checking constellation that have been described elsewhere. Instead, we present a case where the child's primary fears were of harm befalling loved ones and of losing his soul to the devil if he were to refrain from rituals. Such symptoms present several challenges to the therapist. The first of these challenges was to design appropriate imaginal and in vivo exposure while at the same time taking developmental factors into account. A second challenge was how to involve parents in treatment planning and enlist their assistance in helping the child complete between-session exposures. A third challenge was how to make use of the child's interests and knowledge base to create metaphors that help promote understanding of core concepts and engage the child in the treatment process. Such metaphors are inevitably created in the context of the child's age, interests, past treatment history, and intellectual capacity. We illustrate how these were used in this case to help the child confront some particularly distressing feared situations and thoughts.

CHIEF COMPLAINTS

Glenn was a 12-year-old eighth-grader who lived with his mother, father, and three sisters. He had attended Catholic school since first grade, and was about to begin placement testing for academically challenging private high schools. At intake, his primary obsessions were fears of harm befalling his loved ones if he engaged in activities that he found pleasurable (e.g., playing basketball) and fears of losing his soul if he engaged in these activities or if he refrained from certain compulsions (e.g., praying rituals). At intake, it became clear that Glenn was very distressed about these symptoms. In fact, he was able to discuss his fears in detail only after being presented with an extensive discussion about common obsessions and compulsions reported by children and adolescents, and even then, he did so with great trepidation. His parents reported that the prior two years had been particularly difficult. His academic performance was suffering, and he appeared distracted most of the time and tormented on particularly difficult days. At intake, Glenn had a total score of 29 on the Children's Yale-Brown Obsessive-Compulsive Scale (CY-BOCS; Scahill et al., 1997), a clinician-administered instrument that ranges from 0 (no symptoms) to 40 (extremely severe). Glenn's score was indicative of moderately severe symptoms and was slightly higher than the average score for a recent large-scale study of fluvoxamine for pediatric OCD (Riddle et al., 2001). His score of 23 on the Children's Depression Inventory (CDI; Kovacs, 1985) indicated that he was experiencing significant comorbid depressive symptoms, which he reported had largely to do with the OCD-related impairment. At intake, Glenn was on 100 mg of sertraline (Zoloft), which he had been taking for approximately one year. His parents reported slight improvement after the introduction of Zoloft, but Glenn emphasized that the frequency of his obsessions had changed little even though their intensity had decreased somewhat on the whole.

Glenn's OCD symptoms resulted in a substantial decrease in daily enjoyable activities, such as playing sports, eating favorite treats (e.g., mint chip ice cream), and pleasure reading. Because engaging in such activities would prompt obsessive fears about harm befalling family members, he felt it would be "selfish" to take such risks and therefore he refrained from them. He reported that on occasion, he did not have obsessions prior to a pleasurable activity, but that they would then appear immediately after the beginning of the activity. For example, if he were to begin shooting baskets with friends in his driveway, an obsession that one of his sisters would be harmed if he continued to play would intrude, and he would cease playing immediately and go inside. The social consequences of this behavior were quite salient: His friends began to make fun of him for leaving in the middle of games for no apparent reason, and soon they stopped coming over to play altogether. Glenn was quite aware that his OCD made him appear odd to his peers, but felt that he could not risk the possibility that such ball playing may lead to something bad. Thoughts about losing his soul to the devil appeared to be more frequent when he was alone at night; as a result, he would delay going to bed. Some nights he slept on his sisters' floor rather than face the possibility of having the "devil thoughts" alone in his room. He reported that these fears and the required compulsions (e.g., praying rituals, vocalizing the word "No!" in response to devil thoughts) were taking up much of his time, and that he was experiencing nightly difficulty falling asleep because of these fears. The fact that he had to say many of these neutralizing phrases aloud led to considerable disruption of his sisters' sleep as well, followed by arguments and parental involvement in settling things down afterward.

HISTORY

As with so many people with OCD, the severity of Glenn's symptoms had waxed and waned somewhat and had also shifted in content over time. Glenn estimated that his OCD symptoms began in second grade and focused on having to touch certain objects (e.g., back door) repeatedly to prevent family members from being harmed in some way or to court good luck at school that day. These symptoms increased often in conjunction with stressors, until sixth grade (e.g., fewer symptoms during the summer). Severity and related impairment increased considerably when the obsessional fears about harm befalling himself or his loved ones became associated with engaging in pleasurable activities (e.g., playing basketball) and when he began to fear losing his soul if he engaged in these activities. At the beginning of seventh grade, he was finally able to inform his parents about his symptoms, and they scheduled a consultation with a child psychiatrist who was familiar with anxiety problems in children and adolescents. The psychiatrist recommended a trial of sertraline, and Glenn began taking 25 mg/day, gradually building up to a dose of 100 mg. As mentioned above, Glenn's parents reported some reduction in OCD symptoms since pharmacotherapy had been initiated; Glenn acknowledged some symptom reduction, but was concerned that "the medicine wasn't helping enough." In light of Glenn's thin frame and occasional somatic complaints, the psychiatrist was reluctant to increase the dose of sertraline, instead opting for referral to CBT specialists.

BEHAVIORAL ASSESSMENT

An adequate assessment of pediatric OCD includes a comprehensive evaluation of current and past OCD symptoms, current OCD symptom severity and associated functional impairment, and a survey of comorbid psychopathology. In addition, strengths of the child and family should be evaluated, as well as their knowledge of OCD and its treatment.

There are many self-report and clinician-administered instruments that can be used to guide this type of assessment. We typically mail several relevant self-report questionnaires (e.g., CDI; Kovacs, 1985; Multidimensional Anxiety Scale for Children [MASC]; March & Sullivan, 1999) for the family to complete prior to the intake visit, then review these materials prior to meeting with the child. If it is apparent from these materials that comorbid depression or other anxiety problems besides OCD are prominent, we discuss these in the intake. The Anxiety Disorders Interview Schedule for Children (ADIS-C; Albano & Silverman, 1996; Silverman & Nell, 1988) is a semistructured interview that can be used to examine comorbid problems in greater detail; we use the ADIS in our current collaborative study examining the relative efficacy of CBT, sertraline, combined treatment, and pill placebo (Pediatric OCD Collaborative Study Group, 2001).

For surveying history of OCD symptoms and current symptom severity, we use the CY-BOCS checklist and severity scale (Scahill et al., 1997). Before administering this scale, it is important to determine whether the child should be interviewed with or without the parent present. In our randomized controlled trial, we conduct a conjoint interview, directing questions to the child but soliciting parental feedback as well. In nonresearch settings there is more flexibility, and the decision to interview the child alone or with a parent present can be made by discussing these choices with the parent in advance, observing the child's and family's behavior in the waiting area, and even during the interview if necessary. For example, if it becomes clear that a patient is reluctant to discuss certain symptoms with a parent present (e.g., sexual obsessions), the therapist can skip that item on the CY-BOCS checklist and save some time at the end of the interview to revisit these potentially sensitive issues alone with the patient. Our mantra in the clinic is "Get the information," meaning that if parental presence increases the validity of the assessment, then do that; if not, then interview the child alone.

Prior to administering the CY-BOCS, the therapist should explain the concepts of obsessions and compulsions, using examples if the child and/or parent has difficulty understanding. We also take this opportunity to tell children and adolescents about the prevalence, nature, and treatment of OCD, which may increase their willingness to disclose their specific symptoms. Children may be particularly vulnerable to feeling as if they are the only ones on earth with obsessive fears of hurting a loved one, so prefacing the examples with "I once met a kid who . . ." helps to dispel this myth and minimize the accompanying sense of isolation. During the intake, it is also important to observe the child's behavior and inquire if certain behaviors (e.g., unusual movements, vocalizations) are compulsions designed to neutralize obsessions or to reduce distress. Tic disorders are commonly comorbid with OCD, and it is important to try to make a differential diagnosis, as compulsions and tics would be targeted by different treatment procedures. Further, as mentioned above, some children who are aware of their obsessional content may be fearful of saying the fears aloud. Surveying common obsessions with a checklist instead of asking the child to disclose the fears tends to help with this problem, as does encouragement on the part of the therapist (e.g., "Lots of the kids I see have a hard time talking about these kinds of fears"). We have found that flexibility in manner of disclosing the obsession is warranted. Thus, for example, we allow children to write down the fears or nod as the therapist describes examples of similar fears to help them share their OCD problems. In this way, we can convey to the child and family that we recognize the difficulty associated with disclosure. We also use examples from children we evaluated in the past (e.g., "I remember a few months ago when a kid about your age told me she would be scared to touch her dog for fear she might lose control and hurt him"), although we let the children and families know we are careful not to violate confidentiality when citing such examples. Below are brief descriptions of our core assessments:

Children's Yale-Brown Obsessive-Compulsive Scale (CY-BOCS): The primary instrument for assessing OCD is the CY-BOCS, which assesses obsessions and compulsions separately on time consumed, distress, interference, degree of resistance, and control (Goodman, Price, Rasmussen, Mazure, Delgado, et al., 1989; Goodman, Price, Rasmussen, Mazure, Fleischmann, et al., 1989). We use the pediatric version (Scahill et al., 1997) of the CY-BOCS symptom checklist and symptom scale to inventory past and present OCD symptoms, initial severity, total OCD severity, relative preponderance of obsessions and compulsions, and degree of insight. The CY-BOCS is a clinician-rated instrument merging data from clinical observation and parent and child report.

Anxiety Disorders Interview for Children (ADIS): The child and adolescent ADIS is a semistructured interview for assessing *DSM-IV* anxiety disorders in youth that shows excellent psychometric properties for internalizing conditions relative to other available instruments, such as the Diagnostic Interview Scale for Children (DISC; Silverman, 1991). The ADIS uses an interviewer-observer format, thereby allowing the clinician to draw information from the interview and from clinical observations. Scores are derived regarding specific diagnoses and level of diagnosis-related interference.

OCD Impact Scale (OCIS): We also obtain child and parent versions of the OCIS, which shows preliminary evidence favoring psychometric adequacy and sensitivity to change (Jaffer & Piacentini, 2001; Piacentini, Jaffer, Liebowitz, & Gitow, 1992), for use in analyses of functional impairment from OCD. This instrument enables us to estimate whether the CY-BOCS improvements result in normalization as assessed by functional impairment.

Multidimensional Anxiety Scale for Children (MASC): The MASC has four factors and six subfactors: physical anxiety (tense/restless, somatic/autonomic), harm avoidance (perfectionism, anxious coping), social anxiety (humiliation/rejection, performance anxiety), and separation anxiety. It is in use in a variety of NIMH-funded treatment outcome studies. The MASC shows test-retest reliability in clinical (ICC > .92) and school samples (ICC > .85); convergent/divergent validity is similarly superior (March, 1998; March & Sullivan, 1999). There is also the MASC OC Screener, a 20-item questionnaire that surveys OCD symptoms frequently reported by children and adolescents.

Children's Depression Inventory (CDI): The CDI is a 27-item self-report scale that measures cognitive, affective, behavioral, and interpersonal symptoms of depression (Kovacs, 1985). Each item consists of three statements, of which the child is asked to select the one that best describes his or her current functioning. Items are scored from 0 to 2; therefore, scores on the CDI can range from 0 to 54. The CDI shows adequate reliability and validity (Kovacs, 1985). This scale is useful to assess for symptoms of depression, which assists in tailoring the treatment plan.

MEDICAL CONSULTATION

Pediatric OCD patients' medical history should be surveyed, with particular attention paid to presence of recurrent Strep infection. Although children with streptococcal-precipitated OCD (Pediatric Autoimmune Neuropsychiatric Disorders Associated with Streptococcal Infection, PANDAS) may require somewhat different treatment(s), experts agree that the base rate of PANDAS given OCD is currently unknown and that the diagnosis cannot be assigned retrospectively at this juncture (Leonard et al., 1999; Swedo et al., 1998). Current research diagnostic criteria for PANDAS require at least two prospectively documented episodes of exacerbations in OCD and tic symptoms associated with streptococcal infection. Unfortunately, an unambiguous retrospective diagnosis of PANDAS is next to impossible in a clinically referred population of youth with OCD (Giulino et al., 2001). Clinically, children who have unambiguous cases of PANDAS should be referred for appropriate treatment of their group A β-hemolytic streptococcal (GABHS) infection. Once treated for strep, the clinician should then consider CBT and/or SSRI (selective serotonin reuptake inhibitor) pharmacotherapy strategies.

In the case of Glenn, the physician who prescribed and supervised the SSRI and was the referral source was contacted on completion of the intake to coordinate treatment efforts. The physician's concerns about possible side effects (e.g., increased GI symptoms) at a higher dose of sertraline were discussed, and CBT was initiated with the patient remaining on 100 mg. Periodic contacts between the treatment providers were made during the treatment to discuss progress and the aftercare plan. When combined treatment is instituted, it is important that treatment providers discuss the case conceptualization up front and present a united front to the patient and family. In cases where the family is self-referred for CBT augmentation, it is essential that the CBT therapist establish a cordial professional interaction with the treating psychiatrist.

CASE CONCEPTUALIZATION

There are several theoretical accounts of the etiology and maintenance of OCD, some of which underlie the treatments that were implemented in the case we present. Mowrer's (1939, 1960) two-stage theory for the acquisition and maintenance of fear and avoidance behavior was invoked by Dollard and Miller (1950) to explain OCD. Accordingly, a neutral event comes to elicit fear after being experienced along with an event that, by its nature, causes distress. Distress can be conditioned to mental events (e.g., thoughts) as well as to physical events (e.g., floors, bathrooms). Once fear is acquired, escape or avoidance patterns (i.e., compulsions) develop to reduce fear and are maintained by the negative reinforcement of fear reduction. Mowrer's theory does not adequately account for fear acquisition (Rachman & Wilson, 1980), but it is consistent with observations about maintenance of compulsive rituals: Obsessions give rise to anxiety/distress and compulsions reduce it (e.g., Roper & Rachman, 1976; Roper, Rachman, & Hodgson, 1973). Accordingly, we discussed with Glenn and his family this functional relationship between obsessions and compulsions and used this discussion to introduce the rationale for ritual prevention.

Salkovskis (1985) offered a thorough cognitive analysis of OCD. He proposed that five assumptions are specifically characteristic of OCD: (1) Thinking of an action is analogous to its performance; (2) failing to prevent (or failing to try to prevent) harm to self or others is morally equivalent to causing the harm; (3) responsibility for harm is not diminished by extenuating circumstances; (4) failing to ritualize in response to an idea about harm constitutes an intention to harm; and (5) one should exercise control over one's thoughts (p. 579). An interesting implication of this theory is that, whereas obsessive intrusions may be seen by the patient as unacceptable, the mental and overt rituals that they prompt will be acceptable. In Glenn's case, he viewed rituals as essential to prevent his family from being harmed and the loss of his immortal soul, although he did experience obsessions as unwanted and intrusive. Discussion of these cognitive concepts is certainly a part of good CBT, as such information promotes cognitive change in conjunction with the disconfirming evidence gleaned from prolonged and repeated exposure exercises. Glenn and the therapist often discussed these issues, usually in the context of doing exposures but sometimes preceding particularly difficult exposures. Glenn's understanding of the rationale for doing exposure was considered essential in promoting a good outcome for him, as it is for other children and adolescents doing CBT for OCD.

Foa and Kozak (1985) hypothesized that individuals with OCD determine that a situation is dangerous if its safety cannot be proven, and fail to make inductive leaps about safety from information about the absence of danger. For example, to feel safe, an OCD sufferer requires a guarantee that the toilet seat be safe before sitting on it, whereas a person without OCD would sit on the toilet seat unless there were something particular about it indicating danger, such as visible brown spots on the seat. Consequently, rituals that are performed to reduce likelihood of harm can never really provide safety and must be repeated. For other patients with obsessive compulsions, certain harmless stimuli are strongly associated with distress, without regard to harm. For example, some patients reduce distress about disarray by rearranging objects, but do not anticipate any harmful consequences of the disorganization, except that it "just doesn't feel right." Glenn did have feared consequences and, to complicate matters, many of his feared consequences were based in the future, which makes their disconfirmation more difficult. He also came to view the intensity of his physiological reaction to obsessions as evidence for how likely it would be that feared consequences would ensue if he were to refrain. For example, he viewed mildly distressing obsessions that evoked little physiological reaction as "less likely," whereas those that evoked situationally bound panic attacks were seen as extremely serious and highly likely to result in disastrous consequences if rituals were not completed successfully.

Importantly, although exposure therapy for pathological anxiety originated from a learning theory perspective, from the start, exposure and ritual prevention has been construed as a program for modifying mistaken beliefs (Meyer, 1966). In the same vein, to explain efficacy of exposure therapy with anxiety disorders, Foa and Kozak (1986) proposed that exposure exercises are successful to the extent that they include information that corrects the pathological elements of the specific cognitive structure of the patient. To address the hypothesized need for OCD patients to search for complete safety, therapy is presented as an opportunity to learn to tolerate ambiguity about safety. This concept became a core feature of discussions with Glenn during treatment about how his need for a guarantee that his immortal soul and his family were going to be safe perpetuated his fears and avoidances, and that exposure exercises were designed to strengthen his tolerance of doubt about these obsessions.

The prevailing biological account of OCD hypothesizes that abnormal serotonin metabolism is expressed in OCD symptoms. Study of the efficacy of SRIs for OCD as compared to nonserotonergic compounds and to pill placebo has provided a compelling argument for this hypothesis (Zohar & Insel, 1987). Significant correlations between clomipramine plasma levels and improvement in OCD have led researchers to suggest that serotonin function mediates obsessive-compulsive symptoms, thus lending further support to the serotonin hypothesis (Insel et al., 1983). However, studies that directly investigated serotonin functioning in OCD patients have proven inconclusive. For example, serotonin platelet uptake studies have failed to differentiate OCD patients from controls (Insel, Mueller, Alterman, Linnoila, & Murphy, 1985; Weizman et al., 1986). Also inconsistent with the serotonin hypothesis is the finding that clomipramine, a nonselective serotonergic medication, appears to produce greater OCD symptom reduction than SSRIs such as fluoxetine, fluvoxamine, and sertraline (Greist, Jefferson, Kobak, Katzelnick, & Serlin, 1995). Nevertheless, the consistent superiority of SRIs over placebo and over antidepressant medications without serotonergic properties (e.g., Leonard et al., 1989, 1991) suggests that serotonin dysfunction does play a role in the pathology of OCD. Increasingly, OCD is discussed as a neurobehavioral disorder (e.g., March & Mulle, 1998), and UCLA positron emission tomography (PET) scan studies have underscored the effects of CBT on both psychological and biological measures (e.g., Baxter et al., 1992). Glenn was given this rationale as well, and the compatibility of the neurobehavioral model with CBT and pharmacotherapy was discussed.

With respect to other biological theories, research being conducted at the National Institute of Mental Health on PANDAS may ultimately shed light on the role of basal ganglia dysfunction in certain neuropsychiatric conditions, including OCD (Swedo et al., 1998). Some have even proposed that childhood-onset OCD represents a phenomenologically and etiologically distinct subtype of OCD, bearing a close genetic relationship to tic disorders and possibly sharing a common or similar pathogenesis (Eichstedt & Arnold, 2001). Glenn's medical history was inconsistent with a diagnosis of PANDAS, in that he did not experience sudden onset of symptoms in the wake of strep infection and did not evidence the requisite "saw-tooth" pattern of dramatic waxing and waning of symptoms in step with strep infection and recovery. Thus, Glenn's comprehensive treatment plan did not include use of antibiotics.

Other theoretical viewpoints emphasize the role of family psychopathology in the generation of anxiety and other psychiatric symptoms. Indeed, families often become entangled in the symptoms of pediatric OCD sufferers, and the goal of the therapist is to try to help the family play a positive and supportive role in treatment. Earlier psychodynamic and other, more family-oriented theoretical approaches to OCD may have focused in Glenn's case on the meaning of his symptoms, given that they involved harm befalling family members; as a vestige of these theoretical approaches, even the CY-BOCS checklist categorizes such obsessions as "aggressive," suggesting that murderous impulses may be at issue rather than fears. We do not ascribe to this theoretical viewpoint and are quick to educate patients and families about the fact that OCD content does not appear to be a function of interpersonal conflicts, even when symptoms seem to lend themselves readily to such an interpretation. As is often the case when these issues are discussed openly, Glenn and his family were reassured to learn that the content of his fears did not indicate serious family psychopathology that must be addressed rather than the more functionally impairing OCD. In fact, the family described themselves as quite close, and members were demonstrably affectionate and kind to one another during the intake process. Overly involved families may need assistance with allowing the child to experience anxiety while confronting OCD, but we do not believe that the overinvolvement caused the OCD, nor should it be the primary target in treatment.

RATIONALE FOR TREATMENT CHOICE

Treatment choice for pediatric OCD should be informed by a variety of factors, including empirical data, expert recommendation, clinical judgment, and the patient's input. At the same time, practical factors such as availability of local expertise and insurance requirements must also be considered. Below we discuss some of these factors in detail and describe the rationale for choosing combined treatment in the particular case we are presenting.

RESEARCH ON THE EFFICACY OF SEROTONIN REUPTAKE INHIBITORS

Increased recognition of pediatric OCD in the past decade has stimulated psychopharmacological treatment outcome research. Three controlled studies with children and adolescents have evaluated efficacy of clomipramine (CMI; DeVeaugh-Geiss et al., 1992; Flament et al., 1985; Leonard et al., 1989), a tricyclic antidepressant that inhibits serotonin reuptake but also affects other neurotransmitter systems (e.g., DeVeaugh-Geiss, Landau, & Katz, 1989). In the largest of these pediatric CMI studies, DeVeaugh-Geiss et al. (1992) found a mean 37% reduction on the CY-BOCS for CMI versus 8% for placebo in a pediatric OCD sample, which is convergent with findings from the multicenter study on adults (DeVeaugh-Geiss et al., 1989). Thus, CMI is superior to placebo, produces partial symptom reduction on average, and yields similar results in adults and children.

Despite evidence for efficacy of CMI, *selective* SRIs (fluoxetine, fluvoxamine, sertraline, and paroxetine) are more typically used as a first-line treatment of pediatric OCD in clinical practice. This is likely due to their generally more favorable side effect profile in comparison to that of CMI (March et al., 1997). Several SSRIs have been found effective for children and adolescents with OCD in controlled studies. Fluoxetine was found to be superior to placebo in a double-blind, placebo-controlled, crossover study (Riddle et al., 1992). In the largest pediatric OCD placebo-controlled study conducted to date, sertraline was also found superior to placebo (March et al., 1998). A preliminary report from yet another recently completed multicenter study suggests that fluvoxamine is also superior to placebo for pediatric OCD (Riddle et al., 2001). To date, no study has compared the relative efficacy of one SRI versus another using a pediatric OCD sample. Based on the mean CY-BOCS reductions reported in the controlled trials conducted so far, it appears that CMI and the SSRIs are effective treatments for pediatric OCD, with no clear superiority of a particular compound (March et al., 1997). As mentioned above, evidence from these trials consistently suggests that partial response is the rule rather than the exception, although the widespread availability of SRIs and the relative ease of the treatment on families makes pharmacotherapy an attractive first-line treatment for pediatric OCD.

RESEARCH ON EXPOSURE AND RITUAL PREVENTION

Extrapolating from the adult OCD treatment outcome literature, it appears that CBT involving EX/RP is likely to be a highly effective treatment for pediatric OCD. The close parallels between adult and pediatric OCD symptom reductions in response to pharmacotherapy further support this contention, as do several recently published case series examining CBT involving EX/RP in children and adolescents. March, Mulle, and Herbel (1994) found a mean posttreatment CY-BOCS reduction of 50% in 15 children and adolescents following a CBT program that included psychoeducation, cognitive training, EX/RP, and anxiety management training; all but one child received concurrent pharmacotherapy with an SRI. More recently, 14 children and adolescents treated with CBT involving EX/RP evidenced a mean 67% and 62% CY-BOCS reduction at posttreatment and at follow-up, respectively (Franklin et al., 1998). In the largest of the published open trials involving CBT for juvenile OCD, Wever and Rey (1997) reported a mean posttreatment CY-BOCS reduction of 68% in 57 children and adolescents who received CBT and concomitant pharmacotherapy. In addition, de Haan et al. (1998) randomly assigned pediatric patients to treatment with CBT or CMI and found that CBT was superior to CMI in reducing OCD symptoms as measured by the CY-BOCS. Although these findings on the whole are encouraging, much more empirical research is needed before definitive conclusions can be drawn about the relative and combined efficacy of CBT and pharmacotherapy for pediatric OCD. Such studies are indeed underway (Pediatric OCD Collaborative Study Group, 2001; Piacentini, 1999), and when published, they will provide essential information about initial treatments. In the interim, clinical decision making regarding EX/RP treatment for children and adolescents is guided by the few studies mentioned above, case study data (for a review, see March, 1995), and expert consensus (March, Frances, et al., 1997), as well as the extensive adult EX/RP treatment outcome literature.

As noted earlier, Glenn was referred for CBT after having the typical partial response to SRI pharmacotherapy. Rather than switch to another SRI or add an atypical neuroleptic, such as risperidone, which are augmentation strategies commonly used in clinical practice, the treating physician opted for CBT augmentation. Availability of psychologists locally who had expertise in CBT for pediatric OCD made this a viable alternative for referral, and the family's interest in this form of treatment was further stimulated by their reading of two recently published books on CBT for pediatric OCD (Chansky, 2000; March & Mulle, 1998). Glenn's motivation to be rid of OCD also played a role in choosing the augmentation strategy. EX/RP requires a good deal of effort on the part of the family and, mostly, the patient; thus, desire to get better may influence treatment compliance and thereby influence outcome. Glenn had been highly compliant with his medication regimen and had discussed with his physician his strong desire to try other treatments when it became apparent that his SRI pharmacotherapy regimen left him with substantial residual symptoms.

COURSE OF TREATMENT

OVERVIEW

The EX/RP program that we typically employ was published as a book by March and Mulle in 1998 (see Table 15.1 for visit summary). In the context of the randomized controlled outcome study we are currently conducting, this program has been adapted for research purposes to include 14 sessions over 12 weeks in Phase I, with four monthly follow-up sessions conducted in Phase II for patients who responded to EX/RP or to combination treatment. Thus, although the context in which the patient is seen influences session frequency at least in part, the protocol that we use in the research trial is the same one that guides fee-for-service treatment in our respective centers. We present Glenn's treatment by discussion of early, middle, and later sessions, including discussion of the three family sessions that are built into the protocol, to illustrate how early work sets up later discussions and exercises.

As shown in Table 15.1, the CBT protocol consists of 14 visits over 12 weeks that involve (1) psychoeducation, (2) cognitive training, (3) mapping OCD, (4) EX/RP, and (5) relapse prevention. Except for weeks 1 and 2, when Glenn came to the center twice weekly, all visits were one weekly sessions of one hour each. In addition to these in-person visits, a brief telephone contact was conducted after each of the weekly sessions in which the therapist provided encouragement and answered questions about homework assignments. Each session includes a statement of goals, review of the previous week, provision of new

Table 15.1
CBT-Treatment Protocol

Visit Number	Goals
Weeks 1 and 2	Psychoeducation Cognitive training
Week 2	Mapping OCD Cognitive training
Weeks 3–12	Exposure and ritual prevention
Weeks 11–12	Relapse prevention
Visits 1, 7, and 11	Parent sessions

information, therapist-assisted practice (when appropriate), homework for the coming week, and monitoring procedures.

OVERVIEW OF PARENT SESSIONS

Glenn's parents were directly involved in sessions 1, 7, and 11, with the latter two sessions devoted to guiding them about how to assist Glenn with the accomplishment of his homework assignments and with reinforcing his efforts to combat OCD. Sessions 13 and 14 also require significant parental input. Typically, Glenn was brought to the clinic by his mother. She would spend the last five minutes of most of the nonparent sessions checking in with the therapist; they discussed Glenn's homework goals and his progress in treatment. The therapist helped Glenn's parents praise him for resisting OCD, while at the same time refocusing their attention on positive elements in his life, an intervention termed differential reinforcement of other behavior. In some cases, extensive family involvement in rituals and/or the developmental level of the child require that family members play a more central role in treatment than was needed for Glenn, and the CBT protocol provides sufficient flexibility to accommodate variations in family involvement dictated by the OCD symptom picture and by the developmental stage of the child. Decisions about when and how to involve parents are made in clinical supervision, where factors such as the child's ability to discuss his or her symptoms directly with the therapist, the extent to which obsessional content and/or rituals involves parents, and likelihood of successful completion of exposure homeworks and self-monitoring tasks are all taken into consideration.

PSYCHOEDUCATION

The initial parent session involved a detailed discussion of OCD as a neurobehavioral disorder. We described the areas of the brain that may be implicated in the pathophysiology of OCD, the serotonin hypothesis, and the PET scan studies, suggesting that behavioral changes after EX/RP may affect these areas of the brain. We try to help the family view OCD as a medical illness rather than a series of habits that the child/adolescent could stop if he or she tried hard enough. Adopting this view may promote externalizing of OCD and foster the collaborative spirit of the family and therapist in fighting against the illness rather than against the child. It is also important in this first session to explain how the treatment process follows logically from our understanding of the disorder, and that successful CBT will ultimately, but not immediately, require elimination of all rituals and other avoidance behaviors. Glenn's family did not exhibit the common problematic tendency to want to push a child faster than he or she can go, which can damage the child's sense of self-efficacy that is needed to fully engage in the treatment.

Glenn's parents were a bit less informed about CBT for OCD than many families are, and the initial meeting was an opportunity to answer their questions and increase their sense of optimism. Glenn spent much of this first session staring at the floor and making ritualized subvocalizations (e.g., "No") to reduce the chance that his feared consequences would occur. The therapist asked Glenn whether this was typical for him or a function of being in a new situation, and described to him how his treatment team would devise a plan to make the OCD less bothersome and impairing. It is also important to know up front whether the child has contamination fears, as the therapist's extending of a hand to shake upon meeting the patient in the waiting room at the first visit can prompt obsessional distress and arguments among family members (e.g., "Don't you see that the doctor wants to shake hands with you? You shouldn't be so rude!").

Because Glenn was 12, motivated, successful in grasping key treatment concepts, and able to implement exercises between sessions with minimal prompting, the parents were not given a more extensive supervisory role. They were told in advance about the need for Glenn to confront fears pertaining to the devil, and were given examples of the kinds of exposure the therapist wished to conduct to maximize benefit of the treatment. Glenn's parents were both devout Catholics and were raising their children in this faith. Thus, reducing their discomfort about confronting obsessional content pertaining to the devil was essential to successful treatment, and the therapist discussed at length how such exposures were designed and why they were important. After discussing these matters, Glenn's parents were comfortable with the therapist proceeding as planned.

Glenn's love of basketball became apparent in the first session. Quickly recognizing an "in," the therapist was able to make use of the child's keen interest in the sport to foster a common vocabulary that allowed the patient to quickly master the core principles of EX/RP while at the same time having fun in the sessions. As can be seen below, Glenn and the therapist made ample use of these analogies in the conduct of EX/RP; the coaching analogy in particular served as a useful way for Glenn to understand why, at times, the therapist suggested that Glenn push himself in practice to tackle situations and thoughts that were more challenging.

It is important to recognize that psychoeducation takes place throughout treatment rather than just in the first session. The therapist should take advantage of opportunities to point out flaws in OCD's logic and should reinforce the children for mastering key concepts and for designing exposure and ritual prevention strategies on their own based on their understanding of these concepts.

Mapping OCD and Cognitive Training

In sessions 2 through 4, the therapist met with Glenn alone and developed a treatment hierarchy. This hierarchy was created in the form of a map in which OCD themes, their interconnections, and their relative severity were documented. The map would also serve as a reminder of where we started. On Glenn's map there were several loosely connected OCD themes. First, Glenn was afraid that he might get poisoned if he drank liquids, especially water, and thus was reluctant to drink even when thirsty. When he did drink liquids, he would check to see if they contained poison and would occasionally ask his parents if someone might have slipped something toxic into his drink. Items on this hierarchy were ranked relatively low and thus were targeted first. Glenn's more pressing fears pertained to harm befalling his family if he refrained from rituals and, even more distressing, to losing his soul to the devil. On these "islands" Glenn was experiencing less success in resisting OCD. Most if not all of the time, those fears required him to ritualize or avoid in relation to these themes and Glenn would give in. Glenn and the therapist decided together which of the symptoms to target first and what their plan of action should be. Notably, although ritual abstinence was our stated long-term goal, it was not required in the early treatment sessions. Glenn would target a subset of obsessions and functionally connected rituals first, such as his fear that liquids he drank might contain poison and associated reassurance rituals and avoidance of ingesting the feared drinks. He gradually became proficient in confronting these situations and thoughts, and then extended his range to include other themes. This led to his ritual prevention moving closer and closer to complete ritual abstinence, and he was able to examine whether his feared consequences occurred despite successful resistance. It is imperative to convey to the child/adolescent that the treatment will progress at the pace he or she feels is manageable, while at the same time helping him or her recognize that inordinate delays in moving up the hierarchy will slow the much-desired reduction of obsessional frequency/distress.

Cognitive training is also an element of our treatment. The purpose of this training, or learning to "talk back to OCD," is to encourage the child/adolescent to remain in feared situations without ritualizing to promote habituation and a change in core OCD beliefs. Thus, when faced with obsessions about contamination and associated urges to ritualize, a child might say "You're not the boss of me" to encourage himself or herself to stay in the fear-provoking situation. Accordingly, the purpose of the positive self-talk is not to reduce short-term anxiety during exposure but to strengthen the child's ability to stay in the feared situation long enough for short-term and long-term habituation. If children do not understand this function of cognitive training, they may be vulnerable to using these self-statements in a ritualized fashion, that is, to reduce obsessional distress during exposure, which may compromise outcome and actually prolong their difficulties. Therapists should teach children/adolescents the purpose of positive self-talk and pay particular attention that cognitive training is not producing what essentially would amount to new mental rituals. Because some children cannot tolerate distress associated with exposure, positive self-talk and other anxiety management strategies may be necessary to help these children increase exposures even more gradually than is typical.

EXPOSURE AND RITUAL PREVENTION

In accord with Glenn's hierarchy, the first practice exposure conducted during session 4 entailed drinking a dark soda from a clear glass, which was ranked as minimally anxiety-provoking. The therapist demonstrated how he wanted Glenn to conduct such exposure by drinking from a different glass of dark soda, as drinking from the same glass might invalidate the exposure by proving to Glenn that the soda was "safe." The therapist drank from his glass and was careful to demonstrate how to do this quickly to minimize the chance of Glenn's engaging in an automatic olfactory check of the soda. Glenn was able to drink the soda with only a slight increase in his anxiety (Fear Temperature = 3). His fears subsided rather quickly, and within 10 minutes, he was back to his baseline temperature of 1. The therapist and Glenn discussed whether Glenn should repeat and monitor this same exposure during the week preceding session 5 or whether they should step up on the hierarchy to the next level, which would be to drink a clear liquid from a glass. It was decided that the homework should be identical to the in-session in vivo exposure, as the therapist needed to stack the odds in favor of successful completion of the initial trial exposure at home to build momentum for the more difficult tasks to come. Glenn was asked to carry out such exposure daily, to monitor his anxiety reduction over time as was done in the session, and to refrain from all olfactory checking and reassurance seeking pertaining to the soda exposures.

During exposure session 5, Glenn's homework was checked and discussed, and the next step was taken given successful habituation to the previous exposure. Glenn opted to drink clear liquid from a clear glass and, finding that this raised his anxiety only slightly, chose to drink clear liquid from a can, from which his OCD suggested it would be more difficult to detect the presence of poison. Glenn easily completed this exposure and, his thirst for more progress now increasing, suggested that the clear liquid exposures be added as homework to be completed between sessions 5 and 6. He also volunteered to refrain from all poison-related assurance seeking, pronouncing in accord with the basketball theme, "I can hit the 10-footer without a problem now. Maybe I'd better work on the 15-footer."

Glenn's optimism was rewarded, as the poisoning theme had virtually vanished by session 6, as had all reassurance seeking and checking pertaining to ingesting liquids. The therapist asked Glenn if there were any other vestiges of the poisoning theme that needed to be addressed and, convinced that there were not, revisited the hierarchy to select the next target. There had already been some generalization to the fears of harm befalling family members, as Glenn was having more success "doing what I want to do instead of what OCD tells me I have to do" when such fears occurred spontaneously during the week. In session 6, the therapist and Glenn played a hand-held basketball game together that Glenn liked, first without evoking obsessional content and then, when it became apparent that minimal anxiety was being evoked by engaging in this positively reinforcing activity, each shot in the game was preceded with a comment about harm befalling others (e.g., "If I make this basket, then my father will get the flu"). Exposure was titrated from mild to moderately bad outcomes, and Glenn's anxiety peaked at 6 but again returned to 1 after about 15 minutes of such practice. Proceeding cautiously, the therapist assigned the same exposures for Glenn to do daily on his own, and also asked him to refrain from all rituals pertaining to moderate harm befalling family members. Extensive discussions were focused on the fact that the bad outcomes that were raised in the sessions had yet to occur, and that if they did not occur, there may very well be something wrong with the

OCD's logic. Session 7 was a family session (see below), and the therapist wanted to have consecutive sessions to tackle the more difficult exposures pertaining to serious harm befalling loved ones. To ensure that momentum was not lost, the same homework exposures were reassigned after session 7 to keep Glenn working on the OCD formally.

In session 8, the more serious harms were confronted, this time with a combination of imaginal and in vivo exposure. After extensive discussion of the rationale for imaginal exposure, Glenn and the therapist devised stories of how his failure to protect family members via rituals led to their deaths and that he was responsible for this tragic oversight. Glenn and the therapist discussed how reading this story again and again would produce fear reduction and improved ability to distinguish between real and imagined outcomes. In particular, Glenn had come to view signs of anxiety as evidence of forthcoming doom, which further reinforced the need to neutralize obsessions in the context of particularly strong physiological reactions. Because OCD patients may be vulnerable to what Salkovskis (1995) and others have termed "thought-action fusion" and have an exaggerated sense of responsibility, attacking these themes directly via exposure and discussion of mistaken beliefs were core intertwining elements of treatment. Glenn's fears of catastrophes that would occur in the future could not be readily disconfirmed in vivo; these were addressed via imaginal exposure and cognitive techniques focused on discussion of mistaken beliefs, and these treatment elements were introduced again in session 9.

With over 90% ritual abstinence reported by Glenn during the week preceding session 10, the therapist and Glenn agreed to confront the fear of the devil in this session. Glenn was given cultural/historical accounts of evil and the devil to read during the session, which proved very anxiety-provoking (Fear Temperature = 9). Discussion focused on the anxiety he was experiencing, the courage he was demonstrating by confronting this difficult theme, and how OCD used logical tricks to try to convince him to engage in rituals and to avoid feared thoughts and situations ("If I'm superanxious, something bad must be about to happen"). The session finished with Glenn's temperature at 4, which prompted the therapist to reassign the same reading to be done daily, during the day (nighttime was more difficult for devil fears), and to record progress on the usual homework sheets. Session 11 was a family session and Glenn told the therapist about his progress in reading the assigned material, but the therapist wanted to wait for the next in-person exposure session before graduating to more imaginal and in vivo exposures pertaining to the devil fears.

Sessions 12 through 14 focused primarily on continuing to confront fears related to the devil. Because these fears were still quite salient, we conducted in vivo exposures in session that Glenn was asked to repeat daily between sessions. In session 12, for example, the therapist and the patient reviewed the rationale for confronting the "devil thoughts" and testing the hypothesis that bad things would occur in the future if devil thoughts and stimuli were not neutralized. They also discussed the fact that exposure had nothing to do with religion or the practice of Catholicism: They were simply vehicles designed to help Glenn reduce his obsessive fears and, by extension, become more comfortable practicing and strengthening his faith. Following this discussion, the therapist modeled the selected in vivo exposure by typing several sentences on the computer that were more and more directly related to losing his soul. The therapist started with less anxiety-evoking sentences, such as

"If I finish this sentence the devil might take my soul," working toward more anxiety-evoking exposures such as "Dear Satan, I implore you, please, please, take my soul once I have finished typing this sentence, and show me that you have done so by making the walls of the office turn blood red." Next on Glenn's hierarchy were exposures that were not "time-locked" and therefore more difficult to disconfirm: "Please, Satan, take my soul at the end of my life so that I can be with you forever." The rationale for doing this sort of exposure was to increase Glenn's tolerance of uncertainty pertaining to these thoughts; these exposures should also be supported by informal cognitive techniques, such as discussion of whether Glenn's religious teachings were consistent with the idea of losing one's soul simply because of an utterance outside the context of an entire life.

Once the therapist had demonstrated exposure, Glenn was asked to do so similarly. To promote his active involvement in exposure, he was given free rein to change the wording of the sentences he typed according to his own level of comfort and in his own writing style. In session 12, Glenn was able to type the most difficult sentences; he habituated well to having done so, discussed with the therapist the fact that the feared outcomes did not materialize, and was given homework assignments to complete between sessions. He was asked to begin refraining from rituals prompted by devil thoughts and to continue with sentence exposure. Notably, Glenn's spontaneous intrusions typically involved feared consequences in the distant future, yet the exposure exercises in session 12 were written in the present to promote immediate disconfirmation of fears; the fact that he must take the risk that feared future consequences would be incurred was also discussed, although disconfirmation in the present seemed to lessen somewhat his concerns about the future. Session 13 was conducted similarly to session 12, with the exception that content focused exclusively on thoughts about future feared consequences. Sessions 12 and 13 also involved some review of his progress and discussion of relapse prevention.

Session 14 was devoted to further discussion of relapse prevention, a review of his progress, and a small celebration of his having completed the core treatment so successfully. Glenn's mother and sisters were able to attend this final session. In keeping with the theme of not allowing OCD to dictate what kinds of activities Glenn could engage in, his favorite flavor of ice cream was served at this party. During the party, his sisters and mother discussed how much better he was doing now compared to 12 weeks previously, which Glenn appeared to appreciate greatly.

ADDITIONAL PARENT SESSIONS

Glenn's second parent session, session 7 of the protocol, was presented to the parents in the form of a basketball "half-time report." Glenn and his therapist created a mock scoreboard ("Glenn 56, OCD 42"), and described the action in the first half of the treatment by reviewing the treatment's core concepts, describing the initial exposures already completed, and chronicling his successes to that point. In addition, Glenn and the therapist discussed with his parents what to expect in the second half of treatment, such as increasing focus on the more persistent devil fears and the systematic elimination of the few rituals that remained. Glenn's parents were able to share their view about success of the treatment, to discuss his progress, and, most important, to tell their son how proud they were of his efforts and his accomplishments in treatment. Session 11 was cast again in the basketball metaphor, with an "end of the third quarter" report. The report highlighted the fact that Glenn had expanded his lead on OCD by confronting the most difficult items on his exposure hierarchy without resorting to a return to rituals and avoidance behavior. In the context of his tremendous progress in therapy by that point, issues of relapse prevention were discussed with his parents. Glenn was able to discuss with his parents which of their behaviors he found helpful (e.g., gentle reminders to confront OCD wherever possible) and which he found annoying (e.g., assuming that avoidance of certain chores must be OCD-linked). The therapist was able to help the family troubleshoot problematic areas that remained, while at the same time remaining cognizant of the steady progress that Glenn had made.

RELAPSE PREVENTION

Glenn's progress in treatment was quite significant, and the last two sessions of the acute phase and the booster sessions that followed the acute treatment phase included discussion of relapse prevention. In Glenn's case, we were able to use "OCD quizzes" to test his knowledge of key concepts, ability to generalize, and again, to interject some humor into the treatment process. Glenn was advised about the difference between lapses and relapses in accord with discussions from the treatment of other disorders (e.g., Marlatt & Gordon, 1985) and was asked to describe how he would respond if his symptoms crept back in. The therapist and he also began to work on a list of identifiable stressors that might exacerbate his currently subclinical symptoms, and he was advised that the time to work hardest on OCD in the future (e.g., devising exposures, self-monitoring) was when the symptoms were more prevalent and distressing. Initial discussion in these sessions set up discussions during the later termination phase, when Glenn's sessions were reduced from weekly to monthly.

DEVELOPMENTAL CONSIDERATIONS

Clinical observations suggest the importance of flexibility in delivering protocol-driven treatments as a function of developmental factors (Clarke, 1995). We try to promote developmental appropriateness by allowing flexibility in CBT within the constraints of fixed session goals. More specifically, the therapist adjusts the level of discourse to the level of cognitive functioning, social maturity, and capacity for sustained attention of each patient. Younger patients require more redirection and activities to sustain attention and motivation. Adolescents are more sensitive to the effects of OCD on peer interactions, which in turn requires more discussion; cognitive interventions require adjustment to the developmental level of the patient, with adolescents, for example, less likely than younger children to appreciate giving OCD a "nasty nickname." Developmentally appropriate metaphors relevant to the child's areas of interest and knowledge are used to promote active involvement in the treatment process, such as demonstrated above with Glenn. Patients whose OCD symptoms entangle family members require more attention to family involvement in treatment planning and implementation than those without as much family involvement. Nonetheless, although our CBT protocol includes extensive discussion of developmental sensitivity that is specific for each treatment session, the general format and goals of the treatment sessions are the same for all children.

THERAPIST-CLIENT FACTORS

Traditionally given short shrift in writings about cognitive-behavioral treatment, a good therapist-client relationship may very well be necessary but appears not to be sufficient to produce clinically meaningful change in OCD symptoms in adults (Lindsay, Crino, & Andrews, 1997). In pediatric OCD, this is also likely to be the case. In our clinical experience, the mere developing of a warm and caring relationship between therapist and patient is not expected to yield OCD symptom reduction, although it may result in other benefits. At the same time, successfully instituting exposure and ritual prevention require full collaboration of the patient. Thus, establishing a collaborative spirit is essential to good outcome.

Involving the family in the development of this positive and supportive tone is also an important part of the treatment process. Early on in treatment, we try to externalize OCD to promote the sense that patient, therapist, and family are fighting together against a common enemy, OCD, rather than fighting one another. We begin this distancing process by asking the younger children to name OCD, which then allows for the development of a common vocabulary and set of metaphors to illustrate key points throughout treatment. For instance, a 6-year-old patient of ours decided to call her OCD "Tummy Tickle" because of the abdominal symptoms that would so often accompany obsessive thoughts. Using the Tummy Tickle moniker allowed the child to gain some distance from OCD, to view it as something apart from herself to minimize her guilt about involving her parents in so much reassurance seeking, and to seize on this imagery in the conduct of imaginal exposure exercises (e.g., "I see myself saying no to Tummy Tickle"). Fostering a sense of humor about OCD is another way to build rapport and to strengthen the child's resolve when confronted with obsessions and urges to ritualize. With this youngster, sessions involved drawing more and more ridiculous pictures of Tummy Tickle on the office computer and practice talking in Tummy Tickle's silly voices, which enhanced the therapeutic relationship while at the same time allowing the child to confront OCD thoughts without ritualizing. Optimally, the child or adolescent should experience the therapist as accepting and also very knowledgeable about how to win the fight against OCD.

Another useful way to enhance the therapeutic relationship is to spend at least some session time discussing issues that do not pertain to OCD. This strategy allows the therapist to get to know the child's strengths and weaknesses in greater depth, to understand the context in which the child is struggling with OCD symptoms, and to gather grist for later metaphorical mills. For example, a child with a passion for soccer may be more engaged in discussions of core treatment concepts cast in terms of soccer strategies than in more technical discussions; the therapist would know about the child's interests only if he or she fostered such discussion. Discussion of fun topics can be used as rewards for efforts during session; a child recently treated by our group was given 5 to 10 minutes at the end of each treatment session to work with the therapist on a plastic model of the Space Shuttle that she was highly motivated to complete. This time was a reward for hard work, and the therapist was able to use the model building exercise to demonstrate key treatment concepts, such as the importance of systematically ascending a hierarchy of tasks rather than going at OCD willy-nilly.

Another benefit of this less focused discussion is demonstration to the parents of the differential reinforcement of other behaviors, a behavioral technique often brought to bear in the fight to shift child-parent interactions to topics other than OCD. Parents and children are cautioned against letting OCD become the only topic of conversation at dinner; perhaps the best way to assist families in adopting this difficult strategy is to demonstrate it in the office.

COURSE OF TERMINATION

Altogether, Glenn received 14 sessions of CBT conducted over approximately 12 weeks, and had two visits with his psychiatrist during this period. His OCD and depressive symptoms had been substantially reduced from pre- to posttreatment, at which time the aftercare plan was discussed. Given the significant progress he had made and the fact that his symptoms were now subclinical as indicated by his CY-BOCS score of 10, Glenn and his family were offered monthly booster sessions for OCD with the CBT provider, which would consist of check-ins and troubleshooting. It was also decided that remaining on the medication would be prudent, at least for the time being: Glenn's somatic complaints began to subside, and the family was very concerned that "rocking the boat" too much would prove problematic down the line. Glenn was maintained on 100 mg of sertraline during the four months of booster sessions, and he saw his psychiatrist once during that period of time.

Glenn was concerned at posttreatment about two main issues. First, although he clearly saw the benefits of discontinuing therapy at that point and was confident that he knew what to do if OCD were to "mount a comeback," he was somewhat worried that his progress would not last without the regular therapy sessions he had found so helpful. He and the therapist discussed this issue in detail, and the therapist offered to e-mail "OCD quizzes" to keep Glenn sharp during the booster session phase. These multiple-choice questions centered around identifying OCD symptoms, choosing appropriate strategies to confront OCD fears, developing treatment hierarchies, and successfully implementing treatment procedures (see Figure 15.1). As was the case during the acute treatment, the therapist also tried to introduce levity into the process, giving one frivolous answer among the multiple choices. Much of the content of the booster sessions focused on recognizing the important difference between lapses and relapses and in continuing to use the techniques that proved useful during the acute phase whenever the need arose. Many of these discussions were cast in metaphors about basketball, as this method had proven particularly useful in keeping Glenn engaged in the treatment process. For example, Glenn's third booster session began with his making the statement, "They're down by 12 now." The therapist, remembering that Glenn in a previous e-mail referred to the OCD basketball team "trailing him by 25 in the third quarter," recognized that this signified an upturn in OCD symptoms. He quickly called a "timeout" for Glenn to discuss using the strategies that had allowed him to build up such a big lead over OCD in the first place. This more playful approach to discussing OCD minimized alarmist thinking and allowed Glenn to reconnect with the metaphors and strategies he had used so successfully during acute treatment. Glenn's second issue at posttreatment was fears about his soul, which continued to be very bothersome. He and the therapist discussed ways he could work on these fears on his own to reestablish his dominance over OCD. A simply worded e-mail imparted the good news of his success in implementing the strategies discussed in the booster session: "I'm up by 22 again, and they're emptying their bench."

1. You're on the bus when OCD tells you that you have to confess to your mom about one of your scary thoughts. You should:
   a. Rush home and tell her right away.
   b. Tell OCD that this isn't important and that you don't have to confess.
   c. Call the local TV station and tell them too.
2. You're in the schoolyard when you see bird poop on the ground near you. You should:
   a. Run inside and wash your hands and feet in case it got on you.
   b. Throw out your shoes as soon as you go home.
   c. Continue to play in the schoolyard and tell OCD that bird poop isn't a big deal anyway.
3. A kid's OCD tells him that he should check his bookbag over and over again to make sure that nothing fell out. He should:
   a. Take everything out of the bag to make sure that he didn't lose anything.
   b. Realize that this is just OCD up to its old tricks and tell OCD that he doesn't really need to check.
   c. Glue the bag shut so he never ever loses anything.
4. A kid whose OCD makes him retrace his steps should eventually practice:
   a. Shuffling his feet so that OCD doesn't give her a hard time about stepping any more.
   b. Stepping without rituals in order to show OCD who's boss.
   c. Roller skating.

Figure 15.1 Sample OCD Quiz

The booster sessions proved quite useful and appeared to be sufficient. Glenn's symptom changes were maintained at the end of this four-month period, which was followed by an "open door" period in which he was told he could contact the therapist whenever he felt the need, and could do so either via e-mail or telephone; he was also instructed to let his mother and father know if he needed any in-person contact.

Medication was maintained during the four-month period, after which the family and the treatment providers agreed that with Glenn's symptoms remaining subclinical for four months, it was a reasonable time to discontinue pharmacotherapy. The medication taper was done gradually, first reducing to 50 mg for several weeks then to 25 mg for a few more weeks and then to no medication. Glenn did not experience any return of OCD or mood problems during this period, and he was given an "open door" option with his psychiatrist as well. Contacted once by Glenn during the discontinuation phase, the CBT therapist provided occasional e-mailed encouragement during this period, but Glenn did not seek additional booster sessions.

FOLLOW-UP

At one-year posttreatment, Glenn continued to remain well. Most of his OCD symptoms had vanished, although there were still occasional obsessions about the devil that he confronted directly via imaginal and in vivo exposure. His symptoms remained subclinical (CY-BOCS = 10) and his functional impairment was greatly reduced. He remained medication-free, although he and his family continued to be open to the possibility of reinitiating pharmacotherapy if the need arose. At the time of the one-year check-in, significant stressors loomed on the horizon: An academically challenging high school placement would soon begin, basketball tryouts in the fall, and the stress of participating in a highly competitive summer all-star baseball league had led to increased thoughts about the devil and desired outcomes (e.g., "If I get a hit with runners in scoring position, the devil will gain my soul"), which he confronted directly using the methods he learned during treatment. The open door policies of the treatment providers remain in place, and Glenn has received repeated advice about the fact that if OCD symptoms return, he has the tools to get them back under his control.

MANAGED CARE CONSIDERATIONS

In the United States, insurance companies have tremendous influence over the provision of mental health care, including diagnoses that will be considered sufficiently impairing to warrant treatment, selection of providers of the approved treatments, the number of treatment sessions granted, and the percentage of the provider's usual and customary fee that will be reimbursed. As is inevitable when maximizing the company's profit margin is the primary motivator of service provision, clinical decisions are often subservient to the bottom line, and thus patient care is compromised. For example, there are many mental health providers without expertise in CBT for OCD who, by virtue of having endured the inherent burdens of signing up for the company's provider list and listing their specialty areas, are funneled the OCD patients covered by the company's policies. At present, many expert treatment providers are reluctant to become involved in these provider networks because of visit and fee restrictions and the heavy administrative burden involved, which means that their services can be accessed primarily by those who can afford to pay the full fee out-of-pocket or who opt to enroll in ongoing treatment outcome studies. This latter alternative may open the door at least somewhat to families of more modest means. At this point, many families opt to seek treatment outside their insurance company's restrictions to access the best possible care for their children. Unfortunately, without adequate coverage, many families simply cannot afford this alternative and may be forced to make do with less expertise and fewer sessions. Other countries, such as Germany and Spain, have shifted to making empirically based decisions about which treatments should be used for which disorders, which in time ought to force providers to become proficient in these reimbursable techniques. Such a system appears to be far away from our shores, however; thus, access continues to be restricted until experts and insurance companies can collaboratively foster a solution that takes these patients' clinical needs into account.

Given these market realities, one way to improve dissemination of CBT might be to initiate research projects to train insurance companies' preferred providers in CBT treatment techniques so that the empirically supported treatments that seem to work so well for anxiety disorders may actually reach the majority of sufferers seeking care. There may be too few OCD patients in any one system to make OCD-specific training feasible, but perhaps effectiveness studies could focus on training providers in general CBT principles and then providing access to expert supervision of anxiety cases that enter the system. In this way, the insurance companies could continue to manage costs in accord with their mission and patients under their policies may be exposed to the state-of-the-art treatments that so often go underutilized.

OVERALL EFFECTIVENESS

In our case, we have provided an example in which a highly motivated family and child presented for CBT after experiencing partial response to SRI pharmacotherapy. Obviously, effectiveness of CBT in these kinds of cases is probably greater than in cases where the parents must coerce the child into coming to see a therapist, where more severe comorbidity clouds the clinical picture, and where high expressed emotion dominates the family environment (Hibbs et al., 1991). We have demonstrated how to help the child and family actively engage in the treatment process and how to address clinical difficulties that so often arise in the treatment of OCD, such as presence of disastrous consequences in the future rather than in the present. We also discussed how to titrate exposure in a developmentally appropriate manner, taking into account the clinical objectives of the exercise, the family's cultural background, and the child's ability to cope with distress. Further, we believe that use of developmentally appropriate metaphors, which we have highlighted throughout our case presentation, helps foster the collaborative spirit necessary to confront OCD and facilitate the patient's understanding of core treatment concepts. Regarding what can be expected down the road with respect to OCD symptoms, we choose in clinical practice to let children and adolescents who received CBT know that they may remain vulnerable to a return of symptoms in the future but that use of the techniques they learned in CBT greatly increases their chances of keeping OCD at bay. We discuss with children who received combined treatment with SRI that pharmacotherapy may play a significant role in the maintenance of their treatment gains. We do not have cures for this disorder as yet, but the treatments we have developed so far appear to be sufficiently effective to warrant optimism about long-term prognosis for children and adolescents with OCD.

REFERENCES

Albano, A. M., & Silverman, W. K. (1996). *Anxiety Disorders Interview Schedule for DSM-IV: Child version*. San Antonio, TX: Psychological Corporation.

American Psychiatric Association. (1994). *Diagnostic and statistical manual of mental disorders* (4th ed.). Washington, DC: Author.

Baxter, L. J., Schwartz, J. M., Bergaman, K. S., Szuba, M. P., Guze, B. H., Mazziotta, J. C., et al. (1992). Caudate glucose metabolic rate changes with both drug and behavior therapy for Obsessive Compulsive Disorder. *Archives of General Psychiatry, 49,* 681–689.

Chansky, T. (2000). *Freeing your child from Obsessive Compulsive Disorder: A powerful, practical program for parents of children and adolescents*. New York: Crown.

Clarke, G. N. (1995). Improving the transition from basic efficacy research to effectiveness studies: Methodological issues and procedures. *Journal of Consulting and Clinical Psychology, 63,* 718–725.

de Haan, E., Hoogduin, K. A., Buitelaar, J. K., & Keijsers, G. P. (1998). Behavior therapy versus clomipramine for the treatment of Obsessive-Compulsive Disorder in children and adolescents. *Journal of the American Academy of Child and Adolescent Psychiatry, 37,* 1022–1029.

DeVeaugh-Geiss, J., Landau, P., & Katz, R. (1989). Treatment of Obsessive Compulsive Disorder with clomipramine. *Psychiatric Annals, 19,* 97–101.

DeVeaugh-Geiss, J., Moroz, G., Biederman, J., Cantwell, D., Fontaine, R., Greist, J. H., et al. (1992). Clomipramine hydrochloride in childhood and adolescent Obsessive-Compulsive Disorder: A multicenter trial. *Journal of the American Academy of Child and Adolescent Psychiatry, 31,* 45–49.

Dollard, J., & Miller, N. E. (1950). *Personality and psychotherapy: An analysis in terms of learning, thinking and culture.* New York: McGraw-Hill.

Eichstedt, J. A., & Arnold, S. L. (2001). Childhood-onset Obsessive-Compulsive Disorder: A tic-related subtype of OCD? *Clinical Psychology Review, 21,* 137–158.

Flament, M. F., Rapoport, J. L., Berg, C. J., Sceery, W., Kilts, C., Mellstrom, B., et al. (1985). Clomipramine treatment of childhood Obsessive Compulsive Disorder: A double-blind controlled study. *Archives of General Psychiatry, 42,* 977–983.

Flament, M. F., Whitaker, A., Rapoport, J. L., Davies, M., Berg, C. Z., Kalikow, K., et al. (1988). Obsessive Compulsive Disorder in adolescence: An epidemiological study. *Journal of the American Academy of Child and Adolescent Psychiatry, 27,* 764–771.

Foa, E. B., & Kozak, M. J. (1985). Treatment of anxiety disorders: Implications for psychopathology. In A. H. Tuma & J. D. Maser (Eds.), *Anxiety and the anxiety disorders* (pp. 421–452). Hillsdale, NJ: Erlbaum.

Foa, E. B., & Kozak, M. J. (1986). Emotional processing of fear: Exposure to corrective information. *Psychological Bulletin, 99,* 20–35.

Foa, E. B., Kozak, M. J., Goodman, W. K., Hollander, E., Jenike, M. A., & Rasmussen, S. (1995). *DSM-IV* field trial: Obsessive Compulsive Disorder. *American Journal of Psychiatry, 152,* 801–808.

Franklin, M. E., & Foa, E. B. (1998). Cognitive-behavioral treatment of Obsessive Compulsive Disorder. In P. Nathan & J. Gorman (Eds.), *A guide to treatments that work* (pp. 339–357). Oxford, England: Oxford University Press.

Franklin, M. E., Kozak, M. J., Cashman, L., Coles, M., Rheingold, A., & Foa, E. B. (1998). Cognitive behavioral treatment of pediatric Obsessive Compulsive Disorder: An open clinical trial. *Journal of the American Academy of Child and Adolescent Psychiatry, 37,* 412–419.

Franklin, M. E., Tolin, D. F., March, J. S., & Foa, E. B. (2001). Intensive cognitive-behavior therapy for pediatric OCD: A case example. *Cognitive and Behavioral Practice, 8,* 297–304.

Giulino, L., Gammon, P., Sullivan, K., Franklin, M. E., Foa, E. B., & March, J. S. (2001). *Retrospective assessment of pediatric autoimmune neuropsychiatric disorder associated with streptococcal infection.* Manuscript submitted for publication.

Goodman, W. K., Price, L. H., Rasmussen, S. A., Mazure, C., Delgado, P., Heninger, G. R., et al. (1989). The Yale-Brown Obsessive Compulsive Scale. II: Validity. *Archives of General Psychiatry, 46,* 1012–1016.

Goodman, W. K., Price, L. H., Rasmussen, S. A., Mazure, C., Fleischmann, R. L., Hill, C. L., et al. (1989). The Yale-Brown Obsessive Compulsive Scale. I: Development, use, and reliability. *Archives of General Psychiatry, 46,* 1006–1011.

Greist, J. H. (1992). An integrated approach to treatment of Obsessive Compulsive Disorder. *Journal of Clinical Psychiatry, 53,* 38–41.

Greist, J. H., Jefferson, J. W., Kobak, K. A., Katzelnick, D. J., & Serlin, R. C. (1995). Efficacy and tolerability of serotonin transport inhibitors in Obsessive-Compulsive Disorder: A meta-analysis. *Archives of General Psychiatry, 52,* 53–60.

Hibbs, E. D., Hamburger, S. D., Lenane, M., Rapoport, J. L., Kruesi, M. J., Keysor, C. S., et al. (1991). Determinants of expressed emotion in families of disturbed and normal children. *Journal of Child Psychology and Psychiatry and Allied Disciplines, 32,* 757–770.

Insel, T. R., Mueller, E. A., Alterman, I., Linnoila, M., & Murphy, D. L. (1985). Obsessive-Compulsive Disorder and serotonin: Is there a connection? *Biological Psychiatry, 20,* 1174–1188.

Insel, T. R., Murphy, D. L., Cohen, R. M., Alterman, I. S., Kilts, C., & Linnoila, M. (1983). Obsessive-Compulsive Disorder: A double-blind trial of clomipramine and clorgyline. *Archives of General Psychiatry, 40,* 605–612.

Jaffer, M., & Piacentini, J. (2001). The Child OCD Impact Scale (COIS): Clinical applications. In D. McKay (Chair), *Childhood OCD: Bringing research into the clinic.* Paper presented at the World Congress of Behavioral and Cognitive Therapies, Vancouver, BC, Canada.

Kendall, P. C., & Southam-Gerow, M. A. (1995). Issues in the transportability of treatment: The case of anxiety disorders in youths. *Journal of Consulting and Clinical Psychology, 63,* 702–708.

Kovacs, M. (1985). The Children's Depression Inventory (CDI). *Psychopharmacology Bulletin, 21,* 995–998.

Kozak, M. J., Liebowitz, M. R., & Foa, E. B. (2000). Cognitive behavior therapy and pharmacotherapy for OCD: The NIMH-sponsored collaborative study. In W. K. Goodman, M. Rudorfer, & J. Maser (Eds.), *Obsessive Compulsive Disorder: Contemporary issues in treatment* (pp. 501–530). Mahwah, NJ: Erlbaum.

Laidlaw, T. M., Falloon, I. R., Barnfather, D., & Coverdale, J. H. (1999). The stress of caring for people with Obsessive Compulsive Disorders. *Community Mental Health Journal, 35,* 443–450.

Leonard, H. L., Swedo, S. E., Garvey, M., Beer, D., Perlmutter, S., Lougee, L., et al. (1999). Post-infectious and other forms of Obsessive-Compulsive Disorder. *Child and Adolescent Psychiatry Clinics of North America, 8,* 497–511.

Leonard, H. L., Swedo, S. E., Lenane, M. C., Rettew, D. C., Cheslow, D. L., Hamburger, S. D., et al. (1991). A double-blind desipramine substitution during long-term clomipramine treatment in children and adolescents with Obsessive Compulsive Disorder. *Archives of General Psychiatry, 48,* 922–926.

Leonard, H. L., Swedo, S. E., Lenane, M. C., Rettew, D. C., Hamburger, S. D., Bartko, J., et al. (1993). A 2- to 7-year follow-up study of 54 obsessive compulsive children and adolescents. *Archives of General Psychiatry, 50,* 429–439.

Leonard, H. L., Swedo, S. E., Rapoport, J. L., Koby, E., Lenane, M. C., Cheslow, D. L., et al. (1989). Treatment of Obsessive Compulsive Disorder with clomipramine and desipramine in children and adolescents: A double-blind crossover comparison. *Archives of General Psychiatry, 46,* 1088–1092.

Lindsay, M., Crino, R., & Andrews, G. (1997). Controlled trial of exposure and response prevention in Obsessive-Compulsive Disorder. *British Journal of Psychiatry, 171,* 135–139.

March, J., Frances, A., Kahn, D., & Carpenter, D. (1997). Expert consensus guidelines: Treatment of Obsessive-Compulsive Disorder. *Journal of Clinical Psychiatry, 58*(Suppl. 4), 1–72.

March, J., Parker, J., Sullivan, K., Stallings, P., & Conners, K. (1997). The Multidimensional Anxiety Scale for Children (MASC): Factor structure, reliability and validity. *Journal of the American Academy of Child and Adolescent Psychiatry, 36,* 554–565.

March, J. S. (1995). Cognitive-behavioral psychotherapy for children and adolescents with OCD: A review and recommendations for treatment. *Journal of the American Academy of Child and Adolescent Psychiatry, 35,* 1265–1273.

March, J. S. (1998). *Manual for the Multidimensional Anxiety Scale for Children* (MASC). Toronto, Ontario, Canada: Multi-Health Systems.

March, J. S., Biederman, J., Wolkow, R., Safferman, A., Mardekian, J., Cook, E. H., et al. (1998). Sertraline in children and adolescents with Obsessive-Compulsive Disorder: A multicenter randomized controlled trial. *Journal of the American Medical Association, 280,* 1752–1756.

March, J. S., Franklin, M., Nelson, A., & Foa, E. (2001). Cognitive-behavioral psychotherapy for pediatric Obsessive-Compulsive Disorder. *Journal of Clinical Child Psychology, 30,* 8–18.

March, J. S., & Mulle, K. (1998). *OCD in children and adolescents: A cognitive-behavioral treatment manual.* New York: Guilford Press.

March, J. S., Mulle, K., & Herbel, B. (1994). Behavioral psychotherapy for children and adolescents with Obsessive-Compulsive Disorder: An open trial of a new protocol driven treatment package. *Journal of the American Academy of Child and Adolescent Psychiatry, 33,* 333–341.

March, J. S., & Sullivan, K. (1999). Test-retest reliability of the Multidimensional Anxiety Scale for Children. *Journal of Anxiety Disorders, 13,* 349–358.

Marlatt, G. A., & Gordon, J. R. (1985). *Relapse prevention.* New York: Guilford Press.

Meyer, V. (1966). Modifications of expectations in cases with obsessional rituals. *Behavior Research and Therapy, 4,* 273–280.

Mowrer, O. H. (1939). A stimulus-response analysis of anxiety and its role as a reinforcing agent. *Psychological Review, 46,* 553–565.

Mowrer, O. H. (1960). *Learning theory and behavior.* New York: Wiley.

Pediatric OCD Collaborative Study Group. (2001). Recent developments in the treatment of pediatric Obsessive Compulsive Disorder. In S. Taylor (Chair), *New developments in treating Obsessive Compulsive Disorder: Behavior therapy and beyond.* Paper presented at the World Congress of Behavioral and Cognitive Therapies, Vancouver, BC, Canada.

Piacentini, J. (1999). Cognitive behavioral therapy of childhood OCD. *Child and Adolescent Psychiatric Clinics of North America, 8,* 599–616.

Piacentini, J., Jaffer, M., Liebowitz, M., & Gitow, A. (1992). *Systematic assessment of impairment in youngsters with Obsessive-Compulsive Disorder: The OCD Impact Scale.* Boston: AABT Proceedings.

Rachman, S. J., & Wilson, G. T. (1980). *The effects of psychological therapy.* Oxford, England: Pergamon Press.

Riddle, M., Reeve, E., Yaryura-Tobias, J., Yang, H., Claghorn, J., Gaffney, G., et al. (2001). Fluvoxamine for children and adolescents with Obsessive Compulsive Disorder: A randomized, controlled, multicenter trial. *Journal of the American Academy of Child and Adolescent Psychiatry, 40,* 222–229.

Roper, G., & Rachman, S. (1976). Obsessional-compulsive checking: Experimental replication and development. *Behaviour Research and Therapy, 14,* 25–32.

Roper, G., Rachman, S., & Hodgson, R. (1973). An experiment of obsessional checking. *Behaviour Research and Therapy, 11,* 271–277.

Salkovskis, P. M. (1985). Obsessional compulsive problems: A cognitive behavioral analysis. *Behaviour Research and Therapy, 23,* 571–583.

Scahill, L., Riddle, M. A., McSwiggin-Hardin, M., Ort, S. I., King, R. A., Goodman, W. K., et al. (1997). Children's Yale-Brown Obsessive Compulsive Scale: Reliability and validity. *Journal of the American Academy of Child and Adolescent Psychiatry, 36,* 844–852.

Silverman, W. K. (1991). Diagnostic reliability of anxiety disorders in children using structured interviews: Assessment of childhood anxiety disorders [Special Issue]. *Journal of Anxiety Disorders, 5,* 105–124.

Silverman, W. K., & Nelles, W. B. (1998). The Anxiety Disorders Interview Schedule for children. *Journal of the American Academy of Child and Adolescent Psychiatry, 27,* 772–778.

Swedo, S. E., Leonard, H. L., Garvey, M., Mittleman, B., Allen, A. J., Perlmutter, S., et al. (1998). Pediatric autoimmune neuropsychiatric disorders associated with streptococcal infections: Clinical description of the first 50 cases. *American Journal of Psychiatry, 155,* 264–271.

Weizman, A., Carmi, M., Hermesh, H., Shahar, A., Apter, A., Tyano, S., et al. (1986). High-affinity imipramine binding and serotonin uptake in platelets of eight adolescent and ten adult obsessive-compulsive patients. *American Journal of Psychiatry, 143,* 335–339.

Wever, C., & Rey, J. M. (1997). Juvenile Obsessive Compulsive Disorder. *Australian and New Zealand Journal of Psychiatry, 31,* 105–113.

Zohar, J., & Insel, T. R. (1987). Drug treatment of Obsessive-Compulsive Disorder: Drug treatment of anxiety disorders [Special Issue]. *Journal of Affective Disorders, 13,* 193–202.

CHAPTER 16

School Refusal and Separation Anxiety

SARA G. MATTIS and THOMAS H. OLLENDICK

DESCRIPTION OF THE DISORDER

SEPARATION ANXIETY DISORDER (SAD) is identified in the *Diagnostic and Statistical Manual of Mental Disorders*, fourth edition (*DSM-IV*; American Psychiatric Association, 1994) as a disorder specific to childhood with an onset before the age of 18. The primary feature of this disorder is excessive, developmentally inappropriate anxiety regarding separation from the home or from attachment figures (e.g., parents). Because school is a setting that requires such separation, school refusal behavior, often termed school phobia, frequently develops in children with SAD. Indeed, the *DSM-IV* requires the presence of at least three of eight symptoms to diagnose SAD, one of which is "persistent reluctance or refusal to go to school or elsewhere" due to fear of separation. The other seven symptoms of SAD identified by the *DSM-IV* are recurrent distress when separation occurs or is anticipated, excessive worry about harm befalling attachment figures, persistent worry that an untoward event (e.g., being kidnapped) will lead to separation, excessive fear regarding being alone or away from attachment figures at home or in other settings, refusal to go to sleep unless near a major attachment figure or to sleep away from home, repeated nightmares regarding separation, and complaints of physical symptoms (e.g., headaches, nausea) when separation is anticipated. To receive a diagnosis of SAD, the symptoms must be present for at least four weeks, and the disturbance must cause significant distress or impairment in social, academic, or other significant areas of functioning.

The term school phobia was first used to describe extended absences from school presumably motivated, from a psychoanalytic perspective, by overdependency on the part of both mother and child, who each experienced severe anxiety on separation (Johnson, Falstein, Szurek, & Svendsen, 1941). More recently, most researchers and clinicians have acknowledged that school refusal and avoidance can actually be symptoms of a variety of underlying disorders (Kearney & Silverman, 1990; Wachtel & Strauss, 1995). For instance, an adolescent with social phobia may avoid school due to excessive fear of embarrassment in front of peers. In other cases, the fear may focus on a specific aspect of the school environment (e.g., fear of a particular teacher, subject, or classroom), thus reflecting a specific phobia (Wachtel & Strauss, 1995).

It has been reported that approximately three-quarters of clinic-referred children diagnosed with SAD show school avoidance (Last, Francis, Hersen, Kazdin, & Strauss, 1987), often accompanied by somatic complaints (e.g., headaches, stomachaches) either before the child goes to school or during the school day (Wachtel & Strauss, 1995). However, although school avoidance is often a component of SAD, some children exhibit separation anxiety in the absence of school refusal behavior. Likewise, reluctance to attend school may occur without separation anxiety. In an early study of 37 school-refusing children and adolescents, for example, Ollendick and Mayer (1984) found that 13 (35%) of the youths refused school largely for separation anxiety concerns, 15 (41%) refused school largely for school-related fears related to specific aspects of the school itself and not separation concerns (e.g., entering a new school, taking tests, participating in physical education classes, sarcastic teachers, and being teased by peers), and 9 (24%) refused to go to school for concerns related to both separation anxiety and specific school-related fears. In a more recent study, Last and Strauss (1990) identified 63 children and adolescents who refused to attend school. As with Ollendick and Mayer, they reported a range of disorders associated with school refusal: 38% (24) of the youths were diagnosed with SAD, 31% (19) with social phobia, 22% (14) with specific phobia, 6% with Panic Disorder (4), and 3% (2) with Posttraumatic Stress Disorder. Over 60% of the children and adolescents who refused school presented with a primary anxiety disorder other than SAD. Thus, it is important to differentiate school refusal from SAD and not assume that one condition is isomorphic with the other.

In the 1980s and 1990s, several authors suggested the use of the term school refusal behavior to reflect the heterogeneous nature of this problem (Blagg & Yule, 1984; Kearney, 1995; King, Ollendick, & Tonge, 1995). In their research on the functional assessment of school refusal behavior, Kearney and Silverman (1990, 1993) have suggested four primary categories that capture the main underlying reasons for school refusal: (1) avoidance of school-related fearfulness or general overanxiousness; (2) escape from anxiety-provoking social interactions; (3) attention seeking or separation anxiety; and (4) tangible reinforcement. Children in the first category include those with fears of a specific stimulus in the school environment (e.g., fire drills, a teacher) or those with general overanxiousness (e.g., during a test). The second category consists of children with difficult peer relationships or social anxiety regarding evaluation (e.g., answering a question in class). The third category includes children with separation anxiety who might engage in behaviors (e.g., tantrumming) to stay home with an attachment figure. Finally, children in the fourth category stay home for other rewards, such as watching TV, sleeping late, or visiting friends. The remainder of this chapter focuses primarily on the third category, which captures the relationship between school refusal and separation anxiety.

CASE DESCRIPTION

Amanda N. was a 9-year-5-month old Caucasian female who was referred to an anxiety disorders specialty clinic by her school guidance counselor for evaluation and treatment of school refusal and separation anxiety. At the time of referral, Amanda lived with her mother, father, and 6-year-old brother in a suburb of a major city, where she was in the fourth grade at a public elementary school. Amanda's father was employed as an electrical engineer and her mother was a teacher at the local high school. Amanda was referred for assessment following a four-week period during which she had expressed significant distress about leaving her mother to attend school. During this time, she had missed 10 days of school and typically had gone to the nurse's office complaining of nausea on the days when she did attend. The school guidance counselor and Amanda's teachers expressed serious concern about the impact her absences were beginning to have on her peer relationships and academic performance.

Amanda appeared rather shy and withdrawn when she first presented for the assessment. The interviewer met with Amanda and her parents initially to discuss their reasons for coming to the clinic and to review the assessment process. Amanda's mother reported that she had begun noticing that Amanda seemed worried about going to school in the morning about two months earlier, but that it had not become a serious problem until the past few weeks. Amanda's father reported that she had always had difficulty leaving them to go to new places, but that she had seemed "okay" about going to school until the previous month, when she seemed "frightened for some reason." Initially, Amanda would only nod in response to the interviewer's questions; she eventually stated that she felt "scared to leave my mom" on school mornings.

After meeting with Amanda and her parents, the interviewer asked Amanda to meet with her alone while her parents completed some questionnaires in the waiting room. At this point, Amanda became tearful and appeared notably anxious, repeatedly stating "Please don't make me leave my mom." She became slightly more relaxed once the interviewer arranged to conduct the interview in a room with a two-way mirror so that Amanda could see her parents completing their questionnaires in the adjacent room. Initially quite withdrawn and reluctant to answer the interviewer's questions, Amanda gradually became more comfortable and was able to talk about some of her worries and fears. In particular, she reported feeling very worried about her mother for the past two months, particularly that something would happen to her when they were apart so that she would never see her again. She reported worrying that her mother would be in a car accident on her way to work or that someone would "attack my mom's school like those kids did in Colorado" (referring to the Columbine High School murders). She reported that she had nightmares about being away from her mom or "losing her someplace," such as a crowded store, and not being able to find her. Because of these nightmares, Amanda said that it was hard for her to go to sleep without her mother staying in her room with her. She also reported getting stomachaches and feeling nauseous whenever she had to leave her mom to go to school or if her mom had to go somewhere without her. She said that she really liked school and missed seeing her friends, but that it was hard for her to leave her mom to go to school. She reporting wanting to "stop worrying so much" so that she would be able to go to school.

CHIEF COMPLAINTS

The Anxiety Disorders Interview Schedule for *DSM-IV*, Child Version (ADIS-IV, Child Version; Silverman & Albano, 1996) is a semistructured diagnostic interview designed to assess anxiety and related disorders in children. This interview consists of separate child and parent components, which were administered separately to Amanda and her parents to assess the chief presenting concerns and symptoms. Amanda gave a positive response to many of the questions in the Separation Anxiety Disorder section of the interview. For instance, when asked if she felt very scared or worried about being away from her mom or dad, Amanda reported that she felt very worried about her mom when she was away from her and that she often would cry when she knew she had to go to school or if her mom had to go to an appointment without her. She reported worrying that "something bad" would happen to her mom when they were apart, and that she felt afraid to go to school or to a friend's house because of this worry. She also indicated that she did not like to be too far away from her parents even at home, and could not stay alone in her room or fall asleep unless her mom was with her. Finally, she reported having nightmares about being away from her mom, and that she would get stomachaches and feel nauseous whenever she had to leave her. She reported that these worries had gotten worse over the past two months, but that she had always felt somewhat nervous about being away from her mom. When asked how much these worries interfered in her life (e.g., with friends, in school, or at home), Amanda gave a rating of 6 on a 9-point scale.

Amanda's parents also endorsed many of the symptoms of SAD during their portion of the interview. Specifically, Mrs. N. reported that Amanda seemed "very scared" and usually would cry when getting ready for school in the morning. Mr. N. noted that Amanda would start to get upset on Sunday evenings, and often had told him that she worried about "something happening to mom" during the coming week. Both parents reported that Amanda was afraid to be alone in her room and that she needed her mother to stay with her until she fell asleep at night. They indicated that Amanda experienced nightmares about losing them, and that she often complained of stomachaches on school mornings. Amanda's parents also assigned a rating of 6 to reflect the level of interference caused by separation concerns in Amanda's life.

HISTORY

The history of Amanda's separation anxiety dated back to her infancy, when her parents reported that she was quite wary of new people and would fuss when they tried to leave her with a grandparent or other family member. As a result, Mr. and Mrs. N. noted that one of them was almost always with Amanda and that they tended to do many family-focused activities. They reported that during her preschool years, she was a "quiet but friendly" child who enjoyed being with other children and family members. However, Mr. N. reported that she was always anxious about going to new places without them and often would insist that they accompany her on school field trips and visits to friends' houses. The birth of her brother, when Amanda was 3 years old, also seemed somewhat stressful for her, and Mrs. N. noted that it was around this time that Amanda began asking her to stay with her until she went to sleep at night.

Amanda's parents reported that the transition to kindergarten was difficult for her, and that she cried every morning the first week they brought her to school. At that time, they debated whether she was emotionally ready to begin school and considered postponing kindergarten for a year. However, the teacher encouraged them to persist and Amanda gradually became less distressed. Since that time, Amanda reportedly enjoyed school, was a very good student, and had several close friends.

As a younger child, Amanda had always shown concern about her mother's health and well-being, bringing her candy as "medicine" if she had a cold, and worrying that she was "in the hospital" during her brother's birth. However, her parents identified the many news stories about the Columbine High School shootings as the precipitant of Amanda's current level of concern. Following this tragedy, Amanda became very worried about the possibility that someone would shoot her mother at the high school where she taught. She began asking her teachers about whether this could happen in their town, and often would try to call her mother during the day to make sure everything was "okay" at the high school. Although her anxiety gradually dissipated in the months following the Columbine incident, she continued to express concern about her mother's safety when she was at work and whenever she went somewhere without her.

Importantly, Amanda experienced the first significant loss within her extended family 10 weeks prior to the assessment, when her maternal grandmother died quite suddenly following a heart attack. Mrs. N. reported feeling extreme sadness following her mother's death and left for two days to be with her sister and make the funeral arrangements. Amanda reportedly showed a great deal of anxiety about her mother's well-being during this time, as well as sadness due to her grandmother's death. Mrs. N. reported that Amanda had missed three days of school to attend her grandmother's funeral and be with their extended family. The parents noted that Amanda became quite "clingy" and reluctant to be apart from her mother for even brief periods of time during the days following her grandmother's death. On her return to school, she began expressing heightened levels of concern about her mother's safety and well-being. Specifically, she would tell her mom that she wished they didn't have to be apart during the day and would sometimes try to call her at the high school to "check in." According to Amanda's parents, this anxiety gradually worsened over the course of several weeks, until Amanda began "crying hysterically" on many school mornings and complaining of nausea. When she was "too hysterical" to attend school, Mrs. N. reported that she would either call in sick and stay home with her, or leave her with a retired family friend who lived quite close to the high school. Amanda's mother reported feeling guilty that her own grief surrounding her mother's death may have negatively impacted her daughter.

BEHAVIORAL ASSESSMENT

A comprehensive assessment of child anxiety requires the use of multiple methods that gather information across different settings (e.g., school and home) and from several perspectives (e.g., child, parent, and teacher). Such an assessment typically incorporates diagnostic interviews, child self-report, behavioral observations, ratings from parents and teachers, and possibly physiological measurements

(Kendall, Chu, Pimentel, & Choudhury, 2000; Ollendick & King, 1990). As described below for the case of Amanda, thorough assessment can yield valuable information while laying the groundwork for successful treatment.

BEHAVIORAL

As a semistructured diagnostic interview, the ADIS-IV, Child Version (Silverman & Albano, 1996) not only yields important information on the presence and severity of anxious symptomatology, but also provides a critical opportunity for behavioral observation. In Amanda's case, the behavior displayed at the onset of the interview was at least as important in understanding her separation anxiety as was the verbal information obtained. Specifically, the interviewer was able to directly observe Amanda as she became tearful, was visibly trembling, and began pleading with the interviewer to not separate her from her mother. Such observations provided a firsthand account of the separation anxious behaviors reported by Amanda's parents.

Ollendick and King (1990) described the direct observation of a child's behavior in the setting where it occurs as the "hallmark of behavioral assessment" (p. 193). Approximately one week before the beginning of treatment, Amanda's therapist arranged to conduct a home visit on a school morning. During the visit, which lasted about one hour, the therapist remained as unobtrusive as possible, sitting first on a chair in the upstairs hall and then in one corner of the kitchen. The therapist carefully observed and recorded any incidents of separation anxious or school refusal behavior (e.g., verbal protests about going to school or separating from mother, expressing concern about mother's welfare, whining or crying, physical complaints, clinging behavior, refusing to get dressed or leave the house). During the observation, Amanda displayed 10 verbal protests (e.g., "Please don't make me go!") and made six comments regarding concern for her mother (e.g., "What if you get in an accident today?"). The therapist also observed three brief episodes of tearfulness, two complaints of stomach distress, and some reluctance to get dressed, although Amanda ultimately did go to school on that particular morning (perhaps due, at least partially, to the therapist's presence and Amanda's desire to please her). A Behavioral Avoidance Task (BAT) was also conducted at the clinic and is described in detail in the Physiological Assessment section following.

Finally, Amanda and her parents were asked to self-monitor the following behaviors both prior to and throughout the duration of treatment: needing mom to be with her when going to sleep, expressing concern about mom, refusing to go to school, clinging to mom or dad, stomachache or nausea, and crying. Whenever a behavior occurred, Amanda and/or her parents were asked to indicate the date/time, situation or precipitant, response or outcome, and an anxiety rating from 0 to 8 (1 = mild anxiety, little distress; 8 = very severe anxiety, intense distress).

SELF- AND OTHER-REPORT MEASURES

Self-report measures are an important component of a comprehensive assessment because they capture the subjective experience of anxiety from the child's perspective. Likewise, use of parent- and teacher-report measures provides important information on child behavior across different settings (e.g., school and home). Several questionnaire measures exist that allow for the assessment of general anxiety symptoms and/or symptoms of separation anxiety. These include the Revised Children's Manifest Anxiety Scale (RCMAS; Reynolds & Richmond, 1978), the Multidimensional Anxiety Scale for Children (MASC; March, 1997), the Fear Survey Schedule for Children–Revised (FSSC-R; Ollendick, 1983), the Child Behavior Checklist (CBCL; Achenbach, 1991), and the Teacher Report Form (TRF; Achenbach, 1991).

The RCMAS (Reynolds & Richmond, 1978) is a 37-item questionnaire designed to assess anxiety-related symptoms. Amanda's score of 21 on this measure was elevated relative to normative data, suggesting that she was experiencing higher levels of anxiety and worry than most girls her age. She also received an elevated score of 8 on the worry/oversensitivity subscale of the RCMAS. Items endorsed by her on this measure included "I worry about what is going to happen," "Often I feel sick in my stomach," and "I am nervous."

Amanda also completed the MASC (March, 1997), a 39-item questionnaire designed to assess various anxiety dimensions in children and adolescents. She received a total score of 83 (T-score = 71) on this measure, again suggesting a high overall level of anxiety. She also received an elevated score on the Separation/Panic Scale of the MASC, which assesses the tendency to be scared when alone or in an unfamiliar place, and to want to stay close to family or home. Items endorsed by Amanda on the MASC included "I avoid going to places without my family," "I sleep next to someone from my family," and "I feel sick to my stomach."

The FSSC-R (Ollendick, 1983) is an 80-item questionnaire that assesses the extent and nature of a child's fears. Ollendick and Mayer (1984) reported that the FSSC-R discriminated between school-refusing children whose fears were related to separation anxiety and children whose fears were related to specific aspects of the school itself. Children whose school refusal was related to separation anxiety endorsed items such as "getting lost in a strange place," "being left at home with a sitter," and "dark places." In contrast, children whose fears were related to specific aspects of the school itself more frequently checked items such as "giving an oral report," "being sent to the principal," and "taking a test." Interestingly, both groups of children indicated fears of "having to go to school" and "getting sick at school." Last, Francis, and Strauss (1989) and, more recently, Weems and colleagues (1999) reported similar findings related to the differential diagnosis of school-refusing children and adolescents with a variety of anxiety disorders. Amanda's total score of 158 on the FSSC-R was above the mean for girls of her age, and she indicated "a lot" of fear in response to separation-related items (e.g., "being alone," "going to bed in the dark").

Each of Amanda's parents completed the CBCL (Achenbach, 1991), a checklist assessing behavioral problems across both the internalizing (e.g., anxiety, depression) and externalizing (e.g., oppositional behavior) domains. Mr. N.'s score of 21 and Mrs. N.'s score of 26 on the internalizing scale were in the clinical range for children of Amanda's age. Both parents indicated that Amanda seemed "too fearful or anxious" and appeared "nervous, highstrung, or tense." Amanda's primary teacher was asked to complete the TRF (Achenbach, 1991), a version of the CBCL that allows teachers to rate a child's classroom behavior. Her responses confirmed that Amanda worried a great deal while in school and complained frequently of physical symptoms, such as stomachaches.

PHYSIOLOGICAL

Although the physiological assessment of childhood anxiety is a relatively new area of empirical study (Kendall et al., 2000), there is evidence suggesting that at least some anxious children may show greater autonomic reactivity in response to stressful tasks relative to their nonanxious peers (Beidel, 1988). The assessment of physiological indices, particularly heart rate, may therefore add to a comprehensive understanding of a child's pattern of anxiety. The BAT provides a unique opportunity to gather behavioral data, self-ratings of anxiety, and physiological measurements while the child is exposed to a feared situation. During the BAT, the therapist creates a situation in which the child is exposed in a controlled way to the focus of his or her fear. For instance, a child with SAD would be observed while in the same room with the parent, then with the parent down the hall but within sight, and finally, with the parent out of sight (Wachtel & Strauss, 1995).

Prior to beginning treatment, Amanda completed a BAT during which her heart rate was measured using a pulse oximeter. Throughout the BAT, she was asked periodically to rate her anxiety from 0 to 100 (0 = completely relaxed or not at all anxious; 100 = as anxious as she could imagine being). This is known as a Subjective Units of Discomfort Scale (SUDS). The BAT began with a 5-minute baseline period when Amanda was asked to sit quietly and relax while her mother was in the room with her. During the baseline, Amanda gave an average SUDS rating of 15 and evidenced an average heart rate of 72 beats per minute. Amanda's mother was then asked to go to the room next door where Amanda could still see her through a two-way mirror. During this part of the BAT, Amanda gave an average SUDS rating of 25 and her heart rate increased to an average of 84 beats per minute. Next, Mrs. N. was asked to sit in the waiting room, out of Amanda's sight. Amanda reporting feeling "upset" at this point, and gave a SUDS rating of 60. Her heart rate also increased to 91 beats per minute. Finally, Mrs. N. was instructed to leave the building and get a cup of coffee and a soda for Amanda at the bagel shop next door. Amanda became more distressed at this point, asking the therapist to "please let my mom stay in the building." However, she was able to tolerate her mother's brief departure, giving an average SUDS rating of 75. After her mother's departure, Amanda's heart rate increased to 98 beats per minute. When Mrs. N. returned, she and Amanda sat together for approximately 10 minutes while finishing their drinks. Amanda's SUDS ratings during this time were all below 20, and her heart rate gradually decreased to an average of 80 beats per minute. This BAT was thus successful in illustrating the physiological reactivity Amanda experienced when separated from her mother.

MEDICAL CONSULTATION

Medical consultation can play an important role in the assessment and treatment of school refusal and separation anxiety, particularly when the child reports physical symptoms or somatic complaints (e.g., headaches, nausea). Some cases of excessive school absenteeism can be the result of an undiagnosed medical illness, and a thorough physical examination can rule out such underlying problems (Wachtel & Strauss, 1995). In other cases, separation anxiety may exist along with a medical concern, necessitating both medical and behavioral treatment.

After meeting with Amanda and her parents for the initial assessment, the therapist suggested that Amanda visit her pediatrician to rule out the possibility that a medical problem was involved in her frequent episodes of nausea and stomach distress. The therapist also received a signed consent form from Mrs. N. allowing her to speak with Amanda's medical doctor. After conducting a physical examination, Amanda's doctor reported that he did not see evidence of a medical cause for Amanda's stomach distress. However, he did note that she had evidenced signs of lactose intolerance as a younger child, and suggested some moderate dietary changes to reduce her exposure to dairy products containing lactose. Both the therapist and the pediatrician agreed that the stomach distress occurred primarily in separation-relevant situations (e.g., school mornings), suggesting that anxiety played a significant role in this somatic complaint. The pediatrician also suggested the possible use of medication, such as imipramine or Alprazolam, both of which have some empirical support in the treatment of school refusal and SAD (Gittelman-Klein & Klein, 1971; Klein & Last, 1989). However, due to the efficacy of behavior therapy and the risk of potential side effects with medication, it was decided that behavioral treatment would be attempted first and medication would be used only if additional treatment seemed necessary.

CASE CONCEPTUALIZATION

A complete conceptualization of the case of Amanda must begin by examining her temperament and related behaviors as a young child. Specifically, Amanda's parents described her as being quite wary of unfamiliar people and anxious about going to new places without them. Kagan and colleagues (1984, 1987) described behavioral inhibition as a temperamental style characterized by shy and cautious behavior as well as a tendency to experience physiological arousal and to withdraw from unfamiliar situations. Recent research has provided some support for the hypothesis that behavioral inhibition may be linked to the development of anxiety (Biederman et al., 1990; Rosenbaum et al., 1988). Amanda's behavioral inhibition may thus have set the stage for the development of anxiety later in her childhood.

It is important to consider the response of Amanda's family to her particular temperamental style and the role it may have played in the development of her anxiety. Both Mr. and Mrs. N. reported that they responded to Amanda's wariness of new people and places by being sure that one of them was almost always with her and doing many family-focused activities. Ollendick and King (1990) have noted that the behavioral perspective of school refusal and separation anxiety views these problems as a "learned response." Indeed, Amanda's parents may have inadvertently reinforced her tendency to avoid new people and situations by almost always being with her (a response that was likely very positive from Amanda's perspective). At the same time, their reluctance to leave Amanda may have given her the nonverbal message that her safety and comfort depended on their presence, and that she was unable to cope with unfamiliar situations on her own. Furthermore, her parents' willingness to accompany her on school field trips and visits to friends' houses likely prevented her from learning to effectively manage her anxiety in these situations. Finally, Amanda seemed to experience some stress and anxiety around the birth of her brother when she was 3 years old. At this time, she began asking her mother to stay with her until she went to sleep at night, probably due to a desire to regain some of the attention that her parents were bestowing on the new baby. Although it was important for Amanda to continue to receive positive attention from her parents at this time, the fact that this attention became contingent on her experience of anxiety at bedtime only served to reinforce her fear of falling asleep without her mother and set up a long-standing pattern of problematic bedtime behavior/separation anxiety.

Amanda's separation anxiety was clearly evident during her transition to kindergarten. At this time, she showed much reluctance about going to school, crying every morning during her first week of kindergarten. However, with the support of her teacher, Mr. and Mrs. N. were able to help her overcome this anxiety and successfully begin her schooling. Specifically, rather than deciding to postpone kindergarten for a year (which probably would have served to reinforce Amanda's fears), the teacher encouraged them to continue bringing Amanda to school while showing her that they believed she was indeed ready to start kindergarten. This approach was an ideal intervention because it was based on the principle of exposure, a core element in the behavioral treatment of school refusal and other anxiety disorders (Ollendick & King, 1990). By Amanda's continuing to attend school each day, her fear response was gradually extinguished and she learned to cope with the anxiety of leaving her parents to attend school. This successful experience during kindergarten seems to have been instrumental in helping Amanda at last partially overcome her early signs of separation anxiety to establish a positive relationship with school.

Like many children with separation anxiety, Amanda had always shown concern for her mother and tended to worry about her well-being. However, after the Columbine High School tragedy, her concern for her mother escalated to the point that it began to cause excessive anxiety and interfere in her daily functioning. Her parents reported that she became preoccupied with news reports about the shootings at Columbine and developed extreme concern over the possibility that a similar tragedy would happen at the high school where her mother taught. Indeed, the transmission of fear-inducing information has been suggested as one means through which fears may be vicariously acquired in childhood (Ollendick & King, 1990; Rachman, 1977). Interestingly, Amanda did not seem to develop significant fear of a shooting taking place at her own school, nor did she worry excessively about her own well-being. Rather, the Columbine incident seemed to exacerbate her long-standing separation anxiety and concerns about her mother's safety, perhaps due to perceived similarities between Columbine and the school where her mother taught (e.g., both were high schools).

The *DSM-IV* (APA, 1994) states that SAD may develop after the experience of a life stressor (e.g., the death or illness of a relative, a move to a new school or neighborhood). The death of Amanda's grandmother certainly would qualify as such a stressor, which, though it did not trigger Amanda's first episode of separation anxiety, served as the precipitant of her current anxiety symptoms. It is important to note that the birth of her brother when Amanda was 3 years old served as another life stressor for her that seemed to contribute to at least one manifestation of her SAD (i.e., refusal to go to sleep without being near her mother). The death of her maternal grandmother, which occurred quite unexpectedly, may have confirmed her worst fears regarding the possibility of losing her own mother suddenly and without warning. It was also apparent that, although Amanda was certainly sad at the loss of her grandmother, her primary focus at this time was on the well-being of her mother. Seeing her mother in distress and being separated from her for two days prior to the funeral seemed to significantly heighten her separation anxiety. Her reaction to these heightened levels of anxiety was to become "clingy" and reluctant to be apart from her mother for even brief periods at the funeral and during the days that followed. Reduction in anxiety that resulted from this behavior served as a powerful source of negative reinforcement, which only increased Amanda's "clinginess" and desire to be with her mother at all times. As a result, the return to school was extremely difficult for her, leading to increased anxiety accompanied by somatic complaints (e.g., stomach distress) and the development of actual school refusal behavior.

Various sources of reinforcement within the environment outside of school may play an important role in the maintenance of school refusal (Kearney & Silverman, 1990, 1993; Ollendick & King, 1990). For instance, the child who stays home from school may receive a high level of attention from parents or other adults, or may be allowed to watch television, play outside, and so forth. Amanda's case illustrates the role of such reinforcement in maintaining school refusal behavior even when it is the result of underlying SAD. Specifically, Amanda's refusal to go to school always allowed her to maintain proximity with her mother because Mrs. N. would either stay home with her or leave her with a family friend who lived close to the high school. In both cases, Amanda received a great deal of attention from a favored adult, often having a special lunch with her mother or helping the family friend work in her garden. Amanda's mother acknowledged that her feelings of guilt about how her own grief may have negatively affected Amanda had probably led her to be "less strict" than she otherwise might have been about Amanda's school attendance and activities when she was not attending school. Mrs. N. agreed with the therapist that changing the expectations for Amanda's behavior, as well as the reinforcement she received, would be important elements of treatment for her current separation anxiety and school refusal.

RATIONALE FOR TREATMENT CHOICE

Cognitive-behavioral treatment was selected as the intervention of choice for Amanda's separation anxiety and school avoidance. This decision was based on the premise that successful treatment of SAD almost always requires a behavioral program focused on increasing independent behaviors, such as attending school or sleeping alone (Wachtel & Strauss, 1995). Recent research has supported the inclusion of cognitive strategies in child anxiety treatment, with the cognitive-behavioral approach reflecting an integration of behavioral techniques (e.g., relaxation, exposure) and training in the identification and restructuring of anxious thoughts (Kendall et al., 2000; Ollendick & King, 1998).

Ollendick and King (1990) reviewed the primary behavioral strategies that have been used in the treatment of school refusal and separation anxiety. These strategies are based on the principles of classical, vicarious, and operant conditioning, with a particular focus on exposure to feared situations (i.e., those involving separation). Counterconditioning and extinction are the primary treatment strategies based on classical conditioning principles. During counterconditioning, the child is exposed to feared situations in the presence of stimuli that trigger responses that are incompatible with anxiety (e.g., relaxation). Extinction involves repeated exposure to the feared stimuli in the absence of the original unconditioned stimuli (e.g., a negative or unpleasant outcome). This allows the child to learn that there is truly nothing to be afraid of, and the anxiety will gradually dissipate. Systematic desensitization is a counterconditioning technique that has been applied successfully to the treatment of school refusal (Lazarus, 1960). This technique involves teaching the child progressive relaxation, developing a hierarchy of feared situations, and presenting the anxiety-provoking situations together with the relaxation response. Whereas traditionally, the feared stimuli were presented imaginally while the individual was relaxed, the treatment can also be successfully applied by confronting the actual situations in vivo. For instance, the child can be assisted in gradually facing the feared situations on the hierarchy, with the goal of extinguishing the fear. The combination of imaginal desensitization and real-life exposure also has been used effectively in the treatment of separation anxiety (Miller, 1972).

Treatment strategies based on vicarious conditioning principles emphasize observational learning or modeling (Ollendick & King, 1990). Through modeling, the therapist or other relevant person demonstrates nonfearful behavior in the anxiety-provoking situation, thus showing the child an appropriate response for coping with his or her fear. For instance, children with school refusal are usually accompanied by a parent or therapist who models appropriate coping behavior during initial exposure practices focused on reentering the school environment. The principles of operant conditioning also play an important role by reinforcing appropriate behavior such as confronting feared situations and using coping strategies. Operant strategies attempt to increase the reinforcement a child gains for successfully separating from the parent or attending school while decreasing the reinforcement obtained from staying home. Material or social reinforcers may be used initially (e.g., a trip to a favorite restaurant with mom), but it is hoped that natural reinforcers, such as positive peer interactions, will maintain the desirable behavior (e.g., school attendance). Several studies have supported the use of operant procedures, or behavior management, in the treatment of separation anxiety and school refusal (e.g., Ayllon, Smith, & Rogers, 1970).

Use of cognitive techniques in the treatment of separation anxiety and school refusal is based on the premise that the child's anxious behavior is produced or maintained by maladaptive thoughts, beliefs, or self-statements (Wachtel & Strauss, 1995). The first step in changing such thoughts involves helping the child identify self-statements that are associated with his or her anxiety (e.g., "My mom will get hurt in an accident while I am at school today"). The child then can be taught to replace such anxious thoughts with coping statements that reflect confidence in the child's independent abilities (e.g., "I can handle this on my own"), the parents safety (e.g., "My mom is a careful driver who has never had an accident before; she will be fine"), and self-praise (e.g., "I am a very brave girl!"). The use of such cognitive strategies, combined with behavioral techniques, has been shown to effectively reduce school refusal and separation anxiety (King et al., 1998; Mansdorf & Lukens, 1987; Ollendick, Hagopian, & Huntzinger, 1991).

COURSE OF TREATMENT

Amanda and her parents participated in 12 sessions of cognitive-behavioral treatment over a four-month period. Two therapist-assisted exposures were also conducted outside of the clinic during the course of treatment, as described in the following. The treatment sessions generally consisted of the therapist meeting individually with Amanda for about half of the session, followed by meeting with Amanda and her parents to review the material covered in treatment, assess progress, and plan homework assignments for the coming week. Three times during the course of treatment the therapist met individually with the parents to discuss parenting issues (e.g., implementing behavioral strategies, such as reinforcing school attendance).

Treatment began with a psychoeducational focus on the nature of anxiety and the specific treatment strategies that would be introduced. In particular, the therapist described the three components of anxiety: the physical ("What I feel"), the cognitive ("What I think"), and the behavioral ("What I do"). Amanda, her parents, and the therapist discussed the role that each of these components played in maintaining Amanda's anxiety. For instance, Amanda reported that she had many "scary thoughts" when faced with the idea of being separated from her mother, including "What if my mom gets in an accident on her way to school today and I never see her again?" and "I think some of those mean high school kids may be planning to bomb my mom's school." After having such anxious thoughts, she was able to recognize that she usually started to have some uncomfortable feelings in her body, such as feeling that her heartbeat and breathing were faster than usual, feeling stomach distress "like I might throw up," and just feeling "tense all over." Finally, both Amanda and her parents recognized that she would usually try to leave a situation when she was experiencing anxious thoughts and feelings (e.g., going to the school nurse) or to avoid it altogether (e.g., refusing to go to school in the morning). Once she avoided or left the situation, she would quickly feel much better, resulting in the negative reinforcement of her avoidant behavior. The therapist was able to help Amanda and her parents see that only through facing her fears would she ultimately overcome her anxiety and avoidance while increasing her confidence in her ability to cope with separation.

After introducing the three-component model of anxiety, the therapist explained that Amanda would be learning skills during the course of treatment that would target each of the components. The goal by the end of treatment was to provide Amanda with a "toolbox" filled with skills/"tools" that she could use to cope with the feelings, thoughts, and behaviors associated with her anxiety. In particular, she would learn breathing and relaxation strategies to reduce the physical sensations, and also become a "detective" who could question and change her anxious thoughts. Finally, she would gradually face the situations she feared to learn that these situations were not as fearsome as she had imagined and that she could cope with them through the use of her anxiety-management tools. The therapist and Amanda's parents were described as "coaches" who would support and encourage Amanda as she faced her fears and learned to cope with anxiety.

Finally, a behavioral plan was established during Session 2 in which Amanda would earn points for facing feared situations that could be traded for various rewards (e.g., 5 points allowed Amanda to rent a favorite movie; 10 points earned her a family trip to the restaurant of her choice). It was decided that this plan would be used initially to reinforce her attendance at school. Although she already was attending school on some days, she was having difficulty remaining in school for the entire day without going to the nurse or calling her mother. The therapist decided to use a graduated approach in which Amanda would receive a point each day she was able to remain in school for at least two hours without these "escape" behaviors. Once she was able to complete this task for four of five days in a week, she would then begin to earn additional points for remaining in school at least three hours, gradually progressing up to a full school day. It was decided that Amanda would receive an additional half-point for each hour she remained in school beyond the initial two-hour requirement. For instance, three hours earned her 1.5 points, four hours was worth 2 points, and a full six-hour school day earned 3 points. As part of this plan, Amanda's parents also agreed that she would not be reinforced for undesirable behavior (e.g., spending special time with mom during days she refused to go to school). Table 16.1 depicts Amanda's school attendance throughout the course of treatment.

Breathing and relaxation strategies were introduced during Session 3 to target the physical sensations of anxiety (e.g., rapid heartrate/breathing, stomach distress, muscle tension). The goal was to give Amanda some initial tools that she could use independently when she had the urge to avoid or escape from a particular situation (e.g., going to the school nurse with complaints of nausea). Relaxation training began with the therapist explaining to Amanda that many people tend to breathe in a very quick, shallow way and to tense many of their muscles when they are anxious. The therapist demonstrated shallow, rapid breathing and asked her how she thought such breathing would make a person feel. Amanda responded that it would probably make someone feel "pretty stressed out." The therapist then taught Amanda diaphragmatic breathing, asking her to imagine

Table 16.1
Amanda's School Attendance and Ability to Sleep Independently
during the Course of Treatment

	School Attendance		Nights Going to Sleep Independently	
	Number of Partial Days	Number of Full Days	Mother Upstairs	Mother Not Upstairs
Week 1 (session 1)	2	0	0	0
Week 2 (session 2)	3	0	0	0
Week 3 (session 3)	4	0	0	0
Week 4 (session 4)	4	0	0	0
Week 5 (session 5)	4	0	0	0
Week 6 (session 6)	3	1	3	0
Week 7 (session 7)	4	1	5	0
Week 8 (session 8)	3	2	7	0
Week 9 (session 9)	2	3	5	2
Week 10	1	4	3	4
Week 11 (session 10)	0	5	1	6
Week 12	1	4	0	7
Week 13 (session 11)	0	5	0	7
Week 14	0	5	0	7
Week 15	0	5	0	7
Week 16 (session 12)	—	—	—	—

Note: Each week represents the week following a particular session (e.g., week 1 is the week following session 1).

that she had a balloon in her stomach that she was trying to inflate with each breath. Amanda quickly learned to breathe deeply, from her abdomen, and to slow her breathing down to a relaxed and comfortable rate. Following breathing retraining, the therapist introduced progressive muscle relaxation, using imagery to help Amanda relax various muscle groups throughout her body. For instance, the following description was used to teach her to recognize tension in her stomach followed by a relaxation response:

> Imagine that you are playing a game of ball with someone without using your hands. Instead, your friend is throwing the ball to you and you are trying to bounce it back to her using only your stomach! The ball is soft, so it won't hurt, but you'll need to make your stomach very tight in order for the ball to bounce. I want you to make your stomach as tight as you can—good! Now hold it for a few more bounces . . . Excellent. Okay, the game is over and you've done great. You can really relax your stomach now. Just let it go, relax your stomach as much as you can. I want you to really pay attention to how good it feels for your stomach to be relaxed and how different it feels from being all tense.

An audiotape was made of progressive muscle relaxation, and Amanda was asked to practice the breathing and relaxation twice daily over the coming week. She also was asked to begin using her breathing tool in anxiety-provoking situations and to practice relaxing her body whenever she noticed feelings of tension or physical discomfort. Amanda reported feeling happy and surprised that she could relax her body on her own. During the following weeks, she indicated using the breathing and relaxation skills to help her cope with anxiety at times when she would previously have gone straight to the nurse's office or refused to leave her mom.

Session 4 focused on learning to challenge and change anxious thoughts by "becoming a detective." The therapist and Amanda discussed the idea that anxious thoughts often do not turn out to be true, and that it is the job of a good detective to treat these thoughts as "guesses" and to look for clues that show whether or not the thought is true. For instance, Amanda reported believing that her mother was very likely to have a car accident on her way to school. However, when the therapist asked her to be a detective and examine this thought more closely (i.e., "Use your magnifying glass"), Amanda could not find any clues supporting this thought. Instead, she reported that her mother was actually a very safe driver and had never had an accident and that the roads she drove to work were back roads with low speed limits. Similarly, she was able to challenge her fear of an attack at her mother's school by recognizing that there had never been a serious act of violence at the high school or at any of the surrounding schools. Amanda pointed out that Columbine also had been a very peaceful place prior to the tragic shootings, but she recognized that this one example of violence was greatly outnumbered by the thousands of schools that had never experienced violence. In the end, she stated that the likelihood of an attack at her mother's school was "probably not more than the chance of being hit by a comet from outer space, which isn't a very big chance." Amanda also was taught to make coping self-statements whenever she found herself feeling anxious (e.g., "I know that I can use my tools to deal with this"), and to praise herself when she successfully coped with anxiety (e.g., "I got through the whole school day myself. I'm a great detective and I really know how to use my relaxation tools!").

A Fear and Avoidance Hierarchy (FAH) was developed with Amanda during Sessions 3 and 4. This was a list of 10 situations that Amanda identified as a primary focus of anxiety and avoidance. She rated her fear and avoidance of each situation from 0 (no fear/never avoids) to 8 (severe fear/always avoids), as detailed in Table 16.2.

Amanda's FAH was used as the foundation for graduated exposure, which was begun during Session 5. During this session, the therapist met with Amanda and her parents together to discuss the rationale for exposure and develop a plan for Amanda to begin to face the situations on her hierarchy. The therapist explained that exposure was one of the most effective ways of reducing anxiety and was based on the principle that anxiety would gradually diminish when a feared situation was confronted repeatedly in the absence of negative consequences. Because Amanda and her parents loved to ski, the therapist used skiing as a good example of how something that may be scary at first becomes less and less anxiety-provoking with repeated practice. Furthermore, facing feared situations was presented as an ideal opportunity to practice the tools and strategies learned in treatment, thus enhancing Amanda's coping ability. Once the family understood the rationale for exposure, a plan was developed for Amanda to begin practicing the situations on her hierarchy. Beginning with the least anxiety-provoking item, the therapist asked Amanda to plan a visit to a friend's house during the coming week. Once this was completed successfully, they would attempt the next situation by having Mrs. N. stay in her own bedroom next door to Amanda while Amanda went to sleep. After developing this plan, the therapist conducted an imaginal practice during which she had Amanda imagine facing these two situations while successfully using her anxiety-management strategies to cope with them. Amanda's parents were encouraged to give her much support and praise for completing each exposure practice. Amanda also earned points through her behavioral plan for completing exposure tasks.

The therapist met with Amanda and her parents at the beginning of Session 6 to review the exposure practices from the previous week. Amanda reported that she had made three visits to a friend's house, using her breathing, relaxation, and "detective" tools to cope with the moderate anxiety she initially experienced. She reported that she began to feel much less nervous after she had been at her friend's house for awhile, stating, "I was having so much fun I forgot to worry

Table 16.2
Amanda's Fear and Avoidance Hierarchy

Feared Situations	Fear	Avoid
Parents going away overnight	8	8
Sleeping at a friend's house	7	8
Going to sleep without mom at home	7	8
Going on a field trip without parents	7	7
Staying at school all day	6	6
Going to sleep, mom downstairs	5	6
Going to school in the morning	5	5
Mom going to an appointment alone	4	5
Going to sleep, mom in the next room	3	4
Visiting a friend's house	2	3

about my mom." However, she and her parents reported that their efforts to have Amanda go to sleep while mom was in the next room had not gone as smoothly. Specifically, Amanda stated that she had felt very nervous and could not sleep with her mother so far away. The therapist helped the family problem-solve to come up with a plan for breaking this task down into more manageable steps. Because Mrs. N. typically would lie next to Amanda while she fell asleep, the family decided to begin by having Mrs. N. sit in a chair near Amanda's bed until she fell asleep. Once this was successful, Mrs. N. would move the chair closer to the bedroom door, then to the hall right outside Amanda's bedroom, and finally into the room next door. Amanda would earn a point each time she successfully completed one of these smaller tasks. This process, known as shaping the desired behavior, worked very well for Amanda, who was able to go to sleep with her mother in the room next door within two weeks (earning her a family trip to her favorite restaurant!). Table 16.1 depicts changes in Amanda's ability to sleep independently during the course of treatment.

Between Sessions 6 and 7, the therapist conducted an assisted exposure with Amanda to help her successfully confront the fourth situation on her FAH, "Going to school in the morning." The therapist went to Amanda's house on a school morning and helped her use her anxiety-management tools while modeling appropriate coping behavior. Specifically, the therapist helped Amanda identify and challenge anxious thoughts (e.g., "Nothing bad has ever happened to mom at work before, so the chances are really low that she would get hurt today"), while offering praise and examples of coping self-statements (e.g., "I am really good at using my tools now. I know I can go to school today"). Finally, the therapist helped her use her breathing and relaxation strategies when she reported some stomach distress, and talked with her about using these strategies in school as well. Although Amanda was able to go to school during this therapist-assisted exposure, she did go to the school nurse after lunch with complaints of nausea and worries about her mom. Another therapist-assisted exposure was thus conducted after Session 7, although this time, the therapist planned to meet Amanda at school during lunch time with the goal of helping her stay at school all day without a trip to the nurse's office. Again, the therapist coached Amanda in the use of her anxiety-management tools and modeled coping behavior. At the next session, Amanda proudly reported that she had stayed in school all day and felt much more confident about her ability to cope with her anxiety in school. Indeed, this was a turning point for Amanda, who began attending school much more regularly with fewer and fewer visits to the nurse.

The final sessions of treatment were devoted to continued exposure practices and review of Amanda's coping strategies. By the end of treatment, Amanda had three consecutive weeks of perfect school attendance and had completed all but the highest-anxiety situation on her hierarchy. The therapist helped her and her parents plan to complete this exposure and to conduct additional exposures as relevant situations arose. Her parents and the therapist praised Amanda for her bravery in confronting her fears and her mastery of the anxiety-management tools.

THERAPIST-CLIENT FACTORS

The therapist's role in the cognitive-behavioral treatment of school refusal and separation anxiety is that of "educator and facilitator" (Wachtel & Strauss, 1995,

p. 60). For instance, Amanda's therapist served to teach anxiety-management skills while modeling coping behavior and "coaching" Amanda as she faced the feared situations on her hierarchy. The therapist also educated Amanda and her parents about the nature of anxiety and provided guidance as Mr. and Mrs. N. applied behavioral strategies to reinforce Amanda's exposure practice and coping efforts. The therapist's relationship with Amanda proceeded very smoothly, largely due to Amanda's motivation and desire to overcome her anxiety. Amanda reported that she liked learning new "tools" and was pleasantly surprised that therapy involved more than just "talking about stuff" every week. She eagerly embraced the idea of become an expert on her own anxiety and its management, and stated that she was ready to "be my own therapist" by the end of treatment.

In contrast to her relationship with Amanda, the therapist's relationship with Amanda's parents required some effort. Amanda's father, in particular, had expected the therapist to work solely with his daughter and became quite defensive at the suggestion that he and Mrs. N. would play an important role in treatment. The therapist explained that parental involvement was incorporated in cognitive-behavioral treatment because of the critical role parents could play as "coaches," encouraging their child's efforts at facing feared situations and practicing coping skills. Mr. and Mrs. N. also expressed some initial hesitancy regarding the reinforcement of appropriate behavior, stating that it felt like "bribery" for "activities she should be doing anyway." The therapist worked with the parents to find rewards that felt more palatable to them (e.g., family activities rather that material rewards), and explained that reinforcement should be viewed as a "pat on the back" for a job well done. They also discussed the important role of praise and natural reinforcers. The therapist's efforts in working with the parents were very helpful in alleviating their concerns, and both Mr. and Mrs. N. reported feeling very positive about the course of therapy and Amanda's progress.

COURSE OF TERMINATION

A plan for the termination of Amanda's therapy was discussed with the family at Session 8. At this session, both Amanda and her parents reported feeling very pleased with the progress Amanda had made, particularly her success with completing a full school day following the therapist-assisted exposure that had taken place between Sessions 7 and 8. Sessions had been conducted on a weekly basis up to this point, and the therapist suggested that they schedule Session 9 for the following week to ensure that this progress continued. If so, the family and therapist agreed to begin tapering treatment by scheduling Sessions 10 and 11 at two-week intervals. This plan would allow Amanda a greater period of time between sessions to plan and conduct exposure practices, while allowing a more gradual transition for the termination process. During Sessions 10 and 11, Amanda and her therapist began reviewing the skills learned in treatment and discussing the importance of continuing to face feared situations and use her coping tools even after treatment had ended. Amanda reported feeling quite confident that she could do this and was able to plan some future exposure practices (e.g., going to an overnight camp the following summer). The final session was planned for three weeks following Session 11, and termination was made contingent on successful school attendance during this period of time. At Session 12, Amanda proudly reported that she had had three weeks of perfect school attendance and felt ready to continue using the treatment strategies on her own. The therapist helped the family plan an overnight trip for Amanda's parents (the last item on Amanda's FAH). While she prepared Amanda and her parents for the reality that Amanda might experience some episodes of anxiety in the future, particularly when confronting feared situations, the therapist expressed confidence in Amanda's ability to cope with anxiety.

FOLLOW-UP

A follow-up appointment was scheduled for two months following termination of treatment to assess the maintenance of treatment gains and Amanda's continued progress. During the appointment, a shortened version of the ADIS-IV interview was conducted, focused particularly on areas of initial concern (e.g., separation anxiety). Amanda reported that, although she sometimes felt worried about her mother when they were apart, she was able to use her anxiety-management skills to challenge these worry thoughts and reduce her anxiety. Amanda stated that by facing feared situations, she had developed confidence in her ability to separate from her mother; she was now able to attend school and sleep on her own with only mild anxiety. When asked how much her separation anxiety interfered in her life at follow-up, she gave a rating of 3 on a 9-point scale. Amanda's parents also reported notable improvement in her separation anxiety and school refusal, stating that they were particularly pleased with her ability to attend school and use her coping strategies instead of visiting the nurse. Mrs. N. was extremely happy about Amanda's ability to go to sleep on her own. Her parents assigned a rating of 2 to reflect the very mild level of interference currently caused by separation concerns in Amanda's life.

The BAT was also readministered at follow-up to assess Amanda's physiological reactivity, SUDS ratings, and behavioral response to separation tasks. All of Amanda's SUDS ratings during the BAT remained below 30 (on a 100-point scale), and her maximum heart rate was 83 beats per minute (compared to a maximum heart rate of 98 beats per minute on the pretreatment BAT). Amanda reported feeling some mild anxiety when her mother left to get coffee next door, but was able to use her coping strategies to manage this anxiety. Finally, Amanda, her parents, and her teacher completed the same questionnaires used prior to treatment. Amanda's score of 16 on the RCMAS was in the normal range, as was her score of 4 on the worry/oversensitivity subscale of this measure. Similarly, she received a total score of 65 (T-score = 60) on the MASC, suggesting a level of anxiety only slightly above average for girls her age. Her score on the Separation/Panic Scale of this measure was in the average range. Her score of 142 on the FSSC-R was also in the average range for girls her age. Mr. N.'s score of 9 and Mrs. N's score of 11 on the internalizing scale of the CBCL were both below the clinical range. The teacher's responses on the TRF also confirmed reduction in Amanda's worry and complaints of physical symptoms while in school. Overall, Amanda showed notable improvement at follow-up, as evidenced by her reports and those of significant others.

MANAGED CARE CONSIDERATIONS

Managed care issues were not raised by the case of Amanda because she was treated at a clinic that operates via sliding scale fees rather than through insurance reimbursement. However, the case raises some important issues that should be considered when conducting such cognitive-behavioral treatment within a managed care model. First, the case provides support for the efficacy of cognitive-behavioral treatment as well as its ability to produce notable change in a relatively short period of time (e.g., 12 sessions). Use of this type of treatment is often quite appealing to managed care companies with a focus on cost-effective treatments. Second, the cognitive-behavioral treatment of anxiety typically involves the development of concrete goals (e.g., teaching anxiety-management skills, specific exposure practices) and assessment strategies for measuring whether these goals have been achieved. Again, this is important from the perspective of managed care, which often requires a clearly delineated plan for treatment and assessment when authorizing requests for treatment sessions.

One potential problem that might arise when working with a managed care company is receiving reimbursement/authorization for treatment strategies that depart from the traditional, 50-minute therapy session. For instance, therapist-assisted exposure can be a critical component of treatment (as is illustrated by the case of Amanda), yet it takes place outside of the office and can involve several hours of work on the part of both therapist and client. When working with a managed care company, the therapist may need to carefully document the importance of such a treatment strategy in the context of a cost-effective and efficacious treatment plan. Similarly, the case of Amanda illustrates the importance of conducting a thorough behavioral assessment to clearly delineate the presenting problems and develop a focused treatment plan. Such a through assessment often requires more than one visit. For instance, Amanda was assessed over the course of two clinic visits (one of which consisted of the ADIS and self-report measures, and the other involved the BAT), as well as one home visit during which the therapist conducted a behavioral observation prior to initiating the treatment sessions. Managed care companies often are reluctant to pay for more than one assessment visit, and the therapist may need to clearly justify the importance of such thorough assessment within the overall treatment plan. Indeed, such assessment typically increases the efficiency and decreases the length of treatment by allowing therapist and client to clearly delineate goals and appropriate strategies from the outset. Through clear communication, the therapist can develop a positive working relationship with the managed care company with the goal of best serving the client.

OVERALL EFFECTIVENESS

The case of Amanda clearly supports the overall effectiveness of cognitive-behavioral treatment for school refusal and separation anxiety. By the end of treatment, Amanda had developed coping strategies for managing her own anxiety rather than depending on adults, such as her mother or the school nurse, to help her cope. As a result, she was able to confront many of her fears, including participating fully in her school and sleeping on her own. She terminated treatment as a more independent child whose anxiety was causing far less interference in her life. The effectiveness of treatment for Amanda was well-documented in the follow-up assessment that took place two months following termination. At this time, both she and her parents reported that separation concerns were causing far less interference in Amanda's life, and questionnaires completed by Amanda, her parents, and her teacher indicated a level of anxiety that was within the normal range for girls her age. At the end of treatment, Amanda stated that she was ready to "be my own therapist." This comment reflects one of the strengths of cognitive-behavioral treatment, which strives to give individuals tools they can use to cope with anxiety throughout their lives. Amanda's success demonstrates the impact such treatment can have by reducing fear and avoidance, thus improving a child's quality of life.

REFERENCES

Achenbach, T. M. (1991). *Integrative guide for the 1991 CBCL/4–18, YSR, and TRF.* Burlington: University of Vermont.

American Psychiatric Association. (1994). *Diagnostic and statistical manual of mental disorders* (4th ed.). Washington, DC: Author.

Ayllon, T., Smith, D., & Rogers, M. (1970). Behavioral management of school phobia. *Journal of Behavior Therapy and Experimental Psychiatry, 1,* 125–138.

Beidel, D. C. (1988). Psychophysiological assessment of anxious emotional states in children. *Journal of Abnormal Psychology, 97,* 80–82.

Biederman, J., Rosenbaum, J. F., Hirshfeld, D. R., Faraone, S. V., Bolduc, E. A., Gersten, M., et al. (1990). Psychiatric correlates of behavioral inhibition in young children of parents with and without psychiatric disorders. *Archives of General Psychiatry, 47,* 21–26.

Blagg, N. R., & Yule, W. (1984). The behavioral treatment of school refusal: A comparative study. *Behaviour Research and Therapy, 22,* 119–127.

Gittelman-Klein, R., & Klein, D. F. (1971). Controlled imipramine treatment of school phobia. *Archives of General Psychiatry, 25,* 204–207.

Johnson, A. M., Falstein, E. I., Szurek, S. A., & Svendsen, M. (1941). School phobia. *American Journal of Orthopsychiatry, 11,* 702–711.

Kagan, J., Reznick, J. S., Clarke, C., & Snidman, N. (1984). Behavioral inhibition to the unfamiliar. *Child Development, 55,* 2212–2225.

Kagan, J., Reznick, J. S., & Snidman, N. (1987). The physiology and psychology of behavioral inhibition in children. *Child Development, 58,* 1459–1473.

Kearney, C. A. (1995). School refusal behavior. In A. R. Eisen, C. A. Kearney, & C. E. Schaefer (Eds.), *Clinical handbook of anxiety disorders in children and adolescents* (pp. 19–52). Northvale, NJ: Aronson.

Kearney, C. A., & Silverman, W. K. (1990). A preliminary analysis of a functional model of assessment and treatment for school refusal behavior. *Behavior Modification, 14,* 340–366.

Kearney, C. A., & Silverman, W. K. (1993). Measuring the function of school refusal behavior: The School Refusal Assessment Scale. *Journal of Clinical Child Psychology, 22,* 85–96.

Kendall, P. C., Chu, B. C., Pimentel, S. S., & Choudhury, M. (2000). Treating anxiety disorders in youth. In P. C. Kendall (Ed.), *Child and adolescent therapy: Cognitive-behavioral procedures* (2nd ed., pp. 235–287). New York: Guilford Press.

King, N. J., Ollendick, T. H., & Tonge, B. J. (1995). *School refusal: Assessment and treatment.* Boston: Allyn & Bacon.

King, N. J., Tonge, B. J., Heyne, D., Pritchard, M., Rollings, S., Young, D., et al. (1998). Cognitive-behavioral treatment of school-refusing children: A controlled evaluation. *Journal of the American Academy of Child and Adolescent Psychiatry, 37,* 395–403.

Klein, R. G., & Last, C. G. (1989). Anxiety disorders in children. In A. E. Kazdin (Ed.), *Developmental clinical psychology and psychiatry* (pp. 32–34). Newbury Park, CA: Sage.

Last, C. G., Francis, G., Hersen, M., Kazdin, A. E., & Strauss, C. C. (1987). Separation anxiety and school phobia: A comparison using *DSM-III* criteria. *American Journal of Psychiatry, 144,* 653–657.

Last, C. G., Francis, G., & Strauss, C. C. (1989). Assessing fears in anxiety-disordered children with the revised Fear Survey Schedule for Children (FSSC-R). *Journal of Clinical Child Psychology, 18,* 137–141.

Last, C. G., & Strauss, C. C. (1990). School refusal in anxiety-disordered children and adolescents. *Journal of the American Academy of Child and Adolescent Psychiatry, 29,* 31–35.

Lazarus, A. A. (1960). The elimination of children's phobias by deconditioning. In H. J. Eysenck (Ed.), *Behaviour therapy and the neuroses* (pp. 114–122). Oxford, England: Pergamon Press.

Mansdorf, I. J., & Lukens, E. (1987). Cognitive-behavioral psychotherapy for separation anxious children exhibiting school phobia. *Journal of the American Academy of Child and Adolescent Psychiatry, 26,* 222–225.

March, J. S. (1997). *Multidimensional Anxiety Scale for Children.* North Tonawanda, NY: Multi-Health Systems.

Miller, P. M. (1972). The use of visual imagery and muscle relaxation in the counterconditioning of a phobic child: A case study. *Journal of Nervous and Mental Disease, 154,* 457–460.

Ollendick, T. H. (1983). Reliability and validity of the revised Fear Survey Schedule for Children (FSSC-R). *Behaviour Research and Therapy, 21,* 685–692.

Ollendick, T. H., Hagopian, L. P., & Huntzinger, R. M. (1991). Cognitive-behavior therapy with nighttime fearful children. *Journal of Behavior Therapy and Experimental Psychiatry, 22,* 113–121.

Ollendick, T. H., & King, N. J. (1990). School phobia and separation anxiety. In H. Leitenberg (Ed.), *Handbook of social anxiety* (pp. 179–214). New York: Plenum.

Ollendick, T. H., & King, N. J. (1998). Empirically supported treatments for children with phobic and anxiety disorders: Current status. *Journal of Clinical Child Psychology, 27,* 156–167.

Ollendick, T. H., & Mayer, J. A. (1984). School phobia. In S. M. Turner (Ed.), *Behavioral theories and treatment of anxiety* (pp. 367–411). New York: Plenum Press.

Rachman, S. (1977). The conditioning theory of fear acquisition: A critical examination. *Behaviour Research and Therapy, 15,* 375–387.

Reynolds, C. R., & Richmond, B. O. (1978). What I think and feel: A revised measure of children's manifest anxiety. *Journal of Abnormal Psychology, 6,* 271–280.

Rosenbaum, A. F., Biederman, J., Gersten, M., Hirshfeld, D. R., Meminger, S. R., Herman, J. B., et al. (1988). Behavioral inhibition in children of parents with Panic Disorder and Agoraphobia: A controlled study. *Archives of General Psychiatry, 45,* 463–470.

Silverman, W. K., & Albano, A. M. (1996). *Anxiety Disorders Interview Schedule for DSM-IV: Child and parent versions.* San Antonio, TX: Psychological Corporation.

Wachtel, J. R., & Strauss, C. C. (1995). Separation Anxiety Disorder. In A. R. Eisen, C. A. Kearney, & C. E. Schaefer (Eds.), *Clinical handbook of anxiety disorders in children and adolescents* (pp. 53–81). Northvale, NJ: Aronson.

Weems, C. F., Silverman, W. K., Saavedra, L. M., Pina, A. A., & Lumpkin, P. W. (1999). The discrimination of children's phobias using the revised Fear Survey Schedule for Children. *Journal of Child Psychology and Psychiatry, 40,* 941–952.

CHAPTER 17

Social Phobia

CHRISTOPHER A. KEARNEY and KELLY L. DRAKE

DESCRIPTION OF THE DISORDER

ONE OF THE most common types of human anxiety is social anxiety, or psychological discomfort when interacting with others. Mild to moderate amounts of social anxiety are usually considered normal, and perhaps serve adaptively to inhibit inappropriate behavior or to increase alertness during key interactions. More severe or extreme anxiety during social interactions, however, can be quite debilitating and may be linked to social phobia or Social Anxiety Disorder. According to the *Diagnostic and Statistical Manual of Mental Disorders* (*DSM-IV*), the essential feature of Social Anxiety Disorder is a "marked and persistent fear of social or performance situations in which embarrassment may occur" (American Psychiatric Association, 1994, p. 411). Thus, social phobia affects direct human interactions as well as those situations where one is performing or being evaluated before others.

DSM-IV symptoms of social phobia/Social Anxiety Disorder resemble those of a situationally bound or situationally predisposed panic attack. Thus, in social situations, where a person greatly fears that he or she will act in a humiliating or embarrassing way, characteristic physiological (e.g., rapid heart rate, sweating) and cognitive (e.g., worry about losing control) symptoms are likely to occur. *DSM-IV* criteria also mandate that the person understands that his or her fear is unreasonable or excessive. In addition, specific social and/or performance situations must be avoided or endured with great dread, and the person's avoidance and distress must significantly interfere with daily functioning. Furthermore, impairment is not due to substance use or medical conditions.

In children and adolescents, *DSM-IV* makes special provisions with respect to social phobia. First, the child must show a capability for appropriate relationships with familiar people, such as family members or close friends. It is not unusual, for example, for youth with social phobia to carefully restrict themselves to a small group of siblings and one or two friends. Second, social anxiety must occur in peer settings and not simply during interactions with adults. Many children, for example, are nervous about speaking to elders but have no trouble discussing topics with friends. Children with social phobia, however, would have such difficulty. Third, social anxiety in children may be linked to "crying, tantrums, freezing, or shrinking from social situations with unfamiliar people" (p. 417). Fourth, children with social phobia may not recognize their fear as excessive or unreasonable. Finally, duration of social phobia in youth under age 18 years must be at least six months.

Reported prevalence rates for social phobia in youth vary, but generally range from 1% to 4% (Beidel, Turner, & Morris, 1999; Essau, Conradt, & Petermann, 1999; Vasey, 1995). Beidel et al. reported that youth with social phobia fear a wide variety of social situations, especially reading aloud in front of the class, performing musically or athletically, joining or starting conversations, speaking to adults, writing on the blackboard, ordering food in a restaurant, attending nightly social activities (e.g., dances), taking tests, and going to parties. Many feared situations involve those in a school setting, so school refusal behavior and selective mutism may also be seen. Beidel et al. also reported that these children tend to have very few friends, avoid extracurricular activities, and experience high levels of anxiety and somatic complaints. Comorbidity with other anxiety disorders and depression is common (Beidel, 1991; Essau et al., 1999).

The etiology of social phobia in youth remains debatable, but is likely related to a combination of temperamental behavioral inhibition, biological vulnerability to high arousal, social apprehension, high neuroticism and low extroversion, a sense of uncontrollability in social situations, stressful life events, and family factors such as genetic predisposition, modeling perceptions of environmental threat, overprotectiveness, lack of warmth, and disrupted attachment (Beidel et al., 1999; Hudson & Rapee, 2000; Schwartz, Snidman, & Kagan, 1999; Walters & Inderbitzen, 1998). Social phobia likely is maintained by negatively reinforcing escape from aversive social and/or evaluative situations and positively reinforcing factors from family members and others (Kearney, 1999).

CASE DESCRIPTION

Eugene Erickson was a 13-year-old multiracial male who was referred to a childhood anxiety disorders clinic for persistent difficulty interacting with others and for school refusal behavior. Eugene was referred by his mother and school counselor, both of whom reported that he was steadily missing more school days and seemed overly withdrawn in several of his classes. Eugene was an eighth-grade student at a public junior high school, and was referred for assessment in January of the academic year. The referral for assessment was triggered largely by two events. First, he had just missed his fifteenth day of school that year, which violated the school's attendance policy. Both the principal of the school and Eugene's counselor informed the family that his case was likely to be referred to juvenile court, where charges of truancy and educational neglect may surface. The second trigger leading to the referral was a statement by Eugene to his mother that he did not want to live anymore, and that facing certain children each day at school was unbearable. Later assessment revealed no suicidal tendencies, though Eugene was distraught over his situation.

Mrs. Erickson also reported that Eugene's father often traveled out of town and out of the country on business, and that he would not be able to fully participate in Eugene's assessment and treatment. She also speculated during the screening process that her husband's absence may be exacerbating Eugene's distress and refusal to attend school. For example, she revealed that Eugene often mentioned his father's absence and complained that his father was not helping him academically as much as he had in the past. Mrs. Erickson did indicate, however, that her husband would be willing to consult with the therapist via telephone and e-mail if he missed a session.

On talking to Eugene during the screening process, the therapist noted that the boy was somewhat stilted in his conversation. Answers to questions were usually one-word responses or an abject "I don't know." When asked if he would be willing to come in to talk with the therapist, Eugene paused and said he would speak to his mother about this. He then left the conversation. Mrs. Erickson scheduled a time for her and Eugene to meet the therapist, and she was instructed to tell her son that he would not be required to answer any questions he did not wish to answer. In addition, the therapist assured Mrs. Erickson that only she and a student would be present during the initial assessment.

Eugene's school counselor contacted the therapist prior to the assessment session to state that Eugene's school status had worsened. He was now missing a majority of days at school and was in danger of failing classes that required attendance and participation (e.g., physical education, music). She noted that Eugene's mother came to school on those days when her son was absent to collect his homework, and that Eugene, being a bright student, faithfully completed the work at home. The counselor was concerned, however, that Eugene's other classes would have to be made up in the summer.

CHIEF COMPLAINTS

Mrs. Erickson and Eugene, following one postponement, did attend the assessment session. The therapist spoke with each separately and asked each to complete a small series of questionnaires (see Behavioral Assessment). The therapist spoke with Eugene first to build rapport, ensure that most of his answers (outside of harm to self/others) would be confidential, and remind him that he could respond only when desirable. Eugene was well dressed and groomed and seemed of average weight and height for his age. He wore glasses and often looked at the floor when talking. At times, the therapist had to prompt him to speak louder so she could hear him. He was compliant with all requests to improve his communication.

Eugene reported that he often felt sick when going to school and that he was usually nervous. His nervousness would first begin when he awoke in the morning, and took the form of worries about different events during the school day. Specifically, he worried about the quality of his homework, tests, participation in physical education and music classes, and interactions with others. Eugene was especially anxious about talking to peers in school, although discussions with adults were less problematic. He reported having few friends, and often felt alone during transitions to class and during lunch. He also reported being teased by others, but could not give any specific examples. His somatic complaints took the form of stomachaches and shaking, which started in the early morning and increased in intensity during the rest of the morning. His worries and physical distress peaked after lunch during physical education and music class, but subsided greatly in his last class, science. Such sudden lessening of tension was due mostly to his liking for the class and because it was close to the end of the school day.

Mrs. Erickson largely echoed her son's report, but added that his situation may have been aggravated by her willingness to allow him to stay home from school when his anxiety was strong. She was unsure of any other course of action and seemed quite willing to allow the therapist to guide her. She did insist, however, that Eugene was required to complete his homework before experiencing any pleasurable activities during the day.

HISTORY

Mrs. Erickson reported that, even as an infant and youngster, Eugene was typically a "fussy and nervous" child. When asked how Eugene dealt with novel situations as a youngster, Mrs. Erickson replied that he was often "clingy, apprehensive, and somewhat withdrawn." For example, he often would sit near his mother when unknown people (e.g., distant relatives) came to the house. He also took longer than her other child (an adult daughter) to sleep through the night and become more stable in his eating and toileting activities. Other developmental milestones were described as normal, however, and Eugene's language skills were reportedly excellent, even at a young age.

During preschool, Eugene was described as quiet but never tearful or overly inappropriate in his behavior. He did have some preschool friends, although these relationships dissipated once school began. Mrs. Erickson stated that Eugene was shy during this period, and always seemed to warm to adults more quickly than to other children; he did respond, however, when others asked him to play or share materials. In addition, he attended birthday parties and other social events when invited, but rarely initiated extensive contacts. His language skills remained excellent, however, and his basic social skills were good, thus ruling out any type of developmental disability.

During Eugene's early school-age years, a general pattern of shyness and nonproblematic withdrawal took place. Eugene was described as a child who tended to have one or two close friends but who did not interact socially on a wide scale. He attended parties and other social functions but tended to leave early, stay to the side, or participate at some minimal level. His withdrawal was somewhat reinforced by his love for schoolwork and education. He would spend many hours completing his homework and declined some opportunities to engage in socially oriented extracurricular activities. He did play soccer, which he greatly enjoyed, as well as golf and tennis, the latter being more individual efforts.

Mrs. Erickson stated that her son's current problems became more apparent in the previous school year, when he entered middle school for the first time. At the beginning of seventh grade, Eugene was somewhat overwhelmed by many different teachers, classes, peers, and responsibilities. Of particular concern to him was getting lost at school, performing before others in class, and walking the long hallways. She stated that her son had great difficulty going to school in the initial part of that year, but that she and her husband made it clear that nonattendance was unacceptable. Eugene attended school despite the distress it caused, but constantly complained about having to talk in front of others in class, play sports he did not do well (e.g., basketball), and hurry to class. However, he was able to attend classes with one of his close friends from elementary school and continued to excel in his schoolwork.

At the beginning of this academic year, however, Eugene found that he and his one close friend had very different class schedules. Thus, during classes and lunch, Eugene was usually on his own. Although school attendance was not initially problematic, his absences began to mount in mid-October. At this time, according to his and his mother's reports, he was expected to present orally in class and sing or speak a solo performance in music. In addition, he was struggling with math for the first time, and tests in that class became more difficult for him. In conjunction with his social isolation, these events triggered the avoidance and cognitive and physiological symptoms described earlier. At this point, in mid-January, Eugene's avoidance of social situations and school was nearly complete, and his anxiety level was quite high.

BEHAVIORAL ASSESSMENT

BEHAVIORAL

Eugene's assessment consisted of behavioral and self-report measures as well as a brief physiological evaluation. In cases of social phobia, especially in children, it is instructive to observe a person directly to see whether deficient social skills are more relevant than anxiety. In addition, the observation allows a therapist to evaluate level of avoidance, overt distress (e.g., crying, tantrums), receptivity to overtures from others, resistance to help, or other signs of social anxiety. As is true for most cases of direct observation, it is best that the person being observed remain oblivious to that fact, so as to reduce reactivity.

Given that Eugene was not currently attending school, he allowed the therapist to view him during a birthday party for his best friend, the one from elementary school. The party would be attended by his friend as well as others whom Eugene did not know. In addition, Eugene's friend would be preoccupied by many people and events at the party and thus unable to devote all of his attention to Eugene. The party was held in a neighborhood park, which allowed the therapist to watch from afar without being directly involved in the festivities.

During the three-hour party, to which Eugene arrived late, many of the children appeared to be having great fun eating, joking, and playing games. Eugene was typically to the side of these activities, near an adult, and only occasionally participated to a full degree. Instead, he was content to watch, albeit with a sour look on his face. Afterward, he told the therapist that he did not enjoy himself and kept looking at his watch to see when he could go. Interestingly, he also complained that the other children deliberately excluded him from time with his friend and the party activities.

SELF-REPORT

Several self-report measures have been designed for youth with social anxiety, especially the Social Anxiety Scale for Children-Revised (SASC-R; La Greca & Stone, 1993), Social Interaction Self-Statement Test (Johnson & Glass, 1989), Social Phobia and Anxiety Inventory for Children (and for Adolescents; Beidel, Turner, & Morris, 1995; Clark et al., 1994), Loneliness Scale (Asher & Wheeler, 1985), and Test Anxiety Inventory for Children (Sarason, Davidson, Lighthall,

Waite, & Ruebush, 1960). In addition, structured diagnostic interviews are available for children with anxiety, most notably the Anxiety Disorders Interview Schedule for Children (ADIS-C; Silverman & Albano, 1996).

In Eugene's case, the therapist used the ADIS-C during the interview process and asked Eugene to complete the SASC-R in addition to other scales. According to the diagnostic interview, Eugene did meet criteria for Social Anxiety Disorder and Generalized Anxiety Disorder. Specifically, he and his mother endorsed several items from the ADIS-C. For example, both stated that Eugene feared doing something stupid when surrounded by peers, especially not knowing the answer to a question or what to say, or acting in some way that would draw ridicule. In addition, he often felt embarrassed in social situations, especially when seeing others engage in conversation so easily.

On the list of ADIS-C items that probed for socially phobic situations, Eugene endorsed many, but particularly reading aloud in class, gym class, musical performances, starting or joining a conversation, taking tests, and, to Mrs. Erickson's surprise, using the school restroom. Furthermore, Eugene indicated that it did not matter if the social group was mostly male or female or younger or older, although he did prefer interactions with adults and especially those he knew well (e.g., relatives, certain teachers). Finally, significant interference in Eugene's life was indicated by his school absenteeism, low number of friends, and substantial distress.

The SASC-R contains two subscales of social avoidance and distress as well as one of fear of negative evaluation. Eugene scored high on the SASC-R in general, but particularly endorsed those items involving fear of negative evaluation. For example, he strongly endorsed items such as "I worry about being teased," "I'm afraid that other kids will not like me," "I worry about what other kids think of me," and "I feel that kids are making fun of me." He also strongly endorsed items from other subscales, including "I worry about doing something new in front of the kids" and "I get nervous when I talk to kids I don't know very well."

PHYSIOLOGICAL

Physiological methods of assessing childhood anxiety take different forms, the most common being measures of musculoskeletal, electrodermal, and cardiovascular activity (King, 1994). Musculoskeletal activity may be measured via an electromyogram, which evaluates electrical activity in muscle groups most prone to physical tension (e.g., shoulders). Electrodermal activity may be measured via skin conduction and resistance, or speed of transmission of electrical activity in the skin that is affected by perspiration. Cardiovascular activity may be measured via pulse rate, blood pressure, and blood volume and blood volume pulse. In Eugene's case, the therapist found that his pulse rate accelerated at least 10% to 20% in situations that demanded performance before others or when meeting a stranger. This was assessed via analog observations where Eugene read a newspaper article in front of two unknown persons and also conversed with them.

MEDICAL CONSULTATION

In cases of youth with anxiety disorders, it is not unusual to see a plethora of somatic complaints, some of which are genuine and some of which may be exaggerated for positive or negative reinforcement. In any case, however, it is advisable to

refer the family to a pediatrician or medical specialist who can help rule out physical causes of specific symptoms. Physical symptoms of anxiety, for example, may
be caused by any number of medical (e.g., cardiovascular) ailments. In addition,
general somatic complaints such as stomachaches and nausea may be due to an
ulcer or other gastrointestinal problem. In still other cases, the child may have a
medical problem (e.g., asthma) that is worsened by his or her anxiety disorder,
and this should be thoroughly evaluated as well. The main goal of medical consultation with respect to childhood anxiety disorders is to ensure that a true
physical problem is addressed and that psychological treatment will not be harmful or ineffective.

In Eugene's case, Mrs. Erickson was already in the process of having her son
checked medically. Eugene saw both a pediatrician and an internist, and extensive tests were conducted to see if he had any gastrointestinal or other problems.
Tests revealed slightly elevated blood pressure, although this may have been due
to anxiety during the assessment process. In addition, Eugene was found to have
a slightly larger amount of stomach acid than usual, which may have led to his
feelings of malaise in the morning. He was encouraged to eat a more substantial
breakfast and was given over-the-counter medication to control some of his acid
reflux. After several days of this regimen, Eugene reportedly felt better, though
he was still avoiding school and interactions with others.

CASE CONCEPTUALIZATION

Anxiety often is conceptualized as a three-component response system that involves physiological, cognitive, and behavioral elements. In Eugene's case, all of
these elements were certainly active and would need to be addressed. As mentioned earlier, he often had physiological symptoms such as stomachaches and
shaking, cognitive worries of being ridiculed or failing in some way, and behavioral avoidance and noncompliance. He also displayed the behavioral symptom of
excessive reassurance seeking, in which he would repeatedly ask his mother,
teachers, and eventually his therapist the same types of questions. Most of these
questions had to do with possible negative consequences in school and desires to
avoid social and performance-based situations.

When conceptualizing a case of a youth with social anxiety, pinpointing the
primary physiological, cognitive, and behavioral symptoms is only a first step.
The next step often involves examining the specific pattern of anxiety shown by
the child. In many cases, for example, initial cognitive symptoms lead to aversive
physiological experiences. These symptoms may continue to escalate and then
trigger avoidance and other behavioral problems. In other cases, avoidance is a
more immediate response, with concurrent worries about the consequences of
one's actions (e.g., What will happen if I miss that test today?). A key aspect of assessment, and later treatment, is to identify this pattern and help the client gain
insight into his or her own behavior.

In Eugene's case, his anxiety pattern was fairly, though not always, consistent.
Most of the time, his anxiety would begin immediately with physiological symptoms involving his stomach and uncontrollable shaking. He was usually convinced that these symptoms were harmful to him and, worse yet, that they were
clearly noticeable to others around him. As he experienced these symptoms, especially in the morning, he usually began to worry about his ineffectiveness in

certain social and performance situations. Specifically, he worried that his stomach pain would interfere with his ability to concentrate on tests and solo performances, and that his shaking would be so obvious that it would invite ridicule during conversations and other social interactions. These worries were so strong that he preferred to avoid these situations altogether. Thus, his specific pattern of anxiety was usually physiological to cognitive to behavioral. However, given his recent pattern of increased avoidance of school, many days saw a swift progression from physiologically based anxiety to avoidance and refusal to attend class.

In identifying this pattern, the therapist may prioritize symptom targets. In Eugene's case, addressing his initial physiological symptoms was a clear priority because it led to other response systems. In addition, his behavioral avoidance was seen as a top priority given the seriousness of a potential legal situation for his school refusal behavior. However, his cognitive worries would certainly have to be modified as well. The therapist also noticed that Eugene's social skills could stand some improvement. In some cases of youth with social anxiety, extended avoidance can lead to an erosion of social skills and initiative; this may necessitate the use of social skills retraining via modeling, role play, and frequent practice and feedback.

The conceptualization of social anxiety in a particular youth also should involve identifying areas of avoidance and thus targets for later exposures. In Eugene's case, targets included very specific as well as more general areas. Because school reintegration was an immediate target, Eugene was asked to identify those specific areas of greatest concern (i.e., those primarily preventing his attendance). Eugene stated that the required oral presentations and musical solo performance were two situations that he simply could not complete. Close behind were tests, but only those specific to his math class. When asked if he would be willing to initially attend school without attending his language arts, music, and math courses, he hesitated, then cautiously said "Maybe."

The therapist then asked about more generally anxiety-provoking areas that Eugene could identify as most problematic. These areas included interactions with his peers and transitions during school. With respect to interactions, Eugene admitted that he had difficulty starting and maintaining conversations, and that he wished he had more friends. In addition, he fretted continuously about getting to class on time and making sure that the teacher received his completed homework. He worried about the consequences of talking in class (e.g., being placed on detention). Minor areas of concern involved situations he was not actively avoiding but that still provoked anxiety, such as social outings with his friend.

The conceptualization of social anxiety often involves the form of the behavior, including the types and patterns of symptoms. However, a more detailed conceptualization of social anxiety requires a determination of the function of the behavior, or what motivates or maintains the behavior over time. Maintaining variables often take the form of negative and positive reinforcement, or the removal of aversive stimuli and the administration of positive stimuli that increase the frequency of behavior. Each of these behavior processes should be explored in depth via functional analysis.

In Eugene's case, significant negative reinforcement certainly applied. He was very aware that his level of anxiety substantially declined when he removed himself from a social or performance-based situation. He gave several examples of this, including his relief when he came home from school or the party that the therapist observed. In addition, he reportedly felt better once he knew he would be in class on time or once a conversation with an unfamiliar person was ending. He also felt enormous relief when not called on in class. In general, Eugene was well practiced at reducing distress by dodging areas that would draw attention to him. His avoidance, however, conflicted with his desire to attend school, have more friends, and feel more comfortable around his peers.

A more ominous function of Eugene's behavior was the substantial amount of positive reinforcement that he currently received for his avoidance. Mrs. Erickson conceded that she allowed her son much leeway in his daily activities, which often included videogames, television, nonacademic reading, games and conversations with her, telephone calls and online chats with his father, and computer time. In addition, Mrs. Erickson noted that Eugene was getting out of bed at later and later times and would sometimes not dress until midmorning. Although he continued to complete his schoolwork at home, she reported that she was having to "nag" him more and more about getting started on it.

Eugene's case thus involved a complex set of symptoms as well as a family dynamic that acquiesced to, and thus reinforced, his avoidance. In many cases of childhood social anxiety, therapists need to dually address child-based and family-based issues. A complete conceptualization of such cases demands attention to both form and function of behavior.

RATIONALE FOR TREATMENT CHOICE

Given that Eugene's difficulties involved both child-based and family-based issues, a complex treatment approach was chosen to involve Eugene, his parents, school officials, selected peers, and persons affiliated with the therapist's clinic. In addition, treatment components were chosen to address different forms of Eugene's social anxiety and social skill deficit as well as Mrs. Erickson's response to her son's avoidance. The therapist also clarified that Mr. Erickson would need to be more involved with the therapy process, and both parents agreed.

Specific child-based components to the treatment plan included psychoeducation, development of a social anxiety hierarchy, somatic control exercises, cognitive restructuring, modeling and role play, and behavioral exposures. The main goal of this approach was to help Eugene understand, control, and eventually master his social anxiety and reintegrate himself into various social and performance-based situations. The comprehensiveness of these treatment elements was dictated by Eugene's generalized nature of social anxiety. In addition, the therapist planned to introduce these components quickly and concurrently to help Eugene return to school as soon as possible.

Specific parent-based components to the treatment plan included the establishment of clear morning and daily routines, modification of parent commands, development of specific consequences for Eugene's compliance and anxiety-based behavior, and escorting Eugene into school. In Mrs. Erickson's case, her parenting skills and relationship with her son were generally good, so basic contingency management practices were deemed appropriate. In other cases where more problematic family variables apply, more in-depth therapy may be necessary (e.g., responsive parent therapy; Cavell, 2000).

Treatment included significant others in Eugene's life to maximize the effect and generalization of therapy. For example, Eugene's school counselor and teachers were informed of the treatment plan to ensure their cooperation with exposures and assist with Eugene's academic reintegration. In addition, Eugene's close friend and two acquaintances were enlisted for support and social skill practice. Finally, some of the therapist's coworkers served as "props" for initial, in-session behavioral exposures.

The rationale for treatment should be understood by the therapist and communicated clearly to clients. In cases of social anxiety, clients should be made aware of their current difficulties and courses of action (i.e., avoidance). Children and parents should recognize that avoidance is a good short-term strategy for reducing anxiety but that, in the long term, various problems will occur. In addition, clients should be made aware of their current aversive feelings and thoughts. Therapists should convey that treatment is designed to teach a different way of coping with negative feelings and thoughts and alternatives to avoidance. Such a comprehensive treatment will be somewhat difficult initially, but the therapist can convey that persistence in therapy will lead to faster progress and eventual mastery of anxiety (see Kearney & Albano, 2000, for specific rationales).

COURSE OF TREATMENT

Research on treatment for youth with social phobia has advanced substantially in recent years, with many outcome studies lending support to cognitive-behavioral intervention (see Overall Effectiveness section). Some of these studies evaluated a generic approach that targets various children with anxiety disorders; others developed and tested protocols specific to youth with social anxiety. These latter treatments may be administered in individual or group format, but the essential techniques remain the same. Such techniques most often involve psychoeducation regarding the nature of social anxiety; training in social, assertiveness, and problem-solving skills; cognitive restructuring; modeling, shaping, and role play; in vivo exposure; and parent-based training to enhance and support the child-based training. These techniques have been shown to be effective for youth with social anxiety, and served as the basis of treatment for Eugene.

Eugene's therapist spent the initial part of the first treatment session reminding him of the rationale for treatment and asking him to recommit to the therapy process. Eugene agreed that the short-term goal of therapy was to reintegrate him into school, and that the long-term goal of therapy was to integrate him more fully into different social and performance-based situations. He was informed that this process would proceed at a pace set largely by his therapist and parents, but that he would have considerable input as to what he could and could not handle at a particular time. It is important when working with this population to fully inform clients about what will be expected of them, to solicit their agreement regarding treatment techniques, and to encourage their compliance to all homework assignments. Treatment adherence and attendance can sometimes be fragile, so therapists must also play the role of motivator.

Following this recommitment process, Eugene's therapist spent the first treatment session discussing the concept of social anxiety and educating Eugene about its components and patterns. Specifically, Eugene was asked to relist his physiological, cognitive, and behavioral symptoms in detail. He dutifully recounted his feelings of nausea and shakiness in the morning, his worries about interactions with (and before) others as well as being late to class and getting into trouble, and his avoidance of various social and performance-based situations. The therapist gently added another behavior to Eugene's list: excessive reassurance seeking in the form of constant questions and pleas to his mother and therapist. A formal list was made of each of these symptoms in the three categories, and copies were made for Eugene and his parents.

The therapist then reexamined Eugene's pattern of anxiety and used a large piece of paper to list the types of symptoms that triggered one another. She outlined Eugene's physical complaints in a column and then drew a large arrow to his cognitive symptoms. A large arrow was then drawn to a list of behavioral symptoms. Eugene was shown how his physiological symptoms of anxiety initially triggered cognitive symptoms and then behavioral ones. To further illustrate this, the therapist and Eugene discussed several real-life examples. In discussing the birthday party that served as the basis for the behavioral observation, the therapist and Eugene recalled how he generally felt queasy and unsure of himself during the ride to the party, and how these symptoms escalated to a general malaise by the time he arrived late. Eugene then reiterated how he worried that others would notice his uneasiness, and that he might vomit at some point during the party. As he worried about these things, in addition to not knowing what to say to others, he generally withdrew from group activities and felt bad that he could not spend more time with his friend. Other scenarios were discussed as well, especially those particular to school.

The therapist then asked Eugene to develop a social avoidance and anxiety hierarchy in which his most distressing scenarios would be charted. Ratings for this hierarchy were made on a 0 to 10 scale, with 10 being extreme avoidance and anxiety. Eugene listed eight general scenarios, depicted in Table 17.1.

Although many of these items were specific, two represented Eugene's generalized social anxiety. For example, having to start a conversation with an unfamiliar person was a common expectation in middle school and in social situations where Eugene knew few people. In addition, telephoning an acquaintance applied to potential friends as well as errands that his mother needed him to do (e.g., contact a baby-sitter). Eugene was informed that these items would likely require exposure in a variety of settings. For example, he might be asked to start a conversation with people at school, church, and social gatherings. At the end of this session, Mrs. Erickson was shown this list and agreed that they were the major social/performance obstacles for her son.

Table 17.1
Eugene's Social Avoidance and Anxiety Hierarchy

Scenario	Avoidance Rating	Anxiety Rating
Oral presentations/musical solo	9	9
Starting a conversation with an unfamiliar person	8	9
Performing in physical education class	8	9
Sitting in the cafeteria with other kids	7	9
Calling an acquaintance on the telephone	7	8
Volunteering an answer in class	6	7
Getting to class late	6	6
Getting into trouble in class	4	4

The therapist asked Eugene to develop more specific scenarios during the week and to assign avoidance and anxiety ratings to them. He was also asked to begin rating his anxiety during the morning, afternoon, and evening hours on a 0 to 10 scale. Eugene was quite compliant with each of these tasks. The first treatment session ended with a long discussion of what classes Eugene could attend without significant levels of anxiety. He mentioned that his morning classes were more interesting to him, and that lunchtime and his afternoon classes were more problematic. He was instructed to prepare for school in the morning and attend his morning classes, after which he would be allowed the option of returning home and completing schoolwork. In addition, he was told to eat a full breakfast, take his medication, practice relaxation exercises, and tolerate minor stomach discomfort as long as possible.

The therapist and Mrs. Erickson established certain rewards for Eugene's attendance, including permission to do what he wanted after his homework was done and the opportunity to do chores for money. However, noncompliance would be met with a severe restriction on his daily activities, including a ban on television, computer, and videogame time. In addition, Mr. Erickson was asked to rearrange his schedule to bring Eugene to school in the morning and provide support. Between Sessions 1 and 2, Eugene was able to attend his morning classes, but declined to stay longer. His part-time attendance was enough to placate school officials, as they deferred legal intervention until seeing the final therapeutic result.

During Session 2, Eugene reported surprisingly minor anxiety and stomach discomfort during school, and was praised substantially by his parents and therapist. All parties agreed that he should next add lunch to his schedule as well as one afternoon class. However, he would not be required to fully participate in class. Eugene agreed to attend his math class and, between Sessions 2 and 3, also added his music and English classes. This left only his physical education class, which he still strongly avoided. In adding these classes, Eugene's therapist was eliminating an urgent problem as well as building a foundation for later, more complex exposures. She also was building Eugene's compliance with the therapeutic homework assignments.

Session 2 included an introduction to cognitive restructuring, where Eugene was asked to list his major thoughts in socially anxiety-provoking situations. His overriding thought was of being ridiculed in virtually all of his hierarchy scenarios. He feared social rejection and the consequences of being embarrassed or doing "something stupid." When asked for specifics, he said that he primarily worried about being laughed at or ignored when he spoke. He said he often did not know what to say and was convinced that he would be ridiculed in performance-based situations. His worst-case scenario involved speaking before or to others who began laughing uncontrollably.

The therapist delved into Eugene's cognitions in greater depth and asked him to consider alternative scenarios. For example, he was asked to provide evidence that others would not laugh at him during an oral presentation. He stated only that the teacher was very strict about inappropriate comments made by student audience members. The therapist assisted Eugene by suggesting that he may be a very good presenter and that the awful scenario he described had never happened to him before. These alternative scenarios were presented to help Eugene reexamine his problematic thoughts and consider more positive or realistic events. In this instance, for example, Eugene conceded that the chances of his classmates laughing at him were minimal, giving it a probability estimate of just 5%. The therapist informed Eugene that sufficient preparation for an oral presentation would help reduce his anticipatory anxiety, which helped set the basis for an in-session exposure.

During this exposure, Eugene was asked to practice relaxation and then read a newspaper article in front of the therapist. He did so with moderate discomfort, after which the therapist asked him to modify a few aspects of his presentation style (e.g., increase volume, articulation, and audience eye contact). After several tries, Eugene's style improved. The therapist then asked him to read the article to her and two other workers at the clinic who were unknown to him. Again, moderate discomfort and stylistic problems were transformed via feedback to a more effective presentation. The final part of the exposure involved laughter from the small audience as Eugene read the article. Although visibly flustered, Eugene made it through the presentation without stopping or escaping. After several more exposures, he was unfazed by the audience's "rudeness."

Following this exposure, the therapist reinforced the notion that continued exposure to a feared stimulus eventually leads to greater habituation or, in this case, lessened anxiety. Eugene understood this process and was willing to engage in other scenarios as long as they were in session. The therapist asked him to continue his school attendance and reestablish better social contact with those people with whom he was already comfortable. Eugene did reestablish good contact with two friends, including the one from the birthday party.

During Session 3, the therapist noted that Eugene's daily anxiety ratings had gradually declined over time, and pointed this out to him as further evidence of habituation. She asked him to read parts of a book chapter that contained several difficult words, and he was eventually able to do so without much trouble, even before a small audience. Subsequently, however, the therapist required Eugene to speak with clinic workers while she excused herself. The coworkers, who were skilled in treating socially anxious youth, asked Eugene questions and helped him develop appropriate responses. When Eugene was asked about school, for example, the clinic workers challenged him to speak up, make eye contact, and give more detailed answers. He had initial trouble with this and was reportedly anxious, but the clinic workers provided empathy and feedback to help elicit his responses. During this session, Eugene also was asked to say hello to the receptionist, which he did.

Sessions 4 through 6 were largely an extension of this process, as Eugene was required to meet more and more clinic workers, maintain appropriate conversations, and make oral presentations to them. The therapist extended this process by finding other youth near Eugene's age. These were youth who did not attend his school and who varied with respect to their social skills. The therapist worked carefully to shape Eugene's social behavior via modeling, role play, and corrective feedback, and meticulously pointed out that the extreme consequences that Eugene feared never occurred. She also reminded him that his social anxiety ratings generally declined the more he spoke with others. More difficult in-session exposures, such as approaching an unknown peer to start and maintain a conversation, were also conducted.

During this in-session exposure process, Eugene's therapist continued restructuring his cognitions. Specifically, Eugene was asked to challenge and change negative thoughts with the use of "dispute handles," or questions to refute anxious thoughts. For example, Eugene was instructed to ask, "Am I 100% sure this will happen?"; "Can I really know what that person thinks of me?"; "What is the worst that can happen?"; and "Am I the only person that has had to deal with this situation?" Gradually, he was able to incorporate these thought processes into his exposures, which helped reduce his fear of social rejection and ridicule. Over time, his in-session exposures became more challenging, as he was asked to react appropriately to others who were instructed to snicker or ignore him when he spoke.

At Session 7, Eugene was attending school with the exception of physical education class, was interacting with two close friends on a regular basis, and reported minor to moderate amounts of daily anxiety. Mrs. Erickson stated that her son was appropriately preparing for school in the morning and that he was reporting only minor somatic complaints. In essence, Eugene was back to his level of functioning at the beginning of the academic year. Subsequent sessions were designed to enhance his functioning in other social/performance areas.

To do so, the therapist began scheduling formal between-session exposures for Eugene. Given his extensive practice in session, he was now asked to make up his oral presentations for English class. Working with his teacher, Eugene made one oral presentation per week for three weeks to complete his assignment. He reported that the class was generally uninterested in what he had to say, but admitted that this was the case for other student reports as well. Moderate anxiety was reported, but this dissipated. Fortunately, this experience generalized to his music class, where he was allowed to provide a solo narration during a song to fulfill a requirement.

Other between-session exposures concentrated on Eugene's taking the initiative to speak with others, especially at school. He was instructed to ask people for homework assignments, comment on class or lunch, ask to sit next to others, ask others how they were doing, and smile and otherwise be pleasant during interactions. He was reminded that some people would not respond, but that others would respond and perhaps become friends. Following extensive avoidance and then stilted practice, Eugene was able to talk to others on a fairly regular basis and reportedly made three good friends as a result.

As Eugene discovered his ability to make friends, he better understood that his anxiety was gradually abating. He still feared ridicule, but realized that it was not likely to happen. In addition, he felt reasonably confident that he could handle negative responses from others. He was then given other homework assignments such as contacting people via telephone and volunteering answers in class. During the course of therapy, fears of getting to class late and getting into trouble in class spontaneously remitted.

One area of concern that was not resolved was Eugene's adamant refusal to attend physical education class. Despite much cognitive work and other accommodations (e.g., switching class time), he simply would not go to this class. He said that he hated to perform athletically in front of others because of his poor coordination and lack of understanding of the games that were being played. Despite numerous efforts, the therapist was only able to get Eugene to agree to make up the class in the summer, when he could choose most of his activities and do so in a local athletic club that he enjoyed.

Eugene's therapy lasted a total of 17 sessions, during which he was able to interact with others and reduce his anxiety considerably. Treatment terminated near the end of the academic year, and Eugene was invited back for a booster session during August to reinforce his social and anxiety management skills. He continued to enjoy social activities with his new friends with the assistance of his parents, who continued to encourage him to initiate contact and restart activities that he previously had found pleasurable (e.g., soccer).

THERAPIST-CLIENT FACTORS

According to Kendall et al. (1992), therapists who address youth with anxiety disorders must adopt several roles in doing so. A therapist may act as a consultant who helps a child discover the correct strategy in a particular situation; as a diagnostician who collects information about a certain case and makes an informed decision about treatment; and as an educator who stimulates self-thought and who helps correct maladaptive thoughts and actions. As noted in Eugene's case, a therapist may also have to facilitate therapy adherence and compliance. This often involves frequently contacting a child during the week, encouraging the completion of exposures and other assignments, rewarding positive efforts, and providing elongated treatment sessions.

In Eugene's case, the therapist adopted all of these roles. She established a general treatment plan for Eugene and his parents and provided a rationale for that plan at the beginning of and during the therapy process. However, she also solicited input from Eugene and his mother about the nature and rate of the specific exposures. Children with anxiety disorders sometimes require nudging toward certain goals, and this is facilitated by their cooperation in setting up the parameters of the homework assignment. During treatment, the therapist continually challenged Eugene to state what he thought might happen in a given situation and what treatment technique he should rely on to cope. For example, he was often asked what he thought the next stage of treatment should be, what strategies he could use when facing an obstacle, what it meant when his anxiety subsided, and what he could do in future hypothetical situations. Although the therapist was "in charge" of Eugene's case, he remained an active participant in problem solving.

COURSE OF TERMINATION

Termination in cases of anxiety disorders in children must be handled with care. In some cases, there is a tendency for clients to terminate treatment prematurely once a particularly urgent problem is resolved. In Eugene's case, for example, there was some interest on his part in ending therapy once he was back in school full time. However, the therapist reiterated the rationale for treatment and urged Eugene and Mrs. Erickson to continue therapy to increase effective functioning in various social and performance-based situations.

Termination in Eugene's case was a gradual process that began four sessions prior to the formal end of treatment. The therapist introduced the concept of termination and stated that she thought it would be appropriate under certain conditions. These conditions were that Eugene would remain in school full time for the next month, that he would begin to attend more social functions with friends, that he would successfully complete his remaining exposures, and that he would be able to respond correctly to hypothetical anxiety-provoking situations. Both Eugene and his mother agreed to these conditions, and the therapist raised the issue of final termination and remaining goals at each subsequent session.

Eugene continued to progress with respect to school attendance and behavioral exposures. Near the end of treatment, the therapist began to pose theoretical problems that Eugene could face in the future. For example, she asked what he would do if rejected by a potential date, if tempted by his peers to do something illegal, and if faced with an unexpected anxiety reaction in a public place. He was required to work through each scenario and indicate how he would handle it using the treatment techniques he had learned.

FOLLOW-UP

Follow-up for cases of anxiety disorders in children can be key to relapse prevention. Follow-up may involve formal procedures such as booster sessions to review skills or informal procedures such as telephone contact. In either case, the main goals of follow-up are to see if a child or parent (1) is experiencing substantial slips or relapse due to nonpractice of treatment procedures, (2) needs help in solving upcoming problems, (3) desires feedback from the therapist, and/or (4) needs referrals to other agencies or mental health professionals. In Eugene's case, initial follow-up consisted of telephone contact with the therapist every two weeks for two months and then once per month during the summer.

Long-term follow-up with Eugene indicated some degree of stagnation, as he had maintained his group of friends but had not gone out of his way to develop more relationships. Neither he nor his mother considered this overly problematic, however, as Eugene was continuing to attend social functions and speaking with various people there. The end of his academic year and summer were reportedly happy, and Eugene even approached people during his remedial physical education class. The end of the summer, however, revealed a problem that necessitated another formal session with the therapist. Eugene said he was experiencing considerable anticipatory anxiety about the prospect of going back to school and potentially being in classes with none of his friends. The therapist reviewed his skills for approaching people and encouraged him to continue to do so, engaged in cognitive restructuring to dissolve irrational thoughts of deliberate alienation, and arranged to have his schedule sent to him for review. Following this process, Eugene was able to attend school with moderate and later mild levels of social anxiety.

MANAGED CARE CONSIDERATIONS

Several managed care considerations apply to the treatment of youth with social phobia (Albano, Detweiler, & Logsdon-Conradsen, 1999). Of particular concern is overreliance on a medical model at the expense of viewing psychologists and other mental health professionals as primary care providers. Social Anxiety Disorder is often seen as a problem that does not require urgent care. Cases like Eugene's, however, where severe developmental and academic problems are at stake, belie this general expectation. In addition, reliance on medical doctors to diagnose social phobia is problematic given a lack of familiarity with the disorder and a general trivialization of its importance (e.g., "It's just shyness").

Second, managed care often places an emphasis on pharmacological rather than psychological intervention. As a result, persons with social phobia may be more likely to be recommended a specific drug to reduce anxiety rather than a psychological intervention to increase social skill and help them master and control their anxiety level. Finally, managed care tends to place more emphasis on cheaper and less educated therapists. This is unfortunate given that Social Anxiety Disorder has been shown to be a complex problem often comorbid with other disorders such as substance abuse.

In Eugene's case, he was fortunate to have seen a psychologist who specialized in childhood anxiety disorders. Prior to therapy, however, his mother had referred him to a pediatrician and psychiatrist, the latter of whom prescribed an antidepressant medication. This was unsuccessful, however, and created some unwanted side effects. In general, the pharmacological treatment of anxiety disorders in youth has mixed efficacy (Kearney & Silverman, 1998).

OVERALL EFFECTIVENESS

The overall effectiveness of cognitive-behavioral intervention for youth with anxiety disorders has been demonstrated across several studies (e.g., Albano & Barlow, 1996; Albano et al., 1999; Albano, Marten, Holt, Heimberg, & Barlow, 1995; Kendall et al., 1997; Silverman, Kurtines, Ginsburg, Weems, Lumpkin, et al., 1999; Silverman, Kurtines, Ginsburg, Weems, Rabian, et al., 1999). Interventions to improve social skills in youth have been largely effective as well (Cartledge & Milburn, 1995, McFayden-Ketchum & Dodge, 1998). Successful treatment of a particular case of Social Anxiety Disorder often involves a combination of anxiety reduction and skill development, as many children in this population have both problems. This was particularly true in Eugene's case, as his avoidant behavior over time had led to an erosion of his social interaction and performance-based skills.

The most effective component of treatment for youth with social anxiety is likely behavioral exposure and the process of habituation. This was particularly relevant in Eugene's case, as he stated several times that in-session and in vivo practices were instrumental in improving his social functioning. In addition, identifying the functions of social anxiety is important. For example, many youth avoid situations to initially reduce anxiety (negative reinforcement) but, over time, to gain attention or tangible stimuli as well. The development of more contextual therapies that support interactive behavior is a priority. This was also relevant to Eugene's case, as his parents learned over time to maintain their son's exposure to social events and to discourage inappropriate avoidance.

REFERENCES

Albano, A. M., & Barlow, D. H. (1996). Breaking the vicious cycle: Cognitive-behavioral group treatment for socially anxious youth. In E. D. Hibbs & P. S. Jensen (Eds.), *Psychosocial treatments for child and adolescent disorders: Empirically based strategies for clinical practice* (pp. 43–62). Washington, DC: American Psychological Association.

Albano, A. M., Detweiler, M. F., & Logsdon-Conradsen, S. (1999). Cognitive-behavioral interventions with socially phobic children. In S. W. Russ & T. H. Ollendick (Eds.), *Handbook of psychotherapies with children and families* (pp. 255–280). New York: Kluwer Academic/Plenum.

Albano, A. M., Marten, P. A., Holt, C. S., Heimberg, R. G., & Barlow, D. H. (1995). Cognitive-behavioral group treatment for social phobia in adolescents: A preliminary study. *Journal of Nervous and Mental Diseases, 183,* 649–656.

American Psychiatric Association. (1994). *Diagnostic and statistical manual of mental disorders* (4th ed.). Washington, DC: Author.

Asher, S. R., & Wheeler, V. A. (1985). Children's loneliness: A comparison of rejected and neglected peer status. *Journal of Consulting and Clinical Psychology, 53,* 500–505.

Beidel, D. C. (1991). Social phobia and overanxious disorder in school-age children. *Journal of the American Academy of Child and Adolescent Psychiatry, 30,* 545–552.

Beidel, D. C., Turner, S. M., & Morris, T. L. (1995). A new inventory to assess childhood social anxiety and phobia: The Social Phobia and Anxiety Inventory for Children. *Psychological Assessment, 7,* 73–79.

Beidel, D. C., Turner, S. M., & Morris, T. L. (1999). Psychopathology of childhood social phobia. *Journal of the American Academy of Child and Adolescent Psychiatry, 38,* 643–650.

Cartledge, G., & Milburn, J. F. (1995). *Teaching social skills to children and youth: Innovative approaches* (3rd ed.). Boston: Allyn & Bacon.

Cavell, T. A. (2000). *Working with parents of aggressive children: A practitioner's guide.* Washington, DC: American Psychological Association.

Clark, D. B., Turner, S. M., Beidel, D. C., Donovan, J. E., Kirisci, L., & Jacob, R. G. (1994). Reliability and validity of the Social Phobia and Anxiety Inventory for Adolescents. *Psychological Assessment, 6,* 135–140.

Essau, C. A., Conradt, J., & Petermann, F. (1999). Frequency and comorbidity of social phobia and social fears in adolescents. *Behaviour Research and Therapy, 37,* 831–843.

Hudson, J. L., & Rapee, R. M. (2000). The origins of social phobia. *Behavior Modification, 24,* 102–129.

Johnson, R. L., & Glass, C. R. (1989). Heterosocial anxiety and direction of attention in high school boys. *Cognitive Therapy and Research, 13,* 509–526.

Kearney, C. A. (1999). *Casebook in child behavior disorders.* Belmont, CA: Wadsworth.

Kearney, C. A., & Albano, A. M. (2000). *Therapist's guide to school refusal behavior.* San Antonio, TX: Psychological Corporation.

Kearney, C. A., & Silverman, W. K. (1998). A critical review of pharmacotherapy for youth with anxiety disorders: Things are not as they seem. *Journal of Anxiety Disorders, 12,* 83–102.

Kendall, P. C., Chansky, T. E., Kane, M. T., Kim, R. S., Kortlander, E., Ronan, K. R., et al. (1992). *Anxiety disorders in youth: Cognitive-behavioral interventions.* Boston: Allyn & Bacon.

Kendall, P. C., Flannery-Schroeder, E., Panichelli-Mindel, S. M., Southam-Gerow, M., Henin, A., & Warman, M. (1997). Therapy for youths with anxiety disorders: A second randomized clinical trial. *Journal of Consulting and Clinical Psychology, 65,* 366–380.

King, N. J. (1994). Physiological assessment. In T. H. Ollendick, N. J. King, & W. Yule (Eds.), *International handbook of phobic and anxiety disorders in children and adolescents* (pp. 365–379). New York: Plenum Press.

La Greca, A. M., & Stone, W. L. (1993). Social Anxiety Scale for Children–Revised: Factor structure and concurrent validity. *Journal of Clinical Child Psychology, 22,* 17–27.

McFayden-Ketchum, S. A., & Dodge, K. A. (1998). Problems in social relationships. In E. J. Mash & R. A. Barkley (Eds.), *Treatment of childhood disorders* (2nd ed., pp. 338–365). New York: Guilford Press.

Sarason, S. B., Davidson, K. S., Lighthall, F. F., Waite, R. R., & Ruebush, B. K. (1960). *Anxiety and elementary school children.* New York: Wiley.

Schwartz, C. E., Snidman, N., & Kagan, J. (1999). Adolescent social anxiety as an outcome of inhibited temperament in childhood. *Journal of the American Academy of Child and Adolescent Psychiatry, 38,* 1008–1015.

Silverman, W. K., & Albano, A. M. (1996). *The Anxiety Disorders Interview Schedule for Children for DSM-IV, child and parent versions.* San Antonio, TX: Psychological Corporation.

Silverman, W. K., Kurtines, W. M., Ginsburg, G. S., Weems, C. F., Lumpkin, P. W., & Carmichael, D. H. (1999). Treating anxiety disorders in children with group cognitive-behavioral therapy: A randomized clinical trial. *Journal of Consulting and Clinical Psychology, 67,* 995–1003.

Silverman, W. K., Kurtines, W. M., Ginsburg, G. S., Weems, C. F., Rabian, B., & Serafini, L. T. (1999). Contingency management, self-control, and education support in the treatment of childhood phobic disorders: A randomized clinical trial. *Journal of Consulting and Clinical Psychology, 67,* 675–687.

Vasey, M. W. (1995). Social anxiety disorders. In A. R. Eisen, C. A. Kearney, & C. E. Schaefer (Eds.), *Clinical handbook of anxiety disorders in children and adolescents* (pp. 131–168). Northvale, NJ: Aronson.

Walters, K. S., & Inderbitzen, H. M. (1998). Social anxiety and peer relations among adolescents: Testing a psychobiological model. *Journal of Anxiety Disorders, 12,* 183–198.

CHAPTER 18

Anorexia Nervosa

DAVID M. GARNER and CRISTINA G. MAGANA

DESCRIPTION OF THE DISORDER

IN RECENT YEARS, there has been a trend toward understanding anorexia nervosa as multidetermined, as there does not appear to be any single underlying cause that explains all cases. Rather, it is hypothesized that there are cultural, psychological, biological, and familial causal factors that may either act alone or may combine in different ways, leading to the development of eating disorders. Once the disorder has developed, starvation symptoms along with others' reaction to weight loss can perpetuate the disorder.

A key feature of anorexia nervosa is a persistent overconcern with body size and shape indicated by behaviors such as prolonged fasting, strenuous exercise, and self-induced vomiting aimed at decreasing body weight and fat. In anorexia nervosa, the overconcern has been described variously as a relentless pursuit of thinness (Bruch, 1973), a morbid fear of fatness (Russell, 1970), and a weight phobia (Crisp, 1970). For those with anorexia nervosa, body weight or shape becomes the main gauge for self-evaluation. Weight loss erroneously becomes equated with beauty, success, self-esteem, and self-control.

There is general agreement that anorexia nervosa symptoms have psychological and developmental significance. Both individual and family theorists have emphasized that eating disorders often represent a developmental struggle for autonomy, independence, and individuality. These normal development hurdles become flashpoints in adolescence, when the vulnerable individual, parents, or entire family are forced to deal with emergent developmental realities. However, the phenomenology of eating disorders cannot be fully appreciated outside of the context of cultural values. In recent years, there has been intense pressure on women to diet to conform to ultraslender role models for feminine beauty (Garner, 1997; Garner & Garfinkel, 1980). Unfortunately, very few women will ever achieve the admired physical form through restrictive dieting, largely owing to biological limits to achieving permanent weight loss. Nevertheless, constructs such as competence, control, attractiveness, self-worth, and self-discipline continue to be associated with dieting and weight control in our culture. The consequence of the conflict between cultural imperatives and biological realities has been widespread dissatisfaction with body shape and weight that has infected even young girls yet to cross the pubertal threshold (Edlund, Halvarsson, & Sjödén, 1995).

Another aspect of the phenomenology of anorexia nervosa is the ego-syntonic nature of certain symptoms, such as pathological dieting and other extreme weight-controlling behaviors. In contrast to patients with other psychological disorders such as depression or anxiety, most anorexia nervosa patients actively embrace their eating disorder symptoms. It is not uncommon for patients to actually strive for and then cling to an "anorexic identity" due to the disorder's associations with celebrity status and socially desirable traits. The resistance to change seen in anorexia nervosa has obvious implications for treatment and has been a major focus of therapeutic strategies recommended for this disorder (Garner, Vitousek, & Pike, 1997).

The current requirements for a diagnosis of anorexia nervosa according to the *Diagnostic and Statistical Manual of Mental Disorders* (*DSM-IV-TR*, American Psychiatric Association [APA], 2000) are as follows: (1) refusal to maintain body weight at or above a minimally normal weight for age and height (e.g., weight loss leading to maintenance of body weight less than 85% of that expected, or failure to make expected weight gain during period of growth, leading to body weight less than 85% of that expected); (2) intense fear of gaining weight or becoming fat, even though underweight; (3) disturbance in the way one's body weight or shape is experienced, undue influence of body weight or shape on self-evaluation, or denial of the seriousness of the current low body weight; (4) in postmenarcheal females, amenorrhea, that is, the absence of at least three consecutive menstrual cycles (a woman is considered to have amenorrhea if her periods occur only following hormone, e.g., estrogen administration; APA, 2000, p. 589).

The *DSM-IV-TR* (APA, 2000) divides anorexia nervosa into two diagnostic subtypes: restricting type and binge eating/purging type. The restricting subtype is defined by rigid restriction of food intake by dieting, fasting, or excessive exercise without bingeing or purging. The binge eating/purging subtype involves episodes of binge eating and/or purging behavior that can include self-induced vomiting or the misuse of laxatives, diuretics, or enemas. Restricting anorexia nervosa patients have been described as overly compliant, but at the same time, obstinate, perfectionistic, obsessive-compulsive, shy, introverted, interpersonally sensitive, and stoical (Casper, 1990; Hsu, Kaye, & Weltzin, 1993; Strober, 1980). In contrast, patients who regularly engage in bulimic episodes report greater impulsivity, social/sexual dysfunction, substance abuse, general impulse control problems, family dysfunction, and depression as part of a general picture of more conspicuous emotional disturbance compared to patients with the restricting subtype of anorexia nervosa (Garner, Garfinkel, & O'Shaughnessy, 1985; Garner, Garner, & Rosen, 1993; Herzog, Keller, Sacks, Yeh, & Lavori, 1992; Laessle, Wittchen, Fichter, & Pirke, 1989; Rosen, Murkofsky, Steckler, & Skolnick, 1989).

IDENTIFICATION OF THE CASE

B is a 13-year-old, junior high school student who is 5 ft 2 in. tall and weighs 87 pounds. She was referred by a psychiatric hospital, where she had been hospitalized on two separate occasions for symptoms of depression, suicidal ideation, and anorexia nervosa. During her first admission at the psychiatric hospital, B complied with treatment but lost significant weight within two weeks of her first discharge. She was readmitted to the same facility, where the treatment team determined that she needed specialized eating disorder treatment. She was referred to an intensive day treatment eating disorders program designed to assist with nutritional rehabilitation, overcome rigid dietary patterns, and address the psychological problems that led to the development and maintenance of anorexia nervosa.

B's highest weight was 103 pounds 10 months prior to the initial assessment. At her highest weight, B was not engaging in any restrictive eating or dieting behavior. However, around the age of 12, B began to feel bad about herself and started to equate feeling bad with her weight. Some of these associations were triggered by her friends' overconcern with weight and eating. During the same time, B reported significant conflict with her older sister, with whom B was very competitive. In addition, her family was undergoing the stress of having her younger brother placed in a group home for autism. Amid this stress, B began restricting her food intake and reached her lowest weight of 79 pounds six months prior to the initial assessment. Her weight had fluctuated between 80 and 87 pounds since achieving her lowest weight; however, her weight gain was due to the refeeding process at the inpatient psychiatric hospital. B reported that her menstrual periods ceased two months after starting to restrict her food intake. In addition, she experienced depressed mood, psychomotor retardation, and hypothermia.

Prior to her first psychiatric admission, B had been prescribed Zoloft by her pediatrician to address her depressed mood and suicidal ideation. However, her mood continued to be depressed and it was unclear whether her depressive symptoms were primary or secondary to the starvation symptoms and anorexia nervosa (Garner, 1997). It was concluded from the initial assessment that B would be a good candidate for the intensive day treatment program. After the recommendation was given, B reported being terrified at the prospect of weight gain, but was able to see that concerns for weight and shape were interfering with her ability to function as she had previously. Furthermore, she felt that she would not be able to return to school without additional treatment. Another motivating factor for B was the significant guilt that she experienced by the impact of her eating disorder on her family.

At the time of the initial assessment, B lived with her biological parents, an older sister, and a younger brother. Her mother was a 40-year-old school administrator and her father was a 46-year-old detective. B had a few friends and was active in her school's theater program. However, since the onset of anorexia, she had withdrawn socially and was struggling to keep her grades up. She had always been a straight-A student and worked hard to maintain this reputation. Because the current treatment facility was located outside of her home state, B's mother stayed with her in an apartment during the first phase of treatment and her father stayed with her during the second portion.

CHIEF COMPLAINT

At the time of the initial assessment, B consciously attempted to lose weight by skipping meals, eating very small meals, eating meals low in calories and fat grams, and chewing and spitting out food. She also avoided snacks, sweets, fats, and meat. On average, B consumed approximately 800 calories per day. The only exceptions were the times that she was hospitalized, when she was placed on 3,000 calories per day. B reported exercising during her initial attempts to lose weight, but she no longer did so. She also reported intentionally vomiting once but being afraid and ceasing that behavior. She denied any history of binge eating or use of laxatives, diuretics, or diet pills.

B reported a host of physical and psychological symptoms consistent with anorexia nervosa and starvation symptoms. She was emaciated, had severe loss of appetite, and had delayed gastric emptying and constipation. She had amenorrhea for the past seven months. She had dry skin and complained that her skin bruised and bled easily. She experienced headaches and dizziness on a regular basis and had a few fainting spells. She was experiencing hypothermia and chills and often felt fatigued and weak. She experienced significant mood swings with marked negative affect. She appeared withdrawn, and her parents were concerned by her irritability and lack of interest in things.

B reported extreme body dissatisfaction and was terrified of weight gain and being overweight. She reported that her weight and shape greatly impacted the way she felt about herself and at 87 pounds reported feeling extremely fat. She expressed concerns that others would reject her or view her negatively if she were to be fat.

Interpersonally, B reported a great degree of insecurity and maturity fears. She described herself as perfectionistic and a high achiever. Nonetheless, she saw herself as a failure compared to her sister, whose extroverted and confident personality she envied. Socially, B felt inferior because she saw her friends as more attractive, outgoing, and thinner than she. Being thin had become a way of measuring up to her friends' standards. In her home life, there was significant family stress, especially because the family did not openly discuss their feelings regarding her younger brother with autism, who was no longer living at home. B reported feeling that there were things "you just don't talk about." She was not able to express to her parents her feelings, especially those that she perceived as negative. She feared that if she were to express her anger they would perceive her as disrespectful and care less for her.

HISTORY

B described herself as happy and confident until she entered junior high school. Once she started junior high school, she began to feel insecure, especially around her friends, who started to talk about fashion, boys, and weight. B often felt awkward around these conversations because she did not find them interesting. However, she also realized that if she did not engage in these conversations, she had little to contribute. Within a few months, the conversations about weight started to translate into restrictive eating behaviors among B's friends. During lunchtime, her friends started to restrict the types of foods they ate and classified foods as good and bad. B reported wanting to fit in and feeling that her friends rejected her for being "plump." She felt "like a pig" if she ate her meal while her friends watched. She recalled that she also started to eat less of her lunch and eventually was consuming only what she considered to be nonfattening food.

In addition to the social pressures to be thin, B was experiencing significant stress at home. The family was adjusting to her brother's absence, yet no one talked about the emotional impact it had on them. B often felt stifled, without anywhere to turn for support. Controlling her food intake was one way of dealing with the many changes she was enduring. She also reported being terrified of growing up and of the responsibility that entailed.

As B lost weight, she became much less confident and more self-conscious. She doubted what she did and became consumed with worries about what others thought of her. Within a two-month period, B's weight dropped from 103 to 90 pounds. She stopped menstruating and became isolative, irritable, and obsessional, especially around food and schoolwork. Her parents attempted to force her to eat but were generally unsuccessful. They noticed that she appeared depressed and decided to have her see a therapist. The therapist who evaluated B determined that she met criteria for clinical depression and started to treat her in individual outpatient psychotherapy. B attended individual psychotherapy for two months and found that her depression was increasing to the point of feeling suicidal. However, her weight continued to drop; she was approaching 80 pounds. The therapist referred her for a psychiatric evaluation, where she was prescribed Zoloft and was diagnosed with anorexia nervosa. It was agreed that B would continue in outpatient psychotherapy to address her depression and anorexia nervosa.

After another month of individual psychotherapy, it was determined that B be hospitalized in an adolescent inpatient psychiatric hospital because her weight had dropped to 79 pounds. During this hospitalization, she was placed on 3,000 calories per day. She gained weight successfully and reached 89 pounds within three weeks of the hospitalization. With the refeeding process, B's mood significantly improved and she was no longer reporting suicidal ideation. However, she was secretly very angry and resentful at the hospital staff and her parents for forcing her to be fat. She had decided that she was not going to "stay fat" once she was discharged. B was discharged at 90 pounds and was instructed to remain on 2,200 calories per day.

Immediately after discharge, B recommenced her previous restrictive eating habits. Her weight dropped to 80 pounds, and with the weight loss came an increase in her depressed mood. She was readmitted to the same hospital and was placed on the same caloric level. The hospital was successful in having B gain weight to 87 pounds, at which point she refused to comply with treatment. B's parents agreed with the hospital's recommendation that she enter a specialized eating disorder program.

BEHAVIORAL ASSESSMENT

Various approaches to information gathering have been developed for eating disorders, including standard clinical interviews, semistructured interviews, behavioral observation, standardized self-report measures, symptom checklists, clinical rating scales, self-monitoring procedures, and standardized test means. There are three broad areas of focus in the assessment process (Garner et al., 1997): (1) assessment of specific symptom areas that allow the diagnosis of the eating disorder, (2) measurement of other attitudes or behaviors characteristic of eating disorders, and (3) identification and measurement of associated psychological and personality features that are indicative of overall psychosocial functioning.

Behavioral

As with other eating disorder patients, B's initial and ongoing assessment may be divided into two broad areas. The first relates to attitudes toward weight and shape, as well as symptoms fundamental to the eating disorder. The second concerns the various psychological and social factors that are not specific to anorexia nervosa but that may predispose toward or maintain the eating disorder. Accordingly, the initial assessments covered a number of key areas, including (1) weight history; (2) attitudes toward weight and shape; (3) the presence, frequency, and duration of bingeing and vomiting; (4) details of weight-losing behaviors such as dieting, exercise, and abuse of laxatives, diuretics, and appetite suppressants; (5) physical and medical complications; (6) psychological state, with particular reference to depression, anxiety, and personality features; (7) impulse-related behaviors; (8) social and family functioning; (9) reasons for seeking treatment; and (10) motivation for change. Clinicians should be familiar with specific questions or probes aimed at assessing eating disorder symptoms (Garner et al., 1997).

Because B was referred by an inpatient psychiatric hospital, information as to her attitudes toward weight and shape and symptoms fundamental to the eating disorder was available prior to the initial assessment interview. Therefore, the initial session with B focused on her motivation for change and psychological and social factors that were possibly maintaining the eating disorder. B's mother and father attended the assessment session and were able to provide significant information on her premorbid functioning. Her level of depression and possible suicide risk presented a serious concern. Through detailed questioning, it was determined that much of her depressive thought content emanated from a sense of hopelessness about her condition and her low self-esteem. She was reassured at learning that treatment for her condition had a good likelihood of success, and it was determined that the current suicidal risk was low. B's parents stated that there had been significant family stress in dealing with the son with autism. Her mother reported feeling somewhat guilty for spending little time with B. Through this disclosure, it became apparent that feelings were not often communicated within the family. B stated that often, she had wanted to share her feelings with her mother but felt that it would be a burden to do so.

Another important factor was B's relationship with her older sister. B's parents reported that she and her sister had gotten along quite well; however, in the recent past, there was significant conflict. B's sister was outspoken and directive, whereas B was quiet and passive in expressing her needs. They reported not understanding why B felt competitive given that both were very talented academically and in theater.

When discussing peer relationships, B's parents were unaware of the pressures that B was undergoing in trying to fit in. They expressed surprise and dismay at the extreme importance that she and her friends placed on weight and shape as determinants of self-worth.

Self-Report

In many cases, standardized self-report measures can be efficient in gathering information about eating behavior and other symptoms common in those with eating disorders. The Eating Disorder Inventory 2 (EDI-2; Garner, 1991) is a standardized, multiscale measure aimed specifically at assessing a range of psychological characteristics clinically relevant to eating disorders. It consists of three subscales (Drive for Thinness, Bulimia, Body Dissatisfaction) for tapping attitudes and behaviors relating to eating, weight, and shape, in addition to eight subscales (Ineffectiveness, Perfectionism, Interpersonal Distrust, Interoceptive Awareness, Maturity Fears, Asceticism, Impulse Regulation, and Social Insecurity) assessing more general organizing constructs or psychological traits clinically relevant to eating disorders. As part of the assessment process, B completed the EDI-2. She had markedly elevated EDI-2 subscale scores on Drive for Thinness, Body Dissatisfaction, Maturity Fears, and Perfectionism. Findings from this standardized measure confirmed the information derived from the clinical interview. Other self-report instruments indicated that she was experiencing depression, poor self-esteem, decreased ability to perform her daily activities, and interpersonal sensitivity and ineffectiveness.

PHYSIOLOGICAL

The effects of weight loss on psychological as well as physiological functioning are extraordinary, a fact often underestimated by clinicians not familiar with the psychobiology of human starvation (Garner, 1997). Severe psychological symptoms such as depression, mood swings, and apparent personality disturbances ameliorate with stabilization of eating and body weight in those with eating disorders; therefore, nutritional stabilization was a priority in B's treatment, especially due to the multiple physical symptoms she was experiencing. Similarly, reduction in caloric intake and dietary chaos can produce physical changes such as low potassium levels, which can lead to psychological symptoms such as depression. The general assumption in the understanding and treatment of anorexia nervosa is that there is interplay between physical and psychological symptoms. This assumption played a central role in the selection of B's treatment.

MEDICAL CONSULTATION

A medical evaluation of patients with eating disorders may be necessary to identify or rule out physical complications of starvation or those associated with certain extreme weight loss behaviors. Occasionally, a medical evaluation will be necessary to determine if weight loss has been precipitated by an underlying physical disorder. Certain symptoms, such as hypotension, hypothermia, bradycardia, and overall reduced metabolic rate, are common to starvation and may be evident in anorexia nervosa. Self-induced vomiting and purgative abuse may cause various symptoms or abnormalities, such as weakness, muscle cramping, edema, constipation, cardiac arrhythmias, and paresthesia. Additionally, general fatigue, constipation, depression, various neurological abnormalities, kidney and cardiac disturbances, swollen salivary glands, electrolyte disturbances, dental deterioration, finger clubbing or swelling, edema, and dehydration have been reported (Mitchell, Pomeroy, & Adson, 1997) in those who engage in self-induced vomiting and purgative abuse.

Prior to her admission to the intensive day treatment program, B was evaluated by her pediatrician. She determined that B's potassium level was below that expected, but this lab finding did not place her in a position of requiring acute medical intervention. B's reported headaches and dizziness appeared to be secondary effects of her restrictive eating patterns. She was also evaluated by a psychiatrist for medication management throughout treatment.

CASE CONCEPTUALIZATION

As is common with many anorexia nervosa patients, B's disorder can be conceptualized as multidetermined, resulting from the interplay of familial, psychological, sociocultural, and biological factors. Each of these factors may or may not have had etiological significance in B's anorexia nervosa but, in any case, they contribute and/or maintain it. B's sensitivity to weight and shape was heightened when she entered adolescence and was faced with insecurities of not fitting in and fear of rejection. In addition, given her perfectionistic tendencies, it is difficult to differentiate these as primary from symptoms that are secondary to the eating disorder. Furthermore, there is evidence to believe that in B's case, her symptoms of depression and low self-esteem were exacerbated as a direct result of restricting food intake and weight suppression.

B's case conceptualization thus targeted three main areas for intervention:

- Maturity fears.
- Conflict and undue competition with sister.
- Lack of emotional expression in family of origin.

RATIONALE FOR TREATMENT CHOICE

There is now broad agreement that the rationale for cognitive-behavioral therapy (CBT) for eating disorders rests primarily on the assumption that restrictive dieting (largely in response to cultural imperatives to meet unrealistic standards for body weight) is in direct conflict with the internal biological systems responsible for the homeostatic regulation of body weight (Garner et al., 1997). Given the current cultural pressures for thinness, it is easy to understand why women, particularly those with persistent self-doubts, could arrive at the conclusion that personal failings are to some degree related to weight or that the attainment of slenderness would measurably improve self-estimation. It has been asserted that for some who develop eating disorders, the motivating factors do not seem to go beyond a literal or extreme interpretation of the prevailing cultural doctrine glorifying thinness. For others, however, the impetus is more complicated, with a range of psychological and interactional factors playing a role (Garner et al., 1997).

According to the cognitive-behavioral view, the dieter's steadfast attempts to down-regulate body weight leads to myriad compensatory symptoms, including binge eating. Although the cognitive restructuring component of CBT has taken various forms, most rely on Beck's well-known model (Beck, Rush, Shaw, & Emery, 1979) which has been adapted for eating disorders (Fairburn, 1985; Garner & Bemis, 1982; Garner et al., 1997). The initial aim of cognitive restructuring is to challenge specific reasoning errors or self-destructive attitudes toward weight and shape so that the patient can relax restrictive dieting. Behavioral strategies such as self-monitoring, meal planning, and exposure to feared foods serve the overall goal of normalizing food intake. The primary point of emphasis of the cognitive-behavioral view has been the analysis of functional relationships between current distorted beliefs and symptomatic behaviors related to eating, weight, and body shape.

Although it has received relatively little emphasis in theoretical writings, the cognitive-behavioral model is well suited for examining other historical, developmental, and interpersonal themes identified with some eating disorder patients, themes that have been described best by psychodynamic and family theorists. These motifs include fears of separation, engulfment, or abandonment, failures in the separation-individuation process, false-self adaptation, transference, overprotectiveness, enmeshment, conflict avoidance, inappropriate involvement of the child in parental conflicts, and symptoms as mediators of family stability; all involve distorted meaning on the part of the individual, the family, or both. Although the language, style, and specific interpretations may differ sharply between the cognitive-behavioral model and the dynamic models that have generated these respective formulations, it is notable that both orientations are specifically concerned with meaning and meaning systems. Moreover, the respective therapies are aimed at identifying and correcting misconceptions that are presumed to have developmental antecedents (Garner et al., 1997). The marked social deficits observed in anorexia nervosa, the need to involve the family in many cases, and the longer duration of therapy have formed the basis for the explicit integration of interpersonal themes in early descriptions of CBT for anorexia nervosa (Garner et al., 1997). One of the advantages of the cognitive-behavioral approach is that it allows incorporation of developmental and interpersonal themes when they apply to a particular patient but does not compel all cases to fit into one restrictive explanatory system.

There are a number of general treatment principles and issues considered central to this model: (1) giving special attention to the therapeutic relationship; (2) enhancing motivation for change; (3) using a directive style; (4) following a "two-track approach" (track 1 pertains to issues related to weight, dieting, and eating; track 2 addresses beliefs and thematic underlying assumptions that are relevant to the development and maintenance of the eating disorder); (5) recognizing and addressing ego-syntonic symptoms; (6) differentiating starvation symptoms from primary psychopathology; and (7) enlisting special strategies to normalize eating and weight. Because these have been described fully in previous publications (Fairburn, 1985; Garner, 1997; Garner et al., 1997), they will be briefly touched on here to the extent that they pertain to the case material presented.

The treatment chosen for B was admission to the intensive day treatment program, which emphasizes structured eating to achieve nutritional rehabilitation, group psychotherapy, individual CBT, and cognitive family therapy. As stated previously, many of the cognitive-behavioral techniques originally developed by Beck and colleagues (Beck et al., 1979) for the treatment of depressive and anxiety disorders are directly applicable to anorexia nervosa. However, other methods have been developed or adapted to address features that distinguish eating disorders from other diagnostic groups (Garner & Bemis, 1982; Garner et al., 1997).

COURSE OF TREATMENT

The intensive outpatient program consisted of seven hours of treatment five days a week in a private clinic setting. There are between 14 and 20 eating disordered patients participating in the program at any given time, with most needing weight restoration. The therapeutic orientation was cognitive-behavioral and the key components of treatment were supervised eating, meal planning, and psychoeducation. Therapy format is primarily group; however, all patients receive individual therapy with one or more of the program staff. Due to B's living out of state, it was arranged that she and her mother would stay in an apartment while B was attending the intensive day treatment program. B's mother was able to take time off from work while B was in treatment.

B's caloric intake began at 1,800 calories per day, which was increased gradually to 3,200 calories per day to achieve the expected weekly weight gain of two to three pounds. A great deal of care was taken to explain that the goal of treatment was to restore *control* to her life, not simply to gain weight. She was educated about starvation symptoms and the need to eat in a consistent and predictable manner to restore her physical health, emotional well-being, and metabolic functioning. The treatment team assured her that she would not be allowed to gain weight faster than agreed on, as the goal of treatment was predictable change. Her calories would be adjusted either downward or upward to achieve the agreed on rate of weight gain; thus, it was very important to complete all meals and snacks on the meal plan; otherwise, the calculations of caloric need would be meaningless. B ate two meals and one snack at set times each day to normalize her intake and allow her body to adjust to the refeeding process. The primary goals for B were to review starvation symptoms, institute meal planning, provide correct information regarding nutrition, and ensure appropriate weight gain. Her goal weight range was 99 to 102 pounds, which was considered to be a weight approximately 5 pounds above that necessary for resumption of normal menstrual periods (Garner et al., 1997). B had to be coached often with accurate nutritional information to challenge her rigid rules for avoiding all dietary fat. She was extremely fearful that the consumption of dietary fat would turn to body fat that would accumulate on her stomach, hips, and legs.

In the early phases of treatment, B remained extremely anxious and frightened around meal times and when her daily weight was recorded. She required a tremendous amount of support around eating, as she experienced strong feelings of guilt after eating. She found the group atmosphere (with other females recovering from eating disorders) to be of great benefit, as she often questioned the normalcy of her feelings and thoughts throughout the recovery process.

B was reassured by the structure of the treatment program and with the attention to nutritional and dietary details during the refeeding process. She was quickly able to develop a trusting therapeutic relationship with staff and other patients. She was highly compliant throughout the nutritional rehabilitation phase of treatment, even while experiencing many negative feelings about weight gain and consuming feared foods. One of the most reassuring aspects of the renourishment process, especially in the initial phase of treatment, involved the meal-planning component, as the structure provided B with comfort. She rigidly adhered to meal planning while she was in the program and carefully followed through, ensuring that she met her daily caloric and fat intake. Initially, she limited herself to "safe" foods, but over time, she was gradually able to incorporate more of her "feared, forbidden" foods in small amounts and was able to feel more comfortable about eating them. She also was encouraged to keep notes in a journal and record her thoughts and feelings around mealtimes and her reactions in interpersonal situations at school and at the clinic.

B steadily gained weight during her treatment, at a rate of about one to three pounds per week. She struggled excessively with body image-related problems and had great difficulties learning to adjust to the changing shape of her body. During the course of weight gain, she became more aware of the psychosocial function that her eating disorder had served: It allowed her to avoid social expectations related to dating and it deflected her attention away from uncertainties about her future at school and beyond. She was also able to recognize that her feelings toward her family were not quite as harmonious as they had appeared; she was increasingly able to articulate that she felt angry with her father because she saw him as controlling and demanding.

The day after B reached 100 pounds, she started her period. This was particularly difficult for her because it indicated that she was very close to her goal weight range. She feared that at this weight she would be obese. However, with additional support, she remained dedicated to completing her meals and staying on the path of recovery. Once she reached her goal weight range, her calories were slowly decreased to stabilize her weight. She participated in the intensive outpatient program until she reached a weight of 101 pounds.

To test B's ability to sustain improvements outside the intensive day treatment program, it was arranged for her to go home with her family and return to the clinic within three weeks, before transitioning to outpatient treatment. During her time off, B was to continue consuming 2,500 calories per day to maintain her weight gain. She was able to maintain the treatment plan, adhered to her prescribed caloric intake, and had only one day of minimal restriction of calories. However, she was able to call her therapist for help and, after reassurance, was able to adhere to her meal plan completely. She returned to the intensive day treatment program for one week and worked on transitioning back to school and maintaining recovery despite the difficulties she would face at school. Of particular importance was helping B problem-solve how she would address people at school who had questions regarding her absence.

B was discharged from intensive day treatment program and was scheduled to see a counselor on a weekly basis. Her school nurse was to weigh her on a weekly basis and fax her weight to the clinic. B agreed that if her weight fell below her goal range of 99 to 102 pounds, she would return to the clinic. She and her family would also return to the clinic on a monthly basis for family therapy and to continue to improve communication patterns and emotional expression.

B continued in therapy for an additional 11 months; she was increasingly able to address other psychological issues related to self-esteem, perfectionism, expressing her emotions to her parents, competition with her sister, and fears associated with the social expectations of becoming an adolescent that contributed to her eating difficulties. Her weight toward the end of treatment remained within her goal range. She was socializing appropriately in school and had returned to theatrical performances.

Ten months after being discharged from the intensive day treatment program, B returned for two days due to her weight falling below her range. She was feeling competitive toward her sister and started to restrict her food intake. However, she was able to see that when she restricted her level of food, weight preoccupations increased dramatically and she became frightened that she was headed for a relapse. She agreed that she needed to return to the clinic for a couple of "booster sessions." B attended intensive day treatment for two days; the major psychological theme was her insecurity that resulted from comparing herself to her sister. This resulted in her feeling that the only redeeming quality she possessed was her eating disorder. The therapy group provided her with support in identifying other areas of personal competence that she could use in her self-evaluation. B was reassured that periods of vulnerability were common during the course of recovery and that her ability to identify problems early on and make adjustments accordingly was a very positive sign. Reframing and "normalizing" her concerns led to her feeling more confident and committed to the goals of treatment.

Over the next year, B's psychosocial adjustment continued to improve and she was able to find a healthy balance among academic, family, and social activities. She continued in treatment with her school counselor and had monthly telephone contact with the therapist from the intensive day treatment program. Frequency of therapy meetings was gradually reduced, until therapy was terminated. B and her family were encouraged to reinitiate therapy if she developed any concerns about her weight, eating, or psychological issues.

THERAPIST-CLIENT FACTORS

The clinician treating eating disorder patients should possess the accepted qualities of all skilled therapists: warmth, genuineness, empathy, honesty, and acceptance. The fact that many of the symptoms evinced by the eating disorder patient are ego-syntonic requires that the therapist have the ability to be firm, authoritative, and directive, while maintaining a collaborative therapeutic style. It is important for the clinician to be knowledgeable in certain subject domains that are outside typical training in general psychotherapy but are essential in understanding and treating eating disorders. These include (1) the biology of weight regulation, including the effects of restrictive dieting and semistarvation on behavior; (2) physical complications of extreme weight-controlling methods such as vomiting and laxative abuse; (3) attitudes and beliefs toward the body and food that are characteristic of eating disorder patients; and (4) the role of cultural pressures for thinness that impinge on women today and how to meaningfully address cultural issues in psychotherapy.

Establishing a working relationship with the family is essential with the younger patient as well as with some older patients who are living at home. However, family therapy may not always be a realistic option due to the unavailability of experienced therapists, insurance limitations, or the family's unwillingness to participate. Reluctant family members may become motivated to participate in family therapy once they recognize that blame is not being placed on them, or when they find the intervention to be helpful to the overall functioning of the family.

B had a very positive view toward treatment and this aided her in being able to trust the treatment principles that were recommended. Some adolescent patients have less commitment to treatment than that shown by B; however, most become collaborators in treatment as long as developmental issues are being addressed in family meetings. Being in a group setting and seeing other patients recover allowed B to feel validated and also allowed her to trust the treatment process. In addition, her intelligence facilitated her ability to grasp the psychoeducational material presented that aided in dispelling nutritional myths. The commitment that her family showed to her recovery and their respect of the limits set by her allowed B and her family to more appropriately express thoughts and feelings.

COURSE OF TERMINATION

B attended the intensive outpatient program for a total of 34 sessions over the course of a two-month period. At admission, it was determined that discharge from the intensive outpatient program would be contingent on B's reaching her goal weight range and being able to maintain a stable weight without resorting to previous restrictive eating patterns. B reached her goal range and maintained it for two weeks on 2,500 calories per day prior to being discharged from intensive day treatment. At termination, her eating symptoms were completely under control. She was able to (1) increase her caloric intake to an appropriate, "nondieting" level without anxiety, (2) space meals so that food was consumed throughout the day rather than just in the evening, (3) gradually incorporate "forbidden foods" into her diet, and (4) inhibit urges to diet or engage in weight-controlling behaviors. Challenging underlying assumptions related to dieting and obesity was the primary focus early in treatment (Garner & Wooley, 1991). She was able to address her own negative feelings about weight and shape and to recognize that her dislike of her shape was based on assumptions about obesity in general that were inaccurate and inconsistent with her other principles for viewing human worth. Furthermore, B's body image improved with weight restoration and with her ability to define her self-worth independent of weight and shape.

Later, more general themes were explored related to family-of-origin relationships and how they related to self-definition, maturity fears, and expression of thoughts and feelings. B was successful in asserting herself with her parents, especially her father. During family therapy, the family had addressed their difficulty expressing feelings, especially anger and disappointment. Throughout her treatment, B had been able to identify her emotions, define the triggers for these, and then cope with them in appropriate ways. A turning point for her was a family session in which she was able to verbalize her competitive feelings toward her sister. She was able to recognize that her sister also felt competitive toward her and that they each had their own unique strengths. B's sister verbalized that B's anorexia was a way to get attention, and B was able to confront her sister on what purpose anorexia nervosa had served. Following this family meeting, B reported feeling relieved and her mood lifted considerably. She was able to keep her competitive feelings toward her sister from translating into weight control. She also was able to see how her social environment had provided a window through which cultural values toward weight and achievement had been magnified. She discussed ways she might approach her friends that would be conducive to maintaining recovery. She took special pride in being able to challenge her friends' myths about weight, shape, and eating and was optimistic that they would accept her regardless of her weight and shape. Given the possibility that they would not accept her, she discussed ways that she might seek out friends who respected her views on weight and shape.

FOLLOW-UP

B and her family continue to attend family therapy once a month and B continues to see her school counselor. Their communication patterns, especially those dealing with expression of negative affect, greatly improved. B also strengthened her relationship with her sister and is currently playing a lead in a school play while her sister occupies a secondary role. She continues to be weighed weekly by her school nurse and the results are faxed to the clinic. Her goal weight range has been adjusted to account for developmental factors, and her calories were increased due to her increased activity level in school activities.

For the most part, B continues to plan meals but has eaten in restaurants and at holiday dinners without the use of a meal plan. She has discussed gradually weaning herself from formal meal planning, as she now feels much more relaxed toward eating.

B has recognized that her self-worth extends beyond her weight and shape. She now is able to define her self-worth in more appropriate terms. Socially, B has struggled with having to distance herself from friends who have been triggers for potential relapse. She has taken a proactive stance in educating others around her as to the dangers of eating disorders.

MANAGED CARE CONSIDERATIONS

In the past, there were extraordinary economic incentives for inpatient care, surging demands for clinical services, and widespread misinformation regarding optimal treatment. This led to the unnecessary hospitalization of many eating disorder patients who could have been managed easily as outpatients or at a partial hospitalization level of care. Abuse of residential and inpatient treatment was followed by a backlash by the insurance industry, resulting in inappropriate denial of hospital coverage or absurd limitations of coverage for eating disorder patients. Unfortunately, this has put many eating disorder patients at unnecessary risk for chronic illness and death. Part of the problem has been a failure to clearly articulate the different objectives for correcting acute medical complications and comprehensive treatment of eating disorders.

Hospitalization is most appropriate for patients who are in acute medical danger and who require medical stabilization. It can be brief and is not necessary for the majority of patients. When aimed at treating physical complications, hospitalization is a medical priority that does not require a commitment by the patient to recover from his or her eating disorder. In contrast, treatments aimed at "recovery from the eating disorder" have the goals of nutritional rehabilitation, containment of eating disorder symptoms, and addressing the psychological problems that led to the development and maintenance of the eating disorder. In most cases, this can be conducted in a cost-effective manner in a specialized eating disorder program at a partial hospitalization level of care. Partial hospitalization or intensive day treatment programs provide the preferred alternative to inpatient care for most patients. These programs provide structure around mealtimes plus the possibility for intensive therapy, without requiring the patient to become totally disengaged from the supports and therapeutic challenges outside of the hospital. Partial care programs offer the distinct advantage of being more economical than full hospitalization. They also can provide a useful bridge between inpatient and outpatient care. There are various models for day treatment programs that generally share many features with inpatient programs; the major difference is that patients receive the therapeutic services but do not stay overnight. Again, inpatient treatment is still the preferred modality for patients who are seriously emaciated, require close medical monitoring, fail to progress in partial care, or are at serious risk of self-harm.

It is generally pointless to negotiate with patients or insurance carriers around the duration of partial hospitalization treatment required for weight restoration, because the time needed is relatively straightforward and easy to calculate. It is the number of weeks or months required to reach at least 90% of expected weight, gaining at a rate of between two and three pounds a week and assuming optimal compliance with the treatment program. Even though this is a time-consuming and expensive process, it is an economical alternative if it leads to recovery, as a chronic eating disorder inflicts a heavy price, both in monetary and emotional terms.

OVERALL EFFECTIVENESS

Illustrating CBT for eating disorders using the case study format has the primary advantage of providing concrete examples of actual interventions, giving life to otherwise sterile theoretical accounts of treatment. Unfortunately, the case study format has a number of disadvantages that are particularly important in illustrating the treatment of eating disorders. It has repeatedly been emphasized that eating disorders are multidetermined and present with myriad associated forms of psychopathology.

The case presented here demonstrates only one set of presenting problems, underlying assumptions, application of the method, format for delivery, duration of treatment, and resolution among a wide array of possibilities. As was outlined, much of B's initial psychological distress was secondary to her restrictive eating patterns (Garner et al., 1997). Once she reached an appropriate weight and her eating patterns were normalized, she was able to tackle the psychological issues that were maintaining her eating disorder, especially those related to family interactional patterns and cultural pressures for thinness. There are many anorexia nervosa patients whose presentation and course are more straightforward and who respond favorably to brief cognitive-behavioral or educational techniques outlined here and elsewhere. Effective cognitive interventions can be brief in some cases; for others, they assume a lengthy course. Individual, group, and family therapy formats each may be advantageous for certain patients and may be combined in some instances. In B's case, inpatient treatment was necessary to normalize eating and weight, to treat complications, and to disengage the family from ineffective interactional patterns. Many of the nuances of treatment go well beyond the scope of the preceding case presentation but have been described in detail elsewhere (see references).

REFERENCES

American Psychiatric Association. (2000). *Diagnostic and statistical manual of mental disorders* (4th ed., text rev.). Washington, DC: Author.

Beck, A. T., Rush, A. J., Shaw, B. F., & Emery, G. (1979). *Cognitive therapy of depression.* New York: Guilford Press.

Bruch, H. (1973). *Eating disorders: Obesity, anorexia nervosa and the person within.* New York: Basic Books.

Casper, R. C. (1990). Personality features of women with good outcome from restricting anorexia nervosa. *Psychosomatic Medicine, 52,* 156–170.

Crisp, A. H. (1970). Anorexia nervosa: Feeding disorder, nervous malnutrition or weight phobia? *World Review of Nutrition, 12,* 452–504.

Edlund, B., Halvarsson, K., & Sjödén, P. (1995). Eating behaviours, and attitudes to eating, dieting, and body image in a 7-year-old Swedish girl. *European Eating Disorders Review, 3*(111), 1–14.

Fairburn, C. G. (1985). Cognitive-behavioral treatment for bulimia. In D. M. Garner & P. E. Garfinkel (Eds.), *Handbook of psychotherapy for anorexia nervosa and bulimia* (pp. 160–192). New York: Guilford Press.

Garner, D. M. (1991). *Eating Disorder Inventory-2: Professional manual.* Odessa, FL: Psychological Assessment Resources.

Garner, D. M. (1997). Psychoeducational principles in treatment. In D. M. Garner & P. E. Garfinkel (Eds.), *Handbook of treatment for eating disorders* (pp. 145–177). New York: Guilford Press.

Garner, D. M., & Bemis, K. M. (1982). A cognitive-behavioral approach to anorexia nervosa. *Cognitive Therapy and Research, 6,* 123–150.

Garner, D. M., & Garfinkel, P. E. (1980). Socio-cultural factors in the development of anorexia nervosa. *Psychological Medicine, 10,* 647–656.

Garner, D. M., Garfinkel, P. E., & O'Shaughnessy, M. (1985). The validity of the distinction between bulimia with and without anorexia nervosa. *American Journal of Psychiatry, 142,* 581–587.

Garner, D. M., Garner, M. V., & Rosen, L. W. (1993). Anorexia nervosa "restricters" who purge: Implications for subtyping anorexia nervosa. *International Journal of Eating Disorders, 13,* 171–185.

Garner, D. M., Vitousek, K., & Pike, K. (1997). Cognitive-behavioral therapy for anorexia nervosa. In D. M. Garner & P. E. Garfinkel (Eds.), *Handbook of treatment for eating disorders* (pp. 94–144). New York: Guilford Press.

Garner, D. M., & Wooley, S. C. (1991). Confronting the failure of behavioral and dietary treatments for obesity. *Clinical Psychology Review, 11,* 1–52.

Herzog, D. B., Keller, M. B., Sacks, N. R., Yeh, C. J., & Lavori, P. W. (1992). Psychiatric morbidity in treatment-seeking anorexics and bulimics. *Journal of the American Academy of Child and Adolescent Psychiatry, 31,* 810–818.

Hsu, L. K. G., Kaye, W., & Weltzin, T. E. (1993). Are the eating disorders related to Obsessive Compulsive Disorder? *International Journal of Eating Disorders, 14,* 305–318.

Laessle, R. G., Wittchen, H. U., Fichter, M. M., & Pirke, K. M. (1989). The significance of subgroups of bulimia and anorexia nervosa: Lifetime frequency of psychiatric disorders. *International Journal of Eating Disorders, 8,* 569–574.

Mitchell, J. E., Pomeroy, C., & Adson, D. E. (1997). Managing medical complications. In D. M. Garner & P. E. Garfinkel (Eds.), *Handbook of treatment for eating disorders* (pp. 383–393). New York: Guilford Press.

Rosen, A. M., Murkofsky, C. A., Steckler, N. M., & Skolnick, N. J. (1989). A comparison of psychological and depressive symptoms among restricting anorexic, bulimic anorexic, and normal-weight bulimic patients. *International Journal of Eating Disorders, 8,* 657–663.

Russell, G. F. M. (1970). Anorexia nervosa: Its identity as an illness and its treatment. In J. H. Price (Ed.), *Modern trends in psychological medicine* (Vol. 2, pp. 131–164.) London: Butterworth.

Strober, M. (1980). Personality and symptomatological features in young, nonchronic anorexia nervosa patients. *Journal of Psychosomatic Research, 24,* 353–359.

CHAPTER 19

Posttraumatic Stress Disorder

JOSEPH R. SCOTTI, TRACY L. MORRIS,
KENNETH J. RUGGIERO, and JULIE WOLFGANG

DESCRIPTION OF THE DISORDER

TRAUMATIC EVENTS AS defined in the fourth edition of the *Diagnostic and Statistical Manual of Mental Disorders* (*DSM-IV*; American Psychiatric Association [APA], 1994) include experiences that involve "actual or threatened death or serious injury, or a threat to the physical integrity of self or others," and that evoke intense fear, helplessness, or horror (p. 424). The diagnosis of posttraumatic stress disorder (PTSD) is used to classify individuals who have experienced such a traumatic event and endorse at least (1) one trauma-related reexperiencing symptom, (2) three trauma-relevant forms of avoidant behavior, and (3) two symptoms of increased arousal following the event. Although these diagnostic criteria are the same for adults and children, manifestations of symptoms may differ. In the case of young children, disorganized or agitated behavior may appear more prevalent than articulated expressions of fear and helplessness. The diagnostic criteria also specify that nightmares are not required to include recognizable trauma-related content (e.g., monsters) to be considered a reexperiencing symptom among children. Although not included as diagnostic requirements, many clinicians and researchers have noted that trauma-exposed children may exhibit behavioral regression, such as bed-wetting, refusal to sleep alone at night, and difficulty separating from their parents during the day (Perrin, Smith, & Yule, 2000; Saigh, Yasik, Sack, & Koplewicz, 1999).

Portions of this work were supported by a National Institutes of Mental Health research grant (1 R03 MH55533-01) to the first author, which is gratefully acknowledged. The opinions expressed herein are not necessarily those of that agency. This case represents a compilation of several actual cases seen through the Quin Curtis Center for Psychological Research, Training, and Service at West Virginia University. Correspondence may be addressed to Joseph R. Scotti, PhD, Associate Professor and Eberly Family Professor of Outstanding Public Service, Department of Psychology, Post Office Box 6040, West Virginia University, Morgantown, WV 26506-6040. e-mail: jscotti@mail.wvu.edu

Additionally, a substantial body of literature indicates increased risk for psychopathology among children who have experienced traumatic events. Risk for major depression, panic disorder, overanxious disorder, social phobia, and somatoform pain appears to be elevated among trauma-exposed children and adolescents (see review by Saigh et al., 1999). Among children, attention problems (including attention-deficit/hyperactivity disorder) and disruptive behavior (e.g., oppositional defiant disorder and conduct disorder) also have been found to increase following exposure to traumatic events (Saigh et al.).

Several important variables that may mediate or moderate outcomes following trauma exposure have been identified in the literature (Saigh et al., 1999). The greater the perception of threat to one's safety or body integrity, the higher the likelihood that one will experience symptoms of PTSD. Thus, events resulting in physical injury have a higher association with PTSD. Furthermore, the more traumatic events an individual has experienced, the greater the likelihood for PTSD, suggesting a cumulative stressor effect. Degree of social (particularly parental) support following the traumatic event plays a significant role in long-term adjustment, as does the degree of parental psychopathology.

A number of these important child variants of PTSD symptoms, comorbidities, and protective and risk factors are evident in the present case example of PTSD in a child following a motor vehicle accident.

CASE DESCRIPTION

The reader might ask why we have chosen to focus on the aftereffects of a motor vehicle accident (MVA) as a case example of PTSD in a child. The reason is simple: MVAs are exceedingly common events, but often are not considered potentially traumatic events that may lead to PTSD and a host of related psychological symptoms and disorders (e.g., phobias, withdrawal, and other anxiety-related symptoms; depression). Of the 6.8 million motor vehicle crashes in the United States in 1996, approximately one-third (2.3 million) resulted in physical injury to at least one person, and about one percent resulted in the death of at least one person (U.S. Department of Transportation, 1996). These injury figures include some 413,000 children age 15 years and under and 953,000 youth age 16 to 24 years. These latter figures are the reported *physical* injuries from motor vehicle crashes in just one year; they do *not* include the psychological distress that may follow involvement in an MVA. It is this psychological and behavioral distress that is the focus of the present case study.

THE ACCIDENT

As an essential feature in the diagnosis of PTSD is occurrence of a traumatic event, we begin with an overview of the MVA. Keisha, age 3 years, and Terry, age 9, were both in an accident three months prior to their initial presentation at the clinic. Keisha and Terry were backseat passengers in a car that their 35-year-old mother, Mrs. Washington, was driving on a wet road with many sharp turns. A pickup truck was driving uncomfortably close behind them, such that when Mrs. Washington hit the brakes on a sudden sharp turn, the truck hit their rear bumper, sending them off the road, skidding and then coming to a stop in a ditch. The mother's arm was caught between the front seat and the door for some 20 minutes until help arrived. Mrs. Washington's face and arms were dotted with multiple minor pinpoint cuts caused by flying glass from the shattered windshield. Rain poured in as Mrs. Washington sat pinned and blood flowed from her seemingly serious head wounds. Both children screamed in distress until helped arrived. Keisha appeared uninjured. Terry had apparently bumped his head on the window of the side door, receiving a rather large swollen bruise on his forehead, but no lacerations. A trip to the hospital via ambulance revealed that all of the injuries were quite minor and would quickly heal.

THE FAMILY

Background variables are critical features of any case presenting for assessment and treatment, but never more so than in the case of current family dynamics when the clients are young children (see Scotti & Morris, 2000). In this African American family, the mother had been born in South Africa but had been in the United States for over 10 years. Mrs. Washington was not working outside the home. She was seen as very submissive—even passive—especially when her husband, a native of the United States, was present. Mr. Washington, a medical researcher, seemed annoyed by the damage to the vehicle but rather unconcerned, even dismissive, about the continuing distress of his family (he came to only one session). The family was devoutly Christian. Terry attended a church-affiliated school as well as multiple afterschool church-run activities (e.g., bible study and youth groups several times per week). An important feature of this case was the perspective, voiced primarily by Mrs. Washington, that God had played a role in allowing the accident; thus, in her view, prayer and faith would be important aspects of resolving the distress of her children. She was rather unconcerned about herself, although it became evident that she had the most serious symptoms of all involved. The case raises a number of important cultural and ethnic issues that need to be incorporated into the case conceptualization (see Rabalais, Ruggiero, & Scotti, in press).

CHIEF COMPLAINTS

As is often the situation with cases that involve children and, as a result, their families, the presenting complaints did not cover fully what eventually became the behavioral and psychological symptoms that were treated. First, Mrs. Washington denied much distress for herself; however, discussion and a subsequent structured interview with the Clinician-Administered PTSD Scale (CAPS; Blake et al., 1990) showed her to be fully meeting criteria for moderate PTSD as a result of this MVA, as well as a history of anxiety and depression. In separate sessions, the mother was subsequently treated with implosive therapy, an imaginal exposure technique that is an empirically-validated intervention for PTSD (Chambless et al., 1998; see Lyons & Scotti, 1995, and Westrup, Kalish, & Scotti, 1997, for case examples of treating adults with MVA-related PTSD with implosive therapy). Work with Mrs. Washington focused on her symptoms of PTSD, but also her guilt concerning her perception of having caused the accident that led to the current distress of her children. This work, as often happens, led to her revelation of a history of childhood physical abuse and sporadic domestic violence, additional issues then addressed in continuing therapy.

Mrs. Washington reported that, as a result of the accident, both of the children showed signs of distress whenever she was the driver. This was especially the case in rainy weather. However, when the father drove the car, the children were quiet and well behaved. Mrs. Washington noted that Terry was now reluctant to get into a car and that he appeared restless and "fidgety" when riding with her. Of particular concern to her was that Terry now often criticized her driving, frequently exhorting her to be careful. She found this to be distracting, and she worried that it might result in another accident. Of concern to the father was that Terry was coming into the parental bed at night, a "habit" they thought they had "broken" several years earlier.

HISTORY

The history of the problems related to this MVA is a rather brief one, given that the disorder—PTSD, in the case of Terry—stems from the time of the accident, just three months prior to the initial clinical session.

Keisha was reported to have been distressed the evening of the MVA and had some difficulty falling asleep. She also asked her mother several times about the "boo-boos" on her face, but seemed unconcerned when given an honest answer. By the time of our initial sessions, three months postaccident, Keisha seemed to have little to no memory of the accident. She said that she did not remember it, and we had to act on the basis of her self-report. It should be noted that Keisha displayed distressed behavior similar to Terry's when in a car with both her mother and brother. This might suggest a memory for the event when sufficient reminders are present (i.e., car, mother, and brother). However, Keisha's behavior appeared related more to the distressed behavior of her brother; she did not act distressed when in a car alone with her mother or when her father was driving. The operative component appeared to be the agitated behavior of her brother, in response to which she would cry.

Keisha's situation raises the issue of whether one must be able to describe events verbally to be affected by them. Scotti, Ruggiero, and Rabalais (in press) provide a brief overview of work in this area, noting issues such as the apparent difference in the organization and experience of memory in younger versus older children, as revealed through event narratives; the fall-off in recall accuracy over time (as with any memory); and differences in recall accuracy related to age (even between 3- and 4-year-old children). Memory for a traumatic event is a developmental issue, which likely interacts with the characteristics of the event and subsequent psychological vulnerabilities and symptom presentation. For example, Bahrick, Parker, Fivush, and Levitt (1998) found that 3-year-old children reported fewer details than 4-year-old children about their experience of Hurricane Andrew. Additionally, they found that more details were recalled by children who had a moderate level of exposure to the hurricane, as compared to those children with either high or low levels of exposure. Thus, given her age, the mild to moderate severity of the MVA, no prior history of psychopathology, and only intermittent distress that was more likely occasioned by Terry's distress, it is not surprising that Keisha was not able to describe the accident. Thus, after the first two sessions, Keisha was no longer involved in further assessment or therapy sessions.

Terry, on the other hand, slept very poorly for several nights after the accident and appeared fitful in his sleep thereafter. He complained of head and neck pain for several weeks, requiring further medical evaluation (which did not reveal a cause for continuing reports of pain). He became increasingly resistant to entering the family car; he had no difficulty with the school bus. When coaxed with promises of special treats to ride in the car, he was hypervigilant, looking for pickup trucks and sharp bends in the road, and he became distressed by sudden changes in the speed or direction of the vehicle. His distress was evident by yelling out, crying, and general restlessness in the backseat, all of which appeared upsetting to his sister when she was present. He was also highly critical of his mother's driving, making repeated remarks for her to be careful and to keep both hands on the steering wheel at all times (what we refer to as "safety" behaviors). Mrs. Washington alternately complied with his requests and snapped at him to be quiet so that she did not have an accident, mention of which served only to distress him further. None of this behavior was evident when the father was driving the car. Terry reported being quite tense when his father drove, but said that his father would punish him if he and Keisha were not quiet and still, both in the car and generally. (Follow-up on the father's behavior suggested very strict and stern family rules consistent with some stated cultural and religious beliefs, but not to the point of abusive behavior against the children.) By the time of the initial sessions, Mrs. Washington was just beginning to receive written reports from school that Terry was daydreaming in class and not performing academically at his usual high level.

BEHAVIORAL ASSESSMENT

This case was initially seen in response to an advertisement to participate in a grant-funded research project concerning the effects of MVAs on children. Thus, the assessment package was rather more extensive than might usually be possible in the typical clinical setting. Still, the assessment reported here well demonstrates the range of methods that can be used in the assessment of PTSD.

BEHAVIORAL

The information obtained through an unstructured interview on the behavioral features of this case has already been provided in the prior two sections. Additionally, we note the extraordinarily well-behaved and well-mannered behavior of the two children, noteworthy in that it appeared stifled and uncomfortable. Although very pleasant children, ready to talk, play, and otherwise interact with the examiners, they appeared anxious about making mistakes or offending (Terry more so than Keisha), especially in the presence of the father.

As part of the research protocol, Terry completed the *Clinical Stroop Task*. In its original format, the Stroop (1935) color-naming task required naming—as fast and accurately as possible—five different colored inks in which a set of five color names are printed; the color name and the color of the ink in which it is printed are different (e.g., when seeing the word "GREEN" printed in blue ink, the person is to say "blue"). The Clinical Stroop Task involves use of trauma-relevant words printed in different colors; again, the task is to ignore the word and say the color of the ink. In our MVA-relevant Stroop Task, the participant sees the word "ACCIDENT" printed in red ink, for example, and is required to say "red" and ignore the word "ACCIDENT." The rather consistent finding in Clinical Stroop studies is that persons who are both trauma-exposed and distressed (as compared to nondistressed trauma survivors and a nontrauma control group) take significantly longer to complete this task with trauma-relevant words as compared to either stressful (but non-trauma-relevant) or neutral words. This "Stroop effect" is most often accounted for by differences in information processing or selective attention, but we have more parsimoniously conceptualized the effect as behavioral disruption due to conditioned emotional responses (Mullen James, 1999; Scotti, 1992; see Scotti et al., in press, for a review of the Clinical Stroop used with children). As a measure of behavioral disruption, this task is a suitable means of directly observing the effects of the presence of trauma-relevant (i.e., MVA-related) word stimuli on children exposed to MVAs, capturing such features of PTSD as distractibility and concentration difficulties, arousal to event-related cues, and hypervigilance.

At present, the Clinical Stroop Task should be considered a research tool rather than a validated and normed clinical assessment instrument. Thus, we report results of the MVA-related Stroop completed with Terry with due caution. In completing the Clinical Stroop Task, Terry accurately named the colors on the three cards (each containing 50 words) with neutral words (e.g., "POTATO") and one card with school-stress words (e.g., "TEST") all within 5 seconds of each other (an average of 63 seconds across the four cards). However, the card with MVA-related words (e.g., "SEATBELT") took him 25 seconds longer than any of the other cards, and he made multiple mistakes, saying the word (e.g., "CRASH") rather than the ink color (i.e., "blue"). In and of itself, the pretreatment results are not meaningful. They acquire meaning when compared to his posttreatment results, presented later, and when compared to the other children in our research study. He responded similarly (both in terms of time and errors) to children who had been in mild to severe MVAs and were clinically distressed.

SELF-REPORT

In performing a psychological assessment of Terry, we used several self-report measures and interviews focusing on PTSD, anxiety disorders in general, and depression, which often accompanies PTSD. It is also critical with young children to gather information about the parents and the social and family environment, as there is a substantial literature demonstrating the detrimental effects of parental psychopathology on child functioning, and one needs to know about family resources and whether the family functions as a support or an additional stressor for the child.

Thus, the Symptom Checklist 90-Revised (SCL-90-R; Derogatis, 1983) was completed by Mrs. Washington about herself. The SCL-90-R showed clinical elevations (above a T-score of 60) on the Obsessive-Compulsive, Anxiety, Depression, and Hostility subscales, as well as the Global Severity Index (follow-up testing after her course of therapy revealed an elevation on only the Obsessive-Compulsive subscale, with a Global Severity Index in the normal range).

Both Terry and Mrs. Washington independently completed the AcCIdentS (*Ac*cident Characteristics *Ident*ification *S*cale; see Scotti et al., in press), which identifies important features of the MVA (e.g., damage to vehicle, type of collision, extent of injury). Both mother and son rated the MVA in the mild to moderate range, reporting a moderate amount of fear of being injured or killed at the time of the accident, and continuing fear (by Terry) of riding in cars.

The Child Behavior Checklist (CBCL; Achenbach, 1991), completed by Mrs. Washington about Terry, revealed clinical elevations (above a T-score of 65 and ranging as high as 75) on the Internalizing Scale (and all related subscales: Withdrawn, Somatic Complaints, and Anxious/Depressed), as well as Social Problems, Thought Problems, and Attention Problems. There were no elevations on any of the Externalizing scales. In completing the child self-report measures, Terry did not indicate depression (Children's Depression Inventory [CDI]; Kovacs, 1985), but did reveal clinically significant anxiety (Revised Children's Manifest Anxiety Scale [RCMAS]; Reynolds, 1980), including the subscales of Physiological Anxiety, Worry and Oversensitivity, and Concentration Anxiety. Of most relevance to the issue of PTSD, Terry's score on the Impact of Event Scale (IES; Horowitz, Wilner, & Alvarez, 1979) was in the PTSD range, with high levels of both intrusive and avoidant symptoms. Finally, Terry completed the Social Support Scale for Children ("People in My Life"; Harter, 1985), the scores on which were over half a standard deviation above the mean on all subscales (Friend, Classmate, Parent, and Teacher). Thus, Terry reported strong social support, an important factor related to positive outcome in cases of PTSD.

As a final step in this part of the evaluation, both mother and son separately completed the parent and child versions of the Anxiety Disorders Interview Schedule for Children (ADIS; Silverman & Nelles, 1988). Terry's report indicated that he currently met criteria for both separation anxiety (with onset postaccident) and generalized anxiety disorder (GAD; formerly overanxious disorder of childhood, with Terry's concerns being primarily oriented to social and school failure, and having an onset prior to the MVA), as well as PTSD. With regard to PTSD, his most prominent symptoms were those of reexperiencing. Terry indicated that he often thought of car accidents. He denied dreaming of accidents, but did report repetitive play in which he made cars crash into each other (this being a change from prior behavior). He also reported feeling like the accident was happening again, especially when there was any sudden change in the speed or direction of the vehicle in which he was riding. Seeing pickup trucks or fast-moving cars resulted in increased arousal (e.g., heart pounding, hard to breathe). Terry indicated that he did not like to talk or think about accidents; however, he noted that when riding with his mother he spoke frequently of them, warning her of dangers and criticizing her driving. He described how he did not want to get into the family car, especially when his mother was driving, and that he was not as interested in previously enjoyed afterschool activities (in part, it seemed, because staying after school meant that his mother would pick him up in her car, rather than his taking the bus home). Finally, he reported that he was hypervigilant to accident-related cues, was easily startled by loud noises and changes in movement, was having difficulty concentrating on his schoolwork, and was generally more irritable and sleeping fitfully. The mother's report on the ADIS corroborated Terry's reported symptoms of GAD (also noted to be prior to the MVA) and PTSD; she did not see his symptoms of separation anxiety.

Both mother and son agreed that the symptoms of GAD preceded the MVA by several years, indicating a possible predisposing factor. (It is important to define the time course of GAD symptoms as they would otherwise be better accounted for by PTSD if they began after the accident.) Both also admitted, for the first time, when queried during the interview, that Terry had begun wetting the bed at night within a week of the accident (regressive behavior); he met full criteria for nocturnal enuresis.

PHYSIOLOGICAL

In addition to the self-reports that clearly indicate increased physiological arousal, we employed two additional methods for evaluating arousal to trauma-related stimuli. The first is feasible in the typical clinical setting; the second involves rather more extensive experience and specialized equipment. Both, in this case, were completed within our laboratory research protocol.

We first had Terry listen to six brief audiotaped vignettes, two of which described neutral to pleasant activities (a birthday party and a trip to the mall), two that described potentially stressful events at school (forgetting to study for a test and giving an oral report), and two that described a mild and a more severe MVA; the order of the six scenes was randomized. At the midpoint and end of each vignette, Terry rated on a 4-point scale how fearful and how happy the scene made him feel. One school scene (oral report) and both MVA scenes produced ratings of "very fearful" and "not at all happy." All other scenes were rated as "very happy" and "not at all fearful."

Following this, Terry participated in a psychophysiological assessment protocol during which he listened to more extended and more vivid audiotaped vignettes of a pleasant scene (start of summer vacation), a school-stress scene (forgetting to study for a test), and an MVA in which minor injury occurred (in fact, a scene coincidentally quite similar to his own accident). During these scenes and appropriate baseline conditions, heart rate and skin conductance data were continuously recorded. Analyses of these physiological data showed Terry to be responding differentially, with increased heart rate and skin conductance, to the MVA scene in a manner consistent with the group of children in this study who had experienced mild to severe accidents and were displaying symptoms of PTSD (see Scotti et al., in press). His pattern of responding was clearly discriminable from the two control groups: children who had not been in an MVA, and children who had been in an MVA but were not displaying symptoms of PTSD or other distress.

SUMMARY

The multiple methods and sources of information across three response channels (overt behavior, cognition/covert behavior, physiology) were all highly congruent in pointing to responses consistent with a diagnosis of PTSD, with related symptoms of separation anxiety, along with a preaccident history of GAD.

MEDICAL CONSULTATION

As previously noted, the family was transported from the accident scene to the emergency room of a local hospital, where the injuries were described as minor. Hospitalization was not required. Terry, however, reported head and neck pain for several weeks after the accident. Further medical evaluation failed to reveal any significant injury beyond the soreness associated with whiplash. It is critical, however, in the comprehensive assessment and treatment of MVA survivors, that such head injury-related symptoms be thoroughly investigated. An interesting aspect of MVAs that involve a head injury is that the symptoms of PTSD and head injury show considerable overlap, including difficulties with attention and concentration, irritability, loss of interest, sleep disturbance, and anxiety seen in this case, but also memory problems, emotional lability, disinhibited behavior, social avoidance, depression, and fatigue (Davidoff, Laibstain, Kessler, & Mark, 1988; Horton, 1993; Jacobson, 1999; Scotti et al., 1992). The time course of symptoms associated with head injury and PTSD is somewhat different. The symptoms of mild postconcussive head injury are typically of a relatively brief duration, occurring within hours of the event and continuing for several weeks to months. Symptoms of PTSD, on the other hand, by definition have onset after one month (although one may also show signs of acute stress disorder). When the head injury is more severe and thus more extended in time, these differences can easily become blurred (Davidoff et al.). Furthermore, what the lasting effects of even a mild head injury may be on children are largely unknown (Satz et al., 1997). Consequently, it is strongly advised that the clinician who is assessing and treating an MVA survivor ensures that a medical evaluation has been completed, particularly when the client reports any physical injury to the head during the accident. In Terry's case, medical evaluation did not suggest the lingering effects of a head injury (see Scotti et al., in press, for further discussion of this issue as well as the problem of postconcussive amnesia). Additionally, after consultation with the family's personal physician, it was decided that anxiolytic medications would not be prescribed unless therapy was unsuccessful.

CASE CONCEPTUALIZATION

In conceptualizing this case, we applied the integrated *paradigmatic behavioral framework model,* as developed by Arthur Staats and colleagues (Eifert, Beach, & Wilson, 1998; Eifert & Evans, 1990; Staats, 1993) and expanded for application with accident survivors by Scotti and colleagues (Scotti, Beach, Northrop, Rode, & Forsyth, 1995/in press; Scotti et al., in press). Space does not allow a full explication of that conceptual model here; instead, we briefly outline each of the components of the model as we discuss the relevant details of this case and bring the components together into a full clinical functional analysis. The purpose of such a model is to fully integrate the multiple interrelated factors that both set the occasion for and maintain the adaptive and maladaptive responses seen in a clinical case. The framework is a dynamic one that outlines not only the critical variables, but their back-and-forth interplay that results in a case conceptualization with sufficient flexibility to incorporate idiographic differences within a comprehensive framework based on empirical research. Such an analysis assists in the identification of appropriate intervention strategies, as the subsequent section on intervention demonstrates.

Original Learning (Historical Antecedents)

This component of the model represents the individual's learning history prior to the event of interest, in this case, the MVA. Factors of importance include age and developmental history; history of prior trauma; the cohesiveness of the family; education (grade level and achievement); socioeconomic status (as this may reflect family resources available in treatment); ethnic and cultural background; history of psychopathology (child and family); and coping skills. A great deal of this information is gathered in the typical initial clinical interview and information-gathering phase of the assessment, some of which has already been noted. Terry's history was noteworthy only for his symptoms of GAD and for enuresis that continued past the age at which bed-wetting typically ceases for males (see Scotti & Morris, 2000). We initially suspected that there may have been some episodes of sexual abuse because an uncle who lived in Terry's home for a short while was incarcerated for molesting his own 10-year-old daughter; such abuse was denied by Terry and his mother, as were any other traumatic events or serious accidents. Additionally, we investigated suspected physical abuse by the father, as already noted. Thus, we are presented with a child from a middle-class family, with good to excellent educational achievement prior to the MVA, excellent verbal skills (important to our gathering of information and his understanding of the procedures that we eventually used), and a problem-oriented coping style (he was much more interested in what he could do, versus focusing on how he felt).

Very little is known about the relation between aspects of ethnicity and culture and the response to trauma, especially in the case of accidents (Rabalais et al., in press). Thus, it was tempting to consider how the family's religiosity and African American ethnic tradition might contribute as either risk or protective factors in this case. The father's stern manner and expectations of the children could not be attributed specifically to either ethnic background or cultural factors, although it was clearly an important contributor to the expression of trauma-related fears in Terry and Keisha. More critical was the mother's religious perspective of rather passively "leaving it up to God" to resolve the current situation, her most active role being that of daily prayer.

UNLEARNED/GENETIC BIOLOGICAL VULNERABILITY

In the paradigmatic model, this component focuses on genetically based inherited characteristics and biological differences that might play a role in the development of a disorder and thus its treatment. In the case of Terry, it became evident that his mother was quite anxious with her own history of anxiety and depression, including PTSD from the accident at the time of initial presentation. One might speculate that Terry's own history of anxious concerns, especially of somatic complaints, and GAD were related to this family history and thus a predisposing factor in his responding to the MVA with diagnosable PTSD and separation anxiety. Whether this was a biological predisposition (e.g., high autonomic arousal and reactivity, "conditionability") or the result of the mother's modeling anxious behavior and the father's being stern and punitive cannot be known for certain. However, incorporating a possible biological/genetic predisposition into the case conceptualization served to keep us aware that anxiolytic medication might be a useful adjunct to our behavioral intervention, especially if that intervention proved less than fully successful.

A related component of the paradigmatic model is that of *acquired/learned* biological vulnerabilities, such as changes in neurotransmitter and hormonal levels and increased baseline autonomic arousal, particularly in response to extensive physical or brain injury, long-term exposure to trauma, or an extended period between trauma and treatment. This component was considered in the functional analysis; however, due to the very minor physical injuries, lack of evidence of brain trauma, and the short time since the accident, it was seen as not presently relevant in Terry's case.

THE ACCIDENT: TRAUMA LEARNING AND CHARACTERISTICS

This component captures the features of the MVA, the degree of exposure, and the individual's role in it (e.g., active versus passive), features that are included in the overall rating of severity on the AcCIdentS. This MVA might be considered sudden, although somewhat predictable under the circumstances (i.e., being tailgated on a wet, winding road). Although the car was totaled and Mrs. Washington at first appeared severely injured, all three of the passengers quickly recovered from their injuries. However, the children felt quite helpless in the minutes after the accident when they could do nothing to assist their mother. Mr. Washington blamed his wife for the accident (although he could not know the details, as he was not present), adding to her own feelings of responsibility. In a way, Terry also held her responsible; he never said this directly, but his actions and statements when she drove clearly revealed his concern over her driving leading to further accidents.

A critical aspect in this component of the model is those stimuli that have come to be associated with the MVA. In this case, rain, wet roads, sharp turns or sudden movements of the vehicle, squealing brakes, loud noises, and his mother driving were all considered classically conditioned stimuli that subsequently produced arousal (conditioned response) and active (operant) avoidance in Terry.

PRESENT SITUATIONAL FACTORS

Critical elements of this component of the model include presence of MVA-related stimuli and situational factors, including behavioral contingencies and social and family support. As noted, Terry was quite aroused, even fearful, in the presence of accident-related stimuli. It is noteworthy that his arousal and active avoidance were differentially displayed in the presence of his father (with or without his mother) versus when alone with his mother. Terry essentially "suffered in silence" when in a car with his father. One might ask why rides with his father did not then extinguish his conditioned fear response and avoidance behavior. We surmise that continuing discomfort, even fear, in the presence of his father was sufficient to maintain arousal and thus prevent extinction. Additionally, trips with the father were much less frequent than with the mother, and nearly all trips since the accident had been brief. On the positive side of the equation, Terry felt that he had excellent social and familial support, despite the evident strain related to his father's stern behavior, and school (including extracurricular activities) was typically not seen as stressful for him. Thus, the present situational stressors in Terry's life were highly focused around the accident itself.

PSYCHOLOGICAL VULNERABILITY

This component of the model considers the person's deficient and inappropriate behavioral repertoires (i.e., emotional-motivational, language-cognitive, sensory-motor). In the emotional-motivational domain, we include Terry's physiological arousal in the presence of accident-related stimuli and his hypervigilance for accident-related cues. The language-cognitive domain includes his differential response (i.e., selective attention) to accident-related cues (such as seen in his response to the Clinical Stroop Task) and deficits in problem-solving skills, his skill level being that of a typical 9-year-old. Terry did have some features of his mother's view that "God will provide," but he was also more likely to ask what he could actively do about his problems. In the sensory-motor domain, we include his avoidance of riding in vehicles, especially when his mother was driving. Deficits in social skills and social support seeking would also be included here; however, these were not problem or deficit areas for Terry. The key issue in this part of the conceptualization was identifying behavioral patterns and resources/deficits that Terry brought to current situations that would then combine with the other elements of the model, in dynamic fashion, to produce the current symptomatic response, the final component of the model.

PRESENT SYMPTOMATIC RESPONSES

The symptomatic responses (diagnosable as PTSD, in this case) result from the interactions, over time, of the other critical elements in the model: historical learning and biological vulnerabilities that were brought to the moment of the accident, followed by new learning and acquired psychological and biological vulnerabilities that set up the current pattern of symptomatic responses, these in turn being influenced by environmental contingencies (e.g., parental responses, avoidance).

Terry's presenting symptoms fell within the same three response domains noted earlier. First, in the emotional-motivational domain (which overlaps with the avoidant and arousal symptoms of PTSD), we included the symptoms of hyperarousal, irritability, difficulty relaxing, loss of interest in prior activities, and specific accident-related fears. These were all most evident in direct response to the presence of accident-related stimuli, including cars and his mother, the avoidance of which was negatively reinforced by decreased anxiety/arousal and the removal of feared stimuli. We conceptualized the conditioned arousal to accident-related cues as the motivation for his avoidance behavior and for what amounts to escape-related behaviors seen in the car when his mother was driving (i.e., criticizing and warning her repeatedly).

In the language-cognitive domain fall the symptoms of reexperiencing, in the form of intrusive thoughts and feelings that the accident was recurring whenever there were sudden changes in speed or direction. In children, repetitive play (as Terry was doing with toy cars) is seen as a reexperiencing symptom, not unlike that of intrusive thoughts or nightmares. Finally, we include his increasing concentration difficulties, especially apparent at school, in this domain.

Motor restlessness, active avoidance, and his "safety" behaviors in the car fall within the sensory-motor domain, these being posttraumatic symptoms but also being reinforced in several ways. First, behaviors that resulted in his avoiding cars altogether (such as refusing and tantrums) and behaviors that resulted in his mother's driving more cautiously (e.g., "Mom, please keep your hands on the wheel . . . watch out for that truck!") were seen as negatively reinforced by either the removal or reduction of fear-relevant stimuli, thereby decreasing arousal (i.e., emotional-motivational domain). Second, the refusal and criticism behaviors by Terry resulted in attention from his mother by her either cajoling or even "bribing" (such as with candy or toys) him into compliance or by reassuring and soothing statements. Thus, both positive and negative reinforcement were seen as being operative here, with a notable difference in Terry's exhibition of these behaviors when his father was present, a context within which behaviors that the mother reinforced were punished by the father. Finally, we include in this domain the several regressive behaviors that Terry exhibited: the return of enuresis and even his symptoms of separation anxiety. These two symptom patterns co-occurred in his bed-wetting at night, resulting in his being allowed to sleep in his parents' bed for the remainder of the night (which may have positively reinforced bed-wetting, but also resulted in negative reinforcement by a decrease in anxiety/arousal associated with being separated from his parents). Thus, a number of symptoms that may arise from the accident (when viewed as an instance of classical conditioning) have a number of operant components that maintain it (such as by negative reinforcement through escape/avoidance) and even lead to the acquisition of other response functions (such as attention by the mother).

RATIONALE FOR TREATMENT CHOICE

We should note that there is only a very small literature on the treatment of children who have been exposed to traumatic events, the largest share of that literature being focused on children who have been sexually abused (Ruggiero, Morris, & Scotti, 2001). In our review of the PTSD treatment-outcome literature that focuses on children (Ruggiero et al.), we have found only a small number of methodologically rigorous, open trial studies, each offering empirical support for the effectiveness of cognitive-behavioral interventions, including exposure-based procedures (in vivo and imaginal procedures, such as systematic desensitization and graduated exposure) and anxiety-management strategies (e.g., relaxation exercises, role play, and education/information). We also found that nonbehavioral forms of intervention with traumatized children have not been adequately evaluated in methodologically rigorous research studies. Still, the literature does contain a number of single-case reports of successful treatment with child MVA survivors. As reviewed in Scotti et al. (in press), these studies include play therapy as a form of age-appropriate exposure, distraction and redirection techniques, guided imagery and relaxation, in-vivo exposure, and Eye Movement Desensitization and Reprocessing (EMDR). Thus, the literature holds some clues for promising directions for the treatment of child MVA survivors.

Given the above information and the case conceptualization outlined here, it is clear that the first line of attack with this case is most appropriately a combination of anxiety-management, exposure-based procedures, and contingency management procedures. The first set of strategies is important to provide Mrs. Washington and Terry some background information on their situation, that is, to normalize Terry's response to a traumatic incident and to teach him skills that will help him manage anxiety in related situations. The second set of strategies, use of exposure-based procedures, follows from the conceptualization of PTSD as the result of classically conditioned fear to trauma-relevant stimuli and operant avoidance behaviors: the classic two-factor learning model (Mowrer, 1960; see also Lyons & Scotti, 1995). Finally, as other variables had begun to control Terry's behaviors both at home and when riding in cars, some contingency management procedures, to be implemented by Mrs. Washington, were called for.

COURSE OF TREATMENT

TREATMENT SETTING

The treatment of this case occurred at the Quin Curtis Center for Psychological Research, Training, and Service (QCC), which is the training clinic associated with the professional master's and doctoral programs in clinical psychology at West Virginia University. Thus, this case was treated in a somewhat unique situation, different from the typical private practice or community mental health center setting. As noted earlier, the case first came to our attention when the family participated in a grant-funded research project concerning the effects of MVAs on children. During the course of that research protocol, Mrs. Washington asked if there was anything we could do to assist her and her son. We provided a variety of treatment options in the community, including the QCC; when she contacted the Clinic one week later, we agreed to provide treatment. A unique aspect of the QCC is that there are several "vertical teams," each with a focus on a different speciality area (as determined by the faculty coordinator) and with graduate student therapists at varying levels of training. In this case, the PTSD Clinical Team was directed by the first author, and the graduate student therapists included the third and fourth authors. Thus, the family essentially was seen by three therapists, each with different roles and responsibilities in the case. In addition, we had the benefit of extensive assessment results from the family's earlier participation in the research protocol (see Behavioral Assessment).

INITIAL INTAKE

After gathering the usual intake information with regard to names, addresses, insurance provider, and treatment consent forms, the intake process was considerably shorter than usual as we were already familiar with the family and had a substantial amount of information from the research protocol. Thus, in the initial sessions, we were able to focus on determining whether Keisha was in need of treatment and the behavioral contingencies operating with regard to Terry's behavior and the parental response, detailed earlier. Thus, we were able to rather quickly move into the formal intervention phase, which consisted of nine hour-long sessions over a three-month period.

ANXIETY MANAGEMENT

An important first step in this treatment was education: providing Terry and Mrs. Washington with basic information about trauma and the range of effects that can be expected. We stressed that PTSD can be considered "a normal response to an abnormal situation." By this we meant to show the family that when potentially traumatic events, such as their MVA, occur, the response is fairly predictable. We discussed with the family aspects of their accident that made it traumatic *for them*, stressing that such an appraisal can often be idiosyncratic and specific to the person and event. Factors that we (therapists, Terry, and Mrs. Washington) concluded were important in this case included the mother having been trapped in the car and thus unable to comfort her children, the children's reaction to the mother's apparently severe facial injuries, the delay in receiving assistance, and the father's less than supportive behavior in response to the accident. We discussed how these aspects of the accident led to feelings of fear and helplessness in the face of actual minor injuries and perceived/threatened serious injury, two critical features defining a traumatic event in the *DSM-IV* (APA, 1994). Given these event characteristics, we then showed Terry and Mrs. Washington how both of their behavioral responses were part of the expected cluster of symptoms that follow such an event. We further normalized their situation by providing statistics on exposure to trauma in general, rates of MVAs, and the percentage of people who can be expected to have some difficulty after a traumatic event. Finally, as it is a frequent misunderstanding by clients (and all too often by clinicians), we corrected the family's misperception that PTSD only follows exposure to combat—particularly among Vietnam veterans—or sexual assault.

We then indicated that there was much that could be done about their situation. To begin, we focused on skills that could be taught to Terry concerning how to relax himself when feeling anxious and how to distract himself when riding in cars. This approach fit well with Terry's interest in "taking action," but met with some initial resistance in the face of the mother's view that prayer and faith would resolve the situation. Thus, we gently challenged her view by first asking what expectations she had about treatment and why she had sought it, and suggesting the complementary view to her position that "God helps those who help themselves" and that, perhaps, her prayerful consideration had led her to seek an active treatment for herself and her son. This was a comfortable interpretation for her and seemed to lead to her full investment in our intervention protocol.

Terry was then taught deep breathing relaxation. We felt that this would be simpler for him to learn than progressive muscle relaxation (which we were prepared to offer if needed) and rather more portable; that is, he could easily use it immediately in those situations in which he was becoming anxious, our primary focus being travel in cars. To have Terry rate his level of anxiety, arousal, or discomfort, we used a 4-point "Worry Scale" consisting of four line drawings of a boy who, on one end of the scale, appears calm and relaxed (a rating of 1) and on the other end appears very upset and nervous (with worry lines on his face, tension in his muscles, and churning in his stomach; a rating of 4). Terry practiced the deep breathing in session until he was doing it in a manner that was comfortable for him and was associated with decreased ratings on the Worry Scale. He was then asked to practice this further at home, and to use it when riding in cars. Mrs. Washington was given a number of copies of the Worry Scale and was asked to have Terry complete these after riding in a car, indicating the highest level of worry or discomfort that he felt during that trip.

In addition to deep breathing, we wanted Terry to use some distraction techniques, the easiest of which was to simply keep himself busy with favorite activities while riding in a car. Terry volunteered that he liked to draw and color and play with his handheld computer game. He also volunteered that he really liked the superhero action figure that he had found in the clinic's toy box, and that if he had that with him, he would not only be able to distract himself but would feel "safer and stronger." We allowed him to borrow the action figure and used it in subsequent sessions to compare his behavior while riding in cars to that of a fearless superhero.

EXPOSURE

With Terry's newfound relaxation and distraction skills in hand, we began planned *graduated exposure* sessions. First, while in session, this involved Terry drawing pictures of cars and accidents or reenacting accidents with toy cars. We made these age-appropriate imaginal exposure activities fun and playful, used the occasion to model and practice deep breathing relaxation, and asked him to rate his level of worry, which quickly dropped in one session from a rating of 3 to a 1. Terry was then asked to rate his level of worry in response to approaching the family car (rating of 2), getting in the car (rating of 2), starting the engine (rating of 3), and driving away (rating of 4). As a homework assignment, Mrs. Washington was asked to have Terry sit in the family car several times during the coming week, without starting the car or driving away. Terry was to use his relaxation and distraction techniques and remain in the car until his worry rating dropped to a 1. The same procedure was subsequently followed with both Mrs. Washington and Terry sitting in the car with the motor running, but not driving away. Finally, short trips were taken until Terry could use relaxation and distraction to reduce his ratings to a 1. Within four weeks of such assignments, Terry was reliably able to ride in a car with his mother driving and not exceed a rating of 2 during any part of the trip. As a side benefit, he reported that he had begun using relaxation and distraction whenever he felt anxious, including at night when he had difficulty sleeping or at school, such as during a test. We attribute his no longer meeting diagnostic criteria for GAD at the follow-up assessment in part to his unplanned use of these new skills.

CONTINGENCY MANAGEMENT

Although Terry quickly learned and successfully used (and generalized) the relaxation and distraction skills, other contingencies were additionally operating on his "safety" behaviors in the car, as well as on his nighttime behavior of enuresis and coming into the parental bed. Thus, we developed some basic strategies for Mrs. Washington to implement, also informing Terry what these would be.

We determined that Terry may have initially been critical of his mother's driving and frequently asked her to be careful and watch out for perceived dangers as a result of his arousal to accident-related stimuli and his fear that another accident would occur. Mrs. Washington complied with these safety requests, providing a source of negative reinforcement (through decreased arousal) for Terry. However, these safety behaviors by Terry also resulted in a great deal of attention from his mother, including both calming and reassuring statements and requests for him to be quiet. We saw these interactions as positively reinforcing his safety behavior by providing maternal attention that he was not otherwise getting during car rides. Thus, intervention was a matter of acknowledging the positive reinforcement function of these safety behaviors and switching the contingencies such that these behaviors would be ignored and calm talk about any topic unrelated to cars, driving, and accidents received attention in the form of continued conversation with his mother. In theory, this was a simple reversal of contingencies for functionally equivalent behaviors; in practice, it was initially a difficult task for Mrs. Washington to undertake, as she felt she was ignoring her son's distress. By pointing out the logic of the intervention and showing her how Terry's worry ratings actually showed he was not in as much distress as his behavior in the car would seem to indicate, she was able to follow through on this procedure. With consistent ignoring of Terry's safety behaviors, attention for other conversation, and praise for his acting calm, his safety behaviors diminished to zero within several weeks.

Finally, we were left with Terry's return to enuresis, his difficulty sleeping at night (the most prominent symptom of GAD, which existed preaccident), and his coming into the parents' bed (the behavior of most concern to the father). Terry had already initiated, on his own, using relaxation and distraction to assist him with falling asleep at night. We felt that the enuresis could be viewed as a regressive behavior that would very likely cease as his fear of riding in cars diminished. Still, it was sufficiently problematic for the parents and embarrassing for Terry that it called for more immediate action. Thus, we had Mrs. Washington and Terry implement a simple correction procedure when Terry wet the bed: He was to take the wet sheets off the bed, put them in the laundry, and remake his bed. He was then to return to his own bed and, if needed, use relaxation to help him return to sleep. The correction procedure can be viewed as a mild but logically consistent punishment for bed-wetting. His parents were not to assist in this correction procedure, nor were they to allow him to come into their bed, thus removing a potential source of attention (positive reinforcement) for these behaviors. Finally, as nighttime was associated with more worries about separation, which Terry in part responded to by coming into the parents' bed, this procedure also helped Terry relax, distract himself from thoughts about separation from his parents, and extinguish these fears. As a last component, Mrs. Washington praised successful nights (no enuresis or coming into the parental bed), and Terry provided us with a report of his success at our sessions. These combined procedures were associated with a decline in both behaviors within three weeks.

THERAPIST-CLIENT FACTORS

A solid understanding by the therapist of typical child development is necessary both to understand the difference between "developmental lags" and "treatable symptoms" (as in the case of Terry's renewed enuresis) and to provide a positive therapeutic environment. Although Terry was quite a bright and verbal youngster, it is typically important not to err by talking too far above or below the child's level of comprehension. Many novice therapists make the mistake of engaging in detailed cognitive explanations and lengthy discussion with young children. A more directive and behavioral approach tends to be more productive with children, that is, placing an emphasis on "doing" rather than "talking," as worked so well here with Terry. Therapy sessions with children often involve forms of play, useful not only to establish rapport and maintain the child's interest, but also to assist in modeling appropriate behavioral strategies, as when we engaged Terry in drawing and play with cars while practicing deep breathing relaxation, or in the use of the action figure. Establishment of trust was not difficult in this case, especially after providing information that normalized the family's experience, but it can be particularly problematic with children who have experienced certain traumatic events, such as intrafamilial sexual abuse or more gruesome traumatic accidents. In such cases, one should first take time to get to know the child, spending time—perhaps even multiple sessions—talking about the child's life and interests apart from discussion of the trauma.

Treatment success with children also depends greatly on the degree of parental involvement. Therapists will do well to take time to explain to parents the rationale behind and procedural implementation of selected therapeutic strategies, including potential pitfalls and "side effects" (e.g., initial increases in tantrum behavior or distress). Much of the work we do to assist children takes place in the context of explaining the child's symptoms to the parents and assisting the parents in changing their own behavior to promote positive change for the child, as was the case with Mrs. Washington. This raises the issue of exactly who is the "client." Very rarely would we endorse working solely with a child client. The child lives within a system, and that system must be considered in treatment. Therapists do not have sufficient control of antecedents and consequences affecting the child outside the clinic setting. Adults (primarily parents, but often teachers as well) will be called on to monitor and consequate behavior and assist in carrying out homework assignments. Without full parental participation, treatment success will be limited. In our case example, Terry's mother was a cooperative and active participant in treatment. Without her support, Terry may have gone on to experience chronic symptoms of PTSD and restricted social functioning. Ideally, his father would have participated as well, which would have enabled the therapists to address issues of family functioning that went beyond the presenting problem (e.g., marital conflict, the father's stern parenting style). Therapists also must give consideration to cultural issues that may impact treatment. In our case example, the family held strong religious views. The therapists worked within that framework (guiding the client toward the axiom that "God helps those who help themselves"), rather than ignoring or rejecting the client's perspective on the role God played in the accident and subsequent emotional responding.

Finally, it is essential that therapists receive proper training in exposure-based strategies in order that these procedures are implemented properly and that the therapist projects confidence in the procedures, their theoretical basis, and their empirical support. Novice therapists often experience discomfort when conducting exposure trials, even the graduated exposure used here. This is particularly the case when clients have experienced horrific events and the stimuli presented during exposure (whether graduated, systematic desensitization, flooding, or implosion) are necessarily graphic, such as in the case of an MVA involving decapitation (Lyons & Scotti, 1995). Due in part to concerns about client and therapist discomfort, graduated forms of exposure have come to be used more often with children than has traditional implosive therapy.

COURSE OF TERMINATION

The time course of our treatment sessions led to a natural fading out and termination of treatment. The first five sessions were conducted on a weekly basis, the next four were two weeks apart. The final treatment contact was via phone some four weeks after the last face-to-face visit. We intentionally began to space out the treatment sessions after the initial skill training and development of contingency management procedures, as at that point, the active component of the intervention was the work that Terry and Mrs. Washington were doing at home on their own. Several phone calls were needed between some of the sessions to confer about success with the procedures and to problem solve on issues that arose; but the problems were minor and the success was steady.

By the final session, all identified problems were remediated, Terry was feeling quite proud of himself (being most proud of having stopped wetting the bed), and Mrs. Washington was pleased with the outcome. We encouraged them to keep the procedures in effect as needed, and for Terry to continue using his relaxation and distraction skills in any situations in which he felt anxious. We concluded by presenting Terry with a certificate of achievement and allowing him to keep the superhero action figure he had borrowed from the clinic.

FOLLOW-UP

Our initial assessment was conducted three months after the MVA, and therapy continued for a three-month period. Three months after the completion of treatment (now nine months post-MVA), we were able to bring Terry and his mother back for a repeat of the full assessment battery, including the laboratory research components.

Mrs. Washington's scores on the SCL-90-R (completed about herself) were all within normal limits, except for a T-score of 70 on the Obsessive-Compulsive Scale. Recall that she completed her own course of therapy for mild PTSD, the symptoms of which were also diminished (CAPS interview and other relevant psychometrics).

Mrs. Washington's completion of the CBCL about Terry showed all subscales and total scores to be within normal limits (below a T-score of 60), except for Somatic Complaints (which remained at 70). This was consistent with Terry's own report on the RCMAS, which was within normal limits except for Physiological Anxiety. Terry's score on the CDI continued to be within normal limits, although the score was half of what it had been at the initial assessment. Additionally, his score on the IES was now at zero, indicating no trauma-related avoidant or intrusive symptoms, consistent with the reports of both mother and son (on a retest with the AcCIdentS) that Terry no longer had any fear of riding in cars, regardless of who was driving. Finally, evaluation with the ADIS revealed consistent reports by mother and son that Terry no longer met criteria for PTSD, nor for separation anxiety, GAD, or enuresis. Terry also continued to report a high level of social support.

We also were able to repeat the psychophysiological assessment and the Clinical Stroop Task with Terry. On the Clinical Stroop, all of the neutral and school- and MVA-related word cards were completed within eight seconds of each other, with a faster time on the MVA words than one of the neutral cards and the school-related words. Notably, there were no errors on the MVA-related words. Neither format of vignette presentation (audiotaped vignettes to which self-report ratings were given, and extended vignettes during which heart rate and skin conductance were measured) showed any differential response to the MVA scenes. Terry's responses were now more similar to the nondistressed MVA and non-MVA groups in this research protocol than to the distressed MVA group.

Thus, at follow-up, all measures consistently indicated a lack of distress both generally and specifically related to the MVA. Of note, Terry and his mother reported on a trip they had taken to visit relatives who lived a two-day drive away. Terry noted that he was so bored (and unconcerned) on this trip that he slept for much of it, and his mother noted that he did not express any concern (his "safety" behaviors) at all during the trip.

MANAGED CARE CONSIDERATIONS

In our case example, the family was seen for nine sessions over a three-month period. This level of service generally would be covered by most insurance providers. However, the extensive assessment protocol, especially the psychophysiological assessment, conducted here generally would *not* have been covered in full, nor would it likely have been done outside of a research setting. When conducting traditional implosive therapy, in which sessions may span two or three hours in length, or in situations when massed sessions (e.g., daily for 10 days) are expected to have more success than standard 50-minute sessions held once per week, it becomes necessary to seek preauthorization for services. This may require providing substantial documentation to the insurance provider regarding empirical support for the selected treatment strategy (and information related to relative cost benefit). Another reason for the apparent preference of graduated exposure strategies with children versus traditional implosive therapy is that graduated exposure tends to conform more readily to the traditional 50-minute therapy session for billing purposes. Often, treatment plans call for therapist-accompanied in vivo (and off-site) exposure assignments. One must review the provider policy to determine whether sessions conducted outside of the clinic actually qualify for reimbursement.

Apart from billing concerns for treatment conducted off clinic premises, one must consider issues of liability for the client's safety. We advise against transporting a client in the therapist's vehicle. In the case of exposure to MVA-related cues, parents can be provided proper instruction on how to carry out homework assignments, as was the case with Terry and his mother.

We had the luxury of working with this family in a university-based clinic, allowing multiple therapists to assist in carrying out the treatment plan. Such availability of "free" personnel may be useful in setting up certain exposure trials and conducting role plays, but insurance providers generally do not cover costs for multiple therapists. On the flip side, training clinics do come with their own set of billing constraints. Many insurance providers require that the licensed faculty supervisor be present in order to bill for the session.

OVERALL EFFECTIVENESS

Overall, this package of interventions focused on Terry's symptoms of PTSD, but also incorporated into the conceptualization his other anxiety symptoms and enuresis. The package, which included anxiety management strategies, exposure-based procedures, and contingency management, was quite effective in reducing those symptoms, as well as having the unintended effect of reducing his symptoms of GAD, a problem that preceded the MVA. Although this represents a case study, we have successfully used a similar intervention package with other children who have experienced MVAs, as well as with a child who had a severe peanut allergy and significant related fears (Masia, Mullen, & Scotti, 1999). Additionally, the package is based directly on our clinical functional analysis of this case and is supported by empirical research on children exposed to traumatic events (see Ruggiero et al., 2001). Furthermore, the speed of the intervention and long-lasting effects obviated the need to seek further medical consultation for a possible medication trial. Finally, we were able to document with multiple measures (self-report, interview, physiological assessment) a pattern of behavior fitting PTSD and Terry's related anxiety disorders and the return to nonclinical levels of all of his symptoms.

REFERENCES

Achenbach, T. M. (1991). *Manual for the Child Behavior Checklist/4–18.* Burlington: University of Vermont, Department of Psychiatry.

American Psychiatric Association. (1994). *Diagnostic and statistical manual of mental disorders* (4th ed.). Washington, DC: Author.

Bahrick, L. E., Parker, J. F., Fivush, R., & Levitt, M. (1998). The effects of stress on young children's memory for a natural disaster. *Journal of Experimental Psychology: Applied, 4,* 308–331.

Blake, D. D., Weathers, F. W., Nagy, L., Kaloupek, D. G., Klauminzer, G., Charney, D. S., et al. (1990). A clinician rating scale for assessing current and lifetime PTSD: The CAPS-1. *The Behavior Therapist, 18,* 187–188.

Chambless, D. L., Baker, M. J., Baucom, D. H., Beutler, L. E., Calhoun, K. S., Crits-Christoph, P., et al. (1998). Update on empirically validated therapies, II. *The Clinical Psychologist, 51*(1), 3–16.

Davidoff, D. A., Laibstain, D. F., Kessler, H. R., & Mark, V. H. (1988). Neurobehavioral sequelae of minor head injury: A consideration of post-concussive syndrome versus post-traumatic stress disorder. *Cognitive Rehabilitation, 6,* 8–13.

Derogatis, L. R. (1983). *SCL-90-R: Administration, scoring, and procedures manual-II.* Towson, MD: Clinical Psychometric Research.

Eifert, G. H., Beach, B. K., & Wilson, P. H. (1998). Depression: Behavioral principles and implications for treatment and relapse prevention. In J. J. Plaud & G. H. Eifert (Eds.), *From behavior theory to behavior therapy* (pp. 68–97). Boston: Allyn & Bacon.

Eifert, G. H., & Evans, I. M. (Eds.). (1990). *Unifying behavior therapy: Contributions of paradigmatic behaviorism.* New York: Springer.

Harter, S. (1985). *Manual for the Social Support Scale for Children.* University of Denver.

Horowitz, M. J., Wilner, N., & Alvarez, W. (1979). Impact of Event Scale: A measure of subjective distress. *Psychosomatic Medicine, 41,* 209–218.

Horton, A. M., Jr. (1993). Posttraumatic stress disorder and mild head trauma: Follow-up of a case study. *Perceptual and Motor Skills, 76,* 243–246.

Jacobson, R. (1999). Road traffic accidents and the mind: The post-concussional syndrome. In E. J. Hickling & E. B. Blanchard (Eds.), *Road traffic accidents and psychological trauma: Current understanding, treatment, and law* (pp. 89–116). Oxford, England: Elsevier.

Kovacs, M. (1985). The Children's Depression Inventory (CDI). *Psychopharmacological Bulletin, 21,* 995–998.

Lyons, J. A., & Scotti, J. R. (1995). Behavioral treatment of a motor vehicle accident survivor: An illustrative case of direct therapeutic exposure. *Cognitive and Behavioral Practice, 2,* 343–364.

Masia, C. L., Mullen, K. B., & Scotti, J. R. (1999). Peanut allergy in children: Psychological issues and clinical considerations. *Education and Treatment of Children, 21,* 514–531.

Mowrer, O. H. (1960). *Learning theory and behavior.* New York: Wiley.

Mullen James, K. (1999). *Measuring behavioral disruption in children who have been in motor vehicle accidents.* Unpublished doctoral dissertation, West Virginia University, Department of Psychology, Morgantown.

Perrin, S., Smith, P., & Yule, W. (2000). Practitioner review: The assessment and treatment of post-traumatic stress disorder in children and adolescents. *Journal of Child Psychology and Psychiatry and Allied Disciplines, 41,* 277–289.

Rabalais, A., Ruggiero, K., & Scotti, J. R. (in press). Multicultural issues in the response of children to disasters. In A. M. La Greca & W. K. Silverman (Eds.), *Helping children cope with disasters and terrorism*. Washington, DC: American Psychological Association.

Reynolds, C. R. (1980). Concurrent validity of What I Think and Feel: The Revised Children's Manifest Anxiety Scale. *Journal of Consulting and Clinical Psychology, 48,* 774–775.

Ruggiero, K. J., Morris, T. L., & Scotti, J. R. (2001). Treatment for childhood posttraumatic stress disorder: Current status and future directions. *Clinical Psychology: Science and Practice, 8,* 210–227.

Saigh, P. A., Yasik, A. E., Sack, W. H., & Koplewicz, H. S. (1999). Child-adolescent posttraumatic stress disorder: Prevalence, risk factors, and comorbidity. In P. A. Saigh & J. D. Bremner (Eds.), *Posttraumatic stress disorder: A comprehensive text* (pp. 18–43). Needham Heights, MA: Allyn & Bacon.

Satz, P., Zaucha, K., Asarnow, R., McCleary, C., Light, R., & Becker, D. (1997). Mild head injury in children and adolescents: A review of studies (1970–1995). *Psychological Bulletin, 122,* 107–131.

Scotti, J. R. (1992). An analysis of several parameters of conditioned fear in combat-related post-traumatic stress disorder: Serial cues, contexts, conditioning trials, and avoidance behaviors (Doctoral dissertation, State University of New York at Binghamton, 1992). *Dissertation Abstracts International, 53*(2), 1076B-1077B. (UMI No. DA 92–17704)

Scotti, J. R., Beach, B. K., Northrop, L. M. E., Rode, C. A., & Forsyth, J. P. (in press). The psychological impact of accidental injury: A conceptual model for clinicians and researchers. In I. Z. Schultz, D. O. Brady, & S. Carella (Eds.), *The handbook of psychological injuries*. Chicago: American Bar Association. (Reprinted from *Traumatic stress: From theory to practice*, pp. 181–212, by J. R. Freedy & S. E. Hobfoll, Eds., 1995, New York: Plenum)

Scotti, J. R., & Morris, T. M. (2000). Diagnosis and classification. In M. Hersen & R. T. Ammerman (Eds.), *Advanced abnormal child psychology* (2nd ed., pp. 15–32). Mahwah, NJ: Erlbaum.

Scotti, J. R., Ruggiero, K. J., & Rabalais, A. E. (in press). The traumatic impact of motor vehicle accidents on children. In A. M. La Greca & W. K. Silverman (Eds.), *Helping children cope with disasters and terrorism*. Washington, DC: American Psychological Association.

Scotti, J. R., Wilhelm, K. L., Northrop, L. M. E., Price, G., Vittimberga, G. L., Ridley, J., et al. (1992, November). *An investigation of post-traumatic stress disorder in vehicular accident survivors*. Poster presented at the 26th annual convention of the Association for Advancement of Behavior Therapy, Boston.

Silverman, W. K., & Nelles, W. B. (1988). The Anxiety Disorders Interview Schedule for Children. *Journal of the American Academy of Child and Adolescent Psychiatry, 27,* 772–778.

Staats, A. W. (1993). Personality theory, abnormal psychology, and psychological measurement: A psychological behaviorism. *Behavior Modification, 17,* 8–42.

Stroop, J. R. (1935). Studies of interference in serial verbal reactions. *Journal of Experimental Psychology, 18,* 643–661.

United States Department of Transportation National Highway Traffic Safety Administration. (1996). *Traffic safety facts 1996* [Online]. Available from: www.nhtsa.dot.gov /people/ncsa/TSF96Contents.html

Westrup, D., Kalish, K. D., & Scotti, J. R. (1997, November). *MVA-related PTSD treated with implosion: Use of the paradigmatic model*. Poster presented at the 31st annual convention of the Association for Advancement of Behavior Therapy, Miami Beach, FL.

CHAPTER 20

Conduct Disorder

C. NANNETTE ROACH and ALAN M. GROSS

DESCRIPTION OF THE DISORDER

THE FOURTH EDITION of the *Diagnostic and Statistical Manual of Mental Disorders* (*DSM-IV*; American Psychiatric Association, 1994) describes the essential feature of Conduct Disorder as "a repetitive and persistent pattern of behavior in which the basic rights of others or major age-appropriate societal norms or rules are violated" (p. 85). Behavioral symptoms may fall across four general groups: aggressive behaviors resulting in physical harm or the threat of harm to other people or animals, nonaggressive behaviors resulting in property loss or damage, deceitfulness or theft, and serious rule violations. In the first group, aggressive behaviors may include bullying or intimidating others, initiating physical fights, using a weapon with the potential for harm, physical cruelty to people or animals, forced sexual activity, or theft with physical confrontation. In the second group, nonaggressive disruptive behaviors may encompass deliberate fire setting with intention of damage and vandalism via defacing or destroying another's property. The third group of deceitfulness or theft often may include lying to avoid responsibilities or to obtain some goal, minor theft without physical confrontation, or breaking into a building or automobile. Finally, serious rule violations commonly reflect truancy from school, running away from home, or defying household regulations such as staying out at night. The *DSM-IV* requires that three or more of these behaviors have been apparent within the prior year and that at least one behavior has been displayed within the past six months. Characteristic behaviors associated with Conduct Disorder are usually displayed in multiple settings; as such, it is generally possible to demonstrate significant functional impairment in social, academic, and/or occupational functioning. The typical developmental progression is represented by oppositional and defiant behaviors in the early years followed by a gradual increase in the number and severity of problem behaviors throughout adolescence (Loeber, Green, Lahey, Christ, & Frick, 1992). Individuals older than 18 years are not diagnosed with Conduct Disorder unless they clearly do not meet criteria for Antisocial Personality Disorder.

Gender statistics reflect a ratio of 3 to 5 males per female diagnosed, a ratio that decreases with age.

Two subtypes of Conduct Disorder are provided in the *DSM-IV*, distinguished by age of onset. Childhood-Onset type is categorized by evidence of one characteristic behavior displayed prior to 10 years of age. Adolescent-Onset type is categorized by the absence of characteristic conduct-disordered behaviors prior to the age of 10 years. A substantial body of research exists indicating significant differences between these two subtypes in terms of number and severity of behaviors exhibited, developmental course, and prognosis. For example, childhood-onset conduct problems have been associated with higher levels of aggression and neuropsychological deficits in comparison to patterns of conduct problems that do not appear until adolescence (Frick, 1998; Moffitt, 1993b). These longitudinal studies indicate that individuals with adolescent-onset Conduct Disorder may demonstrate a better prognosis for antisocial behavior in adulthood. The *DSM-IV* further delineates subtypes of Conduct Disorder with three severity specifiers. The "mild" specifier is used to describe a small number of characteristic behaviors, resulting in relatively minimal harm to others. The "severe" specifier designates a high number of characteristic behaviors that may result in considerable harm to others. The specifier "moderate" is used to represent an intermediate classification.

Despite common symptoms, the Conduct Disorder diagnosis represents a heterogeneous group in terms of problem behaviors exhibited, contributing factors involved, developmental progression of problem behaviors, and individual response to treatment. Multiple factors across several contexts interact to affect the development and maintenance of conduct problems. Several psychosocial correlates of Conduct Disorder have been examined. Farrington (1991) demonstrated higher prevalence rates of Conduct Disorder among economically disadvantaged families. These findings are consistent with the results of the Great Smoky Mountains Study of Youth, which showed poverty as the strongest demographic correlate of Conduct Disorder, among other psychiatric diagnoses, in populations of both urban and rural children (Costello et al., 1996). Inconsistent and coercive parenting practices have been linked to the development of Conduct Disorder (Patterson, Reid, & Dishion, 1992). Loeber and Stouthamer-Loeber's (1986) meta-analytic review reported parental involvement, supervision, and monitoring as strong, consistent correlates of Conduct Disorder. Not surprisingly, child abuse has been demonstrated as a reliable risk factor for Conduct Disorder (Finkelhor & Berliner, 1995). In addition, children with Conduct Disorder tend to have lower measured levels of intelligence, poor academic achievement, higher incidence of learning disabilities, greater peer rejection, and demonstrated deficits in social cognition and information processing (Kazdin, 1995; Loeber & Keenan, 1994; Moffitt, 1993a).

Individuals with Conduct Disorder are highly likely to meet criteria for other comorbid conditions. Concurrent disorders to be ruled out include mood disorders, anxiety disorders, Attentional Deficit Disorder, Adjustment Disorder, drug and alcohol abuse/dependence, and Posttraumatic Stress Disorder. For example, estimates of comorbid Attention-Deficit/Hyperactivity Disorder have been as high as 90%, with presence of ADHD being associated with a greater severity of aggression, more persistent problem behaviors, and higher levels of peer rejection (Abikoff & Klein, 1992). By contrast, estimates of comorbid anxiety disorders have ranged from 60% to 75%, with anxiety correlated with lower levels of problem severity, fewer police contacts, fewer school suspensions, and lower levels of aggression in comparison with other Conduct Disorder peers (Russo & Beidel, 1994; Walker et al., 1991). Finally, co-occurrence of depression has not been associated with a differing course for Conduct Disorder but has signaled an increased suicidal risk (Capaldi, 1992).

CASE DESCRIPTION

Dewey J., a 9-year-old, Caucasian male, presented to a university outpatient psychology setting accompanied by his biological mother, Sandra J. Sandra and Dewey were referred to the outpatient clinic subsequent to school-based recommendations. Sandra requested evaluation and treatment for Dewey's disruptive behaviors, particularly incidents of fighting and minor shoplifting.

The following history was provided during an initial intake with Sandra and Dewey. Dewey presently resides with his mother (Sandra), sister (Aymee), and maternal grandmother (Gladys M.). Dewey's parents, Sandra and Arnold J., divorced after five years of marriage. Dewey was 4 years old at the time of the divorce; Aymee was 6 months of age. Sandra described the marriage as turbulent, citing instances of verbal and physical abuse on the part of Dewey's father. She added that conflicts frequently arose following her husband's episodes of drinking. Dewey was commonly a witness to these altercations. After the divorce orders were filed, Arnold left the area and has not had subsequent contact with Sandra or Dewey. Due to financial difficulties, Sandra and the children then moved in with the maternal grandmother. Sandra presently works the night shift for a paper plant in an adjacent town and is the sole provider for the family. Family income averages $18,000 annually, supplemented by Gladys's disability checks. The family lives in a well-maintained, low-income housing complex; the neighborhood was described as having a low crime rate. Dewey has his own room, and Aymee presently shares a bedroom with Sandra.

Dewey was born on September 14, following a normal delivery. Sandra did not report any prenatal or perinatal complications. In infancy, he met the developmental milestones for motor skills in a timely fashion. For example, he sat alone at the age of 6 months and began walking at the age of 14 months. However, Sandra described Dewey's verbal skill development as slightly delayed. He began using recognizable words at the age of 12 months, but experienced difficulty constructing meaningful phrases. Sandra reported that Dewey was fully toilet-trained by the age of 3 years, with a few "accidents" in subsequent years. His health during infancy and childhood was reported as "good," marred only by the occasional cold or flu. He has no known allergies. There was no demonstrated history of serious medical injuries or conditions, such as neurological trauma. However, Sandra stated that Dewey commonly comes home with scrapes or bruises, incurred while riding on his bike or climbing in trees. Family medical history revealed a moderate incidence of cancer, heart disease, and high blood pressure. Family history was reportedly negative for attentional disorders, disorders of mood or anxiety, and thought disorders. With the exception of Arnold, there is no known history of substance abuse in either maternal or paternal families.

At the age of 4 years, Dewey began attending a local Head Start Program. He continued attending Head Start until his enrollment in the county elementary school. In elementary school, teachers frequently reported that he experienced academic difficulties. Nonetheless, these difficulties were not sufficiently severe to warrant enrollment in the assisted education programs. He repeated kindergarten, but was evaluated as having successfully completed first and second grade. He continues to attend the same elementary school, where he is currently in the third grade. Dewey's grades presently are within the low-average range (including Cs), with English/language arts consistently representing his weakest area of achievement. He has been spending an average of one hour nightly on homework assignments. Sandra noted that his motivation and tolerance for frustration have declined as his academic struggles have increased. Dewey stated that he often dislikes school and that other children tease him for his reading difficulties. He said his favorite subject is mathematics. In his afterschool hours, he enjoys riding his bicycle and playing basketball, usually unaccompanied by peers. On the weekends, he participates in church activities with his family.

Sandra was self-reported as the sole disciplinarian for Dewey and stated that she used a combination of corporal punishment and restriction of privileges as forms of discipline throughout early childhood. Prior to the divorce, it was reported that Arnold occasionally spanked Dewey, allegedly following bouts of drinking. On one occasion immediately preceding the marital separation, Sandra reported Arnold to the Department of Human Services for allegedly spanking Dewey with a belt. Following DHS investigation and the separation, no legal charges were filed against Arnold. There is no additional evidence of physical abuse, sexual abuse, or neglect. At present, restriction of privileges is the mode of discipline. Sandra reported that, due to her employment, she is often unable to supervise Dewey during the evening hours and that Gladys has had difficulty managing his increasingly disruptive behavior. Despite his noncompliance and tendency toward fighting, Sandra and Gladys both described Dewey as a "lovable if hardheaded" child. Sandra and Gladys similarly described having a positive family relationship. Dewey reported positive feelings for each member of his family, although he stated that he was "always getting in trouble for no reason."

PRESENTING COMPLAINTS

At present, Sandra disclosed that Dewey has been sent to the principal's office on four occasions during the current school year due to fighting. She stated that Dewey's reports of these incidents are frequently incongruent with reports by school personnel. Incidents of fighting do not appear to occur with any particular individual target; Dewey expressed that he is often provoked by others. On one occasion, he was observed to throw a pencil case at another peer; he stated that he did intend to strike this individual with the object. Sandra suspected that Dewey has likewise been fighting with peers in the neighborhood but has observed that fights with his sister occur with low frequency. In discussion, Dewey acknowledged his behavior of fighting in school and in the neighborhood, while generally blaming other peers for instigation of the conflicts. Both Sandra and Gladys stated that Dewey also lies as to completion of household chores or other assigned tasks such as homework.

Sandra has also been concerned that Dewey is engaging in episodes of minor theft. Without Sandra's knowledge, Dewey admitted to a few successful incidents of shoplifting at a local convenience store, in which he "ripped off" candy and magazines. He reported that at least one incident of shoplifting had occurred within the past two months. At this time, he has not been subject to any legal charges or other action.

Finally, Sandra described Dewey's mood of the past six months as frequently withdrawn and/or irritable. He supported this statement and reported that he feels upset and angry at times when he is picked on at school. Sandra stated that he also becomes distressed when he is being punished. Dewey's average level of activity and patterns of eating and sleeping were described as age-appropriate.

HISTORY

Dewey has a history of disruptive behavior problems at home and at school. Sandra described Dewey as a toddler as "fussy." She reported several oppositional and defiant behaviors beginning in early childhood. As early as the age of 3 years, Dewey's favorite word was "no" and he was often noncompliant with parental instruction. For example, when instructed not to touch a hot plate, he immediately touched the plate and burned his finger. Sandra added that Dewey frequently tantrummed when denied a desired object or activity. According to Sandra, these behaviors were consistent with observations of Head Start personnel. Teachers in the Head Start Program had also reported that Dewey was aggressive with peers, such as an incident of biting a classmate, and noncompliant with staff instruction. When reprimanded at home or school, he would deny responsibility for his behavior. Following Aymee's birth, Sandra described, Dewey was excited and eager to interact with his new sibling. At times, however, he has been observed to engage in destructive behavior when prolonged attention was directed at Aymee. For example, Sandra claimed that if visiting guests were focusing on the baby, Dewey would start throwing the cushions off the sofa or tearing up his magazines.

These behaviors persisted into the elementary school setting. Sandra produced report cards that frequently reflected poor marks for conduct. The report cards indicated that Dewey's pattern of behavioral disruption predated his present level of academic difficulty. He currently has a C average in four of his six subject areas, with Bs in the remaining areas. Teachers wrote that Dewey often disrupted the work of others. They described him as sensitive to slight and easily provoked. For example, he knocked the materials off another student's desk and made verbal threats if he perceived a classmate to be teasing him. Placing Dewey's desk apart from the other students was reported to increase his attempts at class disruption. As noted previously, Dewey's episodes of aggression continued during this period. In response to disruptive behaviors, teachers generally used verbal reprimand, and visits to the principal's office were common punishments for Dewey's aggressive behavior. The teachers at the elementary schools had an average-class size of 30 students and reported great difficulty in devoting one-on-one time to Dewey.

BEHAVIORAL ASSESSMENT

Frick (1998) concisely outlined the goals of assessment as evaluating the type and severity of problem behaviors and other psychological factors, assessing multiple aspects of the child's emotional and behavioral functioning, and obtaining a thorough evaluation of individual vulnerabilities as well as elements of the environment that may be incorporated into treatment. In the assessment of conduct disorders, multiple informants and multiple methods strengthen the reliability and validity of the diagnostic evaluation. Information about the conduct problems should be extracted from the perspective of the individual, the family, the school, and potentially the community. As to the context of Conduct Disorder, information may be located even in medical records, police or court documents, and files of human services programs. The importance of these multiple sources of information is found in the frequent difficulty of determining age of onset for covert forms of conduct problems and the common motivation of the client to conceal any incidence of problem behaviors.

CLINICAL INTERVIEWS AND BEHAVIOR RATING SCALES

Two commonly used, multi-informant approaches include behavior rating scales and structured or semistructured clinical interviews. These methods are generally time- and cost-efficient for the clinician while permitting the assessment of multiple aspects of behavior across varying settings. Both techniques have demonstrated utility in evaluating frequency and severity of behavior as well as potential comorbid conditions.

In the case of Dewey, the parent, teacher, and self-report forms of the Behavior Assessment System for Children were administered (Reynolds & Kamphaus, 1992). In addition, information was obtained via a structured interview, the Diagnostic Interview Schedule for Children. Informants included Dewey, Sandra, and two of Dewey's teachers. Sandra and the teachers consistently reported a high number and frequency of problems across the domains of aggression, conduct, and learning. Specific behaviors included threatening to hurt others, bullying others, hitting other children, lying to get out of trouble, getting in trouble, taking others' things, having to stay after school for punishment, worrying about schoolwork, bothering others during work, and reporting that textbooks are difficult to understand. These problem areas were congruent with Dewey's report. Sandra also endorsed behaviors consistent with depression and withdrawal (e.g., complaining about a lack of friends, saying "Nobody likes me," and being sad or irritable); however, neither Dewey's report nor the teachers' ratings were significantly elevated in these areas. Levels of hyperactivity, attention problems, and anxiety were not clinically elevated across measures. Social and study skills were identified by Sandra and the teachers as below average areas of adaptive functioning.

PSYCHOEDUCATIONAL TESTING

Psychoeducational testing was used to evaluate Dewey's academic difficulties. Results of the Wechsler Intelligence Scale for Children, third edition (*WISC-III;* Wechsler, 1991) indicated that Dewey was functioning in the "average" range of ability (39th percentile). Relative strengths were noted in Dewey's visual-spatial skills, such as part-to-whole relationships and psychomotor speed. Results of the Wechsler Individual Achievement Test (Wechsler, 1992) indicated that the majority of achievement scores were commensurate with overall ability. An exception was noted in the domain of reading (9th percentile), with a significant discrepancy between measured ability and achievement. Particularly, Dewey displayed difficulty with word identification. The co-occurrence of Conduct

Disorder diagnoses and significant ability/achievement discrepancy is not uncommon, with estimated incidence of 20% to 25% (Frick et al., 1991). Results of the Conners' Continuous Performance Test demonstrated no clinically significant deficits in attentional capacity.

DIRECT OBSERVATIONS

Behavioral observations from naturalistic or analog settings allow for the functional assessment of behavior and contextual factors in the environment via a trained, theoretically unbiased observer. Several formal coding systems have been developed for use with direct observation. Patterson and colleagues (1992) constructed the Family Interaction Coding System to examine both individual conduct problems and social interactions among family members; this system was subsequently modified for use in the academic setting. Due to the consumption of time and finances involved in the training and implementation of a formal observation coding system, this method was not used in the home. Structured clinical observations were conducted and recorded during psychoeducational testing and in the course of two sessions at the elementary school.

During the course of the assessment, Dewey displayed average attentional capacities and attempted every required task. He was not distracted easily by visual or auditory stimuli and did not generally require repetition of task instructions. Initially, he appeared unwilling to begin the assigned subtests (stating "I don't want to"), but his interest and motivation were engaged with the prospect of performance reward. He responded positively to verbal praise and small reinforcers (e.g., pencils, stickers) following task performance. For example, he smiled when presented with a sticker and expressed a statement of self-praise: "I did a good job." He exhibited a low tolerance for frustration when attempting tasks of moderate to high levels of difficulty and frequently discontinued these tasks prematurely. Reading activities appeared particularly frustrating for him. At these times, he would generally not continue despite verbal prompt and would attempt to gain access to other objects in the testing area or make disruptive noises (i.e., popping or clicking sounds with mouth). These behaviors were ignored by the examiner, and when the next activity was presented, Dewey would resume on-task behavior. He displayed an age-appropriate level of motor activity, neither fidgeting excessively nor leaving his seat without permission.

Prior to initiation of treatment, observations were conducted in the academic setting on two occasions, for a total of six hours. The classroom environment consisted of a primary teacher, teaching assistant, and 28 classmates. During in-class activities, Dewey was observed as disruptive in five incidents. In three episodes, he distracted peers by tearing the paper on his desk and breaking his pencils. At these times, he was nonresponsive to the teacher's attempts at correction and displayed angry facial gestures when verbally reprimanded. On one of these occasions, he verbally threatened a peer who made fun of him for getting in trouble. In the other two instances, he took an item (pencil, eraser) from another student's desktop. When confronted by the peer or teacher, he initially denied having taken the items and appeared angry after the items were located and returned. Prior to three of these episodes, he was engaged in an assigned reading activity. In addition, he received a high amount of negative attention from both teachers and peers in response to his behavior.

Dewey also was observed during two playground sessions, which consisted of a combination of structured games and free play. Across these observations, he engaged in three incidents of aggression. On one occasion, he was competing with another student to gain access to the swing. He successfully got possession after shoving the peer away from the swing. The peer complained to a teacher and the children were generally instructed to take turns with the swings. Dewey was observed in two episodes of verbal aggression (i.e., threatening another with physical aggression), each a response to the perceived slight of a peer. These three episodes all occurred during free play activities.

PHYSIOLOGICAL

The psychobiology of conduct disorders is presently a wide area of study and includes the examination of genetic effects, neurochemical differences, autonomic nervous system differences, and even hormonal differences. Due to the invasiveness of many procedures (e.g., spinal taps, multiple venipunctures), financial costs, and lack of other resources, it is rare for the individual in the clinical setting, such as Dewey, to be referred for neurophysiological evaluation. However, the findings of physiological studies of conduct disorders have implications for the accurate identification of risk factors, selection of treatment (e.g., dietary recommendations or psychopharmacological interventions), and prediction of treatment outcome. For example, some research has indicated that individuals with Conduct Disorder diagnoses demonstrate neurochemical abnormalities such as low levels of serotonin, low levels of epinephrine, and high levels of testosterone (Kreusi et al., 1990; Scerbo & Kolko, 1994). Raine (1993) found that groups with childhood-onset Conduct Disorder exhibited lower baseline heart rates, blood pressure, and skin conductance levels as well as a diminished reactivity to stressful stimuli in comparison with control groups. In contrast, Raine, Venables, and Williams (1995) indicated that groups with adolescent-onset Conduct Disorder demonstrated higher baseline heart rates, blood pressure, and levels of skin conductance in addition to greater reactivity to stressful stimuli. These results indicate that attention to these psychobiological elements is warranted to further understand the phenotypic expression of Conduct Disorder.

MEDICAL CONSULTATION

Following his presentation at the clinic, Dewey was referred for medical consultation and subsequently examined by his general practitioner. Results of vision and hearing testing were within normal limits. As Dewey did not appear to meet criteria for Attention-Deficit/Hyperactivity Disorder or clinical levels for disorders of mood or anxiety, a pharmaceutical regimen targeting such symptoms was not recommended. Results of physical examination and prior medical records were consistent with Sandra's report regarding the absence of neurological injury and disease. Further, the examination did not indicate any present health concerns. In this connection, Dewey was not prescribed any medications. However, his aggressive behavior was monitored closely throughout the course of treatment to assess the potential need for psychopharmacological interventions. Research has examined use of an array of pharmacological treatments with Conduct Disorder, including neuroleptics, stimulants, antidepressants, mood stabilizers (lithium, anticonvulsants), central nervous system depressants, adrenolytic drugs (clonidine, propanolol), and other sedatives such as antihistamines and atypical anxiolytics. When examining these psychopharmacological methods, it is essential to consider clinical effects as well as unwanted effects and potential for abuse.

CASE CONCEPTUALIZATION

According to the information obtained via history and assessment, Dewey met criteria for Conduct Disorder, Childhood-Onset, Mild severity (*DSM-IV* 312.80). He had exhibited all of the following symptoms within the prior six months: initiating physical fights, threatening others, lying to avoid obligations or escape other consequences, and stealing (albeit items of trivial value). Onset of the behaviors had occurred prior to the age of 10 years. In addition, he was experiencing significant impairment in social and academic functioning. Second, Dewey met criteria for Reading Disorder (*DSM-IV* 315.00) as indicated by reading achievement that fell significantly below the level predicted by his chronological age, years of schooling, and measured ability levels.

Although Attention-Deficit/Hyperactivity Disorder is a common comorbid condition with conduct disorders, Dewey had no known history of attentional difficulties, nor were such deficits demonstrated in formal testing. His avoidance of school-related tasks and periodic failure to follow through on household chores appeared related to issues of noncompliance as well as his reading difficulties. Likewise, he did not exhibit a sufficiently high number of hyperactive or impulsive symptoms. Although he admitted to worrying about his schoolwork, this worry did not appear excessive, nor did it seem to generalize to other situations. Neither Sandra nor Dewey's teachers reported clinically significant levels of anxiety in any context. Although he had been exposed to some specific psychosocial stressors (the divorce, the addition of a new sibling), as seen with Adjustment Disorder diagnoses, onset of Dewey's behavioral problems predated these incidents and his particular pattern of symptoms appeared fully accounted for by the Conduct Disorder diagnosis. Finally, with the exception of transient feelings of emotional distress and/or irritation, Dewey and other informants did not endorse additional symptoms of a Major Depressive Episode or Dysthymic Disorder. Nonetheless, given the report of emotional distress and irritability, he was monitored for persistence of these feelings and for development of any new symptoms of depressed mood.

As discussed previously, several factors have been identified as high-risk or indicators for greater stability in the Conduct Disorder diagnosis. Dewey's developmental history was reported as positive for both economic deprivation and physical abuse. Additionally, his early display of aggressive behavior and accompanying lack of positive peer relationships matched factors established as having positive predictive value for higher levels of adolescent delinquency (Kerr, Tremblay, Pagani, & Vitaro, 1997). In contrast, his case also demonstrated elements associated with greater resilience in Conduct Disorder diagnoses. For example, Dewey had positive relationships with his family members, a factor theorized to buffer the child from more severe antisocial behaviors or other environmental stressors (Werner & Smith, 1992). In addition, he displayed interest in some athletics, such as basketball, and participated in church activities. Additional resilience factors under study have included high measured ability levels, easy temperament, empathy or interpersonal skills, strong work habits at school, and areas of competence outside of academics (Rae-Grant et al., 1989).

In summary, Dewey's case provided several target areas for treatment, including aggression and other conduct problems, academic difficulties, and social difficulties. In addition, the function and maintenance of his behaviors varied across multiple contexts and settings. For example, Dewey frequently exhibited disruptive behaviors to escape an aversive task, such as reading. Similarly, he demonstrated disruptive behaviors as an attempt to gain attention, and aggression to obtain access to a reinforcer. As such, treatment was multimodal in nature, following a primary multisystemic treatment goal to provide familial caregivers with the skills and resources to target the innate difficulties of child rearing and to provide youth with the skills and resources to cope with family, peer, school, and neighborhood conflicts (Henggeler & Borduin, 1990).

RATIONALE FOR TREATMENT CHOICE

Dodge (1993) outlined these factors as essential to the effective treatment of conduct disorders: (1) Treatments target multiple factors leading to the individual's conduct problems; (2) treatments are flexible enough to encompass the variability in the needs of the individual; and (3) treatments are prevention-oriented so that high-risk individuals are targeted prior to progression into more severe forms of antisocial behavior. Selection of optimal treatment strategies may be based on a functional analysis of behavior. The following questions are considered: What are the antecedents and consequences of problem behaviors? What factors serve to maintain the problem behaviors? What function do the behaviors serve in the family, classroom, and peer group environments? What level of intervention is necessary to target problem behaviors? Finally, what resources are available? (Horne, Glaser, & Calhoun, 1999). In the past, intervention programs for Conduct Disorder have been largely unidimensional in nature and not focused on these multiple questions, thus ignoring the heterogeneity of the population and limiting treatment efficacy (Kazdin, 1995).

The focus of the present treatment plan was to structure a developmentally appropriate series of specific interventions to target the multiple, interacting systems in Dewey's environment. Coie, Underwood, and Lochman's (1991) comprehensive program for reducing aggressive behavior was selected for targeting Dewey's anger management issues and providing instruction in social skills and problem-solving strategies. Research has indicated significant treatment gains with these program elements (Guerra & Slaby, 1989). To provide additional intervention in these skill areas and increase generalizability, a peer group format using cognitive problem-solving training in the elementary school was recommended. This training program views aggressive behavior to be a result of the individual's cognitive and attributional biases in social situations; related research has shown positive effects for children's social adjustment posttreatment (Lochman & Curry, 1986). In addition, a series of behavior management strategies was structured for teacher implementation in the classroom; such techniques have demonstrated efficacy in the reduction of problem behavior and the enhancement of academic performance (Kazdin, 1987, 1995).

To address patterns of social interaction and provide instruction in behavioral management techniques, elements of parent management training were incorporated in family therapy sessions and home visits. Parent management training promotes greater levels of familial involvement with and therefore supervision of children, the use of positive contingencies to increase adaptive behaviors, and the use of consistent noncorporal discipline to decrease maladaptive behaviors. The original program has expanded to incorporate conflict-resolution skills training and self-control strategies, and has demonstrated clinical efficacy in multiple domains of systemic functioning (Kazdin, 1993; Miller & Prinz, 1990).

Finally, referrals for academic tutoring, extracurricular activities, and community support programs were selected to target other deficit areas (e.g., reading, funding) and to provide additional sources of positive reinforcement for Dewey and his family.

COURSE OF TREATMENT

SESSIONS 1 THROUGH 6

Initial sessions were structured for one hour, twice weekly. Session format varied and involved both individual and family therapy segments with all four family members in attendance. Sandra, Gladys, and Dewey were provided information about the rationale behind the upcoming treatment plan, the structure of treatment, and related activities in the course of treatment, including homework assignments. Sandra and Gladys expressed a strong verbal commitment to the treatment program. In addition, Sandra and Dewey were provided with several referrals and set up for external services. These referrals included Think Fast, a cognitive problem-solving group for peers at the elementary school; the Leap Frog Program, an academic tutoring program conducted by graduate-level education majors during regular school hours; Families First, a community services program providing assistance to low-socioeconomic-status families in need of mental health services; and the local Big Brothers/Big Sisters program. In addition, Sandra and Dewey were encouraged to continue participating in local church activities.

Individual therapy with Dewey began with the program for reducing aggressive behavior, incorporating elements of both social skills training and social problem solving (Coie et al., 1991). As per the anger management and conflict resolution goals, Dewey practiced developing greater awareness of anger feelings, identifying antecedents to feelings of anger, recognizing the negative consequences of inappropriate anger expression, and learning adaptive methods of anger expression. A simplified version of relaxation exercises was also used.

Family therapy sessions were structured, using elements of parent management training to provide training in specific child management techniques as well as general social learning principles (Kazdin, 1987). Sandra and Gladys identified and defined specific behaviors for targeted change: academic performance, stealing, disruption at home and school, and aggression at home and school. In this connection, a token reinforcement system was established in which Dewey would earn stickers (to translate into spending money) for time-limited periods absent problem behaviors (aggression, disruption, stealing) and for the commission of prosocial behaviors (i.e., grade improvements, household chores, homework completion). Initially, Dewey's behavior was evaluated at one-hour intervals in the home. Contingencies of the token system was explained to him. Earned tokens translated into spending money for the local store (Dewey was no longer permitted to frequent this store without adult supervision). Consistent with parent management training guidelines, periodic home visits were scheduled (Session 4 was conducted in the home).

During this phase of treatment, Dewey began participation with the Think Fast group, led by a master's-level therapist. In the group format, he and his peers were taught to recognize problem situations, use self-statements to interrupt impulsive responding, generate multiple solutions to problem situations, evaluate potential consequences of behavioral responses, and practice perspective-taking exercises. The group therapist also conducted periodic classroom observations and subsequently provided behavioral management recommendations to the teachers. Recommendations included increasing the level of structure in classroom and playground activities, increasing the frequency of verbal praise, and implementing random "caught in the act" rewards, where students demonstrating rule compliance were provided coupons for desired activities. The homeroom teacher was informed of Dewey's token economy program and monitored his behavior with stickers. In the playground setting, he was rewarded for 15-minute intervals without aggressive incident. His stickers were reimbursed at home daily. Dewey also started working with his assigned volunteer tutor in the Leap Frog Program, specifically targeting his reading difficulties. Sandra reported having completed the paperwork for the Big Brothers/Big Sisters program and Dewey was awaiting his assigned partner for extracurricular activities.

SESSIONS 7 THROUGH 12

During this treatment phase, individual therapy continued to target anger management and social skills training. Modeling and role-playing techniques were introduced to shape appropriate behavior. In addressing contexts of anger, Dewey and the primary therapist discussed issues surrounding the divorce, marital conflict, the absence of his father, and specific peer conflicts at school. Family therapy sessions continued emphasizing behavioral management techniques, such as the appropriate use of verbal and physical rewards, and ignoring minor disruptive behaviors with an attention-seeking function. In addition, these sessions emphasized self-control strategies such as goal-setting, self-monitoring, and self-reinforcement. To fine-tune the treatment, session 10 was conducted in the home. Dewey continued working with his tutor in the Leap Frog Program. He began his participation in Big Brothers with an assigned volunteer visiting on Saturdays, thus reducing unstructured activity on weekends and providing an additional avenue of reinforcement.

SESSIONS 13 THROUGH 18

Individual therapy progressed according to the reduction of aggressive behavior program, and new skills, such as behavioral rehearsal, were introduced. Dewey's behavior intervals for token reinforcement were lengthened in both home and school settings. Family therapy sessions began to target patterns of communication more intensively, focusing on healthy affective expressions, reflective listening, and negotiation. During this phase of treatment, the focus of the Think Fast cognitive problem-solving training program moved into areas of positive play training and group entry skills. Dewey continued participation in the Leap Frog Program. He was distressed when his assigned volunteer discontinued the Big Brothers program, but was excited to sign up with the community basketball league for youth age 8 to 10 years. He was transported to athletic activities by volunteers from the community services program. Program coordinators reported that he would be repaired with another Big Brother volunteer.

Sessions 19 and 20

Individual therapy and family therapy sessions were both conducted with a review of treatment concepts. Dewey, Sandra, and Gladys were prepared for termination. At this time, Sandra began participation in a support group offered by the community services program for parents of children with problem behaviors.

THERAPIST-CLIENT FACTORS

In the therapeutic relationship with Dewey, trust was difficult to develop. Dewey was naturally reluctant to disclose incidents of behaviors that he identified as "wrong" or illegal. However, he responded well to positive reinforcers, such as verbal praise and activity reinforcers (e.g., playing videogames). Other relationship-building behaviors such as joking, showing concern, and enthusiasm have also been linked to clients' positive evaluation of rapport and treatment satisfaction (Wilner et al., 1977). Research by Alexander, Barton, Schiavo, and Parsons (1976) emphasized two dimensions of therapist characteristics in the treatment of conduct disorders. Their findings revealed that relationship characteristics, such as warmth and humor, accounted for 45% of the variance in treatment outcome and 15% of variance was attributed to structuring characteristics, such as directiveness and self-confidence.

Clearly, there are several factors that must be considered in the therapist-client relationship with this population. Research has indicated that children under the age of 10 years may not provide reliable self-report and, particularly, may underestimate the incidence of their aggressive behavior (Loeber & Schmaling, 1985). The reliability of self-report is further called into question when lying is one of the reported problem behaviors. Additional studies must be conducted to examine the influence of cultural and ethnic factors in the therapeutic relationship and treatment of individuals with Conduct Disorder.

COURSE OF TERMINATION

Having been presented with an explanation of the structure and course of therapy, Sandra appeared well-prepared for termination. While Dewey verbalized mild disappointment, he was becoming increasingly involved in and excited about his extracurricular activities. At this point, the following changes were noted: The frequency of aggressive and disruptive episodes at home and school had decreased and Dewey's grades had improved overall. He maintained a C grade in reading, but his tutor and teacher reported gains in reading skills. He continued to have difficulty with interpersonal skills. Sandra and Dewey were informed of the follow-up schedule and encouraged to contact the clinic if additional sessions appeared warranted.

FOLLOW-UP

As per the treatment guidelines for parent management therapy, "booster sessions" were provided on a regular basis to foster relapse prevention. Dewey and Sandra presented to the clinic for one monthly session in the six months following treatment termination. In addition, a home and school visit were each conducted at three months and six months posttermination. These intervals were designated as research has indicated that treatment gains may begin to erode after three months (Horne et al., 1999). During this six-month period, Dewey continued his participation with the Leap Frog Program, Big Brother services, and community athletic programs. A brief follow-up examination conducted at one-year posttermination indicated continued improvements in levels of physical and verbal aggression, level of classroom disruption, and general academic performance. Dewey continued to exhibit residual problems in reading-related tasks and interpersonal problem solving. Sandra reported increasing levels of confidence in her ability and skills in managing Dewey's problem behaviors, and specifically noted a sense of greater efficacy in conflict resolution.

MANAGED CARE CONSIDERATIONS

Introduction of managed care organizations has had a significant impact on the treatment of Conduct Disorder as well as other mental health services. Managed care restrictions have fostered an emergence of new models for briefer, time-limited psychotherapy and the development of empirically supported treatments founded on research-based intervention programs (Giles, 1991; Hoyt, 1992; Kent & Hersen, 2000). In this connection, managed care organizations have strongly emphasized group therapy approaches as a "clinically proven" and cost-effective way of providing treatment to larger numbers of individuals. Although this change has met with some resistance, McRoberts, Burlingame, and Hoag's (1998) review indicated no significant differences when a specific form of treatment was conducted in the individual versus group format. Other empirical evidence has demonstrated that, whereas group therapy is effective as a general support provision, individual therapy may be essential for active treatment efficacy (Fuhriman & Burlingame, 1990).

With regard to treatments for Conduct Disorder, psychotherapy is generally reimbursed if it is used as treatment for a substantiated *DSM-IV* diagnosis; however, "practice guidelines" are provided by the managed care organization. Outpatient treatment frequently has been recommended and selected in contrast to the current brief inpatient stays of 3 to 10 days with a minimum of follow-up evaluation. A common issue in the provision of mental health services regards medically necessary as opposed to discretionary treatment. In the case of Dewey, a full psychoeducational evaluation was conducted to examine potential learning disorders in addition to attentional or impulse control deficits. Although managed care often provides reimbursement for briefer assessments in the evaluation of Attention-Deficit/Hyperactivity Disorder, the purpose of the full battery in targeting comorbid learning disorders was ruled the responsibility of the school system and not deemed medically necessary. Sandra was subsequently referred to the university assessment services, where testing could be conducted on a sliding-fee scale. The structured individual sessions at the university outpatient clinic were covered by a combination of managed care reimbursement and funding from the community services program. These examples illustrate the importance of considering potential managed care restrictions in the structure and implementation of clinical treatment plans. In the case of Dewey and his family, community and campus resources were employed to offset treatment costs.

OVERALL EFFECTIVENESS

Horne, Glaser, and Calhoun (1999) identified two areas of concern in evaluating treatment efficacy for Conduct Disorder diagnoses: the generalizability of treatment effects across home and school contexts and the long-term maintenance of any demonstrated treatment effects. Overall effectiveness of the implemented treatment for Dewey was assessed across multiple domains, such as academic performance, disruption/aggression at home, disruption/aggression at school, disruption/aggression in the community (particularly stealing), peer relations, and global prosocial behaviors. These areas of functioning were evaluated with several measures: report cards, school records, updated behavior ratings by Sandra and Dewey's teachers, and Dewey's self-report. As noted previously, Dewey's grades demonstrated significant improvement, although he continued to struggle in the area of reading skills. School records indicated a lower incidence of classroom disruption and aggressive behavior; these gains were substantiated by the behavior ratings of Sandra and Dewey's teachers. In addition, teachers, family members, and Dewey reported an increased level of satisfaction and positive experiences in their interactions. Dewey's behavior indicated significant improvement overall, yet the need for continued consistent implementation of behavioral management procedures was strongly emphasized to his family members and teachers.

REFERENCES

Abikoff, H., & Klein, R. G. (1992). Attention-Deficit Hyperactivity and Conduct Disorder: Co-morbidity and implications for treatment. *Journal of Consulting and Clinical Psychology, 60,* 881–892.

Alexander, J. F., Barton, C., Schiavo, R. S., & Parson, B. V. (1976). Systems-behavioral intervention with families of delinquents: Therapist characteristics, family behavior, and outcome. *Journal of Consulting and Clinical Psychology, 44,* 656–664.

American Psychiatric Association. (1994). *The diagnostic and statistical manual of mental disorders* (4th ed.). Washington, DC: Author.

Capaldi, D. M. (1992). Co-occurrence of conduct problems and depressive symptoms in early adolescent boys. II: A 2-year follow-up at grade 8. *Development and Psychopathology, 4,* 125–144.

Coie, J. D., Underwood, M., & Lochman, J. E. (1991). Programmatic intervention with aggressive children in the school setting. In D. J. Pepler & K. H. Rubin (Eds.), *The development and treatment of childhood aggression* (pp. 389–410). Hillsdale, NJ: Erlbaum.

Costello, E. J., Angold, A., Burns, B. J., Erkanli, A., Stangle, D. K., & Tweed, D. L. (1996). The Great Smoky Mountains Study of Youth: Functional impairment and serious emotional disturbance. *Archives of General Psychiatry, 53,* 1137–1143.

Dodge, K. A. (1993). Social-cognitive mechanisms in the development of Conduct Disorder and depression. *Annual Review Psychology, 44,* 559–584.

Farrington, D. P. (1991). Childhood aggression and adult violence: Early precursors and later-life outcomes. In D. J. Pepler & K. H. Rubin (Eds.), *The development and treatment of childhood aggression* (pp. 5–29). Hillsdale, NJ: Erlbaum.

Finkelhor, D., & Berliner, L. (1995). Research on the treatment of sexually abused children: A review and recommendations. *Journal of the American Academy of Child and Adolescent Psychiatry, 34,* 1408–1423.

Frick, P. J. (1998). Conduct disorders. In T. H. Ollendick & M. Hersen (Eds.), *Handbook of child psychopathology* (pp. 213–237). New York: Plenum Press.

Frick, P. J., Kamphaus, R. W., Lahey, B. B., Loeber, R., Christ, M. A., Hart, E. L., et al. (1991). Academic underachievement and the disruptive behavior disorders. *Journal of Consulting and Clinical Psychology, 59*(2), 289–294.

Fuhriman, A., & Burlingame, G. M. (1990). Consistency of matter: A comparative analysis of individual and group process variables. *Counseling Psychologist, 18*(1), 6–63.

Giles, T. R. (1991). Managed mental health and effective psychotherapy: A step in the right direction? *Journal of Behavior Therapy and Experimental Psychiatry, 22*(2), 83–86.

Guerra, N. G., & Slaby, R. G. (1989). Evaluative factors in social problem-solving by aggressive boys. *Journal of Abnormal Child Psychology, 17*(3), 277–289.

Henggeler, S. W., & Borduin, C. M. (1990). *Family therapy and beyond: A multisystemic approach to treating the behavior problems of children and adolescents.* Pacific Grove, CA: Brooks/Cole.

Horne, A. M., Glaser, B. A., & Calhoun, G. B. (1999). Conduct disorders. In R. T. Ammerman, C. G. Last, & M. Hersen (Eds.), *Handbook of prescriptive treatments for children and adolescents* (2nd ed., pp. 84–101). New York: Wiley.

Hoyt, M. F. (1992). Discussion of the effects of managed care on mental health practice. *Psychotherapy and Private Practice, 12,* 79–83.

Kazdin, A. E. (1987). Treatment of antisocial behavior in children: Current status and future directions. *Psychological Bulletin, 102*(2), 187–203.

Kazdin, A. E. (1993). Treatment of Conduct Disorder: Progress and directions in psychotherapy research. *Development and Psychopathology, 5,* 277–310.

Kazdin, A. E. (1995). *Conduct disorders in childhood and adolescence.* Thousand Oaks, CA: Sage.

Kent, A. J., & Hersen, M. (2000). *A psychologist's proactive guide to managed mental health care.* Mahwah, NJ: Erlbaum.

Kerr, M., Tremblay, R., Pagani, L., & Vitaro, F. (1997). Boys' behavioral inhibition and the risk of later delinquency. *Archives of General Psychiatry, 54,* 809–816.

Kreusi, M. J. P., Rapoport, J. L., Hamburger, S., Hibbs, E., Potter, W. Z., Lenane, M. I., et al. (1990). Cerebrospinal fluid monoamine metabolites, aggression, and impulsivity in disruptive behavior disorders of children and adolescents. *Archives of General Psychiatry, 47,* 419–426.

Lochman, J. E., & Curry, J. F. (1986). Effects of social problem-solving training and self-instruction training with aggressive boys. *Journal of Clinical Child Psychology, 15*(2), 159–164.

Loeber, R., Green, S. M., Lahey, B. B., Christ, M. A. G., & Frick, P. J. (1992). Developmental sequences in the age of onset of disruptive child behaviors. *Journal of Child and Family Studies, 1,* 21–41.

Loeber, R., & Keenan, K. (1994). Interaction between Conduct Disorder and its comorbid conditions: Effects of age and gender. *Clinical Psychology Review, 14,* 497–523.

Loeber, R., & Schmaling, K. B. (1985). Empirical evidence for overt and covert patterns of antisocial conduct problems: A meta-analysis. *Journal of Abnormal Child Psychology, 11,* 1–14.

Loeber, R., & Stouthamer-Loeber, M. (1986). Family factors as correlates and predictors of juvenile conduct problems and delinquency. In M. Tonry & N. Morris (Eds.), *Crime and justice* (Vol. 7, pp. 29–149). Chicago: University of Chicago Press.

McRoberts, C., Burlingame, G. M., & Hoag, M. J. (1998). Comparative efficacy of individual and group psychotherapy: A meta-analytic perspective. *Group Dynamics: Theory, Research, and Practice, 2,* 101–117.

Miller, G. E., & Prinz, R. J. (1990). Enhancement of social learning family interventions for childhood Conduct Disorder. *Psychological Bulletin, 108,* 291–307.

Moffitt, T. E. (1993a). Adolescence-limited and life-course persistent antisocial behavior: A developmental taxonomy. *Psychological Review, 100,* 674–701.

Moffitt, T. E. (1993b). The neuropsychology of Conduct Disorder. *Development and Psychopathology, 5,* 135–152.

Patterson, G. R., Reid, J. B., & Dishion, T. J. (1992). *Antisocial boys.* Eugene, OR: Castalia.

Rae-Grant, N., Thomas, F., Offord, D., Boyle, M. H., Thomas, B. H., & Offord, D. R. (1989). Risk, protective factors, and the prevalence of behavioral and emotional disorders in children and adolescents. *Journal of the American Academy of Child and Adolescent Psychiatry, 28,* 262–268.

Raine, A. (1993). *The psychopathology of crime: Criminal behavior as a clinical disorder.* New York: Academic Press.

Raine, A., Venables, P., & Williams, M. (1995). High autonomic arousal and electrodermal orienting at age 15 years as protective factors against criminal behavior at age 29 years. *American Journal of Psychiatry, 152,* 1560–1595.

Reynolds, C. R., & Kamphaus, R. W. (1992). *The Behavior Assessment System for Children.* Circle Pines, MN: American Guidance Service.

Russo, M. F., & Beidel, D. C. (1994). Co-morbidity of childhood anxiety and externalizing disorders: Prevalence, associated characteristics, and validation issues. *Clinical Psychology Review, 14,* 199–221.

Scerbo, A., & Kolko, D. J. (1994). Salivary testosterone and cortisol in disruptive children: Relationship to aggressive, hyperactive, and internalizing behavior. *Journal of the American Academy of Child and Adolescent Psychiatry, 33,* 1174–1184.

Walker, J. L., Lahey, B. B., Russo, M. F., Frick, P. J., Christ, M. A. G., McBurnett, K., et al. (1991). Anxiety, inhibition, and Conduct Disorder in children. I: Relations to social impairment. *Journal of the American Academy of Child and Adolescent Psychiatry, 30,* 187–191.

Wechsler, D. (1991). *Wechsler Intelligence Scale for Children–III.* New York: Psychological Corporation.

Wechsler, D., (1992). *Wechsler Individual Achievement Test.* San Antonio, TX: Psychological Corporation.

Werner, E., & Smith, R. (1992). *Overcoming the odds: High risk children from birth to adulthood.* New York: Cornell University Press.

Wilner, A. G., Braukmann, C. J., Kirigin, K. A., Fixsen, D. L., Phillips, E. L., & Wolf, M. M. (1977). The training and validation of youth-preferred social behaviors with child care personnel. *Journal of Applied Behavior Analysis, 10,* 219–230.

CHAPTER 21

Attention-Deficit/ Hyperactivity Disorder

DAVID REITMAN and STEPHEN D. A. HUPP

DESCRIPTION OF THE DISORDER

FEW BEHAVIORAL DISORDERS of childhood have attained the notoriety of Attention-Deficit/Hyperactivity Disorder (ADHD). Yet despite the reputed "ADHD epidemic," actual prevalence of ADHD in school-age children is estimated to be only 3% to 5% (Barkley, 1998). Considered three to six times more common in males, prevalence estimates vary considerably based on how the disorder is defined (Breen & Altepeter, 1990). The *Diagnostic and Statistical Manual of Mental Disorders* (*DSM-IV;* American Psychiatric Association [APA], 1994) describes ADHD-diagnosed children and adolescents as frequently exhibiting inattentive (e.g., off-task, easily distracted), hyperactive (e.g., out of seat, fidgeting), and impulsive (e.g., interrupts others) behavior. The earliest conceptualizations of ADHD-diagnosed children alleged that their behavioral excesses were a result of neurological insult, and labels such as "minimal brain dysfunction" reflected this bias. Current conceptualizations of ADHD include both environmental and biological influences, although several leading researchers continue to theorize about its neurodevelopmental origins (e.g., Barkley, 1998). The *DSM-IV* now sidesteps much of the earlier debate, focusing on symptoms (i.e., inattention and hyperactivity) and associated diagnostic features of the disorder rather than its ontology.

The *DSM-IV* suggests a two-factor model of ADHD comprising "predominately inattentive" and "predominately hyperactive-impulsive" subtypes. The "combined type" is most commonly observed and includes symptoms of both inattentive and hyperactive-impulsive subtypes. To receive a diagnosis, the child must exhibit at least six of nine behaviors from at least one of the subtypes. Some impairment must be present before age 7 years, and these behaviors must impair social or academic functioning in multiple settings.

Approximately 35% of ADHD-diagnosed children also meet criteria for Oppositional Defiant Disorder (ODD), which is characterized by "negativistic, hostile, and defiant" behavior (Farrington, 1994). High diagnostic comorbidity may be a function of symptom overlap, as many inattentive, hyperactive, and impulsive behaviors are also considered oppositional (e.g., being off-task or frequently out of seat). In addition, up to 50% of ADHD-diagnosed adolescents meet diagnostic criteria for Conduct Disorder, a heterogeneous group of children exhibiting behaviors such as aggression, destruction of property, deceitfulness, and serious rule violations (Biederman, Newcorn, & Sprich, 1991). Internalizing problems also may be associated with ADHD. Approximately 9% to 32% of ADHD-diagnosed children meet criteria for major depression or dysthymia and another 25% meet criteria for an anxiety spectrum disorder (Biederman et al., 1991).

Impairment in either academic or social functioning is required for a diagnosis of ADHD. Using stringent criteria for a learning disorder, Frick et al. (1991) reported that 8% of ADHD-diagnosed children met criteria for a reading disorder and 12% met criteria for a math disorder. Indeed, whether behaviors associated with ADHD impact learning problems or learning problems increase the likelihood of ADHD-related behaviors is hotly debated. Regarding impairment in social functioning, approximately 50% of ADHD-diagnosed children experience peer relationship difficulties due to impulsive and aggressive behaviors. Not surprisingly, many of these children are considered to exhibit poor social skills (Landau, Milich, & Diener, 1998).

CASE DESCRIPTION

Given the high rates of comorbidity between ADHD and other diagnostic classifications, we present a case in which the core symptoms of ADHD are embedded in a cluster of other challenges to assessment and treatment. This chapter illustrates the thorough assessment and treatment of a child exhibiting both internalizing and externalizing problems: the type of complicated ADHD case that appears rarely in the research literature, yet frustrates both student therapists and experienced clinicians. Because no two children diagnosed with ADHD are exactly alike, we highlight the importance of an idiographic assessment and treatment.

Robert was an 8-year-old male of average intelligence, in his second month of second grade at a public elementary school. He was referred to a university psychology clinic for an assessment of disruptive classroom behavior and academic difficulties. Robert lived with his mother (age 25), stepfather (age 29), and half-brother (age 1) in an economically depressed section of a midsize southern city. His mother graduated from high school and worked as a customer service agent for a department store before the birth of her youngest son. Robert's stepfather was a high school graduate and worked as a casino dealer. The mother and stepfather were married two years prior to the intake interview.

Robert's biological father had been incarcerated for theft and had been in treatment for drug abuse intermittently since Robert's birth. As a child, Robert's father was diagnosed with ADHD and Conduct Disorder. Robert's first cousin was also diagnosed with ADHD. According to his mother, the majority of his uncles and cousins on both sides of the family had drug problems and were frequently in jail. Robert's mother denied that either she or her husband had a history of psychological problems.

Robert's mother was the primary caregiver for the children and was very frustrated with him. Since the birth of her second child, Robert had become increasingly difficult to manage. She felt unable to provide adequate supervision during homework. She also was concerned about several recent phone calls and notes from the school regarding his behavioral and academic problems. Robert behaved much better when his stepfather was home, but his stepfather worked up to four nights a week at the casino. On a more positive note, Robert and his stepfather had developed a very close relationship over the past four years. They enjoyed fishing together on the weekends and routinely played with toy cars and other age-appropriate games. Additionally, Robert was a good artist, frequently rode his bike, and liked to hold his little brother.

CHIEF COMPLAINTS

On the initial clinic visit, Robert's mother and stepfather indicated that Robert's most significant problem was extreme hyperactivity. In the classroom, he frequently left his seat to sharpen his pencil, talk to other students, or just "run around the room." His teacher estimated that he was out of his seat several times an hour. Even when seated, he was said to be "fidgety." His high activity level extended to public settings, where he ran around grocery stores, church, and the homes of friends and family. Whenever possible, his mother avoided taking him to public places. Robert's teacher complained that he talked while she was trying to teach and that he usually failed to participate in class discussions. He often distracted students around him.

Most days, Robert did not complete his work at school. Uncompleted work was sent home, and his mother also had difficulty getting him to complete assignments. The combination of unfinished classwork and homework often required more than three hours to complete. Typically, he began by working independently but became distracted after a few minutes, requiring his mother's frequent redirection and encouragement. He very rarely completed work independently. His mother and teacher were deeply concerned about his academic progress, and he received primarily Cs, Ds, and Fs.

Noncompliant and aggressive behavior helped contribute to academic problems and resulted in poor weekly conduct grades. During transitions outside of the classroom, Robert started verbal and physical fights with other students about two times a day. These fights were reportedly in response to other children "bumping into him," and he responded by yelling at them or pushing them back. He had been written up four times for fighting on the school bus on the way to school. He indicated that other children teased him, calling him "stupid" and "ugly." He reported that he sometimes started fights with other students because "they were about to start teasing," and he wanted to "get them first." Robert's mother was concerned that his aggressive behavior negatively impacted his relationships with his teacher and peers. She believed that his teacher did not like him, and that other students in his class had variable responses to him, either "really liking him" or "really hating him." He had two good friends at home but had been prevented from playing with them since the beginning of the school year as a consequence for poor conduct. Robert's mother also was concerned about his increasing tendency to withdraw from the family.

HISTORY

Semistructured or unstructured interviews are typically the first part of a multi-method assessment for externalizing childhood problems (Reitman, Hummel, Franz, & Gross, 1998). A semistructured interview was conducted with Robert's mother and stepfather to obtain information regarding Robert's history and current functioning. In addition to broad questioning about presence of other symptoms (e.g., anxiety or depression), specific information was sought regarding the frequency and duration of ADHD symptoms as well as the circumstances that appeared to influence the appearance of symptoms (e.g., functional analysis; see Sturmey, 1996).

Robert's mother reported an uneventful pregnancy and delivery. Robert reached his motor and speech milestones within normal limits, and his mother denied that he experienced any early feeding, sleeping, or toilet-training difficulties. She indicated that Robert was a very active toddler and "ran all over the house" as soon as he was able. He frequently moved from one activity to the next and appeared to be easily distracted when she played games with him. She often had to repeat herself to get him to follow her directions, and he threw temper tantrums to avoid complying with requests. She reported being concerned about "correcting him too much" and indicated that it was easier to "let him have his way" than to deal with tantrums.

When Robert entered kindergarten, the teacher reported that he was active in the classroom. He wandered around the room during transitions, such as arrival, recess, and lunch. Midway through the school year, he began displaying temper tantrums at school and was noncompliant to teacher requests. He had tantrums at school about once a week, and at home started throwing items and slamming doors when asked to clean up. Despite behavioral problems, he did well academically and appeared to benefit from one-on-one instruction with a classroom aide.

In first grade, his teacher did not have a classroom aide, and she reported that Robert ran around the classroom most of the day. He complied with requests to sit but got back up within a few minutes. He did not complete much work independently in the classroom and was inattentive even when the teacher worked with him individually. Robert's teacher complained that he was poorly motivated; his grades were primarily Ds and Fs. He was aggressive toward the other students, tripping or kicking them at least once a day. The teacher reported that on one occasion, he "tried to cut a girl's ear with scissors." Robert repeated first grade because of concerns about his academic readiness and lack of social maturity.

In his second year of first grade, Robert's new teacher also remarked on his high activity level and inattentive behavior in the classroom. He began fighting on the bus, and reportedly "stuck another child's head in a toilet." During this year, he had fewer temper tantrums but started talking back to teachers, frequently being written up for "being disrespectful." His grades were primarily Cs, yet his teacher believed he could do much better. Robert joined a T-ball team, but the coach "could not control him" during practice, so his mother withdrew him. Since that time, he has not joined any other afterschool or weekend activities.

BEHAVIORAL ASSESSMENT

State-of-the-art assessment for externalizing disorders should employ multiple informants and methods, including interviews, questionnaires, and direct observation (Reitman et al., 1998). Information gathered during the parent and teacher interviews appeared in the previous two sections. Based on interview data, Robert's parents endorsed 7 of 9 inattentive behaviors and 8 of 9 hyperactive-impulsive behaviors listed in the *DSM-IV* for ADHD. Additionally, they endorsed 5 of 8 behaviors listed for ODD. Prior to the first session, they were mailed parent and teacher questionnaires with a letter requesting that all forms be completed before the intake.

The Child Behavior Checklist (CBCL; Achenbach, 1991) is a broad-band parent-report instrument containing both internalizing and externalizing domains, and a similar teacher form (Teacher Rating Form; TRF) corresponds with the parent form. Internalizing subscales include Withdrawn, Somatic Complaints, and Anxious/Depressed. Externalizing subscales include Delinquent Behavior and Aggressive Behavior. Additional subscales include Social Problems, Thought Problems, and Attention Problems. A rating at or above the 95th percentile (i.e., 1.5 standard deviations above the mean) is considered clinically significant. The Attention Problems subscale of the CBCL does not distinguish between inattentive and hyperactive-impulsive behaviors, so we also included the short form of the Conners' Rating Scales–Revised (CRS-R; Conners, 1997) which yields independent ratings for these domains.

The responses of Robert's mother, stepfather, and teacher on the CBCL and TRF showed significant elevations on the Attention Problems and Aggressive Behavior subscales. Additionally, the mother's responses were in the clinically significant range on the Withdrawn, Anxious/Depressed, and Social Problems subscales, and his stepfather's responses were elevated on the Withdrawn subscale. The teacher did not report internalizing problems, but the Social Problems subscale was elevated. Parent and teacher responses to the CRS-R resulted in clinically significant elevations on Oppositional, Cognitive Problems (inattention and academic difficulties), Hyperactivity, and ADHD Index subscales. In summary, questionnaire and interview data indicated that Robert was demonstrating significant ADHD-related and aggressive behaviors in multiple settings. Furthermore, he was demonstrating internalizing problems at home, but these problems were not observed by his teacher at school. His mother and teacher agreed that he had significant social problems.

Following the initial intake with Robert's parents, and prior to the therapist meeting Robert, his teacher was contacted by telephone. At this time, a two-hour school observation was scheduled and Robert was carefully monitored during the hours when he was most likely to exhibit inappropriate behavior. His teacher indicated that he exhibited inappropriate behavior "all day long" but suggested observing him in the afternoon, when he seemed to be most active. The ADHD Behavior Coding System (see Barkley, 1990) was used to monitor behaviors such as being off-task, inappropriate vocalizing, being out of seat, fidgeting, and playing with objects. To gather data as to the possible function (i.e., purpose) of these behaviors, instances of peer attention and teacher attention were also coded. Behaviors were coded during both group and independent seat work in math and language using a 10-second interval time-sampling procedure. During each 10-second interval, the observer alternated between monitoring Robert and five randomly chosen male peers. Thus, Robert's behavior could easily be compared to the behavior of the other boys in the classroom.

During the observation, Robert's behavior did not seem to vary much as a function of task (i.e., language versus math) or setting (i.e., group versus individual seatwork); thus, observations were collapsed across academic subjects. Overall, he was off-task nearly twice as much as his peers (46% versus 23% of the intervals). During the majority of the intervals he was off-task, he was also inappropriately vocalizing (37% of the intervals), while his peers inappropriately vocalized during only 13% of the intervals. Desks in the classroom were arranged by group rather than rows, and the majority of Robert's vocalizations were intended for another boy sitting directly across from him. Robert initiated most of the interactions and the boy frequently responded. Robert was out of his seat during 35% of the intervals and was reprimanded three times for this behavior, whereas his peers were out of their seats during only 10% of the intervals. Robert also fidgeted during 30% of the intervals, and his peers fidgeted during 13% of the intervals. Both Robert and his peers infrequently played with inappropriate objects (i.e., 3% of the intervals each).

Although Robert was frequently off-task and disruptive in the classroom, he was engaged in task-relevant behavior approximately half of the time, and at one point worked independently for approximately 10 minutes. Robert was also observed during a recess. The majority of the boys played kickball together, while Robert and one boy (the same boy that sat across from him) played on a jungle gym. Immediately following the observation, Robert's teacher was interviewed. She indicated that it was a typical day for Robert.

Robert attended the second clinic appointment with his mother and was interviewed individually. During the interview, he appeared much more withdrawn than during the classroom observation. He reported that he was "always in trouble" because of his behavior at school and being bored at home because he was not "allowed to do anything but homework." Regarding his poor schoolwork and fighting, he indicated that he was often "grounded" for these behaviors. During the interview, he completed the Children's Depression Inventory (CDI; Kovacs, 1992) with the therapist. Items he endorsed included "I do not like myself," "I look ugly," "I have to push myself to do my schoolwork," "I never have fun at school," and "I get into fights many times." Endorsement of these items indicated that Robert had a poor self-concept and was aware of his problems at school. He denied eating or sleeping difficulties, and he also denied being sad or exhibiting anxious behaviors.

A curriculum-based measurement (CBM; see Shinn, 1989) was conducted to assess Robert's basic reading, writing, and mathematics skills. For the reading assessment, he read (aloud) a second-grade passage for two minutes, scoring 21 correct words read per minute, well below the second-grade instructional level of 40 to 60 correct words. During a second trial, an incentive (i.e., a toy from a prize box) was offered if he could improve his score by 25% (i.e., 5 words). Robert was unable to significantly improve his score, indicating that his low reading score was likely a skill deficit (i.e., he could not read quickly and accurately) rather than a performance deficit (i.e., he possessed the necessary reading skills but did not use them). He made few errors while reading, but read slowly, indicating problems with reading fluency. A similar writing assessment also suggested poor writing skills, and his writing did not improve when offered a reward. He then participated in a similar math assessment. The second-grade instructional level for math is 20 to 39 correct digits per minute, and Robert completed 11 digits per minute. However, when offered an incentive for improving, he doubled his score, suggesting than his poor math grades could have been a result of low motivation rather than a skill deficit.

During the third clinic session, a brief experimental analysis was conducted to evaluate the function of inattentive and hyperactive behavior during homework (DuPaul & Ervin, 1996). Several five-minute conditions were set up in which Robert was required to independently complete academic seatwork. During each condition, the observer used the ADHD Behavior Coding System (see Barkley, 1990) to monitor ADHD-related behaviors (e.g., off-task, out of seat) from behind a one-way mirror. Conditions included escape, reprimand, differential positive attention, and high demand and low demand seatwork. During the escape condition, Robert's mother was instructed to make him take a 30-second break following 10 seconds of off-task behavior. During the reprimand condition, she reminded him to get back to work following 10 seconds of off-task behavior; during the differential positive attention condition, she praised him every 30 seconds if he was attending to his work. During the high and low demand conditions, Robert was presented math problems at either his frustration level (upper second grade) or mastery level (first grade). Robert's inattentive behaviors were highest during the escape condition and high-demand condition. These conditions, along with the differential positive attention condition, were replicated in the context of a reversal design, depicted in Figure 21.1.

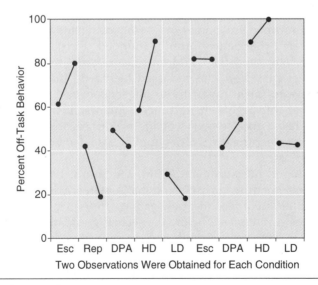

Figure 21.1 Percent of Intervals with Off-Task Behavior during Homework Sessions at the Clinic (*Key to Condition:* Esc = Escape Condition; Rep = Reprimand Condition; DPA = Differential Positive Attention (Praise) Condition; HD = High Demand Condition; LD = Low Demand Condition)

MEDICAL CONSULTATION

One of the gravest dangers confronting child clinicians is a failure to properly consider medical conditions that may mimic psychological symptoms (Morrison, 1997). Consequently, a reasonably thorough medical examination is necessary to assess biological factors that may relate to child behavior problems (Barkley, 1998). A typical examination protocol might include an evaluation of (1) hearing and visual acuity; (2) hyper- or hypothyroidism; (3) presence of lead or other toxic poisons; (4) possible biological insult to the central nervous system (e.g., head trauma); (5) common coexisting medical conditions, such as enuresis and allergies; (6) medication side effects; and (7) contraindications for the medical management of behavior, such as high blood pressure or tic disorders. Robert's pediatrician conducted a complete physical examination and ruled out the above factors as contributing to his hyperactive, inattentive, and aggressive behavior.

CASE CONCEPTUALIZATION

Twin studies support that ADHD-related behaviors are heritable and occur on a continuum of frequency and severity, leading some researchers to conclude that the diagnosis represents the extreme end of a continuum of behavior distributed evenly throughout the entire population, rather than a dichotomy (i.e., disorder present or absent; Levy, Hay, McStephen, Wood, & Waldman, 1997). In addition to genetic influences, environmental factors appear to influence the display of ADHD-related behavior. DuPaul and Ervin (1996) summarized research supporting four possible functions of these behaviors, including escape from aversive tasks, acquisition of peer or teacher attention, obtaining access to highly desirable objects or activities, and self-stimulation (i.e., automatic reinforcement). We believe that functional approaches (i.e., What is the function of the child's behavior?) are crucial for identifying the most effective treatment options for ADHD-diagnosed children, yet traditional structural approaches to assessment (i.e., Does the child's behavior meet diagnostic criteria?) will most certainly remain the norm. Scotti, Morris, McNeil, and Hawkins (1996) have proposed a modification of the current *DSM-IV* multiaxial system that blends traditional and functional assessment in a way that appears to maximize the strengths of each approach. In this model, Axes I and II are unchanged and continue to serve as the foundation for rendering a "traditional" diagnosis. However, Axis III is modified to provide additional information about the individual's strengths and weaknesses and other factors that may enhance or reduce the likelihood of treatment success. Axis IV is reconfigured to provide more detailed information about the function of target behaviors (i.e., functional analysis). Scotti et al.'s modification of the *DSM-IV* Axes III and IV served as the conceptual framework for Robert's case.

According to Axis I diagnostic criteria, Robert's inattentive and hyperactive-impulsive behaviors appeared to produce clinically significant academic and social impairment, and he met diagnostic criteria for ADHD, Combined Type. Robert's noncompliant and aggressive behavior was also serious enough to meet criteria for ODD. Although he had recently been withdrawn from the family and he appeared to have a poor self-concept, criteria were not met for major depression or dysthymia. Neither did he meet diagnostic criteria for an Axis II disorder (i.e., personality disorders or mental retardation) or an Axis III diagnosis using the existing classification system (i.e., general medical conditions). At present, Axis IV registers the psychosocial and environmental problems that may "affect the diagnosis, treatment, and prognosis of mental disorders" (APA, 1994, p. 29). Certainly, Robert's enduring academic and social problems relate to Axis IV and could be coded as V62.30 (academic problem) or V61.20 (parent-child problem). On Axis V, we rated his Global Assessment of Functioning over the past year to be a 55, in the "moderate symptoms" range.

Scotti et al.'s (1996) modifications of the *DSM-IV* require changes only to Axes III and IV, but facilitate the organization of clinical information that might otherwise be overlooked in traditional assessment. On the modified Axis III, Robert had considerable strengths and a few liabilities. For example, he had strong parental support, a close relationship with his stepfather, and had been able to develop a few friendships at home and school. Academically, he was good in math when provided incentives for his work, suggesting that a contingency-based program could play a role in an academic intervention. He had been observed to work independently for at least 10 minutes. He had several hobbies, including drawing, fishing, and biking. His weaknesses included poor language skills and generally poor work habits at home and school. He had few, if any, positive experiences in activities outside of school and had a very poor-self concept. He had frequent conflicts with other children at school, and his mother was concerned that his teacher disliked him. Finally, he had a family history of ADHD, delinquent behavior, and substance abuse, placing him at greater risk for continued problems.

We next considered the antecedents and consequences of Robert's behavior on a modified Axis IV (Scotti et al., 1996). Robert's temper tantrums at a young age were reportedly successful at providing escape from his mother's commands; thus, tantrums could have been negatively reinforced. Despite absence of oppositional behavior on entering school, he became increasingly noncompliant to teacher requests as the year progressed. His aggressive behavior toward adults soon generalized to students. His acts of aggression appeared to provide access to desired objects and activities. Lack of an effective behavior management program at home or in the school environment may have further exacerbated the problem.

He did well academically in kindergarten when he was provided with one-on-one instruction. However, in the absence of individualized assistance, his skills and motivational deficits were quickly apparent. During first and second grade he was frequently off-task and out of his seat. Out-of-seat behavior may have served an escape function, and inappropriate vocalizations were usually preceded by or followed by peer attention. These off-task behaviors certainly inhibited further academic progress, resulting in poor grades and the failure to master academic skills necessary for new, more difficult material. Data from brief experimental analyses conducted in the clinic suggested that his inattentiveness at home was maintained by escape (removal of the task), was more likely to occur during high-demand work, and sometimes produced help (escape through assistance rather than removal of the task). Both differential attention and reprimands appeared to increase his on-task performance.

Robert's academic problems and frequent conflicts with adults and other children may have contributed to his poor self-concept. He has been unable to participate in activities (e.g., sports, Scouts) outside of school because of his hyperactive, noncompliant, and aggressive behavior, making it difficult for him to learn or model appropriate social interactions. Although he had one good friend at school, he has been unable to develop other friendships. Furthermore, he has not been allowed to play with his friends at home because of his poor conduct grades, contributing to his increased withdrawal at home.

RATIONALE FOR TREATMENT CHOICE

In conjunction with Robert's parents, we formulated several treatment goals, including increasing on-task behavior in the classroom, increasing on-task behavior during homework, improving his academic skills in reading and writing, increasing positive social interactions, improving self-concept, and decreasing withdrawal at home.

Stimulant medication is the most commonly used treatment for ADHD-diagnosed children, and approximately 75% of these children demonstrate significantly improved behavioral and academic functioning while taking medication (DuPaul, Barkley, & Conner, 1998). Stimulant medication effectively improves the core symptoms of ADHD, such as increasing attentive skills and decreasing hyperactive behavior. Side effects of stimulant medication are usually mild and include appetite suppression, headaches, stomachaches, and sleep disturbance. However, there are several limitations associated with an exclusive reliance on stimulant medication in the treatment of ADHD-diagnosed children. For example, treatment benefits do not extend to unmedicated conditions (e.g., after school), and associated comorbid problems are not specifically addressed by stimulant medication (e.g., social skills). Neither have the long-term benefits of stimulant medication been established (Pelham, Wheeler, & Chronis, 1998).

Research has demonstrated that using a lower dosage of medication in conjunction with behavioral treatments may be equivalent to a higher dose of medication alone; thus, the two treatments often are used in combination (Pelham et al., 1998). In addition, contingency-based classroom interventions and parent training both meet the criteria for empirically supported treatments for ADHD (Pelham et al., 1998). At school, both classroom modifications (e.g., seating preference) and behavior management programs (e.g., token economies) may improve the on-task behavior of students. Abramowitz and O'Leary (1991) summarized classroom seating arrangement literature, suggesting that row seating was more conducive to on-task behavior than was clustered seating. ADHD-diagnosed children also typically perform better with smaller class sizes. Classroom token economies have been shown to significantly improve on-task behavior and academic achievement (Pelham et al., 1988). Moreover, token economies can be used with entire classrooms or individual students. Points are removed for inappropriate classroom behavior and added for work completion, and points can be exchanged for prizes or privileges. Teachers are trained to provide praise for appropriate behavior.

Much of behavioral parent training consists of extending school-based interventions such as token economies to the home environment (Horn, Ialongo, Greenberg, Packard, & Smith-Winberry, 1990). School-home notes require that teachers rate child behavior at school and parents provide consequences at home. Kelley and McCain (1995) reported that school-home notes increased on-task behavior and the amount of completed academic work, and children were even more likely to exhibit on-task behavior if a response-cost component was added.

For example, the child was required to cross off a "smiley face" if the teacher gave a reprimand. Parents have been used to facilitate social skills training programs for ADHD-diagnosed children (Frankel, Myatt, Cantwell, & Feinberg, 1997).

Recently, sports skills training has been used in combination with social skills training (Reitman, Hupp, O'Callaghan, Gulley, & Northup, 2001). Participation in sports provides ongoing opportunities for social interaction, and greater athletic competence is associated with higher social status (Weiss & Duncan, 1992). The construct "athletic competence" includes not only specific sports skills, but also sportsmanlike behavior, sports knowledge, and attending to important aspects of the game; ADHD-diagnosed children are likely to have difficulties in many of these areas. Hupp and Reitman (1999) demonstrated that basketball skills (e.g., dribbling) could be improved with only a few training sessions. Sportsmanlike behavior and attending skills have been improved during kickball games with ADHD-diagnosed children (Hupp, Reitman, Northup, O'Callaghan, & LeBlanc, 2001; Reitman et al., 2001).

COURSE OF TREATMENT

To address his diverse needs, we recommended a combined pharmacological and behavioral treatment approach for Robert. First, we consulted a local psychiatrist and began a medication evaluation. A placebo and three doses of Adderall (a commonly prescribed stimulant medication) were alternated each day in a counterbalanced design until each level had been administered three times. Robert's parents were provided written instructions for medication administration, a pill box, and a self-monitoring form to keep track of administration. Robert and his teacher were blind to medication status, and his teacher agreed to complete the 28-item short form of the Conners Teacher Rating Scale–Revised (CTRS-R; Conners, 1997) and a brief daily school-home note. The school-home note included the following target behaviors: (1) remain on task, (2) remain seated, (3) raise hand to speak, (4) keep hands and feet to self, and (5) use friendly words. His teacher rated each behavior on a 4-point scale. During the assessment, Robert's parents were instructed not to provide any feedback regarding school behavior, and no home consequences were assigned for good or bad notes at that time. Robert's teacher was told that the data would be used to determine which dose of medication, if any, was the most effective. Finally, after each school day, Robert's mother asked if he had experienced any of the common side effects associated with stimulant medication (e.g., dizziness, loss of appetite).

Results of the medication evaluation are presented in Figure 21.2. Robert's average T-score on the ADHD Index of the CTRS-R during placebo days was 75, which was 2.5 standard deviations above the mean. The T-score ($M = 72$) decreased only slightly when he was taking 5 mg of Adderall. His T-score decreased substantially during both 10 mg ($M = 63$) and 15 mg ($M = 60$) doses of Adderall. Data from the school-home note were consistent with data from the ADHD Index. The only side effect endorsed was decreased appetite. After consultation with the psychiatrist, it was recommended that Robert take 10 mg of Adderall in the morning after breakfast and an additional 5 mg in the afternoon following lunch.

Part of a clinician's job is to seek other services that may benefit the client. During the course of the medication evaluation, we discovered a specialized classroom designed for disruptive children at another school. Although such

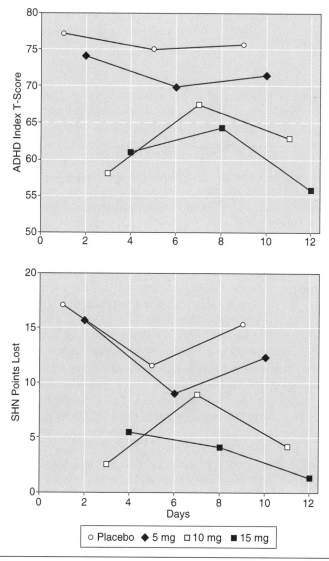

Figure 21.2   ADHD Index T-Scores on the Conner's Teacher Rating Scale–Revised (top panel) and School Home Notes (SHN) Points Lost (bottom panel) during Placebo and Three Doses of Adderall

programs are clearly not available for all ADHD-diagnosed children, the essential components of the program can be incorporated into almost any classroom (see below). Robert enrolled in the program two weeks after the medication evaluation and continued taking the prescribed dose of Adderall.

The classroom was designed for disruptive children and used a structured point system to manage classroom behavior. Students lost points for being off-task, noncompliant, out of their seat, or aggressive (physically or verbally). They earned points for completing assignments and exchanged them for prizes (e.g., pencils, small toys) and privileges (e.g., extra free time) each day. The program had two teachers and only eight students, which made it particularly well suited to Robert's needs. Robert's teachers kept track of his points (0 to 100) on daily monitoring forms, and assigned daily conduct grades based on point values (90–100 = A; 80–89 = B; etc.).

The teachers also developed individualized academic instruction at Robert's instructional level, which helped him practice crucial reading and writing skills that he had failed to master earlier in his academic career. Over the course of the school year, Robert read progressively more difficult first-grade passages. A modeling and practice procedure was used to increase his reading fluency. The teacher's aide first read a passage aloud to Robert, then Robert read the same passage back to the aide and she corrected any errors he made. This process continued until Robert reached the mastery level of the first-grade passages (i.e., 60 words a minute), and then was repeated for second-grade passages. Robert also completed daily writing exercises, and his homework usually included practice in both reading and writing (though he now experienced far more success in attempting these items). An experimental analysis of homework behavior suggested that inattention during homework was largely maintained by escape from high-demand work; Robert's parents reported that he worked much better independently at home because the work was now within his instructional range. By the end of second grade, Robert's reading and writing skills had improved substantially and he was working on grade level.

Daily monitoring forms were sent home every day, and Robert's parents provided privileges contingent on good conduct grades. He earned two hours of outside play time when his conduct grade was an A, one hour for a B, and a half-hour for a C. Additionally, he lost videogame privileges for a D and lost television privileges for an F. He also earned a weekly reward (i.e., a videogame or movie rental) if he had Bs or better all week on his conduct grade. During the first treatment session, the responsibilities of all parties and definitions of key terms (e.g., compliance) were spelled out in a contract signed by Robert and his parents. His parents also provided praise every day for good conduct grades. During the session, the therapist modeled how the parents should respond to good and bad conduct grades, and Robert and his parents practiced each scenario with feedback from the therapist.

During Robert's first week in the program he received Cs and Ds for conduct, followed by As and Bs over the next two months. He was more often on-task, completed more independent seatwork, and displayed far less inappropriate speech. However, he continued to lose points for arguing with other students. During the first month, he lost points for arguing 7 times (approximately 2 times per week), and during the second month he lost points for arguing 23 times (approximately 1 time per day) and attempted to "choke a child" during an argument at recess. At this time, Robert's teacher requested that we intervene, specifically targeting aggressive behavior. A teacher interview revealed that he was most likely to argue during transitions (e.g., to lunch or recess). Robert confirmed that he argued with other students when they tried to get in front of him in line, bumped into him, or teased him by referring to him as "Forrest Gump." He reportedly choked another student because he said "Run Forrest, run" while Robert lined up after recess.

The therapist and Robert discussed functions of teasing, such as the teaser desiring to get him upset or trying to make him laugh. Robert was instructed to interpret teasing as a simple joke, and he was informed that not showing he was upset was the best way to deal with teasing. He was warned that teasing may increase slightly for a short while (i.e., extinction burst) and that this increase indicated that he was doing a good job because the teasers had to try harder. He was assured the teasing would decrease soon after it increased and was provided with two options for showing that he was not upset: He could either ignore the teaser or laugh and joke along with the teaser. Both options were modeled and practiced several times in the session. For example, in response to being called Forrest Gump, Robert actively ignored the therapist by reading or joked along by repeating a line from the movie (i.e., "Life is like a box of chocolates"). He was taught to differentiate between looking upset and looking content, and he practiced making both facial expressions. These same principles were discussed in terms of children bumping him and getting in line in front of him. We also modified Robert's home consequences. He had been able to receive privileges at home based on relatively high conduct grades, even though he lost some points for arguing. Now, to receive his privileges for the day, he was not allowed to have lost any points for arguing. Robert's teachers were also instructed to praise him for appropriate responses to teasing. He continued arguing about one time per day over the next week and lost his home privileges all week. Following that week, arguing behaviors dropped significantly, and he lost points for arguing only about two times a month for the rest of the school year. He continued working hard and doing well academically through the rest of second grade.

During second grade, Robert and his stepfather starting playing baseball together on the weekends, and that spring we recommended that Robert sign up for a baseball team. We conducted one two-hour training session on a large field near the psychology clinic. We encouraged Robert's parents to continue practicing basic baseball skills, and we offered two new skills to be incorporated into practice sessions: attending to the game and sportsmanlike behavior. Attentive behavior was defined as "being in the ready position" while on the field; Robert bent his knees, placing his hands on his thighs, and faced home plate. We practiced several trials with Robert on first base, and the therapist pitched the ball to his stepfather. His mother recorded "ready positions" and provided praise for being ready. Next, sportsmanlike behavior was defined as "cheering for a teammate either verbally or physically, and congratulating a player on another team." Robert practiced cheering for the pitcher, and his mother provided praise for sportsmanlike behavior.

Toward the end of the sports training session, we instructed Robert's parents to monitor attentive and sportsmanlike behavior on a tally sheet during baseball practices and games. We agreed that if Robert displayed at least 10 "ready positions" and 3 "sportsmanlike behaviors" during the first practice, he could choose where they would go for dinner. Following the first practice, the therapist contacted Robert's mother by phone. She indicated that he had a great practice (17 ready positions and 3 sportsmanlike behaviors) and chose pizza for dinner. His parents were encouraged to continue monitoring his attentive and sportsmanlike behavior. Throughout the season, Robert enjoyed playing on the team, and his parents reported being pleased to see him play. They also indicated that he became much less withdrawn at home as he started performing better academically and they believed his positive experience playing baseball helped improve his self-concept.

Following Robert's successful second-grade year, his teacher recommended mainstreaming into a regular education classroom for third grade. He continued

taking the same dose of Adderall (after stopping for the summer), and the original school-home note (designed for the medication evaluation) was reinstated.
Robert's new teacher was instructed to cross off one smiley face for each rule violation (i.e., remain on-task, remain seated, raise hand to speak, keep hands and
feet to self, and use friendly words). Robert could earn up to 20 happy faces
each day and was given a conduct grade accordingly (i.e., 18–20 = A; 16–17 = B;
etc.). A new contract was written explaining the same home consequences that
were used during the previous year. From the beginning of the year, Robert received primarily As and Bs for his daily conduct grade and also received good
grades academically.

One month into Robert's third-grade year, the teacher completed the TRF and
Robert's parent's completed the CBCL. Their ratings are compared to parent and
teacher ratings from the initial assessment in Figure 21.3. Overall, both parents'
scores fell below the clinically significant range across all subscales, and his
third-grade teacher rated him much more positively than his original second-
grade teacher.

THERAPIST-CLIENT FACTORS

This case clearly illustrates the importance of a good working relationship among
all parties involved in Robert's care. Indeed, in cases such as Robert's, there are
actually many "consumers" or "clients." As noted by Baer (1988), therapy may be
regarded as complete when the "complaints" of the individual in treatment
and/or the referral agent have been fully addressed. In this instance, Robert's
complaints centered around punishment and what he considered to be unfair
treatment by others. His parents complained about their difficulty in managing
his behavior at home and harbored serious concerns about his social and academic progress. His teachers complained that his behavior in the classroom setting was unmanageable and shared the parents' concern about his intellectual
and emotional development. To resolve these concerns, it was necessary to establish good communication among all parties, meaning that each person became
aware of his or her responsibilities and maintained a good working relationship
with the therapist. The therapist served as a "coach" and sometimes "broker,"
who facilitated the transmission of information among the parties through
school-home notes, contingency contracts, and the presentation of data used
to inform treatment decisions. Providing information to other professionals (e.g.,
psychiatrist, teachers) also enhanced the effectiveness of their efforts to assist
Robert. In our view, the child behavior therapist is in an ideal position to serve as
a link among the numerous individuals likely to be involved in the treatment of a
child diagnosed with ADHD.

COURSE OF TERMINATION

Our role in Robert's treatment was relaxed substantially after his aggressive behavior decreased in second grade. At that point, the structured classroom, individualized academic instruction, and hard work by Robert and his parents
became the focus of the intervention. Following Robert's successful performance
in second grade, we actively participated in treatment only to assist with his rein-
troduction into athletics and the mainstream third-grade class. We met with

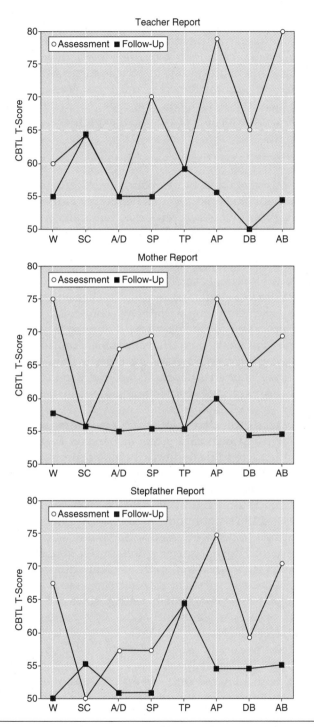

Figure 21.3 T-Scores on the Child Behavior Checklist Based on Teacher (top panel), Mother (middle panel), and Stepfather (bottom panel) Report during Assessment (circles) and 1-Year Follow-Up (squares) (*Key:* W = Withdrawn; SC = Somatic Complaints; A/D = Anxious/Depressed; SP = Social Problems; TP = Thought Problems; AP = Attention Problems; DB =Delinquent Behavior; AB = Aggressive Behavior)

Robert and his parents one month into his third-grade year. They indicated that they were happy with the treatment and agreed that we had met our treatment goals. We recommended termination of our services, and encouraged them to call us if they had any other concerns. We also scheduled a follow-up appointment (three months later) to monitor Robert's social and academic progress. We suggested that Robert join the Art Club at his school to further develop his creative abilities and provide additional positive social experiences.

FOLLOW-UP

Robert's mother was contacted by telephone one week prior to the scheduled follow-up appointment. She reported that he received all As and Bs on his previous report card and continued to receive excellent daily conduct grades. He had not lost any points for arguing in the classroom lately and had several good friends at home and school. He showed no signs of withdrawal from his parents and was excited about playing baseball again in the spring. His parents enrolled him in an art class after school at the local community center. He continued taking his prescribed dose of Adderall, and his mother asked about discontinuing the medication. After consultation with the psychiatrist, it was suggested that he stop taking the medication for the next week without informing his teacher. To control for possible placebo-related effects, Robert's mother gave him a vitamin and told him it was the same as Adderall (the school nurse was informed of the procedure and provided vitamins as well). We instructed Robert's mother to bring the prior four weeks of school-home notes into the clinic on the following week.

Data from the notes indicated that Robert was more off-task and out of seat during the week without medication. We also asked Robert how he felt about taking the medication. He indicated that it helped him work harder, but he did not enjoy going to the nurse after lunch. We monitored the effects of the medication for one more week with Robert taking a 10 mg dose of Adderall in the morning (i.e., discontinuing the 5 mg afternoon dose) and another week of placebo. We evaluated the school-home notes two weeks later. Results indicated that Robert performed better while taking the medication, and he appeared to do as well as before with just a morning dose. After consultation with Robert's mother and psychiatrist, we recommended continuation of the morning dose of Adderall.

MANAGED CARE CONSIDERATIONS

We were fortunate to work with Robert at a university psychology clinic with a sliding-fee schedule. In this setting, we were insulated from many of the constraints associated with managed care. Robert's specialized classroom was part of his school system and the services were provided at no extra cost. His medication was paid for by Medicare.

Perhaps the major limitation of working with a third-party payer is obtaining reimbursement for assessment and treatment in the classroom. Some clinicians negotiate this obstacle by asking clients to pay for school visits. Using well-trained master's or bachelor's level support staff may also help keep these costs low. Moreover, a considerable amount of money may be saved by conducting

CBM, which can be completed in a fraction of the time of traditional psychoeducational testing (though such testing may still be necessary to obtain special classroom accommodations).

OVERALL EFFECTIVENESS

Approximately one year after our first session with Robert's family, he was receiving As and Bs for academic work and conduct. His parents reported that he was also doing better socially and no longer withdrew from the family. Robert's case illustrates the importance of a multimodal assessment and treatment package. Most ADHD-diagnosed children receive some form of pharmacological and behavioral treatment, but the functional assessment of Robert's behavior helped to tailor these interventions specifically for him. The individual treatment components may have effectively reduced some of the presenting problems; however, the combined approach was necessary to address all of our treatment goals.

The in-depth functional assessment also greatly facilitated the selection of treatment options. Observing Robert's behavior in the classroom helped to identify several variables that related to his poor work completion (e.g., peers), and an experimental analysis of homework performance identified additional factors (e.g., task difficulty). The CBM provided a ready assessment of his academic strengths and weaknesses and provided important information regarding skill and performance deficits. Additionally, the CBM probes were completed more efficiently than a traditional psychoeducational assessment (e.g., intelligence and achievement testing). The medication evaluation also proved invaluable in the determination of therapeutic medication dose. Without multimodal assessments of this sort, physicians must rely primarily on parent and teacher reports of dubious validity to assist in their clinical decision making. Finally, Scotti et al.'s (1996) functional modification of the *DSM-IV* multiaxial system guided our assessment and greatly enhanced our case conceptualization.

Stimulant medication frequently plays a pivotal role in the treatment of core symptoms of ADHD, and behavioral techniques enhance treatment by addressing many behaviors associated with the diagnosis. We were fortunate to have access to an intensive behavioral classroom that had a substantial impact on Robert's behavior. Robert's parents and teachers also greatly contributed to treatment success by providing consistency during his transition back into the mainstream classroom. Finally, we considered Robert's participation in athletics to be an important component of treatment, as it provided an opportunity to develop much needed social skills that may translate into better long-term outcome.

REFERENCES

Abramowitz, A. J., & O'Leary, S. G. (1991). Behavioral interventions for the classroom: Implications for students with ADHD. *School Psychology Review, 20,* 220–234.

Achenbach, T. M. (1991). *Manual for the Child Behavior Checklist/4–18 and 1991 profile.* Burlington: University of Vermont, Department of Psychiatry.

American Psychiatric Association. (1994). *Diagnostic and statistical manual of mental disorders* (4th ed.). Washington, DC: Author.

Baer, D. M. (1988). If you know why you're changing a behavior, you'll know when you've changed it enough. *Behavioral Assessment, 10,* 219–223.

Barkley, R. A. (1990). *Attention Deficit Hyperactivity Disorder: A handbook for diagnosis and treatment.* New York: Guilford Press.

Barkley, R. A. (1998). *Attention Deficit Hyperactivity Disorder: A handbook for diagnosis and treatment* (2nd ed.). New York: Guilford Press.

Biederman, J., Newcorn, J., & Sprich, S. (1991). Comorbidity of attention deficit hyperactivity disorder with conduct, depressive, anxiety, and other disorders. *American Journal of Psychiatry, 148,* 564–577.

Breen, M. J., & Altepeter, T. S. (1990). *Disruptive behavior disorders in children.* New York: Guilford Press.

Conners, C. K. (1997). *Conners' Rating Scales–Revised technical manual.* North Tonawanda, NY: Multi-health Systems.

DuPaul, G. J., Barkley, R. A., & Conner, D. F. (1998). Stimulants. In R. A. Barkley (Ed.), *Attention deficit hyperactivity disorder: A handbook for diagnosis and treatment* (2nd ed.). New York: Guilford Press.

DuPaul, G. J., & Ervin, R. A. (1996). Functional assessment of behaviors related to attention-deficit/hyperactivity disorder: Linking assessment to intervention design. *Behavior Therapy, 27,* 601–622.

Farrington, D. (1994). Child, adolescent, and adult features of violent males. In L. Huessmann (Ed.), *Aggressive behavior: Current perspectives* (pp. 215–240). New York: Plenum Press.

Frankel, F., Myatt, R., Cantwell, D. P., & Feinberg, D. T. (1997). Parent-assisted transfer of children's social skills training: Effects on children with and without attention-deficit hyperactivity disorder. *Journal of the American Academy of Child and Adolescent Psychiatry, 36,* 1056–1064.

Frick, P. J., Kamphaus, R. W., Lahey, B. B., Loeber, R., Christ, M. A. G., Hart, E. L., et al. (1991). Academic underachievement and the disruptive behavior disorders. *Journal of Consulting and Clinical Psychology, 59,* 289–294.

Horn, W. F., Ialongo, N., Greenberg, G., Packard, T., & Smith-Winberry, C. (1990). Additive effects of behavioral parent training and self-control therapy with ADHD children. *Journal of Clinical Child Psychology, 19,* 98–110.

Hupp, S. D. A., & Reitman, D. (1999). Improving sports skills and sportsmanship in children diagnosed with attention-deficit/hyperactivity disorder. *Child and Family Behavior Therapy, 21,* 35–51.

Hupp, S. D. A., Reitman, D., Northup, J., O'Callaghan, P., & LeBlanc, M. (2001). *The effects of delayed rewards, token incentives, and stimulant medication on sportsmanlike behavior with ADHD-diagnosed children.* Manuscript submitted for publication.

Kelley, M. L., & McCain, A. P. (1995). Promoting academic performance in inattentive children: The relative efficacy of school-home notes with and without response cost. *Behavior Modification, 19,* 357–375.

Kovacs, M. (1992). *Children's Depression Inventory.* North Tonawanda, NY: Multi-Health Systems.

Landau, S., Milich, R., & Diener, M. B. (1998). Peer relations of children with attention-deficit hyperactivity disorder. *Reading and Writing Quarterly: Overcoming Learning Difficulties, 14,* 83–105.

Levy, F., Hay, D. A., McStephen, M., Wood, C., & Waldman, I. (1997). Attention-deficit/hyperactivity disorder: A category or continuum? Genetic analysis of a large-scale twin study. *Journal of the American Academy of Child and Adolescent Psychiatry, 36,* 737–744.

Morrison, J. R. (1997). *When psychological problems mask medical disorders: A guide for psychotherapists.* New York: Guilford Press.

Pelham, W. E., Schnedler, R. W., Bender, M. E., Miller, J., Nilsson, D., Budrow, M., et al. (1988). The combination of behavior therapy and methylphenidate in the treatment of hyperactivity: A therapy outcome study. In L. Bloomingdale (Ed.), *Attention deficit disorders* (Vol. 3, pp. 29–48). London: Pergamon Press.

Pelham, W. E., Wheeler, T., & Chronis, A. (1998). Empirically supported psychosocial treatments for attention deficit hyperactivity disorder. *Journal of Clinical Child Psychology, 27,* 190–205.

Reitman, D., Hummel, R., Franz, D. Z., & Gross, A. M. (1998). A review of methods and instruments for assessing externalizing disorders: Theoretical and practical considerations in rendering a diagnosis. *Clinical Psychology Review, 18,* 555–584.

Reitman, D., Hupp, S. D. A., O'Callaghan, P., Gulley, V., & Northup, J. (2001). The influence of a token economy and methylphenidate on attentive and disruptive behavior during sports with ADHD-diagnosed children. *Behavior Modification, 25,* 305–323.

Scotti, J. R., Morris, T. L., McNeil, C. B., & Hawkins, R. P. (1996). *DSM-IV* and disorders of childhood and adolescence: Can structural criteria be functional? *Journal of Consulting and Clinical Psychology, 64,* 1177–1191.

Shinn, M. R. (1989). *Curriculum-based measurement: Assessing special children.* New York: Guilford Press.

Sturmey, P. (1996). *Functional analysis in clinical psychology.* New York: Wiley.

Weiss, M. R., & Duncan, S. C. (1992). The relationship between physical competence and peer acceptance in the context of children's sports participation. *Journal of Sport and Exercise Psychology, 14,* 177–191.

CHAPTER 22

Mental Retardation

CYNTHIA R. JOHNSON

DESCRIPTION OF THE DISORDER

THE DIAGNOSTIC CRITERIA and definition of mental retardation have met with much controversy over the past two decades. This has been due in large part to there being different professional groups involved in the shaping of the definition and the criteria used for the definition and diagnostic criteria of mental retardation. Two primary diagnostic systems that have set forth criteria for mental retardation are the *Diagnostic and Statistical Manual of Mental Disorders,* fourth edition (*DSM-IV*; American Psychiatric Association [APA], 1994) and *Mental Retardation: Definition, Classification, and Systems of Support* (American Association on Mental Retardation [AAMR], 1992). Both classification systems list below-average cognitive functioning as the fundamental feature of mental retardation. Deficits in adaptive functioning in skill areas such as communication, self-care, social skills, leisure and work, and personal safety (AAMR, 1992; APA, 1994) are further necessary to make the diagnosis. A third criterion is the onset of developmental delays before the age of 18 years. Prevalence of mental retardation in the United States is around 2% (Watson & Gross, 1997).

Four degrees of mental retardation are used to designate the severity of impairment in *DSM-IV* (APA, 1994). For each level, a corresponding IQ range is assigned. Mild Mental Retardation (IQ level of 50 to 55 to approximately 70), Moderate Mental Retardation (IQ level of 35 to 40 to 50 to 55), Severe Mental Retardation (20 to 25 to 35 to 40), and Profound Mental Retardation (IQ level below 20 to 25) are the four levels included in *DSM-IV*. Mental Retardation, Severity Unspecified is also used in *DSM-IV* for use when mental retardation is strongly suspected but appropriate assessments have not yet been administered or are not available.

These levels or degrees of mental retardation give some predictive value with regard to expected competencies and in planning for appropriate educational, habilitative, and other services. The mild mental retardation group represents the largest number of individuals with mental retardation. It is generally accepted that these individuals are capable of achieving nearly full independence with appropriate instruction and support. Within the moderate range, it is expected that some level of supervision and assistance in the community will be necessary. The expectation for individuals functioning in the severe to profound range of mental retardation is generally that lifelong care will be needed, although mastery of some self-care, survival, and some forms of communication may be attained. It should be underscored that the achievements of individuals vary vastly within all the levels of mental retardation.

This variability may be explained by a number of factors. First, the underlying etiology of mental retardation may impact developmental course and prognosis. Identified causes include chromosomal disorders, metabolic disorders, neonatal disorders, and environmental factors such as toxins and malnutrition. Postnatal potential causes include infections, degenerative disorders, and other, later-onset neurologic disorders. A specific etiology is much more likely to be identified in the moderate and severe/profound ranges, whereas etiology of mild mental retardation is more elusive and unclear. Variability also may depend on when the diagnosis of mental retardation was made. It is now accepted that early intervention services may greatly influence the course of mental retardation (Castro & White, 1993; Innocenti, 1996).

Children with mental retardation often present with concomitant impairments. These include cerebral palsy, seizure disorders, and sensory impairments (visual and hearing deficits). If one of these impairments co-occurs with mental retardation, specific interventions or therapies to address these impairments often are required. Children with a known etiology may present with other medical issues related to the cause of the mental retardation.

CHALLENGING BEHAVIORS AND MENTAL HEALTH DISORDERS IN CHILDREN/ADOLESCENTS WITH MENTAL RETARDATION

Of particular relevance to this chapter are the comorbid challenging behaviors very often observed in children with mental retardation. The presence of behavior and psychiatric disorders may be one of the greatest obstacles to the normalization and education of individuals with mental retardation. While prevalence of behavior and emotional disturbance in individuals with mental retardation has varied greatly, from 7% to 70% (Jacobson, 1990), it has long been accepted that those with mental retardation are at much greater risk for developing behavior and mental health disorders at some point in their life (Bruininks, Hill, & Morreau, 1988; Quay & Hogan, 1999). Although historically, specific behavior problems often were associated with mental retardation, it was debated whether all mental health disorders co-occurred with mental retardation, especially the internalizing disorders (e.g., depression and anxiety). It is now accepted that all mental health disorders may occur in those with mental retardation (Reiss, 1994). These additional challenges not only pose a significant risk to life, health, and property, but they also may disrupt or disable normal family functioning and interfere with participation in habilitative activities. Presence of behavior and emotional problems in individuals with mental retardation and other developmental disabilities greatly influences the level of restrictiveness of educational placement (Singer & Irwin, 1987) and, in later years, is associated with placement decisions and placement failures in living arrangements (Lakin, Hill, Hauber, Bruininks, & Heal, 1983; Vitello, Atthowe, & Cadwell, 1983).

Behaviors often exhibited in individuals with mental retardation include aggression, property destruction, self-injurious behaviors, stereotypies or self-stimulatory behaviors, pica (ingestion of inedible items) and mouthing, oppositional or noncompliant behaviors, and regulatory problems (i.e., in eating, sleeping, and toileting). All of these behaviors are more likely to occur in children with mental retardation (see Benson & Aman, 1999). Further, common childhood disorders such as Attention-Deficit/Hyperactivity Disorder (ADHD) occur more often in those with a diagnosis of mental retardation. Hyperactivity in individuals with mental retardation has been reported to be problematic in 9% to 21% of this population (Jacobson, 1982; Quine, 1986).

CASE DESCRIPTION

At the time of an initial evaluation in a program for children with mental retardation and concomitant behavior and emotional challenges, Raymond was a 10-year-old boy. He had attended specialized schools since school age. At the time of evaluation, he was enrolled in a specialized school serving primarily children and adolescents, ages 5 to 21 years, with mental retardation, often with physical challenges. Raymond lived at home with his parents and older brother.

CHIEF COMPLAINTS

Raymond was seen for this initial evaluation after moving to the area; the primary purpose was to determine his current intervention needs. Although he was receiving educational services that seemed to serve his needs, it was felt that additional support and treatment services were needed to realize this child's potential, optimize levels of independence, address specific behavioral concerns, decrease future level of restrictiveness, and improve family adaptation. Raymond was evaluated to be functioning in the moderate range of mental retardation, who also presented with oppositional and noncompliant behaviors in addition to behavior symptoms consistent with ADHD. Raymond further had great difficulty in home situations when there were additional persons present (i.e., relatives, friends).

HISTORY

For a diagnosis of mental retardation, the history of the disorder is often considered to date back to the prenatal period for etiology causes. In the case of Raymond, pregnancy was unremarkable with no noted risk factors. His birthweight was 8 lbs., 6 ozs. Delivery was equally uneventful, and he was discharged from the hospital with his mother the day after delivery.

Early on, Raymond was a quiet infant who slept for long periods. His mother became concerned when he did not appear to be gazing at her when nursed or when held. This led to a cascade of medical tests and procedures, which eventuated to a diagnosis of optic nerve hypoplasia. This diagnosis is made when there is medical evidence that the optic nerve connections are reduced in number in the occipital lobe of the brain. Individuals with this visual impairment may appear to see, but they experience difficulty with colors, clarity, and details of images. Often, optic nerve hypoplasia co-occurs with nystagmus (involuntary rhythmic movements of the eye). Raymond was diagnosed with both of these visual impairments within the first 5 months of his life. His parents were informed that children with optic nerve hypoplasia often are diagnosed with mental retardation and have a higher incidence of seizures. Hence, unlike children who are diagnosed with mild mental retardation and no other significant medical diagnoses, Raymond's developmental status was brought under scrutiny very early in life. As he failed to achieve common motor milestones, such as rolling over, sitting, and then later, walking, his parents sought out early intervention programs to address skills in the motor domain and then the cognitive domain. A vision specialist was also involved. These services were provided both in the home and in the context of an infant stimulation class. Raymond went on to receive specialized services for preschool children with developmental disabilities. Unfortunately, he began having complex partial seizures around the age of 3½ years. This led to the prescription of anticonvulsant medication for control of the seizures. Phenobarbital, which was prescribed and taken daily, greatly reduced the occurrence of seizures.

BEHAVIORAL ASSESSMENT

Assessment of Raymond included a behavioral interview with his mother. The purpose of this type of interview is to gather specific information about the behavior problems exhibited and behaviors that will be a focus of behavioral treatment. In addition to obtaining an operational definition of "target" behaviors, eliciting possible information about possible antecedents and consequences of the problematic behaviors serves to begin making hypotheses about the environmental influences of the challenging behaviors. This information is further helpful in directing additional behavioral assessment procedures that will be most sensitive in measuring identified behavior problems.

Our interview resulted in the identification of interfering, challenging behaviors, including noncompliance with the daily routine and simple adult requests. For example, Raymond often would refuse and complain about simple daily living activities and chores (dressing, clearing his dishes after a meal, and brushing his teeth). He also protested when making a transition (leaving his afterschool program to go home). Infrequently, he would become aggressive if he were required to do something he did not wish to do; typically, this aggression took the form of pushing or hitting one of his parents or older brother. This behavioral interview identified the antecedents and consequences of these behaviors along with proximal and temporal variables. Interfering behaviors were more likely to occur (1) when there were more people around, (2) when asked to do a less preferred activity, (3) when Raymond was fatigued, and (4) when his routine had been disrupted from a typical situation.

Direct observations were made and the Motivation Assessment Scale (Durand & Crimmins, 1988) was conducted to better ascertain the motivation or function of the interfering behaviors Raymond displayed. This would then inform the development of empirically derived treatments. Both parent and teacher ratings of the Aberrant Behavior Checklist (ABC; Aman & Singh, 1986) and the Conners Rating Scale (CRS;) garnered additional information. The five subscales on the ABC are

Irritability, Agitation, Crying; Lethargy, Social Withdrawal; Stereotypic Behavior; Hyperactivity, Noncompliance; and Inappropriate Speech. Both his parents and special education teacher rated Raymond in the clinically significant range on the Hyperactivity and Noncompliance scales. On the CRS, clinically significant scores were obtained on the Oppositional and ADHD subscales. Together, these assessment tools revealed that Raymond's challenging behaviors were motivated and maintained by social attention (i.e., gaining adult attention) and escape (getting out of doing something) and documented the presence of significant ADHD symptoms.

COGNITIVE ASSESSMENT

Both for diagnostic purposes and to develop appropriate interventions for individuals with mental retardation, cognitive testing is warranted to determine overall level of functioning as well as to discern particular cognitive strengths and weaknesses. Additional neuropsychological testing may be useful in better characterizing an individual's abilities across several domains, including attention, language, and memory in addition to adaptive behavior areas.

Given Raymond's visual impairments, only portions of a traditional IQ test could be administered. On an individual intelligence test, he obtained a Verbal IQ of 46. On a test of language development, he obtained age-equivalent scores at the 4-year to 5-year levels. Additional memory and learning tasks suggested an age-equivalent level of 4 years. In keeping with conventions for the diagnosis of mental retardation, an adaptive behavior inventory was administered and revealed a composite score of 67; this finding suggested adaptive behavior skills higher than his intelligence test but was still significantly below average. It could be stated that whereas Raymond's IQ testing suggested moderate mental retardation, adaptive behavior findings were consistent with mild mental retardation. In this particular case, this difference was attributed to the early intensive services he received, along with his family's efforts in providing him with many integrated opportunities and inclusion in all aspects of family activities.

MEDICAL CONSULTATION

Raymond received consultation services from several medical subspecialty areas simultaneously with the initiation of behavioral services. First, he had an earlier identified seizure disorder for which he was prescribed phenobarbital. This medication apparently controlled the seizure activity prior to the family's recent move, but clinical signs of seizure activity had been noted recently. A neurologic consultation resulted in changes in his anticonvulsant medication; he was placed on a dose of depakote that resulted in greatly reduced seizure activity. It had been presumed earlier that the phenobarbital increased Raymond's inattentiveness and irritability; with discontinuation of phenobarbital, its adverse effects could be eliminated as contributory to his daily behavior. These adverse effects of phenobarbital are documented (Domizo, Verrotti, Ramenghi, Sabatino, & Morgese, 1993).

Given Raymond's small physical stature, association between optic nerve hypoplasia and hormone deficiencies, and family history of hormone abnormalities, a consultation from an endocrinologist was also obtained. Medical testing ruled out a medical difference in this area.

Considering this child's concomitant visual impairment, consultations from an opthamalogist and a special education vision specialist were essential in the discernment of visual abilities and deficits interfacing with his cognitive and adaptive behavior abilities. Though Raymond had had earlier involvement with opthamalogy, consultation was warranted given the family's recent move to the area and his interest in physical activities. Hence, it was extremely important to better discern his visual skills to better plan for realistic leisure skills, training, and community activity goals. From these consultations, recommendations for ongoing low-vision training and orientation and mobility training were made. These services were provided in his special education setting.

Given the prominent ADHD symptoms assessed in this child, along with a positive family history, a psychiatric consultation to determine the appropriateness of a possible pharmacological intervention was pursued. This resulted in a trial of methylphenidate (Ritalin) to address his attention deficits and distractibility. A low dose of Ritalin resulted in improvements in attention and decreased distractibility.

CASE CONCEPTUALIZATION

At the time of referral, Raymond was a 10-year-old child with mental retardation in the moderate range. Specific referral concerns suggested further evaluation of inattention, distractibility, and oppositional behaviors. Additionally, the family was seeking advice concerning his intervention needs and the availability of resources in the area to which they had recently relocated that might appropriately address those needs. As with many children with mental retardation, Raymond had other co-occurring medical complications: optic nerve hypoplasia, nystagmus, and a seizure disorder. These additional medical diagnoses further complicated assessment and treatment approaches.

Based on our assessment, Raymond was diagnosed with ADHD. He displayed significant symptoms consistent with this diagnosis far beyond what might be expected given his delayed developmental level. He further met criteria for Oppositional Defiant Disorder. This diagnosis captured his propensity to be noncompliant with simple adult requests and daily routines. Instead of complying with realistic expectations and specific requests, Raymond would talk back, refuse, or passively engage in other behaviors. On occasion, he became aggressive when he was made to comply with a daily activity. A functional behavior assessment revealed two primary motivations or functions of these behaviors: social attention and escape. That is, these seemingly interfering behaviors served Raymond in gaining adult attention and getting him out of situations or tasks he found undesirable. This was in the context of a child with moderate mental retardation who likely found many tasks he confronted difficult and possibly stressful.

Physical and medical variables further influenced Raymond's behavior. When physically fatigued or ill, he was more likely to be oppositional and noncompliant. Furthermore, he displayed deficits with regard to independent leisure skills, safety skills, self-care skills, and social skills. Hence, as is the typical scenario for treatment of children with mental retardation, intervention focused on a change or decrease in specific areas and the teaching of new skills. Although often discussed in isolation, the interactions between problematic behaviors and lack of skills are well established. In this case, the lack of skills often led to engagement in other, inappropriate behaviors.

In collaboration with his parents and the numerous clinicians and educators involved in this child's care, the following treatment goals were delineated:

1. Increase attention to task and decrease distractibility.
2. Increase compliance to daily routine, adult requests, and household expectations.
3. Increase independent leisure skills.
4. Increase independence in self-care activities.
5. Increase social skills.
6. Increase safety and community skills.
7. Increase maintenance and generalization of skill acquisition.

RATIONALE FOR TREATMENT CHOICE

As with the majority cases where a primary presenting diagnosis is mental retardation, with secondary behavioral and emotional challenges, treatment choices involve multicomponents of behavior treatment, often with psychopharmacological intervention. In the case of Raymond, additional medical issues further influenced both treatment choices and specific implementation procedures. For purposes of clarity in this chapter, the types of treatment used for Raymond are described within the contextual settings where they were a primary focus; in practice, the treatments were more fluidly implemented across settings.

COURSE OF TREATMENT

INTENSIVE HOME-BASED BEHAVIOR INTERVENTION AND PARENT TRAINING

Soon after initial evaluation, home-based services were initiated. These provided both parent training in behavior management as well as direct staff support to provide intervention in Raymond's home and neighborhood for 15 hours a week. Several antecedent management strategies were developed and implemented. Antecedent management strategies refer to strategies that alter the environment either by modifying it or by adding antecedents that decrease the probability that the behavior will occur (Horner et al., 1990). In his home, Raymond's daily routine was altered to allow for more interspersing of preferred tasks with nonpreferred, challenging tasks. His parents and in-home staff followed this newly designed schedule, which was intended to decrease escape behavior as overall stress was decreased. To promote independence in self-care, his environment was altered to ensure his ease in accessing what he needed. For example, "outfits" were organized in drawers, so that each drawer had all the necessary clothing for the day: pants, shirts, underwear, and socks. Additionally, items he was able to use independently were placed in containers he could easily access and open.

To address the goal of increasing compliance to his parents' and other adults' requests, a contingency management system was developed by which Raymond earned stars, then points to be "cashed in" for tangible reinforcers or privileges.

He could earn a point for compliance to adherence to routine requests specified on his card. Loss of a point, a response cost, was included for noncompliance, defined in this case as failure to follow a request after one reminder or prompt. This greatly increased Raymond's compliance to his parents' requests, from 25% before the system began to about 80%. As this change in compliance was observed over time, the schedule of reinforcement as well as the types of reinforcers were adjusted to be more consistent with what typically was available in the home and community.

Once compliance had increased, additional interventions were implemented in the home setting. Rule training was introduced and focused on having Raymond remain in the house while his mother completed essential household tasks. For example, one of the issues raised had been his nightly habit of entering the kitchen while his mother was cooking dinner; this was not only disruptive, it was also dangerous. With in-home staff, Raymond was taught the rule of "boundaries," specifying where he should remain during the time his mother cooked. A correspondence training paradigm (Baer, 1990) was used: The staff stated the rules, then Raymond was asked to verbalize the rules. He was then reinforced for following the rules. At first, he was reinforced by the staff on a frequent basis; this role then was transferred to his mother, with frequency of reinforcement fading systematically to every 10 to 12 minutes. At this point, his mother would simply need to "check on him" and verbally reinforce him for engaging in an activity independently. Fading of the reinforcement was again implemented to promote maintenance of behavior change.

As these gains were made, further steps toward increasing Raymond's independent self-care skills were undertaken. Self-management strategies such as reported in the literature (Burgio, Whitman, & Johnson, 1980) were implemented to promote his independence with the morning routine on school days. The steps of the morning routine were recorded on an audiotape. Raymond was then taught to turn the tape recorder on and follow the steps recorded. As he completed the steps, he was taught to check off the step on a large chart. After completing the sequence of steps successfully, he was reinforced with a special breakfast of his choice. This self-management strategy was extremely effective in not only increasing his level of independence but in decreasing conflict between Raymond and his mother during the morning. Therefore, a similar approach was implemented for the bedtime routine. The end reinforcer for successful completion was extended TV time in his bedroom.

THERAPEUTIC AFTERSCHOOL PROGRAM

After approximately one year of treatment services in the home, Raymond had made gains, but he continued to fail to generalize newly learned skills and behaviors to community settings. He also continued to have tremendous difficulty in social situations; he would either become intrusive and perseverative in his verbal interactions or become passive and fail to participate altogether. He therefore was enrolled in a therapeutic afterschool program with the specific goals of improving his social skills and increasing his repertoire of leisure skills and safety and community skills.

In this program, treatment goals along with methods and procedures to reach these goals were documented. For Raymond, social skill goals included increasing his skills with respect to initiating and conversing on appropriate topics, responding to others, and asking pertinent questions of others. Through direct instruction, role playing, and behavioral rehearsal in the "social group" of this program, Raymond improved in his ability to engage in "to-and-fro" conversation on relevant topics. Through use of video coaching, improving aspects of nonverbal social communication behaviors was undertaken as well. For example, Raymond received feedback about his tendency not to make eye contact with his listener when conversing. Likewise, videotaping him in large groups when he perseverated on a topic and interrupted others helped to illustrate for him when he should refrain from interjecting comments and how to identify times when it would be more appropriate to contribute a comment.

With the operating assumption that many of the children with mental retardation and challenging behaviors enrolled in this afterschool program could benefit from regular physical exercise as well as instruction in relaxation, Raymond also received these interventions. Several studies have demonstrated a decrease in maladaptive behaviors in response to participation in an aerobic exercise program and relaxation training (Baumeister & MacLean, 1984; Calamari, Geist, & Shahbazian, 1987; Kern, Koegel, Dyer, Blew, & Fenton, 1982; McGimsey & Favell, 1988). Specific exercise programs have varied as well as the target subjects; behaviors treated include stereotypies, self-injury, aggression, and negative vocalization. Using this information, a schedule of physical exercise was incorporated in the program. The specific exercise program varied so as not to be monotonous and included lap walking or jogging around a track across the street from the program, riding a stationary bicycle, and an aerobics class. A physical exercise schedule was developed with the input of the child participants. These physical activities were met with enthusiasm on Raymond's part. He was highly motivated to complete the physical activity and responded to verbal reinforcement of his performance to complete the exercises.

As with exercise, participation in relaxation training has been successful in decreasing problematic behaviors in individuals with mental retardation (Calamari et al., 1987; McPhail & Chamove, 1989). Hence, a relaxation group was implemented as a component of this program. A useful resource for conducting relaxation training with children and adolescents with mental retardation (Cautela & Groden, 1978) was consulted to develop specific activities.

The expansion of Raymond's leisure skills, both in group and independent activities, was another important goal with far-reaching implications for his adaptive functioning and well-being. Toward this formidable goal, Raymond participated in specific sport skills training in the afterschool program. In this aspect of the program, specific essential skills were taught using discrete trials, behavior rehearsal, and feedback. Raymond participated in the essential skills of basketball, baseball, and soccer. Additionally, direct instruction in computer and video games was a component of the program. This was then incorporated in the home programming to ensure generalization.

Likewise, the direct instruction of safety skills was undertaken in this afterschool program. First, children enrolled in the program were explicitly taught discrimination between dangerous and safe stimuli, for example, what was safe versus not safe to touch (e.g., flame, stove burner). Then, the more complex skills around safety were undertaken; these included such skills as crossing the street, how to call in case of an emergency, and when to call for assistance. With respect to Raymond, the situations when he should call for an adult's help were a focus, with the goal of increasing his level of independence at home and in community settings.

THERAPEUTIC SUMMER CAMP

Although Raymond had made impressive gains in all areas of functioning, the maintenance of skills when there was a discontinuity in programming remained of concern. This is common in those with mental retardation. For Raymond, lack of continuity of structure and programming in the summer months had led previously to regression in skills as well as exacerbation in challenging, interfering behaviors. To avoid these detrimental effects and offer this youngster new experiences and exposure, Raymond attended a specialized summer camp designed for children with special needs of many types. The treatment goals and treatment plan were shared with the camp personnel to promote carryover of behavior goals. A progress report similar to that used in the afterschool program was further implemented to monitor his progress in this six-week setting. In this setting, Raymond's newly acquired skills were successfully put to use. He enjoyed popularity as a camper given his repertoire of social skills and ability to independently manage most of his self-care needs.

EDUCATIONAL CONSULTATION

Consultation to this educational program was provided on an infrequent basis. A systematic reinforcement system, similar to the system in the afterschool program, was implemented in this setting. The behavior treatment plan was shared with educational personnel. Likewise, Raymond's individual education plans were reviewed by the mental health program.

PHARMACOLOGICAL INTERVENTION

In light of Raymond's significant inattention and distractibility observed across settings, a trial of Ritalin was initiated. An initial dose of 5mg twice a day was prescribed; this was increased to 7.5mg and then to 10mg as Raymond became older and his body weight increased. His ability to focus without being easily distracted by extraneous stimuli was much improved with Ritalin. Moreover, his compliance and willingness to cooperate were enhanced on this stimulant medication.

THERAPIST-CLIENT FACTORS

The therapist in this unique type of clinical case is in actuality many therapists or clinicians working collaboratively to realize the intensive and comprehensive interventions crafted to address the needs in multidomains of adaptive functioning. Raymond's educational needs were addressed by special educators, paraprofessionals, and supportive therapists (occupational, speech, and physical). More intensive intervention was essential in realizing the generalization of adaptive functioning outside of the educational setting. Within the partial hospitalization program (afterschool program), Raymond's primary therapist was the group leader. Goals and treatment objectives were developed for this setting by all team members; a primary therapist determined his progress and discussed needed alterations to the treatment if gains were not realized.

In this clinical case, the therapist-client factors extended to the family members involved in the client's care. As Raymond was not competent to make treatment choices, a relationship with the parents and all involved clinicians was essential in the pursuit of effective treatment course. Appreciation of the family members' course in coping not only with the loss of a "typical" child, but also with the extraordinary needs of a family member with medical, developmental, and behavioral challenges was of utmost importance. Adherence to a philosophy of family-focused care implies recognition of the importance of family as "team members" in the ongoing treatment and intervention process. Family members, including Raymond's older sibling, were included in the treatment team for ongoing planning of his care and interventions. As many components of his care were in the home and community, his family members were important "interventionists" in this capacity.

COURSE OF TERMINATION

Given the chronicity of developmental disabilities, including mental retardation, the termination of intervention is more often than not an unreasonable goal. Instead, ongoing refinement of treatment and intervention objectives is the long-term goal. In this particular case, termination involved reaching the short-term goal to decrease the level of restrictiveness of care. Raymond's treatment was systematically faded to include primary community-based services. Hence, after two years in an intensive therapeutic setting, he was able to participate with minimal supports in community activities for individuals with mental retardation.

FOLLOW-UP

Again, follow-up in the case of mental retardation is somewhat atypical in comparison with other disorders. In this case illustration, this child continues to receive support services and ongoing community interventions, but this is occurring at less restrictive levels. While still on a low dose of Ritalin, Raymond receives all of his intervention services in the community, which allow him now, as a 15-year-old, to participate in many more integrated community activities in addition to prevocational activities. For example, this now adolescent is able to independently attend community programs for individuals with exceptional needs. Further, he is able to participate in prevocational training with minimal supports; for example, he works for a few hours a week in a snack shop in a parochial community center. He is also participating in a workshop that involves sorting clothes for resale for a charity organization a few hours a week. This is in addition to the educational programming, which is now geared to transitioning to adulthood.

Raymond continues to have periods of difficulty in the home setting when there is less structure in his schedule. Despite many gains in his ability to engage in leisure activities, he is likely to become increasingly distressed when not participating in routine, daily activities. Hence, holidays and vacations are often stressful for the family and client. Raymond's family has initiated referrals for placement in a group home setting in their neighborhood community; as this process is typically quite lengthy, a referral at this time is necessary to ensure the availability of an appropriate living situation at the time Raymond's parents decide on this major life transition.

MANAGED CARE CONSIDERATIONS

In most states, individuals with a diagnosis of mental retardation are eligible for special medical insurance allowances. In addition, children with chronic mental health issues typically are eligible for special federal funds for services. This said, it is often the case that children with a disorder considered chronic are excluded from the criteria of third-party payer insurance products. It is a travesty that even young children with a diagnosis of a developmental delay, developmental disorder, or mental retardation may not be eligible for needed services under third-party payer criteria. Nonetheless, intensive services are known to improve outcome and greatly influence the level of restrictiveness and thus decrease cost of care and burden to the family and society as a whole. A further issue is the lack of clarity of who is responsible for the care of these children. Insurance products often do not provide for their comprehensive health and habilitative care needs, and the educational system is also not adequately funded to offer the comprehensive care system needed. States do have mental retardation systems; the services provided under this umbrella vary greatly from state to state and even from county to county within a state. Accessing services through the mental retardation system is further problematic when children are younger and less impaired. Furthermore, children with mental retardation and concomitant behavioral and emotional issues often straddle the mental retardation and mental health systems. This often results in discontinuity of care, dispute of who is responsible for the funding of what aspect of care, and subsequent frustration of family members and caregivers who attempt to manage the care of these children.

The effect of managed care has been selective delivery of treatment in individuals with mental retardation. In some states, special state and federal funds may be managed by a health maintenance organization; this typically results in a regular review of services and a rationalization of the need for the level of intensity. In Raymond's case, as decreases in services were systematically demonstrated, approval of services were received without difficulty. This was achieved with effective case management and ongoing team planning.

OVERALL EFFECTIVENESS

The long-term, multimodal treatment provided this child with mental retardation resulted in tremendous gains in his level of independence, with parallel decreases in challenging and interfering behaviors. As in most long-term treatment cases, it is often unclear what treatments are accountable for the improvements. It can only be presumed that the comprehensive treatment package resulted in gains in adaptive functioning, level of independence, and decreases in challenging and interfering behaviors. The issues of maintenance of behavioral change and generalization of this change to different settings have proved to be particularly problematic in individuals with mental retardation and should be evaluated as indicators of effectiveness. If change fails to generalize to settings other than the treatment setting and with the specific change agent in that setting, maintenance in "real-world" settings may be jeopardized. In Raymond's case, measures to promote maintenance and generalization were undertaken. These included (1) systematic fading of reinforcement to a schedule that is more likely to be maintained; (2) use of reinforcers readily available in the individual's environment; (3) use of multiple "therapists" in the implementation of treatment procedures; (4) training in multiple settings in which treatment is implemented; and (5) use of self-control/self-management procedures to decrease reliance on external control whenever appropriate.

In this particular clinical case, the specific effects of intervention may not be untangled. This case highlights the extraordinary needs of children with mental retardation, the need for coordination of care at multiple levels, the issues that thwart continuity of care, and the resulting putative impact on the client and his parents.

REFERENCES

Aman, M. G., & Singh, N. N. (1986). *Aberrant Behavior Checklist: Manual.* East Aurora, NY: Slosson Educational.

American Association on Mental Retardation. (Ed.). (1992). Diagnosis and systems of support. In *Mental retardation: Definition, classification, and systems of support* (9th ed., pp. 23–34). Washington, DC: Author.

American Psychiatric Association. (Ed.). (1994). Mental retardation. In *Diagnostic and statistical manual of mental disorders* (4th ed., pp. 39–46). Washington, DC: Author.

Baer, R. A. (1990). Correspondence Training: Review and current issues. *Research in Developmental Disabilities, 11,* 379–393.

Baumeister, A. A., & Maclean, W. E. (1984). Deceleration of self-injurious responding by exercise. *Applied Research in Mental Retardation, 5,* 385–393.

Benson, D. J., & Aman, M. G. (1999). Disruptive behavior disorders in children with mental retardation. In H. Quay & A. Hogan (Eds.), *Handbook of disruptive behavior disorders* (p. 559). New York: Plenum Press.

Bruininks, R., Hill, B., & Morreau, L. (1988). Prevalence and implications of maladaptive behaviors and dual diagnosis in residential and other service programs. In J. A. Stark, F. Menolascino, M. Albarelli, & V. Gray (Eds.), *Mental retardation and mental health: Classification, diagnosis, treatment, services* (pp. 3–29). New York: Springer-Verlag.

Burgio, L. D., Whitman, T. L., & Johnson, M. R. (1980). A self- instructional package for increasing attending behavior in educable mentally retarded children. *Journal of Applied Behavior Analysis, 13,* 443–459.

Calamari, J. E., Geist, G. O., & Shahbazian, M. J. (1987). Evaluation of multiple component relaxation training with developmentally disabled persons. *Research in Developmental Disabilities, 8,* 55–70.

Castro, G., & White, K. R. (1993). Longitudinal studies of alternative types of early intervention: Rationale and design. *Early Education and Development, 4,* 224–237.

Cautela, J. R., & Groden, J. (1978). *Relaxation: A comprehensive manual for adults, children, and children with special needs.* Champaign, IL: Research Press.

Domizo, S., Verrotti, A., Ramenghi, L., Sabatino, G., & Morgese, G. (1993). Anti-epileptic therapy and behavior disturbances in children. *Child's Nervous System, 9,* 272–274.

Durand, V. M., & Crimmins, D. B. (1988). Identifying the variables maintaining self-injurious behavior. *Journal of Autism and Developmental Disorders, 18,* 99–227.

Horner, R. H., Dunlap, G., Koegel, R. L., Carr, E. G., Sailor, W., Anderson, J., et al. (1990). Toward a technology of "non-aversive" behavioral support. *Journal of the Association for Persons with Severe Handicaps, 15,* 91–97.

Innocenti, M. S. (1996). *1991–1996 Final report of the effects of early intervention for children with disabilities* (Contract No. HS90010001). Logan: Utah State University, Early Intervention Research Institute.

Jacobson, J. (1982). Problem behavior and psychiatric impairment withing a developmentally disabled population: I behavior frequency. *Applied Research in Mental Retardation, 3,* 121–139.

Jacobson, J. (1990). Assessing the prevalence of psychiatric disorders in a developmentally disabled population. In E. Dibble & D. Gray (Eds.), *Assessment of behavior problems with persons with mental retardation living in the community* (pp. 19–70). Rockville, MD: Department of Health and Human Services, National Institutes of Health, Public Health Service, Alcohol, Drug Abuse, and Mental Health Administration.

Kern, L., Koegel, R. L., Dyer, K., Blew, P. A., & Fenton, L. R. (1982). The effects of physical exercise on self-stimulation and appropriate responding in autistic children. *Journal of Autism and Developmental Disorders, 12,* 399–419.

Lakin, K. C., Hill, B. K., Hauber, F. A., Bruininks, R. H., & Heal, L. W. (1983). New admissions and readmissions to a national sample of public residential facilities. *American Journal of Mental Deficiency, 88,* 13–20.

McGimsey, J. F., & Favell, J. E. (1988). The effects of increased physical exercise on disruptive behavior in retarded persons. *Journal of Autism and Developmental Disorders, 18,* 167–179.

McPhail, C. H., & Chamove, A. S. (1989). Relaxation reduces disruption in mentally handicapped adults. *Journal of Mental Deficiency Research, 33,* 399–406.

Quay, H., & Hogan, A. (1999). *Handbook of disruptive behavior disorders.* New York: Plenum Press.

Quine, L. (1986). Behavior problems in severely mentally handicapped children. *Psychological Medicine, 16,* 895–907.

Reiss, A. (1994). *Handbook of challenging behaviors: Mental health aspects of mental retardation.* Worthington, OH: International Diagnostic Systems.

Singer, G., & Irwin, L. (1987). Human rights review of intrusive behaviors for students with severe handicaps. *Exceptional Children, 54,* 46–52.

Vitello, A. F., Atthowe, J. M., & Cadwell, J. (1983). Determinants of community placement of institutionalized mentally retarded persons. *American Journal of Mental Deficiency, 87,* 539–545.

Watson, G. S., & Gross, A. M. (1997). Mental retardation and developmental disorders. In R. T. Ammerman & M. Hersen (Eds.), *Handbook of prevention and treatment with children and adolescents: Intervention in the real world context* (pp. 495–520). New York: Wiley.

CHAPTER 23

Elimination Disorder

CHRISTA HOLLAND JOHNSON, LARRY L. MULLINS, and C. EUGENE WALKER

DESCRIPTION OF THE DISORDER

ALTHOUGH CHANGES HAVE occurred in the diagnostic criteria, the term *encopresis* has been in use for over 75 years (Walker, Milling, & Bonner, 1988). According to the most recent version of the *Diagnostic and Statistical Manual for Mental Disorders* (*DSM-IV*; American Psychiatric Association [APA], 1994), the diagnostic criteria for encopresis are (1) repeated involuntary or intentional passage of feces into inappropriate places; (2) at least one such event a month for a minimum of three months; (3) the child must be at least 4 years of age; and (4) the disorder cannot be due to the direct effects of a general medical condition other than constipation. The diagnosis of encopresis also requires a distinction between soiling due to constipation or no constipation (APA, 1994). Encopresis is designated "primary" if the child has reached age 4 and has never established fecal continence, and "secondary" if the soiling develops after a period of fecal continence (APA, 1994). Although diurnal encopresis is most common, nocturnal soiling also can occur (Levine, 1975; Walker et al., 1988; Wolters, 1974).

In the literature, encopresis has been primarily used to describe constipation and overflow incontinence; however, Walker (1978) has identified three subtypes of encopresis: retentive, manipulative, and stress-induced. The *retentive* type represents the majority of cases seen clinically, and results from constipation and overflow incontinence. The *manipulative* (resulting from intentional soiling for secondary gain) and *stress-induced* (resulting from anxiety-induced diarrhea) types represent a much smaller number of clinical cases, and are not associated with constipation with overflow incontinence (Ondersma & Walker, 1998; Walker, 1978). Recent literature (McGrath, Mellon, & Murphy, 2000; Stark, 2000) has emphasized the importance of examining each of these subtypes to allow for greater understanding of specific symptoms and treatment approaches to encopresis.

Current incidence estimates indicate that encopresis ranges from 1% in children above the age of 4 (APA, 1994) to 8% in child psychiatric inpatient settings

434

(Geffken & Monaco, 1996; Kisch & Pfeffer, 1984). Encopresis is more common in males, but tends to decrease with age for both sexes (Levine, 1975).

Associated physical features of encopresis include chronic abdominal pain, poor appetite, and lethargy (Levine, 1975). Some studies have indicated that encopresis can have a significant impact on a child's psychosocial functioning, including decreased self-esteem and increased emotional and behavioral problems (Bernard-Bonnin, Haley, Belanger, & Nadeau, 1993; Gabel, Hegedus, Wald, Chandra, & Chiponis, 1986; McGrath et al., 2000). Although some children with encopresis, particularly those in inpatient psychiatric settings, evidence encopresis and psychological/behavioral problems concomitantly, they are not necessarily causally related (Walker et al., 1988). In fact, it may be more common for psychological problems to occur as a result of, rather than being the cause of, encopresis and/or constipation (Abrahamian & Lloyd-Still, 1984).

CONSTIPATION AND ENCOPRESIS

As previously indicated, the majority of cases seen clinically for encopresis present with constipation (Levine, 1975; Walker et al., 1988; Wright & Walker, 1978); however, there is often confusion regarding the role of constipation and fecal soiling in encopresis, particularly as they appear to be opposite functions. Thus, a basic explanation may prove helpful.

Constipation can result from numerous factors, including inadequate fiber intake, underhydration, previous history of painful bowel movements, or a hereditary tendency toward constipation, to name a few. Once a child becomes constipated, a chronic condition can quickly develop, as children are not accustomed to tracking their bowel movements, and parents may lose track of their child's elimination functions once children are toilet-trained or placed in a school setting. Regardless of the initial cause of constipation, soiling occurs in the following manner. As fecal material continues to build and lodges in the colon, it creates a condition known as *psychogenic megacolon*. In this condition, the colon becomes enlarged and loses muscle tone, and the intestine walls become stretched relatively thin. At this point, fluid and liquid wastes collect above the impaction and eventually seep around the impacted fecal material and out the anus, resulting in a pasty stain in the child's clothing. During this process, the child does not experience the sensation to defecate and does not recognize that a bowel movement is taking place until the seepage has already occurred. Occasionally, large masses of the impacted fecal material may loosen and the child may have a spontaneous and extremely large bowel movement. Chronic psychogenic megacolon can result in serious health complications, including damage to the intestinal tract, tearing of the colon, and, with severe impactions, distended abdomen. Fortunately, the colon does have the capacity to regain muscle tone and sensitivity once regular elimination patterns have been regained (Ondersma & Walker, 1998; Walker, 1978, 1995). For further details on the physiology of the colon and the etiology of constipation, the reader is referred to several excellent descriptions provided in the literature (Christophersen & Purvis, 2001; McGrath et al., 2000; Murray, 1994; Ondersma & Walker, 1998; Walker et al., 1988).

Given that encopresis can result in serious medical and psychosocial problems, an immediate and effective treatment approach is often indicated. The literature has identified several probable efficacious treatment approaches for encopresis, including biofeedback, structured behavioral intervention, behavioral plus medical intervention, and medical intervention plus positive reinforcement (Calkins, Walker, & Howe, 1994; McGrath et al., 2000; Ondersma & Walker, 1998). However, it remains unclear which approach is most effective for any given subtype of encopresis.

In the following case description, a combination of behavioral, medical, and systems treatment components were used based on our assessment of precipitating and maintaining variables of the disorder. We believe that this idiopathic approach to the case resulted in a particularly efficacious and cost-effective treatment. However, as many encopresis cases have been reported to be successfully treated solely with a structured behavioral approach, the reader may want to refer to a specific case protocol outlined in Calkins et al. (1994) for a detailed protocol of this type.

CASE DESCRIPTION

Sarah J. is a 7-year-old, White female who was referred to the Pediatric Psychology Consultation Liaison Service by the Surgery Service at a large children's hospital in the Southwest. She was admitted to the surgical unit for the removal of a large fecal impaction. Sarah was admitted two days prior to the referral with significant stomach complaints, which were the result of a large impaction that had been recalcitrant to treatment via traditional means (i.e., use of laxatives, suppositories, and occasional enemas). Thus, surgical removal of the impaction was necessary, which also required that she be placed under general anesthesia. The surgical resident involved in the case requested psychological consultation due to Sarah's three-year history of intermittent encopresis and the serious health problems that had ensued.

Sarah's family was from a small farming community in the southeastern part of the state approximately 250 miles from the hospital. Her parents had been married for 12 years, and Sarah was their only child. The marital relationship was described by Sarah's mother as both "strained" and "routine," particularly in the past several months. Both parents graduated from high school, and each had attended the local junior college. Her father worked as a salesperson for an agricultural chemical supply company, and her mother worked primarily in the home. A few immediate family members lived in adjacent towns, but were far enough away that they did not have regular contact, except for holidays.

From a developmental perspective, Sarah was the product of a normal pregnancy and delivery. However, her mother indicated that she had miscarried twice prior to her pregnancy with Sarah. Sarah was born with an imperforate anus, which required emergency surgery and a subsequent colostomy immediately after her birth. The anal structure was surgically repaired and the colostomy closed within a week of her birth. Other available medical history was benign. By parental report, Sarah met early developmental milestones in an age-appropriate fashion. She had experienced the usual childhood illnesses. Other available family history indicated no significant health problems in any of her immediate family members. However, Sarah's mother indicated that she and one of her sisters had been treated for episodic depression over a 10-year period. There was no history of mental health problems reported for Sarah's father's family. According to her mother, Sarah had never received any form of psychological counseling, although her current teacher had suggested a mental health consultation for her soiling difficulty.

Socially, Sarah was described by her mother as a "precocious child, with many friends." Her mother did note, however, that she was often described by her peers as "bossy" and that she often experienced minor conflicts with the neighborhood children. These conflicts took the form of argumentativeness and disagreements over rules of games and sharing of toys. It was not unusual for Sarah to end up running home in tears, stating, "All the other kids hate me." Notably, many of her closest friends were described as being younger in age than she.

Academically, Sarah had just completed the first grade. Her mother indicated that she did "extremely well in her schoolwork," making high marks in all subjects. However, she also noted that Sarah had occasionally received reprimands from her teacher for minor acts of disrespectfulness (e.g., talking back, refusing to follow class rules about taking turns). Further, her encopretic episodes had begun to lead other children to tease her and call her names. Such name-calling had on occasion erupted into verbal confrontation, with subsequent referral to the principal's office for a "cooling down" period.

CHIEF COMPLAINTS

The primary presenting complaint was episodic encopresis. Sarah reported having "poopy pants" on one or two occasions per day, and her mother described the soiling as consisting of small amounts of soft material, approximately one or two inches in diameter.

Prior to Sarah's hospitalization, a negative pattern had developed between Sarah and her mother that resulted in escalating soiling and behavioral problems. A typical example of this pattern is illustrated in the following scenario. While Sarah was playing, her mother would smell an odor and ask Sarah if she needed to go to the bathroom. Sarah's most common response was no. On checking Sarah's underwear, her mother would find fecal material and confront her daughter about the soiling. At that point, Sarah either became extremely upset or denied the soiling accident. A struggle would then ensue to clean Sarah's clothing, which left Sarah and her mother feeling frustrated and worn out. Sarah rarely went to the bathroom on her own, and attempts to schedule daily toileting led to major temper tantrums. On occasion, Sarah would comply in response to several prompts by her mother, but would sit on the toilet for one or two minutes, jump up, stating "I'm done," and then run off to play. Her mother indicated that these attempts at toileting resulted in success fewer than once every two months, and in fact, only one documented successful toileting experience was reported in the six months prior to Sarah's hospitalization.

As a result of Sarah's toileting difficulties, she became impacted on a regular basis. Typically, treatment at home consisted of laxatives or suppositories, both of which Sarah reportedly "hated." Although these strategies for treating the impaction worked approximately 90% of the time, they were not always successful. For the past two years, the local family physician had encouraged Sarah's parents to resort to an enema to treat the impaction. However, during those treatments, Sarah reportedly became "out of control" to the point that her mother independently decided to stop subjecting her daughter to what she considered a "horrible treatment." As a result, the most recent impaction had occurred, warranting the referral to specialists at the children's hospital.

In addition to the soiling, Sarah's mother indicated that she was increasingly concerned about her daughter's behavioral outbursts and disagreements with her friends. She noted that these problems had worsened in the past six months, coinciding with increased soiling difficulties. She attempted to link the two sets of difficulties, believing that her daughter's stress and frustration with her encopresis were leading to social problems. Although she did not necessarily believe that Sarah was depressed, her own history of mood regulation problems made her much more concerned for her daughter.

Although Sarah's mother did not report marital tension as a major presenting concern, a significant dissatisfaction with the marital relationship was evident in some of her comments. In particular, she repeatedly emphasized that she and her husband did not spend much time together, and that her husband did not appear to understand the stress she was feeling, particularly related to Sarah's soiling and behavioral difficulties. Additionally, she reported that when she and her husband were able to spend time alone, they tended to end up in disagreements and arguments over how to manage Sarah's behavior.

HISTORY

Sarah's mother indicated that her daughter achieved both bowel and bladder control by the age of 2, and maintained that control for one year. At approximately age 3, Sarah began to experience encopretic episodes, as described previously. Notably, these encopretic episodes coincided with her father's losing his job in the oilfield. Shortly after Sarah's third birthday, Mr. J. lost his job and was unemployed for approximately eight months. During this period of unemployment, he spent the majority of his time at home with Sarah and her mother. Because the family was financially unprepared for his unemployment, they came close to losing their home. As a result, Sarah's mother began to work part time at a local grocery store, which she found quite stressful and "embarrassing." With their life savings virtually depleted, Sarah's father reluctantly took a position as a salesperson for a large agricultural supply company. This job resulted in his traveling around the state approximately five days out of the week. Sarah's mother indicated that this time period was emotionally draining and difficult for all of them. Sarah was particularly upset over her father's long absences, as she had become quite attached to him during the eight months of unemployment, in which he primarily stayed at home. Sarah's mother also became depressed during this period and began taking antidepressant medication. By her report, she did not seek psychotherapy at this time for her depressive symptoms, stating, "I could not find a counselor I would be comfortable talking to."

Initially, Sarah's mother attempted to treat Sarah's soiling problem with mild admonishment, thinking it "would go away on its own." After a few months, her scolding became more intense and she would occasionally threaten to spank Sarah. After consulting with her local family physician, she attempted to increase the amount of fiber in Sarah's diet, which was met with great resistance by her daughter, who was immediately aware of the dietary changes. Mineral oil also met with similar resistance, as Sarah often would spit it out and run from the room. Sarah's father had somewhat greater success coaxing her into trying certain foods and taking the mineral oil; however, it not only took great effort but was also episodic, given his lack of availability during the week.

These treatment efforts continued until Sarah reached the age of 4. At this time, Sarah's mother grew so frustrated that she again consulted with her family physician, who recommended laxatives and suppositories. Initially, Sarah was completely noncompliant with such regimens. Eventually, however, her parents found that by promising substantial rewards (e.g., toys, going shopping for a new dress), Sarah would often comply. Her parents continued with these treatment tactics on an intermittent basis between the ages of 4 and 7, with resultant intermittent success.

BEHAVIORAL ASSESSMENT

Behavioral

Sarah was observed on the medical unit over the course of approximately three to four hours following the receipt of the referral. She initially presented as a highly verbal and energetic child who spent much of her time playing in the hallways of the unit and conversing with nurses at the nurses' station. To a considerable extent, these interactions involved asking the nurses to take her to the playroom on the next unit or on visits to the gift store downstairs. Notably, the majority of her behavior involved some form of social interaction. Her visits to the nurses' station began to annoy the staff after a relatively short time, but their attempts to set limits on her visits and interruptions were often met with arguments and other attention-seeking behavior. In the staff's words, "She just won't take no for an answer."

Sarah's mother indicated that these problems were quite consistent with her behavior at home. She noted that Sarah appeared to "crave attention" and demanded a great deal from other people in her environment, to the extent that she would "wear them out." Her mother was obviously embarrassed by her daughter's behavior, but did little to intervene. Occasionally, she would remind Sarah to "let the nurses do their job," but no other consequence was instituted.

Behavioral assessment also included observations of interactions between Sarah and her mother. Mrs. J., who appeared emotionally dysthymic, would interact with her daughter for brief periods of time but often appeared distracted and disinterested. When Mrs. J. allowed her attention to wander or engaged in conversation with another person, Sarah would immediately begin to exhibit minor inappropriate behavior to regain her mother's attention.

Self-Report

Sarah reported that she did not like to talk about her problem with encopresis. When asked about why she was in the hospital, she replied, "I really don't know." When asked for additional information about her procedure, she said, "You need to ask my mommy." Sarah was willing to talk about her friends back home, stating, "I have more friends than anybody else in my class." When asked if her friends ever teased her about anything, she immediately changed the subject and began to show the psychologist her new doll. When asked if she ever got sad, she replied, "Yes, when my daddy leaves to go to his job. I never get to see or talk to him—ever."

Because of Sarah's age, no objective measures were administered. However, her mother was asked to complete a Beck Depression Inventory (BDI; Beck, Ward, Mendelson, Mock, & Erbaugh, 1961) for herself, given her history of depressive symptoms and her current dissatisfaction in her marital relationship. Additionally, Sarah's mother completed the Child Behavior Checklist (CBCL; Achenbach, 1991) for Sarah. Results of the BDI indicated a mild to moderate level of clinical depression. Results of the CBCL were consistent with parental report, confirming a subclinical level of externalizing behavioral difficulties but no elevations on internalizing scales.

PHYSIOLOGICAL

Interviews with both the surgical resident and the attending physician were conducted throughout Sarah's hospitalization. The surgeon noted that medical tests conducted following the reconstruction of the anal area indicated that there was definite neuronal innervation of the tissue. From a medical perspective, they concluded that it was highly unlikely that physiological reasons contributed to the encopretic episodes, especially in light of her success at gaining bowel control at age 2, and maintaining control for one year.

MEDICAL CONSULTATION

Members of the surgical team felt that Sarah's long-standing history of constipation warranted an aggressive medical treatment approach. Specifically, her frequent impactions secondary to constipation led the attending surgeon to conclude that she would need daily suppositories and/or enemas. It appeared that the medical team was quite frustrated by this particular case, especially because a surgical procedure was needed to remove the significant impaction. The medical team also voiced concerns that the parents were not actively involved in the treatment of this particular problem, despite the frequent visits to the specialty clinics at the children's hospital.

Given the somewhat negative sentiments voiced by the surgical team, the Pediatric Psychology Consultation Service was quite concerned that recommendations would be made that ultimately could prove both physically and psychologically harmful to Sarah and her family (i.e., regular enemas). Alternatively, it was our perspective that Sarah's difficulties had a strong learning component and that following medical treatment (i.e., removal of the impaction), she would be a good candidate for a traditional behavioral approach to the treatment of the encopresis. In addition, the psychology team felt that Sarah and her family would benefit from a family/systems approach, to address some of the other maintaining variables and factors inherent in the family interactions and system that may have been contributing to the long history of Sarah's soiling. Thus, we chose to approach the Surgical Service in the following manner. First, we agreed that Sarah's difficulties were quite frustrating, and that although parental efforts may have been well-intentioned, they could have served to maintain the symptoms. Second, we indicated the importance of intervening with the parents to help them understand the treatment protocol and to help them reach optimal compliance in implementing the protocol at home. Finally, we suggested that prior to their beginning an aggressive medical treatment plan, we would like to try a more psychologically and behaviorally based intervention that we believed might be helpful. The surgical team seemed skeptical of the recommended approach, but also seemed relieved that we were taking over primary responsibility for this case.

CASE CONCEPTUALIZATION

Medically, Sarah's case was initially complicated by her history of surgical correction of an obvious physical problem (i.e., the imperforate anus), but whether physical abnormalities contributed to her difficulties remained of some concern. Medical consultation led the team of psychologists involved in her case to conclude that there was sufficient neuronal innervation to allow for normal bowel function. Indeed, her successful bowel training at the age of 2 suggested that her encopresis was secondary to chronic constipation. It was also notable that development of encopresis coincided with major changes in the family system (e.g., Mr. J.'s loss of employment, period of unemployment, and a work schedule that required extensive travel) and that the maintenance of her encopresis had been concomitant with ongoing marital difficulties and tension. Thus, there was some evidence to suggest that other behavioral and systems factors might be involved in this case.

It was also apparent that there was considerable strain between Sarah and her mother. Our observations led us to believe that Sarah had "worn her down" over time, and that limit-setting either was no longer implemented or was inconsistently implemented. Depression and increased parenting stress gradually contributed to Sarah's mother adopting a more passive role, which further led to behavioral difficulties on the part of Sarah.

As indicated, Sarah's mother had made considerable efforts throughout the past three years to manage her child's encopretic difficulties; however, the question arose as to whether the mother's reactions, increased attention, and chosen methods of dealing with Sarah's soiling had come to directly or indirectly reinforce her daughter's encopresis. Given the family's report of recent stressors and relationship strains, there was also the possibility that Sarah's encopresis could be serving a larger function within the family unit (e.g., increased attention or decrease in parental tension) that also needed to be explored at this time.

Based on these observations, several complementary approaches were determined useful in the conceptualization and treatment of this case. First, because Sarah's encopresis was conceptualized in part as a function of traditional encopresis or *retentive* encopresis, which results from constipation and incontinence overflow, a traditional behavioral protocol with medical approaches was instituted. This protocol combines traditional behavioral components such as reinforcement and punishment with medical components such as an initial cleanout phase (often accomplished through use of laxatives) and dietary modifications. Two traditional behavioral approaches have been described in the literature as being highly effective in the treatment of retentive encopresis (Calkins et al., 1994; Walker et al., 1988). The first is a conservative approach, which is recommended as the first choice for treatment of encopresis, and the second is defined as an aggressive approach, which is recommended for more severe cases. The basic components of these two approaches are education, reinforcement for appropriate toileting, scheduled toilet sittings, dietary changes, and, in some cases, mild punishment for soiling (Ondersma & Walker, 1998). Regardless of which approach is used, the first step is to educate the parents and child about the program, with particular emphasis on the fact that in retentive encopresis cases, the child is not intentionally soiling. For the conservative approach, the second step is a cleanout phase, in which enemas may be required to thoroughly evacuate the bowel. Following this cleaning, a high-fiber diet, including fresh fruits and vegetables, fruit juices, and raw bran, are incorporated into the child's diet, along with increased fluids and decreased dairy products. The next step is to implement regularly scheduled toilet sittings to produce bowel movements. Sittings are brief (three to five minutes) and can range from one to four times per day, depending on practicality and severity of the problem. When the child successfully produces a bowel movement, a small, mutually acceptable reward is given to the child. Monitoring and charting of the child's bowel movements is an important component and should be maintained for the length of the program. When this program is implemented in a correct and consistent manner, improvement in the child's toileting and bowel movements should be evident within two to three weeks. Within 12 to 16 weeks, the encopresis should be successfully resolved. Once the child sustains eight weeks of regular toileting, a graduation ceremony should be planned to formally recognize and reinforce the child's success. Also at this time, a special reward (e.g., going to a movie, special trips) can be arranged by the family to signify the successful completion of the program. In Sarah's case, the conservative behavioral approach was chosen to complement the medical treatment protocol.

Given that Sarah's soiling and behavioral difficulties were perceived to result in considerable familial attention, a systems treatment component was deemed necessary. In essence, Sarah had been able to gain a great deal of negative, direct, and immediate attention from her parents as a result of her toileting and behavioral difficulties, rather than gaining positive attention for engaging in appropriate toileting and social behaviors. Additionally, the majority of the family interactions, particularly marital discussions, revolved around the issue of Sarah's encopresis, leaving little time for any type of focus on the marriage or engaging in intimacy. Systems theorists have argued that behaviors such as those displayed by Sarah may well serve the purpose of stabilizing a fragile marital unit, inasmuch as they provide a focus for the family interactions. One goal of a systems approach is to shift the cycle of attention, such that all units in the family receive appropriate attention and reinforcement for positive behaviors. Given these observations, a systems component was added to the protocol and a behavioral-systems approach was used.

RATIONALE FOR TREATMENT CHOICE

As previously indicated, further empirical validation of treatment approaches to encopresis is clearly needed. However, as noted in the literature, combined medical and traditional behavioral approaches to treating retentive encopresis have evidenced a high success rate, ranging from 78.8% to an almost 100% cure rate (Fireman & Koplewicz, 1992; McGrath, Mellon, & Murphy, 2000; Stark, 2000; Stark, Owens-Stively, Spirito, Lewis, & Guevremont, 1990; Wright, 1975). Given the medical and behavioral evidence suggesting that Sarah's encopresis was of the retentive type, a medical-behavioral approach was deemed appropriate and necessary. However, it was also believed that successful treatment would be predicated on addressing systemic aspects within the family, including the marital relationship. Specifically, it was believed that both parents should be involved in the administration of the protocol, and that Sarah's father would need to be available for additional social support to his wife. Additionally, we believed that while the medical-behavioral protocol was being initiated, attention also needed to be paid to the marital and parent-child relationships for the treatment to be ultimately successful. The treatment team realized that this would be a difficult task in light of the considerable distance this family lived from the hospital; in essence, formal therapeutic encounters (i.e., parent training and family therapy) were largely precluded. However, we believed that we could develop a program that would address all of these components, while working within the family's resources and travel constraints.

COURSE OF TREATMENT

Consistent with the implementation of a conservative behavioral treatment approach, as described above, the parents were instructed about the treatment program and provided detailed information about the encopresis protocol. Specifically, they were educated as quickly as possible about the nature of retentive encopresis and the role of constipation in such cases. The parents were informed that the majority of encopresis cases involve chronic constipation, subsequently leading to a lack of tone in the bowel. It was explained that the fecal material found on clothing was the result of seepage around this particular impaction. Next, it was explained that Sarah would need to have regular evacuation of fecal material for treatment to be successful. The parents were encouraged to provide a high-fiber diet for her and to use laxatives, if needed, as a secondary means of evacuating the fecal material.

Next, it was explained that Sarah would need to be on a regular toileting schedule. It was recommended that she be taken to the toilet approximately 10 minutes after each meal and asked to sit on the toilet for a five-minute period of time. If Sarah was able to sit on the toilet without complaining or jumping off, she was to receive a small reward (e.g., piece of candy). If she was successful in having a bowel movement, she was to receive a small toy from a grab bag of gifts that were jointly decided on by Sarah and her mother. Sarah's mother was encouraged to refrain from admonishing or scolding her daughter under any circumstances for failure to sit on the toilet or to have a bowel movement. Further, because of the distance between Sarah's home and the hospital, it was decided that phone consultation would be the most appropriate means of communication. Sarah's mother was asked to make daily calls during the first week of the protocol to report to the psychologist on her daughter's progress.

Throughout this initial discussion of the protocol, several points were emphasized. First, we attempted to minimize blame on the part of Sarah's mother. Our explanation of the encopresis in both physiological and learning terms enabled her to see that her daughter's difficulties were not because she was a "bad mother." In addition, we emphasized that she could master the skills necessary to help her daughter in a short time, and that these skills had proved successful with many other children with similar problems. Further, we gently encouraged her to increasingly set limits with her daughter, and in this regard, "take control" of not only the encopresis problem but other behavioral difficulties as well. Finally, based on Sarah's mother's BDI score, previous reports of depressive symptoms, and a family history of depression, we recommended that she pursue psychological treatment to address her depressive symptoms, and we provided an appropriate referral for a mental health professional in her area.

Phone consultation was arranged to summarize the treatment conceptualization for Sarah's father, who had not been able to come to the hospital during this most recent hospitalization. Our initial phone calls were aimed primarily at eliciting his support and developing a sense of trust in the treatment team. The nature of the protocol was then explained to him in similar fashion and his help was solicited. Both mother and father were informed that he was to call Sarah on a daily basis while on the road and to praise her for her efforts in working on this problem. In this manner, it was hoped that the father would be able to play a more active role in his daughter's success.

Finally, the parents were instructed to arrange for a date night for themselves on the father's return to the home on the weekends. They were requested to get a baby-sitter for Sarah so that they could spend time together and "catch up." It was further requested that they not talk about Sarah's encopresis during this time, with the rationale provided that they "needed a break" from discussion of this issue.

Sarah was discharged from the hospital to her home the day after this intervention was described to her mother. Prior to their leaving, a final conference was held during which all aspects of the treatment protocol were discussed again and a written outline was presented to Sarah's mother. Emphasis was placed on the need for continued communication, particularly in light of the distance this family lived from the medical center.

Mrs. J. was diligent in contacting the therapist on a daily basis at a prescribed time. She noted that although Sarah exhibited some minor tantrum behaviors on the first day home, Sarah quickly realized that she would receive rewards by going to the bathroom. Three days after discharge, Sarah reportedly had a successful bowel movement in the toilet. Her mother was elated at this turn of events, and noted that her husband was not only delighted as well but was maintaining regular communication with her and her daughter as per our recommendations. By day 7 of the protocol, Sarah had successful bowel movements on five occasions, with only one occasion of encopresis. Such success was in dramatic contrast to the previous six months. At that point, it was decided that the mother could begin to make phone calls every other day, with the stipulation that if she felt there was a setback, she should call immediately. The psychologist involved also contacted the father at the end of the first weekend to review his role in helping his daughter with her difficulties. At the end of week 2, Sarah had no further encopretic episodes and the decision was made to taper phone consultation to once a week. In addition, it was agreed that the family would meet with the psychologist during their next visit to the GI clinic at the hospital. This visit occurred at approximately one month's time. No further episodes of encopresis were then noted. Indeed, the parents noted that Sarah's behavior had improved overall. A graduation ceremony, in which Sarah was able to take a day-long trip to the zoo, was planned with the family so that Sarah could receive final recognition for her work and success.

Although a formal evaluation of the marital relationship was not conducted, Sarah's mother reported that the increased social time spent with her husband was going well and resulted in some "improvements" in their relationship. She also reported that both she and her husband had come to "really looked forward" to their dates and increased interactions.

THERAPIST-CLIENT FACTORS

The current case exemplifies a common problem encountered by the pediatric psychologist who works on a consultation-liaison service (i.e., having a very brief period of time to establish a therapeutic relationship with a distraught client and implement a treatment protocol that may be foreign to the average individual). In Sarah's case, pressures existed to provide treatment recommendations and to discharge her as soon as possible. Thus, it was critical that the pediatric psychologist quickly establish rapport and instill hope, while at the same time providing technical information to the family. Sarah's mother's level of distress was sufficiently high at the time of consultation that establishing a trusting relationship was relatively easy, guaranteeing that the parents would follow through with the treatment protocol. However, following discharge, treatment was more challenging. We believe that it helped considerably to build regular, daily communication into the protocol and to reassure Sarah's parents that they could call at any time for clarification of the protocol or if they experienced some type of crisis. We also felt that it was critical to the success of the case to work with the current situation, even if it meant that the majority of contact was administered by phone. We found that the parents responded very well to the structure of the treatment protocol and that they came to trust us wholeheartedly as we assisted them in following the protocol.

COURSE OF TERMINATION

A graduated course of termination was employed for this case. As noted above, Sarah achieved substantial treatment success after seven days of the implementation of treatment. Although this success allowed for a shorter than expected treatment program, it did not diminish the need for monitoring to ensure long-term treatment gains. Thus, the therapist maintained weekly contact with the family for the next three weeks. As Sarah continued to maintain her 100% success rate for toileting behaviors over these three weeks, the therapist terminated telephone contacts, and a face-to-face contact was scheduled in the next month. On the report that Sarah had maintained her treatment gains for two full months, termination was instituted and a graduation ceremony was planned. Thus, termination of treatment for this case was achieved within two months of the initiation of treatment.

FOLLOW-UP

Sarah was seen in the GI clinic at a hospital on a monthly basis for three months following termination of treatment. At those times, the psychologist met with her and her mother briefly to ascertain the effectiveness of the program. Sarah seemed delighted that she was no longer experiencing episodes of encopresis. In addition, her mother's affect seemed much more positive, with less evidence of depression, despite the fact that she had not followed through on the recommendation for psychological treatment of her previous depressive symptoms. She indicated that her husband was looking for other employment so that he would not have to travel as often. She indicated that she and her husband continued to spend more time together and had been regularly attending various church and social events. Further, she stated that Sarah appeared to be getting along better with her as well as her peers. During the second clinic visit, Mrs. J. reported that Sarah's teacher had actually sent a note home the week prior saying that she appeared to be much less obstinate and that there had been fewer behavioral episodes with her peers.

MANAGED CARE CONSIDERATIONS

Despite the fact that numerous encopresis cases have been treated successfully through behavioral techniques, primary care physicians are the providers most typically sought out to treat elimination disorders. The current case exemplifies how a relatively treatable pediatric problem, first identified in a primary care setting, can result in significant medical cost, particularly when hospitalization is required. In fact, cost of hospitalization and outpatient visits to various specialty clinics for this case is estimated to be at least three times the cost of a behavioral treatment protocol implemented by a doctoral-level psychologist, not to mention the cost in time and resources for the family and all professionals involved in the care of this case. Yet, successful treatment of this case through the use of a behavioral-medical approach precluded further hospitalizations and visits to specialty clinics, resulting in a substantial cost reduction to the family, to health care professionals, and to health insurance companies. Such a case exemplifies the cost-effective nature of behavioral interventions with elimination disorder cases, but also the importance and feasibility of incorporating a systems perspective when needed.

This case also points to the importance of prevention efforts. It is highly plausible that if a behavioral or mental health specialist were involved earlier in the course of this case, hospitalization might not have been required; certainly, fewer visits to specialty clinics would have been needed. Both of these would have substantially decreased the cost incurred by this case. It remains to pediatric psychologists to continue to educate both medical professionals and managed care companies on the effectiveness of behavioral techniques for elimination disorders and other common pediatric problems.

OVERALL EFFECTIVENESS

In recent reviews of the literature (Houts & Abramson, 1990; McGrath et al., 2000; Ondersma & Walker, 1998), it has been well documented that treatment outcome research for encopresis has significantly lagged behind that of enuresis and other pediatric-based problems. One particular deficit noted is the lack of research on the various subtypes of encopresis, which has prohibited any systematic exploration of treatment-specific protocols. Additionally, methodological limitations have been noted in sample selection, such as reliance on convenience samples and small sample size (Stark, 2000). Despite these empirical limitations, there is evidence of high levels of success in the treatment of encopresis with medical and behavioral interventions, particularly when a medical condition can be ruled out (Fireman & Koplewicz, 1992; McGrath et al., 2000; Ondersma & Walker, 1998; Stark, 2000; Walker, 1995; Wright, 1975). We posit that this case provides additional evidence of the effectiveness of a combined medical-behavioral treatment approach to retentive encopresis. In particular, the appropriate medical treatment, including purgative therapy, was applied while Sarah was in the hospital to remove all impaction. Success of this medical treatment set the groundwork for the implementation of dietary and behavioral interventions, including increased fiber intake, establishment of regular bowel movements, and positive reinforcement of appropriate toileting behavior.

However, inclusion of a systems treatment should not be underestimated. Although systems therapy typically has not been noted in the literature as a component of encopresis protocols, we hypothesize that it proved to be a very effective treatment component in this case, and may have served to expedite the success of the concomitant behavioral and dietary interventions. In particular, helping this family to recognize some of the dysfunctional relationship patterns that had formed and modifying the circumstances in which Sarah received attention and praise were critical to the success of this program. Once Sarah learned how to gain appropriate reinforcement and attention, she no longer needed to gain attention through inappropriate mechanisms. Also, once her parents began to refocus their relationship on each other, they found ways to interact with one another that did not involve discussion of Sarah's toileting behavior, particularly once Sarah became successful at toileting. As familial or systems factors can play a significant role either in the etiology or exacerbation of the disorder and may be important in the implementation of treatment, a systems approach may warrant further investigation within the literature for some types of encopresis cases.

Another treatment component that may have contributed to the success of this case is the adaptation of protocol to accommodate Sarah's parents and resources. Of particular note is the fact that the majority of therapeutic contacts were done by phone, indicating the flexibility created in the treatment protocol. We believe that working with a patient's current resources is critical to the success of any type of treatment, and certainly contributed to Sarah's family being able to maintain an active protocol despite distance.

Other factors that warrant consideration in the success of this case include the reported decrease in Mrs. J.'s depressive symptoms, an increased readiness on both parents' part to implement a more structured treatment protocol for Sarah, and Sarah's age, which may have helped her to recognize the advantages of adhering to a treatment protocol.

REFERENCES

Abrahamian, F. P., & Lloyd-Still, J. D. (1984). Chronic constipation in childhood: A longitudinal study of 186 patients. *Journal of Pediatric Gastroenterology and Nutrition, 3*, 460–467.

Achenbach, T. M. (1991). *Manual for the Child Behavior Checklist/4–18 and profile.* Burlington: University of Vermont Department of Psychiatry.

American Psychiatric Association. (1994). *Diagnostic and statistical manual of mental disorders* (4th ed.). Washington, DC: Author.

Beck, A. T., Ward, C. H., Mendelson, M., Mock, J., & Erbaugh, J. (1961). An inventory for measuring depression. *Archives of General Psychiatry, 4*, 561–571.

Bernard-Bonnin, A., Haley, N., Belanger, S., & Nadeau, D. (1993). Parental and patient perceptions about encopresis and its treatment. *Developmental and Behavioral Pediatrics, 14*, 397–400.

Calkins, D. L., Walker, C. E., & Howe, A. C. (1994). Elimination disorders: Psychological issues. In R. A. Olson, L. L. Mullins, J. B. Gillman, & J. M. Chaney (Eds.), *The sourcebook of pediatric psychology* (pp. 46–54). Boston: Allyn & Bacon.

Christophersen, E. R., & Purvis, P. C. (2001). Toileting problems in children. In M. C. Roberts & C. E. Walker (Eds.), *Handbook of clinical child psychology* (3rd ed., pp. 453–469). New York: Wiley.

Fireman, G., & Koplewicz, H. S. (1992). Short-term treatment of children with encopresis. *Journal of Psychotherapy, Practice and Research, 1,* 64–71.

Gabel, S., Hegedus, A. M., Wald, A., Chandra, R., & Chiponis, D. (1986). Prevalence of behavior problems and mental health utilization among encopretic children: Implications for behavioral pediatrics. *Developmental and Behavioral Pediatrics, 7,* 293–297.

Geffken, G. R., & Monaco, L. (1996). Assessment and treatment of encopresis. *Journal of Psychological Practice, 2*(3), 22–30.

Houts, A. C., & Abramson, H. (1990). Assessment and treatment for functional childhood enuresis and encopresis: Toward a partnership between health psychologists and physicians. In S. B. Morgan & T. M. Okwumabua (Eds.), *Child and adolescent disorders: Developmental and health psychology perspectives* (pp. 47–103). Hillsdale, NJ: Erlbaum.

Kisch, E. H., & Pfeffer, C. R. (1984). Functional encopresis: Psychiatric inpatient treatment. *American Journal of Psychotherapy, 38*(2), 264–271.

Levine, M. D. (1975). Children with encopresis: A descriptive analysis. *Pediatrics, 56,* 412–416.

McGrath, M. L., Mellon, M. W., & Murphy, L. (2000). Empirically supported treatments in pediatric psychology: Constipation and encopresis. *Journal of Pediatric Psychology, 25*(4), 225–254.

Murray, R. D. (1994). Elimination disorders: Medical issues. In R. A. Olson, L. L. Mullins, J. B. Gillman, & J. M. Chaney (Eds.), *The sourcebook of pediatric psychology* (pp. 42–45). Boston: Allyn & Bacon.

Ondersma, S. J., & Walker, C. E. (1998). Elimination disorders. In T. H. Ollendick & M. Hersen (Eds.), *Handbook of child psychopathology* (3rd ed., pp. 355–378). New York: Plenum Press.

Stark, L. J. (2000). Treatment of encopresis: Where do we go from here? *Journal of Pediatric Psychology, 25*(4), 255–256.

Stark, L. J., Owens-Stively, J., Spirito, A., Lewis, A., & Guevremont, D. (1990). Group behavioral treatment of retentive encopresis. *Journal of Pediatric Psychology, 15,* 659–671.

Walker, C. E. (1978). Toilet training, enuresis, and encopresis. In P. Magrab (Ed.), *Psychological management of pediatric problems* (Vol. 1). Baltimore: University Park Press.

Walker, C. E. (1995). Elimination disorders: Enuresis and encopresis. In M. C. Roberts (Ed.), *Handbook of pediatric psychology* (2nd ed.). New York: Guilford Press.

Walker, C. E., Milling, L. S., & Bonner, B. L. (1988). Incontinence disorders: Enuresis and encopresis. In D. K. Routh (Ed.), *Handbook of pediatric psychology* (pp. 363–397). New York: Guilford Press.

Wolters, W. H. G. (1974). A comparative study of behavioural aspects in encopretic children. *Psychotherapy and Psychosomatics, 24,* 86–97.

Wright, L. (1975). Outcome of a standarized program for treating psychogenic encopresis. *Professional Psychology, 6,* 453–456.

Wright, L., & Walker, C. E. (1978). A simple behavioral treatment program for psychogenic encopresis. *Behaviour Research and Therapy, 16,* 209–212.

CHAPTER 24

Child Sexual Abuse

EUGENIA HSU, GEORGANNA SEDLAR, MARY F. FLOOD, and DAVID J. HANSEN

DESCRIPTION OF THE PROBLEM

CHILD SEXUAL ABUSE is a disturbingly prevalent problem that has received increased attention from researchers, clinicians, and the general public during recent decades. Incidence studies from the 1990s provide the best estimate of the numbers of children and families affected by this problem, but even the advancement in comprehensive and methodologically sophisticated efforts are believed to underestimate the problem. The Third National Incidence Study of Child Abuse and Neglect estimated that in 1993, approximately 217,700 children nationwide had experienced harm from sexual abuse, and that sexually abused children accounted for 29% of the total number of children who suffered any form of child maltreatment (i.e., physical, sexual, and emotional abuse and neglect; National Center on Child Abuse and Neglect, 1996). Child protective service agencies in the United States reported that in 1998, 1.6 children per 1,000 children experienced sexual abuse, with approximately 75% involving girls as victims (U.S. Department of Health and Human Services, 2000). Underreporting and failure to substantiate actual cases of abuse are likely to influence these figures, leading to widespread speculation that they are substantial underestimates of actual occurrence.

A considerable body of research has examined the effects of sexual abuse on children and documented its generally deleterious consequences (Kendall-Tackett, Williams, & Finkelhor, 1993; Paolucci, Genuis, & Violato, 2001; Wolfe & Birt, 1995). Most studies have focused on relatively short-term correlates of childhood sexual abuse and found a notable range and variability in behavioral and emotional responses associated with sexual abuse. The research indicates that symptoms vary in intensity, number, and character. Some children exhibit no to minimal symptoms, whereas other children display a combination of symptoms (Finkelhor & Berliner, 1995; Hecht & Hansen, 1999; Kendall-Tackett et al., 1993). Kendall-Tackett et al. reviewed 45 studies examining the impact of sexual abuse on children and found a diverse array of symptoms in different age groups. Their review indicates that inappropriate sexual behavior, anxiety, and nightmares were the most common symptoms of sexually abused preschool-age children and that both preschool-age and school-age victims frequently experienced symptoms of Posttraumatic Stress Disorder (PTSD), such as nightmares and reexperiencing the event (Kendall-Tackett et al., 1993). School-age children also reported experiencing fear, academic problems, aggression, and hyperactivity (Kendall-Tackett et al., 1993). Adolescent victims tend to have poor self-esteem and display maladaptive behaviors, such as running away, engaging in promiscuous behaviors, committing illegal acts, abusing substances, engaging in self-injurious behaviors, and attempting suicide (Gil, 1996; Hecht & Hansen, 1999; Kendall-Tackett et al., 1993). Depressed mood is a symptom common to all age groups (Kendall-Tackett et al., 1993; Paolucci et al., 2001). Despite such breadth of prominent psychological consequences across age groups, sexually abused children do not appear more symptomatic than clinically referred nonabused children, with the exception that sexually abused children exhibit more PTSD symptoms and sexualized behavior than do other referred children (Friedrich et al., 2001; Kendall-Tackett et al., 1993; Wolfe & Birt, 1995). In addition, no typical "profile" or diagnostic syndrome uniformly applies to the majority of sexual abuse victims (Finkelhor & Berliner, 1995; Wolfe & Birt, 1995).

Researchers have examined incident characteristics of the abuse and contextual factors in the child's life and environment to explain the variability in symptomatology and the lack of a single diagnostic profile for child victims of sexual abuse. Characteristics of the abuse experience, such as severity (e.g., fondling, penetration), identity of the perpetrator, duration and frequency of sexual contact, and use of force are thought to influence the type and severity of children's symptoms (Kendall-Tackett et al., 1993; Wolfe & Birt, 1995). Contextual factors that contribute to variation in symptom presentations include age at the time of the assessment, other child variables (e.g., gender, children's attributions about the abuse), familial relationships (e.g., quality of parent-child relationship, maternal support), the presence of multiple forms of maltreatment (e.g., physical abuse, neglect), and offenders' responses to abuse allegations (Friedrich, 1998; Kendall-Tackett et al., 1993; Saunders & Meinig, 2000). Despite variability in specific symptoms, sexual abuse appears to impact three broad areas of adjustment and functioning: the individual or self (e.g., self-esteem, internalizing feelings); relationships (e.g., social interactions, externalizing problems with peers and family); and sex (i.e., sexual knowledge and abuse-related issues; Futa, Hecht, & Hansen, 1996; Hansen, Hecht, & Futa, 1998).

CASE DESCRIPTION

This chapter describes the case of two adolescent girls who were living in foster care with their maternal aunt and her family, the Kraller family.[1] The girls and their aunt and uncle participated in Project SAFE, a university-based program for

---

[1] Identifying information on the case was altered to protect the Kraller and Smith families' confidentiality.

sexually abused children and their nonoffending caregivers, which is described in detail in the Course of Treatment section. The Kraller family was referred to Project SAFE by the local Child Advocacy Center. Miriam Kraller contacted the Child Advocacy Center when she learned that her two nieces (her younger sister's daughters), Gina (age 14) and Suzy (age 13), had been sexually abused and were moving in with her and her family due to their mother's inability to care for them. Both Gina and Suzy reportedly had experienced sexual abuse while living with their mother (Abigail Smith) in Alabama. Mrs. Kraller sought help because she was concerned about the impact of the sexual abuse on her nieces.

Miriam and Matthew Kraller had been married for 13 years at the time of the referral to Project SAFE. Mrs. Kraller worked as a human resources manager in a local business corporation and Mr. Kraller worked as a production worker in a local factory. Mr. and Mrs. Kraller had one son (Travis, age 9) and one daughter (Stephanie, age 15).

Gina and Suzy were living with a family friend in Alabama when they came to the attention of child protective authorities because they and the friend's children were engaging in illegal, unsupervised activities (e.g., driving a car). Gina and Suzy were removed from their home and placed in foster care. The girls disclosed experiences of sexual abuse during the time they were receiving child protective services in Alabama.

Mrs. Kraller's first contact with Project SAFE was a request for information made before her nieces arrived in her home. She indicated that she would contact Project SAFE again after her nieces had time to adjust to their new living arrangements. A few months after the initial telephone call, Mrs. Kraller contacted Project SAFE to set up an intake appointment. Mr. Kraller was unable to attend the intake assessment, yet both Mr. and Mrs. Kraller were highly motivated to participate in treatment.

CHIEF COMPLAINTS

During the intake assessment, Mrs. Kraller said that she had had little time to get to know Gina and Suzy and expressed concerns that her caregiving style would be different from that of her sister. She also feared that the girls would engage in future risky behaviors because of their prior history. Both Gina and Suzy displayed sexualized behaviors (e.g., being overly friendly with men they did not know well, talking in a flirtatious manner, asking to look at sexually explicit TV shows) on a regular basis, according to their aunt. Mrs. Kraller also identified distinct concerns and strengths for each of the girls. She described Gina as having some difficulties getting along with others (including her sister, cousins, and other children). According to Mrs. Kraller, Gina did not have any close friends and was socially isolated from her peers outside of school. Mrs. Kraller was most concerned about Gina's lack of interest in her academic achievement and shared that Gina was previously diagnosed with a learning disability in reading. When asked about Gina's best qualities, Mrs. Kraller responded that Gina was sensitive, patient, and had a good sense of humor. For Mrs. Kraller, the most concerning aspects of Suzy's behavior were her low self-esteem and inability to calm down. Mrs. Kraller described Suzy's positive attributes as her happy demeanor and her devotion to her sister.

HISTORY

Mrs. Kraller provided information about Gina's and Suzy's abuse histories at the initial assessment session. Although the case was being handled out of state, Mrs. Kraller was considered to be a good historian regarding characteristics surrounding the abuse incidents.

According to Mrs. Kraller, Abigail (Ms. Smith) arranged for Gina to be "married" to a male acquaintance (age 36) when Gina was 12 years old. According to Mrs. Kraller, Gina believed that she was this man's legitimate wife for a period of time. Reportedly, no force was used during the abuse. Mrs. Kraller reported that the abuse included vaginal intercourse, but she was uncertain if other types of abuse occurred. Mrs. Kraller also believed that multiple offenders were involved. The abuse occurred over the course of approximately one year. Law enforcement was involved after Gina reported the abuse when she was in foster care, but there was no court or trial involvement because the alleged perpetrator could not be located and was believed to have left the country.

Suzy's abuse was disclosed at the same time as Gina's, although details about Suzy's abuse were less clear. According to reports, Suzy was abused by her mother's boyfriend when she was approximately 7 or 8 years old. Mrs. Kraller believed fondling and exposure were involved and vaginal penetration was suspected. Suzy was treated for a bladder infection 10 months prior to the assessment. Mrs. Kraller believed that Suzy had experienced more abuse incidents than were initially disclosed. In treatment, however, Suzy reported experiencing abuse on only one or two occasions.

BEHAVIORAL ASSESSMENT

A comprehensive assessment relying primarily on self- and parent-report measures was conducted to assess the effects of sexual abuse on the children and to identify co-occurring family issues. Assessment information was gathered from multiple informants (i.e., child and parent) and conducted at key time periods: pretreatment, posttreatment, and three months following treatment. A brief description of the child and parent measures is provided below. These measures were previously reviewed and have adequate psychometric properties (see Hansen et al., 1998, for more detailed descriptions of the measures). Weekly rating forms were also completed to monitor progress in treatment and are described in the Course of Treatment section.

At the intake session, both girls were relatively quiet. They were attentive during the description of the treatment program and cooperative in completing the intake measures.

CHILD SELF-REPORT

Child self-report measures assessed multiple domains of child functioning, particularly internalizing problems and self-esteem. The Children's Depression Inventory (CDI; Kovacs, 1992) is a 27-item measure used to assess recent cognitive and somatic symptoms of depression. Each item on the CDI has three choices reflecting severity of the symptoms: 0 = absence of symptom, 1 = mild symptom, and 2 = definite symptom. The Hopelessness Scale for Children (HSC; Kazdin,

Rogers, & Colbus, 1986) is a 17-item scale (true-false format) that measures feelings of hopelessness and negative expectations about the future. The Revised Children's Manifest Anxiety Scale (RCMAS; Reynolds & Richmond, 1985) is a 37-item measure (yes-no format) that assesses general anxiety, with a Total Anxiety score comprising physiological, subjective, and motor symptoms of anxiety. The Self-Esteem Inventory (SEI; Coopersmith, 1981) contains 58 items (like me-unlike me format) that measure children's attitudes about themselves in social, academic, family, and personal areas of experience. The Children's Loneliness Questionnaire (CLQ; Asher & Wheeler, 1985) is a 24-item questionnaire (5-point Likert-type scale) that assesses children's feelings of loneliness, social adequacy, and subjective estimations of peer status. The CDI and RCMAS utilize T-scores with a mean of 50 and standard deviation of 10. Range of scores on the other measures are as follows: HSC (0 to 17), SEI (0 to 100 without the Lie Scale), and CLQ (16 to 80 without eight items that are not included in the score).

At the beginning of treatment, Gina and Suzy displayed different clinical presentations. In general, Gina reported substantial problems in many areas of adjustment, whereas Suzy reported problems in only a few areas. Gina reported moderate levels of depressive symptoms (CDI T-score = 62). She indicated that she felt like crying many days, had trouble sleeping many nights, felt alone many times, and was not sure that things would work out for her. Gina's self-report measure responses were consistent with feelings of hopelessness and negative expectations about the future (HSC score = 8). For example, she endorsed feeling that she should give up because she could not make things better for herself. She exhibited clinically significant anxiety-related symptoms (RCMAS T-score = 69). Although all three domains on the RCMAS were elevated, she was reporting very high levels of physiological manifestations of anxiety (e.g., often feeling sick in her stomach, hands feeling sweaty, waking up scared some of the time). Her responses suggested that she was experiencing feelings of loneliness and social inadequacy (CLQ score = 47), as she did not have anyone to talk to in her class, felt alone at school, and found it hard to make friends at school. Her self-esteem score on the SEI (Total score = 58) suggested that she had a poor self-concept in social, academic, family, and personal areas of experience. In particular, Gina described especially low self-esteem in the school and academic settings (e.g., finding it very hard to talk in front of the class, often getting discouraged at school, not doing as well in school as she would like to, and her teachers making her feel that she was not good enough). Her self-report was consistent with Mrs. Kraller's concerns that she displayed a lack of interest in school, had some difficulties academically due to the previously diagnosed learning disability, and was socially isolated from her peers.

In contrast to Gina's scores, Suzy's self-report scores at intake did not reflect maladjustment in most areas of functioning. However, her Lie scores on two instruments were elevated, suggesting that she may have tried to present herself favorably or downplay her distress. Evaluation results for Suzy must be considered in light of her response style. For example, Suzy's SEI score reflected a high self-concept, but her Lie score was 6 (with a maximum score of 8). Similarly, her RCMAS score fell within the normal range, but her Lie score was in the 84th percentile. Her self-report suggested much below average level of depressive symptoms (CDI T-score = 34) and she did not endorse feelings of hopelessness about her future (HSC score = 1). Furthermore, she appeared to view herself as being socially adequate and experiencing few feelings of loneliness in peer interactions (CLQ score = 24).

Gina and Suzy completed two measures of abuse-specific reactions in addition to the measures of internalizing problems and self-esteem issues. The Children's Fears Related to Victimization (CFRV) is a 27-item subscale of the Fear Survey Schedule for Children–Revised (FSSC-R; Ollendick, 1983). The CFRV lists situations that sexually abused children seem to find particularly distressing (e.g., people not believing me, being lied to by someone I trust, people knowing bad things about me), and children rate how afraid they are of the situation using the options none, some, or a lot. Scores on the CFRV range from 27 to 81. The Children's Impact of Traumatic Events–Revised (CITES-R; Wolfe, Gentile, Michienzi, Sas, & Wolfe, 1991) is a 78-item semistructured interview developed to measure the impact of sexual abuse from the child's perspective across areas of posttraumatic stress, abuse attributions, social reactions, and eroticism. Children rate each statement on the CITES-R as very true, somewhat true, or not true. The 26-item Posttraumatic Stress subscale assesses intrusive thoughts, avoidance, hyperarousal, and sexual anxiety (with a range of scores from 0 to 52); this subscale provided the most salient information about Gina's and Suzy's needs.

Gina reported posttraumatic stress symptoms (e.g., trying to stay away from things that remind her of what happened to her, thinking about what happened to her even when she did not want to, hoping she never had to think about sex again, and sometimes feeling very scared when she is reminded of what happened; CITES-R, PTSD scale score = 30) and some fear about situations that sexually abused children typically find distressing (CRFV score = 58). Despite her reluctance to report internalizing and self-esteem problems, Suzy's responses to the measures of abuse-specific symptoms were similar to those of her sister. Suzy reported experiencing posttraumatic stress symptoms (PTSD scale score on the CITES-R = 29), such as trying to forget what had happened to her, being upset when she thought about sex, sometimes wanting to cry when she thought about what happened, and wishing that there was no such thing as sex. She also experienced fears in situations that sexually abused children seem to find distressing (CFRV Score = 55).

PARENT SELF-REPORT

Mrs. Kraller completed the pretreatment assessment measures that provided information about Gina's and Suzy's functioning. The Child Behavior Checklist–Parent Report Form (CBCL; Achenbach, 1991) is a 113-item checklist used for the assessment of parents' perceptions of social competence and behavioral problems of their children ages 4 to 18 years. The widely used CBCL uses T-scores for interpretation. The Child Sexual Behavior Inventory (CSBI; Friedrich et al., 1992) is a 35-item inventory of the frequency of various sexual behaviors such as sexual aggression, self-stimulation, gender-role behavior, and personal boundary violation observed in children ages 2 to 12. Each item is rated along a 4-point scale and the scores range from 0 to 105.

Mrs. Kraller's responses to the assessment instruments indicated that both Gina and Suzy were exhibiting significant behavioral symptoms. Gina was experiencing pervasive emotional and behavioral problems (CBCL Total T-score = 85), with clinically significant problems in internalizing (CBCL T-score = 88) and externalizing (CBCL T-score = 76) domains, according to her aunt's report. Similarly, Mrs. Kraller reported pervasive behavioral problems for Suzy, as most of the CBCL subscales were in the clinically significant range and the CBCL Total T-score was clinically significant (T-score = 71). Particularly, Mrs. Kraller noticed severe attention problems (T score = 81) in Suzy. She reported significant sexual behavior problems for both Gina and Suzy, as shown by her responses on the CSBI (scores of 35 and 26, respectively). Gina reportedly imitated the act of sexual intercourse, made sexual sounds, talked about sexual acts, hugged adults she did not know well, and was overly aggressive, whereas Suzy was overly friendly with men she did not know well, talked in a flirtatious manner, and seemed very interested in the opposite sex.

Family functioning across multiple domains was assessed through parental self-report instruments as well. The Family Adaptability and Cohesion Evaluation Scales (Olson, 1986) is a 20-item self-report measure that assesses adaptability, cohesion, and family satisfaction. The Family Crisis Oriented Personal Evaluation Scales (F-COPES; McCubbin, Olson, & Larsen, 1987) is a 30-item measure used to assess effective problem-solving coping attitudes and behavior (e.g., seeking spiritual support, passive appraisal) used by families in response to problems or difficulties. Two dimensions of family interactions are assessed by the F-COPES: internal family strategies and external family strategies. The Dyadic Adjustment Scale (Spanier, 1976) is a 32-item instrument that assesses the quality of a dyadic relationship (in this case, Mr. and Mrs. Kraller's marital relationship) and four specific aspects of the relationship: dyadic satisfaction, dyadic cohesion, dyadic consensus, and affectional expression. The Symptom Checklist-90–Revised (Derogatis, 1983) is a 90-item multidimensional symptom inventory that provides a global measure of psychological distress based on respondents' ratings of the degree of distress experienced for various symptoms. These measures did not indicate that the Krallers were experiencing significant problems at intake in these areas, nor did these measures show significant changes over the course of treatment for the Kraller family. Therefore, they are not discussed further.

MEDICAL CONSULTATION

Project SAFE treatment does not include a medical consultation or examination. Families are typically referred to Project SAFE by community and state agencies such as a local child advocacy center and the Department of Health and Human Services. Necessary medical examinations are provided prior to families' contact with Project SAFE. For example, the local child advocacy center provides a child-friendly environment where medical examinations and forensic interviews are conducted.

In Gina's and Suzy's cases, sexual abuse was discovered when they were living in foster care in another state and medical examinations were not conducted at the time of disclosure. Nevertheless, medical practitioners have an important role in diagnosing and treating sexually abused children. DeJong (1998) summarized four main reasons for conducting medical examinations: (1) to reassure child victims and their parents that they are normal and healthy; (2) to detect, prevent, and treat abuse-related medical conditions (including sexually transmitted diseases and pregnancy); (3) to collect and provide verbal and physical evidence for protection of the abused child; and (4) to collect and provide verbal and physical evidence to help prosecute the abuser. General guidelines have been published by the American Academy of Pediatrics (1999) for physicians evaluating childhood sexual abuse. Practice guidelines recommend obtaining a history (including behavioral changes and a clear statement about the abuse), performing a physical examination, and using laboratory data. Physical examinations typically include a medical history, a complete physical exam, and a thorough examination of the genitalia using a colposcope. Colposcopes are used with either still or video cameras to photographically preserve any signs of trauma, and resulting photographs or videotapes are given to law enforcement as part of a criminal investigation (Levitt, 1998). Medical examinations also may involve laboratory tests, forensic collection, and treatment of medical conditions. Despite advances in medical technology, medical evidence of sexual abuse is hard to obtain and "a high percentage of children with well-documented abuse will have normal physical examinations" (Jenny, 1996, p. 200). Specific signs and symptoms of sexual abuse include rectal or genital bleeding, sexually transmitted diseases, and developmentally unusual sexual behavior. Two high-probability physical indicators of child sexual abuse are pregnancy in a child and venereal disease in a child younger than age 12 to 14 (Faller, 1993).

CASE CONCEPTUALIZATION

The variability of symptom presentation following sexual abuse makes generalizations about the effects of child sexual abuse difficult; however, several models have attempted to identify mediating and moderating variables in the adjustment process. Two widely recognized models are the traumagenic dynamics model (Finkelhor & Browne, 1985) and the transactional model (Spaccarelli, 1994). Because detailed review and critique of these models are beyond the scope of this chapter, readers are referred to other sources for additional conceptualizations and perspectives (e.g., Cicchetti & Toth, 2000; Conte, 1990; Hansen et al., 1998; Wolfe & Birt, 1997).

The traumagenic dynamics model (Finkelhor & Browne, 1985) views the extent of a child's symptoms following child sexual abuse as dependent on the child's experiences of four trauma-causing factors, known as "traumagenic dynamics": traumatic sexualization, betrayal, stigmatization, and powerlessness. An application of the traumagenic dynamics model helps account for Suzy's and Gina's adjustment at intake. *Traumatic sexualization* describes a variety of processes by which a child's sexuality (including both sexual feelings and sexual attitudes) is shaped in a developmentally inappropriate manner (Finkelhor & Browne, 1985). According to Suzy, her offenders told her they were doing nothing wrong and were teaching her to have sex. This message may have contributed to Suzy's belief that abuse happens to all girls. These experiences may have changed her view about herself sexually and therefore may account for her increase in sexualized behavior and potentially risky behavior reported by Mrs. Kraller over the course of treatment. Although Gina displayed problematic sexual behavior at intake, this behavior substantially subsided over the course of treatment and follow-up, consistent with the model's position that traumagenic processes are open to change over time.

Betrayal occurs when the child realizes that a trusted person has manipulated him or her and caused him or her harm. Therefore, the closeness of the relationship between the offender and the child is likely to affect the degree of betrayal experienced by the child (Finkelhor & Browne, 1985). Betrayal processes may account for some of Suzy's and Gina's difficulties after the abuse. Suzy reported that prior to the abuse, she felt safe, happy, and comfortable with the offenders. Suzy's offenders did not admit that they did anything wrong and, in fact, blamed someone else for the abuse. Gina's perpetrators did not admit to any wrongdoing, either, and it appears that Gina may have believed she was married to one of the perpetrators for a time. Therefore, Suzy and Gina are likely to have felt betrayed by the perpetrators' actions and unwillingness to acknowledge the abuse incidents.

Stigmatization refers to the negative messages about the self, such as feelings of shame or guilt, that are communicated to the child during and after the sexual abuse (Finkelhor & Browne, 1985). Stigmatization processes seemed to contribute to Gina's adjustment difficulties, particularly her poor self-image, as evidenced by her low scores on the SEI. Besides not admitting to any abuse, Gina's offenders told her never to tell anyone about the abusive incidents. Such messages, particularly the instruction to keep the abuse a secret, may have increased Gina's sense of stigma and, subsequently, been incorporated into her self-image. Gina indicated that if the abuse had not happened, then maybe she would not feel "weird." She also expressed a desire to stop putting herself down in the future. Overall, her presentation was consistent with the traumagenic model's proposition that victims may view themselves as "spoiled goods."

Powerlessness occurs when the child's will and sense of efficacy are repeatedly contravened, and the child experiences violence, coercion, and threat to life and body (Finkelhor & Browne, 1985). Both Gina and Suzy reported posttraumatic stress symptoms, suggesting that they may have experienced a certain sense of powerlessness and fear during the abuse. For example, Suzy described her abuse as "scary," "gross," and "painful." Similarly, Gina indicated that after the abuse, she thought that she could have stopped it, but she was not sure how.

The transactional model (Spaccarelli, 1994) contributes additional understanding about Gina's and Suzy's adjustment following sexual abuse. According to the transactional model (Spaccarelli, 1994), children's development progresses through a series of person-environment transactions that influence healthy or psychopathological outcomes. Children's environments are considered to be continually changing, which affects their development and available resources. In addition to external resources, children also possess internal resources that can influence their organization of the environment. In this model, the impact of sexual abuse on the child's family and community environment is as important as the characteristics directly associated with the abusive events (e.g., seriousness, frequency, duration, and coerciveness).

The model's emphasis on environmental factors is particularly relevant for understanding Gina and Suzy. The transactional model starts with the belief that victims of sexual abuse encounter a series of stressors (Spaccarelli, 1994). Based on the background information provided by Mrs. Kraller, the girls were experiencing environmental stressors prior to and concurrent with the abuse. These stressors may have contributed directly to the occurrence of sexual abuse, or they may have created an underlying family system that allowed sexual abuse to occur. Once the abuse began, it may have exacerbated the other environmental stressors as well.

The transactional model predicts that a victim's risk for poor mental health outcomes increases as a function of the total abuse stress across three categories of stressful events: abuse, abuse-related, and public disclosure events (Spaccarelli,

1994). Among the salient abuse-related events, the girls' family environment was key. Prior to moving in with the Krallers, the girls were faced with a lack of family stability. Numerous friends and partners of their mother came in and out of the household. Gina's "marriage" was allegedly arranged to help her mother financially. Additionally, when the girls were found by law enforcement, they were riding around town unsupervised, with an unlicensed, underage driver. Gina and Suzy encountered multiple changes in living environments over a relatively short period of time: living with their mother, followed by living with their friend's family, then temporary foster care, and finally settling in with the Kraller family. Although the children may have lacked maternal support subsequent to law enforcement involvement, Mr. and Mrs. Kraller's unwavering support and timely responding helped to buffer against prior negative experiences. In addition to family dysfunction, the girls also endured many public disclosure events. These events included police involvement and interviews in Alabama, removal from their home, and contact with the local child advocacy center. Although the girls did not have to appear in court for any criminal or civil cases directly associated with the sexual abuse (e.g., perpetrator court case), they did participate in the hearing that terminated their mother's parental rights.

Mr. and Mrs. Kraller provided substantial environmental resources for Gina and Suzy. After a considerable period of chaos and instability, they provided a secure and stable environment. The type and amount of support the girls received was an important environmental factor in their adjustment. A prime example of the Krallers' support was their timely involvement in treatment. Their participation in group treatment was an admirable way to convey their support. Although information on the girls' individual functioning prior to the abuse was limited, the transactional model supports the notion that differences in their abuse experiences, developmental stages, and prior functioning most likely played a role in their adjustment.

The transactional model suggests that children's cognitive appraisals and coping strategies mediate the effects of sexual molestation and related life events and function as the immediate causes of symptoms. Spaccarelli (1994) emphasized that sexually abusive events are likely to lead to negative cognitive appraisals and problematic coping strategies, although not all children develop such appraisals or use maladaptive coping strategies. The model posits a bidirectional influence for appraisals and symptoms, in which children's psychological symptoms influence cognitive appraisals and coping strategies as well as being influenced by them.

Both Gina and Suzy expressed negative cognitive appraisals of themselves and their role in the abuse. For instance, Gina believed that if the abuse had never happened, she would not feel "weird" and would be able to make friends easier. Gina assumed responsibility for the abuse, believing she could have stopped it. Suzy's belief that abuse happens to all girls is a cognitive appraisal that may have contributed to her relatively higher self-esteem. Alternatively, her belief may have led her to feel vulnerable and frightened. The coping strategies employed by Gina and Suzy appear to have included some risk-taking behaviors and avoidance. For example, Gina used humor and cartoon-like voices when she was nervous or anxious during sessions, suggesting an attempt to avoid dealing with her feelings. Despite this initial avoidant coping strategy, Gina began to use support from her aunt and uncle as an alternative coping mechanism strategy during the course of treatment.

RATIONALE FOR TREATMENT CHOICE

Finkelhor and Berliner (1995) concluded from their review of treatment literature that, "taken as a whole, the studies of sexually abused children in treatment show improvements that are consistent with the belief that therapeutic intervention facilitates children's recovery" (p. 1414). Children who are not treated may exhibit difficulties in areas of daily functioning (e.g., school, peer, and familial relationships) and have a significant chance of being revictimized (Browne & Finkelhor, 1986; Kendall-Tackett et al., 1993). Therefore, it is important to assess sexually abused children's needs carefully and offer treatment to children with behavioral and emotional problems associated with the abuse.

Several treatment modalities (e.g., individual, group, family) have been implemented with child sexual abuse victims; however, empirical evidence supporting the different approaches is limited (King et al., 1999). The current trend in clinical psychology is to depart from nondirective supportive therapy and shift toward the use of empirically validated treatment protocols (Ollendick, 1999; Weisz, Weiss, & Donenberg, 1992). Despite this movement, standardized treatment programs are underutilized with child sexual abuse victims and their families. Studies have shown preliminary support for using abuse-specific therapy to decrease related symptomatology (e.g., Berliner & Saunders, 1996; Deblinger, Lippmann, & Steer, 1996; Deblinger, Steer, & Lippmann, 1999). Cohen and Mannarino (1998) found that sexual abuse-specific cognitive-behavioral therapy was more effective in decreasing depressive symptomatology and improving clinical presentation than nondirective supportive therapy. The inclusion of nonoffending parents has also been identified as an integral part of positive treatment outcome for sexually abused children (Celano, Hazzard, Webb, & McCall, 1996; Damon & Waterman, 1986).

Research findings suggest that group therapy is a potentially beneficial treatment modality for sexual abuse victims. Reeker, Ensing, and Elliott (1997) analyzed literature on group therapy and found that "effective group treatments for sexually abused children do exist" (p. 695). They reported that the greatest advantage of group treatment is that participants have the opportunity to share with others who have had similar experiences. Another benefit of group therapy is its high cost-effectiveness and low labor involvement (Reeker et al., 1997). However, additional research is needed to identify the characteristics of effective group treatments. In the Reeker et al. review, multiple treatment modalities were included, providing little clear direction on group structure or content.

Most nonoffending parents do not have their own support system, and a supportive environment may be beneficial for parents to process what has happened to their child and family. Group treatment has been suggested for treating nonoffending parents because it provides parents a supportive atmosphere where they can give and receive support with other parents who share similar experiences and resolve stressful issues (Landis & Wyre, 1984). Group therapy offers additional benefits to parents not available in individual therapy. Group therapy gives the parents a greater opportunity to develop social skills and to participate in role modeling and role playing (Sgroi & Dana, 1982). Groups also help parents regain a sense of belonging to something, develop supportive friendships, and decrease the isolation that usually occurs after disclosure of abuse (Schonberg, 1992; Sgroi & Dana, 1982). To date, only one known cognitive-behavioral group treatment outcome study for nonoffending mothers and their sexually abused children has been completed (Stauffer & Deblinger, 1996). Parallel groups were conducted with 19 nonoffending mothers and their young sexually abused children, ages 2 to 6. Results indicate that following treatment, mothers experienced lower levels of general distress, exhibited less avoidance of abuse-related thoughts and feelings, and responded more appropriately to their children's behaviors and abuse-related issues (Stauffer & Deblinger, 1996). Project SAFE is unique as a parallel, standardized group treatment for sexually abused children *and* adolescents and their nonoffending caregivers (Futa et al., 1996; Hansen et al., 1998; Hecht, Futa, & Hansen, 1996).

COURSE OF TREATMENT

Project SAFE is a standardized group treatment program for sexually abused children (ages 7 to 16) and their nonoffending parents or caregivers. Project SAFE is operated through the Psychological Consultation Center at the University of Nebraska–Lincoln (UNL), a clinic for research training and service.

Separate groups are conducted simultaneously for children and parents. Groups meet for 90-minute sessions for 12 consecutive weeks, covering 10 modules. Each group is cofacilitated by two therapists who are doctoral students in the clinical psychology program at UNL. The same topics are covered in the sessions for children and parents, incorporating education and strategies to prevent future sexual abuse.

Project SAFE groups are generally small, usually with 3 to 4 children and 4 to 6 parents. The group in which Gina and Suzy participated had one other 13-year-old girl. Similarly, the parent group included Mr. and Mrs. Kraller and the parents of the other child.

The treatment protocol was developed from a systematic review of the literature on treatment programs for sexually abused children and their nonoffending parents. The intervention was designed to address three critical target areas impacted by sexual abuse: the individual or self (self-esteem, internalizing feelings); relationships (social interactions and externalizing problems with peers and family); and sex (sexual knowledge and abuse related issues; Futa et al., 1996; Hansen et al., 1998). Procedures used in sessions are psychoeducational, skill building, problem solving, and supportive. Different protocols are used for younger children and adolescents to address the children's developmental levels appropriately. The treatment overview of Project SAFE and descriptions of the modules below are focused on the adolescent's group, given Gina's and Suzy's ages. Specific details about techniques used in Project SAFE can be obtained by referring to a chapter by Hansen et al. (1998) or by contacting the authors for a copy of the treatment manual.

Each child group began with Circle Time, when each child shared with the group how her previous week went, and ended with a Free Time, when the children and therapist named one good thing that each group member did during the session. This latter structured activity, led by one of the therapists, promoted the girls' positive self-esteem, helped the session end on a positive note, and allowed the lead child therapist an opportunity to check in and talk to the parents. Each parent group began with a brief discussion of the child's behaviors at home during the previous week and ended with the lead child therapist joining the group to discuss how the children reacted to that week's session and to answer any questions the parents may have. This check-in period was useful in providing parents reassurance about how their children were doing in treatment; it also provided the parents an opportunity to discuss any concerns they had about their children directly with the child therapist. Additionally, the check-in period allowed the parents to be informed on the upcoming session and address any related concerns.

TREATMENT MODULES

Module 1: Welcome and Orientation   The goals of Module 1 were to introduce the purpose and intent of group, to discuss issues of confidentiality, to establish group rules, and to promote rapport building and group cohesion (e.g., describe unique qualities about themselves and the meaning of being a part of a group). Parents were given basic information about sexual abuse (e.g., prevalence, definition) and the importance of parental support in their children's treatment.

Module 2: Understanding and Recognizing Feelings   Module 2 focused on helping the children to identify feelings in themselves and others; to encourage the expression of feelings; to examine possible causes and consequences of feelings; and to understand the range and multidimensionality of feelings. Parents were encouraged to identify how they respond to feelings, learn more appropriate and effective ways to express emotions, and learn ways to help their children express their feelings. Furthermore, parents discussed how their children express their feelings through their behavior, and how at times, the behavior might not seem to match the feeling. Parents were also encouraged to generate and discuss adaptive coping skills (e.g., engage in relaxing activities, seek social support).

Module 3: Learning about Our Bodies   Module 3 included learning correct information about developing bodies, sexual development, and gender differences; discussing issues related to dating and decisions about sex; increasing comfort with dialogue in the family about sex-related issues; and improving the children's self-image and correcting misperceptions about themselves as "damaged goods." The parents' group focused on increasing the parents' ability and comfort in discussing sexuality and other sex-related issues with their children. In addition, a discussion was held about their children's body image at their stage of development and how sexual abuse may affect body image. Specific ways to enhance their children's body image and self-esteem were identified.

Module 4: Standing Up for Your Rights   The purpose of Module 4 was to empower the children, to prevent future abuse by appropriately asserting themselves, to identify a plan (e.g., whom to call, what to do) if abuse does happen again, and to enhance support networks. In the parent group, a brief discussion of assertiveness was conducted to help parents distinguish among assertion, aggression, and defiance in their children. Additionally, prevention issues were discussed and parents generated ways to prevent future abuse of their children.

Module 5: My Family   Module 5 was intended to identify the strengths within the family, to discuss the effects of disclosure on the family, to address special concerns when the offender is a family member or close family friend, and to discuss supportive family members and other sources of support. A main goal of this module was to reduce feelings of isolation through identification of family strengths and sources of social support. Additional topics in the parent group included identifying the effects of disclosure on the parents' behavior toward the child and siblings (e.g., overprotectiveness) and how the family (e.g., relationships) may have changed.

Module 6: Sharing What Happened, Part I   This module was conducted in two sessions focused on reducing feelings of isolation and stigmatization about the abuse through disclosure to the group. Other topics included dealing with others' reactions to disclosure, identifying feelings related to the abuse and disclosure, and encouraging expression of these feelings. When disclosing their abuse, adolescents were given the option to complete a summary sheet (modified from deYoung & Corbin, 1994) with various responses about different aspects of the abuse (e.g., where the abuse took place, how they felt about the abuser before the abuse) that served as a nonthreatening, structured way to disclose their abuse to others. Each group member decided whether she wanted to read her responses off the sheet or share her story in her own way. Therapists focused on normalizing these feelings and addressing any faulty assumptions or cognitive distortions that the children expressed. The parents were informed that the children were discussing difficult material and that they might be upset after the session and even during the upcoming week. A discussion was conducted on possible "regression" (e.g., return of problematic behaviors) that may result from talking about the abuse, and parents discussed ways to problem-solve should this occur. Parents were reminded to be sensitive listeners and to encourage their children's expression of feelings regarding the abuse. They were also reminded about the importance of being supportive of their children and being available to talk with them about these difficult topics.

Module 7: Sharing What Happened, Part II   Module 7 was an extension of Module 6, focusing on the offender. The goals included educating the adolescents on why offenders offend, placing the responsibility and blame on the offender, and dealing with issues involved in the offender's relationship to the family. Children were asked to talk about their feelings about their own offender and how their feelings might have changed from before the abuse. Similarly, parents were asked to describe their own feelings about the offender and how their feelings might have changed from preabuse to postabuse. Parents were given support and ideas about how to be sensitive to their children's feelings surrounding the abuse, and how to deal with their own strong reactions of anger or guilt.

Module 8: Understanding My Feelings about What Happened to Me   Module 8 was designed to assist the children in understanding their feelings surrounding the abuse and enhance their positive self-image. Feelings that were targeted include stigmatization, guilt, and shame surrounding the abuse. Effects of these feelings on behaviors were discussed. Children were encouraged to channel negative feelings into an appropriate outlet (e.g., be angry at the offender and not at themselves) and to identify positive peer relationships. Parents explored the extent to which they shared the same feelings as their children (e.g., guilt, shame, anger) and were encouraged to remain sensitive to their children's feelings. The stages of grief within the context of child sexual abuse (i.e., shock/denial, anger, guilt/depression, bargaining, acceptance) were also discussed.

Module 9: Learning to Cope with My Feelings　Module 9 was conducted in two sessions and focused on reducing present feelings of anxiety and depression, exploring the relationship between mood and behavior, and identifying coping skills, such as problem solving and relaxation training. Parents generated a list of coping techniques they found useful when they experience distress. Coping techniques included problem-focused coping (e.g., problem solving, finding more information), tension reduction and relaxation techniques (e.g., engaging in pleasurable activities, exercise), and using social support systems (e.g., friends, family, church, mental health professionals).

Module 10: Summary and Goodbye　The goal of Module 10 was to provide a summary of the group experience and to discuss ways of maintaining gains and dealing with separation. Children reviewed content and information from group in a game format. Parents also reviewed the major themes of the group and were asked to focus on the changes they have seen in their children and themselves. If necessary, referrals for additional services were discussed with families. At the end of session, parents and children joined together for a party to celebrate how hard the members worked and to help provide closure for the session.

BEHAVIORAL OBSERVATIONS

Both Gina and Suzy attended all twelve group sessions. Overall, both girls actively and appropriately participated in treatment. At the outset of treatment, both appeared nervous and uncomfortable about participating in treatment activities. Suzy appeared particularly uncomfortable when group discussion focused on self-perceptions since the abuse (Module 3). When she was uncomfortable or nervous, she frequently fidgeted and became restless (e.g., played with her sister's foot, played with clock on a table). She also pulled her hair in front of her face to cover her eyes. She was silent for much of the discussion about bodies and sex, although she was attentive and interested in the discussion and other group members' comments. At the beginning of treatment, Gina was nervous and seemed more comfortable interacting with her sister than with group leaders. As treatment progressed, she appeared more comfortable with the group. At times, she indicated that she felt she was talking too much, although her comments were appropriate in length. She dealt with her discomfort through the use of jokes and laughter; in fact, she frequently spoke in an immature, cartoon-like voice.

Both girls were quiet during the session focusing on disclosure (Module 6). They avoided eye contact, spoke softly, and covered parts of their face (e.g., with their hair or covered their mouth with their hands). Gina expressed that the "sharing what happened" portion of the session was difficult for her, and she remained extremely quiet during the discussion. As treatment progressed, both Gina and Suzy became more comfortable, as evidenced by their increased interaction with the group facilitators and participation in group activities. They were respectful to the other group member, who was visibly uncomfortable and reluctant to participate in treatment activities.

Mr. and Mrs. Kraller were active and interested participants in the parent group. Mr. Kraller missed only one group session due to working overtime. Throughout treatment, the Krallers demonstrated good insight and sensitivity about Gina's and Suzy's behaviors. During the initial group sessions, they expressed concerns to the group about not being the parents of Gina and Suzy; however, this difference did not affect how they were viewed by other group members. In discussing the girls' abuse, both Mr. Kraller and Mrs. Kraller expressed feelings of anger and frustration. Mrs. Kraller felt an additional burden because her sister was the perpetrator. She expressed anger toward her sister for not protecting Gina and Suzy from the sexual abuse. She also expressed guilt for not intervening earlier to help them. The therapists were able to normalize her mixed feelings and assure her that her feelings were common among caregivers of sexually abused youths. Mrs. Kraller's mixed feelings also provided an opportunity to draw parallels to many different feelings sexually abused children might have about their abuse. This approach seemed to enhance her understanding and empathy for the girls. Mr. and Mrs. Kraller's willingness to be emotionally open and honest facilitated their therapeutic progress.

During Module 3, Learning about Our Bodies, Mrs. Kraller disclosed that she had been sexually abused as a child. She was worried about the impact of her abuse history on her ability to be appropriately responsive to the girls' questions about sex-related matters. Her abuse history came up at other points during treatment. For example, she commented that she was able to relate to discussions that paralleled those held in the adolescent group about their feelings related to the abuse and offenders. The potential implications of her abuse history on treatment were addressed. For instance, the therapists validated her experiences and facilitated her understanding about how this experience, just as with her other experiences, may influence how she responded to Gina's and Suzy's feelings and behavior. Again, her acknowledgment of her feelings and questioning the relationship of her experiences to how she managed the girl's behavior was important to the therapeutic process.

Weekly Assessments

Weekly rating forms were completed by the Kraller family, including Gina and Suzy, to monitor their progress in treatment. These forms were developed specifically for Project SAFE (Futa, 1998) with the intent of being sensitive to ongoing changes over the course of treatment. The child form consisted of statements (e.g., "I feel sad," "I get along with my friends") and choices of seven responses on a scale from 0 (never) to 6 (all of the time). Gina and Suzy marked the response that best described their feelings and interactions during the previous week. The weekly rating form completed by parents was parallel to the rating form for the children. Mr. and Mrs. Kraller were presented with 15 statements about Gina's and Suzy's behaviors (e.g., "During the past 7 days my child appeared unhappy, sad, or depressed") and were asked to rate each statement on a scale from 1 (always) to 10 (never). During the course of treatment, Mr. Kraller completed these weekly rating forms for Gina and Mrs. Kraller completed them for Suzy. Both parent and child weekly rating forms consisted of a Total Problem Scale and five subscales of child and family functioning: negative mood, problem behavior, problem interactions with others, abuse-related emotional and communication problems, and problem family functioning.

Over the course of treatment, Gina reported a moderate decline of total problematic behaviors, with the most substantial change in lower negative moods (e.g., sad and worried). Mr. Kraller's ratings were consistent with Gina's self-report over the course of treatment, as he also reported an overall decline in problems. He also described one week (preceding Session 9) when Gina exhibited an increase in her negative moods, problematic interactions with others, abuse-related emotional and communication problems, and difficulties in family functioning. This increase in difficulties may have reflected Gina's anxiety about her anticipated trip to Alabama (to appear in family court to terminate her mother's parental rights). Mr. Kraller also reported that subsequent to Module 6 (i.e., sharing her abuse experiences), Gina was more unwilling to discuss abuse-related topics. However, by the end of treatment, Gina was not displaying any significant difficulties in this domain. Suzy's weekly ratings showed a global trend similar to her sister's, in that she reported a decline in overall problems over the course of treatment. In general, Suzy reported minimal problematic behaviors in all areas of personal and family functioning. Mrs. Kraller also indicated that over the course of treatment, Suzy's overall problematic behaviors decreased.

THERAPIST-CLIENT FACTORS

Treatment with sexually abused children involves important therapist-client factors. One factor is the sex of the therapist. Traditionally, therapists working with sexually abused youth were the same sex as the group members. The rationale for using same-sex therapists was to avoid predominantly female group members from feeling threatened by a male therapist. Project SAFE has used a variety of combinations of cotherapists' sex throughout its development, and clinical experience indicates value in using both male and female therapists. A male and female therapist cofacilitated the group in which Gina and Suzy participated. Presence of a male therapist provided both girls an opportunity to relate to an adult male in a safe and healthy manner. Further, interactions between the male and the female therapist as well as with the girls allowed modeling of healthy relationships (i.e., mutual respect, appropriate boundaries) between men and women. Gina and Suzy appeared to approve of this arrangement, as they reported liking the therapists. The parent group therapists were both male due to therapist availability. The presence of two male therapists in the parents' group may have influenced Mrs. Kraller's reluctance to disclose her abuse history, as this information was shared when the female child therapist checked in at the end of a session.

Although communication and trust within the groups were essential, communication and rapport between the parents and the child therapists were also very important to treatment. A key strategy to facilitating this communication and rapport was for one child therapist to check in with the parent group at the end of each session. While helping facilitate rapport between parents and therapists, this check-in portion incorporated some important therapist-client factors, including trust, engagement, and credibility. First, the check-in period provided the parents with a brief summary of the children's group without violating the girls' confidentiality. The check-in also allowed Mr. and Mrs. Kraller to express any concerns to the child therapists about the girls' behavior or changes in the family (e.g., upcoming visit to Alabama). Similarly, the child therapists were able to prepare the Krallers for possible behavioral changes in response to session and address any questions or topics that might arise in the coming week (especially around the disclosure sessions). This exchange of information facilitated the Krallers' active participation in treatment and helped them to feel empowered in their parenting role. The Krallers were very attentive during the check-in and also shared relevant information with the child therapists. Finally, the check-in enhanced the credibility of the child therapists and reflected a team approach to treatment. The parallel groups in general and the check-in portion in particular sent a clear message to Mr. and Mrs. Kraller that they were integral to the girls' treatment and progress. This message was important for them to receive, given their expressed concerns about not being Gina's and Suzy's biological parents and their relatively recent involvement in the girls' lives.

COURSE OF TERMINATION

Although consistency in informants is important, issues of practicality were considered. The pretreatment assessments of both Gina's and Suzy's functioning were completed by Mrs. Kraller; however, Mr. Kraller was present for the posttreatment and three-month follow-up assessments. Therefore, Mr. Kraller completed measures on Gina and Mrs. Kraller completed them on Suzy. Although different informants were used to assess Gina's adjustment, Mr. and Mrs. Kraller had generally demonstrated consensus in their views about the children's adjustment during the group process.

By the end of treatment, Gina was reporting less depressive and anxious symptomatology, as evidenced by her decreased CDI and RCMAS scores (T-score = 47 and 55, respectively). In addition, she reported fewer feelings of hopelessness (HSC score = 3). Although her feelings of loneliness and social inadequacy did not change after treatment (CLQ score = 47), her SEI scores increased to 78 at the end of treatment, showing improvement in her self-attitude. Mr. Kraller's report on the CBCL was consistent with Gina's self-report, as her Internalizing scale scores fell within the normal range (CBCL Internalizing Scale T-score = 49). Mr. Kraller also reported substantial decreases in Gina's externalizing problems (CBCL Externalizing Scale T-score = 42). Her PTSD scale score on the CITES-R dropped to 20, whereas there were no significant changes in her fears about situations (CFRV score = 56). Another remarkable change occurred with Gina's sexual behavioral problems: At posttreatment, these had essentially stopped (CSBI score of 2).

Suzy's self-report scores remained essentially the same. At the end of treatment, her PTSD scale score dropped to 19, reflecting a reduction in posttraumatic symptoms. Mrs. Kraller reported decreases in Suzy's global externalizing behaviors (e.g., aggression), as indicated by the CBCL (Externalizing Scale T-score = 64) and in sexual behavior (CSBI score decreased from 26 to 20).

At the posttreatment assessment session, Mrs. Kraller was referred for individual therapy at the clinic where Project SAFE was being held. She was experiencing increased stress related to her family and parenting roles. In addition, she had a history of depression and fibromyalgia, a syndrome distinguished by chronic pain in the muscles, ligaments, tendons, or bursae around joints. She expressed concern that she was at increased risk for experiencing another depressive episode.

She recognized that she might benefit from assistance to deal with the adoption and anticipated stressors associated with integrating her nieces into the household on a permanent basis.

Toward the end of treatment, changes had occurred in the family environment. Both Gina and Suzy began seeing an individual therapist in the community. They were dealing with their mother's forfeit of her parental rights and the loss of this part of their family, as well as adjusting to the adoption and establishing a permanent place within the Kraller family. Interestingly, at the end of treatment, Gina and Suzy began calling Mr. and Mrs. Kraller "Dad" and "Mom." Project SAFE cannot anticipate all of the complex issues that arise in sexual abuse cases, but treatment attempts to provide children with opportunities to process their abuse experiences and learn effective ways to cope with stress and future difficulties.

FOLLOW-UP

After group treatment ended, the Kraller family was seen for a three-month follow-up assessment. Overall, they reported that the family was functioning well. The girls had terminated individual therapy based on their therapists' recommendation that treatment was no longer clinically warranted. Mrs. Kraller remained in individual therapy at the clinic to continue addressing stressors associated with family matters. The adoption of Gina and Suzy was still in process.

At follow-up, Gina and Suzy were reevaluated with the same measures used at earlier time points (i.e., intake and posttreatment). Gina's scores from both parent- and child-report measures (e.g., CDI, CBCL) remained essentially unchanged from posttreatment, suggesting her treatment gains were maintained at follow-up. Her score on the CFRV decreased from 56 at posttreatment to 49 at follow-up, indicating that she was experiencing less fear about situations that many sexually abused children may find distressing. Her SEI score returned to pretreatment level, dropping from 78 at posttreatment to 58 at follow-up. This score suggested that she was experiencing a poor self-concept in social, academic, family, and personal areas. Given that her scores on other measures fell within the normal range and remained stable over time, this decrease was unexpected. However, this score may be accounted for by situational factors (e.g., recent termination of her mother's parental rights) rather than a permanent change in her self-attitude. Alternatively, it is possible that the improvement in her self-attitude at the end of treatment was transient, and self-concept may take more than 12 weeks of group treatment to improve. Gina did indicate during treatment that in the future she would like to be able to stop putting herself down. Therefore, her high posttreatment SEI score may be a result of situational factors (e.g., felt accomplished at finishing group). Her increase in her SEI score at posttreatment may have been more transient and her self-esteem would continue to be bolstered after more successful experiences and a longer period of family stability.

Consistent with results at intake, Suzy and Gina displayed divergent clinical presentations at follow-up. While Gina's posttraumatic stress responses remained essentially unchanged, Suzy showed a continued decrease in scores on the PTSD subscale of the CITES-R (PTSD subscale score = 10). Most notable among the differences between them were Suzy's continued internalizing and externalizing behavioral problems. On the CBCL, Mrs. Kraller reported that Suzy was displaying attention problems (T-score = 69) and delinquent behavior (T-score = 70). Mrs. Kraller also observed signs of withdrawal, anxiety, and depression in Suzy's behavior. Whereas Gina's sexual behavior problems substantially diminished by follow-up (CSBI score of 24), Suzy's sexual behavior increased (e.g., tries to kiss adults and other children on the mouth). This shift in the girls' problems was also reflected in Mrs. Kraller's verbal description of the girls toward the end of treatment. She described Gina as someone who liked to stay at home, whereas she had more concerns about Suzy's potentially risky behavior (e.g., flirting with boys at a local convenience store).

MANAGED CARE CONSIDERATIONS

Project SAFE is a university-based research and clinical intervention project, and so participating families are not charged for services. Therefore, managed care considerations did not impact the Kraller family's access to Project SAFE, nor did managed care influence decisions about modality of service, length of treatment, or assessment of progress. If treatment for Gina and Suzy were offered in a community setting, however, managed care demands would be important factors. The Project SAFE model has some advantages over traditional outpatient therapy in the managed mental health care environment. The 12-session protocol is consistent with the brief treatment model that Kent and Hersen (2000) identified as the key factor in managed mental health care. The cost efficiency and clinical efficacy of group treatment have led a number of managed mental health care programs to emphasize the group modality over individual therapy (Kent & Hersen, 2000). In addition, the assessment completed prior to initiating treatment offers objective data for a managed care company to use in a preauthorization process. In some cases, assessment results are likely to present a strong rationale for authorizing services. For instance, Gina's intake assessment results suggested clinically significant problems that many companies would value as a justification of the need for treatment. Finally, Project SAFE measures outcomes at treatment completion and three-month follow-up, offering objective support for claims of goal accomplishment.

Despite these positive considerations, implementation of Project SAFE in the managed care environment is likely to share the challenges faced by other child and family treatment programs. For example, the full cost of the Project SAFE assessment procedures is unlikely to be covered in a pretreatment authorization process, even though such thorough assessment is indicated by the increased risk of behavioral and emotional problems associated with child sexual abuse and the diversity of clinical presentations seen among child survivors of abuse (Chaffin, 1998). Many behavioral health care management companies employ independent screeners who use their own assessment procedures, which are typically brief and involve limited interaction with the client. Some psychologists have suggested that part of the function of such screening evaluations is to restrict access to treatment, but there is also evidence that screening may select participants less likely to discontinue treatment early (Howard & Bassos, 2000). Gina and Suzy were both quiet during the discussion of abuse-related issues in Project SAFE, covering their faces, averting their eyes, and generally indicating uneasiness with disclosure. It seems highly probable that they, like many sexual abuse victims and families, would find a preauthorization screening evaluation by an independent screener threatening. After a medical examination and a child protective/law enforcement investigation, interacting openly with a screener whom they are unlikely to see again may be intimidating.

Authorization of Project SAFE services would not necessarily be assured in all managed mental health care environments. First of all, sexual abuse is not a mental disorder (Chaffin, 1998) and, thus, does not independently suggest that treatment is medically necessary. Although Gina's initial assessment results indicated a treatment need, many of Suzy's responses suggested few problems in functioning, despite her endorsement of symptoms of PTSD on the CITES-R and CFRV. Even if Gina's and Suzy's participation in the adolescent group of Project SAFE was authorized by their managed care company, their aunt's and uncle's participation in the parallel treatment group for nonoffending parents might not be authorized. Frequently, managed care companies reimburse only services provided directly to the identified patient and not to family members, especially when the identified patient is not an active participant in the family intervention.

OVERALL EFFECTIVENESS

Childhood sexual abuse presents a variety of stressful challenges to the victims and their families. Treatment of sexually abused children has received increased attention in research domains and clinical practice as improved incidence studies in recent decades have revealed disturbing information about its occurrence (National Center on Child Abuse and Neglect, 1996; U.S. Department of Health and Human Services, 2000). Group treatment has been recommended as one of the preferred modalities in working with child victims of sexual abuse (e.g., Hansen et al., 1998; Reeker et al., 1997), and the involvement of nonoffending caregivers in treatment has been identified as an integral part of positive treatment outcome for sexually abused children (e.g., Celano et al., 1996; Damon & Waterman, 1986). In addition to its therapeutic benefits, a time-limited, standardized group treatment protocol is a promising option in managed care environments. The present chapter documents a parallel group treatment for Gina and Suzy and their nonoffending caregivers, Mr. and Mrs. Kraller.

In general, the group treatment of Project SAFE was effective in reducing Gina's and Suzy's emotional and behavioral symptoms following disclosure of their sexual abuse experiences, and the Kraller family believed that treatment was helpful and pertinent to their situation. At the end of treatment, Gina reported fewer internalizing (i.e., depressive and anxious symptoms, feelings of hopelessness) and posttraumatic stress symptoms. Mr. Kraller reported similar reductions in Gina's emotional problems as well as noticeable decline in her externalizing and sexual behavioral problems. Although Suzy did not self-report difficulties in most areas of functioning during the intake assessment, there was a decrease in her report of posttraumatic stress symptoms over the course of treatment. Suzy did indicate that she learned not to blame herself for the abuse after completing Project SAFE treatment. Mrs. Kraller also reported that Suzy's externalizing and sexual behavioral problems decreased at the end of treatment. Improvements in functioning generally continued at follow-up and no further treatment for the girls was indicated.

This case study suggests that caregivers' involvement is an important treatment factor from both the children's and caregiver's perspectives. Gina and Suzy said that one of the best things about Project SAFE was participation of Mr. and Mrs. Kraller in the simultaneous group for nonoffending caregivers. Mrs. Kraller shared similar feelings, stating that she liked how she and the girls were attending the groups simultaneously. Mr. and Mrs. Kraller noted that another strength of the Project SAFE group format was the opportunity to share with other caregivers who had similar experiences. Overall, the supportive treatment empowered them in their new role as caregivers to Gina and Suzy by helping them learn that they could manage their parenting roles and by facilitating communication with the girls as well as each other.

The current case study suggests several directions for future clinical practice and research. The importance of thorough assessment is indicated by the different presentation of symptoms for Gina and Suzy, as well as by the diverse constellation of emotional and behavioral symptoms found in literature on sexually abused children. Future research should use such comprehensive assessment data to improve understanding of symptom profiles associated with sexual abuse and related contextual factors, and the relation of these profiles to treatment approach and response. The complex needs and positive responses to treatment of Gina, Suzy, and Mr. and Mrs. Kraller argue strongly that future research and practice should continue efforts to better understand and improve the adjustment of victims and families following disclosure of sexual abuse. Additionally, it is important to comprehensively evaluate standardized treatment protocols for sexually abused children and their families that may be broadly disseminated and replicated.

REFERENCES

Achenbach, T. M. (1991). *The Child Behavior Checklist manual.* Burlington: University of Vermont.

American Academy of Pediatrics. (1999). Guidelines for the evaluation of sexual abuse of children: Subject review (RE9819). *Pediatrics, 103,* 186–191.

Asher, S. R., & Wheeler, V. A. (1985). Children's loneliness: A comparison of rejected and neglected peer status. *Journal of Consulting and Clinical Psychology, 53,* 500–505.

Berliner, L., & Saunders, B. (1996). Treating fear and anxiety in sexually abused children: Results of a controlled 2-year follow-up study. *Child Maltreatment, 1,* 292–309.

Browne, A., & Finkelhor, D. (1986). Impact of child sexual abuse: A review of the research. *Psychological Bulletin, 99,* 66–77.

Celano, M., Hazzard, A., Webb, C., & McCall, C. (1996). Treatment of traumagenic beliefs among sexually abused girls and their mothers: An evaluation study. *Journal of Abnormal Child Psychology, 24,* 1–17.

Chaffin, M. (1998, July). *Assessment, triage, and treatment in a world of managed care.* Paper presented at the Sixth APSAC Colloquium, Chicago.

Cicchetti, D, & Toth, S. L. (2000). Developmental processes in maltreated children. In D. J. Hansen (Ed.), *Motivation and child maltreatment: Vol. 46 of the Nebraska Symposium on Motivation* (pp. 85–160). Lincoln, NE: University of Nebraska Press.

Cohen, J. A., & Mannarino, A. P. (1998). Interventions for sexually abused children: Initial treatment outcome findings. *Child Maltreatment, 3,* 17–26.

Conte, J. R. (1990). Victims of child sexual abuse. In R. T. Ammerman & M. Hersen (Eds.), *Treatment of family violence: A sourcebook* (pp. 50–76). New York: Wiley.

Coopersmith, S. (1981). *Self-esteem inventories*. Palo Alto, CA: Consulting Psychologists Press.

Damon, L., & Waterman, J. (1986). Parallel group treatment of children and their mothers. In K. MacFarlane & J. Waterman (Eds.), *Sexual abuse of young children* (pp. 244–298). New York: Guilford Press.

Deblinger, E., Lippman, J., & Steer, R. (1996). Sexually abused children suffering post-traumatic stress symptoms: Initial treatment outcome findings. *Child Maltreatment, 1,* 310–321.

Deblinger, E., Steer, R. A., & Lippmann, J. (1999). Two-year follow-up study of cognitive behavioral therapy for sexually abused children suffering post-traumatic stress symptoms. *Child Abuse and Neglect, 23,* 1371–1378.

DeJong, A. R. (1998). Impact of child sexual abuse medical examinations on the dependency and criminal systems. *Child Abuse and Neglect, 22,* 645–652.

Derogatis, L. R. (1983). *The SCL-90-R: Administration, scoring, and procedures manual-II*. Baltimore: Clinical Psychometrics Research.

deYoung, M., & Corbin, B. A. (1994). Helping early adolescents tell: A guided exercise for trauma-focused sexual abuse treatment groups. *Child Welfare League of America, 73,* 141–154.

Faller, K. C. (1993). *Child sexual abuse: Intervention and treatment issues*. Washington, DC: U.S. Department of Health and Human Services.

Finkelhor, D., & Berliner, L. (1995). Research on the treatment of sexually abused children: A review and recommendations. *Journal of the American Academy of Child and Adolescent Psychiatry, 34,* 1408–1423.

Finkelhor, D., & Browne, A. (1985). Traumatic impact of child sexual abuse: A conceptualization. *American Journal of Orthopsychiatry, 55,* 530–541.

Friedrich, W. N. (1998). Behavioral manifestations of child sexual abuse. *Child Abuse and Neglect, 22,* 523–531.

Friedrich, W. N., Fisher, J. L., Dittner, C. A., Acton, R., Berliner, L., Butler, J., et al. (2001). Child Sexual Behavior Inventory: Normative, psychiatric, and sexual abuse comparisons. *Child Maltreatment, 6,* 37–49.

Friedrich, W. N., Grambsch, P., Damon, L., Hewitt, S. K., Koverola, C., Lang, R. A., et al. (1992). Child Sexual Behavior Inventory normative and clinical comparisons. *Psychological Assessment, 4,* 303–311.

Futa, K. T. (1998). *The development and initial evaluation of Project SAFE: A group treatment for sexually abused children and their non-offending parents*. Unpublished doctoral dissertation, University of Nebraska, Lincoln.

Futa, K. T., Hecht, D. B., & Hansen, D. J. (1996, November). Working with sexually abused children and their non-offending parents: A conceptualization and treatment. In J. R. Lutzker (Chair), *Child abuse and neglect: The cutting edge*. Symposium conducted at the meeting of the Association for the Advancement of Behavior Therapy, New York.

Gil, E. (1996). *Treating abused adolescents*. New York: Guilford Press.

Hansen, D. J., Hecht, D. B., & Futa, K. T. (1998). Child sexual abuse. In V. B. Van Hasselt & M. Hersen (Eds.), *Handbook of psychological treatment protocols for children and adolescents* (pp. 153–178). Mahwah, NJ: Erlbaum.

Hecht, D. B., Futa, K. T., & Hansen, D. J. (1996, November). *Group treatment of sexually abused children and their nonoffending parents: Development and initial evaluation of a standardized treatment protocol*. Poster session presented at the Association for the Advancement of Behavior Therapy Convention, New York.

Hecht, D. B., & Hansen, D. J. (1999). Adolescent victims and intergenerational issues in sexual abuse. In V. B. Van Hasselt & M. Hersen (Eds.), *Handbook of psychological treatment with violent offenders: Contemporary strategies and issues* (pp. 303–328). New York: Kluwer Academic/Plenum.

Howard, R. C., & Bassos, C. A. (2000). The effect of screening versus nonscreening on treatment authorization in a managed care setting. *Professional Psychology: Research and Practice, 31,* 526–530.

Jenny, C. (1996). Medical issues in sexual abuse. In J. Briere, L. Berliner, J. A. Bulkley, C. Jenny, & T. Reid (Eds.), *The APSAC handbook on child maltreatment* (pp. 196–205). Thousand Oaks, CA: Sage.

Kazdin, A. E., Rogers, A., & Colbus, D. (1986). The hopelessness scale for children: Psychometric characteristics and concurrent validity. *Journal of Consulting and Clinical Psychology, 54,* 241–245.

Kendall-Tackett, K. A., Williams, L. M., & Finkelhor, D. (1993). Impact of sexual abuse on children: A review and synthesis of recent empirical studies. *Psychological Bulletin, 113,* 164–180.

Kent, A. J., & Hersen, M. (2000). An overview of managed mental health care: Past, present, and future. In A. J. Kent & M. Hersen (Eds.), *A psychologist's proactive guide to managed mental health care* (pp. 3–19). Mahwah, NJ: Erlbaum.

King, N. J., Tonge, B. J., Mullen, P., Myerson, N., Heyne, D., & Ollendick, T. H. (1999). Cognitive-behavioral treatment of sexually abused children: A review of research. *Behavioural and Cognitive Psychotherapy, 27,* 295–309.

Kovacs, M. (1992). *Children's Depression Inventory.* Toronto, Ontario, Canada: Multi-Health Systems.

Landis, L. L., & Wyre, C. H. (1984). Group treatment for mothers of incest victims: A step by step approach. *Journal of Counseling and Development, 63,* 115.

Levitt, C. (1998). Further technical considerations regarding conducting and documenting the child sexual abuse medical examination. *Child Abuse and Neglect, 22,* 567–568.

McCubbin, H. I., Olson, D. H., & Larsen, A. S. (1987). F-COPES: Family Crisis Oriented Personal Evaluation Scales. In H. I. McCubbin & A. I. Thompson (Eds.), *Family assessment inventories for research and practice* (pp. 259–270). Madison: University of Wisconsin.

National Center on Child Abuse and Neglect. (1996). *Third national incidence study of child abuse and neglect.* Washington, DC: U.S. Department of Health and Human Services.

Ollendick, T. H. (1983). Reliability and validity of the revised Fear Survey Schedule for Children (FSSC-R). *Behaviour Research and Therapy, 21,* 685–692.

Ollendick, T. H. (1999). Empirically supported treatments: Promises and pitfalls. *Clinical Psychologist, 52,* 1–3.

Olson, D. H. (1986). Circumplex model VII: Validation studies and FACES-III. *Family Process, 25,* 337–350.

Paolucci, E. O., Genuis, M. L., & Violato, C. (2001). A meta-analysis of the published research on the effects of child sexual abuse. *Journal of Psychology, 135,* 17–36.

Reeker, J., Ensing, D., & Elliott, R. (1997). A meta-analytic investigation of group treatment outcomes for sexually abused children. *Child Abuse and Neglect, 21,* 669–680.

Reynolds, C. R., & Richmond, B. O. (1985). *Revised Children's Manifest Anxiety Scale manual.* Los Angeles: Western Psychological Services.

Saunders, B. E., & Meinig, M. B. (2000). Immediate issues affecting long-term family resolution in cases of parent-child sexual abuse. In R. M. Reece (Ed.), *Treatment of child abuse: Common ground for mental health, medical, and legal practitioners* (pp. 36–53). Baltimore: Johns Hopkins University Press.

Schonberg, I. J. (1992). The distortion of the role of mother in child sexual abuse. *Journal of Child Sexual Abuse, 1,* 47–61.

Sgroi, S. M., & Dana, N. T. (1982). Individual and group treatment of mothers of incest victims. In S. M. Sgroi (Ed.), *Handbook of clinical intervention in child sexual abuse* (pp. 191–214). Lexington, MA: Lexington Books.

Spaccarelli, S. (1994). Stress, appraisal, and coping in child sexual abuse: A theoretical and empirical review. *Psychological Bulletin, 116,* 340–362.

Spanier, G. B. (1976). Measuring dyadic adjustment: New scales for assessing the quality of marriage and similar dyads. *Journal of Marriage and the Family, 38,* 15–28.

Stauffer, L. B., & Deblinger, E. (1996). Cognitive behavioral groups for nonoffending mothers and their young sexually abused children: A preliminary treatment outcome study. *Child Maltreatment, 1,* 65–76.

United States Department of Health and Human Services. (2000). *Child maltreatment 1998: Reports from the States to the National Child Abuse and Neglect Data System.* Washington, DC: U.S. Government Printing Office.

Weisz, J. R., Weiss, B., & Donenberg, G. R. (1992). The lab versus the clinic: Effects of child and adolescent psychotherapy. *American Psychologist, 47,* 1578–1585.

Wolfe, V. V., & Birt, J. (1995). The psychological sequelae of child sexual abuse. In T. H. Ollendick & R. J. Prinz (Eds.), *Advances in clinical child psychology* (pp. 233–263). New York: Plenum Press.

Wolfe, V. V., & Birt, J. (1997). Child sexual abuse. In E. J. Mash & L. G. Terdal (Eds.), *Assessment of childhood disorders* (3rd ed., pp. 523–569). New York: Guilford Press.

Wolfe, V. V., Gentile, C., Michienzi, T., Sas, L., & Wolfe, D. A. (1991). The Children's Impact of Traumatic Events Scale: A measure of post-sexual abuse PTSD symptoms. *Behavioral Assessment, 13,* 359–383.

CHAPTER 25

Alcohol and Drug Abuse

HOLLY BARRETT WALDRON and SHARON M. FLICKER

DESCRIPTION OF THE DISORDERS

ALCOHOL AND DRUG use disorders represent two of the most serious health issues facing society today, with as many as 34% of youth meeting criteria for a diagnosis of alcohol abuse or dependence and 23% meeting criteria for a substance use diagnosis for *any* substance prior to reaching adulthood (Cohen et al., 1993; Reinherz, Giaconia, Lefkowitz, Pakiz, & Frost, 1993). The impact for those youth who are engaging in problematic substance use can be devastating. Alcohol and drug use can have negative effects on physical and psychological development and family relationships, and has been associated with conflicts with authority figures, school failure, criminal behavior, comorbid psychiatric disorders, unwanted pregnancy, HIV sexual risk behaviors, fatal and nonfatal accidents and injuries, emergency room admissions, homicides, and suicides. This chapter provides an overview of adolescent alcohol and drug abuse, focusing on the course and treatment of the disorder in a referred adolescent and providing a detailed description of the intervention implemented.

Although substance use and related problems have received greater attention in mental health fields in recent years, researchers and clinicians continue to struggle with fundamental conceptual and empirical issues (cf. Winters, 2001). Because the vast majority of substance-involved youth do not develop substance-related problems and do not go on to abuse as adults, the distinction between use and abuse is a central issue. The complicated array of factors influencing development of substance abuse, the varied presentation of the disorder, the similarities and differences between adolescent and adult abuse, and the comorbidity of substance abuse with other psychiatric disorders add to the perplexing nature of substance use disorders. In short, substance abuse is not a unitary concept, but a complex phenomenon with heterogeneous patterning and multiple determinants. Moreover, substance use is a covert behavior. In the absence of reliable, valid, and practical definitions for the disorders, failure by parents, teachers, or other health professionals to detect signs of use contributes to substance abuse being a commonly missed or misdiagnosed problem. Moreover, research and clinical efforts to identify adolescents in need of assessment, preventive care, and treatment are hampered. As in other areas of child and adolescent psychopathology, however, problem behaviors that are intense (i.e., quantity), frequent, and chronic and that cluster with other related problems will fit the concept of abuse. In addition, age of the adolescent, developmental progression of use, specific drugs used and their effects, number and combinations of drugs used, and severity of consequences resulting from use must be considered (Winters, 2001).

Also, adolescent abuse differs from adult abuse in important ways that have implications for treatment. For example, White and Labouvie (1989) found that adolescents drink less frequently than adults and consume less alcohol overall, but consume larger amounts at one time. Such opportunistic binging, based on sheer availability, suggests that although adolescents may be less likely than adults to develop dependence, managing high-risk situations is a critical component of intervention for most youth. Some researchers have reported that 70% to 98% of adolescents in treatment abuse multiple substances, whereas reports of adult polysubstance use have been considerably lower, and the types and patterns of withdrawal symptoms among adolescents appear unique (Martin, Kaczynski, Maisto, Bukstein, & Moss, 1995; Stewart & Brown, 1995). Adolescents also have a higher likelihood of certain negative social consequences, given their position of dependence and lower status in family and social systems (White & Labouvie, 1989). Interventions targeted at peer and family relationships are also likely to be especially important for adolescents.

DIAGNOSIS

The *Diagnostic and Statistical Manual of Mental Disorders*, fourth edition (*DSM-IV*; 1994) makes no distinction between adolescent and adult use. The two categories of substance use disorders, substance abuse and substance dependence, each require for diagnosis a maladaptive pattern of use with clinically significant impairment. Substance abuse diagnoses further require one or more of the following in a 12-month period: failure to fulfill major role obligations, recurrent use in physically hazardous situations, recurrent legal problems, and continued use despite recurrent social or interpersonal problems related to use. Dependence diagnoses require three or more of seven criteria occurring in a 12-month period: tolerance, withdrawal symptoms, taking larger amounts or over a longer period than intended, failed efforts to control use, much time spent obtaining the substance, activities given up because of use, and continued use despite knowledge of having recurrent physical or psychological problems stemming from use.

Substance abuse disorders in adolescents have a high prevalence of comorbidity with other psychological disorders. For example, Bukstein, Glancy, and Kaminer (1992) found that 62% of adolescents receiving inpatient treatment for substance abuse or dependence were dually diagnosed. DeMilio (1989) found that 42% of adolescents presenting for treatment of substance abuse also met criteria for Conduct Disorder, the most common disorder co-occurring with substance abuse, and 35% also had a Major Depressive Disorder. The comorbidity issue adds a level of complexity to understanding substance abuse. Whether substance abuse is primary or occurs secondary to another disorder, and how the interaction of coexisting disorders influences the onset, identification, course, and treatment of substance abuse problems remain in question.

ETIOLOGY

Researchers have identified a broad spectrum of factors that appear to place youth at greater risk for substance abuse, including poverty, existence of laws and social norms favorable to substance use, availability of drugs, neighborhood disorganization, lack of social support, parent and sibling use, parent attitudes toward drug use, parenting practices, parent-adolescent conflict, poor coping skills, associating with peers who use, early/persistent problem behavior, drug use expectancies, and psychophysiological vulnerability to drug effects (Hawkins, Catalano, & Miller, 1992; Newcomb, 1995). Researchers also have identified a variety of protective factors across the cultural/social, interpersonal, and intrapersonal domains that decrease the likelihood of substance use initiation or reduce the current level of drug use. These factors may moderate the relationship between risk factors and use/abuse or may have a direct effect on reducing drug involvement (Newcomb, 1995). Sanctions against drug use, family support, self-acceptance, and religiosity are a few of the protective factors that have been identified (cf. Hawkins et al., 1992).

The factors influencing substance abuse are likely interdependent and bidirectional. For example, Dishion, Patterson, and Reid (1988) found that parental drug use had both a direct effect, believed to result from modeling and opportunities for use, and an indirect effect, resulting from impaired parental control when parents were under the influence of drugs or alcohol. Similarly, findings of increased stress, increased conflict, highly charged negative affect, lack of openness, and poor cohesion in families, as well as the tendency of adolescents to seek support in relationships outside the family, may all have reciprocal influence. Although the mechanism by which risk and protective factors exert causal influence is poorly understood, Bry, McKeon, and Pandina (1982) and colleagues found evidence that substance abuse derives from the sheer number of risk factors rather than the presence of any one factor or particular set of factors. McGee and Newcomb (1992) also found that exposure to more risk factors was not only correlated with use, but predicted increasing drug use over time, providing support for a multiple etiological pathway model of drug use. The risk and protective factor model is a useful one for predicting which youth may develop substance abuse problems and for identifying specific targets for intervention.

CASE DESCRIPTION

Ray was a 17-year-old male with a three-year history of abusing multiple substances, predominantly marijuana. He was referred for treatment by his probation officer to an outpatient substance abuse treatment program for adolescents, following a charge of possession of marijuana and failing a subsequent urine drug screen. Although Ray did not think he needed therapy and did not want to participate in the sessions, the conditions of his probation were such that failure to attend therapy likely would result in a jail sentence.

CHIEF COMPLAINTS

Ray lived with his mother, Debbie, and his two younger brothers, James, age 15, and Andrew, age 12. Ray had had limited contact with his father since his parents' divorce five years before. At the intake interview, which was attended by both

Debbie and Ray, Debbie complained about Ray's increasingly difficult behavior since he began high school at the age of 14. She reported that he had been arguing more with her and her other sons. He refused to listen to her house rules, including disregarding curfews, not completing chores, and not spending time with the family. Despite her requests to find a job, Ray had not yet done so. Debbie was overwhelmed by her inability to manage her son and worried that he would negatively influence her other children. She was ready to give up on Ray and concentrate her parenting efforts on James and Andrew.

HISTORY

Ray had experienced difficulties at school since he was a young child. He had a learning disability that had gone undiagnosed for several years, and during that time, he struggled to keep up with the rest of his class. When his learning disability was diagnosed in fifth grade, he received extra assistance in school and was taught additional tools to help him learn. Despite this assistance, however, he never gained much confidence in his academic abilities. In high school, he was suspended from school twice for fighting with other students and had numerous absences. In the first two months of his senior year, Ray had accumulated 10 days of unexcused absences from school, and his teachers had reported that he was not turning in his homework. At the point he entered treatment, he was at risk for having to retake all his classes for the semester.

Debbie also reported significant personality changes in Ray since he began high school. He had become increasingly sullen and withdrawn. She lamented that whereas he had once shared everything about his life with her, he now seemed to resent even the most superficial questions about his day. After numerous rejections, his brothers had stopped inviting him to spend time with them. Throughout his childhood, Ray had been very active in sports and had been the star of both his soccer and baseball teams in the neighborhood leagues. He had half-heartedly completed the soccer season in his freshman year, and he had adamantly refused to participate in sports after that. His interest in building model planes, which had been his favorite hobby, had disappeared. Debbie reported that, when not with his friends, Ray spent all of his time alone in his room, often sleeping. She had also noticed changes in his eating habits: At times, he ate little, and at other times, he appeared ravenous.

In the area of social functioning, Debbie reported that Ray's group of friends changed when he began his freshman year. Until then, Ray had always been a shy child and had the same three close friends since elementary school. Debbie knew the families of these boys and the boys spent a lot of time at her house. When Ray entered high school, he began spending time with friends of whom Debbie did not approve. His friends from junior high school informed her that some of his new friends were known drug dealers. They smoked cigarettes and did not show Debbie what she felt was an appropriate amount of respect. Ray mostly socialized with his new friends outside of the home, making it difficult for Debbie to monitor his behavior.

Debbie was especially concerned about Ray's substance use due to a significant history of substance abuse in her family. Her father had been an alcoholic and would physically abuse her and her mother when he drank. Ray's father also drank a lot, which had been a contentious issue in Debbie's relationship with him. She feared that his inherited predisposition to substance abuse would put Ray at serious risk.

Ray confessed to his mother that he used marijuana on occasion, but felt that his mother was overreacting to the situation. According to Ray, school had nothing to offer him, and he did not see a need to put effort into something that promised no benefit. Although he admitted that his recent legal troubles were regrettable, he had no intentions of repeating his mistakes and felt that he should be allowed to live his life as he wished. His main problem, as he saw it, was an overinvolved, overprotective mother.

BEHAVIORAL ASSESSMENT

As in all behavioral approaches to intervention, careful attention to measurement of Ray's problem behaviors prior to and following the intervention was integral to evaluating treatment effectiveness. Some assessment approaches for adolescent alcohol and drug abuse involve only narrow inquiry into substance use behavior. However, substance use typically clusters with other problem behaviors and social dysfunction and, thus, should not be evaluated in isolation from the larger picture of life adjustment. For this reason, broad, multifaceted assessment approaches that address use patterns, problem consequences, other aspects of use (e.g., drug use expectancies, normative beliefs, readiness to change), and functioning across multiple domains (e.g., school, family, leisure time) often are warranted (Winters, 2001).

The main source of assessment information is usually the adolescent, although collateral information is often obtained from parents or others in the social environment (i.e., teachers, siblings, peers). Almost all measures of substance use behavior focus on some type of direct self-report of frequency (e.g., on how many days per month use occurred) and intensity (e.g., number of drinks consumed). The majority of adolescents referred for treatment use multiple substances, necessitating inquiry about the quantity and frequency of use of each drug. Although the validity of adolescent self-report of use has been questioned, studies have shown that direct self-report measures have high sensitivity in detecting substance use problems and compare favorably to biomedical measures such as blood tests and urine toxicology screens (Sobell & Sobell, 1995).

Although many self-report instruments provide summaries of use, they often are scaled in a way that precludes detailed assessment of use (e.g., 0 times, 1 to 2 times, or 3 times or more per week). As a result, such measures fail to capture the pattern of use that could preclude detection of pre- to posttreatment differences, especially among very heavy users who might make meaningful reductions in use while not achieving abstinence. An alternative method is the Timeline Followback procedure (cf. Sobell & Sobell, 1995), a structured interview technique that samples a specific time period, using a monthly calendar and memory anchor points to reconstruct daily consumption during the period of interest. A number of studies have compared quantity/frequency and timeline followback measures and have reported generally similar estimates. In principle, the timeline followback may offer the most sensitive assessment for adolescents, having the advantage of assessing the widely variable drinking patterns that often characterize teen drinking and that might not be modeled adequately by the averaging approaches (Waldron, Slesnick, Brody, Turner, & Peterson, 2001).

Another important tool for assessing adolescents is a functional analysis of substance use behavior. A functional analysis is a structured interview that examines the antecedents and consequences of a specific behavior, such as drinking or using drugs (Meyers & Smith, 1995). This information is integral for identifying stimulus cues associated with higher risk for substance use and identifying the positive and negative consequences the adolescent experiences with respect to substance use and restraint from use. The functional analysis may be useful in a number of other ways as well. For example, the assessment may be used to identify goals that are appropriate and attainable with the individual client. In addition, the functional analysis may be used to explore prosocial behaviors that would help the adolescent in establishing a healthier lifestyle. In general, developing alternative methods of coping with high-risk situations without using alcohol or drugs involves learning specific skills and strategies. Once the situations and problems that contribute to the individual's use are known, the coping strategies and other skills needed to manage those situations can be identified and skills training can begin.

Questions the therapist might ask as part of the functional analysis include in what kinds of situations the adolescent uses; typical triggers for use, such as when, where, and with whom; thoughts and feelings associated with use; what the adolescent dislikes about using; and what some of the positive results of use might be. The therapist may then ask the client to complete a self-monitoring record and demonstrate its use for the adolescent by recording on it the responses to the questions just asked. The therapist summarizes for the client the apparent determinants of substance use and confirms these determinants by asking for other examples.

RAY'S HISTORY AND ASSESSMENT FINDINGS

The assessment began with an interview, first with Ray and his mother to discuss the presenting problems, and then with Ray alone while Debbie completed several self-report questionnaires concerning his behavior and the family relationships. Debbie reported that Ray exhibited high levels of externalizing behaviors. She also indicated problems in her relationship with him, with many areas of dissatisfaction with his behavior noted, and high conflict and low cohesion reported regarding the family environment. Later, she was interviewed separately and asked about Ray's substance use and other problems without Ray present.

The history and severity of Ray's substance use were assessed using a Timeline Followback (TLFB; Sobell & Sobell, 1995) interview, a calendar-based semistructured interview used to reconstruct Ray's substance use on a daily basis during the prior three months and to obtain a lifetime history of use. A semistructured diagnostic interview for alcohol and drug use disorders was also conducted. A urine drug screen was used to confirm self-reported use. Other questionnaires such as a depression inventory and family questionnaires were completed to assess Ray's functioning in other domains. Finally, a functional analysis was conducted to more closely examine the role of substance use in his life.

When his mother left the room, Ray appeared more at ease and was more candid about his current circumstances. Although unhappy to be there, he was cooperative and open in discussing his substance use. This was important because his mother did not know many details of his substance use, and her collateral report significantly underestimated his use, compared to Ray's own report. Her own lack of confidence in her answers was an acknowledgment of her limited information.

During the interview, Ray reported that he tried alcohol for the first time when he was 14 years old and that drinking quickly became a weekly event. Information collected from his TLFB indicated that he drank alcohol on approximately 20% of the days in the previous three months before the intake. He noted that the amount he needed to drink to get drunk had significantly increased since he first began drinking. At the time of the intake, he often drank three or four beers and a couple of shots of liquor at parties on weekend nights. He reported that this amount of alcohol was sufficient to make him "feel good," but on occasion (e.g., once a month), he would drink significantly larger amounts to get drunk. These episodes typically consisted of 8 to 10 shots of liquor and several beers. Ray reported that he would drink when he was with his friends, almost always at parties, though occasionally in the car while they were cruising. Based on a *DSM* semistructured interview, Ray was diagnosed with alcohol abuse. He had continued drinking despite increasing problems with his mother as a result and had driven while under the influence. Although he did not meet criteria for alcohol dependence, he also endorsed two of three required dependence symptoms: tolerance and often drinking more than he had intended. Ray tested negative for alcohol on his urine screen, which corroborated his report of not drinking on the weekdays.

Not long after his first drinking experience, Ray also began using marijuana. During his freshman year, he used about once or twice a month, but his use slowly increased to using several times a day at the time of his initial assessment. During the TLFB interview, Ray indicated that he had smoked marijuana every day for the previous three months. He frequently used with his friends both during and after school, but also used by himself on occasion. About a year before the initial assessment, he had begun to buy his own marijuana and began selling it to support his habit. He met criteria for both cannabis abuse and dependence, endorsing the following symptoms: recurrent absences and poor performance at school, legal problems, continued use despite problems between him and his mother, marijuana taken in larger amounts and over a longer period of time than he had intended, previous unsuccessful attempts to cut down on his use, spending large amounts of time in activities necessary to obtain and use marijuana, and using marijuana instead of playing sports or spending time with family. Ray's urine screen tested positive for cannabis, validating his report of marijuana use within the few weeks prior to the assessment.

Ray reported experimental use of hallucinogens and cocaine in the prior year, also at parties. Specifically, he has used LSD two times, mushrooms four times, ecstasy twice, and cocaine twice. Ray did not meet *DSM-IV* criteria for substance abuse or dependence for any of these drugs and tested negative for each, substantiating his report of infrequent use.

During the functional analysis assessment, Ray was able to identify that when he used marijuana at school, he was typically feeling frustrated or upset with his performance in class and was expecting that the marijuana would help him to relax. Conversely, when he drank at parties, he was usually feeling good and wanting to lose control with his friends. He also thought that drinking would help him loosen up and be more adept at talking with girls. He was able to list both positive and negative consequences of his alcohol and marijuana use. Positive consequences of his marijuana usage included feeling more relaxed and spending time with friends; negative consequences included being less able to concentrate during his next few classes and getting caught with marijuana and charged with possession. Positive consequences of drinking included having a good time at parties, fitting in, and feeling more comfortable when talking with girls; negative consequences included feeling hungover the next day and getting in trouble with his mother.

MEDICAL CONSULTATION

Typically, medical consultation is indicated when a question arises about a comorbid, psychiatric condition for which medication may be required or when inpatient hospitalization or medical detoxification for substance use is indicated. Ray's report on the depression inventory indicated that he was experiencing some mild symptoms of depression, but not at the level that would suggest formal psychiatric evaluation. Although marijuana withdrawal does not generally require medical supervision, Ray's alcohol abuse might have indicated medical intervention for alcohol detoxification. However, his alcohol use was not sustained or heavy, and he had significant periods of abstinence. Thus, no medical consultation was obtained for depression or substance detoxification.

CASE CONCEPTUALIZATION AND RATIONALE FOR TREATMENT CHOICE

On the basis of the initial assessment, the therapist determined that Ray could benefit from outpatient treatment for his substance use and related problems. Ray's lack of motivation for treatment suggested that strategies to enhance his readiness to change would need to be addressed early in treatment. His substance use was sufficiently heavy that he was likely to experience urges and cravings to use, challenging whatever change efforts he would make. Therefore, his treatment needed to include strategies to help him cope with urges and cravings. In addition, his functional analysis indicated that stress or anxiety and social activities with friends were triggers for use. Thus, interventions to promote more adaptive coping with negative emotions and to facilitate his ability to refuse his friends' offers to use drugs or alcohol would be needed. Ray also appeared to need better social, communication, problem-solving, and leisure skills to improve his family and peer relationships and help him use his free time more productively. To address his family and school problems, a multisystemic family intervention was indicated.

The intervention identified for Ray was a family-based intervention called integrative behavioral and family therapy (IBFT; Waldron, Brody, & Slesnick, 2001). This multisystemic intervention combines two common treatment approaches for adolescent substance abuse: family systems therapy and individual cognitive-behavioral therapy (CBT). The rationale for combining family therapy with individually based interventions into an integrated model derives from empirical findings that lend support to both treatment approaches, and from the distinct theoretical formulations concerning the etiology of substance abuse of these two treatment modalities. CBT approaches to the treatment of substance abuse are based on the assumption that drinking and drug use are largely learned behaviors and include elements derived from classical and operant learning principles established in experimental psychology. For example, research examining the classically conditioned acquisition of preferences and aversions for alcohol and drugs, toler-ance, and physiological and psychological urges and cravings has demonstrated that many aspects of addictions appear to be under stimulus control (Sherman, Jorenby, & Baker, 1988). Often, the sight or smell of a particular substance, the presence of drug paraphernalia, the time of day, or the setting is sufficient to trig-ger thoughts of using. Interventions based on classical learning focus on helping clients anticipate and avoid high-risk situations to facilitate sobriety (Monti et al., 1999).

Operant and social learning approaches view the development and mainte-nance of alcohol and drug use behaviors in the context of the antecedents and consequences surrounding the behavior. Both animal and human studies amply demonstrate the responsiveness of drug-taking behavior to positive and negative contingencies. Moreover, therapeutic strategies derived from an operant model have shown promise in treating drug problems for adults (Higgins et al., 1995) and for adolescents (Gilchrist & Schinke, 1985).

The social learning model incorporates conditioned and operant learning, but is expanded to allow for cognitively mediated learning through observation and imi-tation of models (e.g., parents, siblings, peers) who use substances (Bandura, 1997). Modeling, social reinforcement, the anticipated effects of the substance, the direct experience of alcohol's effects as rewarding or punishing, the self-efficacy to re-frain from use, and physical dependence all influence the acquisition and mainte-nance of drinking and drug use behaviors (Abrams & Niaura, 1987). Developing alternative coping behaviors to replace drug use and having sufficient self-efficacy to perform newly acquired coping behaviors are key to successful intervention. Many CBT interventions that have been developed using social learning theory as a foundation have involved multiple treatment components. Self-monitoring, avoid-ance of stimulus cues or triggers, altering reinforcement contingencies, coping skills training to manage and resist urges to use, social skills training (e.g., problem solving, assertiveness), mood regulation (e.g., relaxation training, anger manage-ment, modifying cognitive distortions), and relapse prevention (e.g., drug and alco-hol refusal skills) are all potential components of treatment (Monti et al., 1999).

The traditional initiation of CBT with motivational induction is well supported by trials showing specific efficacy of motivational counseling as a stand-alone in-tervention or as a prelude to substance abuse treatment for adults and adolescents (Monti et al., 1999). As motivation for change is strengthened, the focus shifts to negotiating a treatment plan, including adolescent self-selection of change strate-gies from a CBT menu. Moreover, the CBT treatment approach allows for individ-ual tailoring or treatment so that clients may focus on any problem or issue of concern, regardless of its perceived relationship to drug use. Ultimately, the client is helped to recognize the connection between achievement of self-identified goals (e.g., remaining in school, obtaining employment) and reductions in drug use.

Family therapy has been a widely accepted and empirically supported treatment for adolescent substance abuse. In family systems models, substance abuse and de-pendence are viewed as behaviors that occur in response to problems with existing family relationships and that have a specific meaning in the context of the family. All families are presumed to establish an equilibrium along a continuum of adap-tive and dysfunctional behavior, characterized by observable and repeated pat-terns of family interaction. Moreover, the behaviors of family members are viewed as reciprocally determined, such that the behavior of each member influences and, in turn, is influenced by the behavior of every other member. The essential core and distinguishing feature of systems models, then, is that the locus of problem behavior is systemic, transcending the individual, and therefore the focus of treatment should be relational.

Alcohol and substance abuse, therefore, are conceptualized as maladaptive behaviors expressed by one or more family members but reflecting dysfunction in the system as a whole. The goal of family systems therapy is to correct faulty family interaction patterns and other aspects of family functioning. Family systems interventions are designed to effect change in a number of substance-use risk and protective factors, including parent and sibling drug use, ineffective supervision and discipline (monitoring), negative parent-child relationships, and family conflict. In general, however, changing family interactions and improving relationship functioning are key to reducing adolescents' involvement with alcohol and other drugs. Communication and conflict resolution skills training are commonly used to enhance families' behavioral repertoires and allow them to resolve problems independently. The increased positive interactions they experience when putting such skills to use are presumed to reinforce the likelihood that the new behaviors will become established patterns.

The IBFT model, based on the recognition that substance use and other related problem behaviors derive from many sources of influence and occur in the context of multiple systems, is designed to be effective for adolescents presenting for treatment within the broad spectrum of substance abuse and dependence diagnoses and related problem behaviors. Consistent with Bronfenbrenner's (1979) theory of social ecology, this model views the individual as being nested within a complex array of interconnected systems that encompass individual, family, and extrafamilial (e.g., peer, school, neighborhood) factors. The combination of CBT and family therapy in the IBFT model targets change in adolescent substance use at the level of the individual, while also placing heavy emphasis on the various substance-use risk and protective factors directly associated with the family. In IBFT, then, treatment is directed toward assessing these multiple influences and intervening so that change is supported throughout a number of systems affecting the problem behavior, including the individual adolescent, the family, peers, the school system, and the community.

COURSE OF TREATMENT

The IBFT model is conceptualized as a moderate-intensity, predominantly office-based, relatively brief outpatient intervention that can be conducted in 10 to 16 sessions. Multisystemic family therapy typically includes sessions or parts of sessions held conjointly with the adolescent and other family members, but may also include individual sessions targeting decision making, emotion regulation, or other intrapersonal factors that may be influencing substance use. Actual techniques implemented during treatment are generally drawn from other family models, including family systems and behavioral perspectives, and from intervention approaches in the general psychotherapy literature. Therapists work to evaluate factors in the youth's and family's ecological environment that may be contributing to identified problems. They then plan treatment to include individual and family work in the context of traditional therapy as well as meet with staff in other systems as needed to implement interventions at the broader levels.

The basic objectives of the IBFT intervention for families of substance-abusing members are twofold: (1) to reduce or eliminate substance use and other problem behaviors, and (2) to improve family relationships. These objectives are met in the three phases of the IBFT model. The first phase focuses on both the family and the individual. The initial family sessions focus on engaging the family in treatment, enhancing the family's motivation for change, and assessing aspects of the family relationship to be targeted for change. The initial individual session with the adolescent involves conducting a functional analysis of behavior and then using the functional analysis to guide identification of targets for skills training. At this early juncture, a menu of treatment options is discussed with the adolescent, and intervention components are selected and incorporated into the treatment plan tailored to the individual adolescent's needs and treatment goals. The middle phase of therapy focuses primarily on establishing behavioral changes in the family, but is designed so that portions of each session are spent with the adolescent to reinforce implementation of newly acquired skills. The last phase of therapy focuses on generalization of new family and individual behaviors to the natural environment, with an emphasis on independent problem solving within the family and substance abuse relapse prevention. Implementation of the three phases of the IBFT model with Ray and his family are described in the sections below.

EARLY FAMILY THERAPY SESSIONS

The family-based component of the IBFT approach with Ray began with two sessions focusing on treatment engagement, motivation, and family relationship assessment. Ray and his mother both engaged in high rates of blaming toward the other; Ray's brothers contributed little to the discussion. The therapist asked for each person's perspective on why he or she was there and attempted to create positive expectations for change by normalizing their problems, addressing strengths, and offering encouragement for potential to change. The therapist also focused on motivational enhancement within the family by focusing on an alternative, less negative, and relationship-based definition of the problem that would predispose the family to accept systemic change. Two main strategies for motivating the family included relabeling and focusing on the relational aspects of family members' behaviors. The therapist's use of warmth, empathy, and humor in responding contingently and nonconfrontationally to family members in implementing these strategies was important. The therapist's goals were for family members to experience the interconnectedness of their behaviors and to understand that no one person in the family was at fault or to blame for the problems they were facing.

A final task of the therapist in the first two sessions was to begin the process of assessing family functions. The concept of the interpersonal or relationship function of behavior refers to the way each family member attempts to regulate relationships within the family and the interpersonal outcome or payoff that such maladaptive behaviors and patterns achieve (Waldron, Brody, & Slesnick, 2001). If a behavior is associated with repeated interaction patterns in families that result in their experiencing significant physical or psychological separation from one another, then the outcome (i.e., function) of the behavior is distance. By contrast, if the outcome of a behavior is that family members experience greater connection or interdependency, then the function of the behavior is closeness. In some relationships, family members consistently exhibit elements of both separation and closeness; this blending is referred to as midpointing.

The assessment for Ray and his family, then, was intended to determine what specific changes were necessary (e.g., drug use, nonproductive use of time, or family conflict) and how the behavior change should occur to maintain the functions currently served by the problem behavior within the family. Using both sets of information, the therapist devised a plan taking into account Ray's individual needs and the fit between these needs and the function of his behavior for his relationships with his mother and brothers.

During the early family sessions, it appeared that Ray's behavior was associated with significant physical and psychological separation and distance from his mother, spending time alone in his room, talking less often with her, and spending significant periods of time away from home. The therapist also noted elements of both separation and closeness (i.e., midpointing) with his brothers. Ray would exclude his brothers from most of his activities but have regular fights with them that appeared to provide a source of contact. At the same time, the therapist observed that Ray's brothers would tell tales to Debbie about Ray, by way of getting more closeness with her while at the same time promoting her efforts to make additional contact (i.e., closeness) with Ray. The therapist used the information concerning functions to develop a treatment plan that involved substituting adaptive behaviors for maladaptive ones. That is, the therapist looked for positive ways of increasing Debbie's contact time with Ray's brothers to lessen their need for attention and for positive ways of maintaining Debbie's closeness with Ray, while also providing him with more psychological space apart from her.

Concurrent Individual Therapy Sessions

To maximize the momentum of Ray's motivation as developed in family sessions, individual therapy sessions were held concurrently with the family sessions in the first three weeks of therapy. Using Ray's functional analysis, the individual sessions began with motivational enhancement (see Therapist-Client Factors) to increase Ray's readiness to change, and continued with interventions aimed at coping with cravings and urges to use and peer refusal skills. Coping with cravings and urges involves helping adolescents recognize that cravings and urges usually last only a few minutes at a time and that they become less frequent and less intense as coping skills are used. Ray was assigned a simple self-monitoring task to identify triggers of urges and cravings between sessions. During sessions, the therapist helped him identify when he could avoid the triggers, how to manage the triggers he could not avoid (e.g., getting involved in a distracting activity, talking it through with friends or family members, and challenging/changing thoughts), and how to use imagery to focus systematically on the urge to use until it would pass. The latter strategy, called "urge surfing" (Kadden et al., 1992), involved having Ray imagine himself as a surfer riding the "wave" of the urge like an ocean wave until it grew, peaked, and finally crashed. Ray also needed to be prepared to assert himself with his friends when they would pressure him to use. The therapist advised Ray directly to use avoidance strategies whenever possible for those situations and people associated with drug use. The therapist then presented strategies for refusing substances, modeled them, and rehearsed them with

Ray during the session to help him respond confidently and quickly when the need arose.

THE MIDDLE PHASE OF THERAPY

The next five sessions of therapy in the IBFT model consisted of a combination of both family therapy and individual therapy. For the first 15 minutes of each weekly session, the therapist met individually with Ray to monitor his progress in acquiring and practicing the cognitive-behavioral skills discussed earlier and began to focus on problem-solving school performance problems and developing plans for using free time more effectively. An important and unique benefit of the IBFT approach was that these 15-minute sessions also enabled the therapist to provide individual support and modeling for Ray to communicate better in the family session that immediately followed, thus facilitating communication about spending time with his paternal grandparents and other topics that he was initially reluctant to address with his mother.

The primary goal of the family sessions in this phase was to establish new behaviors and patterns of interaction to replace maladaptive ones that had characterized the family prior to treatment. The therapist focused on treatment strategies and behavior change techniques that would likely benefit Ray's family, such as communication training, contingency management, negative mood regulation, and increasing rewarding shared activities. The particular way the techniques were applied, however, depended on how well the intervention strategy fit each family member's interpersonal function with every other family member. For example, Ray could continue to earn privileges of using the car and staying out late when he checked in frequently with Debbie to let her know where to reach him and when he came home at the agreed-upon hour. In this way, he could retain age-appropriate independence from his mother while allowing her to maintain contact and monitor his behavior more effectively.

THERAPIST-CLIENT FACTORS

Client motivation, or lack thereof, is generally acknowledged to be a significant issue in addressing adolescent substance abuse. Ray's initial resistance to treatment, minimizing his own problems and attending therapy sessions only after being remanded by the court, was typical. A number of therapist behaviors also have been shown to influence client motivation. In particular, therapist support, empathy, and reframing have been related to client cooperation and subsequent improved outcomes in individual and family therapy, whereas therapist confrontation and defensive style have been related to less favorable outcomes.

To address Ray's resistance, the family sessions and early individual sessions included motivational enhancement techniques. Motivational enhancement strategies specifically target client resistance and have as their primary goal the mobilization of clients' commitment to change (Miller & Rollnick, 1991). Several strategies are prescribed to defuse and decrease resistant client behavior, including avoiding argumentation, expressing empathy, and providing the client with choices in therapy. Other strategies are applied to evoke clients' own self-motivational statements of problem recognition, concern, need for change, and self-efficacy.

COURSE OF TERMINATION

As behavioral changes were established, the focus of treatment shifted toward generalization of the new behaviors across other contexts, establishing the family's independence from the therapist, and anticipating substance-use relapse and other potential problems. The therapist encouraged the family to take responsibility for solving problems on their own, bolstering their self-efficacy by reinforcing independent problem-solving behavior. One session was held with Ray alone to plan for emergencies, review how to manage high-risk situations, and anticipate coping with substance-use lapses. Another session was held with all family members to review treatment gains and identify areas needing continued attention.

The therapist may ask the client to describe one or more situations (e.g. breaking up with a girlfriend/boyfriend) that could lead to craving for drugs or to a lapse. Adolescents may be asked to consider how these events might affect their behavior and interactions with others. The adolescent should be encouraged to draw on skills discussed in previous sessions and examine what specific strategies could be used to cope with high-risk situations. The therapist and adolescent should prepare a generic emergency plan for coping with any number of possible stressful situations that might arise unexpectedly. Strategies such as problem-solving skills, calling people for support, and cognitive coping strategies should be identified for each anticipated situation. In the immediate aftermath of a substance use episode, the adolescent should be instructed to leave the situation, call someone for help, and get rid of the drugs. In the event of a longer-term substance use episode, the adolescent should be encouraged to examine the slip with someone, analyzing possible triggers and considering expectations for use. The adolescent must beware of catastrophizing thoughts, for if allowed to proceed unchecked, these reactions can contribute to further substance use episodes.

To develop independence, the therapist gradually took a less active role in intrafamily processes. As family members experienced short-term changes, they were helped to consider alternative ways to continue positive changes. In addition, issues involving Ray's school problems and probation status were discussed. The therapist may interact directly with legal and educational systems on behalf of the family and help the family independently interact more effectively within these systems (Waldron, Brody, et al., 2001). In addition, the therapist may help the family anticipate stressors and problems, exploring solutions to those future difficulties.

Therapy moved toward termination when Ray's drug and alcohol use seemed to be decreasing significantly and when adaptive interaction patterns and problem-solving styles had emerged in the family. Debbie and her sons appeared to have the necessary motivation, skills, and resources to maintain a positive clinical trajectory without the support of ongoing services. They came in for one booster session three months after termination for help resolving a dispute between Ray's brothers, but at that time, Ray was still reporting success in limiting his use, and his grades in school were continuing to improve.

FOLLOW-UP ASSESSMENT AND
OVERALL EFFECTIVENESS

Considerable empirical evidence has been found for the efficacy of family-based interventions for adolescent substance abuse and dependence. Reviews of formal clinical trials of family-based treatments have consistently found that more drug-abusing adolescents enter, engage in, and remain in family therapy than in other treatments, and family therapy produces significant reductions in substance use from pre- to posttreatment (cf. Stanton & Shadish, 1997; Waldron, 1997). In two randomized clinical trials comparing family-based and CBT interventions, Waldron and colleagues (2001) found greater immediate benefits of family-based interventions compared to individual or group interventions alone. In addition, they suggest that integrating family therapy with CBT may be particularly effective in maintaining treatment gains over time. These findings are consistent with other studies providing support for combining family and individual cognitive-behavioral skills training strategies (Dennis et al., 2000; Liddle et al., in press). Thus, combining family therapy with cognitive-behavioral skills training approaches may provide significant advantages over either approach alone, as different risk factors are addressed in each treatment modality and combining treatments increases the number of factors addressed.

Ray's outcome was fairly typical of those undergoing IBFT for outpatient adolescent substance abuse treatment. He and his mother were assessed once again at therapy termination by a member of the treatment center's assessment team to evaluate change. Ray's report on the TLFB indicated that he had significantly cut down on both his drinking and marijuana use and that he had not used any other drugs during that time. During the period corresponding to Ray's last month of treatment, he reported that he had only one drinking occasion, during which he had two beers, a substantial decrease from his pretreatment drinking pattern of at least five or six drinks per occasion once or twice a week. In keeping with the harm-reduction strategies introduced by his therapist, Ray decided that he would plan his drinking episodes to avoid driving while under the influence. He also reduced his marijuana use from several times daily to two times a week. Importantly, he no longer used marijuana before or during school, and his school attendance and performance subsequently improved. Ray's teachers reported to Debbie that he was participating more in classes and was consistently completing and turning in his homework assignments.

An important finding was that Debbie now felt more aware of Ray's behavior outside of the home. She reported on the details of her son's current and previous substance use with more confidence, and her report of his substance use closely matched Ray's self-report. Debbie's responses on the behavior checklist and the family questionnaires showed that Ray's externalizing behaviors had improved, that Debbie and Ray were more satisfied with each other, and that their family was experiencing less conflict and was more cohesive. Debbie also reported that Ray argued with her and his brothers less frequently and completed his chores with less struggle. They seemed to have a mutual understanding of the other's good intentions, and problems thus engendered less defensiveness and were more easily resolved. Ray was willing to spend more time with his family, and these positive interactions helped establish an amicable environment in which concerns could be addressed and resolved within the family as they arose.

When Ray was assessed with the diagnostic interview at follow-up, he met criteria for cannabis abuse, but no longer met diagnostic criteria for alcohol abuse or cannabis dependence. He still used despite his mother's wishes; however, the negative impact on his life, especially academically, socially, and legally, had been greatly reduced. It is important to note that, although none of the measures demonstrated complete remittance of Ray's problem behaviors, the improvement was such that both Ray and Debbie recognized progress and felt happy and encouraged by the changes.

REFERENCES

Abrams, D. B., & Niaura, R. S. (1987). Social learning theory. In H. T. Blane & K. E. Leonard (Eds.), *Psychological theories of drinking and alcoholism* (pp. 131–178). New York: Guilford Press.

American Psychiatric Association. (1994). *Diagnostic and statistical manual of mental disorders* (4th ed.). Washington, DC: Author.

Bandura, A. (1997). *Self-efficacy: The exercise of control.* New York: Freeman.

Bronfenbrenner, U. (1979). *The ecology of human development: Experiments by nature and design.* Cambridge, MA: Harvard University Press.

Bry, B. H., McKeon, P., & Pandina, R. J. (1982). Extent of drug use as a function of number of risk factors. *Journal of Abnormal Psychology, 91,* 273–279.

Bukstein, O. G., Glancy, L. G., & Kaminer, Y. (1992). Patterns of affective comorbidity in a clinical population of dually diagnosed adolescent substance abusers. *Journal of the American Academy of Child and Adolescent Psychiatry, 31,* 1041–1045.

Cohen, P., Cohen, J., Kasen, S., Velez, C. M., Hartmark, C., Johnson, J., et al. (1993). An epidemiological study of disorders in late childhood and adolescence. I: Age and gender-specific prevalence. *Journal of Child Psychology and Psychiatry, 31,* 851–867.

Dennis, M. L., Babor, T. F., Diamond, G., Donaldson, J., Godley, S. H., Tims, F., et al. (2000). *The Cannabis Youth Treatment (CYT) experiment: Preliminary findings.* Rockville, MD: Substance Abuse and Mental Health Services Administration, Center for Substance Abuse Treatment. Available from www.samhsa.gov/centers/csat/content/recoverymonth/000907rtpcover.html

DeMilio, L. (1989). Psychiatric syndromes in adolescent substance abusers. *American Journal of Psychiatry, 146,* 1212–1214.

Dishion, T. J., Patterson, G. R., & Reid, J. R. (1988). Parent and peer factors associated with drug sampling in early adolescence: Implications for treatment. In E. R. Rahdert & J. Grabowski (Eds.), *Adolescent drug abuse: Analyses of treatment research* (pp. 69–93, NIDA Research Monograph 77). Rockville, MD: National Institutes of Health.

Gilchrist, L. D., & Schinke, S. P. (1985). Preventing substance abuse with children and adolescents. *Journal of Consulting and Clinical Psychology, 53,* 121–135.

Hawkins, J. D., Catalano, R. F., & Miller, J. Y. (1992). Risk and protective factors for alcohol and other drug problems in adolescence and early adulthood: Implications for substance abuse prevention. *Psychological Bulletin, 112,* 64–105.

Higgins, S. T., Budney, A. J., Bickel, W. K., Badger, G. J., Foerg, F. E., & Ogden, D. (1995). Outpatient behavioral treatment for cocaine dependence: One-year outcome. *Experimental Clinical Psychopharmacology, 3,* 205–212.

Kadden, R., Carroll, K., Donovan, D., Cooney, N., Monti, P., Abrams, D., et al. (1992). *Cognitive-behavioral coping skills therapy manual* (Vol. 3). Rockville, MD: National Institute on Alcohol Abuse and Alcoholism.

Liddle, H. A., Dakof, G. A., Parker, K., Barrett, K., Diamond, G. S., Garcia, R., et al. (in press). Multidimensional family therapy for adolescent drug abuse: Results of a randomized clinical trial. *American Journal of Drug and Alcohol Abuse.*

Martin, C. S., Kaczynski, N. A., Maisto, S. A., Bukstein, O. G., & Moss, H. B. (1995). Patterns of alcohol abuse and dependence symptoms in adolescent drinkers. *Journal of Studies on Alcohol, 56,* 672–680.

Meyers, R. J., & Smith, J. E. (1995). *Clinical guide to alcohol treatment: The community reinforcement approach.* New York: Guilford Press.

Miller, W. R., & Rollnick, S. (1991). *Motivational interviewing.* New York: Guilford Press.

Miller, W. R., Zweben, A., DiClemente, C. C., & Rychtarik, R. G. (1992). *Motivational enhancement therapy manual: A clinical research guide for therapists treating individuals with alcohol abuse and dependence* (Vol. 2, Project MATCH Monograph Series) Rockville, MD: National Institute on Alcohol Abuse and Alcoholism.

Monti, P. M., Colby, S. M., Barnett, N. P., Spirito, A., Rohsenow, D. J., Myers, M., et al. (1999). Brief intervention for harm reduction with alcohol-positive older adolescents in a hospital emergency department. *Journal of Consulting and Clinical Psychology, 67,* 989–994.

Newcomb, M. D. (1995). Identifying high-risk youth: Prevalence and patterns of adolescent drug abuse. In E. Rahdert & D. Czechowicz (Eds.), *Adolescent drug abuse: Clinical assessment and therapeutic interventions* (pp. 7–37, NIDA Research Monograph 156). Rockville, MD: National Institutes of Health.

Reinherz, H. Z., Giaconia, R. M., Lefkowitz, E. S., Pakiz, B., & Frost, A. K. (1993). Prevalence of psychiatric disorders in a community population of older adolescents. *Journal of the American Academy of Child and Adolescent Psychiatry, 32,* 369–377.

Sherman, J. E., Jorenby, D. E., & Baker, T. B. (1988). Classical conditioning with alcohol: Acquired preferences and aversions, tolerance, and urges/cravings. In C. D. Chaudron & D. A. Wilkinson (Eds.), *Theories on alcoholism* (pp. 173–287). Toronto, Ontario, Canada: Addiction Research Foundation.

Sobell, L. C., & Sobell, M. B. (1995). Alcohol consumption measures. In J. P. Allen & M. Columbus (Eds.), *Assessing alcohol problems: A guide for clinicians and researchers* (pp. 55–74, NIAAA). Rockville, MD: National Institutes of Health.

Stanton, M. D., & Shadish, W. R. (1997). Outcome, attrition, and family/couples treatment for drug abuse: A review of the controlled, comparative studies. *Psychological Bulletin, 122,* 170–191.

Stewart, D. G., & Brown, S. A. (1995). Withdrawal and dependency symptoms among adolescent alcohol and drug abusers. *Addiction, 90,* 627–635.

Waldron, H. B. (1997). Adolescent substance abuse and family therapy outcome: A review of randomized trials. In T. H. Ollendick & R. J. Prinz (Eds.), *Advances in clinical child psychology* (Vol. 19, pp. 199–234). New York: Plenum Press.

Waldron, H. B., Brody, J. L., & Slesnick, N. (2001). Integrated behavioral and family therapy for adolescent substance abuse. In P. M. Monti, S. M. Colby, & T. A. O'Leary (Eds.), *Adolescence, alcohol and substance abuse: Reaching teens through brief interventions* (pp. 213–243). New York: Guilford Press.

Waldron, H. B., Slesnick, N., Brody, J. L., Turner, C. W., & Peterson, T. R. (2001). Treatment outcomes for adolescent substance abuse at 4- and 7-month assessments. *Journal of Consulting and Clinical Psychology, 69,* 802–813.

White, H. R., & Labouvie, E. W. (1989). Towards the assessment of adolescent problem drinking. *Journal of Studies on Alcohol, 50,* 30–37.

Winters, K. (2001). Assessing adolescent substance use problems and other areas of functioning: State of the art. In P. M. Monti, S. M. Colby, & T. A. O'Leary (Eds.), *Adolescence, alcohol and substance abuse: Reaching teens through brief interventions.* New York: Guilford Press.

Author Index

Aasland, O. G., 182
Abelson, J. L.,78
Abikoff, H., 384
Abrahamian, F. P., 435
Abramowitz, A. J., 409
Abramowitz, J. S., 24
Abrams, D. B., 189, 193, 482, 485
Abramson, H., 446
Abramson, L. Y., 256
Achenbach, T. M., 245, 310, 367, 440, 454
Acierno, R., 107, 114
Action, R. R., 450
Adson, D. E., 351
Agras, W. S., 151
Albano, A. M., 280, 307, 309, 331, 335, 341, 342
Albin, R. W., 243
Alessi, N. E., 272
Alexander, J. F., 395
Allyon, T., 315
Alm, T., 81–82, 86
Alterman, I., 284
Altpeter, T. S., 400
Alvarez, W., 367
Amado, D., 98
Aman, M. G., 422–423
Anderson, C. M., 242–244, 250
Anderson, J., 258, 272, 426
Andreski, P., 107, 110
Andrews, B., 107
Andrews, G., 295
Andrews, J., 256
Angold, A., 384
Annas, P., 76
Annis, H. M., 186
Antonuccio, D. L., 4, 27
Apter, A., 284
Arnold, S. L., 285

Arnow, B., 151
Asarnow, R., 369
Asher, S. R., 330, 453
Aterino, M., 26
Ault, M. H., 243

Babcock, J., 8
Babor, T. F., 182, 488
Badger, G. J., 482
Baer, D. M., 415
Baer, R. A., 427
Bagarozzi, D. A., 234
Bahrick, L. E., 364
Baker, M. J., 363
Baker, R. C., 8
Ballenger, J. C., 107, 116, 122
Bandura, A., 482
Barkley, R. A., 400, 404, 406, 407, 409
Barlow, D. H., 10, 23, 24, 25, 30, 31, 53, 57, 62, 71, 94, 126, 129, 199, 342
Barnett, N. P., 482
Barnfather, D., 276
Barrett, K., 488
Barrios, B. A., 250
Bartko, J., 276
Barton, C., 395
Basson, N., 207
Bassos, C. A., 468
Baucom, D. H., 93–94, 96, 243, 252, 363
Baugher, M., 26, 256, 264
Baum, A., 110
Baumeister, A. A., 428
Baxter, L. J., 284
Beach, B. K., 369
Beck, A. T., 7, 9, 10, 23, 32, 37, 43, 44, 48, 58, 67, 94, 111, 129, 256, 440, 353
Beck, J. S., 46, 48
Becker, C. B., 177

Becker, D., 369
Beer, D., 282
Beidel, D. C., 90, 93, 94, 118, 311, 327, 330, 385
Belanger, S., 435
Bellack, A. S., 23
Bemis, K. M., 352, 353
Bender, M. E., 409
Benjamin, L., 163
Bennett Johnson, S., 50
Benson, D. J., 422
Berg, C. J., 286
Berg, C. Z., 276
Bergaman, K. S., 284
Berliner, L., 384, 449, 450, 459
Berman, P. S., 3
Bernard-Bonnin, A., 435
Besk, S. J., 250
Best, C.L., 107, 114
Beutler, L. E., 363
Bickel, W. K., 482
Bickerton, W. L., 256
Biederman, J., 286, 312, 401
Bien, T. H., 196
Bijou, S. W., 243
Birchler, G. R., 220, 222–223, 232
Birmaher, B., 256, 264, 271
Birt, J., 449, 450, 456
Black, D. W., 26
Blackburn, I., 49, 50
Blagg, N. R., 305
Blais, F., 132
Blake, D. D., 110, 122, 363
Blew, P. A., 428
Bogardis, J., 195
Boisvert, J. M., 126, 132
Bolduc, E. A., 312
Bonifazi, D. Z., 145
Bonne, O., 113
Bonner, B. L., 434, 435
Boone, M. L., 91, 95
Booth, R., 82
Borduin, C. M., 392
Borkovec, T. D., 23, 125–126, 129, 132–133, 141
Bowers, W., 26
Boyle, M. H., 392
Bradlyn, A. S., 8
Brain, K. L., 164
Brandberg, M., 81–82, 86
Braukmann, C. J., 395
Bray, J., 216
Breen, M. J., 400

Breitholz, E., 81–82, 86
Brent, D. A., 26, 256, 264
Breslau, N., 107, 110
Brewin, C., 107
Bridge, J., 26, 256, 264
Briere, J., 245
Bright, P., 68
Brody, J. L., 478, 481, 484, 487, 488
Brogan, M. M., 27
Bromet, E., 106, 107, 114
Bronfenbrenner, U., 483
Brow, K. A., 250
Brown, G. K., 9, 32, 44, 58, 94, 129
Brown, S. A., 475
Brown, T. A., 57, 129, 133
Browne, A., 449, 456, 457, 459
Bruch, H., 345
Bruch, M. H., 240, 244
Bruininks, R. H., 421, 422
Bruynzeel, M., 81–82
Bry, B. H., 476
Budney, A. J., 482
Budrow, M., 409
Buitelaar, J. K., 278, 286
Bukstein, O. G., 475
Burgio, L. D., 427
Burlingame, G. M., 396
Burnman, B., 217
Burns, B. J., 384
Butler, J., 450
Butler, L., 256

Caddell, J. M., 23, 110, 113
Calamari, J. E., 428
Calhoun, G. B., 392, 396, 397
Calhoun, K. S., 363
Calkins, D. L., 436, 441
Cantor, J. J., 71, 72
Cantwell, D. P., 286, 410
Capaldi, D. M., 385
Caputo, G. C., 9, 32, 58, 62
Carey, M., 199
Carlson, G. A., 257
Carmi, M., 284
Carmichael, D. H., 342
Carpenter, D., 278, 286–287
Carr, E. G., 426
Carroll, K., 485
Carter, L. E., 91, 95
Cartledge, G., 342
Cashman, L., 286
Casper, R. C., 346

Castonguay, L. G., 4
Castro, G., 421
Catalano, R. F., 476
Cautela, J. R., 428
Cavell, T. A., 334
Celano, M., 459, 469
Cerreto, M. C., 222
Chaffin, M., 468, 469
Chambless, D. L., 3, 9, 23–24, 32, 50, 58, 62, 363
Chamove, A. S., 428
Chandra, R., 435
Chansky, T. E., 287, 340
Chapman, T. F., 76
Charney, D. S., 111–111, 122, 363
Chauncey, D. L., 163
Cheslow, D. L., 284, 286
Chilcoat, H., 107, 110
Chiponis, D., 435
Choudhury, M., 309, 311, 314
Christ, M. A. G., 383, 385, 389, 401
Christensen, A., 227–228, 232, 234
Christophersen, E. R., 436, 441
Chronis, A., 409
Chu, B. C., 309, 311, 314
Ciccehetti, D., 456
Claghorn, J., 279, 286
Clark, D. A., 240–241
Clark, D. B., 330
Clark, E., 256
Clarke, C., 312
Clarke, G. N., 256, 263, 294
Clum, G. A., 26
Coats, K. I., 256, 264, 270
Cochran, B. N., 169, 175
Cohen, J. A., 459, 474
Cohen, P., 474
Cohen, R. M., 284
Cohen, S. D., 59, 78
Coie, J. D., 392, 393
Colbus, D., 452
Colby, S. M., 482
Cole, E., 256
Coles, M., 286
Comtois, K. A., 161, 164, 169–171, 175, 177–178
Cone, J. D., 243
Conner, D. F., 406, 407, 409
Conners, K., 286
Connors, C. K., 404, 410
Connors, G. J., 195
Conradt, J., 327
Constantino, M. J., 4

Conte, J. R., 456
Cook, E. H., 286
Cooley-Quille, M. R., 93
Cooney, N., 189, 193, 485
Cooper, A. M., 241
Coopersmith, S., 453
Corbin, B. A., 462
Cormier, B., 7, 10
Cormier, S., 7, 10
Costello, E. J., 23, 125, 133, 135, 141, 384
Cottraux, J., 49, 50
Coverdale, J. H., 276
Cowley, D. S., 164
Craighead, L. W., 25
Craighead, W. E., 25
Craske, M., 23, 30, 31, 60, 62–63, 71–72, 81–82, 126
Crimmins, D. B., 243, 423
Crino, R., 295
Cris-Cristoph, P., 363
Crisp, A. H., 345
Crowther, J. H., 145
Cucherat, M., 49, 50
Curry, J. F., 392
Curtis, G. C., 78

Dakof, G. A., 488
Damon, L., 454, 459, 469
Dana, N. T., 459
Dancu, C. V., 23, 94
Danton, W. G., 4, 27
Davey, G. C. L., 80
Davidoff, D. A., 369
Davidson, J., 42, 112
Davidson, J. R., 107, 116, 122
Davidson, K. S., 330
Davidson, R., 185
Davies, M., 276
Davis, G. C., 107, 110
Deblinger, E., 459, 460
de Haan, E., 278, 286
Deitweiler, M. F., 341, 342
DeJong, A. R., 455
de Jong, P. J., 76
De La Fuente, J. R., 182
Delahanty, D., 110
Delgado, P., 281
DeMillo, L., 475
Dennis, M. L., 488
Derby, K. M., 250
Derogatis, L. R., 78, 111, 164, 366, 455
De Veaugh-Geiss, J., 286
de Vries, S., 78, 81–82

DeYoung, M., 462
Diamond, G. S., 488
DiClemente, C. C., 26, 195
Diener, M. B., 401
Dietz, S. G., 257
Dimeff, L. A., 165, 169, 177
DiNardo, P. A., 57, 129
Dinnel, D. L., 91
Dinsmoor, J. A., 96
Dirmaher, B., 26
Dishion, T. J., 384, 389, 476
Dittner, C. A., 450
Dobson, K. S., 23, 32, 43, 49
Dodge, K. A., 342, 392
Dollard, J., 283
Dominzo, S., 424
Donaldson, J., 488
Donovan, D., 195, 485
Donovan, J. E., 330
Dorsey, M. F., 243, 252
Dougall, A., 110
Dougher, M. J., 244
Doumas, D. M., 223
Drost, L., 81, 82
Drum, D. J., 49
Duer, K., 428
Dugas, M. J., 125–126, 129–130, 132–133, 141
Dunbar, G., 185
Duncan, S. C., 410
Dunlap, G., 426
Dunner, D. L., 164
DuPaul, G. J., 406, 407, 409
Durand, V. M., 243, 423

Edell, W. S., 164
Edlund, B., 346
Eells, T. D., 239–241, 251–252
Eichstedt, J. A., 285
Eifert, G. H., 93, 101, 369
Eldridge, K., 232, 234
Ellingson, S. A., 250
Elliot, R., 459, 469
Elliot, S., 210
Emery, G., 10, 23, 43, 48, 67, 353
Emmelkamp, P. M. G., 76, 78, 80–82, 84
Emslie, G. J., 256, 271
Ensing, D., 459, 469
Epstein, N., 58
Erbaugh, J., 58 ,440
Erkanli, A., 384
Ervin, R. A., 406
Eshleman, S., 76, 125

Essau, C. A., 257, 327
Estes, A. M., 250
Eth, S., 113
Evans, I. M., 244, 369
Evans, M. D., 26

Fairburn, C. G., 151, 158, 352, 353
Faller, K. C., 456
Falloon, I. R., 276
Falsetti, S., 111
Fals-Stewart, W., 222–223, 232
Falstein, E. I., 305
Fanselow, M. S., 65
Faragher, B., 116, 118
Faraone, S. V., 312
Farmer, M. E., 186
Farrington, D. P., 384, 418
Favell, J. E., 428
Fehan, C., 256
Feinberg, D. T., 410
Felten, M., 80–82
Fenton, L. R., 428
Fichter, M. M., 346
Fines, S., 257
Finkelhor, D., 384, 449, 450, 459
Fireman, G., 442
First, M. B., 6, 78, 163–164, 182, 261
Fischer, H., 76
Fisher, J. L., 450
Fisher, W. W., 248, 250
Fivush, R., 364
Fixsen, D. L., 395
Flament, M. F., 276, 286
Flannery-Schroeder, E., 342
Flemming, M. F., 189
Foa, E. B., 23, 24, 106–107, 114–116, 118, 120, 122, 135, 277–278, 283–284, 286
Foerg, F. E., 482
Follette, W. C., 13
Fontaine, R., 286
Forsyth, J. P., 369
Foulette, W. C., 245
Foy, D., 116, 115, 118, 120
Frances, A., 278, 286–287
Francis, G., 305, 310
Frankel, F., 410
Frankenburg, F. R., 163
Franklin, M. E., 277–278, 282, 286
Frederikson, M., 76
Freeman, K. A., 242, 243, 244, 250
Freeman, R. K., 21
Freeston, M.H., 125–126, 129–130, 132–133, 141

Frick, P. J., 383, 384, 385 387, 389, 401
Friedman, M., 112
Friedman, R., 256
Friedrich, W. N., 450, 454
Friman, P. C., 242, 251
Frost, A. K., 474
Frueh, C., 118
Fruehling, J. J., 271
Fruzzetti, A. E., 23, 172
Fuhriman, A., 396
Futa, K. T., 450, 456, 460, 469

Gabel, J., 26
Gabel, S., 435
Gaffney, G., 279, 286
Gagnon, F., 129, 133, 141, 199
Galensky, T. L., 250
Gallagher, R., 58
Gammon, P., 282
Garcia, R., 488
Garfinkel, P. E., 346
Garlinhouse, M. A., 250
Garner, D. M., 144, 346, 347, 349, 350, 351,
    352, 353, 354, 359
Garner, M. V., 346
Garvey, M., 282, 284
Gatsonis, C., 256
Geffken, G. R., 435
Geist, G. O., 428
Gentile, C., 454
Genuis, M. L., 449, 450
Gersten, M., 312
Getka. E. J., 82
Giaconia, R. M., 474
Gibbons, M., 6, 78, 163–164 , 182, 261
Gilchrist, L. D., 482
Giles, T. R., 396
Gillis. M. M., 23–24
Ginsburg, G. S., 342
Gitlin, M. J., 59
Gitow, A., 282
Gittelman-Klein, R., 312
Giulino, L., 282
Glancy, L. G., 475
Glaser, B. A., 392, 396, 397
Glass, C. R., 330
Glass, D. R., 82
Glick, P., 216
Gloaguen, V., 49, 50
Godley, S. H., 488
Goff, B. C., 172
Goldfried, M. R., 25
Goldstein, I., 198

Goodman, W. K., 276, 279–281
Gordon, J. R., 176, 294
Gorman, J. M., 25
Gorsuch, R. L., 94
Gosselin, P., 129
Gotlib, I. H., 23
Gottman, J. M., 8, 167, 232
Gould, R. A., 25, 26
Gracely, E. J., 9, 32, 58
Graham, E., 116, 118
Grambsch, P., 454
Grant, M., 182
Grattan, E., 256
Green, S. M., 383
Greenberg, G., 409
Greist, J. H., 278, 284, 286
Grey, S., 59
Groden, J., 428
Gross, A. M., 420
Guerra, N. G., 392
Guevremont, D., 434, 442
Gulley, P., 410
Gullone, E., 245
Gulotta, C. S., 248
Gunderson, J. G., 163
Gursky, D. M., 53, 58
Gusman, F. D., 111
Guze, B. H., 284

Haddock, C. K., 21
Hagopian, L. P., 315
Haines, J., 164
Haley, G., 258
Haley, N., 435
Halperin, G. S., 4
Halperin, K. M., 7
Halvarsson, K., 346
Hamburger, S., 276, 299, 390
Hanley, G. P., 248, 250
Hansen, D. J., 449, 450, 456, 460, 469
Harada, N., 91
Hardi, S. S., 25
Harrington, R., 256
Hart, E. L., 389, 401
Hart, J. H., 84
Harter, S., 367
Hartmann, D. P., 250
Hartmark, C., 474
Hauber, F. A., 422
Hawkins, J. D., 476
Hawkins, R. P., 239, 242, 407, 408
Hay, D. A., 407
Hayes, S. C., 13, 239, 242, 245

Haynes, S. N., 239–240, 242–243
Hazzard, A., 459, 469
Heal, L. W., 422
Heard, H., 161, 169
Hearst-Ikeda, D., 118
Hecht, D. B., 449, 450, 456, 460, 469
Hegedus, A. M., 435
Heiman, J., 213
Heimberg, R. G., 93, 96, 342
Hellstrom, K., 76
Hembree, E. A., 23
Henggler, S. W., 392
Henin, A., 342
Heninger, G. R., 281
Hennon, C. B., 216
Herberman, H., 110
Herman, J. B., 312
Hermesh, H., 284
Hersen, M., 23, 25, 272, 305, 396, 468
Herzog, D. B., 346
Hetherington, E. M., 216
Hewitt, S. K., 454
Heyne, D., 315, 459
Hibbs, E., 299, 390
Higgins, J. D., 482
Hill, B. K., 421, 422
Hill, C. L., 164
Hill, R., 59
Himmelhoch, J. M., 23
Hineline, P. N., 94, 97
Hirshfeld, D. R., 312
Hiruma, N., 91
Hoag, M. J., 396
Hoffman, P. D., 172
Hofmann, S. G., 96
Hogan, A., 421
Holder, D., 256, 264
Hollander, E., 276
Hollon, S. D., 3, 26, 43, 44, 50
Holt, C. S., 342
Hoogduin, K. A., 278, 286
Hope, D. A., 93
Hopkins, M. B., 126
Hops, H., 256
Horn, W. F., 409
Horne, A. M., 392, 396, 397
Horner, R. H., 243, 248, 426
Horowitz, M. J., 367
Horton, A. M. Jr., 369
Hortt, J. W., 8
Houts, A. C., 13, 446
Howard, R. C., 468
Howe, A. C., 436, 441

Hoyt, M. F., 4, 396
Hsu, L. K. G., 346
Hudson, J. L., 145, 327
Hudson, M., 145
Hughes, C. W., 271
Hughes, M., 76, 106, 107, 114, 125
Hulsbosch, L., 78, 81–82
Humphreys, L., 116, 120
Huntzinger, R. M., 315
Hupp, S. D. A., 410

Ialongo, N., 409
Inderbitzen, H. M., 327
Innocenti, M. S., 421
Insel, T. R., 284
Inslicht, S., 110
Inz, J., 135
Irwin, L., 421
Iverson, G. L., 242
Iwata, B. A., 243, 252

Jackel, L., 126
Jackson, R. L., 53
Jacob, R. B., 330
Jacobson, J., 421, 422
Jacobson, N. S., 8, 23, 43, 44, 50, 227–228, 231–232, 234
Jaffer, M., 282
Jarrett, R. B., 15, 369
Jasin, S. E., 9, 32, 58
Jaycox, L. H., 23
Jefferson, J. W., 284
Jenike, M. A., 276
Jenny, C., 456
Jenson, W. R., 256
Johnson, A. M., 305
Johnson, J., 474
Johnson, M. R., 427
Johnson, R. L., 330
Johnson, V., 198–199
Johnston, H. F., 271
Jones, K. M., 251
Joy, S. P., 164
Judd, L. L., 186
Juster, H. R., 93–94, 97

Kaczynski, N. A., 475
Kadden, R., 189, 193, 485
Kagan, J.,116, 312, 327
Kahn, D., 278, 286–287
Kahn, J. S., 256
Kalikow, K., 276
Kalish, K. D., 363

Kaloupek, D. G., 110, 111, 122, 363
Kaminer, Y., 475
Kamphaus, R. W., 388, 389, 401
Kamphuis, J. H., 79–80, 82
Kane, M. T., 340
Kanfer, F. H., 252
Kanter, J. W., 161, 177
Kaplan, H., 96, 198
Kasen, S., 474
Kaslow, N. J., 256
Katz, L. F., 167
Katz, R., 286
Katzelnick, D. J., 284
Kaye, W., 346
Kazdin, A. E., 272, 305, 392, 393, 452
Keane, T. M., 23, 110, 113
Kearney, C. A., 305, 314, 327, 335, 342
Keenan, K., 384
Kehle, T. J., 256
Keijsers, G. P., 278, 286
Keith, S. J., 186
Kelleher, W. J., 21
Keller, M. B., 271, 346
Kelley, M. L., 409
Kendall, P. C., 276, 309, 311, 314, 331, 340, 342
Kendall-Tackett, K. A., 449, 450
Kendler, K. S., 15
Kennard, B. D., 256
Kent, A. J., 396, 468
Kern, L., 428
Kerr, M., 391
Kessler, H. R., 369
Kessler, R. C., 76, 107, 110, 116, 122, 125
Keysor, C. S., 299
Kilpatrick, D.G., 111, 107, 114
Kilts, C., 286
Kim, R. S., 340
Kim, S. A., 172
King, D., 110
King, L., 110
King, N. J., 245, 305, 309, 310, 311, 312, 313, 314, 315, 331, 459
King, R. A., 279–281
Kirigin, K. A., 395
Kirisci, L., 330
Kirk, M., 107
Kirschenbaum, D. S., 8
Kisch, E. H., 435
Klatt, K. P., 248
Klauminzer, G., 110, 122, 363
Klein, D. F., 312
Klein, R. G., 271, 312, 384

Kleinknecht, E. E., 91
Kleinknecht, R. A., 91
Klerman, G. L., 263
Klesges, R. C., 148
Kobak, K. A., 284
Koby, E., 284, 286
Koch, W. J., 26
Koegel, R. L., 426, 428
Koerner, K., 166–167, 169, 177
Kolko, D. J., 26, 256, 264, 390
Kopelwicz, H. S., 361, 362, 442
Koselka, M., 23
Kovacs, M., 256–257, 272, 279–280, 282, 367, 405, 452
Koverola, C., 454
Kowatch, R. A., 256
Kozak, M., 114, 135, 276, 283–284, 286
Kratochwill, T. R., 245
Kreusi, M. J. P., 299, 390
Krijn, M., 78, 81–82
Kurowski, C., 263
Kurtines, W. M., 342
Kutcher, S. P., 271

Labouvie, E. W., 475
Lacey, C., 248
Lachance, S., 129
Ladouceur, R., 125–126, 129–130, 132–133, 141
Laessle, R. G., 346
La Greca, A. M., 330
Lahey, B. B., 383, 385, 389, 401
Laibstain, D. F., 369
Laidlaw, T. M., 276
Lakin, K. C., 422
Lambert, M. J., 164
Lancioni, E., 248
Landau, P., 286
Landau, S., 401
Landis, L. L., 459
Lang, R. A., 454
Larsen, A. S., 455
Last, C. G., 272, 305, 310, 312
La Taillade, J. J., 8
Laumann, E., 198–199
Lavori, P. W., 346
Lawrence, E., 232, 234
Lazarus, A. A., 315
LeBlanc, M., 410
Lecrubier, Y., 107, 116, 122
Lefkowitz, E. S., 474
Leger, E., 133, 141

Leiblum, S., 199, 213
Lejuez, C. W., 93–94
Lenane, M., 276, 284, 286, 299, 390
Leon, G. I., 195
Leonard, H. L., 276, 282, 284, 286
Lerew, D. R., 53
Leskin, G., 116
Lester, L. S., 65
Letarte, H., 129
Levine, M. D., 434, 435
Levinsky, E. R., 164, 169–171, 175, 178
Levitt, C., 459
Levitt, M., 364
Levy, F., 407
Lewinsohn, P. M., 23, 256, 263
Lewis, A., 434, 442
Liddle, H. A., 488
Lidren, D. M., 26
Liebowitz, M. R., 109, 278, 282
Light, R., 369
Lightall, F. F., 330
Lin, S., 216
Lindsay, M., 295
Linehan, M. M., 160–161, 164–172, 175, 177–178
Links, P., 163
Linnoila, M., 284
Lippman, J., 459
Litz, B., 110
Livanou, M., 116, 120
Lloyd-Still, J. D., 435
Lochman, J. E., 392, 393
Locke, B. Z., 186
Loeber, R., 383, 384, 389, 395, 401
Logsdon-Conradsen, S., 341, 342
Longabaugh, R., 186, 195
Lougee, L., 282
Lovell, K., 116, 120
Lue, T., 198
Lukens, E., 315
Lumpkin, P. W., 310, 342
Luschene, R. E., 94
Lyons, J. A., 363, 373
Lyonsfields, J. D., 132

Mace, F. C., 243
Maclean, W. E., 428
Magen, J., 272
Maisto, S. A., 475
Mannarino, A. P., 459
Mansdorf, I. J., 315
Mar, C. M., 169, 175

March, J. S., 277–278, 282, 284, 286–287, 310
Mardekian, J., 286
Margolin, G., 217, 231
Mark, V. H., 369
Marks, I., 59, 116, 120
Marlatt, G. A., 176, 294
Marriage, K., 258
Marshall, R., 109
Marten, P. A., 342
Martin, C. S., 475
Martin, G., 186
Mash, E. J., 250
Masia, C. L., 91, 95
Masters, W., 198–199
Mawson, D., 59
Maxwell, W. A., 8
Mayer, J. A., 305
Mayes, T. L., 271
Mazure, C., 281
Mazziotta, J. C., 284
McBurnett, K., 385
McCain, A. P., 409
McCall, C., 459, 469
McCarthy, B., 198–199, 202, 204, 207, 209–210
McCarthy, E., 199, 202, 208
McCleary, C., 369
McComas, J. J., 243
McConnaughy, E. A., 26
McCubbin, H. I., 455
McCullough, J. P., 23
McDavid, J., 165
McDermott, C., 116
McFayden-Ketchum, S. A., 342
McGee, R., 258, 272
McGimsey, J. F., 428
McGivern, J. E., 245
McGlashan, T. H., 257
McGonagle, K. A., 76, 125
McGrath, M. L., 434, 435, 436, 442, 446
McKeon, P., 476
McLean, P. E., 26
McMahon, R. J., 250
McNally, R. J., 53, 58, 80
McNeil, C. B., 407, 408
McNeil, D. W., 90–91, 93–95
McPhail, C. H., 428
McRoberts, C., 396
McStephen, M., 407
McSwiggin-Hardin, M., 279–281
McTeague, L., 110

Meadows, E. A., 23, 106, 115–116, 118, 120, 122
Meier, S. T., 240–242
Meinig, M. B., 450
Melamed, B. G., 84
Mellman, T., 112
Mellon, M. W., 434, 435, 436, 442, 446
Mellstrom, B., 286
Meminger, S. R., 312
Mendelson, M., 58, 440
Merkelbach, H., 76
Meston, M., 213
Metzger, R. L., 129
Meyer, L. H., 252
Meyer, T. J., 129
Meyer, V., 284
Meyers, M., 482
Meyers, R. J., 479
Michael, J., 247
Michael, R., 199, 241
Michael, S., 199
Michienzi, T., 454
Miezitis, S., 256
Milburn, J. F., 342
Milich, R., 401
Miller, G. E., 393
Miller, I. J., 49
Miller, J. Y., 409, 476
Miller, K. J., 156
Miller, M. L., 110, 129
Miller, N. E., 283
Miller, P. M., 315
Miller, W. R., 186, 196, 486
Milling, L. S., 434, 435
Miltenberger, R. G., 247, 249–250
Mirrabella, R., 118
Mitchell, J. E., 351
Mitton, J. E., 163
Mizes, J. S., 148, 156
Mock, J., 58
Moffitt, T. E., 383
Mohlman, J., 82
Mokros, H. B., 256
Monaco, L., 435
Monahan, P., 26
Monroe, S. M., 76
Monti, P. M., 189, 193, 482, 485
Moore, A., 256
Moreau, D., 263
Moretti, M., 258
Morgese, G., 424
Moroz, G., 286

Morreau, L., 421
Morris, S. J., 240
Morris, T. L., 327, 330, 373, 380, 407, 408
Morris, T. M., 363, 370
Morrison, J. R., 15, 407
Moss, H. B., 475
Mowrer, O. H., 80, 283, 373, 380
Mueller, E. A., 284
Mufson, L., 263
Mulle, K., 284, 286–287
Mullen J., 366
Mullen, P., 459
Murkofsky, C. A., 346
Murphy, D. L., 284
Murphy, L., 434, 435, 436, 442, 446
Murray, R. D., 435
Myatt, R., 410
Myerson, N., 459

Nadeau, D., 435
Nagy, L., 110–111, 122, 363
Nathan, P. E., 25
Nelles, W. B., 280, 367
Nelson, A., 278
Nelson, C. B., 76, 106, 107, 114, 125
Nelson, R. O., 239
Newcomb, M. D., 476
Newcorn, J., 401
Newman, M. G., 133, 141
Newton, J. S., 243
Nezu, A. M., 23
Niaura, R. S., 482
Nilsson, D., 409
Norcross, J. C., 9, 26
Norris, F. H., 111
Northrup, J., 410
Northrup, L. M. E., 369
Noshirvani, H., 116, 120
Nurcombe, B., 257
Nutt, D., 107, 116, 122

O'Callagan, P., 410
Oest, L. G., 23
Offord, D. R., 392
Ogden, D., 482
O'Leary, S. G., 409
Ollendick, T. H., 305, 309, 310, 311, 312, 313, 314, 315, 454, 459
Olson, D. H., 455
Ondersma, S. J., 434, 435, 436, 442, 446
O'Neill, R. E., 243
O'Reilly, M. F., 248

Orst, S. I., 279–281
O'Shaughnessy, M., 346
Ost, L. G., 76, 81–82, 86
Otto, M. W., 25, 59
Owens-Stively, J., 434, 442

Packard, T., 409
Padma-Nathan, H., 198
Pagani, L., 391
Paik, A., 198
Pakiz, B., 474
Pandina, R. J., 476
Panichelli-Mindel, S. M., 342
Paolucci, E. O., 449, 450
Parker, J. F., 286, 364
Parker, K., 488
Parson, B. V., 395
Patrick, J., 163
Patterson, G. R., 384, 389, 476
Paz, G., 116
Peck, S. M., 250
Pelham, W. E., 409
Penick, E. C., 257
Perlmutter, S., 282
Perri, M. G., 23
Perrin, S., 361
Perry, K. J., 118
Perry, S., 241
Persons, J., 42, 240, 244–245
Petermann, F., 257, 327
Peterson, R., 53, 58, 243
Peterson, T. R., 478, 481, 484, 487, 488
Pfeffer, C. R., 435
Phillips, E. L., 395
Piacentini, J., 282, 287
Piazza, C. C., 248, 250
Pike, K., 346, 349, 352, 353, 354, 359
Pilgrim, H., 118
Pimentel, S. S., 309, 311, 314
Pina, A. A., 310
Pirke, K. M., 346
Plaud, J. J., 4
Pollack, M. H., 25, 59
Pomeroy, C., 149, 351
Pope, H. G., 145
Pope, K. S., 50
Potter, W. Z., 390
Pozanski, E. O., 256–257
Price, L. H., 281
Printz, R. J., 393
Pritchard, M., 315
Prochaska, J. M., 27

Prochaska, J. O., 9, 26, 27
Provencher, M. D., 126, 129, 141
Purvis, P. C., 436, 441

Quay, H., 421
Quine, L., 422

Rabalais, A., 370
Rabian, B., 342
Rachman, S., 82, 84, 283, 313
Rae, D. S., 186
Raeburn, S. D., 151
Rae-Grant, N., 392
Raine, A., 390
Raistrick, D., 185
Ralabais, A. E., 364, 366, 368, 369
Ramenghi, L., 424
Ramm, E., 59
Rapaport, M. H., 71–72
Rapee, R. M., 93, 126, 133, 327
Rapoport, J. L., 276, 284, 286, 299, 390
Rasmussen, S., 276, 281
Raue, P. J., 25
Razran, G., 54
Reeker, J., 459, 469
Reeve, M., 279, 286
Regier, D. A., 186
Rehm, L. P., 256, 263
Reich, J., 91
Reid, J. B., 384, 389
Reid, J. R., 476
Reinecke, M. A., 272
Reinherz, H. Z., 474
Reis, B. J., 91–92
Reiss, A., 421
Reiss, S., 53, 58, 80
Reitman, D., 403, 404, 410
Rescorla, R. A., 96
Resick, P. A., 111, 115, 118, 120
Resnick, H., 107, 111, 114
Resnick, J. S., 312
Rettew, D. C., 276, 284
Rey, J. M., 286
Reynolds, C. R., 310, 367, 388, 453
Reynolds, M., 116, 118
Reynolds, W. M., 256, 257, 260–261, 264, 269–270
Rheaume, J., 126, 129, 132
Rheingold, A., 286
Riad, J., 111
Richman, D. M., 250
Richman, G. S., 243, 252

Richmond, B. O., 310, 453
Riddle, M., 279–281, 286
Riggs, D. S., 24
Roberts, J., 250
Robinette, C. D., 15
Rode, C. A., 369
Roemer, L., 126
Rogers, A., 452
Rogers, M., 315
Rohde, P., 263
Rohsenow, D. J., 482
Rollings, S., 315, 486
Ronan, K. R., 340
Roper, G., 283
Rose, S., 107
Rosen, A. M., 346
Rosen, J. C., 151
Rosen, L. W., 144, 346
Rosen, R., 198–199, 213
Rosenbaum, A. F., 312
Roth, C., 26
Roth, W. T., 82
Rothbaum, B. O., 118, 120
Rouse, L. W., 263
Roy-Byrne, P. P., 164
Ruebush, B. K., 330
Ruef, A., 110
Ruggiero, K. J., 364, 366, 367, 368, 369, 370,
    373, 380
Rush, A. J., 10, 12, 23, 43, 48, 353
Rushe, R. H., 8
Russell, G. F. M., 345
Russo, M. F., 385
Rutman, J., 257
Ruyter, J. M., 248
Ryan, N. D., 271

Saavedra, L. M., 310
Sabatino, G., 424
Sabatino, S. A., 59
Sack, W. H., 361, 362
Sacks, N. R., 346
Sadock, B., 96
Safer, D. J., 271
Safferman, A., 286
Saigh, P. A., 361, 362
Sailor, W., 426
Salkivskis, P. M., 283, 292
Salusky, S., 23
Sanderson, W. C., 25, 50, 126
Santiago, H., 23
Sarason, S. B., 330
Sas, L., 454

Sasso, G. M., 250
Satz, P., 369
Saunders, B. E., 107, 114, 450, 459
Saunders, J. B., 182
Scahill, L., 279–281
Sceery, W., 286
Scerbo, A., 390
Scheel, K. R., 169
Schiavo, R. S., 395
Schinke, S. P., 482
Schmaling, K. B., 23, 395
Schmidt, N. B., 23, 53
Schneider, J. A., 151
Schneider, R. W., 409
Schonberg, I. J., 459
Schuemie, M. J., 78, 81–82
Schulte, D., 101
Schultz, D. D., 242
Schultz, L., 107, 110
Schultz, S. E., 242
Schut, A. J., 4
Schwartz, C. E., 327
Schwartz, J. M., 284
Schwartz, L., 220
Scotti, J. R., 242–244, 250, 252, 363, 364,
    366, 368, 369, 370, 373, 380, 407, 408
Seligman, M. E. P., 256
Serafini, L. T., 342
Serlin, R. C., 284
Sgroi, S. M., 459
Shadick, R. N., 126
Shadish, W. R., 488
Shafer, C. L., 144
Shahar, A., 284
Shahbazian, M. J., 428
Shalev, A., 113
Shaw, B. F., 10, 23, 43, 48
Shaw, B. J., 353
Shaw, J. A., 258
Sheldon, J. B., 248
Sherman, J. A., 248
Shinn, M. R., 405
Sholam, V., 50
Silverman, W. K., 280–281, 305, 307, 309,
    310, 314, 331, 342, 367
Singer, G., 421
Singh, N. H., 423
Sipperelle, R., 116
Sjoden, P., 346
Skinner, B. F., 17, 242
Skinner, W., 195
Skolnick, N. J., 346
Slaby, R. G., 392

Slesnick, N., 478, 481, 484, 487, 488
Slifer, K. J., 243, 252
Smith, D., 315
Smith, J. E., 479
Smith, P., 361
Smith, R., 391
Smith, R. G., 243
Smith-Winberry, C., 409
Snidman, N., 312, 327
Snyder, C. R., 7
Sobell, L. C., 185, 188–189, 191, 195–196,
    478, 479
Sobell, M. B., 185, 188–189, 191, 195–196,
    478, 479
Sommerfield, C., 116, 118
Sonnega, A., 106, 107, 114
Sorrell, J. T., 93, 94
Southam-Gerow, M., 276, 342
Southwick, S., 112
Spaccarelli, S., 456, 457
Spanier, G. B., 222, 455
Speilberger, C. D., 94
Spencer, P. M., 164
Spirito, A., 434, 442, 482
Spitzer, R. L., 6, 78, 109, 163–164, 182, 261
Sprague, J. R., 243
Sprich, S., 401
Staats, A. W., 369
Stallings, P., 286
Stangle, D. K., 384
Stanley, M. A., 94
Stanton, M. D., 488
Stark, K. D., 256, 263
Stark, L. J., 434, 442, 446
Stauffer, L. B., 460
Stavosky, J. M., 23
Stavynski, A., 98
Steckler, N. M., 346
Steenbarger, B. N., 26
Steer, R. A., 7, 9, 32, 44, 58, 94, 129, 459
Stern, A., 110
Stevens, M. J., 240
Stewart, D. D., 475
Stober, M., 346
Stone, W. L., 330
Storey, J., 23
Storey, K., 243
Stouthamer-Loeber, M., 384
Strauss, C. C., 305, 310, 311, 314, 320
Street, G. P., 23
Stricker, G., 5, 8
Stricker, J. M., 250
Strober, J., 132, 135, 271

Stroop, J. R., 365
Stuart, G. L., 26
Stuart, R. B., 231
Sturmey, P., 243, 403
Sullivan, K., 280, 282, 286
Sullivan, L., 257
Svendsen, M., 305
Swedo, S. E., 276, 282, 284, 285–286
Swenson, C. R., 172
Szuba, M. P., 284
Szurek, S. A., 305

Taft, C., 110
Talcott, G. W., 21
Tarrier, N., 116, 118, 120
Taylor, K. L., 110
Taylor, L. J., 91
Taylor, S., 26, 96
Teasdale, J. D., 256
Telch, C. F., 151
Telch, M. J., 79–80, 82
Terdal, L. G., 250
Thibodeau, N., 133, 141
Thomas, B. H., 392
Thomas, F., 392
Thomas, M., 4, 27
Thomkins, M. A., 241
Thrasher, S., 116, 120
Tims, F., 488
Tolin, D. F., 277
Tompkins, M. A., 240, 244–245
Toneatto, T., 185
Tonge, B. J., 315, 459
Tonigan, J. S., 186, 196
Toth, S. L., 456
Trakowski, J., 23
Treat, T. A., 26
Tremblay, R., 391
Trierweiler, S. J., 5
Tulloch, H. L., 26
Turk, C. L., 91, 93, 95
Turner, C. W., 478, 481, 484, 487, 488
Turner, S. M., 90, 93–94, 118, 327, 330
Tweed, D. L., 384
Tyano, S., 284

Underwood, M., 392, 393

van der Mast, 78, 81–82
Van Hasselt, V. B., 25
van Hout, W. J. P. J., 80, 82, 84
van Reekum, R., 163
Vasey, M. W., 327

Velez, C. M., 474
Velicer, W. F., 26
Venables, P., 390
Verbrugge, L. M., 217
Verrotti, A., 424
Violato, C., 449, 450
Vitaro, F., 391
Vitousek, K., 346, 349, 352, 353, 354, 359
Vogeltanz, N. D., 4
Vollmer, T. R., 243
Vostanis, P., 256

Wachtel, J. R., 305, 311, 314, 320
Wacker, D. P., 250
Wade, W. A., 26
Wagner, A. R., 96
Wahler, H. J., 222
Waite, R. R., 330
Wald, A., 435
Waldman, I., 407
Waldron, H. B., 478, 481, 484, 487, 488
Walker, C. E., 434, 435, 436, 441, 442, 446
Walker, J. L., 385
Walker, P., 252
Walters, K. S., 327
Ward, C. H., 58, 440
Warman, M., 342
Waterman, J., 459, 469
Watkins, P. L., 26
Watson, G. S., 420
Weathers, F. W., 110–111, 122, 363
Webb, C., 459, 469
Wechsler, D., 388
Weems, C. F., 310, 342
Weinberg, W. A., 256–257
Weiss, M. R., 410
Weiss, R. L., 222
Weissman, M. M., 263
Weizman, A., 284
Weltzin, T. E., 346
Werner, E., 391
Wesner, R., 26
Westrup, D., 363
Wetzler, S., 25
Wever, C., 286
Wheeler, T., 409
Wheeler, V. A., 330, 453
Whitaker, A., 276
White, H. R., 475
White, K. R., 421

Whitman, T. L., 427
Wicker, P., 198
Wik, G., 76
Wilheim, K. L., 369
Wilhelm, F. H., 82
Williams, C., 9, 32, 58, 164
Williams, J. B. W., 6, 78, 163–164, 182, 261
Williams, L. M., 449, 450
Williams, M., 390
Wilner, A. G., 395
Wilner, N., 367
Wilson, G. T., 151, 283
Wilson, G. V., 164
Wilson, K. G., 242
Wilson, P. H., 369
Wincze, J. P., 199
Winters, K., 474, 475, 478
Wittchen, H. U., 346
Wolf, M. M., 395
Wolfe, B. E., 25
Wolfe, D. A., 454
Wolfe, V. V., 449, 450, 454, 456
Wolkow, R., 286
Wolters, W. H. G., 434
Wood, A., 256
Wood, C., 407
Woody, S., 26
Woolaway-Bickel, K., 23
Wright, L., 435, 442, 446
Wyre, C. H., 459

Yang, H., 279, 286
Yaryura-Tobias, J., 279, 286
Yasik, A. E., 361, 362
Yeh, C. J., 346
Yehuda, R., 164
Young, D., 315
Yule, W., 305, 361
Yurgelun-Todd, D., 145

Zanarini, M. C., 163
Zarcone, J. R., 243
Zaucha, K., 369
Zayfert, C., 177
Zhao, S., 76, 125
Zimering, R. T., 23, 113
Zinbarg, R. E., 82
Zito, J. M., 271
Zohar, J., 284
Zweben, A., 189

Subject Index

Accidents Characteristics Identification
    Scale (AcCIdentS), 366
Acrophobia Questionnaire (AQ), 78
Acrophobic Cognitions Inventory (ACI),
    78
ADHD. *See* Attention deficit/
    hyperactivitydisorder
Adolescent Psychopathology Scale (APS),
    261
Agoraphobia. *See* Panic disorder and
    agoraphobia
Agoraphobia Cognitions Questionnaire,
    58
Alcohol abuse in adulthood, 181–197
    case illustration of, 182–196
        assessment, 184–187
            functional analysis, 185
            psychiatric comorbidity, 186–187
            self-report, 185
        course of treatment, 189–194
        effectiveness, 196
        follow-up, 195–196
        history, 183–184
        managed care considerations, 196
        medical consultation, 187
        presenting complaint, 183
        termination, 195
        therapist-client factors, 194–195
        treatment rationale, 188–189
    description of, 181–182
Alcohol and drug abuse in childhood and
    adolescence, 474–490
    case illustration of, 476–489
        assessment, 478–481
        case conceptualization, 481–483
        course of treatment, 483–486
        effectiveness, 487–489
        follow-up, 487–489
        history, 477–478
        medical consultation, 481
        presenting complaint, 476–477

termination, 487
therapist-client factors, 486
description of, 474–476
Anorexia nervosa, 345–360
    case illustration of, 359–364
        assessment, 349–351
            behavioral observation, 349–350
            physiology, 351
            self-report, 350–351
        case conceptualization, 352
        course of treatment, 353–356
        description of, 345–346
        effectiveness, 359
        follow-up, 357–358
        history, 348–349
        managed care considerations, 358–359
        medical consultation, 351
        presenting complaint, 347–348
        termination, 356–357
        therapist-client factors, 356
        treatment rationale, 352–353
Anxiety Disorders Interview Schedule for
    Children (ADIS-C), 280, 281, 309
Anxiety Disorders Interview Schedule for
    DSM-IV (ADIS-IV), 57
Anxiety Sensitivity Index (ASI), 58
Areas of Change Questionnaire (ACQ),
    222
Assessment, 6–20, 40–42, 57–59, 77–79,
    94–95, 110–112, 129–130, 147–149,
    163–165, 184–187, 201–203, 220–223,
    260–262, 280–282, 308–311, 330–331,
    349–351, 365–368, 387–390, 404–406,
    423–424, 439–440, 452–455, 478–481
    alcohol abuse, 184–187
    alcohol and drug abuse in childhood
        and adolescence, 478–481
    anorexia nervosa, 349–351
    attention-deficit/hyperactivity disorder,
        404–406
    borderline personality disorder, 163–165

Assessment (Continued)
  bulimia nervosa, 147–149
  child sexual abuse, 452–455
  clinical interview, 6–7
  conduct disorder, 387–390
  contextual factors, 14–20
    recent context, 16–20
      functional analysis, 17–20
    remote context, 14–16
      drugs, 16
      genetic factors, 15
      learning and modeling, 14–15
      physical factors, 15–16
      sociocultural factors, 16
  depression in childhood and
    adolescence, 260–262
  diagnosis, 13–14
  elimination disorders, 439–440
  generalized anxiety disorder, 129–130
  major depressive disorder, 40–42
  marital dysfunction, 220–223
  mental retardation, 423–424
  obsessive-compulsive disorder, 280–282
  panic disorder and agoraphobia, 57–59
  posttraumatic stress disorder in
    adulthood, 110–112
  posttraumatic stress disorder in
    childhood and adolescence, 365–368
  self-monitoring, 8
  separation anxiety disorder, 308–311
  sexual dysfunction, 201–203
  social phobia in adulthood, 94–95
  social phobia in childhood and
    adolescence, 330–331
  specific phobia, 77–79
  standardized self-report instruments, 7
Attention-deficit/hyperactivity disorder
    (ADHD), 400–419
  case illustration of, 401–417
    assessment, 404–406
    case conceptualization, 407–409
    course of treatment, 410–415
    effectiveness, 417
    follow-up, 416
    history, 403
    managed care considerations, 416–417
    medical consultation, 407
    presenting complaint, 402–403
    termination, 415–416
    therapist-client factors, 415
    treatment rationale, 409–410
  description of, 400–401
Attitude Toward Heights Questionnaire
    (ATHQ), 78

Beck Anxiety Inventory (BAI), 7, 58
Beck Depression Inventory (BDI), 58, 440
Beck Depression Inventory II (BDI-II), 9,
    41, 94, 111, 129
Behavioral Avoidance Task (BAT), 309, 311
Behavioral case conceptualization for
    adults, 3–36, 42–43, 60–62, 79–80,
    96–98, 112–115, 130–132, 150–151,
    166–168, 188, 203–205, 223–226
  alcohol abuse, 188
  borderline personality disorder, 166–168
  bulimia nervosa, 150–151
  generalized anxiety disorder, 130–132
  major depressive disorder, 42–43
  marital dysfunction, 223–226
  panic disorder and agoraphobia, 60–62
  posttraumatic stress disorder, 112–115
  sexual dysfunction, 203–205
  social phobia, 96–98
  specific phobia, 79–80
  steps of scientific inquiry, 4–33
    case illustration of, 8–32
      developing hypotheses, 20–30
      observation, 6–20
        data collection methods, 6–8
        identifying target behaviors, 9–10
        identifying treatment targets,
          10–13
        diagnosis, 13–14
        time line, 12
      observing outcome, 32
      revising hypotheses, 32
      testing hypotheses, 30–31
Behavioral case conceptualization for
    children and adolescents, 239–255,
    263–264, 283–285, 312–314, 332–334,
    352, 369–373, 391–392, 407–409,
    425–426, 440–442, 456–458, 481–483
  alcohol and drug abuse, 481–483
  anorexia nervosa, 352
  attention-deficit/hyperactivity disorder,
    407–409
  child sexual abuse, 456–458
  components of, 244–251
    assessing remote context, 246
    defining the problem, 244–246
    developing hypotheses, 249
    development, 250
    functional analysis, 246–249
      antecedents, 246–247
      consequences, 248–249
      establishing operations, 247–248
    research, 250–251
  conduct disorder, 391–392

definition of, 240–241
depression, 263–264
elimination disorders, 440–442
functional assessment and, 243–244
general considerations for, 241–242
mental retardation, 425–426
obsessive-compulsive disorder, 283–285
posttraumatic stress disorder, 369–373
separation anxiety disorder, 312–314
social phobia, 332–334
theoretical foundation of, 242–243
Behavioral couples therapy (BCT), 218–234
Behavioral theory, 242–243
Behavior Assessment System for Children, 388
Body Sensations Questionnaire (BSQ), 58
Borderline personality disorder, 160–180
case illustration of, 161–179
assessment, 163–165
functional analysis, 164
physiology, 164–165
self-report, 164
case conceptualization, 166–168
course of treatment, 170–174
effectiveness, 178–179
follow-up, 177
history, 162–163
managed care considerations, 177–178
medical consultation, 165–166
presenting complaint, 162
termination, 176–177
therapist-client factors, 174–176
treatment rationale, 169–170
description of, 160–161
Brief Symptom Inventory (BSI), 164
Bulimia nervosa, 144–159
case illustration of, 145–159
assessment, 147–149
functional analysis, 147–148
physiology, 149
self-report, 148–149
case conceptualization, 150–151
course of treatment, 152–155
effectiveness, 158–159
follow-up, 157
history, 146–147
managed care considerations, 157–158
medical consultation, 149
presenting complaint, 146
termination, 156–157
therapist-client factors, 156
treatment rationale, 151–152
description of, 144–145

Child Behavior Checklist (CBCL), 310, 367, 404, 440, 454
Children's Depression Inventory (CDI), 367, 452–453
Children's Impact of Traumatic Events-Revised (CITES-R), 454
Children's Loneliness Questionnaire (CLQ), 453
Children's Yale-Brown Obsessive-Compulsive Scale (CY-BOCS), 280–281
Child sexual abuse, 449–473
case illustration of, 450–470
assessment, 452–455
child self-report, 452–454
parent self-report, 454–455
case conceptualization, 456–458
course of treatment, 460–465
effectiveness, 469–470
follow-up, 467–468
history, 452
managed care considerations, 468–469
medical consultation, 455–456
presenting complaint, 451
termination, 466–467
therapist-client factors, 465–466
treatment rationale, 459–460
description of, 449–450
Child Sexual Behavior Inventory (CSBI), 454
Clinician Administered PTSD Scale (CAPS-1), 110
Cognitive therapy, 82
Conduct disorder, 383–399
case illustration of, 385–397
assessment, 387–390
behavioral observations, 389–390
clinical interview, 388
physiology, 390
psychoeducational testing, 388–389
case conceptualization, 391–392
course of treatment, 393–395
effectiveness, 397
follow-up, 396
history, 387
managed care considerations, 396–397
medical consultation, 390–391
presenting complaint, 386–387
termination, 395
therapist-client factors, 395
treatment rationale, 392–393
description of, 383–385

Conners' Rating Scales-Revised (CRS-R), 404
Curriculum Based Measurement (CBM), 405–406

Depression in childhood and adolescence, 256–275
  case description of, 259–272
    assessment, 260–262
      clinical interview, 261–262
      self-report, 261
    case conceptualization, 263–264
    course of treatment, 264–270
    effectiveness, 272
    history, 260
    managed care considerations, 271–272
    medical consultation, 262
    presenting complaint, 259–260
    termination and follow-up, 270–271
  description of, 256–259
Diagnosis. *See Diagnostic and Statistical Manual of Mental Disorders (DSM-IV)*
Diagnostic and Statistical Manual of Mental Disorders (DSM-IV), 37–38, 39, 52–53, 75, 90, 106–107, 125, 144, 160, 181, 216–217, 257–258, 276–277, 304, 326–327, 345–346, 361, 383–384, 400–401, 420, 434–435, 475
  agoraphobia, 53
  alcohol abuse, 181
  alcohol and drug abuse in childhood and adolescence, 475
  anorexia nervosa, 345–346
  attention-deficit/hyperactivity disorder, 400–401
  borderline personality disorder, 160
  bulimia nervosa, 144
  conduct disorder, 383–384
  dysthymic disorder, 258
  elimination disorders, 434–435
  generalized anxiety disorder, 125
  major depressive disorder, 37, 257–258
  major depressive disorder, recurrent, 39
  major depressive episode, 38
  marital dysfunction, 216–217
  mental retardation, 420
  obsessive-compulsive disorder, 276–277
  panic attack, 52
  panic disorder, 52–53
  posttraumatic stress disorder in adulthood, 106–107
  posttraumatic stress disorder in childhood and adolescence, 361
  separation anxiety disorder, 304
  sexual dysfunction, 198
  social phobia in adulthood, 90
  social phobia in childhood and adolescence, 326–327
  specific phobia, 75
Drinker Inventory of Consequences (DRINC), 186
Drug abuse. *See* Alcohol abuse in adulthood, Alcohol and drug abuse in childhood and adolescence
Dyadic Adjustment Scale (DAS), 222

Eating Disorders Inventory (EDI), 148–149
Eating Disorder 2 (EDI-2), 350–351
Effectiveness studies. *See* treatment effectiveness
Elimination disorders, 434–448
  case illustration of, 436–447
    assessment, 439–440
      behavioral observations, 439
      physiology, 440
      self-report, 439–440
    case conceptualization, 441–442
    course of treatment, 443–445
    effectiveness, 446–447
    follow-up, 445–446
    history, 438–439
    managed care considerations, 446
    medical consultation, 440–441
    presenting complaints, 437–438
    termination, 445
    therapist-client factors, 445
    treatment rationale, 442–443
  description of, 434–436
Exposure and response prevention, 150–152
Exposure therapy, 81, 83–84, 115–120, 286–287

Family Crisis Oriented Personal Evaluation Scales (F-COPES), 455
Fear Survey Schedule for Children-Revised (FSSC-R), 310
Functional Analytic Interview, 7

GAD. *See* generalized anxiety disorder
Generalized anxiety disorder (GAD), 125–143
  case illustration of, 126–141
    assessment, 129–130
      functional analysis, 129
      physiology, 130
      self-report, 129–130

case conceptualization, 130–132
course of treatment, 133–138
effectiveness, 141
follow-up, 140
history, 128–129
managed care considerations, 140–141
medical consultation, 130
presenting complaint, 127–128
termination, 139–140
therapist-client factors, 138–139
treatment rationale, 132–133
description of, 125–126

Hopelessness Scale for Children (HSC), 452–453

Intolerance of Uncertainty Scale (IUS), 129
Inventory of Drug-Taking Situations, 186
Inventory of Rewarding Activities (IRA), 222

Loneliness Scale, 330–331

Major depressive disorder, 37–51, 256–275
case illustration of, 39–50
assessment, 40–42
functional analysis, 40–41
physiology, 41–42
self-report, 41
case conceptualization, 42–43
chief complaints, 39
course of treatment, 44–47
effectiveness, 49–50
follow-up, 49
history, 39–40
managed care considerations, 49
medical consultation, 42
termination, 48
therapist-client factors, 48
treatment rationale, 43–44
in childhood and adolescence, 256–275
description of, 37–39
Managed care considerations, 49, 71–72, 86, 103, 121, 140–141, 157–158, 177–178, 196, 213, 234, 271–272, 298, 322–323, 341–342, 358–359, 380, 396–397, 416–417, 431, 446, 468–469
alcohol abuse, 196
anorexia nervosa, 358–359
attention-deficit/hyperactivity disorder, 416–417
borderline personality disorder, 177–178
bulimia nervosa, 157–158

child sexual abuse, 468–469
conduct disorder, 396–397
depression in childhood and adolescence, 271–272
elimination disorders, 446
generalized anxiety disorder, 140–141
major depressive disorder, 49
marital dysfunction, 234
mental retardation, 431
obsessive-compulsive disorder, 298
panic disorder and agoraphobia, 71–72
posttraumatic stress disorder in adulthood, 121
posttraumatic stress disorder in childhood and adolescence, 380
separation anxiety disorder, 322–323
sexual dysfunction, 213
social phobia in adulthood, 103
social phobia in childhood and adolescence, 341–342
specific phobias, 86
Marital dysfunction, 216–235
case illustration of, 217–234
assessment, 220–223
communication sample, 221–222
self-report, 222–223
case conceptualization, 223–226
course of treatment, 227–231
effectiveness, 234
follow-up, 233–234
history, 219–220
medical consultation, 223
presenting complaint, 218–219
termination, 232–233
therapist-client factors, 231–232
treatment rationale, 226–227
description of, 216–217
Marital Relationship Assessment Battery, 222
Marital Status Inventory (MSI), 222
Medical considerations, 42, 60, 79, 96, 112, 149, 187, 262, 282, 311–312, 331–332, 351, 368–369, 407, 424–425, 440–441, 455–456, 481
alcohol abuse and, 187
alcohol and drug abuse in childhood and adolescence and, 481
anorexia nervosa and, 351
attention-deficit/hyperactivity disorder and, 407
bulimia nervosa and, 149
child sexual abuse and, 455–456
depression in childhood and adolescence and, 262

Medical considerations *(Continued)*
  elimination disorders and, 440–441
  generalized anxiety disorder and, 130
  major depressive disorder and, 42
  mental retardation and, 424–425
  obsessive-compulsive disorder and, 282
  panic disorder and agoraphobia and,
    60
  posttraumatic stress disorder in
    adulthood and, 112
  posttraumatic stress disorder in
    childhood and adolescence and,
    368–369
  separation anxiety disorder and,
    311–312
  social phobia in adulthood and, 96
  social phobia in childhood and
    adolescence and, 331–332
  specific phobia and, 79
Mental retardation, 420–433
  case illustration of, 422–432
    assessment, 423–424
      behavioral observations, 423–424
      cognitive assessment, 424
    case conceptualization, 425–426
    course of treatment, 426–429
    effectiveness, 431–432
    follow-up, 430–431
    history, 422–423
    managed care considerations, 431
    medical consultation, 424–425
    presenting complaint, 422
    termination, 430
    therapist-client factors, 429–430
    treatment rationale, 426
  description of, 420–422
Minnesota Multiphasic Personality
  Inventory (MMPI), 148
Mizes Anorectic Cognitions questionnaire
  (MAC), 148
MMPI. *See* Minnesota Multiphasic
  Personality Inventory
Mobility Inventory Questionnaire, 58
Modified PTSD Symptom Scale (MPSS),
  111
Motivation Assessment Scale, 423
Multidimensional Anxiety Scale for
  Children (MASC), 280, 282, 310

Obsessive-compulsive disorder (OCD),
  276–303
  case illustration of, 277–299
    assessment, 280–282

case conceptualization, 283–285
    course of treatment, 287–294
      developmental considerations, 294
      relapse prevention, 294
    effectiveness, 299
    follow-up, 297–298
    history, 279–280
    managed care considerations, 298
    medical consultation, 282–283
    presenting complaint, 278–279
    termination, 296–297
    therapist-client factors, 295–296
    treatment rationale, 285–287
  description of, 276–277
OCD. *See* Obsessive-compulsive disorder
OCD Impact Scale (OCIS), 282
Outcome Questionnaire-45 (OQ-45), 164

Panic disorder and agoraphobia, 52–74
  case illustration of, 54–73
    behavioral assessment, 57–59
    case conceptualization, 60–62
    course of treatment, 63–69
    effectiveness, 72–73
    follow-up, 70–71
    history, 56–57
    managed care considerations, 71–72
    medical consultation, 59–60
    noncompliance, 69–70
    presenting complaint, 55–56
    termination, 70
    treatment rationale, 62–63
  description of, 52–54
Penn State Worry Questionnaire (PSWQ),
  129
Pharmacological treatments. *See*
  Pharmacotherapy
Pharmacotherapy, 59–60, 82, 149, 163–165,
  187, 271, 282–283, 285–286, 312,
  390–391, 409, 429
  alcohol abuse, 187
  attention-deficit/hyperactivity disorder,
    409
  borderline personality disorder,
    163–165
  bulimia nervosa, 149
  conduct disorder, 390–391
  depression in childhood and
    adolescence, 271
  mental retardation, 429
  obsessive-compulsive disorder, 282–283,
    285–286
  panic disorder and agoraphobia, 59–60

separation anxiety disorder, 312
specific phobia, 82
Posttraumatic stress disorder (PTSD) in
adulthood, 106–124
case illustration of, 108–122
behavioral assessment, 110–112
case conceptualization, 112–115
course of treatment, 117–120
effectiveness, 115, 122
follow-up, 121
history, 109–110
managed care considerations, 121
medical consultation, 112
presenting complaint, 108–109
termination, 121
therapist-client factors, 120–121
treatment rationale, 115–116
description of, 106–107
Posttraumatic stress disorder (PTSD) in
childhood and adolescence, 361–382
case illustration of, 362–381
assessment, 365–368
behavioral observations,
365–366
physiology, 368
self-report, 366–367
case conceptualization, 369–373
course of treatment, 374–377
effectiveness, 380–381
follow-up, 379
history, 364–365
managed care considerations, 380
medical consultation, 368–369
presenting complaint, 363–364
termination, 378–379
therapist-client factors, 377–378
treatment rationale, 373–374
description of, 361–362
Project SAFE, 460–469
PTSD. *See* Posttraumatic stress disorder, in
adulthood, in childhood and
adolescence

Response to Conflict Scale (RTC), 222
Revised Children's Manifest Anxiety
Scale (RCMAS), 310, 367, 453
Reynolds Adolescent Depression Scale
(RADS), 261
Ritual prevention treatment, 286–287

SAD. *See* Separation anxiety disorder
School phobia. *See* Separation anxiety
disorder

School refusal. *See* Separation anxiety
disorder
Self-Description Inventory (SDI), 222
Self-Esteem Inventory (SEI), 453
Separation anxiety disorder (SAD),
304–324
case illustration of, 306–324
assessment, 308–311
behavioral observation, 309
measures, 309–310
physiology, 311
case conceptualization, 312–314
course of treatment, 315–320
effectiveness, 323–324
follow-up, 322
history, 307–308
managed care considerations, 322–323
medical consultation, 311–312
presenting complaint, 307
termination, 321–322
therapist-client factors, 320–321
treatment rationale, 314–315
description of, 304–305
Sexual dysfunction, 198–215
case illustration of, 199–214
assessment, 201–203
case conceptualization, 203–205
course of treatment, 205–209
effectiveness, 213–214
follow-up, 210–213
history, 200–201
managed care considerations, 213
presenting complaint, 200
termination, 209–210
therapist-client factors, 209
treatment rationale, 205
description of, 198–199
Short-form Alcohol Dependence Data
Questionnaire, 185
Social Anxiety Scale for Children-Revised
(SASC-R), 330–331
Social Interaction Self-Statement Test,
330–331
Social Phobia and Anxiety Inventory
(SPAI), 94
Social Phobia and Anxiety Inventory for
Children (SPAI-C), 330–331
Social phobia in adulthood, 90–105
case illustration of, 91–104
assessment, 94–95
behavioral tests, 95
physiology, 95
self-report, 94

Social phobia in adulthood (Continued)
    case conceptualization, 96–98
    course of treatment, 99–101
    effectiveness, 103–104
    follow-up, 103
    history, 93–94
    identifying information, 91–92
    managed care considerations, 103
    medical consultation, 96
    presenting complaint, 92–93
    termination, 101–103
    therapist-client factors, 101
    treatment rationale, 98–99
    description of, 90–91
Social phobia in childhood and
        adolescence, 326–344
    case illustration of, 327–342
        assessment, 330–331
            behavioral observations, 330
            physiology, 331
            self-report, 330–331
        case conceptualization, 332–334
        course of treatment, 335–340
        effectiveness, 342
        follow-up, 341
        history, 329–330
        managed care considerations,
            341–342
        medical consultation, 331–332
        presenting complaint, 328–329
        termination, 340–341
        therapist-client factors, 340
        treatment rationale, 334–335
    description of, 326–327
Specific phobia, 75–89
    case illustration of, 76–87
        assessment, 77–79
            functional analysis, 77–78
            measures, 78–79
            self-report, 78
        case conceptualization, 79–80
        chief complaint, 77
        course of treatment, 82–84
        effectiveness, 86–87
        follow-up, 86
        history, 77
        managed care considerations, 86
        medical consultation, 79
        termination, 86
        therapist-client factors, 85–86
        treatment rationale, 80–82
    clinical picture, 75–76
    course, 76

prevalence, 76
prognosis, 76
Stages of Change and Treatment
        Eagerness Scale, 186
Stroop task, 365
Structured Clinical Interview for the
        DSM-IV (SCID-IV), 6–7, 164, 182
Suicidal Ideation Questionnaire (SIQ), 269
Symptom Check List 90 Revised, 78, 111,
        366, 455

Test Anxiety Inventory for Children,
        330–331
Treatment, 43–47, 62–69, 80–84, 96–101,
        115–120, 132–138, 151–155, 169–174,
        188–194, 205–209, 226–231, 264–270,
        285–294, 314–320, 334–340, 352–356,
        373–377, 392–395, 409–415, 426–429,
        442–445, 459–465, 483–486
    alcohol abuse, 188–194
    alcohol and drug abuse in childhood
        and adolescence, 483–486
    anorexia nervosa, 352–356
    attention-deficit/hyperactivity disorder,
        409–415
    borderline personality disorder, 169–174
    bulimia nervosa, 151–155
    child sexual abuse, 459–465
    conduct disorder, 392–395
    depression in childhood and
        adolescence, 264–270
    elimination disorders, 442–445
    generalized anxiety disorder, 132–138
    major depressive disorder, 43–47
    marital dysfunction, 226–231
    mental retardation, 426–429
    obsessive-compulsive disorder, 285–294
    panic disorder and agoraphobia, 62–69
    posttraumatic stress disorder in
        adulthood, 115–120
    posttraumatic stress disorder in
        childhood and adolescence, 373–377
    separation anxiety disorder, 314–320
    sexual dysfunction, 205–209
    social phobia in adulthood, 96–101
    social phobia in childhood and
        adolescence, 334–340
    specific phobia, 80–84
Treatment effectiveness, 49–50, 72–73,
        86–87, 103–104, 115, 122, 141, 158–159,
        178–179, 196, 213–214, 234, 272, 299,
        323–324, 342, 359, 380–381, 397, 417,
        431–432, 446–447, 469–470, 487–489

alcohol abuse, 196
alcohol and drug abuse in childhood
    and adolescence, 487–489
anorexia nervosa, 359
attention-deficit/hyperactivity disorder,
    417
borderline personality disorder, 178–179
bulimia nervosa, 158–159
child sexual abuse, 469–470
conduct disorder, 397
depression in childhood and
    adolescence, 272
elimination disorders, 446–447
generalized anxiety disorder, 141
major depressive disorders, 49–50
marital dysfunction, 234
mental retardation, 431–432
obsessive-compulsive disorder, 299
panic disorder and agoraphobia, 72–73
posttraumatic stress disorder in
    adulthood, 115, 122
posttraumatic stress disorder in
    childhood and adolescence,
    380–381
separation anxiety disorder, 323–324
sexual dysfunction, 213–214

social phobia in adulthood, 103–104
social phobia in childhood and
    adolescence, 342
specific phobia, 86–87
Treatment planning, 20–31
    development of plan, 28–30
        case example, 29
        goals, 28
        interventions, 28
        measurements, 28
    hypotheses, 20–27
        causes, 20–21
        maintenance, 21–24
    implementation, 30–31
    treatment, 24–27
        case example, 27
        empirical literature, 25–26
        functional relationships, 24–25
        pragmatic concerns, 26–27

Virtual reality therapy, 81, 82

Wechsler Intelligence Scale for Children,
    third edition (WISC-III), 388
Worry and Anxiety Questionnaire (WAQ),
    129